# Herding Cats

# Herding Cats

*Multiparty Mediation in a Complex World*

**Chester A. Crocker**
**Fen Osler Hampson**
**Pamela Aall**
*editors*

UNITED STATES INSTITUTE OF PEACE PRESS
Washington, D.C.

The views expressed in this book are those of the authors alone. They do not necessarily reflect views of the United States Institute of Peace.

United States Institute of Peace
1200 17<sup>th</sup> Street NW
Washington, DC 20036

First published 1999

Printed in the United States of America

The paper used in this publication meets the minimum requirements of American National Standards for Information Sciences—Permanence of Paper for Printed Library Materials, ANSI Z39.48-1984.

**Library of Congress Cataloging-in-Publication Data**
    Herding cats : multiparty mediation in a complex world / edited by Chester A. Crocker, Fen Osler Hampson, and Pamela Aall.
        p. cm.
    Includes bibliographical references and index.
    ISBN 1-878379-93-3 (hardback : acid-free paper). — ISBN 1-878379-92-5 (pbk. : acid-free paper)
    1. Mediation, International. 2. Pacific settlement of international disputes. I. Crocker, Chester A. II. Hampson, Fen Osler. III. Aall, Pamela R.
    JZ6045.H47  1999
    327.1'7—dc21                      99-35750
                                                    CIP

# Contents

# Foreword

*Herding Cats* is a serious-minded book on a subject of the utmost importance to the lives of millions of people in conflict situations throughout the world. It is also a fascinating volume full of unforgettable characters, unpredictable plots, desperate situations, and significant diplomatic achievements. This combination is, to say the least, rare. By marrying sober analysis with captivating narrative, *Herding Cats* may encourage readers who tend to shy away from more serious tomes to engage with the important ideas presented herein; by the same token, it may remind an academic audience that concepts of conflict management and conflict resolution are anything but abstract in their application. In *Herding Cats*, the bridge between theory and practice is open for all to cross.

Much of the credit for this volume's ability to speak to practitioners as well as scholars, and to generalists as well as to specialists, belongs to its editors, Chester A. Crocker, Fen Osler Hampson, and Pamela Aall. Building on the success of their 1996 volume, *Managing Global Chaos: Sources of and Responses to International Conflict*, this gifted team has assembled a distinguished cast of international mediators to recount and reflect on their experiences. Crocker, Hampson, and Aall have framed those reflections with insightful assessments of key concepts and strategies, common threads and points of contention, and policy-relevant findings.

No less of the credit for the multifaceted appeal of this volume, of course, is due to the authors themselves, who have furnished thoughtful and compelling accounts of their individual experiences as mediators on the frontlines of international conflict. Their wisdom and candor are bound to be invaluable to those who will follow in their footsteps and to the governments and organizations, both governmental and nongovernmental, who will support future mediation efforts.

The mediation of contemporary conflict is an activity that typically involves throwing well-intentioned individuals into a lion's den of conflicting interests, beliefs, and forces. The mediator is usually asked to do no less than persuade the lions to lie down with one another, and though the onlookers customarily shout out encouragement and instructions, the hapless mediator is rarely armed with much more than quick wits, seasoned judgment, and dedication. It is, to be sure, a situation rich in dramatic possibilities—hence the opportunities for engrossing narrative. It is also a situation in which the odds are stacked so heavily against the mediator that any kind of success is not easy to explain—hence the need for intellectual sophistication.

Such sophistication is also needed if we are not only to understand why a particular attempt at mediation succeeded or failed but also to detect general patterns in an endeavor that, despite its complexity and unique challenges, is becoming increasingly popular as an approach to dealing with international conflicts. Mediation is hardly a recent invention, but in the past twenty years, and particularly since the end of the Cold War, mediation has become both much more common and much more complex. The increase in the number of efforts to mediate interstate and intrastate conflicts owes much to the disappearance of the constraints previously imposed by the rival superpowers on both warmaking and peacemaking among and within their respective client-states. The discipline of the bipolar order has crumbled, leaving many states vulnerable to the reassertion of old antagonisms among contending national, religious, and especially ethnic groups. As conflicts have multiplied and escalated, the opportunities for external mediators to intervene have proliferated.

The increasing complexity of mediation is the product of several factors. Some of these are more or less unrelated to the demise of the Cold War—for instance, the advent of almost instantaneous global coverage of crises and conflicts by the transnational media. Many of today's negotiations, however, reflect the sea change in the international order. Surely, the most notable of these latter factors is the above-mentioned proliferation in the number and types of third-party intervenors. As the somewhat provocative title of this volume makes graphically clear, it is rare that a mediator undertakes a peacemaking effort alone. For instance, the parties to a conflict may wish to engage more than one mediator for the effort, or may not agree on the same choice of mediator, or may jump from one third party to another during the course of a negotiation. Even when the conflict parties are in accord, outside institutions may decide to provide a mediator: the UN secretary-general appoints a special representative, as does the United States and perhaps a former colonial power; the neighboring states and local regional organization intervene to protect their interests and keep the conflict from spreading; a nongovernmental organization (NGO) with a long-term relationship with the area tries to help out; an eminent person, acting on his or her own initiative, decides to become involved.

The following chapters cast much new light on how this multiplicity and diversity of players can impede or assist the process of effective mediation. For instance, by focusing on the mediating institutions rather than on the intervention itself, the book illuminates such underexplored aspects of mediation as the comparative advantage of different mediators and mediating institutions, and the strategic effect that any third-party intervention, whether official or private, has on international peace and security.

*Herding Cats* does justice not only to the complexity of multiparty mediation but also to its variety, presenting an extraordinarily broad range of actors and an equally wide array of conflicts, each of which is itself the stage for a multilayered drama involving numerous actors and issues. As a glance at the table of contents reveals, the chapters cover four continents and almost two dozen conflicts, they take us from televised gatherings of world leaders to meetings cloaked in complete secrecy, from academic workshops in quiet universities to the basements of besieged embassies, from churches to jungles to war-scarred hotels and mountains; and they deal with all stages in the life cycles of conflict, from prevention through efforts to halt ongoing hostilities to attempts to reach and implement lasting settlements.

Given this variety of experiences, it is not surprising that the authors of these chapters come from a wide array of backgrounds. Here, diplomats and politicians rub shoulders with generals and academics. Some have acted in their private, personal capacities, some have represented governments, others have worked for NGOs, still others have pursued careers within international organizations such as the United Nations and the Organization for Security and Cooperation in Europe. What one might not expect, however, is the eloquence and immediacy with which they communicate not only the details of their work but also the often powerful emotional and psychological tensions in the mediation process. To judge from these accounts of the ebb and flow of negotiation and violence, of optimism and pessimism, one might add "storyteller" to the numerous other skills required of today's mediator.

Few, if any, of the authors acquired these skills through formal training. Some skills were in-born, some were developed during careers, and some were acquired during the experience of mediation itself. Although they come from a wide variety of institutions, the authors have all had to develop special skills as part of their mediation effort, learning to differentiate between the long-term sources and the proximate causes of the given conflict; to receive and decipher the messages sent by parties in contention; to deliver effective messages of their own—both to the antagonists and to their home institutions; and to recognize and use resources at hand to weave together a credible peacemaking process.

The lessons learned from these experiences go to the heart of the work of the United States Institute of Peace. Dedicated to promoting a better understanding of international conflict and to enhancing the abilities needed to prevent or resolve such conflict, the Institute supports a wide variety of research on the causes, types, trajectories, and management of disputes that threaten international peace and stability. Many other Institute publications have directly or indirectly addressed the subject of mediation. Some have focused on the tools and skills required to safeguard or restore peace: for instance, *Preventing Violent Conflicts* by Michael Lund, *Building Peace* by John Paul Lederach, and *Peacemaking in International Conflict,* edited by I. William Zartman and J. Lewis Rasmussen. Several others have focused on specific conflicts: for instance, *Mozambique* by Richard Synge, *Angola's Last Best Chance for Peace* by Paul Hare, and *Somalia and Operation Restore Hope* by John L. Hirsch and Robert B. Oakley.

The fundamental assumption behind these works, behind *Herding Cats,* indeed behind all the work of the Institute, is that conflicts do not always need to burn themselves out on the battlefield. There are steps that can be taken to prevent and manage them that do not involve the use of force. Equally important, in the response to conflict situations, many different individuals and institutions—local civic organizations as well as governments, NGOs, regional organizations, and the United Nations—can play vital roles, especially if they support one another. This book provides hard evidence that these assumptions are well-founded. It does not conceal the difficulties and dangers facing a mediator. It does not pretend that intervention always works. It does not shy away from the uncomfortable fact that mediation may sometimes make things worse. But it shows—with candor, eloquence, and a sharp analytical eye—what mediators can accomplish and why so many people have benefited from their efforts.

Richard H. Solomon, President
United States Institute of Peace

# Preface

This book grew out of a desire to unravel the complexities of the frequent third-party interventions in the violent conflicts of the 1990s. We decided to approach the topic by examining how third-party institutions involved in the international response—the United Nations, regional organizations, individual states, groups of "friends," NGOs, and others—had interacted or had failed to interact in carrying out their missions. That confusion and a lack of teamwork dominated the playing field had been amply illustrated by Somalia, Rwanda, and Bosnia, and we wanted to identify ways to lessen that confusion. As we looked at these interventions, a common element emerged: the key role that individual mediators played in providing coherence to the third-party peacemaking efforts and the enormous challenges— not least from their own and other third-party institutions—that these mediators faced in creating this coherence. Our project on intervention became focused on mediation in general, and on multiparty mediation in particular.

In the eyes of most people, mediation practiced in the international sphere remains an obscure activity performed by little-known individuals mysteriously appointed to broker an agreement in some remote corner of the globe. Occasionally, these mediators do make headlines, as George Mitchell and Richard Holbrooke did in Northern Ireland and in Bosnia, respectively. More often, however, the names of individual mediators appear only toward the end of news articles, as the mediators serve up matter-of-fact assessments of progress or the lack thereof in peace processes struggling to end seemingly endless conflicts. The real stuff of mediation—what it entails and what tempests and shoals it encounters—often goes unreported in media accounts and unnoticed in academic analyses. And yet, for complex political, social, economic, and moral reasons, mediation is becoming a common tool of international relations, a means by which the international community tries to extinguish violent conflict or to prevent it from igniting.

To capture the world of present-day mediation, we have developed a book with three components. First, to help us grasp the nature of multiparty mediation, we asked almost two dozen mediators who had worked in very different circumstances and for very different institutions to write about their experiences. These experiences, which furnish a rich fund of new perspectives, insights, facts, and lessons learned, constitute the heart of this book. Second, we situated these first-person accounts within the context of current academic research and analysis, thus creating the conceptual framework for this book. Third, we identified the strategic and operational recommendations that grow out of this academic framework and the lessons distilled by practitioners. These recommendations are found in the concluding chapter. The result is a book that is much longer than we originally intended, but one that will serve, we hope, as a guide for both official and nonofficial peacemakers, as well as a powerful resource for teaching and research in conflict management and resolution.

For their willingness to take time from their busy lives to engage in this project, we thank first and foremost the authors of the case studies collected in the volume. Mediators do not normally seek the limelight; often their success depends on providing a quiet diplomacy that emphasizes not their own efforts but rather the efforts and contributions of the parties to the conflict. For this volume, however, the authors were kind enough to step further toward center stage and into the analytical spotlight. Their accounts give us an insider's perspective on the mediation process, and the authors were particularly generous in helping to pinpoint lessons learned and in creating a road map for future mediators and their sponsoring institutions. Special thanks go to those authors who came to Washington in September 1998 to engage with us in an intense and enlightening discussion of multiparty mediation. Their deliberations, captured in chapter 3, added depth to this project.

The United States Institute of Peace, and particularly its president, Richard H. Solomon, has been very supportive of this project. The Institute, which straddles the academic and the operational worlds, is deeply immersed in the question of how to create an enduring peace. With its many substantive resources and wide-ranging contacts, the Institute has provided an excellent milieu and appropriate home for this project. We are also grateful to Dick Solomon for the title of this book—the picturesque phrase appears in Dick's chapter in this volume and seems to us to capture the difficulty of coordinating independent third parties.

A number of other experts in mediation and conflict intervention have offered helpful advice along the way. Early on in the project, we asked several people to review our initial research design; for their wise suggestions, we are grateful to Antonia Handler Chayes of the Conflict Management Group, Alexander George of Stanford University, Harriet Hentges of the United States Institute of Peace, Andrew Natsios of World Vision, Robert Pastor of Emory University, Peter Schoettle of the United States Institute of Peace, Astri Suhrke of the Christian Michelsen Institute, and I. William Zartman of the Nitze School of Advanced International Studies. Bill Zartman also played an important role at the September 1998 authors' meeting, spinning general conclusions out of a wealth of personal observations and proving that, if one has sufficient breadth of vision, there need be no gap between the academic community and the practitioners' world.

A book of this nature is a challenge to publish, and we greatly appreciate the close attention, care, and wise counsel we received from members of the Institute's Publications program: Dan Snodderly, Joan Engelhardt, Kay Hechler, Marie Marr, Mike Chase, and Michael Sonesen. In this regard, there is the inestimable contribution of our managing editor, Nigel Quinney, who shepherded this book through the publication process. Providing direction, clarity, perspective, and good humor, he kept us on track and focused, and produced a very fine text. In its own way, it was an act of multiparty mediation and, like the case authors in this book, he succeeded admirably.

Much research and administrative support goes into the creation of a book this size. Janice Hoggs and Camilla Pessima have provided a great deal of appreciated administrative support, which may have been hidden from the rest of the world but which was essential to the smooth functioning of this complicated project. We would also like to acknowledge the contributions of Greg Maruszecka of Carleton University, Michael Taylor of Georgetown University, and Louis Klarevas and James Rae of the United States Institute of Peace. Lou saw the book off to a good start, tracking down written material and UN special representatives with zeal and skill, while offering excellent suggestions on many topics. James Rae deserves special recognition for keeping this project going on a daily basis, checking facts, collecting data, communicating with authors, and making sure that we, the editors, understood what we needed to do next and stayed on schedule. In addition, James wrote the summaries that precede each of the case studies, and thus he has contributed a valuable reference tool to the book. He also served as the research assistant for Richard Solomon's chapter on Cambodia. In fact, James has been involved in every aspect of this book, and we are deeply in his debt.

# Contributors

**Chester A. Crocker** is the James R. Schlesinger professor of strategic studies at Georgetown University and chairman of the board of directors of the United States Institute of Peace. From 1981 to 1989 he was assistant secretary of state for African affairs; as such, he was the principal diplomatic architect and mediator in the prolonged negotiations among Angola, Cuba, and South Africa that led to Namibia's transition to democratic governance and independence, and to the withdrawal of Cuban forces from Angola. He is the author of *High Noon in Southern Africa: Making Peace in a Rough Neighborhood,* and coeditor of *Managing Global Chaos: Sources of and Responses to International Conflict* and *African Conflict Resolution: The U.S. Role in Peacemaking.* He is also an adviser on strategy and negotiation to U.S. and European firms.

**Fen Osler Hampson** is professor of international affairs and associate director of the Norman Paterson School of International Affairs, Carleton University, Ottawa, Canada. He is the author of *Nurturing Peace: Why Peace Settlements Succeed or Fail; Multilateral Negotiations: Lessons from Arms Control, Trade, and the Environment; Unguided Missiles: How America Buys Its Weapons;* and *Forming Economic Policy: The Case of Energy in Canada and Mexico.* He is also editor or coeditor of sixteen volumes on international affairs, including *Managing Global Chaos: Sources of and Responses to International Conflict; Earthly Goods: Environmental Change and Social Justice; A Big League Player: Canada among Nations, 1999;* and *Leadership and Dialogue: Canada among Nations, 1998.* Professor Hampson was a peace fellow at the United States Institute of Peace in 1993–94.

**Pamela Aall** is director of the Education Program at the United States Institute of Peace and has been acting director of the Education and Training Program at the Institute. Before joining the Institute, she was a consultant to the President's Committee on the Arts and the Humanities, and to the Institute of International Education. She held a number of positions at the Rockefeller Foundation and has worked for the European Cultural Foundation and the International Council for Educational Development. Her research has focused on conflict management and resolution, nongovernmental organizations, and third-party institutions that respond to conflict. She is coeditor of *Managing Global Chaos: Sources of and Responses to International Conflict,* and coauthor of *A Guide to the Military, NGOs, and IGOs: A Handbook for Practitioners.*

\* \* \*

**Aldo Ajello** is the special envoy of the European Union for the Great Lakes region of Africa. From October 1992 to February 1995, he served as under-secretary-general of the United Nations and special representative of the UN secretary-general for peacekeeping operations in Mozambique (ONUMOZ). Before joining the United Nations, he was a member of the Italian and European Parliaments.

**Dame Margaret Anstee** served the United Nations from 1952 to 1993, rising to under-secretary-general in 1987. She directed field operations in all developing regions, mostly in economic and social development, but also in major disaster relief. After occupying senior positions as assistant secretary-general in New York, she became director-general of the third UN headquarters in Vienna in 1987, with responsibility for all UN programs related to social policy and development and to narcotic drugs. From February 1992 to June 1993, she served as the UN secretary-general's special representative in Angola and headed the second UN Angola Verification Mission (UNAVEM II).

**Paul Arthur** is professor of political science at the University of Ulster, and was a senior fellow at the United States Institute of Peace in 1997–98. Since 1990, he has mediated an unofficial workshop process between political leaders in Northern Ireland.

**James A. Baker III** is honorary chairman of the James A. Baker III Institute for Public Policy at Rice University and a member of the Rice University Board of Governors. From January 1989 to August 1992, he served as U.S. secretary of state in the Bush administration. In this position, he mediated the Madrid peace conference and facilitated the Middle East peace process.

**Andrea Bartoli** founded the SIPA International Conflict Resolution Program at Columbia University and currently holds the chair of the Columbia University Seminar on Conflict Resolution. He has been the special representative of the Community of Sant'Egidio (a Catholic international lay association) to the United Nations since Sant'Egidio mediated a settlement of the Mozambique civil war in 1990–92.

**John de Chastelain** is chairman of the Independent International Commission on Decommissioning for Northern Ireland. A retired Canadian general, he is a former head of the Canadian forces and was Canada's ambassador to the United States in 1993.

**Alvaro de Soto** is assistant secretary-general for political affairs at the United Nations. As the secretary-general's personal representative for the Central American peace process, he was the UN mediator in the El Salvador peace negotiations. He is an ambassador on special leave from the Peruvian diplomatic service.

**Hasjim Djalal** is ambassador-at-large for Law of the Sea and Marine Affairs of Indonesia. He was an influential participant at the Third United Nations Conference of the Law of the Sea and continues to play an important role in the implementation of the resulting United Nations Convention on the Law of the Sea. He devised the Workshop Process in the South China Sea, and directs the initiative with Professor Ian Townsend-Gault.

**Jan Egeland** is a special adviser with the Inter-American Development Bank, the United Nations, the Norwegian and International Red Cross, and the International Peace Research Institute of Oslo. From 1992 to 1997, he served as state secretary in the Norwegian Ministry of Foreign Affairs. In this capacity, he helped to facilitate the Oslo peace process.

**Luigi R. Einaudi** works on multilateral governance and on conflict resolution as a senior visiting fellow at the Inter-American Dialogue in Washington, D.C. He was the U.S. special envoy for the Ecuador-Peru peace process from its inception in 1995 to its conclusion in 1998. From 1989 to 1993, he was U.S. ambassador to the Organization of American States.

**Fabienne Hara** is a political analyst and the project coordinator for the International Crisis Group's Central Africa program. She received her M.A. and predoctoral degree in international relations from the Institut d'Etudes

Politiques de Paris. Since 1995, she has been analyzing the Great Lakes of Central Africa in various capacities: as a research associate with the Center for Preventive Action at the Council on Foreign Relations, and as a head of mission with Doctors of the World. She has been an observer to the Arusha peace process and has published a number of articles on Burundi.

**Paul J. Hare** was a senior fellow at the United States Institute of Peace in 1996–97, and is now executive director of the United States–Angola Chamber of Commerce. He served as the U.S. special representative for the Angolan peace process from 1993 to 1998.

**John Hay,** a former journalist, is a consultant in foreign policy and international affairs in Ottawa. Supported in part by the Canadian Centre for Foreign Policy Development, he conducted an extensive case study of the attempted multilateral intervention in eastern Zaire in 1996.

**Richard Holbrooke** is U.S. ambassador and permanent representative to the United Nations. He served as U.S. assistant secretary of state for European and Canadian affairs from 1994 to 1996. In this capacity, he was the chief architect of the Dayton Peace Accords.

**The Honourable Barbara J. McDougall** is president of the Canadian Institute of International Affairs. From 1991 to 1993, she served as secretary of state for external affairs in the Canadian government. In this capacity, she played an activist role in the Organization of American States' mediation process for Haiti.

**Robert A. Pastor** is Goodrich C. White professor of political science at Emory University. He was the founder and director of the Latin American and Caribbean Program at the Carter Center (1985–98), where he organized international missions to monitor elections in twenty countries in the hemisphere and the world. He was the senior adviser to Jimmy Carter, Sam Nunn, and Colin Powell on their mission to Haiti in September 1994, and is the author or editor of twelve books on U.S. foreign policy, Latin America, and democracy, including *A Century's Journey: How the Great Powers Shape the World,* published in 1999.

**Harold H. Saunders** is director of international affairs at the Charles F. Kettering Foundation, where he engages in nonofficial dialogue to change relationships among people in deep-rooted ethnic, racial, or communal conflicts. Since March 1993, he has helped to facilitate the Inter-Tajik Dialogue within the Framework of the Dartmouth Conference. He was assistant secretary of state, 1978–81.

**Daniel Serwer** is director of the Balkans Initiative at the United States Institute of Peace, which focuses on Balkans regional security. He served as U.S. special envoy and coordinator for the Bosnian Federation from 1994 to 1996.

**Gordon Smith** is director of the Centre for Global Studies at the University of Victoria and chairman of the board of the International Development Research Centre. He was Canada's deputy minister of foreign affairs when Canada led efforts to dispatch a multinational military force to alleviate the crisis in eastern Zaire in 1996.

**Richard H. Solomon,** president of the United States Institute of Peace, was assistant secretary of state for East Asian and Pacific affairs from 1989 to 1992. In that role, he led the U.S. effort to negotiate a peace process for Cambodia and begin normalization of relations with Vietnam. For his efforts, he received awards from the Cambodian community in the United States, the Government of Thailand, and the U.S. Department of State.

**Max van der Stoel** is the first High Commissioner on National Minorities appointed by the Organization for Security and Cooperation in Europe. A former member of Parliament in the Netherlands, he has served as that country's foreign minister and as its permanent representative to the United Nations, and is a longtime human rights advocate.

**Ian Townsend-Gault** is a law professor and director of the Centre for Asian Legal Studies at the University of British Columbia Faculty of Law. He has worked on ocean and resource issues in the Asia-Pacific, North America, and Europe. He is codirector of the Workshop Process in the South China Sea with Ambassador Djalal.

# PART I

## MULTIPARTY MEDIATION

Concepts, Issues, Strategies, and Actors

# 1

# Introduction

CHESTER A. CROCKER, FEN OSLER HAMPSON, AND PAMELA AALL

## WHY A STUDY OF MULTIPARTY MEDIATION?

Since the early 1990s, the nature of warfare has changed radically. The proxy battles—fought between armed troops—that characterized the Cold War have given way to bloody civil and intercommunal conflicts in such places as Haiti, Somalia, Sudan, Rwanda, Congo/Zaire, Congo-Brazzaville, Liberia, Bosnia, and Central Asia. Yet at the same time as these internecine conflicts have increased in number, there has also been an increase in the appetite for negotiated settlements, as witnessed in Northern Ireland, El Salvador, Guatemala, Haiti, South Africa, Namibia, and Mozambique. Together, these two developments have inspired a third: namely, a growing role for the international community in peacekeeping and peacemaking, and especially in mediating political agreements in seemingly intractable conflicts.

This book examines the nature of third-party mediation in violent conflict as perceived by individuals who have worked to bring peace or prevent war in conflict zones around the world. Recognizing the changing complexion of both war and peacemakers, the volume includes official and non-official attempts to mediate conflicts in circumstances of great complexity—

with complexity understood to be not just a function of conflict, with its many causes and consequences, but also a function of the response.

The international response to conflict often entails multiple mediators as well as other third-party actors such as peacekeeping forces, development agencies, nongovernmental organizations (NGOs), and lone operators. Such a profusion of actors has often made peacemaking efforts messy, difficult, and even chaotic. The vicious nature of many contemporary conflicts, however, and the high costs for the international community of failing to prevent or end war make it critical to manage these third-party interventions—to understand current mediations, their consequences, and the requirements for leadership and cooperation in these joint, or at least contiguous, ventures.

Management in these circumstances is not a matter of establishing a line of command and responsibility. Organizing the diverse third-party peacemaking entities is a lot like organizing cats. As anyone who has lived with them can tell you, cats cannot be organized. Independent beings, they will do what they choose to do, gazing at your efforts to organize them with mild curiosity, or simply ignoring you. Gaining a cat's cooperation is a complicated matter of setting a course the cat might find reasonable and employing incentives (food often works) that persuade it at least to give your idea some thought. The volume's title, *Herding Cats*, is borrowed from Richard Solomon's chapter on Cambodia. The title refers to the challenge facing any principal mediator entering into a conflict: how to make a cohesive whole out of the independent third-party peacemaking initiatives, building on the positive results of earlier mediations, keeping simultaneous interventions by different actors from canceling each other out, bringing along the many interests that lie behind the third-party endeavor, organizing the handoff to a successor. In this aspect of his or her work, the mediator faces an array of highly autonomous individuals and organizations, such as special representatives of powerful states or of the UN secretary-general, high-level politicians, and committed individuals who are privately funded and accountable to no government or international organization. Like cats, these independent agents rarely feel an obligation, or even a desire, to cooperate and they retain the ability to walk away from the mediation or to launch competing initiatives. The mediator cannot force these other third parties to collaborate but must persuade them to enter into a working relationship that reinforces rather than undermines the peacemaking mediation.

The wealth of willing third parties may be a boon to international peacemaking, but it raises serious management issues about how and why these multiparty interventions come about; whether and how they are coordinated;

who provides leadership; what determines the level of commitment in terms of human and financial resources; and who is responsible for keeping an already mediated settlement on track and preventing the collapse of the agreement lest it become orphaned.

The presence or availability of different mediators at varying stages of a conflict raises another series of questions. Are some mediating agents particularly effective during one phase of the conflict and less effective during other phases? Do these mediation efforts during different phases of a conflict—assuming that there is more than one—build on one another? Or do they constitute a series of ad hoc attempts at peacemaking whose success depends not on any cumulative effort but on the effectiveness of the mediator or the weariness of the different warring factions?

As more countries and institutional actors become involved in mediation, a judicious assessment is required not only of their comparative institutional strengths and weaknesses, but also of how to encourage complementary efforts and how to coordinate the process when one actor or institution is handing off the responsibilities for mediation to others. In addition, we need to know more about the main obstacles to achieving coordination and coherence among different mediators in such settings and the means to overcome the problems faced by multiple mediators working without a common script to mediate a negotiated resolution to conflict.

## THE CHANGING ENVIRONMENTS OF MEDIATION EFFORTS

As Thucydides' account of the Peloponnesian War reminds us, mediation has a long history in international relations.[1] The Greeks frequently resorted to mediation to avert violent conflict. So too did the Romans and the Italian city states of Renaissance Italy. The Treaty of Westphalia (1648), which led to the origins of the modern state system, arguably increased the need for mediation because of the anarchical nature of international society and the obvious limitations of international law as an instrument for resolving disputes between states.[2]

The past fifty years have seen an increase in the demand for mediators, partly because the international system changed profoundly during that period: the end of World War II, the emergence of the bipolarity of the Cold War, the rapid decolonization of vast areas of the globe, and the shift to the post–Cold War era. During the Cold War, mediators were used to positive effect in a number of major international crises. Over the years, the United States played a key role in successive mediation attempts to end the conflict between Israel and her Arab neighbors[3] and in various regional crises around the globe such as southern Africa.[4] The Soviet Union was only sporadically involved in mediation, notably in Tashkent in 1966 when it attempted to broker a settlement between India and Pakistan over Kashmir.[5]

Representatives of international and regional organizations also used their "good offices" on occasion to mediate an end to various conflicts, as in the efforts of the secretary-general of the United Nations to mediate an end to the Iran-Iraq war or successive rounds of UN mediation in Cyprus.[6] Even middle powers such as Canada and Algeria had their moments as mediators on the world stage. Canada played an important intermediary role in the 1956 Suez crisis. Algerian representatives played a vital role in helping to mediate an end to the U.S. hostage crisis in Iran.[7] But these instances of middle-power mediation tended to be the exception rather than the norm. At the same time, mediated interventions by the United Nations or regional organizations were hampered by the U.S.-Soviet rivalry.[8]

During the Cold War there were also various instances of mediation carried out by nongovernmental officials or representatives of various religious or secular institutions. The Vatican, for example, played a key role in mediating an end to the century-long dispute between Argentina and Chile over the Beagle Channel.[9] The International Committee of the Red Cross (ICRC) and the Quakers were involved in various humanitarian mediations in Africa's civil wars in the 1960s and 1970s.[10] However, mediated interventions of this kind were rare and generally confined to humanitarian objectives such as negotiating a temporary cease-fire that would allow food and medicine to be ferried to those in need.

A number of important developments in international politics have changed both the content and the nature of international mediation. Some of these developments can be traced to the end of the Cold War and bipolarity, but others are reflective of a more general trend of civil society engagement in the processes of international conflict management and resolution. First, the end of the Cold War has freed to some extent international organizations from their bipolar constraints and allowed them to take on new roles in mediation and conflict management.[11] Regional organizations, and coalitions of small and medium-sized powers, have also become more active as mediators, facilitators, and conflict managers.[12] Even in those situations in which great powers have intervened as a result of domestic political pressure or threatened national interests, there is seemingly a greater willingness to share the costs of intervention—military and political—with other states and international actors.[13]

Second, the widespread presence of religious, humanitarian, and development NGOs in countries and regions of conflict has created a third tier of actors beyond states and international organizations. NGOs not only seek to alleviate the plight of refugees and other victims of violent conflict but also see themselves as having the capacity, expertise, and knowledge to initiate a process of dialogue between warring parties and factions.[14] In some instances, outside governments, wishing to intervene politically to stop the fighting, are willing to support these groups because they offer an entry point into the conflict.

Third, the renewed interest in mediation as an instrument of conflict management is prompted by the recognition that civil or intercommunal conflict is not easily dealt with by other modes of conflict management, such as international legal tribunals, arbitration, or even the use of force, which is costly and has obvious limitations as an instrument of third-party intervention.[15] Mediation represents a relatively low-cost alternative between the choices of doing nothing and large-scale military intervention.[16]

Finally, it is arguably the case that international norms are changing. There does appear to be a growing sentiment that something must be done to prevent further eruptions of wide-scale intercommunal violence that threaten regional stability. Some of these sentiments are fueled by the media and the publicity given to the victims of genocide and civil war on television.[17] But there is also a growing sense of moral responsibility premised on the recognition that the international community has an interest in advancing human rights, democracy, and the rule of law because strengthening them will contribute to the development of a more peaceful and stable international order.[18]

## THE ELUSIVE DEFINITION OF MEDIATION

Definitions of mediation are as various as mediators themselves. Most, however, include the idea of a process undertaken by an outside party to bring or maintain peace. Some concentrate on the negotiation process itself. I. William Zartman and Saadia Touval state that "mediation is best thought of as a mode of negotiation in which a third party helps the parties find a solution which they cannot find by themselves."[19] Richard Bilder differentiates between the relatively passive activity of providing good offices and the more proactive role of the mediator: "Good offices and mediation are techniques by which the parties, who are unable to resolve a dispute by negotiation, request or agree to limited intervention by a third party to help them break an impasse. In the case of good offices, the role of the third party is usually limited simply to bringing the parties into communication and facilitating their negotiations. In the case of mediation, the mediator usually plays a more active part in facilitating communication and negotiation between the parties and is sometimes permitted or expected to advance informal and nonbinding proposals of his or her own."[20]

In his attempt to define mediation, Jacob Bercovitch puts forward a wide interpretation while still linking it to the negotiation process: "Mediation is . . . a process of conflict management, related to but distinct from the parties' own negotiations, where those in conflict seek the assistance of, or accept an offer of help from, an outsider (whether an individual, an organization, a group, or a state) to change their perceptions or behavior, and to do so without resorting to physical force or invoking the authority of law."[21]

James Laue broadens the reach of the mediator to include assisting "the parties in their negotiations or other problem-solving interaction,"[22] a theme that Christopher Mitchell takes up in his definition of mediation as "intermediary activity . . . undertaken by a third party with the primary intention of achieving some compromise settlement of the issues at stake between the parties, or at least ending disruptive conflict behavior."[23]

The same range of definition appears in discussions of negotiation, and the activities that lead to negotiation. I. William Zartman uses the term "prenegotiation" to describe the activities engaged in after one party has decided that negotiation is an option but before the actual negotiation takes place.[24] This term has the virtue of delimiting by time and activity actions directly relevant to a negotiation. However, prenegotiation does not capture all the practices undertaken before and after a negotiation by official and nonofficial bodies to bring parties to a realization that negotiation is an option, and to keep them committed to the negotiated agreement after it has been reached. Harold Saunders's neologism, "circum-negotiation," defined as "the tasks apart from negotiation that have the purpose of beginning, sustaining, and nourishing a process by changing relationships and paving the way for negotiation or other peaceful steps to resolve conflict,"[25] attempts to encompass these many practices. Pertinent to this volume, many of the tasks he identifies are precisely those undertaken by third parties in order to support movement toward and commitment to a settlement.[26]

The question of which organization makes the most effective mediator at which point in the conflict cycle is addressed in depth in the next chapter of this book. It is important to point out, however, that the answer to that question depends in part on which definition of mediation is used. For instance, if the definition of mediation includes a broad array of actions to build a constituency for peace, then many organizations, including nonofficial actors, are important to the mediation effort at every phase of the conflict cycle. If, on the other hand, the definition includes an ability to mobilize international resources and political will and to offer incentives and threats to warring parties to change their behavior, then state actors will be the principal players with nonofficial organizations operating at the margins.

## MULTIPARTY MEDIATION

One of the reasons that scholars continue to debate the definition of mediation and its range of activities is that the practice of mediation is evolving in response to changing circumstances. The increase in peacemaking efforts and in the variety of organizations and individuals who undertake them has stretched the meaning of mediation. A U.S. president appoints a special envoy for East Africa who may play a valuable role in preventing conflict by embodying both great power and international interest in keeping the peace and by using that leverage to stop an escalation in violence. A humanitarian NGO, using a combination of education, persuasion, and focused deployment of resources, plays a pivotal role in inducing local agencies to implement portions of a peace treaty. While these may not be examples of mediation in the narrow sense, they are political interventions between warring parties in support of political solutions to contested issues.

Along with an expansion in the numbers and activities of third-party intervenors in conflict, there has been a rise in what we call "multiparty mediation"—situations involving multiple mediators, whether sequential, simultaneous, or "composite" mediatory actors such as the United Nations or the Organization for Security and Cooperation in Europe. This aspect—the added layers of complexity for all the parties involved in a mediated negotiation—complicates any mediator's job, raising the question of who is in charge of the mediation and offering parties alternative venues for their lobbying. It can also, however, mean opportunity for moving a peace process forward, as using an alternative channel may allow stalled talks to restart or may serve to develop support for already negotiated options.

Multiparty mediation refers in this volume to attempts by many third parties to assist peace negotiations in any given conflict. These attempts may occur sequentially—one institution at a time—over the life of the conflict, or may occur simultaneously, involving many different mediators with various institutional bases on the ground at the same time, as happened in 1997 in Zaire. Diplomatic interventions by intergovernmental organizations or coalitions are in themselves multiparty mediations. In these circumstances, the mediation is on behalf of a number of sovereign states, each of which has its own objectives, interests, priorities, and domestic constraints.

Multiparty mediation may also refer to a number of attempts at mediation by different actors over the life cycle of the conflict. In the early stages of a conflict, for example, nonofficial groups may be the only third parties active in the attempt to bring groups together or to alert the international community to the need for preventive diplomacy or some kind of action. If the conflict has escalated to full-scale violence, however, mediation may be undertaken by an international organization or by a representative of a national government who has the necessary influence and ability to move the parties to the conflict toward a negotiated solution. After a conflict is over or a negotiated settlement has been reached, many outside organizations may be involved in a postconflict situation, sustaining implementation of agreements reached by the parties, as has been the case in Bosnia.

To recap, multiparty mediation may be undertaken by international or regional organizations, national governments, and nongovernmental organizations. It may also be undertaken by a collective body such as a coalition of states that represent more than one set of national interests. The mediations undertaken by a range of institutions may occur simultaneously or sequentially, and may involve a variety of mediators who intervene in the conflict at different times. Our definition of multiparty mediation therefore includes an important temporal component and is intended to suggest that more than one mediator may be involved in a conflict at any given point in time or over the total life cycle of the conflict itself. The concept of multiparty mediation refers to simultaneous interventions by more than one mediator in a conflict, interventions by composite actors such as regional organizations or contact groups, as well as sequential mediated interventions that again involve more than one party.[27]

The term "multiparty," therefore, has a triple meaning, and we recognize at the outset that the range of issues associated with multiparty interventions in a sequential setting may well differ from those where various mediators intervene in the same conflict at the same time. That being so, we also recognize that some conflicts may include mediated interventions that comprise both components, that is, simultaneous and sequential interventions that occur during more than one phase of the conflict.

## Practitioner Case Studies in Multiple Mediation

The case studies in this volume reflect a wide range of real, hands-on experience about mediation in complex settings and, through this experience, aim to provide answers to theoretical and practical questions.

Our hope is that such cases will serve to illustrate how multiple mediation works or does not work, and to stimulate further attention to the special requirements and best practices attendant on success. In looking to lessons about multiparty mediation, we have tried to promote a dialogue between practitioners and academics on the obstacles and achievements of multiparty mediation. In doing so, we have posed a number of questions to the practitioners, asking them to reflect on their mediation experience.[28]

Some of those questions were pragmatic and related to institutional settings and various political and bureaucratic constraints on the mediator. Other questions, in varying degrees, were intended to shed light on some of the broader debates in the policy and scholarly literature about mediation bargaining strategies, operational and organizational settings, and effectiveness.

The case studies were selected for the insights that they could give into the complexities of mediating in a multiparty setting. There is a broad geographical sweep, extending from Peru and Ecuador, El Salvador, and Haiti through Northern Ireland, Bosnia, Tajikistan, the Middle East, Angola, Zaire, Mozambique, and Burundi to Cambodia and the South China Sea. To reflect our belief that mediation can be an effective peacemaking mechanism throughout the conflict cycle, we have also selected examples that show how diplomatic intervention can (a) prevent conflict from erupting, (b) intervene in an active conflict in order to bring about a settlement, and (c) facilitate the implementation of a negotiated agreement.

The cases also include a variety of institutional bases for the mediation effort. A number are cases of political intervention by a single state, using all the persuasive and dissuasive resources available to a unitary actor, well illustrated by James Baker's description of putting together the Madrid peace talks. Others, such as the Zairean and Cambodian cases and the Lusaka phase of the long Angolan conflict, describe the mediation from the point of view of a coalition of single states acting alone or in support of a UN effort. In these cases, the resources of the individual states still affect the mediation, but more indirectly. Although they can be effective, these coalitions also run the risk of breaking down over differences among the coalition partners and often depend, as the Namibia/Angola case shows, on the commitment and determination of a single state to carry the effort forward.

Some of the chapters describe mediation by international actors composed of—and ultimately representing—member states, as was the case with the United Nations in El Salvador, and Aldo Ajello's experience in Mozambique. These organizations often compensate for a lack of actual resources through their moral suasion and their access to powerful member states. How credible this position is depends on many factors: how important it is to the conflict parties to have a multilateral—not state-based—stamp of approval; the mediator's ability to satisfy the organization's member states; and their capacity to move their sometimes cumbersome organizations along. And finally, some of the cases—for instance, Harold Saunders's chapter on the nonofficial dialogue process in Tajikistan—illustrate the powerful, but mostly indirect, role that nongovernmental organizations can play in mediation, reflecting their ability to use their long-term relationship building to give voice—and sometimes action—to a civil desire for peace.

Chapter 2 will outline two basic conceptions of mediation—as third-party-assisted negotiation and as a force for change of perception on both individual and societal bases. Those two conceptions permeate the cases in this volume. While a number of the writers, for instance, James Baker, Paul Hare, and Alvaro de Soto, reflect an understanding of mediation as outside assistance to a negotiation, tied specifically to the prenegotiation and negotiation periods, several other writers, including Harold Saunders, Paul Arthur, Andrea Bartoli, Max van der Stoel, and Hasjim Djalal and Ian Townsend-Gault, reflect a broader interpretation of the mediator's role and the essential tasks performed by mediating bodies. Although most of the writers do indeed concentrate on a negotiation process, they evince an awareness that a mediated settlement is only partly achieved inside the negotiation chamber, and that many an agreement has fallen apart because the mediator and the parties failed to prepare their publics for peace.

That said, this volume represents the collective experience of individuals who were involved in a specific type of conflict intervention, that is, the part that operationally intervenes as mediator directly between warring parties or between others who are closely connected to the warring parties. We are not in this project attempting to cover the entire range of potential conflict management interventions, many of which feature lead roles for track-two groups and individuals with potential impact on all phases of the conflict. Rather, we are focusing on multiparty mediation efforts of the track-one variety—involving official organizations—or of a variety that might be termed "track-one-and-a-half," which would involve nonofficial organizations acting with the blessing and tacit or open support of the track-one—or the official—effort.

We are also not attempting to join the debate on the ethics of mediation. Serious ethical considerations are involved in the decision to offer or to accept to provide mediation services in someone else's conflict as well as in the decision not to intervene, especially for those actors who are in a position to make a real difference. Equally, ethical consequences are involved in the formulation of the mediation strategy, in the composition of the mediation team, in the selection of which parties to include in the negotiations, or in the broader activities that sometimes fall under the heading of mediation. Many chapters in this book do take up these issues, either directly or indirectly. The lessons drawn from the individuals reacting to specific circumstances in specific conflicts demonstrate the choices that have to be made between peace and justice, between punishing warmongers and gaining their support for the negotiations, between sticking with a messy negotiation and walking away from a potentially explosive peace settlement, between personal inclination and the unpalatable alternatives that many conflicts present.

These ethical questions, as well as the hundreds of strategic and practical decisions that the case studies describe, highlight a fact that is lost when reading about these mediatory efforts in the media or in scholarly journals. Mediation is a very personal activity and reflects not only the individual capabilities of the mediator or the mediation team, but also the personal credibility and relationships that the third party develops with the parties to the conflict. Although we focus in this book on the institutional capacity to mediate conflicts, we are always aware that it is the personal attributes of the individual mediators plus their interaction with their institutions that really define the mediation effort.

One of the important subthemes of this volume is the importance of the exchange between academics and practitioners in understanding mediation. The insights that come out of the case studies are lessons learned by individuals who struggled with similar questions and situations. They arrived at their answers not in the abstract but through developing strategies and testing their ideas in the high-stakes laboratory of conflict intervention. Scholars, however, have added a great deal to our understanding about mediation and the mediation process, including possible intervention points and appropriate techniques. The volume, therefore, will move between these two worlds. Chapter 2 will review the scholarly literature, examining some of the main analytical approaches to the study of mediation and developing some of the ideas that arise from this scholarly research. The third chapter is different from the second, returning to the practitioner world. It has its origin in a daylong discussion among chapter authors on important elements of mediation. The juxtaposition of chapters 2 and 3 illustrates the different perspectives and interests of the academic and practitioner communities, but also points to a few areas of convergence and many areas for further research. At the end of the volume, chapter 25—the conclusion—will take up themes from both chapters and offer our thoughts on requirements for effective mediation in a multiparty setting.

In between the introductory chapters and the conclusion lie the case studies. Chapters 4 through 24 contain a wealth of stories, insights, and reflections from individuals who have worked and continue to work to bring peace to conflicts around the world. This collection of cases constitutes a rich source of material for both academics and practitioners, providing the basis for further inquiry and research into the practice of peacemaking, as well as inspiring and instructing mediators in the difficult craft of making peace in complex international conflicts.

In order to emphasize the point that there are many opportunities for third-party mediation in the course of a conflict, we have broken the cases into three groups: mediation to prevent conflict from breaking out, mediation during or after hot conflict to assist in the actual peace negotiations, and mediation during the settlement and postconflict phase to help in the implementation of a peace agreement. A number of chapters straddle the lines defined by the table of contents, treating, for instance, both the mediation of a settlement and implementation issues. However, our tripartite structure allows us to examine when and why different third-party mediators are able to gain entry and play effective peacemaking roles over the entire life cycle of a conflict, and thereby adds to our understanding of what works and what does not work in a multiparty mediation. In addition, in order to allow the reader to quickly grasp key elements, a short summary precedes each case history, describing the context of the intervention, the principal players, and significant outcomes.

## NOTES

1. Thucydides, *History of the Peloponnesian War,* trans. Thomas Hobbes (Chicago: University of Chicago Press, 1989).

2. Jacob Bercovitch, J. Theodore Anagnoson, and Donnette L. Willie, "Some Contextual Issues and Empirical Trends in the Study of Successful Mediation in International Relations," *Journal of Peace Research* 28, no. 1 (1991): 7–17.

3. Efraim Inbar, "Great Power Mediation: The USA and the May 1983 Israeli-Lebanese Agreement," *Journal of Peace Research* 28, no. 1 (1991): 71–84; Sidney Dawson Bailey, *Four Arab-Israeli Wars and the Peace Process* (London: Macmillan, 1990); Saadia Touval, *The Peace Brokers: Mediators in the Arab-Israeli Conflict, 1948–1979* (Princeton, N.J.: Princeton University Press, 1982); Jeffrey Z. Rubin, ed., *Dynamics of Third-Party Intervention: Kissinger in the Middle East* (New York: Praeger, 1981).

4. Chester A. Crocker, *High Noon in Southern Africa* (New York: W. W. Norton, 1992); David R. Smock and Chester A. Crocker, eds., *African Conflict Resolution: The U.S. Role in Peacemaking* (Washington, D.C.: United States Institute of Peace Press, 1995); Stephen Chan and Vivienne Jabri, *Mediation in Southern Africa* (London: Macmillan, 1993).

5. Thomas Perry Thornton, "The Indo-Pakistani Conflict: Soviet Mediation in Tashkent, 1966," in *International Mediation in Theory and Practice*, ed. Saadia Touval and I. William Zartman (Boulder, Colo.: Westview Press, 1985), 141–171.

6. Diane Bendahmane and John MacDonald, eds., *Perspectives on Negotiation* (Washington, D.C.: Foreign Service Institute, 1986).

7. Bousetta Allouche, "La mediation des petits états: Retrospective et perspective," *Etudes Internationales*, no. 25 (June 1994): 213–236; Gary Sick, "The Partial Negotiator: Algeria and the U.S. Hostages in Iran," in *International Mediation in Theory and Practice*, ed. Touval and Zartman, 21–66; Warren Christopher et al., *American Hostages in Iran: The Conduct of a Crisis* (New Haven, Conn.: Yale University Press, a Council on Foreign Relations Book, 1985).

8. Raimo Vayrynen, "The United Nations and the Resolution of International Conflicts," *Cooperation and Conflict* 20, no. 3 (1985): 141–171; Oran Young, *The Intermediaries: Third Parties in International Crises* (Princeton, N.J.: Princeton University Press, 1967).

9. Thomas Princen, *Intermediaries in International Conflict* (Princeton, N.J.: Princeton University Press, 1992).

10. C. H. Mike Yarrow, *Quaker Experiences in International Conciliation* (New Haven, Conn.: Yale University Press, 1978); David P. Forsythe, "Humanitarian Mediation by the International Committee of the Red Cross," in *International Mediation in Theory and Practice*, ed. Touval and Zartman, 233–250.

11. Barry M. Blechman, "Emerging from the Intervention Dilemma," in *Managing Global Chaos: Sources of and Responses to International Conflict*, ed. Chester A. Crocker and Fen Osler Hampson, with Pamela Aall (Washington, D.C.: United States Institute of Peace Press, 1996), 287–296; J. William Durch, ed., *The Evolution of UN Peacekeeping: Case Studies and Comparative Analysis* (New York: St. Martin's Press, 1993); J. William Durch, *UN Peacekeeping, American Policy, and the Uncivil Wars of the 1990s* (New York: St. Martin's Press, 1996); Kjell Skjelsbaek, "The UN Secretary-General and the Mediation of International Disputes," *Journal of Peace Research* 28, no. 1 (1991): 99–115.

12. Ruth Wedgwood, "Regional and Subregional Organizations in International Conflict Management," in *Managing Global Chaos*, ed. Crocker and Hampson, with Aall, 275–286.

13. Amitai Etzioni, "Mediation as a World Role for the United States," *Washington Quarterly* 18, no. 2 (summer 1995): 75–87.

14. Thomas G. Weiss, *The United Nations and Civil Wars* (Boulder, Colo.: Lynne Reinner, 1996); Christopher Mitchell, "The Process and Stages of Mediation," in *Making War and Waging Peace: Foreign Intervention in Africa*, ed. Chester A. Crocker and David R. Smock (Washington, D.C.: United States Institute of Peace Press, 1994), 139–159; Hizkias Assefa, *Mediation of Civil Wars: Approaches and Strategies—the Sudan Conflict* (Boulder, Colo.: Westview Press, 1987); I. William Zartman, ed., *Elusive Peace: Negotiating an End to Civil Wars* (Washington, D.C.: Brookings Institution, 1995).

15. Jacob Bercovitch and Allison Houston, "The Study of International Mediation: Theoretical Issues and Empirical Evidence," in *Resolving International Conflicts: The Theory and Practice of Mediation*, ed. Jacob Bercovitch (Boulder, Colo.: Lynne Reinner, 1996), 11–35;

Richard B. Bilder, "Adjudication: International Tribunals and Courts," in *Resolving International Conflicts*, ed. Bercovitch, 155–190; Michael Brown, *International Dimensions of Internal Conflict* (Cambridge, Mass.: MIT Press, 1996).

16. Jacob Bercovitch, *Social Conflicts and Third Parties: Strategies of Conflict Resolution* (Boulder, Colo.: Westview Press, 1984); Jacob Bercovitch, "International Mediation: A Study of the Incidence, Strategies, and Conditions of Successful Outcomes," *Cooperation and Conflict* 21, no. 3 (1986): 155–168.

17. Warren P. Strobel, *Late Breaking Foreign Policy* (Washington, D.C.: United States Institute of Peace Press, 1997).

18. David Cortright, *The Price of Peace: Incentives and International Conflict Prevention* (Lanham, Md.: Rowman and Littlefield, 1997); Lori Fisler Damrosch, *Enforcing Restraint: Collective Intervention in Internal Conflicts* (New York: Council on Foreign Relations, 1993); Tom Hadden, "The Role of International Agencies in Conflict Resolution: Some Lessons from the Irish Experience," *Bulletin of Peace Proposals* 18, no. 4 (1987): 567–572.

19. I. William Zartman and Saadia Touval, "International Mediation in the Post–Cold War Era," in *Managing Global Chaos*, ed. Crocker, Hampson, and Aall, 446.

20. Richard Bilder, "International Third-Party Dispute Settlement," in *Approaches to Peace: An Intellectual Map*, ed. W. Scott Thompson and Kenneth M. Jensen, with Richard N. Smith and Kimber M. Schraub (Washington, D.C.: United States Institute of Peace, 1992), 198.

21. Jacob Bercovitch, "Mediation in International Conflict," in *Peacemaking in International Conflict: Methods and Techniques*, ed. I. William Zartman and J. Lewis Rasmussen (Washington, D.C.: United States Institute of Peace Press, 1997), 130.

22. James Laue, "Contributions of the Emerging Field of Conflict Resolution," in *Approaches to Peace*, ed. Thompson and Jensen, with Smith and Schraub, 314.

23. C. R. Mitchell, *The Structure of International Conflict* (New York: St. Martin's Press, 1981), 287.

24. I. William Zartman, "Prenegotiation: Phases and Functions," in *Getting to the Table: The Processes of International Prenegotiation*, ed. Janice Gross Stein, (Baltimore, Md.: Johns Hopkins University Press, 1989), 1–17.

25. Harold Saunders, "Prenegotiation and Circum-negotiation," in *Managing Global Chaos*, ed. Crocker and Hampson, with Aall, 421.

26. These tasks include being "instigator, communicator, persuader, organizer, precipitator, legitimizer, convenor, moderator, manager, funder, teacher, idea formulator." Ibid., 425.

27. For further discussion, an excellent synopsis of the challenges of multiparty mediation can be found in Louis Kriesberg, "Coordinating Intermediary Peace Efforts," *Negotiation Journal* 12, no. 4 (October 1996): 341–352. Clive Archer, "Conflict Prevention in Europe: The Case of the Nordic States and Macedonia," *Cooperation and Conflict*, no. 29 (December 1994): 367–386; Victor H. Umbricht, *Multilateral Mediation: Practical Experiences and Lessons* (The Hague: Martinus Nijhoff, 1989).

28. These questions include:
    • What were the aims and objectives of the mediated intervention and at what points in the conflict cycle did it occur?

- How and why did the individual or organization get involved in this particular conflict?
- What were the practical difficulties, dilemmas, or obstacles in the third party's efforts to carry out its mandate and meet its objectives?
- In the case of intergovernmental mediations, how did the involvement of a number of different governments affect the mediation effort?
- Did the objectives change during the course of the mediated intervention and why?
- Which actors or parties did the mediator work with most closely?
- How did that mediator see his or her role in relation to other third parties who were involved in the conflict? To the extent there was collaboration or cooperation, was it successful or not?
- Was mediation successful or not and why? What broader lessons about the conditions for successful mediation can be drawn from the case at hand and from the particular experience of that third party?

# 2

# Multiparty Mediation and the Conflict Cycle

CHESTER A. CROCKER, FEN OSLER HAMPSON, AND PAMELA AALL

**C**hapter 1 introduced this volume of case studies with a general discussion of the book's purposes, the changing context for mediation, the concept of multiparty mediation, the question of defining mediation, and the reasons why the editors have assembled a distinguished group of practitioners to prepare the cases. In this chapter, we develop further the volume's analytic and theoretical underpinnings in a more extended discussion of key issues in mediation theory. The purpose here is not to put forward a "new theory of mediation," but to situate the multiparty mediation phenomenon—a classic case of improvised and transitional policy practice—in the academic literature. The problems posed by multiparty mediation are, at one level, essentially problems of managing complexity, coordinating the use of comparative advantages, maximizing leverage, avoiding crossed wires and conflicting agendas, and maintaining focus and coherence. Stated another way, they are problems of leadership, whether of the intellectual, entrepreneurial, or structural variety, to use the terminology of Oran Young.[1]

At the same time, however, the problems posed by multiparty mediation can also help us explore under new light the categories and paradigms prevailing in this field. Rather than reinvent the wheels of mediation theory, we seek in this chapter to explore the possibility that multiparty mediation may add further weight to the need for a synthesis between what might be called the structuralist and social-psychological paradigms of mediation. We look at multiparty mediation from the standpoint of timing and conflict cycles, and seek to explore how the comparative contributions of different actors may unfold and what the strengths of different mediators are. But these ideas represent simply a suggestive and exploratory probe of an emerging phenomenon, one illustrated in rich variety and contextual detail in the ensuing case studies. The chapter concludes with a more general discussion of the particular practical and operational challenges posed by multiparty mediation and the implications for policy—a theme that is developed in chapter 3 and the chapters that follow.

## Two Paradigms of Mediation

Analyzing mediation raises some basic questions about what third parties can do in a conflict, under what circumstances, and to what effect. Oversimplified, the debate over these issues can be classified into two major paradigms: the structuralist and the social-psychological.[2] These two paradigms involve alternative assessments about appropriate bargaining strategies and entry points, as well as about comparative advantage, coordination, and leadership of different kinds of mediators. Each paradigm also points to a different set of conclusions about the possibilities for effective mediation when there is more than one mediator and the kinds of bargaining strategies that are likely to be most effective in a multiparty setting.

These paradigms are presented, however, with a lively awareness that in the real world, negotiators generally find themselves with a foot in each approach, and that choices are rarely as stark as suggested by each school's proponents. Furthermore, viewing the conflict in terms of a life cycle marked by different phases or stages opens up a wider range of possibilities for mediated interventions by a more inclusive set of actors and institutions than is contemplated by either school.

### The Structuralist Paradigm of Mediation

The structuralist paradigm is based on a belief that through the use of persuasion, incentives, and disincentives (i.e., a costing process), parties to a conflict can be led to and through a negotiated settlement. This paradigm, which is anchored in a rational choice view of the world, treats the causes of conflict as objective—as opposed to subjective—issues that can yield to negotiation. It is premised on the familiar notions of "ripeness" and "hurting stalemate" as advanced in the work of I. William Zartman, Richard Haass, and others. As defined by Haass, ripeness is associated with "the prerequisites for diplomatic progress, that is . . . particular circumstances . . . conducive for negotiated solution or even progress. Such prerequisites may include characteristics of the parties to a dispute as well as considerations about the relationship between or among parties."[3] Of the various factors that may make resolution more attractive, thereby enhancing the prospects for successful third-party intervention, Zartman suggests that the prime "condition" is if neither side in a conflict feels it can win a conflict and the parties perceive the costs and prospects of continuing war to be more burdensome than the costs and prospects of settlement.[4] The prospects for a negotiated settlement to a dispute are thus greater when war weariness has set in among the parties and a conflict has reached a plateau or hurting stalemate in which unilateral solutions are no longer believed to be credible or achievable.

Timing, of course, is all important if mediated interventions are to be successful and potential mediators are well advised, according to the theory of ripeness, to wait until the parties are sufficiently "exhausted" on the battlefield to push for a negotiated political settlement.[5] It may well be that in some circumstances the issue of who does the mediating is less important than the matter of timing and ripeness of the conflict itself.

In stressing the importance of timing, ripeness theory has its greatest utility in setting up benchmarks and signposts that help mediators calibrate their strategies to help ripen the conflict. Parties have to be coaxed or cajoled to the bargaining table through a combination of carrots and sticks, and skilled mediators use a variety of ripening agents: coaching, discrediting, legitimizing, making themselves indispensable, leaning and shifting weight, exploiting changes in military balance, exploiting changes in party leadership, as well as promises of resources or threats of withdrawal.[6]

Mediation therefore involves more than just assisting highly motivated parties in reaching a negotiated solution to their disputes. It also requires the use of various side payments and/or penalties and sanctions to get the parties to the dispute to change their cost-benefit calculations about the utility of a negotiated settlement.[7] Thus, what is required in some situations is what Saadia Touval calls "mediators with muscle."[8] According to this formulation, impartiality and objectivity are less important to achieving influence than "power potential considerations."[9] The ability to exercise leverage may also be positively influenced by close ties between a mediator and one or more parties to the dispute, thus allowing the mediator to elicit cooperative behavior and concessions.[10] The less "muscle" a mediator has, and the more removed or distant the mediator is from the conflict, the weaker will be the mediator's efforts.[11] How much leverage mediators must exercise to bring about a negotiated settlement before mediation strays into the realms of coercive diplomacy and, in effect, ceases to be mediation is a matter of some contention.[12]

Structuralists are generally silent on the question of whether one mediator is better than many. However, great powers are considered to be at an advantage when it comes to mediation because leverage depends on persuasion, extraction, termination, manipulation, and the ability to offer and withhold resources. Acting in concert, a coalition of great power mediators should in principle be able to exert greater leverage than a single state, but this assumes that the members of the coalition share similar goals and are willing to work together and not at cross-purposes. International organizations can potentially play an effective mediation role provided they enjoy the backing of key members and are not overwhelmed by other tasks. However, some argue that their ability to do so has been hampered by divisions among their most powerful members and ongoing problems of inadequate credibility and resources.[13]

### Social-Psychological Approaches

The second paradigm of third-party intervention in conflict focuses on the processes of communication and exchange as a way to change perceptions and attitudes. This approach to mediation centers on providing a forum in which parties can explore options and develop solutions, often outside the highly charged arena of a formal negotiating structure. The approach also involves appeals to superordinate goals and values. It plays on the parties' aspiration for legitimacy and their desire to be part of the broader political community. In this approach, the use of moral suasion and symbolic rewards or gestures is important. To this school, the establishment of a dialogue, of a pattern of exchanges and contacts between and among official parties or other influential representatives, helps set the stage for a lasting peace built on an agreement developed by the parties in a collaborative process. A key to this process is often the involvement in the dialogue not just of the principal political authorities but of a wider group of civil and opinion leaders whose support is essential for the long-term sustainability of the peace process.

One of the driving assumptions behind the social-psychological approach is that although parties identify specific issues as the causes of conflict, conflict also reflects subjective, phenomenological, and social fractures and, consequently, analyzing "interests" can be less important than identifying the underlying needs that govern each party's perception of the conflict.[14] Because much of human conflict is anchored in conflicting perceptions and in misperception, the contribution of third parties lies in changing the perceptions, attitudes, values, and behaviors of the parties to a conflict.[15] This process begins with interventions that allow conflict parties to glean a better understanding of the different dimensions of the conflict and works to develop means to allow them to recognize mutual gains and craft joint strategies toward a solution. Attitudinal change can be fostered through a variety of instruments including, for example, consultative meetings, problem-solving workshops, training in conflict resolution at the communal level, and third-party assistance in developing and designing other kinds of dispute resolution systems that are compatible with local culture and norms and are directed at elites at different levels within society.[16]

The objective of the problem-solving workshop is to create more open channels of communication that allow participants to see their respective intentions more clearly and to be more fully aware of their own reactions to the conflict.[17] Workshops are aimed at cultivating respect and objectivity so that the parties develop a mutual commitment to cooperative exchanges in their relationship. Based on findings that show that individuals are more disposed to cooperative behavior in small, informal, intergroup activities, the problem-solving workshop establishes relations among significant players who may be in a position to influence the parties to the conflict and, in so doing, to contribute to the de-escalation of conflict. The approach seems to work best if individuals are middle-range elites such as academics, advisers, ex-officials, or retired politicians who continue to have access to those in power. By helping to establish communications between parties at the subelite level, these workshops help to undermine "we-they" images of conflict, establish linkages among influentials, begin a discussion of framework solutions, identify steps that will break the impasse, and in general create an understanding of these steps and processes that participants can feed back into the track-one effort where actual decisions are made.

A somewhat different kind of premediation activity is third-party-assisted dialogue, undertaken by both official and nongovernmental structures. This activity is directed at ethnic, racial, or religious groups who are in a hostile or adversarial relationship.[18] Like "circum-negotiation," this dialogue occurs at a quasi-official level around or before the formal peace process.[19] Dialogue is directed at both officials and civic leaders, including heads of local nongovernmental organizations, community developers, health officials, refugee camp leaders, ethnic and religious leaders, intellectuals, and academics. This dialogue process can be assisted by specialized training programs that are directed at exploring ways of establishing and building relationships, furthering proficiency in facilitation, mediation, and brokering, data collection, fact-finding, and other kinds of cooperative decisionmaking. As Louis Kriesberg notes, much of this activity is focused on developing "constituency support for peace efforts."[20]

The practice of dialogue and communication is not confined to the nongovernmental sector, but in fact underlies the attempts of a number of regional organizations at mediation. In some instances lacking the resources of individual states or the United Nations, and in other instances reluctant to use the resources they have, regional organizations have used consultation, problem solving, dialogue, and a kind of moral example to shift perceptions and change attitudes among conflict parties. A prime example of the use of this approach is found in the conflict prevention work of the Organization for Security and Cooperation in Europe's High Commissioner on National Minorities, which is the focus of Max van der Stoel's chapter in this volume.

Social-psychological approaches to mediation attempt to find ways of establishing communication channels between different groups in society, initiating discussions of framework solutions to problems of mutual concern, identifying steps for breaking impasses, developing new norms, and creating an understanding of the kinds of decision-making processes that can lead parties out of conflict. In these kinds of activities, third parties are supposed to play a neutral and essentially facilitating role, enabling and encouraging a mutual-learning process rather than guiding or still less influencing and directing the parties to mutually acceptable approaches to problem solving. Their involvement is based on their expert and/or reputational authority or on their ability to represent a normative or real community to which the combatants aspire.

## TOWARD A SYNTHESIS OF PERSPECTIVES

The value of establishing paradigms is that they allow us to isolate and analyze the different assumptions and beliefs and consequent conclusions and patterns of behavior each school embraces. For instance, both structuralist and social-psychological approaches offer different insights into appropriate mediation intervention strategies. The structuralist school places considerable importance on the dynamics of conflict and the interests of the parties, arguing that mediated interventions that are not timed to coincide with hurting stalemates run a real risk of failure. Even so, there is a general consensus that ripeness is more of a cultivated and not just an inherited condition. In fact, mediators can deploy a myriad of techniques and measures to foster the ripening process in order to move the parties from a hurting stalemate to a political settlement. In addition to timing, it is crucial to have a strategy of peacemaking and mediation, to know how to move the parties, to have a sense of how they can be engaged in a process and how unripe conditions can be modified into riper ones, that is, to understand the dynamics of the conflict cycle and the point at which the mediator decides to enter it.

Social-psychological approaches stress the importance of changing attitudes and the creation of new norms in moving parties toward reconciliation. Early intervention, according to this formulation, is preferable because once relations have deteriorated because of violence, and attitudes are embedded in "we-they" images of the enemy, it becomes much more difficult for mediators to move the parties toward sober reflection about their real-world choices and to change perceptions.[21] These interventions, however, may take place at any point in the conflict cycle, because part of their function is to reach beyond elites to the level of civil society by creating mobilized domestic constituencies who are supportive of the peace process and are in a position to influence the policies and positions of those who hold power.

The trouble with establishing paradigms, on the other hand, is that they rarely translate well into reality. Another shortcoming of paradigms is that they can imply that one approach will be more successful than the others in dealing with all of the issues and events of the conflict cycle. The fact that more than one set of factors are at play in any given conflict argues against an intervention strategy that is directed at a single cause or at alleviating only one set of social or political pressures. As Charles King observes, there is a wide range of obstacles to settlement of civil wars.[22] He concludes that there is no single formula for all conflict, and external powers are likely to be more effective at reducing some obstacles (influencing key leaders, leveling organizational and status imbalances, and overcoming security dilemmas) than others. Similarly, Loraleigh Keashly and Ronald Fisher point out that protracted or intercommunal conflicts contain a large number of constituencies with different demands, interests, and belief systems. "With such a large number of elements, it seems unreasonable to expect that a single intervention strategy could deal with all of them. It seems more useful to envision intervention . . . as a coordinated series of concurrent and consecutive strategies directed towards the long-term goal of resolving the conflict."[23]

Such a sequencing strategy, which lends support to the proposition that more than one mediator may be required to help manage an ongoing conflict, is premised on the notion that most conflicts—even protracted ones—have a life cycle of their own, characterized by various phases or stages.[24] These include a period of rising tensions between or among parties, followed by confrontation, the outbreak of violence, and the escalation of military hostilities. In the postagreement or postsettlement phase, a conflict may go through several de-escalatory phases as well, such as a cease-fire, followed by a formal settlement, rapprochement, and eventual reconciliation. And in unfortunate cases, as the situation in Angola in the late 1980s and 1990s reminds us, some conflicts reverse themselves, doubling back into violence even in the implementation stage.[25]

During these various phases or stages of conflict, the intensity of the security dilemma among rival communal groupings is likely to vary. Parties will tend to feel more secure in their relations with other groupings when the level of violence is low, formal ties exist between different groups, and institutionalized channels of communication, though perhaps frayed, are still available. At this stage of the conflict cycle, there may well be more chances for mediation because attitudes and perceptions have not hardened and parties are still willing to talk to each other.[26] As Princen notes, negotiation at this stage is a relatively low-risk strategy for the disputants "because it is not equated with conceding."[27] The downside is that negotiated solutions will seem less attractive because the parties, having not yet experienced the full cost and limits of what can typically be achieved on the battlefield, may consider violence in support of unilateral goals to be a viable alternative to compromise and politically based solutions. This will tend to limit the mediator's leverage over the parties.

As violence increases, different groups start to arm themselves, and factions become increasingly aware of the real-power asymmetries that exist between themselves and other groups, the security dilemma will become more acute and the desire for peaceful and cooperatively based strategies of conflict will weaken.[28] This will tend to reduce the likely effectiveness of most potential mediators unless their mediation is linked to instruments of outright strategic leverage and coercive diplomacy, as was the case in orchestrating both the Madrid peace talks and the Namibia-Angola settlement.[29] Once violence has reached a threshold where no further escalation is possible without major costs, the disputants may be willing to consider other alternatives than the use of force. At this point, the alternatives to mediation have worsened. Although mediators may experience difficulty gaining entry to the conflict because of the sustained pattern of violence, once they do gain entry they will tend to have greater leverage—sometimes termed "procedural control"—over the negotiating process.[30]

However, for conflicts that fall within the middle range of the escalation curve—that is, violence is ongoing and episodic but not sufficient to make the idea of a political solution an attractive alternative to the status quo—mediators will have to work harder to convince parties to accept mediation and to develop the credibility and leverage to engage the parties in a meaningful exploration of options. Such conflicts are sometimes referred to as "protracted social conflicts" because they are marked by self-sustaining patterns of hostility and violence with no apparent end in sight.[31] Lacking any apparent deadline, impending disaster, or sense of time shifting to the other side's advantage, these conflicts can be sustained for years. For third parties intent on offering their mediation services and other "good offices," it may be difficult to identify a formula or pattern in which issues can be resolved in order to lend momentum to the peacemaking process. And in situations that get frozen by previous interventions—Cyprus is an obvious case in point—there must be an intervening shock to the system to drive the parties out of the comfort zone, or it may be necessary to wait for a change in leadership or for broader attitudinal change.

In sum, the notion of a conflict cycle suggests that while the level of violence is low (a condition that may occur at the beginning and at the end of a conflict cycle), there are greater opportunities for a variety of mediators to engage both the parties and the larger society in a wide range of activities. These conditions, however, present fewer opportunities for a real movement toward settlement on disputed issues. As one approaches higher levels of violence, the opportunities for mediators to engage the parties may diminish, but the likelihood of mediation success, that is, helping the parties to negotiate an agreement, may well increase as the conflict reaches a plateau or what Zartman calls a hurting stalemate (see table 1). The escalatory and de-escalatory dynamics of the conflict cycle therefore suggest that there is an inverse relationship between opportunities to engage the players in a political dialogue and opportunities to give direct assistance to a peace negotiation process.

In examining this table, it is important to remember that mediators gain or fail to gain entry into a conflict for a variety of reasons besides the level of violence and the hardening of attitudes. Outside actors, particularly great powers, also may not want to intervene because the costs and risks of intervention outweigh any perceived potential political benefits for them.[32] The parties themselves may wish to exclude international organizations and great powers from mediation at low levels of conflict because they fear that interventions by these actors will complicate the issues and raise the stakes in ways that further polarize attitudes.[33] Equally, if parties consider interventions

Table 1. Entry Points in the Conflict Cycle

| Level of Violence | Number of Potential Entry Points | Barriers to Entry | Opportunity to Exercise Procedural Control |
|---|---|---|---|
| Low | Many<br><br>(Perceptions and attitudes have not hardened.) | Low–Medium<br><br>(Parties are open to consultation with many different third parties; may avoid high-level mediators.) | Low<br><br>(Parties are not yet prepared to eschew violence if demands cannot be met through negotiation.) |
| Rising | Declining<br><br>(Perceptions and attitudes are hardening.) | Medium–High<br><br>(Parties perceive increasing risks of negotiation, coupled with status and legitimacy concerns.) | Low<br><br>(Parties still believe that they have the option of escalating conflict and/or accepting resulting costs/losses.) |
| High | Few<br><br>("We-they" images of the enemy have hardened.) | High<br><br>(Parties are locked into a continuing struggle.) | Moderate-High<br><br>(Alternatives to mediation have worsened as conflict reaches a plateau or "hurting stalemate.") |
| Declining in the aftermath of a peace settlement | Rising<br><br>(Perceptions and attitudes may be softening.) | Low–Medium<br><br>(The settlement provides openings for a variety of third-party mediators.) | Moderate–High<br><br>(Parties may be more willing to sustain the negotiation process at different levels, but danger of spoilers persists.) |

to be unwarranted intrusions in the internal affairs of a state, the mediator's possibilities for action may also be limited.[34] This is not to say that great-power intervention is undesirable or should be avoided at lower rungs on the escalatory ladder—sometimes, a dramatic intervention or shock is just what is needed to bring the parties to their senses and avert violent conflict and effectively to engage the parties in a process that limits their options—

but there may well be some resistance to early mediated interventions by the parties themselves depending on who is doing the mediating.

## COMPARATIVE ADVANTAGE OF DIFFERENT KINDS OF MEDIATORS

What are the implications of this hypothesis of the inverse relationship between mediator opportunity and mediator effectiveness? Do some mediators have a greater comparative advantage over others in gaining entry, initiating dialogue, and/or bringing the parties to settlement at different points along the escalation curve? And if so, what does this mean for the multiparty mediation in which many actors may be trying to influence the course of peacemaking?

Jeffrey Rubin has suggested that there are several different kinds of resources and influence that mediators can bring to the negotiating table and that these are related to six different bases of power:

- reward power, when the mediator has something to offer to the parties such as side payments in exchange for changes in behavior;
- coercive power that relies on threats and sanctions to carry those threats out, again with the intention of changing the behavior of the parties;
- expert power that is based on the mediator's greater knowledge and experience with certain issues;
- legitimate power that is based on certain rights and legally sanctioned authority under international law;
- referent power that is based on a desire of the parties to the conflict to maintain a valued relationship with the mediator; and
- informational power that works on the content of the information conveyed as in the case of a go-between or message carrier.[35]

As Rubin and others have argued, whereas private individuals and nongovernmental mediators are low in reward and coercive power capabilities, they may be strong in expert and referent power capabilities.[36] The scholar-practitioner also tends to enjoy high levels of reputational authority, which itself creates its own form of legitimacy. Regional and international organizations tend to enjoy legitimate power because they speak with the authority of their members,[37] but they also tend to be weak on the reward and coercive power dimensions.[38] The most powerful states in the international system generally tend to have strong reward and coercive power capabilities, although their hegemonic status may, in some instances, weaken their legitimacy and informational power capabilities because they are not trusted by one or more of the parties.

How an organization is structured and to whom or what it is ultimately accountable also have consequences for the efficacy of the mediation effort.

Johannes Botes and Christopher Mitchell perceive a "paradox" in which a mediator's flexibility and freedom from constraints imposed by internal structure and constituency demands shape both the methods and the potential effectiveness of a mediation: the absence of constraint widens the choice of possible conflicts to be tackled, entry points, tactics, and approaches. Yet at the same time, this absence of constraint is generally associated with an absence of capacity and, hence, flexibility, to bring influence to bear on the conflicting parties.[39]

These remarks highlight the varying bargaining capabilities and resources as well as perceived legitimacy of different mediators. They also point to the importance of the mediator's own organizational environment and institutional setting—a theme that is developed in the conclusion to this volume. Such differences, however, may enable disparate organizations to perform widely varying roles depending on where the conflict stands on the escalation curve or conflict life cycle. When violence is low, parties may handle disputes on their own or consider interventions by a wide range of mediators, including various nonstate actors. However, the extent to which parties to the conflict are willing to resort to violence if negotiations fail limits mediator leverage, and these third parties will face an uphill struggle keeping the negotiations on course. Mediation efforts at this level should therefore be directed at "lengthening the shadow of the future"[40] by dramatizing the long-term costs of violence to the parties if negotiations fail. Ideally, they should also be directed at changing the attitudes of the parties by creating domestic constituencies that are supportive of negotiation and political as opposed to military options. This analysis therefore points to the real potential of a multiple-track mediation strategy that is directed at both elites and various factions and groups within civil society, that is, a series of simultaneous mediated interventions by governmental and nongovernmental mediators that are targeted at different groups in the conflict.[41]

The middle range of the conflict curve is typically resistant to entry because the conflicting parties' attitudes and perceptions have hardened toward each other with the escalation of violence. Opportunities to exercise effective leverage by would-be mediators is limited because the conflict has not yet reached a level where the parties are prepared seriously to explore negotiation as a viable option to a continued unilateral pursuit of military options. Where sovereignty and recognition issues lie at the heart of conflict, one of the main challenges is to establish direct communication between the parties in order to initiate a process of prenegotiation. Various nongovernmental actors and scholars-practitioners may enjoy a comparative advantage in this sort of task because they can help to establish informal channels of communication without compromising the interests of the parties or formally committing them to a politically risky course of action.

That being said, once entry is gained and communication between the parties involving some kind of mutual recognition is established, mediators who exercise reward and coercive power will likely have to be brought into the formal negotiating process. This is because offers of side payments, or coercive threats such as sanctions and the use of force by an external third party, and the full panoply of leverage-based diplomatic mediation techniques may be required to change the cost-benefit calculus of warring parties away from violence to a consideration of various political alternatives.[42] Absent these externally induced incentives, parties will have little incentive to come to the table and may, in fact, be willing to escalate the conflict in the hope of achieving their objectives. It is at this stage of conflict when entry points are few and leverage is limited that a combined strategy that draws on the different resources and influence of different kinds of mediators may be most valuable.

In situations of medium to high levels of protracted conflict and violence where parties are deadlocked and yet worried enough to consider direct communication without preconditions, track-two initiatives by small powers or nongovernmental organizations (NGOs) can assist with prenegotiation processes and negotiation as in the case of Norway's role in the Oslo peace talks between Israelis and Palestinians (see Jan Egeland's chapter in this volume). But such interventions, if they are to be translated into concrete agreements, require concerted engagement and follow-up by states or groups of states.

The use of sanctions and side payments may also be required to bring the parties to the table. Creative uses of shifting military balances on the ground can become a key ingredient in the arsenal of this kind of mediation. As in the case of NATO air strikes in Bosnia, discussed later, the use of force against recalcitrant elements who refuse to come to the table may be critical to prenegotiation strategies[43] and even to formal negotiations as in the case of the Carter-Nunn-Powell mediation in Haiti, which is the subject of Robert Pastor's chapter in this volume.

At the upper end of the escalation curve, a different kind of mediator with muscle may be called for as the mediator is required to develop and deploy those pressures and inducements that keep the mediation moving forward and present or deter parties from exiting or blowing up the process. Also, mediators will often be expected to come up with innovative and credible ideas for confidence-building measures, cease-fire monitoring, verification proposals to assure that commitments are being carried out, and other forms of political guarantee that help address the most difficult security dilemmas faced by the parties.

Where further escalation is not possible, or at least not possible without greatly raising costs, the warring parties' alternatives to a mediated solution may appreciably, perhaps dramatically, worsen. Success depends on mediators who can exercise effective procedural control and carry out the following tasks: meeting with stakeholders to assess their interests, helping to choose spokespersons or teach leaders, identifying missing groups or strategies for representing diffuse interests, drafting protocols and setting agendas, suggesting options, identifying and testing possible tradeoffs, writing and ratifying agreements, and monitoring and facilitating the implementation of those agreements.[44]

It would be wrong to suggest that these kinds of skills are tied to the capabilities and resources of a single kind of actor in international politics. Great powers, middle- and small-sized powers, and international and regional organizations have all at one time or another played this kind of role although demonstrable qualities of leadership are essential.[45] Given the complexity of the assignment, organizational capacity, staying power, and flexibility are also key to the multitasking needs of this kind of mediation.

Based on the preceding analysis, table 2 links mediators to activities that they may undertake effectively at different levels of violence.

This classification of mediators, entry points, and their respective comparative advantage should not, however, be taken too literally. That more than one set of factors are at play in any given conflict argues against a mediation intervention strategy that is directed at a single cause or at alleviating only one set of social or political pressures. The list of causes in any conflict is long, and different third-party intervenors may enjoy different kinds of comparative advantage depending on the actual situation at hand and the specific issues that lie at the heart of a particular dispute. Furthermore, some situations may be more ripe for certain kinds of intervention than others, depending on who does the intervening. The kinds of confidence-building measures set in motion by mediators will also vary from one setting to another depending on the intensity of the conflict and the pressures that are brought to bear on the disputants themselves.

As noted previously, it is important to recognize that effective third-party mediation also depends on the mediator's capabilities and leverage, as well as the linkage between the third party and the conflict and the extent to which the mediators see themselves as stakeholders. Those third parties that are not stakeholders in the conflict or do not have a relationship with the parties may have greater difficulty engaging them than those who do. It

Table 2. Type of Third-Party Assistance and the Conflict Cycle

| Level of Violence | Type of Third-Party Assistance | Mediators | Multiparty Initiative |
|---|---|---|---|
| Low | Track-two diplomacy is coupled with track-one diplomacy. | Eminent private persons, scholar-practitioners, NGOs, international and regional organizations. | Simultaneous |
| Rising | Track-two diplomacy gains entry and assists with prenegotiation-negotiation followed by track-one "mediation with muscle." | Scholar-practitioner, NGOs for pre- and postnegotiation; great powers or coalitions for formal negotiation. | Sequenced |
| High | Track-one diplomacy, and much more rarely track-two organizations, gain entry and conduct mediation. | Great powers, international and regional organizations for formal negotiation; occasionally, eminent private persons, scholar-practitioners, and NGOs. | Sequenced |
| Declining | Track-two diplomacy, especially at civil society level, is coupled with continuing need for track-one diplomacy. | NGOs, international and regional organizations, and/or other mediators involved in earlier peace process. | Simultaneous |

may well take several false starts to figure out what works, what does not, and who has the most to offer as a third-party mediator. Most conflicts may, in fact, cry out for more than one set of hands at the tiller. The fact that more than one mediator may be involved in a conflict as it moves through the various stages of the conflict life cycle also suggests that maintaining coherence, coordinating and sequencing initiatives, and having staying power are essential in any sort of multiparty mediated intervention. These are operational aspects that have hitherto received relatively little attention in the mediation literature but which are the focus of the discussion in chapter 3.

## THE WARS IN THE BALKANS: AN ILLUSTRATION

The wars in the Balkans since 1991 illustrate some of the points this paper has made: the difficulty of mediation when so many voices are speaking at the same time; the difficulty of keeping a multiparty mediation on track;

the comparative advantage of different third-party institutions at different times during the conflict; and the particular qualities a powerful state brings to the mediation process when disputants are at their most intractable. It should not be taken, however, as the best or only illustration of the validity of the foregoing statements. Mediation is a multifarious activity that calls on all of the powers that Rubin lists. The Bosnian case shows that both reward and coercive power, provided finally by the United States in late 1995, were needed to help stop the fighting. The case of the Community of Sant'Egidio in Mozambique in this volume (see chapter 11) shows how a nonofficial organization can borrow the necessary skill and leverage, as well as exercise its own referent power, in order to become an effective mediator. The case of Norway in the Oslo process (see chapter 20) is an example of a small, relatively powerless—in every sense that Rubin employs—state turning these characteristics to good advantage in facilitating an agreement when other channels were blocked.

Conflict in the former Yugoslavia, especially the Serbian-Croatian war in 1991–92 and the Bosnian war in 1992–95, provides a good example of multiparty mediation in several senses of the definition. First, there were a number of third parties that offered their services or more or less compelled the parties to accept them as intermediaries: the United Nations, the European Community/European Union, the United States, and in a private capacity, former president Jimmy Carter. These concerted interventions were by and large sequential: first the European Community (now the European Union), then the United Nations, then a joint effort by the United Nations and the European Union, the brief Carter-negotiated cease-fire in late 1994–early 1995, and then the United States. A number of the interventions also represented mediations by institutions—the United Nations and the European Union—that are composed of governments with high degrees of sovereignty in the foreign policy arena. Consequently, notwithstanding the European Union's attempt to create a common foreign policy among its member nations, both institutions are subject to strong, often contradictory expressions of national interest among its membership. As discussed earlier in this chapter, these interventions by intergovernmental organizations are included in our definition of multiparty mediation because the mediator, whether UN special representative Yasushi Akashi or the Vance-Owen team, is subject to the multiple pressures of the organization's membership. And finally, some of the mediation efforts were simultaneous. Jimmy Carter's effort to arrange a cease-fire occurred while Owen and Stoltenberg were still active and the U.S. government, in the person of Robert Frasure, was negotiating with Milosevic to end the sanctions in return for recognition of Bosnia.[46]

The conflict in the former Yugoslavia was in part a by-product of the end of the Cold War. The regime of Josip Broz Tito, who ruled over a unified Yugoslavia for thirty-five years, had repressed ethnic identification as part of campaign to build a nation-state out of the disparate communities of Bosnia, Croatia, Macedonia, Montenegro, Serbia, and Slovenia. Even the traditional enmity between Serbs and Croats, intensified by the activities of the Croatian Ustashe and the Serbian Chetniks during World War II, seemed to fade into competition for political and economic power between the two largest Yugoslav states. Intermarriage among the ethnic groups became common. When Bosnian Muslims mobilized in the 1960s and 1970s, they did so as a political force, rather than as a religious grouping, in order to strengthen their position against the larger states of Serbia and Croatia.[47] Yugoslavia seemed to support several anomalies: an open communist system and a unified ethnically diverse state. Unnoticed by the outer world, this model developed cracks along ethnic and political faultlines before Tito died in 1980 but really started to crumble after his death and accelerated with the fall of the Berlin Wall and the political transitions that overtook Eastern and Central Europe as a consequence. In the midst of this political transition in Yugoslavia, politicians such as Slobodan Milosevic and Franjo Tudjman began to use ethnic nationalism as a political platform to increase their own power base.

The Yugoslavian wars began in 1991 with the conflict first between Slovenia and Belgrade, and then between Croatia and Belgrade. The trigger for the latter's turn to mass violence was Croatia's declaration of independence. This declaration coincided with Slovenia's declaration of independence, provoked in both cases by a Serbian refusal to recognize a Croat as head of the rotating federal presidency. Belgrade failed to subdue the Slovenians militarily and so turned to Croatia. Compared with the later Bosnian conflict, this was a short war. The Croats, poorly armed and vulnerable to the UN arms embargo on Yugoslavia, and the well-equipped and trained Serbian federal army fought for four months. During this time, the Croats found ways around the arms embargo and were recognized internationally as a sovereign state. These changes strengthened the Croatian position against the Serbs and may have contributed to Serbs' understanding that this early conflict was headed for an impasse, a hurting stalemate that increased the parties' willingness to negotiate rather than continue military action.

The international response to this war and the later Bosnian war, which were simultaneously intrastate and interstate, was equally a product of the post–Cold War period. After its attempts to stop the dissolution of Yugoslavia had failed, the United States claimed that European institutions should take responsibility for this European conflict. The European Community (later the European Union) agreed and stepped up to the challenge, first enlisting Henry Wijnaendts as the European Community's envoy to Yugoslavia and later appointing Lord Peter Carrington, former British foreign minister, to intervene on its behalf. The European Community then teamed up with the United Nations to negotiate a peace in the former Yugoslavia in 1991. Former U.S. secretary of state Cyrus Vance, acting for the United Nations, was successful in negotiating a cease-fire in Croatia but the end to the war came about because of changes on the battlefield and in international recognition for Croatia's independence. Lord Carrington on behalf of the European Community had a more difficult time in getting the Yugoslav republics to negotiate a joint future,[48] an effort undercut by the German recognition of Croatian independence. From these first third-party attempts at intervention, the deleterious effects of multiple voices making conflicting statements were already apparent in this complex conflict.

The problems caused by competition among the peacemakers were even more apparent in the diplomatic interventions in the war in Bosnia. In the spring and summer of 1992, the war in Bosnia began, sparked in part by the profoundly different political futures the three ethnic groups envisioned for Bosnia. While the Croats and the Serbs wanted to carve Bosnia up along ethnic lines, the Muslims wanted to keep the nascent country together. Again the United Nations and the European Union were teamed as the agents of third-party intervention. A stronger duo is hard to imagine. Cyrus Vance again represented Secretary-General Boutros Boutros Ghali, bringing with him years of experience and a gloss of U.S. involvement in addition to the moral authority of the United Nations. Former British foreign secretary David Owen was appointed as envoy on behalf of the European Union, representing the collective power of Yugoslavia's close neighbors and largest trading partners.

The joint mediating team painstakingly put together a proposal for the resolution of the conflict, a plan that involved recognizing Bosnia-Herzegovina as a decentralized state composed of ten provinces and the eventual demilitarization of the whole country. The proposal was accepted as a basis for negotiation by all three parties, although both Muslim and Serbian authorities had strong reservations about it. Its reception in the United States, however, was mixed. *Time* magazine claimed that the plan clearly favored the Serbs[49] and a critical opinion piece by Anthony Lewis in the *New York Times*, entitled "Beware of Munich,"[50] drew parallels between the Vance-Owen peace plan and Chamberlain's negotiations with Hitler in 1938. While members of the departing Bush administration were cautiously supportive, the new secretary of state, Warren Christopher, expressed doubts on the day following Bill Clinton's inauguration that the plan would work.[51] His ambivalence developed into skepticism by mid-February and set the pattern for U.S. reluctance to engage with the European Union–United Nations mediation effort, a pattern that continued until the United States put its weight behind the creation of the Federation of Bosnia-Herzegovina in March 1994. This agreement ended the war between the Croats and the Muslims in Bosnia, and was the result of an intensive effort by Charles Redman, appointed by Christopher as the Bosnian negotiator during this period. The agreement was important, although as Daniel Serwer (the U.S. special envoy and coordinator for the federation) notes, the State Department remained ambivalent about devoting the attention and resources needed to make the agreement a success (see chapter 21).

A private effort occurred in December 1994 when former president Jimmy Carter traveled to Pale and Sarajevo and managed to secure an agreement among the parties for a four-month cease-fire. How private this effort was is not clear. Certainly, in carrying out his initiative, Carter acted independently of the American diplomatic corps. On the other hand, he may have had White House backing—or at least tacit support—for his work.[52] On the official side, the United States was becoming more involved in the peacemaking effort, principally through a quiet—and ultimately unsuccessful—series of negotiations between U.S. special envoy Robert Frasure and Milosevic.[53]

As public criticism about U.S. unwillingness to play a role in ending the war in the former Yugoslavia increased, pressure mounted for the Clinton administration to do something. Rumors of a massacre at Srebrenica and the horrifying mortar attack on a Sarajevo market in late August 1995 seemed to galvanize the administration.[54] NATO bombing of Serb positions around Sarajevo and then more generally around western and northern Bosnia started on August 30. At the same time, a Bosnian-Croatian military advance, supported by the Muslim authorities and by the Croatian army, streamed into the Krajina region, pushing back Serbian forces on the ground while the international community was pounding them from the sky. Changes in the military equation on the ground, and in the third parties' willingness to use force quickly altered the reckoning for the Serbs. Ripening in this case occurred when the Serbs overplayed their hand and a previous military imbalance (favoring the Serbs) was transformed by the Croat-

Muslim advance and the use of NATO air power. This created for the first time a mutually hurting stalemate that mediators could manipulate to bring the Bosnian Serbs and their patron, Slobodan Milosevic, to the table.

The Dayton Accords that followed this changed understanding of the costs and benefits of continued fighting was an agreement imposed by the United States on three reluctant ethnic groups. The full engagement of the United States gave the U.S. mediator, Richard Holbrooke, a tremendous amount of leverage—both positive and negative—with which to impress upon the parties the absolute necessity of coming to settlement. The mediation took every ounce of leverage that the superpower could bring to bear,[55] including the personal attention of the president and the offer of 60,000 peacekeeping troops available for the implementation phase. The reemergence of the United States, however, changed this mediation from a diffuse multiparty peacemaking effort to a much more focused, single-party one. The Europeans were frozen out of the key decision-making processes and the United Nations was thrust to the background, replaced in the implementation by the nascent OSCE and the newly established Office of the High Representative.

What does the Bosnian case tell us about the complexities of multiparty mediation? The first and most costly lesson in terms of human lives is that the propensity of individuals and institutions to try to run the show themselves—as the Europeans did in the early years of the Yugoslav wars—works only if they have the necessary willingness, resources, and persuasiveness to back it up. The European Union–United Nations mediation had resources in the member states that compose the institutions but found it difficult to marshal them. Individual states, protecting and pursuing their own interests, effectively diluted the mediation effort, and the mechanism to compel them to act concordantly was lacking. Further, the failure to engage—or to convince—the United States lost valuable leverage for the European Union–United Nations effort and meant that member states added to their balance ledgers the possibility of antagonizing the United States: a minor cost to some but more significant to Germany and Britain.

On the American side, it proved possible to muster both willingness and resources to gain entry and to impose a settlement—in one sense a measure of a high degree of effectiveness. The American reluctance, however, to support the Vance-Owen plan undercut these early mediators and led to a long period of mutual recriminations. The Europeans blamed the United States for its unwillingness to commit troops on the ground and its propensity to criticize the European Union–United Nations plan without offering an alternative. The Americans blamed the Europeans for a failure of nerve and an incompetency that allowed the Serbs to commit atrocities under the noses of the peacekeepers.

Bosnia also presents some interesting reflections on when institutions—no matter which they are—can intervene effectively. During the long war, while the Serbs were winning on the battlefield, they were uninterested in considering the possibility of negotiating. This posture changed only when the combined force of the Croatian offensive and NATO bombing attacks changed the situation on the ground. Does this mean that the Bosnian war was ripe for resolution in the fall of 1995? In a sense, yes. The Serbs, the most aggressive party to the conflict at this late stage in the war, had to refigure in these new circumstances the costs and the benefits of continuing to lose soldiers, territory, prestige, and the patronage of Slobodan Milosevic. On the other hand, however, it seems that the Croats had more fight in them and were prepared to pursue a military victory. In addition, the Muslims became more eager to exploit the change in the military balance rather than to negotiate a deal. This is hardly the definition of a mutually hurting stalemate.

The role of the third-party intervenors in managing this situation, in changing the Serbs' perceptions, and in restraining the Croats was critical to developing a state of ripeness. The combination of the use of force and the figurative (and one wonders if it was at times literal) strong-arming of Milosevic to bring his clients to the negotiating table provides an extreme example of the use of leverage to change the parties' appreciation of costs. Only a very powerful state, capable of pulling along a military alliance such as NATO and of providing incentives and disincentives could have played this role in 1995. It does not mean that, given another constellation of circumstances—including a unity of purpose and coordination among the third-party actors—the European Union–United Nations effort was incapable of bringing peace at an earlier stage. These efforts, however, were stymied as third parties looked for scapegoats among allied partners and undercut their own—and all other—efforts. And this raises a final point that this case illustrates: In order for multiparty mediation to succeed, political will among the intervenors to end the conflict and to forge the necessary coordination and unity of purpose is an essential element all too often missing from joint international engagements.

## CHALLENGES OF MULTIPARTY MEDIATION

As we have argued earlier in this chapter and in the brief discussion of the Bosnian multiparty mediation experience, when more than one mediator is involved in a conflict there is clearly a need not only to time and sequence interventions so that the right mix of skills and resources is being brought to bear on the parties to the conflict, but also to ensure that interventions by different parties are pursued consistently and coherently over time in order to move the parties to an agreement. Where direct leverage is limited it may have to be borrowed from others.[56] Episodic interventions in conflicts that have not ripened to the point where parties are willing to consider mediated alternatives to a continuing campaign of violence will offer outsiders little chance to gain leverage. Sometimes it may take external military intervention or major shifts in the military situation on the ground to create fresh openings for mediation, as was the case in Bosnia. Needless to say, in a complex or multiple mediation setting, this requires the careful orchestration of carrots and sticks to create leverage between the mediating party and those who have the ability to exercise force or offer side payments.

As illustrated by the case studies that follow, it is also readily apparent that different mediators have to be aware that the parties will be more disposed to play mediators off one another in particular sets of circumstances, for example, if the conflict has not ripened and the potential for escalation is rife or, on the other hand, when they face the toughest choices and the discussion is edging closer to bottom-line positions. Even at the point of ripeness when escalation is no longer considered a viable option by the parties to the conflict, opportunities to intervene and exercise effective procedural control will be missed if different mediators are sending mixed signals and there is no clear delegation of authority. Such mismanagement only invites "forum shopping" and other unhelpful behavior.

Ideally, the party or parties that mediated the settlement should stay engaged in the peace process in the postsettlement or postimplementation phase.[57] But this may not be possible because of restrictive third-party mandates, and changing personnel, or because other actors and institutions have the responsibility for implementation. In this case, coordination and properly timed handoffs are essential. Negotiation and implementation phases of the peace process are overlapping, intertwined, and mutually interdependent. Failure to recognize the interdependence of mediation roles and functions during the de-escalation phase may lead to an unraveling of the peace process as rival factions or "spoilers" attempt to undermine the settlement in question.[58]

There is almost an inverse relationship between the number of participants and issues in a multiparty mediation and the likelihood of developing and sustaining a coordinated intervention strategy. The larger the number of participants—as in a mediation undertaken by a coalition of states—the greater the likelihood of conflicting interests and positions, and the more complex the interconnections among the parties concerned. But as this review of the mediation literature also suggests, mediation by multiple parties has some obvious advantages if the differing strengths and comparative advantages of different kinds of mediators can be capitalized on to gain entry to the parties to the dispute, create leverage, and propel the negotiation process forward.

Even so, clear lines of delegation and authority that are obviously critical to simplifying the negotiation process so as to avoid confusion may be difficult to achieve in practice. Just what are the desirable operational conditions for effective multiparty mediation is the subject of the next chapter and the case studies that follow. They point to the inescapable conclusion that successful multiparty mediation depends on a complex set of conditions being fulfilled, including close links between the group and the party doing the mediating; coordination and coherence not just on the ground but at the level of strategy and policy; mediator autonomy (or delegated authority) so that the mediator has some leeway to make independent decisions during the actual course of negotiations; and sensitivity to those elements discussed in this chapter that clearly affect the dynamics of the negotiation process, including the phase of the conflict, the interest of the parties in a political settlement, the timing of the intervention, and the resources and sources of leverage available to the mediator.

## NOTES

1. Oran R. Young, "Political Leadership and Regime Formation: On the Development of Institutions in International Society," *International Organization* 45, no. 3 (summer 1991): 281–308.

2. P. Terrence Hopmann, "Two Paradigms of Negotiation: Bargaining and Problem Solving," *Annals of the American Academy of Political and Social Science*, no. 542 (November 1995): 24–47.

3. Richard N. Haass, *Conflicts Unending: The United States and Regional Disputes* (New Haven, Conn.: Yale University Press, 1990), 232.

4. I. William Zartman and Saadia Touval, "International Mediation: Conflict Resolution and Power Politics," *Journal of Social Issues* 41, no. 2 (1985): 27–45; and I. William Zartman, *Ripe for Resolution: Conflict and Intervention in Africa* (New York: Oxford University Press, 1989).

5. Jeffrey Z. Rubin, ed., *Dynamics of Third-Party Intervention: Kissinger in the Middle East* (New York: Praeger, 1981).

6. Chester A. Crocker, *High Noon in Southern Africa: Making Peace in a Rough Neighborhood* (New York: W. W. Norton, 1992), 469–472.

7. Saadia Touval, "Coercive Mediation on the Road to Dayton," *International Negotiation* 1, no. 1 (1996): 547–570; and "Lessons of Preventive Diplomacy in Yugoslavia," in

*Managing Global Chaos: Sources of and Responses to International Conflict,* ed. Chester A. Crocker and Fen Osler Hampson with Pamela Aall (Washington, D.C.: United States Institute of Peace Press, 1996) 403–418.

8. Saadia Touval, *The Peace Brokers: Mediators in the Arab-Israeli Conflict, 1948–1979* (Princeton, N.J.: Princeton University Press, 1982).

9. Saadia Touval and I. William Zartman, eds., *International Mediation in Theory and Practice* (Boulder, Colo.: Westview Press, 1985), 256.

10. Thomas Princen, "Camp David: Problem Solving or Power Politics as Usual?" *Journal of Peace Research* 28, no. 1 (1991): 57–69.

11. Zartman and Touval, "International Mediation"; and Zartman, *Ripe for Resolution.*

12. Edward E. Azar and John W. Burton, eds., *International Conflict Resolution: Theory and Practice* (Sussex, U.K.: Wheatsheaf Books, 1986); and John W. Burton, *Resolving Deep-Rooted Conflict: A Handbook* (Lanham, Md.: University Press of America, 1987).

13. Saadia Touval, "Why the UN Fails," *Foreign Affairs* 73, no. 4 (1994): 44–57.

14. L. W. Doob, *Intervention: Guides and Perils* (New Haven, Conn.: Yale University Press, 1993); and John Paul Lederach, *Building Peace: Sustainable Reconciliation in Divided Societies* (Washington, D.C.: United States Institute of Peace Press, 1997).

15. Louis Kriesberg, "Preventing and Resolving Destructive Communal Conflicts," in *The International Politics of Ethnic Conflict: Theory and Evidence,* ed. David Carment and P. James (Pittsburgh, Pa.: University of Pittsburgh Press, 1997), 232–251; and Kriesberg, *International Conflict Resolution: The U.S.-USSR and Middle East Cases* (New Haven, Conn.: Yale University Press, 1992).

16. Lincoln P. Bloomfield, "Why Wars End: A Research Note," *Millennium: Journal of International Studies* 26, no. 3 (1997): 709–726.

17. Herbert C. Kelman, "The Interactive Problem-Solving Approach," in *Managing Global Chaos,* ed. Crocker and Hampson with Aall, 501–520; and Kelman, "Social-Psychological Dimensions of International Conflict," in *Peacemaking in International Conflict: Methods and Techniques,* ed. I. William Zartman and J. Lewis Rasmussen (Washington, D.C.: United States Institute of Peace Press, 1997), 191–238.

18. Paul Wehr and John P. Lederach, "Mediating Conflict in Central America," *Journal of Peace Research* 28, no. 1 (1991): 85–98.

19. Harold H. Saunders, "Prenegotiation and Circum-negotiation: Arenas of the Peace Process," in *Managing Global Chaos,* ed. Crocker and Hampson with Aall, 419–432.

20. Louis Kriesberg, "Varieties of Mediating Activities and Mediators in International Relations," in *Resolving International Conflicts: The Theory and Practice of Mediation,* ed. Jacob Bercovitch (Boulder, Colo.: Lynne Rienner Publishers, 1996), 228.

21. Paul Wehr and John P. Lederach, "Mediating in Central America," in *Resolving International Conflicts,* ed. Bercovitch, 55–74.

22. Charles King, *Ending Civil Wars, Adelphi Paper* no. 308 (London: International Institute of Strategic Studies, 1997).

23. Loraleigh Keashly and Ronald J. Fisher, "Towards a Contingency Approach to Third-Party Intervention in Regional Conflict: A Cyprus Illustration," *International Journal* 45, no. 2 (spring 1990): 425–453.

24. Michael S. Lund, "Early Warning and Preventive Diplomacy," in *Managing Global Chaos,* ed. Crocker and Hampson with Aall; Jacob Bercovitch and Jeffrey Langley, "The Nature of the Dispute and the Effectiveness of International Mediation," *Journal of Conflict Resolution* 37, no. 4 (1993): 670–691; and Christopher Mitchell, "The Process and Stages of Mediation," in *Making War and Waging Peace: Foreign Intervention in Africa,* ed. David R. Smock (Washington, D.C.: United States Institute of Peace Press, 1994), 139–159.

25. Fen Osler Hampson, *Nurturing Peace: Why Peace Settlements Succeed or Fail* (Washington, D.C.: United States Institute of Peace Press, 1996).

26. Carnegie Commission on Preventing Deadly Conflict, *Preventing Deadly Conflict: Final Report* (New York: Carnegie Corporation of New York, 1998), Bruce D. Jones, "Intervention without Borders: Humanitarian Intervention in Rwanda, 1990–94," *Millennium: Journal of International Studies* 24, no. 2 (summer 1995): 225–49; Lund, "Early Warning and Preventive Diplomacy"; and Howard Adelman and Astri Suhrke, "Early Warning and Response: Why the International Community Failed to Prevent the Genocide," *Journal of Disaster Studies and Management* 20, no. 4 (1996): 295–304.

27. Thomas Princen, *Intermediaries in International Conflict* (Princeton, N.J.: Princeton University Press, 1992).

28. David A. Lake and Donald Rothchild, "Containing Fear: The Origins and Management of Ethnic Conflict," *International Security* 21, no. 2 (1996): 41–75.

29. Jane Corbin, *The Norway Channel: The Secret Talks That Led to the Middle East Peace Accord* (New York: Atlantic Monthly Press, 1994); Crocker, *High Noon in Southern Africa;* Hampson, *Nurturing Peace.*

30. Princen, *Intermediaries in International Conflict,* 54.

31. Edward E. Azar, *The Management of Protracted Social Conflict: Theory and Cases* (Dartmouth, U.K.: Aldershot, 1990); and Cecilia Albin, "Negotiating Intractable Conflicts: On the Future of Jerusalem," *Cooperation and Conflict* 32, no. 1 (March 1997): 29–77.

32. C. R. Mitchell and K. Webb, eds., *New Approaches to International Mediation* (New York, Greenwood Press, 1988).

33. Diana Chigas with Elizabeth McClintock and Christopher Kamp, "Preventive Diplomacy and the Organization for Security and Cooperation in Europe: Creating Incentives for Dialogue and Cooperation," in *Preventing Conflict in the Post-Communist World,* ed. Abram Chayes and Antonia Handler Chayes (Washington, D.C.: Brookings Institution, 1996), 25–98.

34. Abram Chayes and Antonia Handler Chayes, *The New Sovereignty: Compliance with International Regulatory Agreements* (Cambridge, Mass.: Harvard University Press, 1995).

35. Jeffrey Z. Rubin, "International Mediation in Context," in *Mediation in International Relations,* ed. Jacob Bercovitch and Jeffrey Z. Rubin (New York: St. Martin's Press, 1992).

36. Donald Rothchild and Caroline Hartzell, "Great and Medium Power Mediations: Angola," *Annals of the American Academy of Political and Social Science,* no. 518 (November 1991): 39–57.

37. Thomas Perry Thornton, "Regional Organizations in Conflict Management," *Annals of the American Academy of Political and Social Science,* no. 521 (1992): 132–142.

38. Kjell Skjelsbaek and Gunnar Fermann, "The UN Secretary-General and the Mediation of International Disputes," in *Resolving International Conflict,* ed. Bercovitch, 74–104;

Kjell Skjelsbaek, "The UN Secretary-General and the Mediation of International Disputes," *Journal of Peace Research* 28, no. 1 (1991): 99–115; Ruth Wedgwood, "Regional and Subregional Organizations in International Conflict Management," in *Managing Global Chaos*, ed. Crocker and Hampson with Aall, 275–286; Samuel G. Amoo and I. William Zartman, "Mediation by Regional Organizations: The Organization of African Unity (OAU) in Chad," in *Mediation in International Relations*, ed. Bercovitch and Rubin, 131–148; Frank Edmead, *Analysis and Prediction in International Mediation*, UNITAR Study (New York: UNITAR, 1971).

**39.** Johannes Botes and Christopher Mitchell, "Constraints on Third-Party Flexibility," *Annals of the American Academy of Political and Social Science*, no. 542 (November 1995): 168–184.

**40.** Robert Axelrod, *The Evolution of Cooperation* (New York: Basic Books, 1984).

**41.** Kumar Rupesinghe and Michiko Kuroda, eds., *Early Warning and Conflict Resolution* (New York: St. Martin's Press, 1992); John Marks and Eran Fraenkel, "Working to Prevent Conflict in the New Nation of Macedonia," *Negotiation Journal* 13, no. 3 (July 1997): 243–252.

**42.** Mohamed Rabie, *U.S.-PLO Dialogue: Secret Diplomacy and Conflict Resolution* (Gainesville, Fla.: University Press of Florida, 1995); and Janice Gross Stein, "Structures, Strategies, and Tactics of Mediation: Kissinger and Carter in the Middle East," *Negotiation Journal* 1, no. 1 (1985): 331–347.

**43.** Richard C. Holbrooke, *To End a War* (New York: Random House, 1998).

**44.** Jacob Bercovitch, *Resolving International Conflicts*; and Peter J. D. Carnevale, "Strategic Choice in Mediation," *Negotiation Journal* 2, no. 1 (1986): 41–56. See also the chapters by Chester A. Crocker (chapter 10) and Richard H. Solomon (chapter 12) in this volume.

**45.** Margaret G. Hermann, "Leaders, Leadership, and Flexibility: Influences on Heads of Government as Negotiators and Mediators," *Annals of the American Academy of Political and Social Science*, no. 542 (November 1995): 148–167.

**46.** Holbrooke, *To End a War*, 63.

**47.** Noel Malcolm, *Bosnia: A Short History* (New York: New York University Press, 1996).

**48.** Warren Zimmerman, *Origins of a Catastrophe: Yugoslavia and Its Destroyers* (New York: Times Books, 1996), 161.

**49.** Bruce W. Nelan "Serbia's Spite," *Time*, January 25, 1993, 48.

**50.** Anthony Lewis, "Beware of Munich," *New York Times*, January 8, 1993.

**51.** David Owen, *Balkan Odyssey* (New York: Harcourt Brace, 1996), 94–101.

**52.** Ibid., 310.

**53.** Holbrooke, *To End a War*, 63.

**54.** Ibid., 74, 93.

**55.** Ibid.

**56.** Chester A. Crocker, "The Varieties of Intervention: Conditions for Success," in *Managing Global Chaos*, ed. Crocker and Hampson with Aall, 183–196.

**57.** Hampson, *Nurturing Peace*, 227.

58. Stephen John Stedman, "Spoiler Problems in the Peace Process," *International Security* 22, no. 2 (1997): 5–53.

# 3

# The Practitioner's Perspective

CHESTER A. CROCKER, FEN OSLER HAMPSON, AND PAMELA AALL

Chapter 2 concentrated on issues of concern to scholars involved in analyzing mediation: approaches to conflict management, the conflict cycle and barriers to entry, institutional comparative advantage. Although the practitioner also finds these issues important, he or she is interested in them as they affect the strategic and operational aspects of mediation.

In order to examine these issues from a practitioner's perspective and to help untangle the complexities of multiparty mediation, the United States Institute of Peace gathered some of the contributors to this volume for an informal one-day meeting. The purpose of the meeting was to encourage candid, cross-case discussion on their experiences and lessons learned and thereby create a road map for mediators and their institutions, and to clarify the requirements for successful interventions on behalf of peace. The meeting provided a rare opportunity for individuals with deep knowledge of mediation to develop some general principles about third-party intervention. The day produced interesting discussion and unexpected convergence on some key points about what are the elements of an effective mediation. Equally compelling, it also illuminated other areas in which the individual perspectives—particularly between track one and track two—were quite different. More striking than the areas of agreement or disagreement, however, were some personal characteristics shared by participants: commitment, engagement, quick-wittedness, patience, creativity, thoughtfulness, humor, and a strong entrepreneurial spirit.

Although not all the authors were able to attend, those who did represented several different institutional bases. Paul Hare, Gordon Smith, John Hay, Richard Solomon, Jan Egeland, Daniel Serwer, and Chester Crocker had managed or were reporting on mediations by individual states. Luigi Einaudi, Alvaro de Soto, and Margaret Anstee brought a multilateral perspective to the proceedings; the latter two had acted on behalf of the United Nations. Paul Arthur, Hasjim Djalal, Ian Townsend-Gault, Fabienne Hara, and Andrea Bartoli had participated in or witnessed efforts by nongovernmental organizations (NGOs) to bring peace to a conflict. These categories have fairly clear demarcations, but it is worth noting that track-one-and-a-half examples were also well covered. Even though Hasjim Djalal, Ian Townsend-Gault, and Andrea Bartoli acted on behalf of nonofficial bodies, they borrowed a great deal from other, more official agencies; equally, Jan Egeland's Norway example is another case of cooperation between government entities and civil organizations.

Meeting participants also represented mediation cases at different points of the conflict cycle. Although most had been engaged in bringing parties to the table during intense conflict, Hasjim Djalal and Ian Townsend-Gault have been engaged in conflict prevention, and Margaret Anstee and Daniel Serwer mediated the implementation of agreements rather than the negotiation of the peace settlement, though the former had to start mediating a new peace agreement when the original one collapsed into renewed war after elections. The editors also invited I. William Zartman, one of the foremost scholars of mediation, who brought to the meeting both a strong conceptual understanding of the process of peacemaking and an ability to clarify links between the academic and practitioner perspectives.

The principal topics considered by the conference revolved around the conditions under which mediation is currently occurring, the varying roles that mediators play, the strengths and weaknesses of different institutional bases for mediation, the relationship between mediation and the use of force, coordination issues, and gaining entry as mediators. This chapter will not do justice to the richness of debate but will serve to point out the areas of convergence and divergence about the complex terrain that these authors are mapping.

## THE CHANGING GLOBAL CONTEXT OF MULTIPARTY MEDIATION

The transformation of the international system from the Cold War period to the post–Cold War period has affected every individual and institution involved in mediation. Such systemic change has not altered the art of mediation, as reflected in experience from Bosnia and El Salvador to the Middle East and Southern Africa, but it has altered the context of such efforts. The evaporation of the Cold War structure produced or coincided with the boiling over of vicious, identity-based conflicts in Europe, Africa, and Central Asia while it has also shifted the structure of regional balances in a number of places such as East, Southeast, and South Asia and the Middle East. These changes, taken together, have raised a new set of opportunities for, and challenges to, a broadened range of mediating entities.

At the meeting, Luigi Einaudi noted that other factors, such as changes in information technology, population patterns, and economic relationships have also had an impact on the nature of conflict and efforts to resolve it through mediation. Conflicts that may have raged unreported in the days before satellite phones, electronic communication, and faxes now are known (if not acted on) across the world. Population movements—whether voluntary migrations from rural to urban centers or forced migrations caused by violence or hardship—result in pressures on resources or ethnic tensions that flame into conflicts. Economics also affects the propensity for conflict, forging functional ties that may reduce the potential for conflict in some instances and causing social dislocation that raise the potential for conflict in others, as has happened in the former Soviet Union and Indonesia.

At the most basic level, the removal of Cold War rigidities has opened up a range of conflicts to entry and political participation by previously excluded or marginal actors. An occasionally confusing welter of actors has become involved in mediation and conflict resolution. The Soviet collapse translated into a changed strategic calculus for erstwhile Soviet allies, greater apparent global consensus and support for political means of managing conflicts and for experimenting with expanded UN roles, and an ironic rise in the risk-adverse behavior by major powers even as the barriers to entry into conflict management roles have fallen. At times, we have witnessed major powers simply hand conflicts off to the United Nations. At other times, they have shown a short-term determination to pressure warring parties into negotiated solutions without necessarily intending to remain engaged to help manage the long process of implementation. In sum, the

Soviet collapse has not translated into sustained and predictable U.S. or Western engagement.

Despite the turmoil of the early post–Cold War era, a number of positive developments have occurred. The difficulties over peacekeeping did not prevent the United Nations from becoming involved in a number of successful mediations, among them El Salvador and the implementation of peace agreements in Namibia and Mozambique. Even in a more intractable case such as Angola, the United Nations played a lead role for nearly a decade until obliged to withdraw in 1999, following the resumption of full-scale war. The recognition that the support of the United Nations confers some kind of international legitimacy has increased the likelihood that it will be involved in mediation efforts. It is not the same institution, however, that it was in the post–World War II period, when the five permanent members of the Security Council (China, France, the Soviet Union, the United Kingdom, and the United States) represented the dominant world powers. As a number of participants pointed out, Japan, Germany, and the European Community are becoming more significant players, both on regional and international scales; South Africa and Nigeria are other examples of powerful regional actors. Security Council decisions that lack these voices will not represent the most relevant players—in terms of resources and the will to act—in a number of conflicts and consequently will not fully represent the voice of the international community when it comes to conflict intervention.

At the same time, the end of the Cold War opened up opportunities for other actors to play mediating roles. Some states that had been active in peacekeeping operations for many years, such as Canada and Norway, became more active in other kinds of conflict intervention, at times—according to Jan Egeland and confirmed by the Canadian case—with the encouragement of larger powers. However, Norway has also pursued its own initiatives, having made a post–Cold War policy decision to play a major role in international peacemaking, and has been active not only in the Middle East, but in Guatemala, the Balkans, and Colombia as well. Nonofficial organizations have assumed roles once reserved only to sovereign powers. The Community of Sant'Egidio's contribution to Mozambique led to another, less successful effort in Algeria, and to the only political agreement among the warring sides in Kosovo before the outbreak of the 1999 war.

Discussion at the meeting of the changing geopolitical and structural context featured Richard Solomon's presentation of the Cambodian settlement, which occurred during the shift from the Cold War to the post–Cold War period in the early 1990s. This settlement process itself became an agent of systemic change, serving to redefine relations between China and Vietnam, Russia and China, and the United States and all of Indochina. In this set of circumstances, the role of the mediators was to encourage and focus transformations that were already waiting to happen. Solomon suggested that the third parties in the Cambodian negotiations acted as a catalyzing force, providing the cover and momentum for the normalization of relations between Hanoi and Beijing. Without this redefinition of bilateral relations, no amount of third-party intervention would have moved the process forward, but without the catalytic agencies of the Association of Southeast Asian Nations, Australia, the United Nations, and the United States, the China-Vietnam relationship may have remained frozen for a number of years to come. Likening the Cambodian process to the peeling of overlapping layers of an onion, Solomon described the interaction among outer layers that all, increasingly, wanted to end the conflict so they could exit, normalize, and enjoy détente with old adversaries. Least "ripe" for the settlement were the Khmer factions at the center of the conflict who were pressured into it.

The Cambodian case illustrated another characteristic of the current mediation environment: the possibility that civil strife will move beyond national borders in a regionalization of domestic conflict. Hasjim Djalal noted that the regional actors around Cambodia worried that the conflict there would spread to the rest of Southeast Asia, including the South China Sea, a concern that contributed to the support that regional players gave to the UN peace process. The possibility that conflict will spread has provided the rationale for a number of international interventions, but the list— including Rwanda, Zaire, and Bosnia—also points to another feature of the current climate for mediation: the confusion of objectives, approaches, and instruments employed by the international community in the response to conflict may cause more harm than good.

The Permanent Five's unusual level of cooperation and willingness to act in concert were critical to the Cambodian settlement. Could the degree of international consensus shown in the Cambodian case occur almost a decade later, in these more fractured times? It can be argued that this case features a special chemistry and an idiosyncratic, fleeting moment that not only cannot be replicated in Southeast Asia but that has vanished globally. Can broader conclusions or lessons be drawn from such a special set of circumstances? One lesson, surely, is that unique historical turning points have the potential to become powerful moments for peacemakers. Cambodia's subsequent evolution suggests, as well, that these moments may not last long and that sustained engagement in peacemaking is less common but more important than is usually realized when settlements are drawn up in the heady spirit of a "special moment." The context of peacemaking efforts may deserve greater weight than it is generally accorded.

## THE CHANGING ROLE(S) OF MEDIATORS

Along with the changes in international, regional, and local systems which have affected mediation, the roles of mediators have evolved. Andrea Bartoli and others noted at the meeting that the supply of individuals who are willing to take on mediation has grown along with the acceptance of mediation as an option in the resolution of conflict. Pointing out that there is a growing professionalization of mediation, Bartoli cited a number of qualities that are essential to an effective mediator. Among these qualities is the ability to recognize that the mediator is part of the entire process and as such may be required to play many roles: offering mediation in order to get parties to think about the possibility of a political settlement, assisting the parties with the negotiations once they begin, and helping with the implementation. He also noted that institutions may encourage and support, but in contrast to individuals, they do not mediate.

What role the mediator plays in the peace process depends in good part on his or her relationship to the parties and the objective of the mediation. There was general recognition at the meeting that mediators could impose a settlement on parties to a conflict when the mediators had access to overwhelming force and were willing to use it, as happened in Bosnia, or when there was a well-organized and generalized external consensus favoring settlement, as happened in Cambodia. In most other cases, however, the mediator enters into a complex dance with the combatants. Meeting participants differed on whether the successful mediator followed or led the parties in this dance. Bartoli insisted that the parties must lead the process, as only they can determine the best alternatives, decide the main points of agreement, and finally settle.

Although a number of participants agreed that in the best of all possible worlds parties would be in the lead, they pointed out that at times this situation was not practical or possible. I. William Zartman suggested that the mediator's role in such cases was to lead parties to lead the process. In support of this observation, Alvaro de Soto noted that the mediator acts to level the playing field between disputants so that some negotiating relationship can develop. In so doing, the mediator uses whatever tools are available: threats of sanctions, promises of trade relations, international law, pressure from neighboring states, and in some cases, providing arms and resources to build up the weaker side, all with the objective of providing parties with incentives to talk rather than fight. Margaret Anstee remarked that the willingness to allow the parties to lead the process is more appropriate during the negotiation phase than during the implementation period. In her experience in Angola, it would not have been possible always to let the parties lead, as at times the differing objectives of the rebels and the government simply canceled each other out. In the implementation period, she found her role de facto was that of arbiter and referee rather than convener and facilitator, all of which, in any case, went well beyond the original restricted UN mandate of merely "observing and verifying."

In Luigi Einaudi's eyes, maintaining unity among the various third parties in the Peru-Ecuador conflict was one of his key functions as a mediator. He also pointed out, however, that achieving and maintaining this sense of unity can be difficult, as the mediator deals not only with the parties to the conflict, but also with his own domestic constituencies. It is hard, for instance, for the U.S. State Department to promote a unified approach in the face of its own tendency to discuss and disagree internally about appropriate responses, as well as of the protracted nature of interagency and executive-legislative debates. The mediator's challenge in maintaining unity grows more severe when the policy debates become more politicized. As the Cambodia and Namibia-Angola chapters suggest, the congressional disputes about U.S. policy toward Southeast Asia during the Cambodian peace process and the broader public arguments about U.S. policy toward southern Africa in the 1980s could have served to undercut the authority of the mediators by seeming to offer different venues—as well as different priorities and different leanings—to the parties in conflict. These two were extreme cases of mediating in the limelight, both subject to intense public scrutiny, but the sense of exposure and the possibility of serving as a scapegoat for a failed peacemaking effort are constant factors in a mediator's equation.

The roles that mediators assume in the course of assisting parties toward peace include many others besides those of catalyst for transformations, shepherd for holding the mediation mechanism itself together, and punching bag when efforts appear to go awry. Mediator as risk taker, as inventor, as stage director, as mendicant, as visionary: every mediator will play a bit of all these roles, depending on the situation. Hasjim Djalal introduced another kind of relationship between the mediator and the parties: that of informal convener or moderator. In the case of the working group on the South China Sea, the mediators play informal roles, keeping the process going but taking a hands-off approach to the various parties. Although a number of the participants are officials, none attend in their official position and are under no obligation to act officially. This flexibility allows them to consider ideas and take risks that would be difficult under more formal circumstances. Djalal did note, however, that despite the dis-interested role that he and Ian Townsend-Gault play in the process, suspicions about the mediators' motives arise among the parties. The mediator needs to recognize and address those suspicions as part of moving the dialogue along.

Meeting participants accepted as a given that the roles mediators play depend on the situation, meaning not only the global systemic state of affairs, but also the mediators' relationship to the parties and to each other as well as to the internal situation within the mediating party or institution. To this list, we should add once again the reminder that for mediating parties, the act of mediation is itself a policy linked to the broader fabric of that entity's foreign relations or institutional strategy. Roles have many roots. In the discussion of roles, however, it is important to remember—as Paul Hare reminded the group—that no matter what role the third-party mediator plays, or what resources or leverage he or she brings to bear, or in which phase of the conflict the mediator gains entry, the influence of outsiders is finite. Whether the parties lead, or are led to lead, the final decision to stop fighting and on what terms belongs to them.

## INSTITUTIONAL STRENGTHS AND WEAKNESSES

As explained in chapter 2, a major objective of this volume is to examine the question of whether certain institutions have a comparative advantage over other institutions as third-party mediators in violent conflict. The practitioners at the meeting took a slightly different approach to this topic, examining institutional strengths and weaknesses rather than comparative advantage. In his reflections on this subject, Alvaro de Soto returned to the theme of changes in the post–Cold War period, observing that where superpower conflict had prevented third-party mediation, now new actors including governments, international organizations, and NGOs are involved. The international organizations essentially divide into two sets of actors: the United Nations and regional organizations, both of which, in his view, bring advantages and disadvantages to mediation work.

He noted that the strengths of a regional organization include being closer to the problems and consequently having a better understanding of the sources, dynamics, and possible points of intervention in the conflict. This proximity, however, may also impair the ability of regional organizations to intervene effectively, because they are too close: witness, for example, the uneven ability of the Economic Community of West African States (ECOWAS) in peacekeeping in Liberia. Seen from the perspective of the

United Nations, regional organizations are weaker in general resources than the United Nations. For instance, the multimember Organization for Security and Cooperation in Europe (OSCE) shares with the United Nations a problem in developing consensus but the regional organization also lacks the United Nations' establishment and traditions. However, in situations in which communications are open and transparency is established early on in the process, these different kinds of mediating organizations can work together, arriving at a modus vivendi and establishing an informal division of labor. De Soto remarked that an example of this division of responsibility exists in Central Asia, where the United Nations has taken the lead in Georgia, Abkhazia, and Tajikistan while the OSCE has been leading the peace efforts in Armenia/Azerbaijan/Nagorno-Karabakh and Moldova.

De Soto also reflected on the strengths and weaknesses of another kind of mediating mechanism. The Friends of the Secretary-General—informal groups of countries in support of the secretary-general's initiatives on specific conflicts—is an arrangement that offers a sounding board and a source of diplomatic backup (i.e., leverage and practical support), and often can be counted on to finance the cost of peace. As advantageous as this arrangement can be for the United Nations, it seems to be even more attractive to the states that make up the Friends' groups, which gain a sense of role and participation and the ability to demonstrate that they are "doing something." The consequence is that these groups are proliferating even in cases in which they are not needed, adding to the distraction of multiple third parties in peacemaking roles.

Paul Arthur put the question in a broader perspective, asking what now constitutes the international community, and in this international community, what is the role of the United Nations? If the Permanent Five (P-5) do not represent all of the dominant global decisionmakers, how and where can decision making take place? Margaret Anstee raised the point that although much has changed in the global context of mediation, states still have—and actively pursue—national interests. In her eyes, the result is that the UN Security Council is encouraged or permitted by its dominant members—the P-5—to come up with unworkable compromises based on member states' conflicting interests. This presents real problems for mediators who are acting on behalf of the United Nations, especially in those cases when they need to summon unambiguous support in order to oblige parties to comply with agreements they have already signed.

Summoning this kind of leverage is more difficult for NGOs. As their relationship to the power holders is more removed—being less integrated in the international community and lacking the capacity to implement or oversee—than either regional organizations or the United Nations, they depend on their relationships with the governmental and intergovernmental players and borrow political leverage where they can: from the Norwegian government in the Oslo process and from the Italian government in the case of Sant'Egidio in Mozambique. However, NGOs bring other strengths to the process. Andrea Bartoli noted that in Mozambique, Sant'Egidio became part of the political landscape and the role that it played in the mediation was to offer space to the parties in conflict. Space—be it physical or psychological—is often an important component of the process that allows parties to conceive and accept alternatives to their hardened positions. By offering this space, Sant'Egidio helped to create, in Bartoli's words, "a mental path to peace for the participants." Hasjim Djalal's description of the work of the informal working group on the South China Sea confirms the usefulness of this role of providing space and the opportunity to collaborate on functional issues toward the goal of letting parties get used to working with each other. In thinking about the interrelationship between different institutional bases for mediation, Jan Egeland suggested that as far as the Norwegian government is concerned, NGOs provide cover for the state and a means for it to avoid acknowledging involvement in sensitive matters unless and until the official institutions are ready to claim an overt role in the mediation.

Both Ian Townsend-Gault and Luigi Einaudi raised the possibility of using international law as the institutional base for mediation. In Townsend-Gault's example, he suggested the slow accretion of agreements on common issues such as environmental degradation, fishing, and navigation rights leading to a final accord on the central source of the conflict—the ownership of the Spratly Islands. Einaudi described a different kind of legal framework, provided in the case of the Peru-Ecuador negotiations, in which the functional equivalent of the group of Friends—Argentina, Brazil, Chile, and the United States—were the guarantors of the 1942 Rio Protocol. In this case, the legal arrangement provided the trigger for entry, the international institutional base for the mediation, the long-term commitment on the part of the mediators, and the potential for leverage: all important components of a mediation effort.

## USE OF FORCE AND OTHER LEVERAGE

Most of the discussion on how to identify, mobilize, and apply leverage referred to the use of political resources. However, military and economic resources were also considered as potent sources of leverage. The actual or potential use of force was a topic that engendered some discussion. Daniel

Serwer proposed that fear could be a key element in bringing parties to the table or inducing them to implement agreements they have signed. In the Bosnia case, fear was provided by the United States and its willingness to couple its mediation efforts with NATO bombing. A number of other participants, among them Luigi Einaudi and Margaret Anstee, agreed that being able to call on military support—whether the option was exercised or not—was an extremely useful tool for a mediator. The ability to use force lends credibility to the mediation and allows the mediator to level the playing field in situations of uneven power distribution. In terms of bringing this credibility to the table, individual states have far more capacity to marshal the human and financial resources needed to include the use of force as a weapon in the mediator's arsenal. In this regard, the United States stands apart from the rest of the world. As Paul Hare pointed out, the United States is currently the dominant world actor and, as such, the role it elects to play—including that as the user of force—will shape the mediation.

Jan Egeland pointed out that there are other means to persuade antagonists to begin negotiations. Using funds established especially for the purpose, Norway has established a kind of venture capital fund for peacemaking, which can be used to pay the day-to-day costs of mediation, including salaries of the intermediaries and travel costs for the parties. The presence of these funds gives Norway a flexibility in responding to requests for help, but also allows it to decide to participate as an active mediator based on the merits of the individual case rather than on the funding available for it.

## COORDINATION, OR THE PRICE OF DISUNITY

The term "coordination" has become the focus of innumerable conferences and addresses on the weaknesses of the international response to humanitarian disaster or internal conflict. The dire lack of a coordinated response, a sharing of resources, and a willingness to subordinate particular national or institutional goals to an overriding peacemaking agenda has hampered or destroyed several peace operations, including those in Somalia and Rwanda. The criticisms about coordination have generally been targeted at the operational institutions: the UN humanitarian agencies, the military, and NGOs. However, it is also apparent that the lack of unity in an effort to prevent conflict, to bring parties to the table, or to impel them to act on what they have agreed weakens the peace negotiations.

What is needed in a mediation—whether in support of conflict prevention, peace talks, or implementation—is somewhat different from this sense of making sure that intervening parties do not trip over each other in attempting to carry out the same objective. Coordination in a mediation involves the careful crafting of a coherent political strategy, building support and finding resources for that coherent strategy, and diminishing the possibility that other third parties—and interested outsiders—will undermine the peace process by pursuing their own agendas. The mediator, Chester Crocker noted, creates coherence through many means: by adapting what has worked in other circumstances to the situation at hand, by helping the third parties develop a common objective, and by applying imagination, persuasion, and sheer will to bring all the parties—both direct parties to the conflict and other third parties—along with his or her vision of life after a political settlement.

According to Richard Solomon, coordinating the actions of diverse participants in a complex multiparty mediation is similar to the frustrating— and quite often futile—job of herding cats, whence comes the title of this volume. Wary of losing their independence and driven by diverse national or organizational interests, the many governments, international organizations, or NGOs that may become involved in mediation resist coordination and may even balk at information sharing. Therefore, the ability to provide a single focus of the mediation effort is essential, or in Paul Hare's words, that "clear point of control you must have in any mediation or you will have chaos."

An example of the chaos was the international response to Zaire during the struggle between Mobutu and Laurent Kabila: mediation attempts were undertaken by the joint United Nations–Organization of African Unity special representative for the Great Lakes, a U.S. special representative and a U.S. special presidential envoy for democracy, the deputy foreign minister of South Africa, and the president of Togo. The distraction caused by multiple parties was augmented by the numbers of humanitarian and nonofficial institutions caught in the middle of the refugee crises and the rebels' march toward Kinshasa. As Gordon Smith remarked, in Zaire the NGOs allowed themselves to be manipulated by the combatants. Coordination was further strained because the field staff of these organizations did not necessarily represent the views of headquarters. And the news that came out was not always informative as journalists were not well versed in the complexities of the conflict. The result was confusion and miscalculation on the part of the international community, which responded to a humanitarian emergency that never developed while the possibilities of a political settlement withered from the absence of international support or even attention.

Coordination among parties can also be vital in moving between stages of a peace process, from the political settlement to the implementation of an agreement. Difficulties during the implementation period, when the consequences of the hard or ambiguous decisions taken during the peace negotiations become apparent, can undermine or destroy the peace. As Jan Egeland pointed out, parties are not as willing to cooperate as they were during the agreement stage—and recent experiences in Angola, Bosnia, the Middle East, and particularly Cambodia offer ready evidence of the dangers of backsliding. Despite understanding these dynamics, the international community often hands over implementation tasks to institutions and people that were not involved in the settlement—Daniel Serwer noted that the responsibility for the Bosnian settlement had moved from the United Nations to the United States and then back again during the implementation stage to the United Nations, the OSCE, and the Office of the High Representative—without provision for handoff among the mediating institutions. The resulting settlements fall apart, either because they are orphaned by the international community or because they are forced to shuttle between one foster home and another.[1]

## THOUGHTS ON GAINING ENTRY

Meeting participants did not address directly the challenges of gaining entry into a conflict in order to serve as mediator, but this issue did underlie much of the discussion during the day. The consensus seemed to reflect Jan Egeland's assertion that a mediator could engage in a conflict at any point, based on the invitation and willingness of the combatants. It is here, perhaps, that the institutional sponsor rather than the individual makes the largest difference, often allowing state-based mediators to insert themselves into the process using the state's standing, clout, bilateral ties, and other forms of relevant influence, whereas a track-two institution will typically depend more on long-term relationships built on trust and an absence of real stakes in the conflict.

However, this distinction broke down in the discussion as it became clear that there were other factors at play in gaining entry. The United Nations, obliged as it is to take all cases that come to it, provided the model of "emergency room" mediation, declining—in de Soto's words—to check the credit rating or past history of the patient before offering treatment. Andrea Bartoli described a "free market" in mediation, a field liberated from Cold War constraints. It is not practical, he argued, for anyone to impose leadership and coordination in this new environment; we may need to learn to live with a variety of third-party contributions, some positive and some less so. In Burundi, external actors moved beyond standard humanitarian and development programs, as NGOs began to focus more on conflict resolution activities. Yet Fabienne Hara pointed out how these private actors splintered the international reaction to Burundi and reduced the effectiveness of the diplomatic response.

Jan Egeland agreed that variety and even competition are helpful, but he warned of "ambulance chasers" and the need for some sense of "best practice" and quality control in the proffering of mediation services. Mediators also need to be able to filter out tactical from legitimate requests for mediation. At times, parties may request mediation as part of a tactical ploy to appear willing to negotiate; however, their real intentions may be to manipulate public opinion, gain sympathy for their cause, or simply to continue—by other means—to obstruct the movement toward peace. In the case of individual states gaining entry as mediator, Norway provides a very different model from that of the United States. Norway generally enters into a mediation on the basis of an invitation by the parties, thanks in part to its perceived impartiality and absence of national interests in many conflicts. Mobilizing political will and resources is not a problem, as Norway has taken a policy decision to become active in peacemaking on a global scale and has set aside moneys for the implementation of this decision in its venture capital fund for peace.

The United States, with its much vaster resources, actively shapes whatever mediation it engages in. Mediator impartiality is not an option available to parties that engage the United States in a mediation, and often this is the point. On those occasions when the United States is able to muster the political will to intervene diplomatically, it is always possible that the United States might back its political intervention through other means—aid, trade packages, military assistance, use of force. This latent power means that the United States is sometimes sought after by the parties (the Middle East) and sometimes avoided (El Salvador). At other times the parties have no choice, and are obliged to accept the self-appointed mediator as the United States simply pushes its way into a peacemaking role, as it did in Bosnia.

## CONCLUSION

An inescapable conclusion that arose from the discussion is that mediation is an art rather than a science. As a number of participants suggested, it depends on the individual's ability to shape the proceedings, to create—seemingly at times out of nothing—the means to prevent escalation, to structure the peace agreement, or to bridge the social and political divides caused by war. The mediator's dexterity with the materials at hand, including the home institution, monetary and other resources, the willingness of "friends" to provide leverage, and so forth, is as important as the materials themselves.

The art of mediation encompasses a multitude of valid approaches to peacemaking. Success in this medium depends on understanding the forces and the factors at work in any given conflict, and designing a response accordingly. If this is the case, the ad hoc nature of mediation raises the question of whether any of the cases are replicable, either in whole or in part. This question—sharpened by the practitioner's insistence on the special qualities of each situation and the academic's search for generalizable principles—is central to this volume, and the answer from this group of practitioners seemed to be that lessons can be transferred from one experience to another, but only with great care; in other words, it depends.

What makes it so complicated is the number of possible variables at play during these procedures. A number of factors can change the choices, strategy, and effectiveness of a mediation effort: the type of conflict; the phase of the conflict; the readiness of the combatants to come to a political settlement and to cooperate; the mediator's relationship to the parties; the political, military, economic, and moral resources that the mediator can deploy; the relationship to the mediator's home base; and, in these complex, multilayered interventions, the relationship with the other third-party intervenors, and whether the mediation is seen as an isolated event or as part of a larger policy.

However, a number of factors do not change from situation to situation: that there is—or there is a high possibility of—an intense, violent conflict; that there has been a decision at some level to seek a political solution; that the mediator has become involved in this conflict; that the mediator needs to create both the plan and the momentum to carry the plan forward; that the mediator will have to juggle a number of relationships, including the direct parties to the conflict, other influential individuals surrounding the conflict, his or her own host institution, and other third parties—some benevolent, some malevolent, and some simply annoying; and finally that the mediator is an agent of change and as such can represent both a threat and a promise to all involved in the conflict.

Therefore, while these experiences may not be replicable, they do point to certain patterns. Chester Crocker, in closing the proceedings of the day, suggested that the discussion had surfaced a typology of approaches to mediation—the superpower, the venture capitalist for peace, the UN emergency room, treaty-based arrangements (Peru/Ecuador), mediation through developing functional ties (Spratly Islands), and mediation at critical turning points in order to produce a credible exit strategy for the big powers and the international community (Cambodia). Other typologies could be developed that would allow some generalization to occur: for instance, a typology that addressed the particular cultural context of the conflict, a typology of the kinds of conflict situations, a typology of the intersection of the policy priorities of intervening third parties and the mediation. Examining these typologies for similarities and differences may serve to guide mediators in future peacemaking efforts while providing the basis for some contingent generalizations that may serve to guide the scholar.[2] The sorts of "lessons" sought by the practitioner may not lend themselves in all cases to the building of "theory" in the scholarly sense; the practitioner and the scholar often look for different things and have different interests. But given the high stakes of third-party intervention and the fragile nature of most negotiated peace agreements, it must be a plus if they are listening to each other's insights into what works, when, and how in the complex world of mediation.

## NOTES

1. Fen Osler Hampson, *Nurturing Peace: Why Peace Settlements Succeed or Fail* (Washington, D.C.: United States Institute of Peace Press, 1996).

2. Alexander L. George, *Bridging the Gap: Theory and Practice in Foreign Policy* (Washington, D.C.: United States Institute of Peace Press, 1993), 19–30.

# PART II

# CONFLICT PREVENTION AND MANAGEMENT

## Background to Chapter 4

## The Role of the OSCE High Commissioner in Conflict Prevention

With its fifty-five member-states, the Organization for Security and Co-operation in Europe (OSCE) is one of the largest regional security organizations in the world, spanning an area that extends from Central Asia through Europe to North America. The organization has come to play an important role in restoring or maintaining stability and in promoting democracy and the development of civil society in many parts of Eastern Europe and the former Soviet Union. While the OSCE as a whole works to foster peace, security, prosperity, and respect for human rights through an emphasis on conflict prevention and early warning mechanisms, the organization's High Commissioner on National Minorities focuses on volatile situations associated with the assertion or repression of minority rights in member-states. As part of this work, the High Commissioner has been mandated to assume a proactive preventive role. In a number of cases, the High Commissioner—acting as an independent, nonstate entity but with the political support of member-states—has played the part of an external mediator, helping governments and minorities to reach mutually acceptable solutions to their conflicts. This depoliticized, multilateral approach allows the High Commissioner to employ cooperative, noncoercive problem-solving techniques; to examine and address the underlying social and economic sources of ethnic tensions; and to help construct secure interethnic relationships by promoting reforms in education and the use of minority languages.

## MAJOR ACTORS

- Organization for Security and Cooperation in Europe (OSCE)—formerly called the Conference on Security and Cooperation in Europe (CSCE)
- OSCE High Commissioner on National Minorities (HCNM)

## IMPORTANT DATES

- August 1, 1975: CSCE Final Act formally creates the conference to cooperate on security, economic, technical, and humanitarian concerns
- November 21, 1990: Charter of Paris for a New Europe refocuses the CSCE on post-Cold War issues
- July 8, 1992: CSCE Helsinki Summit meeting creates the office of HCNM
- January 1, 1995: The CSCE becomes the OSCE, reflecting the adoption of a more formal and structured role

## EXAMPLES OF CASES MEDIATED

- Hungarian-Romanian relations, leading to historic treaty of friendship
- Crimean autonomy arrangement
- Interethnic relations in transitional societies of the Baltic States

## PRINCIPAL AIMS OF THE HCNM's MEDIATION

- Increased dialogue between ethnic groups within states
- Development of decentralized decision-making bodies with wide participation
- Growing recognition of the importance of minority rights in majoritarian democracies

# 4

# The Role of the OSCE High Commissioner in Conflict Prevention

MAX VAN DER STOEL

## CONFLICT PREVENTION IN THE OSCE CONTEXT

The Organization for Security and Cooperation in Europe (OSCE) is one of a number of security-oriented intergovernmental organizations in Europe. Although their aims overlap in some instances, these organizations each have a clear role to play, and their boundaries have been gradually determined by the states involved. The OSCE applies the concept of "comprehensive security," which it understands as directly relating peace, security, and prosperity to the observance of human rights under democratic governance and the market economy. Of all security organizations in Europe, the OSCE is probably best placed to engage in conflict prevention and conflict transformation in the wider sense, meaning not only the immediate prevention of violent conflict but also the process of establishing security and stability in the region. Indeed, one could say that the development of this wider, nonmilitary security role has allowed for an evolution in the purpose of the OSCE, and that striving to achieve the broad goal of conflict prevention has become one of its core activities.[1]

To achieve this comprehensive approach to security, the OSCE has embarked on developing various organs and institutions. The post–Cold War instability born of various disintegrative processes (e.g., the bloody dissolution of the former Yugoslavia) revealed the need for an independent and impartial actor with the power of initiative who could work quietly, behind the scenes, to address some of the underlying problems relating to national minorities and to settle the root causes of interethnic disputes before they could lead to more heated tensions or erupt into open conflict. Ethnic conflict is one of the main sources of large-scale violence in Europe. Strains in interethnic relations, and particularly tensions between majority and minority populations, have often been a prologue to conflict and violence. To address this aspect of conflict, and to develop a process of early warning and preventive diplomacy, the Conference on Security and Cooperation in Europe (the CSCE, as the OSCE was formerly known) established the High Commissioner on National Minorities (HCNM), the mandate for which was adopted at the CSCE Helsinki Summit Meeting in July 1992.[2]

## THE HIGH COMMISSIONER'S MANDATE

The HCNM's function is to identify and seek early resolution of ethnic tensions that might endanger peace, stability, or friendly relations between participating states of the OSCE. The HCNM's function is described in paragraphs 2 and 3 of the mandate, included in a separate chapter of the 1992 Helsinki Document, as follows:

> (2) The High Commissioner will act under the aegis of the CSO and will thus be an instrument of conflict prevention at the earliest possible stage.

> (3) The High Commissioner will provide "early warning" and, as appropriate, "early action" at the earliest possible stage in regard to tensions involving national minority issues which have not yet developed beyond an early warning stage, but, in the judgement of the High Commissioner, have the potential to develop into a conflict within the OSCE area, affecting peace, stability or relations between participating States, requiring the attention of and action by the [Ministerial] Council or [Senior Council].

The HCNM's mandate contains five innovative and important elements for the OSCE, the first three of which are essential for the effective functioning of any instrument of conflict prevention. First, an external third party can become involved at the earliest possible stage of a potential conflict.

Second, such involvement is at the third party's own discretion: approval from the Ministerial Council, the Senior Council, or the state concerned is not needed. Third, the third party has far-reaching competencies, including the right to enter a participating state without that state's formal consent or the explicit support of other participating states. Fourth, and most revolutionary, the third party is a nonstate entity that can operate independently. Finally, the OSCE has developed an early warning and early action capacity sensitive to the volatile problems involving national minorities.

While these elements are significant to the wider OSCE community and its operations, the following aspects are of more specific importance to the HCNM in carrying out the duties involved. The HCNM mandate provides two principal instruments for conflict prevention: early action and early warning. Within the first instrument, the HCNM may collect information, conduct on-site fact-finding missions, and issue recommendations to the governments concerned in order to contain and de-escalate tensions involving national minorities. The second instrument consists of issuing an early warning to OSCE participating states (in practice through the Permanent Council in Vienna)[3] when there exists a serious risk of violence that the HCNM does not have the means to contain.

In addition to obtaining firsthand information from the parties concerned, the HCNM may promote dialogue, confidence, and cooperation between them. In my work as HCNM, I collect and receive information on national minority issues from a very wide variety of sources, including the media, nongovernmental organizations, individuals, central governments, political parties, representatives of national minorities, cultural organizations, academic centers, and all manner of institutions of civil society. Moreover, I travel to areas where the minority in question is particularly sizable, where problems may be acute, or where the local situation may be indicative of a broader problem. I meet with local authorities, minority representatives, and other relevant personalities, often constituted as political opposition. However, as prescribed by the mandate, I do not communicate with any person or organization that practices or publicly condones terrorism or other forms of violence. Indeed, I am expressly precluded from considering situations involving organized acts of terrorism. Nor may I act on the basis of one person's complaint alone. In this connection, it should be noted that the situations with which I have had to deal do contain many human rights aspects, and my activities may have some positive effect on implementing the rights of persons belonging to national minorities and building respect for human rights in general. But this is not the purpose of the HCNM's work: my task is to try to prevent violent conflict.

The HCNM's mandate contains general guidelines for determining whether or not involvement in a particular situation would be appropriate and provides the necessary freedom to initiate involvement. Importantly, it allows the HCNM to operate with the essential amount of *independence*. As a result, I may act swiftly—as is often necessary. This independence of action is crucial to the timing of my involvement. The sooner third-party conflict prevention is initiated, the greater the chance that the dispute will not reach a high level of tension and that the parties may still be willing (and politically able) to find compromises and accommodate each other's demands. Early action, that is, action taken before tensions become acute or political positions have been staked, is much more likely to be welcomed by all parties concerned. The longer the HCNM waits, the more difficult the HCNM's work becomes. In terms of process, then, lack of independence would imply the necessity for time-consuming consultations and political accords.

There is also a vital substantive aspect to the HCNM's independence. The independence that the HCNM enjoys from the political interests of individual OSCE participating states (and that is denied to many other security mechanisms) reflects the belief of some OSCE states that drafted the HCNM's mandate that conflict prevention must be carried out in the absence of the narrow political interests of individual states.[4] In my view, the HCNM's independence follows naturally from the logic of international public interest that underlies the concept of comprehensive security. Indeed, I believe it is now well established that the multilateralism that created and sustains the HCNM offers opportunities to address highly charged and potentially violent situations in a somewhat depoliticized manner—at least at arm's length through an impartial intermediary.

In the course of my work I may decide to bring before the government in question a report with recommendations. Indeed, in most cases I have issued several recommendations, each one building on my past ones. Consistency in terms of involvement and recommendations is important in order to persuade governments about the necessity of solving certain problems and to gain their support for proposed solutions. Of course, although the mandate allows the HCNM to operate with a large degree of independence, it is clear that he or she could not function properly without the *political support* of the participating states. Such support is crucial whenever the HCNM presents reports and recommendations to the state concerned and, afterward, to the Permanent Council of the OSCE where all participating states are represented. At this stage it becomes clear whether there is sufficient support for the HCNM's activities and recommendations, and whether states are willing to conduct their own follow-up where needed. To avoid acting in isolation, I maintain close contact with the chairman-in-office (the presiding foreign minister) to whom I report in strict confidence after visiting an OSCE state. By expressing their appreciation and support for the HCNM's activities, reports, and recommendations, the participating states give the HCNM the necessary political backing to influence governments in dispute with a national minority.

However, it can be difficult to balance wide political support for my work with the confidentiality and low profile required for conflict prevention. This can be critical when a particularly sensitive negotiation process cannot be talked about openly for fear of inviting counterproductive publicity, but for which more international diplomatic pressure would be welcome.

In certain situations my efforts are strengthened by organizations such as the Council of Europe and the United Nations that share my concerns and publicly support my conclusions and recommendations. It is therefore necessary to *coordinate* efforts among organizations to maximize the effectiveness of outside involvement—and to avoid the duplication of efforts and the consequent waste of resources. Coordination may entail an organization deciding to refrain from addressing a situation that it might otherwise have engaged in, or it may entail several organizations mobilizing their resources and persuasive power in support of a common aim. As HCNM, I have been able in some cases to mobilize different international organizations and gain their political support, in particular the Council of Europe and the European Union. Where our mandates overlap, we have generally sought to coordinate our positions and sometimes have acted jointly. A significant example is the joint HCNM–European Commission–Council of Europe dialogue with the Slovak government regarding language legislation.

The HCNM's mandate also emphasizes strict *impartiality*, which works to my advantage. It is essential for the effectiveness of the HCNM as a third party to preserve at all times a reputation of impartiality. Because I must often address sensitive political issues, I cannot afford to be identified with the parties in a dispute. As paragraph 4 of the HCNM's mandate stipulates, "the High Commissioner will work in confidence and will act independently of all parties involved in the tensions." Of course, this does not preclude me from finding credible and meritorious various positions held by one or other of the parties. Indeed, though I seek to reduce tensions by reconciling conflicting positions, I may well have to discern the better of competing claims that are mutually exclusive in substance. Strict impartiality allows me to do this, preserving my vitality as a third party insofar as my impartiality is recognized by government authorities, minority representatives, and other relevant persons.

The condition of *confidentiality* results in a generally low profile for the HCNM. Among other things, this allows me to work diplomatically and avoid drawing media attention to my activities—attention that might be counterproductive insofar as it escalated tensions. Parties directly involved often feel they can be more cooperative and forthcoming if they know that the content of their discussions will not be revealed to the outside world; it gives them more space for political maneuvering to achieve mutually beneficial ends. Electoral politics is such that parties, fearful of appearing irresolute in the eyes of voters, may make much stronger statements in public than they would in private. On the other hand, in some instances I have considered it necessary to make public statements to prepare the public in different countries to understand and accept a certain situation and to support an envisaged policy or measures previously agreed by the politicians.

For example, after visiting Romania at the end of August 1995 amid the controversy surrounding the recently adopted Law on Education, I issued a statement in which I shared various clarifications and assurances that I had received from the government.[5] I intended my statement to dispel some popular misunderstandings and to reduce tensions. For another example, I issued two statements in the autumn of 1998 about the controversial efforts of the governing coalition in Romania to reach a compromise for the difficult problem of providing tertiary-level education in the languages of national minorities (mainly the Hungarian and German languages).[6] Again, I intended these statements to dispel popular misunderstandings that were causing tension and undermining the political confidence required to solve the problem. A more unusual example was my decision to issue a public statement incorporating my recommendations for a comprehensive program to improve interethnic relations in the former Yugoslav Republic of Macedonia. I issued this statement on November 6, 1998, to help the newly formed government and the wider society focus their attention on solving matters that I believe are essential for the development of peaceful and constructive interethnic relations in their country and the region.[7]

Lastly, the *cooperative, noncoercive, and problem-solving nature* of the HCNM's involvement is also important. Durable solutions are possible only if there is a sufficient measure of goodwill and consent from the parties directly involved. I always endeavor to find such solutions and to bring the parties to a consensus. I always try to find mutually agreeable solutions and to offer my assistance in implementing measures. I am there to assist

OSCE participating states that are experiencing difficulties, and I work together with the parties on the basis of their good faith and their mutual interest in settling difficulties with a view to enjoying a more peaceful and prosperous life together.

## THE HCNM'S EXPERIENCE AND OBSERVATIONS

There exist many minority-related problems, and each problem has to be assessed in light of its particular aspects and circumstances. Nevertheless, I am able to make some general observations based on my own experience. First, the resolution of a dispute between a government and a national minority or between two states is primarily in the long-term interest of the state or states concerned. As such, the protection of persons belonging to national minorities has to be seen as essentially in the interest of the state and of the majority. As a rule, peace and stability are best served by ensuring that persons belonging to national minorities can effectively enjoy their rights. If the state shows loyalty to persons belonging to minorities, it can expect loyalty in return from those persons who will have a stake in the stability and well-being of that state. Therefore, it is better to pursue an inclusive rather than an exclusive approach to minority-related problems. Moreover, solutions that allow for the full realization of the aspirations of persons belonging to minorities should be sought as much as possible within the framework of the state itself. Such development need not necessarily require a territorial arrangement, and may instead be realized through legislation promoting development and preservation of the identity of the minority in, for instance, the fields of culture, language, education, or self-administration on a nonterritorial basis. In such fields, social integration can take place through wide accommodation.

Substantive and constructive dialogue is essential in resolving disputes between majority and minority, as is effective participation by minorities in public affairs. Dialogue and participation need to be available and encouraged. Disputes frequently arise because of insufficient mechanisms for dialogue at the national level. This is why I have supported dialogue involving majority and minority representatives. Specifically, I have promoted the development of structures for dialogue and the establishment of other instruments for democratic discussion and decision making. Dialogue can occur in standing councils, round tables, and other fora where majority and minority representatives gather regularly to discuss issues of mutual interest or particular concern. I have recommended creating or strengthening standing interethnic councils in Croatia, Estonia, Kazakhstan, Latvia, the former Yugoslav Republic of Macedonia, and Romania. In addition, I have initiated ad hoc round tables or consultations regarding specific issues of concern to governments and national minorities (see the later description of the Noordwijk round table on Crimean autonomy). Conclusions reached at such meetings can be submitted to authorities as recommendations, and can thus become an integral part of policymaking in their countries. The development of such institutions and processes of dialogue demonstrates, on the one hand, that authorities are willing to listen to minority concerns and, on the other hand, that minorities are willing to participate in the political life of the country in which they live. Moreover, in reaching compromises and finding solutions the whole society is able to move forward in pursuit of social and economic development.

The complexities and peculiarities of local problems often require wide consultation with all interested and affected persons, since persons belonging to national minorities are vulnerable to unaccommodating majoritarian decision making. In fact, insofar as disputes frequently involve problems of limited subject-matter jurisdiction for which centralized decision-making processes are not always best equipped, it is often the case that lower-level (i.e., decentralized) decision-making processes respond better to minority concerns. This follows from the notion of subsidiarity, that is, that decisions affecting a group at a lower legislative or administrative level should be taken at that level, or at least not without the group's consent.[8] The decentralization that is thus needed may be achieved either territorially (e.g., in the form of devolution of authority through local self-government) or through distribution of limited powers of jurisdiction on a personal or community basis (so-called functional or cultural autonomy). In any case, it is an evident requirement of good and democratic governance that persons affected should be involved in decision making, at least in the form of consultative participation. These are ways in which persons belonging to minorities can be meaningfully integrated into political processes with a view to improving overall governance.

In 1998 I organized, together with the OSCE's Office for Democratic Institutions and Human Rights and the Swiss government, an international conference entitled "Governance and Participation: Integrating Diversity." The conference, held in Locarno, Switzerland, on October 18–20, placed special emphasis on the positive correlation between the principles of self-determination and respect for sovereignty, territorial integrity, and the inviolability of internationally recognized borders. We demonstrated that these principles are not irreconcilable—that while "external" self-determination through secession is fraught with the potential for conflict, there is a great variety of solutions available to accommodate the vital interests and aspirations of various communities within the state through "internal" self-determination. This last idea amounts to a developed regime of democratic governance,[9] including respect for minority rights (especially guarantees of effective participation in public decision-making processes), with carefully constructed electoral processes and special linguistic, educational, and cultural protections. These would include various forms of autonomy. There is, in fact, a wealth of positive experience among OSCE participating states, which was apparent at Locarno. However, it was also apparent that the international community could benefit from the further elaboration and specification of the various alternatives that promote integration of diversity within the state. To this end, I requested a group of internationally recognized independent experts to create a set of recommendations to which states could refer when developing the most appropriate and effective policies for their own situations. This has resulted in *The Lund Recommendations on the Effective Participation of National Minorities in Public Life*, which suggest various ways in which persons belonging to minorities can have a say in, or control over, matters affecting them.[10]

With regard to recurrent issues, I have found that education and the use of minority language(s) are extremely important for the maintenance and development of the identity of persons belonging to national minorities. Certainly, there are important international standards that must be taken into consideration when developing policy and law in these areas. However, these standards are not always sufficiently precise for domestic policymakers and legislators to decide on appropriate application. Therefore, I initiated a series of consultations among internationally recognized experts from various pertinent disciplines to discuss the educational and linguistic rights of persons belonging to national minorities in the OSCE region. The consultations resulted in *The Hague Recommendations Regarding the Education Rights of National Minorities* (which address comprehensively the use of minority language or languages in education and issues regarding minority education more generally) and *The Oslo Recommendations Regarding the Linguistic Rights of National Minorities* (which address the use of minority languages in all other fields).[11] These recommendations (and the explanatory notes attached to them), which are based on independent assessment of current international standards and which reflect the experts' knowledge of the range of possibilities and the most effective practices, essentially constitute balanced and practical guidelines that government officials and minority representatives can use. To the extent that these recommendations may usefully guide governments in developing and implementing appropriate and acceptable policies and laws on minority languages and education, they will serve to resolve or at least to diminish significant sources of interethnic tension. Several states have already referred to *The Hague Recommendations* in national discussions. For example, in early April 1997, a conference in Riga discussed reform of the Latvian policy and law on education with special attention to minority education. At the conference, the minister of education stated that *The Hague Recommendations* would form the basis for Latvian policy and law in education. This statement was well received by minority representatives and, if translated into practice, will remove a major source of tension between the majority population and national minorities, in particular the large ethnic Russian population.[12] Through this kind of modest initiative, much can be done to respond to the root causes of interethnic tensions.

When addressing situations falling within my mandate, I have supported the conclusion of bilateral treaties confirming existing borders and guaranteeing the protection of minorities. One example is the Treaty between the Republic of Hungary and the Republic of Romania on Understanding, Co-operation and Good Neighborliness, concluded in Timisoara on September 16, 1996. In this treaty the two countries laid down a number of important principles regarding minorities. In particular, they recognized "that national minorities constitute an integral part of society of the state where they live," and they committed themselves to "promote a climate of tolerance and understanding among their citizens of different ethnic, religious, cultural and linguistic origin," to "condemn xenophobia and all kinds of manifestations based on racial, ethnic or religious hatred, discrimination and prejudice," and to apply international standards for the protection of persons belonging to national minorities and the development of their identities.[13] Great importance is to be attached to the latter point because it stresses the duty of the state to protect and even to promote the maintenance and development of the identity of minorities, while rejecting the notion that minorities can maintain their identities only by isolating themselves as much as possible from the society surrounding them.

A variety of means are available to me to pursue my work, with different tools appropriate for different situations. Much of my work involves direct human contacts with decision makers, public authorities, and relevant minority representatives. Visits to countries and meetings help me to understand a situation better and to build confidence and trust with the relevant persons. Simply put, talking is important. In fact, in some situations the parties in dispute have no direct line of communication and so they are constantly "reading" (and often misreading) each other through distorted reports in the media. As I have emphasized, establishing structures for dialogue facilitates the exchange of honest and candid opinions. Sometimes it has been necessary for me to help the parties formulate and better articulate their positions, separating the emotional from the substantive. Beyond this, I have endeavored to aid the parties in finding specific solutions to their disputes; sometimes I have suggested new solutions, and sometimes I have encouraged the parties to make compromises in response to their own suggested solutions.[14]

An example was my role in helping the governments of Hungary and Romania to overcome an impasse and conclude their 1996 bilateral treaty, mentioned earlier. Blocking conclusion of this historical treaty (which, inter alia, committed the two states to recognize definitively, and to respect, each other's frontiers and territorial integrity) was a dispute over the applicable standards for treatment of national minorities. This was a classic case of contiguous states with national or ethnic "kin" permanently living in the territory of, and being citizens of, the next (so-called territorial) state. Without conclusion of such a basic treaty, there persisted uncertainty about status and intentions, which particular interests could exploit for their own political purposes. My contacts with the two governments convinced me that they were serious about concluding a basic treaty that would be, in the words of the Romanian government, "a mutually acceptable, viable, and ratifiable treaty which constitutes a real point of convergence."

The main issue in dispute was a possible reference to Council of Europe Parliamentary Assembly Recommendation 1201 of February 1, 1993. The Hungarian government insisted on inserting a reference to the recommendation within the treaty, while the Romanian government resisted. Article 11 of Recommendation 1201 seeks to confer on persons belonging to a national minority "in the regions where they are in a majority" the right to "appropriate local or autonomous authorities." The Romanian government felt uncomfortable about the reference to "autonomous authorities," fearing it might portend a secessionist movement. To overcome this impasse, in the spring and the summer of 1996 I embarked on a kind of shuttle diplomacy between Hungary and Romania. I worked separately with the respective foreign ministers to learn their exact views (and the strength with which they were held), to help clarify each party's views to the other, to explain to both parties certain matters, and finally to propose my own compromise formula, which was accepted by both governments and ultimately led to the conclusion of the treaty. One source of instability in Europe was therefore settled as fears were removed and the foundation was laid for enduring cooperation and mutually beneficial bilateral relations.

I have also engaged in what might be called facilitative mediation or quasi-directed conciliation. An example is the way in which I helped the relevant parties overcome the impasse concerning adoption of a new constitution for the Autonomous Republic of Crimea in Ukraine. In March 1996 I invited the main personalities from the Ukrainian government and parliament in Kiev and the Crimean government and parliament (including Crimean Tatar leaders) to meet with me in a hotel in the Dutch seaside resort of Noordwijk. I thus provided the opportunity for the relevant parties to focus (out of public view and away from the distractions of their offices) for three days on the persistent problem of the basic constitution of Crimea. To further assist the parties, I invited three well-respected independent experts on international law, minority rights, and economics to join the meeting. By structured dialogue and direct contact, the parties were able to move much closer to a resolution of their differences. I relied on the available expert advice to propose my own solutions. I also proposed to move forward on the many issues for which accord was at hand and to leave aside the others to be settled later. Ultimately, the main issues were settled and on April 4, 1996, the Ukrainian parliament adopted a new constitution for the Autonomous Republic of Crimea.[15]

In addition to these aspects of conflict prevention diplomacy, in the last few years I have become increasingly engaged in or actively supported special humanitarian or economic development activities within states. This follows from my observation that interethnic disputes may arise from or be exacerbated by material needs and disparities. Humanitarian or development projects that contribute materially to solving specific problems may alleviate pressures. For example, in Kyrgyzstan I have arranged for new schoolbooks to be published, including in a minority language. In Ukraine, I have acted with the United Nations Development Programme (UNDP) and the United Nations High Commissioner for Refugees (UNHCR) to stimulate projects and to raise the necessary funds to assist with the material needs of the formerly deported peoples who have now returned in substantial numbers to Crimea. Recently, I have been in contact with the World Bank and the European Bank for Reconstruction and Development with a view to suggesting how their planned investments could be targeted to diminish interethnic tension (and certainly to avoid exacerbating it). These "tension-reduction projects" are all relatively small in financial terms, but they may make major contributions as they build confidence among people.[16]

Although the resolution of some sources of tension requires material resources, it is my experience that many of the root causes of interethnic tensions and conflict concern issues that may be largely addressed through appropriate and inexpensive policy formulation.[17] For example, it costs relatively little to resolve disputes over citizenship. Similarly, the adoption of policies assuring the freedom for everyone to maintain and develop their own identity, to pursue their own cultural interests, and to participate effectively in public affairs is fairly cost free. Certainly, some investment in the building of institutions and political structures may well be necessary; similarly, material resources may be required to implement measures aimed at helping persons belonging to minorities to enjoy their rights to the same extent that persons belonging to majorities do. But beyond these still relatively modest costs, the idea of good governance leads to meaningful solutions within the budget of every state. In any event, settlement of the root causes of conflict merits public expenditure since the alternative may well be to let the sparks of interethnic conflict ignite into extremely costly hot wars.

## Long-Term Conflict Prevention

The present support enjoyed by the HCNM in general and in relation to specific situations—especially the wide acceptance of my recommendations by OSCE states—is not enough to resolve underlying problems and settle disputes in the long run. The present progress of conflict prevention work and the results my office has achieved are not sufficient to ensure long-term comprehensive security. This is primarily because there is a general lack of international financial support for societies in transition and, more particularly, for the socioeconomic needs of persons belonging to minorities, who need help in developing a civic identity within the country in which they live. Much more attention must to be given to the deeper causes of conflict that often underlie interethnic tensions. If people are unemployed, if they have little or no possibility for education, if no decent housing is available, if the prospects for their future are gloomy, they will be dissatisfied. In many countries in the OSCE area this situation is exacerbated by ongoing fundamental societal changes. Frequently, people in these countries are faced with huge problems in their day-to-day lives and an uncertain future. Past ideologies have failed them and new ideologies with tailor-made answers are not at hand. This is a condition of general insecurity.

It goes without saying that trying to prevent a conflict amid general insecurity is not an easy task. It can be a tedious process requiring considerable investment over a long period. Such expenditure of energy and time will usually have to be matched by a significant investment of financial capital as well as political capital. For example, the HCNM has developed a number of activities in Ukraine, in particular concerning the position of the Crimean Tatar population in the Autonomous Republic of Crimea. The Tatars (and other smaller populations who have returned from their deportation to Central Asia under Stalin) are facing considerable difficulties in trying to build a future for themselves and their families. There are very few jobs, almost no housing, and limited opportunities for education. If these problems are not tackled, Tatar discontent might destabilize the situation in an area where other political problems have begun to show some improvement. Significant financial investment and assistance are required, but the Ukrainian authorities lack the necessary resources. The international community should be made aware of its responsibility and should step in with considerable financial aid. I am trying to mobilize the resources of international humanitarian, developmental, and financial organizations as well as national governments to support different tension-reduction projects and to assist in better-focused deployment of available resources. I have been working with the UNDP and the UNHCR to provide shelter, employment opportunities, job training, general education, and so on. So far, we have had modest success. As long as these needs persist there remains the potential for tensions to flare. Effective conflict prevention requires a genuine commitment over time through carefully designed and targeted tension-reducing projects.

Even more fundamental, however, is the serious and sustained application of the values to which all OSCE participating states have committed themselves. Beginning with the decalogue of principles in the 1975 Final Act of Helsinki and continuing through the 1990 Charter of Paris for a New Europe, the shared values of the OSCE are articulated in the developed standards of democratic governance and the free market under the rule of law with full respect for human rights, including those of persons belonging to national minorities. It is European experience that conflicts may be prevented only through the development of such democratic societies throughout the region. But security, stability, and prosperity do not flow automatically from declarations or the mere establishment of institutional frameworks. Constant vigilance is required in daily governance and in policymaking and lawmaking of all kinds. Too often, governments fail or hesitate to draw the necessary conclusions for policy and law, or they fail to invest the necessary political and material resources to build peace and prosperity in Europe. In particular, while governments remain prepared to commit billions in U.S. dollars for the purchase of expensive weapons to fight wars, they shy away from committing paltry sums for the prevention of such wars. It may be noted that the budget of the OSCE for 1999 is about $50 million, with only about 20 percent of that available for the Office of Democratic Institutions and Human Rights and a mere $1.4 million available for the Office of the OSCE High Commissioner on National

Minorities. If OSCE participating states really are serious about preventing conflicts in the future, they will surely have to do better than this.

## CONCLUSIONS

When communism collapsed in Europe, the prevailing expectation was that the continent was entering an era of peace, stability, and respect for democratic values. However, in the years since the Berlin Wall came down, more blood has been shed than during the preceding decades of communist oppression in Central and Eastern Europe. The danger of war between European states has receded. But we have learned the bitter lesson that internal tensions can also lead to armed conflicts. Interethnic conflicts presently constitute the main threat to security in Europe. The problem is exacerbated by extreme nationalism, which has proven to be a potent force in many states. Extreme nationalism characterized by feelings of ethnic superiority and refusal to respect the legitimate concerns of other ethnic groups has led to the contemporary horrors of "ethnic cleansing."

The manifold challenges of making the transition from communist states to free and democratic states, and some of the ugly turns that this process of transition has taken in parts of Central and Eastern Europe, should not lead us to despondency or to the fatalistic conclusion that interethnic conflict is as unavoidable as natural disasters. Many good experiences show that interethnic conflict can be avoided if energetic efforts to prevent it are undertaken at an early stage, if sufficient resources are available, and if the necessary external pressures are applied.

This brings me back to the particular role my office has to perform. It is not enough to identify the danger of interethnic conflict in general or in specific situations. There is also the equally vital task of trying to find solutions. The work of the HCNM may not be mediation in the classic sense of the concept, but it certainly has the same essential aim of finding solutions for conflicting interests that take into consideration the reasonable concerns of both sides and it seeks to convince the parties that, whatever their differences, they share a common interest in avoiding escalation and, therefore, in finding accommodations. To the extent that the HCNM has been able to keep tensions from boiling over into violence, perhaps to bring disputing parties to some workable arrangement, and possibly even to resolve the root causes of certain tensions, then the HCNM has fulfilled his mandate of preventing conflict. If such efforts should fail, then the HCNM may still perform a valuable function by sounding an early warning of rising tensions and possible violence. I am convinced that the sustained commitment of the international community to this approach based on a consistent understanding and effective application of our shared values is an important instrument not only for conflict prevention but also for building enduring peace and prosperity in the OSCE area.

## Notes

1. For a fuller understanding of the OSCE, see Arie Bloed, ed., *The Conference on Security and Cooperation in Europe: Analysis and Basic Documents, 1972–1993* (Dordrecht, The Netherlands: Martinus Nijhoff, 1993); Arie Bloed, ed., *The Conference on Security and Cooperation in Europe: Basic Documents, 1993–1995* (The Hague: Kluwer Law International, 1997); Michael Bothe, Natalino Ronzitti, and Allan Rosas, eds., *The OSCE in the Maintenance of Peace and Security: Conflict Prevention, Crisis Management, and Peaceful Settlement of Disputes* (The Hague: Kluwer Law International, 1997); Victor-Yves Ghebali, *L'OSCE dans l'Europe post-communiste, 1990–1996; Vers une identité paneuropéenne de sécurité* (Brussels: Etablissements Emile Bruylant, 1996); and Walter Kemp, *The OSCE in a New Context: European Security towards the Twenty-First Century* (London: Royal Institute of International Affairs, 1996).

2. For a comprehensive description and analysis of the mandate, see Rob Zaagman, "The CSCE High Commissioner on National Minorities: An Analysis of the Mandate and the Institutional Context," in *The Challenges of Change: The Helsinki Summit of the CSCE and Its Aftermath*, ed. Arie Bloed (Dordrecht, The Netherlands: Martinus Nijhoff, 1994), 113–175.

3. The Permanent Council, the OSCE's principal forum, meets weekly in Vienna with delegations headed by permanent representatives at ambassadorial rank.

4. On the drafting history, see Rob Zaagman, "The CSCE High Commissioner on National Minorities: Prehistory and Negotiations," in *Challenges of Change*, ed. Bloed, 95–111.

5. The text of my statement is found in OSCE document HC/6/95, September 1, 1995.

6. The text of my statements is found in OSCE documents HCNM.INF/4/98, September 10, 1998, and HCNM.INF/6/98, October 8, 1998.

7. The statement is found in OSCE document HC/10/98, November 11, 1998. For a summary of the HCNM's work in the former Yugoslav Republic of Macedonia, see John Packer, "The Role of the OSCE High Commissioner on National Minorities in the Former Yugoslavia," *Cambridge Review of International Affairs* 12, no. 2 (spring-summer 1999): 169–184.

8. For an explanation and discussion of relevant OSCE commitments that generally support decentralization and inclusive public decision-making processes, see John Packer, "The OSCE and International Guarantees of Local Self-Government," in *Local Self-Government, Territorial Integrity, and Protection of Minorities*, proceedings of the UniDem Seminar organized in Lausanne on April 25–27, 1996 (Strasbourg: European Commission for Democracy through Law, Council of Europe, 1996), 250–272.

9. See Allan Rosas, "Internal Self-Determination," in *Modern Law of Self-Determination*, ed. Christian Tomuschat (Dordrecht, The Netherlands: Martinus Nijhoff, 1993), 225–252.

**10.** The *Lund Recommendations* are available through the Foundation on Interethnic Relations, Prinsessegracht 22, 2514 AP The Hague, The Netherlands; e-mail: fier@euronet.nl.

**11.** The texts of the two sets of recommendations are available from the Foundation on Interethnic Relations. *The Hague Recommendations* have been reproduced, together with related articles and speeches, in a special issue of the *International Journal on Minority and Group Rights* 4, no. 2 (1996–97). *The Oslo Recommendations*, together with related articles, have also been reproduced in a special issue of the same journal: vol. 6, no. 3 (1999).

**12.** For a description and an analysis of the work of the HCNM in the Baltic States (principally Estonia and Latvia), including educational matters, see Rob Zaagman, *Conflict Prevention in the Baltic States: The OSCE High Commissioner on National Minorities in Estonia, Latvia, and Lithuania*, monograph no. 1, European Centre on Minority Issues (Flensburg, Germany: European Centre on Minority Issues, 1999).

**13.** For the texts of relevant bilateral treaties, together with some scholarly analysis, see Arie Bloed, ed., *The Protection of Minority Rights through Bilateral Treaties: The Case of Central and Eastern Europe* (The Hague: Kluwer Law International, 1999).

**14.** For a good summary of my approach in general and in relation to dialogue, see Stefan Vassilev, "The OSCE High Commissioner on National Minorities: A Non-Traditional Approach to Conflict Prevention," in *The New Yalta: Commemorating the Fiftieth Anniversary of the Declaration of Human Rights in RBEC Region*, comp. United Nations Development Programme (New York: United Nations Development Programme, 1998), 140–145, especially 143.

**15.** For a fuller description of my work in relation to Crimean autonomy, see John Packer, "Autonomy within the OSCE: The Case of Crimea," in *Autonomy: Applications and Implications*, ed. Markku Suksi (The Hague: Kluwer Law International, 1998), 295–316, especially 306–315.

**16.** For some further thoughts on "tension-reduction projects," see Jonathan Cohen, *Conflict Prevention Instruments in the Organization for Security and Cooperation in Europe: An Assessment of Capacities* (The Hague: Netherlands Institute of International Relations, 1998), 49–51.

**17.** For a brief summary of issues recurring in the work of the HCNM, see John Packer, "The OSCE High Commissioner on National Minorities," in *Human Rights Monitoring Procedures: A Textbook on How to Petition and Lobby International Organizations*, ed. Gudmundur Alfredsson, Goran Melander, and Bertrand Ramcharan (The Hague: Kluwer Law International, 1999).

## Background to Chapter 5

## Canada and the Crisis in Eastern Zaire

The Great Lakes region of Africa became an exceptionally dangerous and unstable place in the 1990s. Tutsi massacres of Hutus in Burundi and the 1994 genocide of Tutsis in Rwanda prompted the flight of vast numbers of refugees to neighboring countries, especially Zaire (now the Democratic Republic of Congo). In 1996, the distress, and that of the refugees living within Zaire, deepened as a foreign-assisted rebellion began in Zaire's eastern provinces. To quicken the slow pace of the international response to the resulting humanitarian crisis and to the bloodletting, a Canadian diplomat was mandated by the United Nations to try to end the hostility, promote a peace conference for the Great Lakes region, and consider the future UN role in the area. The UN secretary-general's special envoy, Raymond Chrétien (the Canadian ambassador to the United States), met African and international leaders, and subsequently the Canadian government sought to establish a multinational force to assist refugee repatriation. Chrétien's mission, however, was to a significant extent overtaken by Zairean rebel attacks on the camps—which led to a mass exodus of refugees back to their native countries—and ultimately foundered in the absence of international political support.

## MAJOR ACTORS

- Zairean government: led by President Mobutu Sese Seko
- Zairean rebels: led by Laurent Kabila, and including Rwandan and Zairean Tutsis supported by President Museveni of Uganda
- Raymond Chrétien: UN special envoy to the Great Lakes region
- Steering Group: a fifteen-member group convened to administer a multinational force to be led militarily by Lt. Gen. Maurice Baril of Canada

## IMPORTANT DATES

- 1994: Genocide takes place in Rwanda
- October 31, 1996: Chrétien becomes UN special envoy to the Great Lakes region
- November 4, 1996: Cease-fire is declared in Zairean conflict
- November 9, 1996: Security Council Resolution 1078 calls on members to prepare for possible military intervention in eastern Zaire
- November 12, 1996: Canadian team meets NSA Anthony Lake at White House to discuss integration of U.S. forces into a multinational force (MNF)
- November 15, 1996: Resolution 1080 authorizes Canada to lead the MNF
- November 19, 1996: Baril arrives in Africa
- December 10, 1996: Baril recommends that the MNF stand down
- December 13, 1996: Final Steering Group meeting is held in New York
- Mid-December 1996: Owing to lack of international support, the mission is aborted
- December 31, 1996: The MNF is officially terminated

## KEY AGREEMENT REACHED

- Canada authorized to lead a multinational force, facilitate aid distribution, and facilitate refugee repatriation to Rwanda

## PRINCIPAL OUTCOMES

- Kabila's rebel movement enabled many Hutu refugees to return to Rwanda, though others may have fled deeper into Zaire and perished
- Resolution 1080 helped to prompt rebel attacks on refugee camps

# 5

# Canada and the Crisis in Eastern Zaire

GORDON SMITH AND JOHN HAY

Television images of human suffering—the squalid refugee camps, the corpses of mothers and babies, the ferocity of ethnic warfare—can now be counted among the determinants of foreign policy conduct in a democracy. They can affect government decisions as powerfully as the calculus of trade or the balance of political interest (or the professional advice of diplomats or soldiers). Public opinion, stirred by those images and by the energies of nongovernmental organizations (NGOs), rises with passionate demands on governments to "do something," to relieve the despair and stop the fighting.

But if the so-called CNN Effect operates to stimulate intervention, there was evident in Washington in late 1996 a corollary force that just as effectively inhibited action. Call it the Somalia Effect: the reluctance to commit U.S. troops to a humanitarian mission of the kind that degenerated, again on television, in the dirty streets of Mogadishu. The object in this chapter is to explain how Canada, of all countries, came therefore to take the lead in attempting an armed intervention in eastern Zaire. It will describe the challenges of middle-power management of a multistate coalition, the confusion of facts on the ground in a complex emergency, and the lessons that might flow from the ambiguous conclusion of this unusual episode.

The key events of the case can be quickly retold. On November 9, 1996, in the face of bloody conflict in eastern Zaire that was starving Rwandan refugees of essential aid, the UN Security Council passed Resolution 1078, calling on members to prepare for a possible military intervention. On November 12, Canadian prime minister Jean Chrétien asserted Canada's leadership of the multinational force (MNF), which the Security Council formally authorized on November 15 with Resolution 1080. Just as the council was adopting Resolution 1080, however—and maybe because of it—attacks on the camps by Zairean rebels caused the sudden movement of several hundred thousand Hutu refugees back toward Rwanda. Despite continuing reports of privation and atrocities, and despite commitments from the United States and others, Canada was thereafter unable to secure deployments to the MNF from any other government. In mid-December, the attempt was abandoned. To this day, nobody is certain of the number, fate, or identity of the many Rwandans who never made it out of Zaire.

The first point to make is that the assertion of leadership of a military intervention in Central Africa marked an extraordinary event in Canada's foreign relations: notwithstanding its strong tradition of multilateralism and UN activism, Canada had never before led a multinational force formed under Chapter VII of the UN Charter. In the conventional Canadian view, coalition leadership and MNF command were properly the work of other states with bigger armies. But that was more than a departure in the execution of Canadian policy. It immediately raised crucial questions about the political and military capacities of *any* middle power in the present age to manage the kind of intervention heretofore led by great powers or (usually) the superpower. In this respect, the case of eastern Zaire might tell us something of how lives may be saved, and conflicts resolved, in future humanitarian crises of this kind.

## THE BACKGROUND IN BRIEF

The deeply complicated history of conflict and diaspora in Central Africa has been told and interpreted elsewhere.[1] Enough to say here that the source of the conflict in eastern Zaire in 1996 can be found in the Rwandan genocide of 1994—itself a complex outcome of ethnic division exacerbated by German and Belgian maladministration and postcolonial misrule, compounded by economic hardship and inequality. Although popularly depicted in 1994 as a chaotic "tribal" or ethnic bloodletting between the majority Hutu and the minority Tutsi, what happened in Rwanda was something even more sinister. In the words of a later international study, "The planned, deliberate effort to eliminate the Tutsi population of Rwanda that culminated in the massive slaughter of April–July 1994 fully meets the definition of genocide," as articulated in the 1948 Genocide Convention.[2] Conservative estimates of that slaughter suggest that between 500,000 and 800,000 people were killed (out of a population of perhaps 7 million). Nearly all the victims were Tutsi, the rest generally described as "moderate" Hutus insufficiently ardent in the killing of their neighbors. As Tutsi forces ultimately overcame Hutus, more than 2 million people (mostly Hutu) fled as refugees across Rwanda's borders.

For Canadian decision makers in the fall of 1996, the Rwandan catastrophe remained relevant in at least two respects. First, according to the United Nations High Commission for Refugees (UNHCR), as many as 1.1 million Rwandan refugees (along with 144,000 Burundians) had settled in camps in eastern Zaire. Among them lived more than 10,000 and as many as 40,000 soldiers of the Forces Armées Rwandaises, known as ex-FAR, the army of the deposed Hutu regime in Rwanda. Also in the camps were an uncertain number of Hutu militiamen and a still less certain number of civilian instigators of the genocide. But those ex-FAR soldiers, militias, and other *génocidaires* were not simply mixed into the refugee population; they were, in effect, governing it. The UNHCR, following its standard practice, had facilitated aid distribution in the camps by leaving governance to the refugees themselves. And in practice, that meant the genocidal regime that had escaped Rwanda was replicated in the Zairean camps along Rwanda's border. The camps became centers of violence and sources of conflict between Zaire and Rwanda.

The second relevance of the 1994 Rwandan genocide for Canadian authorities was their belief that the tragedy had been preventable—that the international community could have expected the killing, had warnings of it, and was therefore culpable. The Joint Evaluation of Emergency Assistance to Rwanda, which was led by the Danish foreign aid agency and included Canadian representation, concluded that "through hesitations to respond and vacillation in providing and equipping peacekeeping forces, the international community failed to stop or stem the genocide, and in this regard shares responsibility for the extent of it."[3] That report reached the highest levels of the Canadian government. Prime Minister Chrétien and Foreign Affairs Minister Lloyd Axworthy publicly and privately expressed the conviction that the disaster in Rwanda must not be repeated and that the international community bore an obligation at least to try to prevent such a repetition. "We have all seen the disturbing images from Eastern Zaire in recent days," the prime minister said at a news conference announcing the Canadian intervention initiative on November 12, 1996.

"Innocent men and women and children are dying, human beings going without food and water for days and days. None of us can be blind to the consequences. If the world does not act, more than a million lives are at stake."

In truth, the images from eastern Zaire were appalling. Sadako Ogata, the UN high commissioner for refugees, warned in late October of "a catastrophe greater than the one we knew in 1994." Emma Bonino, the European Union's humanitarian coordinator, spoke of 1 million people in Zaire at risk of dying and accused the world of standing aloof. Stephen Lewis, a former Canadian ambassador to the United Nations with a long personal knowledge of Africa, saw the threat of "the worst human disaster on the continent."

The violence had been escalating throughout 1996, although the identities and objectives of the combatants frequently bewildered even close observers. There was the recurring conflict between the undisciplined Zairean army—and the kleptocratic political leadership in Kinshasa—and local Tutsi populations, including the Banyamulenge of South Kivu province, who had existed in eastern Zaire for some two hundred years. In September and October 1996, local Zairean officials threatened Zairean Tutsis with expulsion to Rwanda; their insecurity was all the more acute because Zairean authorities had denied them Zairean citizenship.

There was also rising violence between Zairean Tutsis, on one side, and Hutu militias and ex-FAR troops in the refugee camps, on the other side. Those were indigenous Tutsis retaliating with increasing force against the encroaching Hutu refugees. Finally (if only to simplify the real confusion), there was an alliance of forces led by Laurent Kabila, who enlisted Tutsi fighters in the rebellion that would overthrow the Mobutu regime only a few months later. What is clear now, but was not so obvious to us then, is that Rwandan army officers and troops were reinforcing Kabila's rebellion and his alliance with the Zairean Tutsis.

By mid-October, thousands of Hutu refugees had been forced by the fighting (and by the intimidation of Hutu gunmen) either to flee the UNHCR camps or in any case submit to the gunmen's rule. In both cases, UN and NGO agencies were forced to withdraw personnel from danger and suspend deliveries of food, water, and medical help. By the end of October, several hundred thousand refugees—some in makeshift camps, some hiding in the hills—were cut off from all aid. The Zairean government, fighting the rebellion, described itself in a state of war with Rwanda, which it accused of attacking and occupying Zairean territory in support of the Tutsis. Television coverage of frightened refugees intensified throughout

October, along with dire accounts and warnings from NGOs in the field. "Now we are confronted by a new genocide," declared the UN secretary-general, Boutros Boutros-Ghali, on November 8, 1996. "I call it a genocide by starvation. . . . So we must act, and we must act immediately."

## THE INTERVENTION

In Ottawa, there was by then a growing sense that "something" had to be done. On Saturday, October 25, 1996, Boutros-Ghali called Robert Fowler, Canada's UN ambassador, to ask if Canada (one of three countries he was considering) would nominate a high-ranking public figure to be his personal envoy to the African Great Lakes region. Why a Canadian? Boutros-Ghali apparently reasoned that a Canadian might be available who was fluent in French and English, with some international reputation, and without the political-historical associations that other governments carried in Central Africa. After discussions between Foreign Affairs Minister Axworthy and Prime Minister Chrétien, I (Smith) replied to Fowler that Canada recommended the name of Raymond Chrétien, who was the Canadian ambassador to the United States, a former ambassador to Zaire, Rwanda, and Burundi—and a nephew of the prime minister. Within twenty-four hours, the secretary-general accepted the nomination. (It may also have occurred to Boutros-Ghali by some point that Ambassador Chrétien's appointment offered him an unforeseen advantage. At a moment when Boutros-Ghali's own reputation in Washington was suffering—he was then in a losing struggle for reelection as secretary-general—Chrétien and his embassy enjoyed ready access and good relations in the Washington foreign policy community.) On October 31, Ambassador Chrétien went to New York to meet and agree to terms with Boutros-Ghali.

Ambassador Chrétien accepted a threefold mandate: to negotiate if he could an end to hostilities in eastern Zaire; to promote a regional conference on peace, security, and development in the African Great Lakes area; and to explore the potential for a longer-term UN presence in the region, beginning with the possible appointment of a UN special representative. But Boutros-Ghali also accepted Chrétien's recommendations: the mission would be short, and in any event finished by Christmas; it would be high profile, attended by full media coverage; Chrétien would be subjected to minimal interaction with UN Secretariat bureaucrats in New York; and he would have an airplane, security, and communications provided by the Canadian forces.

Chrétien left Washington on November 5 (election day in the United States, as it happened) and flew first not to Central Africa but to the south of France. There, he visited President Mobutu, convalescing at his Riviera villa after prostate surgery. Mobutu assured Chrétien that he would not impede efforts to consolidate a cease-fire in eastern Zaire (which had been declared, not altogether convincingly, by the rebels on November 4). The president went on to express at least conceptual acceptance of a regional summit conference and support for the deployment of a multinational, "neutral" force that other African leaders had just endorsed at a summit in Nairobi.

Almost as important, in Ambassador Chrétien's view, was Mobutu's agreement to join Chrétien in front of photographers and camera crews after their meeting. That not only served as a public display of Mobutu's political commitment to the special envoy's mission, it went some way to solidify confidence in Kinshasa, where Mobutu's illness and continuing absence were undermining coherence and resolve inside the regime. The ambassador would repeat this procedural precedent—"photo ops" and, when he could achieve it, a joint news conference with the head of state or government—at each of his stops in the following weeks.

Ambassador Chrétien's strategy in this public part of his diplomacy was designed with two mutually reinforcing objectives: First, it was to establish his own standing and the seriousness of his mission in the minds of the parties to the conflict. Second, it was to secure public commitments from regional leaders so as to discourage backsliding from agreements, however incomplete they may have been. That part of the diplomacy was nothing if not public. In little more than five weeks Chrétien conducted more than a hundred media interviews, twenty-five photo ops, and more than twenty-five formal and informal news conferences. His mission was reported extensively by African, European, and North American media.

His private diplomacy was similarly determined and grew more complex as events rapidly outran his original mandate. One of those complexities, which Ambassador Chrétien took care to control from the start, was the mediator proliferation that had already occurred in the region. The European Union, the United States, and the UN secretary-general himself had earlier dispatched special envoys to Rwanda, Burundi, Zaire, and/or the region generally. Several UN agencies, including the UNHCR and the World Food Program, conducted more or less continual negotiations with governments on refugee and aid matters. Members of the Organization of African Unity (OAU) in several combinations, and its secretary-general, Salim Salim, had also been pursuing mediatory roles.

The November 5, 1996, Nairobi summit drew together leaders from Ethiopia, Eritrea, Kenya, Rwanda, Tanzania, Uganda, and Zambia and the foreign minister of Cameroon (the Mobutu government choosing not to attend) to consider the Rwanda-Zaire conflict. Ambassador Chrétien at the start of his mission cast a positive light on those activities, suggesting they reflected a "convergence of interests and political will" in the pursuit of peace. But before leaving New York, he secured Boutros-Ghali's agreement that his would be preeminent among the many mediation missions. By his own energy, and by a skillful conduct of media relations, the ambassador was largely successful in distancing his own diplomacy from the others. While Chrétien periodically briefed ambassadors accredited in the region and heard their views, there was little interference from other mediation activities during his travels.

The ambassador's quickening fears for the fate of the refugees in early November were soon communicated to the Canadian prime minister. But in their telephone conversations, it was the prime minister, not the ambassador, who first mentioned possible Canadian leadership of an international military intervention. Meanwhile, of course, there were other and more formal pressures working on Canadian policy decisions.

On Friday, November 8, I received a phone call from Peter Tarnoff, undersecretary of state for political affairs in the U.S. State Department. In the course of that conversation, he asked me "if I would fall off my chair" if Canada were asked to lead a multinational humanitarian intervention into eastern Zaire. The Clinton administration, it seemed, believed action was necessary but was constrained by domestic political resistance against bearing the risks of leadership. The U.S. State Department regarded Canada as skilled and experienced in UN peacekeeping, unencumbered by postcolonial history or ambition, as well as a reliable (and compliant?) ally. Still seated, I replied that I would report the question immediately to the prime minister, and did so. I took Tarnoff's question as more than idle curiosity but less than a formal proposal; it was a serious feeler. But it was as startling as it was significant—the U.S. government implying that it would commit forces to an intervention led by another government.

At 2 A.M. the next day, the UN Security Council passed Resolution 1078, calling on member states "to prepare the necessary arrangements" for the immediate return of humanitarian agencies and aid to the camps in Zaire and a voluntary, safe repatriation of refugees. Describing the crisis in eastern Zaire as a threat to regional peace and security (but without citing Chapter VII), the council also directed the secretary-general to prepare plans "for a humanitarian task force, with military assistance if necessary." Resolution 1078 was an obvious compromise. France with a few others had pushed hard for authorization of an immediate military intervention, and the United States had refused. The upshot was an invitation to the willing to assemble an intervention if they could and if the council subsequently agreed.

So these were among the factors influencing the prime minister on November 9 as he reached his decision to assert Canadian leadership: conversations with Raymond Chrétien in Africa; knowledge of the Tarnoff call (and a similar conversation earlier that week between White House national security adviser Anthony Lake and Jim Bartleman, the prime minister's adviser on foreign and defense policy); the inconclusive language of Resolution 1078; evident absence of leadership from the United States or anyone else; and the awful pictures of refugees terrified and dying in the rains of Zaire. By then too, Ambassador Chrétien was finding that French leadership of a multinational force would be unacceptable to key regional actors, not least Rwanda, Burundi, and Uganda.

Indeed, Ambassador Chrétien's mediatory role proved to have dynamic effects on the evolution of Canadian government policy from mediation sponsorship to intervention leadership. First, the sight of his ambassador on television every night undoubtedly fastened the prime minister's attention on the crisis. Second, the mediation activity immediately engaged the foreign policy community in Ottawa; the foreign and defense ministries were providing the special envoy with diplomatic and logistic support, and eastern Zaire instantly became the subject of daily briefings for senior departmental managers and ministers. Third, the ambassador's mission may have entered Clinton administration calculations about Canada's suitability as MNF leader. And fourth, his high-level meetings throughout Africa as the UN secretary-general's personal representative reinforced Canada's standing as a credible interlocutor, both in the region and at the United Nations.

The prime minister was further encouraged by a characteristic exercise of personal diplomacy—he had earlier spoken with President Clinton, and he spent the weekend on the phone to Chancellor Kohl, Prime Minister Major, President Chirac, Boutros-Ghali, and others, canvassing their views. On Monday, November 11, Prime Minister Chrétien and his cabinet formally decided to propose Canada's leadership of the MNF, and on November 12 he publicly announced it.

Canada had never before led a coalition of this kind. Nor had Canada ever commanded an MNF under Chapter VII. So there were doubts—not least in the Canadian Department of National Defence—that Canada was capable of success. It must be said too that there was an unsettling element of surprise in the prime minister's decision: Prime Minister Chrétien's conduct of foreign policy had been consistently modest and cautious until now; this was an entirely atypical initiative carrying considerable risk and attracting intense public attention.

The first and essential challenge was to enlist U.S. collaboration in the intervention—to win the required legal authority from the Security Council, of course, and to secure active operational U.S. participation with troops on the ground in Zaire. That latter purpose deserves special emphasis. In the first place, the United States was very nearly the only country in the world with the aircraft, intelligence assets, and other apparatus to deploy a large-scale intervention (in this case, a planned 10,000 troops from all the contributing countries). But the real necessity of U.S. participation lay rooted in a political fact: the Canadian military, and the governments of Western Europe expressing conditional commitments to participate, would not join without prior U.S. commitment to deploy its forces in Zaire. That gave the Clinton administration an effective veto over the entire operation; if the United States did not commit forces to the MNF, the MNF would not be created. The first Canadian diplomatic objective, therefore, was to secure that U.S. undertaking. But while the United States was inviting Canada to take the lead, the United States had given no assurances that it would follow.

Indeed, Canada-U.S. negotiations throughout November and December were defined by that tension in the U.S. position—the tension between sponsoring Canada's leadership in the MNF while doubting that leadership, testing it, and trying to manipulate it. Canadian officials embarked on what would soon prove to be a daunting effort to satisfy stringent, sometimes vague, and frequently frustrating U.S. demands for the design of a political-decision-making structure within the coalition, for military command-and-control provisions, and for a clear and declared exit strategy. And in dealing with the Americans, one could feel their remembered experience in Somalia, images of which were aired repeatedly on U.S. television screens throughout this period. The lack of enthusiasm among U.S. military commanders was palpable, as was the skepticism among many of the civilians in the rest of the administration.

Satisfying those demands was all the more difficult because the U.S. administration, as ever, was itself divided. Generals from the Pentagon gave every sign of unwillingness to participate in any military way; at the very least, they sought assurances against the familiar fear of mission creep and held to the customary U.S. stricture against placing U.S. troops under foreign command. Secretary of State Warren Christopher (contending at the time with conflicts in Bosnia and the Middle East) remained almost wholly silent, although there were advocates of intervention within his department. It was left largely to the White House national security adviser, Anthony

Lake, both to negotiate terms with Canada and other coalition members and to broker consent inside the administration.

The inevitable problem of integrating U.S. military forces under foreign command arose at the very start of the negotiations, when I and a senior Canadian team met with Lake and other U.S. officials on November 12 in the White House. It was an issue that had already been argued out at great length in the case of Bosnia, but in that instance, its resolution was facilitated by the confidence and experience of nearly fifty years of shared commands in NATO. The intended MNF in Central Africa would include forces not only from NATO members such as the United States, Great Britain, France, and Canada, but also from Africa, Latin America, and non-NATO Europe. In the end—although the agreement was never tested in the field—U.S. authorities agreed to a rather straightforward arrangement: The MNF would function under the operational control of a Canadian commander, Lieutenant General Maurice Baril, with a U.S. deputy interposed between the commander and U.S. troops. U.S. forces in any event would deploy under the national command of their president. And at U.S. insistence, a steering group, consisting of major troop-contributing countries (and others providing MNF financing), would give political direction to the MNF under UN Security Council authority.

On November 15, with at least the outlines of those understandings in place, the Security Council authorized the formation of the MNF with Resolution 1080. Based on a Canadian draft, and citing Chapter VII, Resolution 1080 welcomed efforts to establish "a temporary multinational force" that would facilitate the restoration of aid to the refugees and their voluntary repatriation to Rwanda, along with the safe return of displaced Zaireans. The resolution specified that the MNF would terminate on March 31, 1997, unless the Security Council decided otherwise. As for the MNF's actual operations, participating states were authorized to use "all necessary means"—but were themselves to decide what that meant. The coalition was required to report to the Security Council through the secretary-general at least twice monthly.

What Resolution 1080 emphatically did *not* authorize was an MNF that would attempt by force to separate armed combatants from the refugees they controlled in eastern Zaire. In the eyes of many in the NGOs and UN agencies, this represented a fatal failure of will among MNF participants and Security Council members. But there was simply no consensus on the council in support of fighting or disarming Hutu soldiers or militias; several countries, including Canada and the United States, expressly and publicly opposed any such mandate.

It has since been suggested that an overarching U.S. priority in those weeks was to see Kabila's rebellion advance across Zaire and so extinguish the corrupt and weakened Mobutu dictatorship. Officials in the French government certainly believed U.S. objectives to be unrelated to humanitarian relief. Reciprocally, some U.S. officials thought the French were acting to reestablish their influence in Central and West Africa. Zaire's rich endowment of mineral resources was assumed also to enter the calculations of various Western governments and potential coalition partners. Whatever truth there was to those ulterior interests and unspoken objectives (or to suspicions of U.S.-Rwandan coordination), the conflicting perceptions complicated the work of organizing and managing the intervention coalition. The complications were aggravated by the antipathy of several key African governments to any French leadership role in the MNF.

The Canadian government accepted early on the need for a prominent African presence in the intervention force and ultimately the value of active participation by the OAU in finding a political settlement of Central Africa's conflicts. Indeed, achieving African collaboration in the intervention became one of Ambassador Chrétien's objectives in his weeks of travel in the region; in that and other efforts, officials at the United Nations could not have been more supportive. Engaging African leaders was also the objective of much energy invested by the Canadian government. Prime Minister Chrétien conducted hours of telephone diplomacy with African counterparts, two Canadian ministers visited Africa in the same period, and Foreign Affairs Minister Axworthy lent considerable effort to the same end.

Regrettably, success here was impeded by at least two factors. The first was Canada's own scarce diplomatic resources in Central Africa. Several Canadian embassies in Africa had been closed or severely curtailed in recent years. At the time, Canada had in the field only one officer in Kinshasa, a small aid office in Kigali, and no resident officers in Bujumbura or Kampala. The second factor obstructing progress was the complexity and ambivalence of relations among African states themselves. Neighboring states such as Uganda and Tanzania were in some sense parties to the conflict by reason of the presence of tens of thousands of refugees from earlier Central African conflicts. The Museveni government in Kampala was something of a patron to the Tutsi-dominated government in Kigali and to Tutsis in Zaire. The Rwandan government, unambiguously after November 15, opposed an MNF deployment. There remained, moreover, an enduring (and understandable) objection in African states to the very principle of armed intervention, especially intervention by non-Africans. When African leaders agreed at their Nairobi summit on November 5 to recommend a neutral intervention in eastern Zaire, they meant it to be a UN intervention—under direct UN command—not a UN-authorized mission under the command of foreign governments. The final terms of Resolution 1080—calling for a multinational force under Canadian command—therefore became a lasting grievance to African states resistant to North Americans and Europeans intervening by force of arms in African troubles.

With all of these equivocations—U.S. hesitations, European suspicions, African sensitivities—it was expectedly difficult for a country of Canada's middle-power influence to coordinate and manage the MNF and its directing coalition of willing partners. Although several heads of government were quick to promise their forces to the operation, when the Canadian Foreign Ministry or Defence Department called back for specific troop commitments, they were answered with steadfast waffle by ministers and generals. Among other things, that proved the rule that the military in many countries are far less eager for armed intervention than their civilian political leaders. But the tendency to temporize was strengthened by the dramatically changing and often baffling conditions on the ground as the crisis developed. More on that later.

To compensate for Canada's own modest capacities for launching an intervention of this kind, to answer U.S. concerns for limiting and managing the mission mandate, and to open the whole project to as many governments as possible, a series of consultative meetings began in New York even before the passage of Resolution 1080. The fifteen-member steering group first met formally on November 29. The preparatory stage was chaired by a Canadian from the Department of Foreign Affairs (with the prospect of another state taking the chair once the MNF actually deployed); membership was extended to governments committing major troop contributions, and to Japan in respect of its promise of MNF financing. But almost all that can be said of the steering group is that it served as a forum where Canadian officials repeatedly pleaded for firm commitments of forces and where representatives of other governments just as repeatedly refused to deliver on those commitments.

The original plan for the MNF—the plan that at least some members of the Security Council had in mind when they unanimously passed Resolution 1080—was for forces to occupy and protect the airports at Goma and Bukavu to facilitate aid distribution, then if necessary (and only in what the military called "a permissive environment") to create safe corridors from the camps to the Rwandan border. (The U.S. mission, in the early planning, was to include control of the Goma airport and the road eastward to Rwanda.) The language of the resolution, however, was notably less specific:

it simply described the two-part purpose of enabling the distribution of aid and facilitating repatriation to Rwanda (and, in much smaller numbers, to Burundi). However, none of that happened.

On November 15, a sudden attack by the Kabila forces accomplished what diplomacy had not—it separated the ex-FAR soldiers and Hutu militias from the general population of refugees. No longer under the intimidation of the Hutu gunmen, refugees by the hundreds of thousands thronged toward the Rwandan border east of Goma. Within days, most of the 1.1 million Rwandan refugees who had been in Zaire had returned to their home country. Kabila, meanwhile, had established his control of Bukavu and Goma.

That turn of events, though welcome, left two questions of controversy and doubt. The first was whether Kabila and the Banyamulenge had suddenly attacked the camps precisely because of Resolution 1080—the imminent arrival of disciplined foreign troops jeopardizing the rebels' control of territory in eastern Zaire, thus interrupting the campaign that would eventually dethrone Mobutu. That question can now be answered: Paul Kagame, the Rwandan defense minister and vice president, has since acknowledged that the timing of the attacks on the camps was determined in part by the passage of Resolution 1080. The second and more troubling question was the bleak issue of numbers: How many of those 1.1 million refugees walked not homeward but westward, deeper into the Zairean jungle? Twenty thousand? Two hundred thousand? More to the point, did they flee westward in confusion and fear—or because they were the killers (and their families) active in the genocide of 1994, not so much refugees as fugitives?

That was and remains a worrying question. And it stirred strong emotion among government officials and humanitarian agencies at the time, for an obvious reason. If large numbers of innocent victims were somehow trapped and lost in the Zairean forest, there surely was some obligation on the international community to find and help them. But if so, how? For military commanders (even the boldest and least skeptical among them), it was one thing to arrange for aid deliveries to known and accessible refugee camps and a far more dangerous thing to search out, identify, and provide aid to unknown numbers of people who could not even be found with any confidence—all to be done in the midst of a widening war against a collapsing Zairean army.

In short, with only a few hundred Canadian headquarters personnel yet deployed under MNF command (Lieutenant General Baril arrived in Africa on November 19), the original rationale for the force itself began to dissolve.

In the capitals of Africa, Ambassador Chrétien immediately detected the loss of international enthusiasm for the intervention. In arduous discussions with coalition partners, Canadian ministers and their officials in Ottawa, New York, and Washington sensed the same change of opinion. The transformation was made explicit when military leaders (including Baril) assembled at the U.S. airbase near Stuttgart on November 22 to decide the MNF's operational mandate. After long and contentious debate, it became clear to the Canadians there that no consensus remained among key coalition members for any large-scale military action. All that could be agreed in Stuttgart was to establish the Entebbe headquarters that Baril had already begun, although the Canadian government tried to strengthen that option with a proposal to prepare (but not deliver) airdrops of aid to refugees still in Zaire. In subsequent days, it was obvious that the necessary political and material support for even that modest mission did not exist.

On December 10, with the refugee movement continuing albeit at a slower rate, and with no steering group consensus forthcoming, Lieutenant General Baril recommended to the Canadian government that the MNF be stood down: "It is my assessment that the MNF mission has largely been accomplished and therefore the mandate should come to an end," he wrote. "For those Rwandan refugees who remain in eastern Zaire, and who may not want to return for security reasons, needed assistance can be provided by the humanitarian relief agencies in cooperation with local authorities, in due course, and as the security situation permits."

Two days later, Boutros-Ghali sent Ambassador Chrétien's final report on to the Security Council. With the return of 600,000 or more refugees, the report said, "the need for the deployment of a multinational force . . . has changed." It also pointed out that Rwanda, with the large return of refugees, had withdrawn its earlier (ambivalent) support for MNF deployment. Ambassador Chrétien noted that a new outbreak of fighting between Zairean and Ugandan forces did "not bode well for peace and stability." And he found little regional support for an early peace summit, observing that the basic causes of regional conflict remained to be addressed. There was not much here to dissuade those who had already decided to wind up the MNF. In Washington that day, the Pentagon announced it had pulled out half the 450 soldiers it had deployed to Central Africa in the crisis.

The Canadian position, one can say, was now in flux. Prime Minister Chrétien was being urged by Foreign Affairs Minister Axworthy to carry on the intervention; his defense minister, Doug Young, advocated a prompt withdrawal. The argument had not been resolved even as the steering group gathered in New York on December 13 for its second (and, as it turned out, final) meeting. That naturally presented a problem for Paul Heinbecker, the senior and very experienced Canadian diplomat who would take the chair at that meeting. The problem was made no easier by the telephone message Heinbecker received from Ottawa: Your prime minister wants the MNF wound up now, he was told, and your minister of foreign affairs wants to keep it going; good luck. In the end—and after Lieutenant General Baril had briefed the steering group with his own recommendation for withdrawal—Heinbecker wisely told the meeting that Canada agreed with Baril's assessment. Canada would end its own involvement in the MNF on December 31.

What followed was for the most part a recitation of familiar views. The French argued for some continued effort. Britain accepted Canada's recommendation. South Africa was equivocal. The only surprise was the U.S. suggestion—offered by George Moose, assistant undersecretary for African affairs at the State Department—that a skeleton MNF headquarters be kept in place to monitor events. Heinbecker responded that Canada after all was the only country with forces in the MNF and Canada was leaving; no other government took up Moose's proposal. Later that day, Canadian ambassador Fowler formally reported to Boutros-Ghali with the recommendation that the MNF be terminated on December 31, 1996. And so it was.

## LESSONS AND REFLECTIONS

Many in the international NGO community, including those in Canada, judge the attempted intervention in eastern Zaire to have been a disappointing failure, if not a tragic fiasco. That may be too harsh. Without the impending deployment of the MNF, it is unlikely that Kabila and his allied forces would have been moved so quickly to attack the Hutu forces ruling the refugee encampments; the refugees, in other words, would have remained in terrible straits, cut off from food, water, and medicine. It is dreadful that so many died trying to return home or to lose themselves in the jungle. It is painfully tragic that international action was not taken to save more of them—or at least to try. Nonetheless, the return of many hundreds of thousands to Rwanda was an achievement not to be dismissed, even if it was less than what the Canadians and so many others set out to achieve.

But there were and remain unsettling implications in the experience. Once again, U.S. domestic divisions and institutional frictions worked against timely, effective military intervention, even when the political risks of coalition leadership were accepted by another government. And leaving aside the familiar reluctance of the superpower in this case, what of the other permanent members (China, France, Russia, and the United Kingdom) of the UN Security Council? They no doubt still have greater capacity to conceive and deploy successful humanitarian interventions in general—but not always when it comes to particular cases. In this case, for example, France was unwelcome in Central Africa (except arguably in Zaire). The United States was suspected in Zaire of pursuing self-serving interests and neglecting the plight of an old ally. China remained hostile to intervention generically. Russia was consumed by domestic travails. And the British were skeptical in principle (and compromised, perhaps, by the stresses of reconciling French and U.S. attitudes) and anyway unforthcoming.

Canada, by contrast, was generally welcomed among most African states as a disinterested, able, and well-intentioned intervenor. But we were disadvantaged by our own slight military capacity: It was difficult to secure commitments for a planned force of 10,000 troops from others when we were plainly prepared to deploy only about 1,500 of our own. We had sparse diplomatic representation in the crisis region. And we came with no record of commanding a large MNF. These are all characteristics that any other middle power is likely to exhibit in a future crisis.

In short, the geopolitical specifics of such emergencies might sometimes disqualify P-5 powers from directing humanitarian interventions, and the political and military demands of MNF formation and management tend to disqualify everybody else. This is not a comfortable paradox.

We advance these generalizations guardedly. As we said at the start, this was undeniably an unusual episode with ambiguous outcomes. And like every complex emergency, this one displayed complexities all its own: the ambivalent and unusual U.S. proffer of Canadian MNF leadership; a particular tension between U.S. and French objectives; Canada's modest military capacity and its relative absence from the diplomatic history of Central Africa; and the intricacies of the region's own civil and interstate conflicts.

Still, it is reasonable to suppose that the disadvantages Canada experienced in this case might well adhere to any middle power attempting to lead some similar intervention in the future. The asset of geopolitical disinterestedness, for instance, may commonly be offset by the liability of regional irrelevance. Good intentions, reputation, and exceptional diplomatic skill can qualify a middle power to provide constructive mediation; history supplies a gratifying number of examples, from Suez to Oslo. But leading a large Chapter VII multinational force imposes different demands, for which middle powers most of the time are less well equipped.

These same considerations, among others, go far to explain Canada's active support for improving the United Nations' own capacities in mounting

Chapter VII operations—to mitigate the disadvantages of small and middle powers. The Canadian study of and recommendations for a rapid reaction capability and Denmark's proposed SHIRBRIG (Standby Forces High Readiness Brigade) count as important innovations.

What more can be learned from this episode? It should first be said that we all arrive at such emergencies with some historical burden. In fact, Canada during the weeks of crisis in eastern Zaire was experiencing its own Somalia Effect—televised hearings by a royal commission inquiring into a number of killings and beatings of Somalis by Canadian soldiers in 1993. The impact of this on the Department of National Defence was both cautionary and demoralizing; it inspired no enthusiasm for another humanitarian mission in a remote and confusing African conflict.

The conflict teaches us again that almost any use of military personnel in the midst of hostilities—indeed, even the mere expectation among combatants of military intervention—will have political consequences on the ground.[4] That makes the design and management of an intervention consensus all the more complicated, especially if the consequences are unpredictable or variously anticipated. Differing interests, objectives, and expectations, in the coalition and among combatants, obstructed agreement on intervention, even though its proclaimed purpose was altogether "humanitarian." To repeat, Canada remained in a military sense a lesser player in the coalition, without the influence to direct the MNF where its larger partners would not go.

While considering interests, it also bears recalling that humanitarian agencies have interests too—sometimes political interests. In an emergency when information is scarce, confused, and contested, governments need to understand those various interests and the effects they have on the reliability of information that humanitarian agencies provide. That is especially so when policy perspectives are shaped in part by media reports inspired by agency activities. Even when motivated by all the best intentions, leaders of humanitarian agencies may find themselves overdrawing the problem at the start—or denying a solution when it has occurred.

Indeed, the confusion of rumor, misinformation, and secrecy that prevailed in eastern Zaire throughout this crisis remains one of the most disturbing elements of the case. British broadcaster Nik Gowing, in an extraordinary study of information management and media coverage in eastern Zaire,[5] describes an "information vacuum" largely devised and enforced by Paul Kagame, the Rwandan defense minister. (As he told Gowing in an interview, Kagame had learned at least some of his information-warfare techniques during a U.S. Army training course at Fort Leavenworth.) By severely restricting access for NGOs and reporters in the war zone, Rwandan and Kabila forces in some measure controlled how the international community would define the crisis and respond to it. Their control over information was obviously not complete, but much of what they did not control was muddle and rumor.

Not least because of this burden of gathering and assessing conflicting information, it has to be said as well that forming and leading a coalition of this kind consumes enormous bureaucratic and political energies. The degree to which Canada's initiative preoccupied senior members of the Defence and Foreign Affairs Departments cannot be overstated. The work simply consumed all the time and attention of all the top people in both departments for weeks on end—and would have seriously undermined the departments' operations if the crisis had lasted much longer. This issue of limited resources represents another and practical impediment to middle-power leadership of big multinational interventions.

Nor is this resource limitation likely to be relaxed significantly, even in the longer run. The investments in airlift, staffing, and intelligence (to cite just three of the costly requirements) that would be needed to equip a country of Canada's size for large-scale military interventions of this kind are simply improbable in any realizable future. This is not to say that Canada's actions lacked popular support. To the contrary, domestic public opinion favoring intervention probably outlasted even the prime minister's eagerness for it. The government's intervention policy on the whole attracted support from all parties in Parliament (although their support was never put to the test of a large deployment). Domestic politics may have encouraged the prime minister suddenly to assert intervention leadership, but it would be a mistake to conclude that politics forced him ultimately to abandon it.

Ambassador Chrétien's experience in the crisis points to the value of minimizing the potential interference effect of multiple and simultaneous mediations. To the extent that he was able to advance the work of a peace in Central Africa, it was in part precisely because he was not encumbered by associations with old conflicts and failed bargains or by suspicions of a hidden purpose.

Canada's national experience trying to organize and manage a large MNF was less reassuring—and teaches prudence to any middle power similarly honored by an invitation to lead a future intervention. But that is not to say it was a mistake for us to make the attempt. A terrible tragedy seemed imminent; "something" had to be done. Prime Minister Chrétien was right to believe that this represented an opportunity—and even an obligation—for Canada to accept the risks and take the initiative.

### NOTES

1. See, for example, Glynne Evans, "Responding to Crises in the African Great Lakes," *Adelphi Papers*, no. 311 (London: International Institute of Strategic Studies, August 1997); and Gérard Prunier, *The Rwanda Crisis*, rev. ed. (New York: Columbia University Press, 1997).

2. Joint Evaluation of Emergency Assistance to Rwanda, "Synthesis Report," in *The International Response to Conflict and Genocide: Lessons from the Rwanda Experience* (Copenhagen: Steering Committee of the Joint Evaluation of Emergency Assistance to Rwanda, 1996), 9.

3. Ibid., 11.

4. For this and other useful observations by two Canadians involved directly in the execution of Canadian policy in this case, see James Appathurai and Ralph Lysyshyn in *Canadian Foreign Policy* 5, no. 2 (winter 1998): 93–105.

5. Nik Gowing, "New Challenges and Problems for Information Management in Complex Emergencies" (paper prepared for the conference "Dispatches from Disaster Zones," London, May 27–28, 1998). The problems this kind of information management poses for the international community tend to be aggravated by technology. Satellite communication intensifies pressures on journalists to deliver fresh stories many times a day, without the independent fact-checking that only time allows. But satellite transmission of broadcast material, telephone calls, or NGO e-mail is also vulnerable to interception by combatants and others, who can use the stolen information for their own purposes. Warns Gowing: "The issues of information control and the intercepting of satellite communications are potentially the most explosive for the future management of conflicts."

## Background to Chapter 6

## Managing Potential Conflicts in the South China Sea: Informal Diplomacy for Conflict Prevention

The South China Sea is the scene of numerous conflicting claims to own-ership of the islands that dot its waters and to the living and nonliving resources of the sea and seabed. These disputes over sovereignty and juris-diction have occasionally flared into violence and have long been conducted even in the diplomatic sphere with a vehemence that has precluded the possibility of reaching a compromise solution. In a preventive effort to fos-ter dialogue among the East and Southeast Asian states involved and ulti-mately to reach a mutually acceptable solution to their conflicting claims, an informal workshop process was launched in 1990. Participants in the workshops are drawn from senior levels of government, or have close con-tact with those levels, yet they attend the workshops in their own "personal capacity." As such, they enjoy much greater latitude to discuss matters on which their governments have inflexible public positions. This track-two initiative, which is intended to develop new ideas and cooperative approaches and channel them into current and future track-one negotiations, has in-creasingly focused on more substantive issues and has spawned several work-ing groups to address specific topics in a wide variety of fields.

### MAJOR ACTORS

- Regional states or authorities: Brunei Darussalam, Cambodia, Indonesia, Laos, Malaysia, the People's Republic of China, the Philippines, Singapore, Taiwan, and Vietnam

- Canadian International Development Agency (CIDA), which provides core funding for the project
- Pusat Studi Kawasan Asian Tenggara, directed by Hasjim Djalal, and the South China Sea Informal Working Group, directed by Ian Townsend-Gault

## IMPORTANT DATES

- 1990: First Workshop (including the six ASEAN countries) held in Indonesia
- 1991: Second Workshop (including all regional states/authorities except Cambodia) held in Indonesia
- 1993: First Technical Working Group (TWG) established to deal with specific issues
- 1995: Full project of six meetings per year established
- 1998: Ninth Workshop held in Indonesia (thirty-second project meeting since inception)

## EXAMPLES OF ISSUES DISCUSSED AND AGREEMENTS REACHED

- Agreement reached on proposals for protecting biodiversity, monitoring rises in sea level, and exchanging data and research on marine life in the South China Sea
- Proposals are being formulated for monitoring the marine environment, standardizing education and training standards for mariners, and exchanging hydrographic data and information
- Statement issued urging the peaceful resolution of disputes; served as a precursor to the formal ASEAN Declaration on the South China Sea

# 6

# Managing Potential Conflicts in the South China Sea

*Informal Diplomacy for Conflict Prevention*

HASJIM DJALAL AND IAN TOWNSEND-GAULT

**M**uch of this volume concerns exercises in mediation. Our work focuses on the stage before mediation may be required—on prevention, in our case through the promotion of cooperative security and by means of informal diplomacy. Our reasons for adopting the informal or track-two approach are explained later, and it will be seen that the degree of informality attending our efforts is sometimes a matter of perception and degree. Our work can be regarded as "preventive diplomacy" as defined in the book *Agenda for Peace* (1996) by former UN secretary-general Boutros Boutros-Ghali, who emphasized the need to prevent disputes from arising, to prevent existing disputes from escalating into conflicts, and to limit the spread of conflicts when they occur.

In Southeast Asia, preventing disputes from arising means managing potential conflicts by promoting multifaceted cooperation among the states or authorities[1] in the region, thus fostering confidence and cohesion so that any problems that do arise can be solved peacefully. The Association of Southeast Asian Nations (ASEAN) has been playing this preventive

109

role for the past thirty years and has scored many successes. When, despite ASEAN's best efforts, disputes have nonetheless arisen, they have been handled in the "ASEAN way," through quiet negotiation to reach a consensus. The effectiveness of the ASEAN way suggests that it should be followed in disputes not only among ASEAN member states but also between them and non-ASEAN members.

The goal of limiting the spread of conflicts when they occur can be illustrated by developments over the past decade in the southern Philippines, in Indochina, and in the South China Sea. Although the situation in the Southern Philippines has been regarded primarily as an internal matter, it has also caught the attention of the Organization of Islamic Countries. Indonesia has been able to play a significant role in finding a solution to the problems in the southern Philippines, thus reducing the likelihood that neighboring countries would be drawn into the dispute. In Indochina, ASEAN devoted more than ten years to helping the warring parties in Cambodia reach a peaceful settlement. And our own ongoing efforts, the series of informal Workshops on Managing Potential Conflicts in the South China Sea, have led to the formulation of various cooperative efforts to convert potential conflicts into areas of cooperation. These efforts are the subject of this chapter.

## THE PROBLEM: TERRITORIAL DISPUTES AND OVERLAPPING CLAIMS TO MARITIME JURISDICTION

The potential for conflict in the South China Sea arises from a complex series of overlapping or multiple claims both to the islets and rocks that dot the southern part of that sea and to jurisdiction in the sea areas around these features. Disputes over jurisdiction are fueled in part by the belief that the seabed and subsoil possess substantial valuable natural resources. This belief, it should be noted, is not necessarily well founded—and thus we face a position that is rooted partly in fact and partly in myth. To explain the context for our work, some background on the South China Sea and its resources is required.

### The South China Sea and Its Resources

The South China Sea is surrounded by countries that, though most of them are independent (Macao is still under foreign rule but this status will soon change), differ considerably from one another. The land sizes of the countries surrounding the sea vary markedly—the smallest being Singapore (633 square kilometers) and the largest China (9.5 million square kilometers). Their population sizes also vary greatly, the smallest being that of

Brunei Darussalam (about 300,000) and the largest China (around 1.2 billion). Their GNPs per capita also vary, with the lowest being that of Cambodia ($215) and the highest that of Singapore ($26,400). Brunei has the lowest number of people employed in fisheries whereas China and Indonesia have the highest (there are more than 2 million fishermen in Indonesia alone). Brunei has the lowest fish catch while the highest are those of China (17.5 million tons in 1993) and Thailand (3.4 million tons in 1993). The consumption of fish per capita among the nations around the South China Sea also differs markedly, Indonesia having the lowest per capita consumption of fish of about 17 kilograms per year and Hong Kong the highest at about 50 kilograms per year.

The South China Sea is one of the most strategic waterways in the world. The approaches to the South China Sea, especially the Malacca-Singapore, Sunda-Karimata, Balabac, Mindoro, Bashi, and Taiwan Straits, are located in noncommunist countries. These approaches are important for the passage of military and commercial vessels including tankers. In the past, the Soviet Union placed great importance on the right of "transit passage" through the Strait of Malacca and the Singapore Strait as well as through the surrounding waters in the South China Sea area, primarily because these passages were important for communication between western and eastern Russia through the warm waters of the South Seas. The Russian Federation may revive this interest in transit passage once it overcomes its current political and economic difficulties.

For Japan, the South China Sea and its most important approaches, especially the Strait of of Malacca and the Singapore Strait, are economic and strategic lifelines, with more than 80 percent of Japan's oil imports being transported through these waterways. These waterways are also extremely important to Japanese shipping in its trade with Southeast Asia, South Asia, Africa, the Middle East, and Europe. Japanese interest in the preservation of peace and cooperation in the South China Sea may also grow as a result of its new orientation toward increasingly intensive relations with the countries of Southeast Asia.

The People's Republic of China (PRC), although basically still a continental country, has also begun—for economic, political, and strategic reasons—to pay increasing attention to the South China Sea and to promote its interests in the area more assertively. Recent efforts by the PRC to develop its naval capabilities may be spurred, at least in part, by a desire to strengthen its claim to some islands in the area.

The South China Sea is rich in natural resources. Its waters are home to numerous short-lived species of fish—so numerous, indeed, that large-scale fishing of one type of species is difficult. It is not uncommon for two hundred species to be netted in a single trawl haul, four-fifths of which are of little or no commercial value. There are more than twenty-five hundred fish species in the Indo-Malay region alone.

The subsoil of the seabed of the South China Sea is thought by some experts to contain extensive deposits of hydrocarbon and fossil oil, including natural gas, especially in the shelf area on the western and southern sides and in shallow patches of the South China Sea Basin. Oil exploitation conducted by Malaysia and Indonesia in their own continental shelves, as well as by the Philippines in the Reed Banks, supports such speculations. However, there is no independent evidence of significant accumulations of hydrocarbons in the area around the Spratly Islands group.

## Competing Claims in the South China Sea

Both China and Vietnam claim territorial sovereignty over the Paracel group of islands situated southeast of China. The Paracel group was occupied by the former regime of South Vietnam until the PRC took the islands by force in 1974. Vietnam still maintains its claim over the Paracels despite the Chinese occupation. Both the PRC and Vietnam rely on historical records to support their respective territorial claims to the Paracel Islands. Except for its impact on the situation in the South China Sea as a whole should it lead to armed conflict, the Paracel issue is generally regarded as a bilateral matter between China and Vietnam.

The other territorial conflict over islands is related to the Spratly Islands group, which lies several hundred miles south of the Paracels. Some of the islands, rocks, and reefs that make up the group are presently occupied by Vietnam (which holds 22), the Philippines (11), China (14), Malaysia (10), and Taiwan (1). Brunei Darussalam claims certain portions of the nearby sea as its exclusive economic zone (hereinafter EEZ)[2] or continental shelf,[3] but does not occupy any island. The occupiers are exploiting fishery resources and conducting intensive and extensive exploration for oil and gas in the area.

China justifies its claim to the Spratly Islands by reference to a map of the South China Sea published by the Republic of China in 1947. The map features nine rather broad, discontinuous dotted lines, each located close to the coasts of the other littoral states. Since 1947, China has claimed all the islands encompassed by these lines, although it began to occupy some of them only quite recently. This claim was restated in 1958, when China proclaimed a 12-nautical-mile territorial sea[4] and declared that "no foreign vessels for military use and no foreign aircraft may enter China's territorial sea and the airspace above it without the permission of the government of the PRC." At the same time, Bohay Bay (Yellow Sea) and the Chiung Chow Strait (between Hainan and mainland China) were declared "inland waters" of China in which no right of innocent passage was recognized. Some maps have appeared—for instance, maps published by the U.S. Department of State—that join up the dotted lines (possibly misinterpreting the Chinese purpose), but the PRC insists that the 1947 map is definitive. However, the lines remain ill defined and no coordinates have ever been given, and thus the legality and the precise locations of the lines are far from clear. It is *presumed*, however, that China claims the islands, the rocks, and perhaps the reefs but not the whole sea encompassed by the dotted lines.[5]

Taiwan's claim in the South China Sea is similar to the PRC's. Indeed, the positions of workshop participants from the PRC and Taiwan have sometimes been much alike. Taiwan occupied Itu Aba Island more than two decades ago but does not appear to have occupied any other features.

Vietnam claims the whole of the Spratly Island group and all its continental shelf, as well as an extensive area of the South China Sea. The limits of the claim have not been clearly identified by coordinates, however.

The Philippines' claim is based on the so-called proximity principle and on "discovery" of the islands concerned by a Philippine explorer, Thomas Cluma, in the 1950s. Unlike the Chinese claim, the Philippine claim is clearly defined by coordinates. However, the coordinates are not measured from base points on land, but from fixed positions at sea, which seem to have been chosen rather arbitrarily. It is therefore unclear whether the Philippine claim is limited to islands or rocks within the area bounded by those lines or whether it also includes the whole sea within that area.

The Malaysian claim is clearly defined by coordinates showing the extent of its claim to continental shelf in accordance with international law. It claims those islands that it considers to be situated on its shelf.

Brunei's claim likewise is to an area of continental shelf, although its boundary lines are simply drawn perpendicularly from two extreme points on Brunei's coastlines.

Most of these claims overlap with one or more other claims.

Indonesia is not a claimant to any islands or rocks in the Spratly group. However, if the dotted lines drawn by China in 1947 were to be connected, then the Chinese and Taiwanese claims might be interpreted as intruding on the Indonesian EEZ and continental shelf as defined in the Law of the Sea Convention of 1982 and as demarcated in the Indonesian-Malaysian Agreement of 1969. The Chinese, however, have assured Indonesia that they do not have maritime boundary problems with Indonesia in the South China Sea.

As we have noted, all the claimants except Brunei have occupied numerous islets, rocks, and reefs, and although there is no clear geographic pattern of occupation, the various conflicting claims evidently amount to a scramble for territory and resources.

## THE ORIGINS OF THE WORKSHOP PROCESS

In the late 1980s and early 1990s, the foremost issue on the security agenda of Southeast Asia—namely, the Cambodian conflict—seemed to be moving toward settlement. With the prospects for peace and cooperation in the region looking brighter than ever before, attention turned to focus on the next item on the regional security agenda: the South China Sea. The South China Sea featured so prominently for several reasons:

- Clashes between China and Vietnam had taken place as recently as 1988, when three Vietnamese vessels were sunk and more than seventy persons were killed near Fiery Cross Reef, very far from mainland China and deep in the heart of Southeast Asia.
- There existed multiple claims to territory, islands, and maritime jurisdiction in the South China Sea, particularly in and around the Spratly Islands group.
- The countries around the South China Sea have a very long history of conflict and very little experience of cooperation.
- Economic development of the countries around the South China Sea was proceeding rapidly, spurring a scramble for control of the natural resources of the South China Sea, living and nonliving.
- The South China Sea was strategically significant not only for countries that bordered it but also for more distant states, whose interests could not be ignored.
- The South China Sea was important as a line of communication and transportation for both regional and world trade.
- Problems of pollution and safety of navigation were increasing, as was the need to protect the marine environment and ecosystem in the South China Sea.

Whereas the Cambodian problem had been more or less confined in geographical terms, a major confrontation in the South China Sea threatened to be more serious in that it could not only involve many countries directly but also involve nonregional states directly or otherwise. Therefore, it was essential to seek ways and means of preventing potential conflicts from erupting into armed conflagration. Since negotiations were unlikely to prove successful in the short to medium term, and since the states concerned were unlikely to seek third-party settlement of their various disputes, a different approach was required. It was necessary to find a way of building confidence and promoting a sense of community in the South China Sea area. Part of the challenge here was to encourage the process of evolution from the "old" law of the sea to the "new" regime encapsulated in the Law of the Sea Convention of 1982.

The most salient shift of emphasis in the law of the sea as it developed from 1945 to 1975 was the qualification of previously enjoyed unilateral rights (akin to but distinct from those of sovereignty over land) by concepts that called for various forms of collaboration or cooperation. In other words, states had to come to terms with the fact that their rights were qualified by obligations, often to neighboring states. Nowhere were these obligations more tangible than between the littoral states of a semi-enclosed sea. This concept, like that of single ecoystem management, was developed by marine scientists and posed new challenges for lawyers and policymakers. The most pertinent elements of the 1982 convention addressing the need (or obligation) for different forms of cooperation are those provisions dealing with the regimes of the Exclusive Economic Zone (Part V, Articles 61–67) and the Enclosed or Semi Enclosed Seas (Part IX, Article 123). The problem of implementing the convention was not merely one of habituating governments to notions of cooperation (sometimes between neighbors whose relations were far from cordial) but of helping governments to comprehend just what these obligations might entail. So far as the South China Sea was concerned, the convention was clearly going to come into force (October 1994), and would be ratified by all the littoral states, just when jurisdictional issues were moving to center stage on the regional security agenda.

## Testing the Waters

Thus, by the late 1980s, the consensus was that disputes concerning sovereignty over the Paracels and the Spratlys were becoming prominent issues that could threaten Southeast Asian security. Hasjim Djalal, a former Indonesian diplomat, was among those who had foreseen the possible escalation of a dangerous situation and had conceived of the possibility of convening informal meetings to discuss not sovereignty and jurisdiction but confidence building and cooperation. In part, Djalal was drawing on his experiences with the Fisheries Task Force of the Pacific Economic Cooperation Council (PECC), of which he was a leading member, in facilitating cooperation among the states of Southeast Asia, the Pacific islands, and Pacific Latin America, where formal intergovernmental initiatives had foundered. While working together on a workshop on petroleum joint development in Southeast Asia, Djalal and Ian Townsend-Gault, a Canadian academic, developed Djalal's idea into a concept document that was submitted to the Canadian Department of Foreign Affairs. This led to modest but sufficient financial support from the Canadian International Development Agency for the first (and obviously somewhat experimental) phases of the initiative.

The first step in our project was to investigate the receptiveness of the ASEAN countries to such an initiative. With the blessing and guidance of the Indonesian foreign minister, Ali Alatas, we visited the ASEAN capitals in late 1989 to test the waters. It turned out that (1) nearly everybody we met thought that we should do something; (2) there was apprehension that territorial disputes could pose major difficulties in developing cooperative efforts; (3) in view of difficult and sensitive territorial issues, it would be better if the approach were informal, at least at the initial stage; and (4) there was a notion that ASEAN member states should coordinate their views and positions first before they engaged non-ASEAN states in such efforts.

Consequently, we decided that regardless of the territorial disputes, we should try to find an area or areas in which everyone could agree to cooperate, no matter how small the area or areas might be or how slow or insignificant progress might seem to come. We also aimed to develop confidence-building measures or processes so that the various claimants would become comfortable with one another and would thus be able to address their territorial or jurisdictional disputes within a cordial and constructive atmosphere. If we could help participants from different states work together, we might transform the habit of confrontation into the habit of cooperation. We were guided by the idea that every instance of conflict contains an opportunity for cooperation—an opportunity that we all have an obligation to discover and to develop for the benefit of all.

On the basis of support evinced during the meetings we held in 1989, we organized the First Workshop on Managing Potential Conflicts in the South China Sea, which took place in Bali in January 1990 and was opened by Foreign Minister Alatas. Participation was restricted to members of the (then six) ASEAN countries. In addition to inviting the participants to engage in free discussion, we identified six specific areas for discussion: territorial and sovereignty issues; political and security issues; marine scientific research and environmental protection; safety of navigation; resources management; and institutional mechanisms for cooperation. On the Spratlys and the Paracels, in view of the extremely sensitive nature of the disputes, we limited the forum to five minutes for each participant to express his or her views without entering into discussion. In the end, we found out that there were quite a lot of things on which the participants wanted to cooperate. We also discussed whether and how to include in future workshops non-ASEAN countries, particularly Cambodia, China, Laos, Taiwan, and Vietnam. In his opening remarks as the convener of the workshop, Djalal emphasized that "the workshop is intended as a platform for policy-oriented discussions, not only for academic exchanges of views." Leading participants from each of the ASEAN countries prepared papers on an assigned topic. No statement was issued, but the Canadian workshop secretariat prepared an informal set of proceedings and made it available to governments and experts.[6]

## Participants versus Delegates

The workshop process could not have been initiated, much less developed, had there been any attempt to establish it as an official activity taking place on an intergovernmental basis. The most obvious problem with creating an official process would have been the PRC's objection to the participation of Taiwan, and any intergovernmental meeting would probably have involved only the littoral states (those invested with any rights over the South China Sea), and not the entire region. The most formidable obstacle, however, would have been the attitude of officials. Each claimant government would no doubt have declared at the outset of such a meeting that "our claims are just, clear, and unambiguous, and therefore the only issue worthy of discussion is the adjustment of the position of everyone else to accord with ours." Governments in other marine areas where overlapping claims to jurisdiction exist would not necessarily take such an uncompromising position. However, in the South China Sea these claims have been maintained and promoted with an assiduity that amounts to virulence, and they dominate any meeting at which any aspect of South China Sea activities is discussed. Those who have participated in purely academic meetings on issues pertinent to the South China Sea (or to the Gulf of Thailand, for that matter) will appreciate this point immediately.

Everyone participating in a meeting held under the aegis of the workshop process does so in his or her personal capacity: no one is a delegate or representative. Far from removing the process from the attention of senior officials, this device allows such officials to attend and participate.[7] The "personal capacity" designation can wear rather thin, but this does not matter. What does matter is that the region is meeting and senior people are at the table, not only indicating the status of the gathering but also providing the essential link to the governments and authorities concerned.

In preparing the Second Workshop, we thought it would be helpful to invite China and Taiwan, given that both have claims in the South China Sea. China, though, was reluctant to enter into the discussion, primarily because China considered that South China Sea issues should not be "internationalized" and that China would discuss whatever problems it had directly and bilaterally with the countries concerned. In China's view, its claims to sovereignty over the South China Sea islands were "indisputable." In addition, China would not sit down with Taiwan in a formal international meeting. However, because of the informal nature of our workshop process, and because sovereignty and jurisdiction were not issues for discussion, China did attend.

As it turned out, the Second Workshop, held in Bandung, Indonesia, in 1991, brought into the workshop process not only China and Taiwan but also Vietnam and even landlocked Laos. (Cambodia was invited subsequently, after the UN-sponsored elections resulted in a government that was accorded international recognition.) At the Second Workshop in Bandung we went into more detail than before on the various topics identified at the First Workshop; we also discussed the roles of major non-South China Sea powers in the region, as well as confidence-building measures. Participants were invited to make statements on jurisdiction over the Spratlys and the Paracels, though once again, no discussion was permitted. More technical discussions took place on the issues of marine scientific research, marine environmental protection, and safety of navigation as well as on resources management. Ideas were floated about establishing a secretariat and formalizing the meetings. More significantly, the participants attending the Bandung meeting agreed to issue a statement declaring that disputes in the South China Sea should be settled peacefully, that force shall not be used to settle the disputes, and that parties to the disputes shall exercise restraint in order not to exacerbate the potential conflicts. This statement was a precursor to a much more formal ASEAN Declaration on the South China Sea in Manila issued in 1992, which has come to be regarded as a set of guiding principles for efforts to manage potential conflicts in the South China Sea through cooperation.

## THE EMERGENCE OF THE TECHNICAL WORKING GROUPS

By the Third Workshop, held in Yogyakarta, Indonesia, in 1992, discussions on various topics became so detailed that we decided to create specific technical working groups and experts groups to devise cooperative projects. The meeting in Yogyakarta agreed to establish two technical working groups (TWGs): the TWG on Marine Scientific Research (TWG-MSR) and the TWG on Resources Assessment (TWG-RA).

Some participants continued to urge the creation of a secretariat for the workshop process and to call for the formalization of the process, but many participants opposed those ideas, not least because they believed that discussion of ideas could flow more freely in an informal setup. In addition, there were many technical impediments to the establishment of a secretariat, and it was generally felt that the Center for Southeast Asian Studies (Pusat Studi Kawasan Asia Tenggara), based in Jakarta and directed by Djalal, should continue to be the focal point for the workshop process.

At the Fourth Workshop, held in Surabaya, Indonesia, in 1993, participants agreed that non-South China Sea countries would be allowed to participate on a case-by-case basis to implement specific agreed programs of cooperation. In the meantime, the TWG-MSR had already began discussions in Manila and the TWG-RA had been convened in Jakarta. The Surabaya meeting discussed the results and recommendations of these two TWG meetings, agreed to convene follow-up meetings of the TWG-MSR in Singapore, agreed to establish a TWG on Marine Environmental Protection (TWG-MEP) and a TWG on Legal Matters (TWG-LM), and discussed the possibility of establishing a TWG on Safety of Navigation, Shipping, and Communications (TWG-SNSC). Finally, the participants also indicated that the workshop series had "reached a stage where it would have to concretize programs or projects to realize cooperative efforts on the basis of a step-by-step approach."

The Fifth Workshop, held in Bukittinggi, Indonesia, in 1994 approved some specific projects for cooperation formulated by the TWGs, particularly a program for cooperation on the study and conservation of biodiversity in the South China Sea. The Bukittinggi workshop further agreed to authorize Djalal to seek support and funding for the project proposal on biodiversity; to convene another meeting of the TWG-MSR to finalize proposals on the monitoring of sea levels and tides monitoring, and on database creation, information exchange, and networking; and to convene the first meeting of the TWG-LM in Thailand. The workshop also discussed confidence-building measures.

## A SUMMARY OF RESULTS FOR 1990–98

As of January 1999, thirty-two meetings have taken place under the aegis of the workshop process.[8] These meetings have been held in every part of the South China Sea region except Taiwan, and it is hoped that it will be possible to accept the offer from Taipei to host a meeting there in the future. Four agreed project proposals have been approved, one has been approved in principle, and three others are in an advanced stage of preparation.

Inevitably, several areas remain to be explored, and other areas await more detailed assessment. Even so, it is fair to say that the workshop process has engendered a remarkable range and number of ideas and proposals for cooperation. In a great many cases, these ideas might not have emerged if the workshop process had not offered a forum for airing them. In choosing which ideas to pursue, we have been guided first and foremost by expert opinion. It should be emphasized that we have succeeded in attracting the participation of a great number of the most senior experts in the region in a variety of fields: marine science, ecology, marine environmental protection, navigational safety, hydrography, geology, law, and so on. Many of the participants in the Group of Experts Meeting (GEM) on the Exchange of Hydrographic Data and Information are the preeminent hydrographers in their respective countries. The fact that regional authorities facilitate their participation is further evidence of the degree to which the region is committed to the search for peace in the South China Sea.

The Seventh Workshop, held in Batam, Indonesia, in 1996, discussed the modalities of implementing the agreed project proposals. The most salient problems are financial support and the transformation of the perception of political obstacles into political will. Another, less obvious issue was identified in 1998: capacity. This in turn can be subdivided, and in our opinion the question of domestic capacity to participate is less problematic than the lack of domestic capacity to comprehend why cooperation is necessary at all. States and their officials tend to be instinctively hostile to the notion of cooperation and hide their inaction behind a smokescreen of vaguely defined economic and political obstacles to participation. Almost all countries in the South China Sea have indicated a willingness to participate in the implementation of the agreed-upon programs, providing either expertise, facilities, or even financial resources. Yet there is also a school of thought that holds that implementation should be left to national institutions, because of the sensitive nature of issues that touch on territorial and sovereignty claims.

Only at the Eighth Workshop, held in Pacet, Puncak, Indonesia, in 1997, did participants agree to seek and promote joint implementation of the agreed programs for cooperation. In his keynote address, Foreign Minister Alatas recommended that participants approach this issue with a new sense of purpose. This theme was taken up by Gary Smith, then Canadian ambassador to Jakarta. Speaking on behalf of the Canadian International Development Agency (CIDA), Ambassador Smith not only added his voice to those urging a focus on implementation, but also indicated that CIDA was willing to make available "modest support." Accordingly, Djalal was asked to continue to approach various international, regional, and national agencies, governmental and nongovernmental, in search of support. Our activities have attracted the interest of a large number of organizations, governmental and nongovernmental, domestic and international, many of which have indicated a willingness to play a role in the workshop process. Beginning in 1999, we are devoting additional resources to the task of marrying their priorities and interests to our own.

No direct link exists between our work and a variety of other fora that address issues relevant to the South China Sea—such as the ASEAN-China Dialogue, the informal talks within ARF and in CSCAP (Committee for Security and Cooperation in the Asia-Pacific),[9] and the discussions in ASEAN-ISIS[10]—but such a link is not necessary. After all, the participating personnel overlap, thus ensuring a two-way exchange of views and information.

Despite the progress we have made on many fronts, we should note that as of early 1999 open discussion on territorial and jurisdictional issues, as well as on the more intractable political and security matters, has stalled because of the reluctance of certain participants in the workshops to continue discussion of sensitive issues. We referred earlier to the question of capacity and several shades of meaning connoted by this term. The Law of the Sea Convention has been part of the international landscape—in draft and in final form—for so long that, paradoxically, we are inclined to take it for granted while also being inclined to see implementation as a task for the undefined future. In the South China Sea, however, the time for implementation is at hand. The convention is a treaty in force among all the states of the region except Cambodia and Thailand, and both of those states intend to ratify. Arguably, implementation has commenced, but if so, it is a process that has focused to date on states' rights, not on their obligations. However, once a state ratifies the convention, it is bound by *all* the provisions of the treaty, many of which relate to cooperation.

This is perhaps where problems arise. What forms of cooperation? Under what rules? To what end? In the workshop process, as with all other meetings in the region on marine affairs, official and otherwise, one is struck by the vast disparity in levels of knowledge, experience, and expertise displayed not only from country to country but also from agency to agency within one state. These weak links in the chain—domestically and internationally—must now be helped to come to grips with the realities of the convention to which they have freely subscribed. Our workshop process can assist with this process. Indeed, a start was made with the Study Group on Zones of Cooperation in 1998, which created a framework (supported by a 400-page set of materials) within which participants could absorb information from experts, ask questions, and—most important of all—volunteer information. We have seldom held a meeting marked by such a high degree of collegiality and success. We need hardly say that we learned much from this experience.

The Law of the Sea Convention enjoins cooperation on all coastal states, but especially on the littoral states of an enclosed or semi-enclosed sea. Article 123 (d) of the convention states that "States bordering on enclosed or semi-enclosed sea should co-operate with each other in the exercise of their rights and in the performance of their duties . . . [and] to this end, they shall endeavour to invite, as appropriate, other interested states or international organizations to co-operate with them." Much debate has centered on whether or not the South China Sea constitutes an "enclosed or semi-enclosed sea" within the meaning of this article, and a number of countries have produced highly legalistic textual analyses in support of one position or the other.

Surely this is besides the point. Article 123 attempts to put in legal language a concept that derives from single ecosystem management,[11] and hence the requirement to cooperate is functionally driven. The legal-political element arises from the natural state of the body of water in question, not the other way around. This is not the place for detailed analysis of Article 123, but we raise the issue to illustrate the problem. The workshop process, along with other initiatives focusing in policy, management, and law, must assist the authorities within the region in coming to a better understanding of the relationship between the norms of the law of the sea and the human security–food security imperatives in confronting the challenge of ocean management in the South China Sea. To put it bluntly: We need less politics and more substance.

## CONFIDENCE BUILDING

A second area in which our work focuses is the promotion of confidence-building measures (CBMs) or a confidence-building process (CBP). As mentioned earlier, at the Second Workshop we issued a statement that emphasized the need to resolve any territorial or jurisdictional disputes in the South China Sea by "peaceful means through dialogue and negotiation," that declared "force should not be used to settle territorial and jurisdictional disputes," and that urged "the parties involved in such disputes . . . to exercise self-restraint in order not to complicate the situation." This statement was adopted as the ASEAN Declaration on the South China Sea in Manila in July 1992—thus offering one illustration of how accomplishments in track-two diplomacy can find their way into track-one fora.

In the course of workshop discussions over the years, various CBMs and CBPs have been proposed. Some participants regard the workshop process itself as an important CBM. At the Fifth Workshop, we took up the need for "non-expansion of existing military presence." This principle was supported by many participants but opposed by a few, who argued that this was not an appropriate matter for the workshop to discuss. During the Sixth Workshop, we talked about establishing more contacts between nationals of the littoral authorities stationed in the South China Sea, and initiating an "exchange of military commanders" responsible for the security of the contested areas within the Spratly Islands group. Again, this suggestion elicited a mixed response. There was general agreement, however, that some transparency of the activities in the disputed area was needed. We will continue our efforts to identify mutually acceptable CBMs and CBPs.

If our process is truly informal, can we really place any limit on what can be discussed at the workshops? In theory, the answer is probably no. However, ours is a consensual process and we try to steer the debate into areas where all participants feel free to exchange views. At the same time, we have no desire to enforce overly strict limits, because to do so would undermine the value of the workshops as a venue where senior officials can discuss politically sensitive matters without fear of compromising the official positions of their governments. We have noted that issues regarded as taboo one year can appear on the agenda with the support of all participants one or two years later.

As of early 1999, the pace of discussion of CBMs has slowed. No consensus has yet been reached on the need to prevent the expansion of the existing military presence in the Spratly Islands group or on the need for more contacts and greater transparency among local military and administrative authorities in the disputed areas. Fortunately, there is still agreement to continue discussion on these matters.

## DIALOGUE AMONG THE PARTIES

A third, and more recent, focus for our work is that on encouraging discussion and dialogue among the parties to the territorial disputes with the aim of finding the basis for a solution acceptable to all concerned. China's position has been that the settlement of territorial disputes can be accomplished only by the parties concerned negotiating on a bilateral basis, not regionally or multilaterally or internationally. If it appears that this position is shared by the parties concerned, then all that we can do is to encourage them to seek ways and means to solve their problems peacefully. It is encouraging to note that bilateral dialogues have in some instances yielded positive and concrete results. For instance, the PRC and the Philippines have agreed upon an eight-point code of conduct and the Philippines and Vietnam have agreed upon a nine-point code of conduct. Our TWG-LM has made tentative steps toward exploring elements for a possible code of conduct in the South China Sea.

In any discussion concerning the jurisdictional difficulties in the South China Sea, the subject of joint development arises sooner rather than later. Premier Li Peng of China suggested that his country might be interested in such an arrangement as early as 1990. Much has been written on this topic, which seems to be touted by some international lawyers as a panacea for any and all maritime boundary problems. On the other hand, some imaginative and sophisticated proposals have also been developed for the South China Sea. Comparatively few commentators appear to realize that joint development arrangements must provide a firm basis for resource exploitation and must therefore be an integral part of a resource management regime throughout its existence, which might be as long as fifty years. Furthermore, all such arrangements are essentially sui generis and comparatively untried and untested.

Our own work on joint development, through the TWG-RA and the Study Group on Zones of Cooperation, led to agreement on three points:

- that the joint development concept has excellent potential for application in the South China Sea, especially given the statement by Li Peng in Singapore in 1990, and repeated since, expressing China's willingness to shelve territorial or sovereignty claims in favor of joint development;
- that we should study the various concepts or models of joint development around the world and consider which aspects of these experiences could be usefully applied to the South China Sea area; and
- that we should apply the joint development concept to a "zone to be defined" (the problem is how to define the "zone" for the joint development or joint cooperation).

Sooner or later, agreement on the following four points will also be required:

- the zone within which cooperative or joint activities are to take place;
- the nature or subject of the agreement;
- the mechanism for joint development, which might be an authority or a loosely structured coordinating organization or arrangement; and
- who will participate in joint development or joint cooperation activities.

Agreement on these four points is essential for serious consideration of the possible role of joint development arrangements in the South China Sea. Following the first meeting of the TWG-RA, Djalal suggested a possible "zone" in which every participant, or at least those participants having overlapping claims, could cooperate on the basis of the Law of the Sea Convention of 1982. Some claimants responded favorably to the suggestion, while others said that although they might have some reservations about the idea, they would be willing to examine and discuss it. But one claimant did not want to talk about the proposed "zone" at all, although it expressed its willingness to cooperate.

Joint development is one of those concepts that means different things to different people, and some of these ideas have little basis in reality. We see the work of the Study Group on Zones of Cooperation as helping a number of participants to gain a clearer understanding of the possibilities and shortcomings of the concept and its application to all fields of maritime activities, not merely petroleum operations.

## CONCLUSIONS

### Preconditions for Conflict Prevention in the South China Sea

The preconditions for conflict prevention in the South China Sea have not changed since we began our work. They can be summarized as follows:

- The parties to the disputes must realize that the outbreak of armed conflict will not settle their disputes or benefit them—that it is in fact inimical to the interests of all. (The parties to the disputes appear to recognize this.)
- The parties must develop the political will to settle their disputes peacefully and to take measures to prevent conflict and to focus on their responsibilities with respect to the South China Sea and its vulnerable resources. (The parties appear to be moving in this direction, but much more needs to be done to encourage them to do so.)
- The parties must refrain from legislative acts and unhelpful or provocative acts, and should try to shift public opinion away from support for a hard line and toward support for a more accommodating stance based on the need for cooperation. (This process has barely begun.)

- Transparency—the willingness to engage in public debate and to avoid secrecy as a matter of course—in national policy, legislation, and documentation must be increased; the legal officers of the countries in the region must meet more frequently to exchange documentation and information and to inform one another of planned legislation. (There is still a lot to be done to increase transparency.)
- Preventive diplomacy must be undertaken by all parties that have an interest in the solution of the region's problems. Solutions that take into account national as well as regional interests but that ignore the interests of states outside the region may not be effective in the long term. (This has yet to happen.)

Our experience suggests that to facilitate the achievement of these preconditions, the following lessons must be learned:

- Larger countries should be mindful of the views of their neighbors and take steps to ensure that they are not perceived as trying to dominate or bully their smaller neighbors.
- Participation in cooperative programs should be broadened and linked to mutual economic development. The approach should be inclusive rather than exclusive.
- More emphasis should be placed on regional and common interests, and on the benefits to a state that accrue from the pursuit of regional interests. The countries of the region should learn to pursue their national interests within the regional context.
- The furthering of national resilience and self-confidence should promote regional resilience and cohesion.
- The countries in the region should abandon outmoded concepts of national sovereignty. A growing range of issues once seen as essentially national are acquiring an increasingly regional character or have regional implications that cannot be ignored.
- A new emphasis should be placed on the oriental concept of good neighborliness, which calls for a nonconfrontational approach and the avoidance of rhetoric designed to increase tension and highlight divergences.
- The countries of the region should refuse to participate in an arms race. Instead, they should focus on coordinating their defense needs, thus bolstering regional harmony and the mutual confidence that comes from increased transparency.
- Major external powers should take every opportunity to support the development of an atmosphere in the region that is supportive of peace, stability, and progress—for example, by insisting on adherence to the law of the sea.

- Countries in the region should exercise preventive diplomacy to avoid aggravating, widening, or escalating their disputes into armed conflict.
- Countries in the region should continue to develop various fora for dialogue, bilateral and multilateral, formal and informal. These fora should seek to produce eventual agreement on a code of conduct for the region.
- Countries in the region should pursue various avenues toward the peaceful settlement of disputes through bilateral or multilateral negotiation.
- Third-party mechanisms should be used for dispute settlement, including good offices, mediation, arbitration, and, if necessary, adjudication through the International Court of Justice or the Law of the Sea Tribunal. The High Council established by the Treaty of Amity and Cooperation (TAC)[12]—signed by the original members of ASEAN after their first summit in Bali in 1976—had already formulated certain mechanisms for dispute settlement among ASEAN countries; a new mechanism for the Asia-Pacific region as a whole should be considered, either by drawing from the TAC or from other models.
- The countries in the region should do everything possible to settle their land, maritime, and jurisdictional boundaries as soon as possible and to respect the agreed-upon boundaries.
- Various models of joint development should be considered as interim measures adopted pending an agreement on delimitation as recommended by Articles 74 and 83 of the Law of the Sea Convention.
- Track-two approaches to jurisdictional issues should be inventive and imaginative and transferable to track-one diplomacy.
- The interests of nonregional countries should be taken into account, as should their potential to contribute to the resolution of jurisdictional issues and the promotion or facilitation of cooperation.
- Finally, the parties could make a positive contribution to peace and stability in the South China Sea region if they pledged to adhere to the principles of international law, particularly to the Law of the Sea Convention of 1982, and declared their willingness to submit to adjudication if negotiations between the parties concerned do not bring a solution within a reasonable time or if the disputes persist to the degree that they endanger peace and stability in the South China Sea region.

### Indicia of Progress in the Workshop Process

After almost ten years' experience with the workshop process, what can we say in response to questions such as the following?

- What value do participants ascribe to the process, and how can the ascribed value be measured?

- How can we be sure that the process has not been taken over by one or more countries to create a cooperative smokescreen behind which they can continue their confrontational activities?
- Do regional track-one activities take account of the work of the work-shop process?

Our responses would certainly refer to five points:

1. Countries continue to send to the workshops participants of appropri-ate rank (for example, foreign ministry officials of ambassadorial rank) and leading subject experts, and remain willing to host project meetings.
2. Those countries ineligible to receive CIDA funds meet the full cost of sending participants. Most countries eligible to receive CIDA funds meet the full cost of sending participants in addition to those funded by the project budget. Thus the CIDA contribution covers only a proportion of the entire cost of holding a meeting.
3. Matters of substance (and even controversial matters) are placed on meet-ing agendas and are discussed.
4. Serious consideration is given to acting on meeting recommendations and to implementing proposed projects.
5. There is a growing awareness of the range of issues at stake in the South China Sea, such as marine environmental quality, the sustainability of the fishery, navigational safety issues, the inadequacies of research, and that the confrontational approach is not only inimical to addressing these matters but is itself unlikely to produce satisfactory results. Similarly, there is growing awareness in the region that it may be time to de-emphasize the military-naval option in settling South China Sea disputes.

Regarding point 4, we should note that participating authorities seem to be reluctant to act on the basis of a workshop recommendation until they see concrete evidence of a commitment on the part of other regional authorities and a funding agency to implement that recommendation. This is perhaps a chicken-and-egg situation. Thus, a recommendation resulting from the workshop process may have greater force if it can be shown that it is possible to devise projects for cooperation and bring them at least to the brink of implementation by securing funding, identifying implementing agencies, and so forth.

With respect to point 5, the continuing dispute between the PRC and the Philippines over Mischief Reef and the events that led up to it are hardly evidence of growing trust among regional states and a decline in the role played by their armed forces in interstate disputes. Nevertheless, we would point out that we have always seen the workshop process as but one element of a multifaceted effort at confidence building; the workshop process is intended to complement activities on the formal track, not replace them. The continuing impasse at the track-one level forces attention on track two and the workshop process, which is being asked to assume a greater burden than had been envisaged at the outset.

It has been suggested that our work is promising much but delivering little, that meetings are essentially anodyne exercises and amount to no more than a "talking-shop." We, however, don't see what's wrong with a talking-shop. What is the objection to a forum that brings people together? If the region's experts are not to meet face to face at our meetings, then where? Some critics also charge that significantly more could have been achieved under our banner than has been the case. We are not sure we agree: with secured funding (not as much as we would like, but certainly enough to work with), our only constraints have been political. We are now working in five sectors simultaneously, but we had to build up to this level of activity. It would not have been possible to have launched the process in 1990 with an agenda of eight meetings per year.

Progress will continue to be gradual and essentially piecemeal until states recognize that the obsession with sovereignty issues is essentially a dead end and until they learn to appreciate the negative consequences of maintaining the status quo and the benefits (and imperatives) of the cooperative approach. Continued progress with implementation, confidence building, and avoidance of confrontation depends first and foremost on maintaining political will and on the ability of the initiative to respond to and reflect the changing wishes and priorities of participants.

This is not to say that the absence of a threat to peace and security in the South China Sea would render the workshop process unnecessary or would obviate the need to implement cooperative projects that have been painstakingly discussed and formulated. In the first place, preventive diplomacy is a long-term, continuing process, and we have no wish to halt our work until one or more disputes erupt into armed conflict. Second, we should not forget that cooperation is being employed not merely as a device to encourage confidence and good relations but also because it is the sine qua non of optimum maritime management in a semi-enclosed ocean area such as the South China Sea. A final note: Commentators should hesitate before they assume that the truths of maritime cooperation are self-evident. Implicit in the workshop process is the requirement that participants leave at the door some of their most cherished beliefs and aspirations. They are being asked to think around a regional problem that is inextricably linked to the potent and inflammatory issues of sovereignty and access to natural resources. Few issues pose such challenges or rouse such passions to such an extent. Participants cannot be expected to put aside such concerns easily or swiftly.

As this chapter goes to press, we are planning at least nine meetings in 1999 on zones of cooperation, illegal acts at sea, search and rescue, environmental legislation, other legal matters, marine scientific research and marine environmental protection, nonliving nonhydrocarbon resources, and of course the Tenth Workshop. Our funding is secure until at least 2001, and it appears that this support will continue while we continue to make progress. We have given some indications of how that progress might be measured and how the value of the workshop process might be assessed. Ultimately, the future of our work depends on the attitudes of the authorities of the South China Sea region: How and in what ways do they value this initiative? How and in what ways do they wish to use it? How and in what ways can it be used, now and in the future?

Our initiative is a functional instrument. The workshop process may be compared to a ship that, although it is headed in one general direction, shifts course from time to time as different hands vie for control of the wheel and seek to pilot the ship according to a variety of different and often contradictory charts. The workshop process has defined at least a part of its niche in the regional security landscape and we have learned many lessons from the past nine years. We do not consider the process has yet achieved its full potential: it should evolve, just as our current role has developed. With these caveats in mind, we can say that we are perhaps now sailing somewhat more confidently than before through the dangerous waters of the South China Sea.

## NOTES

1. Because of the involvement in the workshop process of participants from Taiwan, we tend to use the term "authority," rather than "government," to avoid raising issues that have nothing to do with the South China Sea per se.

2. This is the marine area extending seaward 188 nautical miles from the edge of the 12-nautical-mile territorial sea within which coastal states exercise sovereign rights for the exploration for and exploitation of living and nonliving resources, as well as for other economic purposes.

3. The continental shelf is more or less coextensive with the EEZ as regards the nature and extent of state rights, except that it applies to seabed and subsoil only and extends beyond 200 nautical miles where the continental margin of the coastal state does so.

4. The territorial sea is the marine area extending 12 nautical miles from the coast or straight baseline within which the coastal state exercises sovereignty over the water column, seabed and subsoil, and superjacent airspace, subject only to the right of innocent passage available to foreign merchant vessels.

5. It is hard to believe that in 1947, when general international law still recognized only a 3-nautical-mile territorial sea, China would claim the entire South China Sea. A careful

reading of its law of February 25, 1992, likewise suggests that the PRC's claims are more modest, although some recent Chinese writers do seem to imply that China also claims the "adjacent sea" of the islands and rocks.

The concept of "adjacent sea" has not been clearly defined and therefore it is difficult to understand its legal meaning. The concept is foreign to the Law of the Sea Convention of 1982, and this raises the question of the compatibility of this concept with China's international obligations as a state party to this treaty.

The Law of the Sea Convention of 1982 defines only internal waters, archipelagic waters, territorial seas, contiguous zones, exclusive economic zones, continental shelves, high seas, and international seabed area, and stipulates that those waters or zones should be measured by connecting base points on land, or appropriate baselines, to legitimate points, and not by arbitrarily drawing them at sea.

**6.** We have assembled internal reports on each meeting, comprising a detailed summary prepared by rapporteurs from the South China Sea IWG, all conference papers (presented or tabled), the meeting agenda, a list of participants, any statements issued, and so forth.

**7.** Participants from the South China Sea claimant states usually include senior foreign ministry officials (such as the directors of departments concerned with international law and treaties).

**8.** The following summaries illustrate the range of work undertaken by the TWGs.

*TWG on Marine Scientific Research.* As of January 1, 1999, the TWG-MSR has met six times: Manila in June 1993; Surabaya in August 1993; Singapore in April 1994; Hanoi in June 1995; Cebu in July 1996; and Manila again in November 1998 (technically, this was a joint meeting with the TWG-MEP). In addition to the proposed project on biodiversity protection, this TWG has developed two other projects of cooperation: Study on Tides and Sea-Level Change and Regional Cooperation in the Field of Marine Science Data and Information Network in the South China Sea. These proposals were adopted by the Sixth Workshop in Balikpapan in 1995. Contributions by the governments of Brunei Darussalam, Indonesia, and Singapore have made it possible to begin implementing the project on biodiversity protection, but its full implementation will require major funding; negotiations to obtain such support were in an advanced stage when this book went to press.

*TWG on Marine Environmental Protection.* This TWG has met three times: Hangzhou, China, in 1994; Hainan, China, in 1997; and Manila in 1998 (the joint meeting with TWG-MSR). We convened a Group of Experts Meeting on Environmental Protection in Phnom Penh in 1997. This TWG has formulated a cooperative project to establish a training program for ecosystem monitoring in the South China Sea. The project was approved in principle by the Eighth Workshop, in Pacet, Puncak, Indonesia, in December 1997. At the joint meeting in Manila in 1998, it was agreed that an ad hoc group of five or so experts would meet to revise the proposal in light of comments, and that a final version should be reconsidered and adopted in 1999.

*TWG on Resources Assessment.* This TWG has met twice, both times in Jakarta, first in 1993 and then in December 1998. The 1993 meeting agreed to appoint three coordinators: Indonesia, for the study of the geological basin with regard to hydrocarbon potentials; Vietnam, to prepare a study on hard minerals in the South China Sea; and Thailand, to prepare a study on living resources. The efforts of Indonesia and Vietnam were largely frustrated by sensitivities regarding territorial and jurisdictional issues. Thailand, however, was able to prepare a proposal for a stock assessment in the South China Sea, which was discussed at meetings of the TWG on Legal Matters as well as the workshops. Thailand was requested to continue with preparations for the study on stock assessment and a program for its implementation.

The 1998 meeting considered a proposal from Indonesian experts to compile a database on nonliving nonhydrocarbon resources of the South China Sea, in which the Committee for the Coordination of Offshore Prospecting in Bangkok would be invited to collaborate. This proposal was adopted by the meeting, and then by the Ninth Workshop held in Jakarta in 1998. We believe that it will be possible to implement this project fully with our existing resources and hope to commence this process in 1999.

*TWG on Safety of Navigation, Shipping, and Communications.* This TWG has met three times: Jakarta in 1995; Brunei Darussalam in 1996; and Singapore in 1998. The work of this TWG has concentrated on four areas:

- Cooperative efforts regarding hydrographic data and mapping. The first Group of Experts Meeting (GEM) on the Exchange of Hydrographic Data and Information was convened in Kuching, Malaysia, in 1997. The second meeting took place in Singapore in 1998, and a third is planned for 1999. These meetings have been examining two initiatives: a proposed agreement on the exchange of hydrographic data and information, a draft of which was produced by Malaysia; and a proposal drafted by the Philippines to undertake a joint hydrographic survey of a part of the South China Sea (the area in question has no islands or similar features). It is hoped that both initiatives will be finalized in 1999.
- Developing training programs for seafarers and mariners. Singapore was entrusted with the job of developing this topic, and accordingly a GEM was organized in Singapore in 1997. While several promising opportunities for cooperation were identified, it was thought that a second meeting should not be convened until activities in other fora had been concluded, enabling us to see which ideas could be pursued fruitfully.
- Developing cooperative efforts against unlawful activities at sea, and cooperation on search-and-rescue operations. The Ninth Workshop agreed to convene GEMs on both topics in 1999.
- Cooperative efforts regarding environmental protection and the development of contingency plans against marine pollution in the South China Sea. China was entrusted with the task of preparing cooperative programs on this topic.

*TWG on Legal Matters.* The TWG-LM has met three times: Phuket, Thailand, in 1995; Chiang Mai, Thailand, in 1997; and Pattaya, Thailand, in 1998. Numerous legal issues involved in developing the cooperative efforts have been discussed. It has been agreed that legal officers of the South China Sea countries should exchange information and documentation as well as collect various legislation regarding the South China Sea, particularly on environmental matters. A fourth meeting of the TWG-LM, proposed for 1999, will focus on environmental legislation.

A new activity, which falls loosely under the heading "legal matters," was commenced in 1998, when the Study Group on Zones of Cooperation was convened in Vientiane, Laos, in May of that year. This idea arose from a proposal made at the Eighth Workshop. The reasoning behind this proposal was that "joint development" was a much-used phrase, but that not all participants were aware of the many different arrangements that fell into this category. The title "Zones of Cooperation" was adopted to allow the full range of cooperative jurisdictional arrangements at sea to be addressed, including joint fishing zones, cross-boundary oil fields, and the like. A comprehensive set of materials was prepared, including the texts of relevant treaties as well as academic commentaries; presentations covered developments in all parts of the globe. This meeting was adjudged a considerable success, and its results discussed at the Pattaya meeting of the TWG-LM as well as the Ninth Workshop. The latter agreed to convene a second meeting of the study group in 1999.

9. CSCAP is an informal network of government officials, academics, and other experts from the Asia-Pacific and North America that undertakes studies on a variety of topics involving cooperation in the promotion of regional security. Of particular relevance here is the Maritime Cooperation Working Group, of which the authors are members.

10. This refers to the network of institutes dealing with strategic and international matters (the exact names vary slightly) in the ASEAN countries.

11. Single ecosystem management is an ocean management concept applied to a marine area that, according to oceanographers and other experts, has characteristics that distinguish it from surrounding ocean space (the Gulf of Maine is a good example). The littoral states should disregard jurisdictional boundaries for some purposes and agree to cooperate in collective policymaking and management for the unit or system as a whole.

12. The Treaty of Amity and Cooperation was signed at the conclusion of the First ASEAN Summit Conference in Bali, Indonesia, on February 4, 1976, by the original ASEAN members: Indonesia, Malaysia, Philippines, Singapore, and Thailand. All subsequent members of ASEAN have been required to acede to it.

## Background to Chapter 7

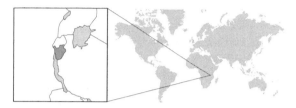

## Burundi: A Case of Parallel Diplomacy

Following the catastrophic violence throughout the Great Lakes region in Africa during the early 1990s, attempts were made to secure a negotiated peace in Burundi. A few months after the assassination of the first democratically elected Hutu president in October 1993, a Tutsi-Hutu coalition government was formed; it failed, however, to establish lasting peace, and civil war soon broke out. With states and intergovernmental organizations unable by themselves to mediate an end to the impasse, various nongovernmental organizations have played a significant role in Burundi, launching numerous projects that focus on political, humanitarian, and conflict resolution problems. These groups have effectively worked in parallel with the diplomacy practiced by the United Nations and sovereign states and have sometimes combined their efforts in a successful division of labor. However, the profusion of players in Burundi, each with its own agenda and favored solution, has undermined the coherence of the international community's response and led to competition among various Burundian factions and NGOs for recognition and support.

### Major Actors
- Pierre Buyoya: president of Burundi, 1987–93; returned to power in July 1996 following a coup
- Léonard Nyangoma: leader of the Hutu rebel movement CNDD-FDD
- FRODEBU (Front for Democracy in Burundi): political party that won the 1993 elections
- UPRONA (Union for National Progress): political party

- Various NGOs, including Search for Common Ground, Synergies Africa, the Community of Sant'Egidio
- United Nations: represented by, among others, Ahmedou Ould-Abdallah, UN secretary-general's special envoy for Burundi, 1993–95, and Mohamed Sahnoun, UN and OAU special envoy for the region, 1996–97
- Organization of African Unity (OAU)
- Julius Nyerere: former Tanzanian president and head of the mediation effort by the "Arusha Group" of regional states
- Jimmy Carter: former U.S. president and active as a mediator in 1995–96
- Various states, including Canada, South Africa, United States, and members of the European Union

## IMPORTANT DATES

- October 1993: Melchior Ndadaye, first democratically elected Hutu president of Burundi, is assassinated
- 1993–99: Civil war claims between 200,000 and 300,000 lives
- September 1994: Power-sharing agreement known as "Convention of Government" leads to a government with a Hutu president and a Tutsi prime minister
- November 1995: Cairo Conference on Burundi cosponsored by Jimmy Carter (first of two conferences that leads to the creation of the Arusha Group)
- March 1996: Tunis Conference on Burundi attended by the regional heads of state; Julius Nyerere is appointed lead negotiator for the Burundi peace talks
- July 1996: Buyoya leads coup against Convention of Government's regime; Great Lakes states impose sanctions on Burundi
- May 1997: Buyoya and Nyangoma sign a pre-cease-fire agreement
- June 1998: Buyoya government and the National Assembly agree to an Internal Partnership for Peace; Burundi Peace Negotiations resume in Arusha under the auspices of Nyerere

## KEY AGREEMENTS REACHED

- 1994: Convention of Government, signed by almost all Burundian political parties
- 1997: outline agreement, reached between Buyoya's government and Hutu rebel leader Nyangoma
- 1998: Internal Partnership for Peace, a transitional agreement between Buyoya government and the National Assembly

**PRINCIPAL OUTCOMES**

- International and regional pressure has forced Burundi to take various steps toward democratization and the negotiation of a peace settlement, but to date (May 1999) externally mediated agreements have not endured or produced peace
- Since the genocide in Rwanda, Burundi has become a laboratory to test conflict resolution and conflict prevention techniques; many sentimentally motivated programs, however, have failed to address the root causes of the conflict or to contain violence

# 7

# Burundi

## A Case of Parallel Diplomacy

FABIENNE HARA

This chapter examines the expansion of private actors into the diplomatic field and the increased attention that the foreign policy elite is now devoting to the concepts of conflict prevention, conflict resolution, and "track-two" or "parallel diplomacy."[1] This new trend has been especially visible in Burundi, which, after the Rwandan genocide, became a test case for post–Cold War intervention in a domestic conflict. In Burundi, external actors initiated a large number of explicitly conflict-oriented activities, in addition to the more standard humanitarian and development programs. However, although nongovernmental organizations (NGOs) proved to have competitive advantages in dealing with the conflict and had accomplishments to their credit, they also augmented the fragmentation of the international response. The competing definitions of the problems and the resulting mismatch of responses led to a general misdiagnosis of the conflict's most critical forces. The experience of Burundi also shows that efforts by private actors, however well intentioned, cannot substitute for strategic commitment by states to deal with the issue of violence.

\* \* \*

The spotlight was turned on parallel diplomacy in May 1997, when news came that an outline agreement on inter-Burundian negotiations had been signed between President Pierre Buyoya's government and Burundi's Hutu rebel leader, Leonard Nyangoma. The story was newsworthy not only for the signing of the accord itself but also for the role played by a private agent in the secret negotiations, namely the Community of Sant'Egidio. This Catholic group based in Rome had already played a mediation role in several peace processes, including the Mozambique peace process.[2]

Has diplomacy entered a new age? The Great Lakes region in Africa has certainly set new precedents in the variety and volume of activities geared toward conflict management and resolution, and in the sheer numbers of official and private diplomatic agents that have been involved. These activities have reflected a commitment to explore new avenues in internal conflict resolution, even as they have highlighted the ineptitude of traditional diplomacy in single-handedly solving conflict. The expansion and decentralization of the diplomatic field to include private entities has fostered the emergence of a "parallel" diplomacy, a sure sign that today's international system has become a lot more than a system of states.

In terms of international rights, the Great Lakes regional crisis is indeed a "judicial monster," totally at odds with any codification within the Westphalian system of states. The agendas of the different agents interconnect like dominoes laid out on a table, creating an odd assortment of coalitions. For instance, in 1996, during an operation by the Alliance of the Democratic Forces for the Liberation of Congo-Zaire (Alliance des forces démocratiques pour la libération du Congo-Zaire), the government of Rwanda formed an alliance with Kinyarwanda-speaking members of the Tutsi elite, "denationalized" by Zaire. They were financed by American, Canadian, and South African mining companies and backed militarily by troops from Angola, Burundi, Eritrea, and Uganda. Opposing them was a coalition trained by ex-Forces armées rwandaises (Rwandan Armed Forces, or FAR) and members of the Interahamwe militia,[3] disguised as refugees, fed and sheltered by a sympathetic international humanitarian community, armed by private British and South African companies and the army of Zaire, and aided by Belgian, Croat, French, and Serb mercenaries. When fighting ended, the Hutu rebels from Burundi, who once enjoyed refuge in

Zaire under Mobutu's regime, were forced to move their bases from that country into Tanzania. As this brief description illustrates, there is within the region a total disregard for frontiers and for the policy of noninterference in a state's internal affairs. As if to underline the point, in August 1998 the Kabila government that had replaced the Mobutu regime was attacked by a coalition of government and nongovernment actors, each with its own agenda. In the Great Lakes region it is all too clear that the dynamics of intrastate conflicts lead them to become interstate conflicts, and inversely, that states wage war against each other by interfering in their neighbors' affairs through such means as support for guerrilla groups.

Orphaned from the Manichaean system of policies and references of the Cold War, the superpowers find it difficult to perceive the link between these conflicts and their own national interest, and to identify their intervention responsibilities. By the same token, the resurgence of death, suffering, and genocide on television screens makes it impossible for the superpowers to justify their passivity in the eyes of public opinion. At first, the lack of action on the part of the major powers in response to these bloody post–Cold War crises meant that private humanitarian organizations assumed, de facto, the responsibility of launching an international response. However, the rapidly increasing cost of the different operations, along with the manipulation of humanitarian aid programs by the fighters, forced the international political elite and the financial sponsors to consider ways to prevent the escalation of violence by early political intervention. By 1992, UN secretary-general Boutros Boutros-Ghali, in his *Agenda for Peace,* had defined prevention as a new axis in international policies, while stressing in an addendum that the United Nations had neither the mandate nor the capacity to intervene in cases of civil war.

The field of conflict prevention and resolution has since become a subject of study and experimentation. Mediation and conflict resolution techniques were originally developed in the United States in the 1980s, first in the area of social conflicts and later in the judicial[4] and environmental fields. Universities then became interested in these new concepts,[5] and consultants went selling their expertise abroad, particularly in South Africa. Appropriating and readapting the technique, South Africans became the best advertising agents for this new type of action. Interest shown by many nations, including the United States and the Scandinavian countries, as well as by several major American think tanks, has led to the merging of the prevention and conflict resolution fields. New NGOs have sprouted, offering new skills and creative projects, and others—including groups active in the fields of humanitarian relief, human rights, and democracy building—

have partly modified their mandates to better integrate the dynamics of conflicts with their approach.

This multipolar and private practice of diplomacy has undoubtedly had its moment of glory in Burundi. This tiny nation has, since 1993 and more particularly since 1994, attracted a multitude of activities and international agents in the field of conflict resolution, a number out of proportion with Burundi's relative strategic value. Impelled by a mixture of guilt toward the Rwandan genocide, genuine indignation in light of the massacres' scope and cruelty, and an oversimplified view of the Burundi problem, the international community became obsessed with the threat of impeding genocide in Burundi. Many members of the international community also saw Burundi as a laboratory to test these new conflict resolution and prevention approaches. Burundi's apparently genuine commitment to pursue peace negotiations with the international community might have created the illusion that a reconciliation was possible. In contrast, the inflexibility of Rwanda and Congo/Zaire (whether before or after the Rwandan genocide and before or after the fall of Mobutu's regime) in the face of international pressure has hindered parallel diplomacy in these two countries.

NGOs have often found themselves playing almost governmental roles in Burundi. They sit as partners at the negotiation table, promoting dialogue and enjoying access to a wealth of resources and to the international media. Overall, their comparative advantages have clearly diversified and enriched the international system's ability to manage the Great Lakes conflicts. But to give a private entity a diplomatic role also leads to numerous quandaries. Should the effectiveness of parallel diplomacy be measured against the yardstick used for official diplomacy? Diplomacy may have been split into two tracks, but neither track is homogenous or exclusive. In fact, the reverse is true, hence the fact that nearly a dozen official special envoys have worked alongside private mediators in the Great Lakes region. Are their initiatives complementary or contradictory? Does the quasi-statelike role of private agents imply that international responsibility for the protection of victim populations can be privatized?

\* \* \*

On October 21, 1993, the first democratically elected Hutu president, Melchior Ndadaye, was assassinated by Tutsi officers from the Burundi army, in power since independence. After a wave of interethnic massacres and several months of negotiations, the various parties, including the Front for Democracy in Burundi (Front pour la démocratie au Burundi,

FRODEBU) agreed on the establishment of a coalition government by January 1994 with a Hutu president and a Tutsi prime minister, which, in September 1994, led to the signing of a "Convention of Government." However, a Hutu faction opposed to power sharing decided to create an armed force, the National Center for the Defense of Democracy–Forces for the Defense of Democracy (CNDD-FDD), which was officially formed in September 1994. The conflict soon escalated into civil war, claiming between two and three hundred thousand lives, and causing hundreds of thousands of people to flee. On July 25, 1996, Major Pierre Buyoya, Burundi's president from 1987 until 1993 (when he lost elections he himself organized), reclaimed power through a coup backed by the army. On July 31, the states of the Great Lakes region imposed sanctions on Burundi. Since then, various dialogue initiatives have taken place: the Arusha process, involving all the protagonists of the conflict and hosted by the former president of Tanzania, Julius Nyerere; the Sant'Egidio process; and the internal dialogue initiative between Pierre Buyoya's government and FRODEBU, which led to the 1998 Internal Partnership for Peace, a transitional agreement between the Buyoya government and a National Assembly dominated by FRODEBU parliamentarians.

From its onset, the Burundi crisis gave rise to all sorts of official mediations, including that of the United Nations, led by the special representative of the secretary-general, Ahmedou Ould-Abdallah, which thrived from 1993 to 1995 and oversaw the negotiation of the Convention of Government; that of the Organization of African Unity, which sent military observers; that of the states of the Central and East Africa region, led by Julius Nyerere, which first offered a peacekeeping force to the Convention of Government regime, later imposed sanctions on the Buyoya government, and has been sponsoring the Arusha inter-Burundi negotiations since June 1998; and those of the European Union, the United States, Canada, South Africa, and Kenya, which all began to appoint special envoys in 1996.

Although coordination efforts are officially part of each official mediator's agenda, the sheer number of special envoys reflects the diversity of their agendas and motivations, and tends to jeopardize the official claim that the international community wants peace, or at least the same peace, for the region. In the eyes of private organizations and churches, the launching of their own reconciliation and dialogue initiatives is a way to compensate for the states' cynicism, and to give priority to the interests of the population. Indeed, the mandate of special envoys is, by definition, to represent the interests of the institutions or governments giving them authority. Amid the various popularity contests between the nations of the region and the superpowers, the struggle for influence between France and the United States, and the geopolitical and economic interests of the countries in the region, all official mediators have been suspected of partiality. Keeping brief their visits to the political elite in each country, and sometimes skipping that step altogether as in the case of Julius Nyerere since July 1996, official mediators find that their work has not been backed by intermediaries working diligently to build mutual trust among warring factions. Various attempts to impose drastic solutions, to hurl them forward with no consideration of political logic, and to claim effectiveness based on symbolic rather than concrete results have resulted in failures, slowly eroding the local populations' faith in the international community. NGOs have identified these problems and have attempted to rectify them on two levels: by conflict resolution programs and by "assisting" in official mediation.

By expanding the field of parallel diplomacy to include a wide variety of activities specifically geared toward conflict resolution, NGOs have tried to reintroduce the elements of time and psychology into the mediation process. (See table 1 on pp. 153–157 for examples of the kinds of projects under way in Burundi since 1995.) They have fostered mediation and dialogue programs in the field to include all sectors of the population, both in cities and in rural areas. Acutely conscious of the tragedy in Rwanda, the NGOs have sought to monitor the Great Lakes region, and particularly Burundi, for signs of any genocidal plans—in effect, serving as the international community's eyes and ears. For example, the International Crisis Group, an American NGO based in Brussels, created a program to monitor the political, economic, and military situation, the internal negotiation process between the government and rebels, and the Arusha peace process. Some of the many and varied NGO efforts have included "Education for Peace" campaigns, reconciliation workshops, initiatives to educate elites and publics about the role of parliament, and the provision of aid to local NGOs and to Hutu and Tutsi youth dialogue groups.

A key element of the NGO contribution has been to introduce Burundians, by way of trips and training seminars, to political figures experienced in conflict resolution in South Africa and other countries in transition. Using similar techniques, some NGO programs have focused on the long term and have sought to change antagonism into cooperation by having Hutus and Tutsis work together on common projects and by building "common ground." Since 1995, International Alert has been committed to the development of the Apostles of Peace Committee (Comité des apôtres de la paix), a local NGO composed of Burundian dignitaries trained after their return from a trip to South Africa. In 1995, Search for Common

Ground, an American NGO, started a radio station in Bujumbura with the dual purpose of providing the public with an independent source of information within the national broadcasting network, and of training a team of Hutu and Tutsi journalists. Meanwhile, Search for Common Ground backed the lengthy and methodical mediation activities of a South African parliamentarian, and opened a Burundi women's peace initiative support center. Through their partnership with civil society and the communities, NGOs bring a unique element to international response, one that most state-led diplomatic initiatives ignore.

In rural areas or in the capitals, the agents of parallel diplomacy have enjoyed tremendous autonomy and direct or indirect influence on the management of the Great Lakes region's many conflicts. The number, commitment, and competence of these track-two players have allowed them a "cognitive" role in the definition of government agendas. In Washington, D.C., for example, the exchange of information and analysis between the State Department and NGOs was institutionalized with the Great Lakes Policy Forum, which has convened twice a month since 1995. Alarmed by massive human rights violations and the overall security breakdown in that region, certain forum members persistently pushed the United States to play a more active role in the region, suggesting, for example, the nomination of a U.S. special envoy for Central Africa, a step that was taken a few months later with the appointment of Howard Wolpe. Some NGOs have even played the role of watchdog of official policies. In April 1998, for example, the International Crisis Group established a presence in Burundi, called for the lifting of sanctions, and denounced official policies of unconditional support for the strategy being pursued by the Central and East African states.

In the end, such actions clearly helped the different private and public actors face up to their responsibilities, forcing governments to be accountable to an informed constituency, as well as these same NGOs to one another.

In many cases, parallel diplomacy in the Great Lakes region has worked alongside official mediations and complemented state diplomacy. Some high-level representatives from multinational organizations, particularly the United Nations, realizing they could capitalize on NGO creativity, flexibility, and skill, have fostered partnerships and a synergy of unparalleled strength between government and the private sector. For instance, the UN secretary-general's special envoy for Burundi, Ahmedou Ould-Abdallah, sought to ensure that most of the mediation activities being undertaken in Burundi by NGOs complemented his own efforts, and he apportioned the diplomatic workload according to his own strategy. During negotiations for the Convention of Government, for example, he encouraged external entities to offer certain individuals funds to cover the costs of travel and other activities, thus giving Ould-Abdallah some leverage and allowing him to establish an informal penalty-and-reward system for those who hindered or helped the peace process. During his two-year mandate, from 1993 to 1995, Ould-Abdallah developed a practical method of cooperation and subcontracting between public and private sectors.

In a similar vein, Mohamed Sahnoun, at the beginning of his term as Organization of African Unity (OAU) and UN special envoy for the region, worked closely with Synergies Africa, which sponsored talks with all the region's mediators and special envoys, as well as political forums involving civil society leaders from Congo.

At certain times since 1993, NGOs have literally taken over the official mediation process in Burundi. Mediation activities have been pluralist in nature, with a numerous and diverse cast of mediators, official and private, operating sequentially or simultaneously. The mediation focal point has changed several times. At first, mediation centered on the United Nations and the OAU; then the focus shifted to the official-private tandem of the Carter Center and Julius Nyerere; then to the Community of Sant'Egidio working in parallel to the efforts of the regional states; and then back to the Arusha process and Nyerere, who has worked in coordination with the European Union and the United States. Meanwhile, parallel processes of internal dialogue have been actively supported by private actors such as Synergies Africa, and official actors such as UNESCO and the Vatican.

Certain private agents have successfully jump-started parallel political negotiations on a head-of-state level. Decentralization and the splitting of negotiation levels have "depoliticized" outside contributors, giving them a comparative edge in terms of access to the parties in conflict. On the basis of his good offices, former president Jimmy Carter, with the help of the former president Amadou Toumani Toure of Mali and Archbishop Desmond Tutu of South Africa, successfully brought together leaders of warring countries and those of neighboring nations to address the Burundi situation, a first of its kind. Cochaired by Julius Nyerere and sponsored by the Carter Center, the Cairo and Tunis summit talks (held in November 1995 and March 1996, respectively) heralded a dynamic regional policy, giving birth to a coalition of regional states while forcing the international community to recognize the conflict's regional character. However, the overthrow of the coalition government in Burundi following a July 1996 coup led by Major Buyoya has brought the Nyerere-sponsored negotiations, which began with the Tunis conference, to a stalemate. The decision by the regional states to impose sanctions on Burundi's new government has strained relations between them.

In contact with the conflict's different protagonists since 1995, the Community of Sant'Egidio saved the peace process by presenting the helpless international community with a genuine alternative to the stalled Arusha process. The decision to pursue secret negotiations in Rome with the new regime, and to initiate a dialogue with Léonard Nyangoma, head of the Hutu rebellion, led to the signing of an outline agreement, made public in May 1997, that called for the suspension of all hostilities, the restoration of constitutional order, and a commitment to multilateral negotiations. Unfortunately, news of the accord triggered a wave of violent reaction among Burundi's Tutsis, forcing the government to interrupt the process.

The comparative advantage of NGOs over official diplomats in facilitating dialogue is also highlighted by the example of Synergies Africa, an African NGO based in Geneva. Involved in mediation missions and numerous brainstorming sessions on Burundi since 1994, Synergies Africa helped set up UNESCO's conference on peace in Burundi in September 1997 and, with the Swiss Federalism Institute, sponsored a seminar in Switzerland on governance and democracy models in March 1998. Both conferences were organized while the Arusha regional process was in a stalemate, and proved that the parties involved in the conflict did not mind being seen together or meeting elsewhere than in Arusha. From then on, Synergies Africa became a discreet point of contact between the government, the National Assembly, and key individuals within FRODEBU,[6] and helped initiate negotiations between those parties. That process led to the signing of an Internal Partnership for Peace in June 1998 and the establishment of a transitional government. For the FRODEBU signatories—members of FRODEBU who had remained in Burundi after the 1996 coup but who had been largely excluded from the regional peace process—the agreement offered an alternative to marginalization. For the government, the agreement offered both recognition of the regime's legitimacy and an end to the threat of regional isolation or even of a regional military intervention.

Unlike seasoned politicians such as Nyerere and Carter, who act according to the logic of the political world, private entities are usually driven by a variety of quite different motivations. The Community of Sant'Egidio, for example, bases its international commitment on religious research into what unites humankind. Its philosophy of peace is to help transform an armed conflict into a political one, and a warrior into a politician, by a constructive approach that emphasizes dialogue and trust. For Synergies

Africa, the objective is, on the one hand, to bridge the gap between the international community and the local actors in the conflict, and, on the other hand, to strengthen African skills in the area of conflict prevention and resolution and to help create a new African elite committed to African peace and development.

The idea that parallel diplomacy and conflict resolution techniques can effectively, discreetly, and economically help prevent the escalation of conflicts and human tragedies, and thus forestall the need for expensive humanitarian operations, has attracted financial donors. A number of American organizations—such as the Carnegie Corporation, the Council on Foreign Relations, the United States Institute of Peace, and the Winston Foundation for World Peace—have spearheaded efforts in this field. The U.S. Agency for International Development (USAID) and the European Union (EU) have sponsored numerous mediation and conflict resolution projects in the Great Lakes region, although the allotted budgets for these preventive initiatives remain far below the budgets earmarked for humanitarian operations. The Scandinavian, Dutch, Japanese, and German governments are also among the major contributors to these programs. It is interesting to note that by funding NGOs from other countries, some states are emerging as new, nontraditional agents in the international diplomatic scene. For example, Sant'Egidio's mediation process was partly financed by an American foundation and partly by the government of Norway.

However, the high hopes and funds that some officials have invested in these innovative approaches tend to conceal contradictions and hesitations in the international response to the Great Lakes crisis. Private agents have certainly been eager to compensate for official diplomatic mistakes, but their initiatives, despite being widely and enthusiastically applied, not only have failed to solve the problems of communication gridlock but also have contributed to the harmful cacophony of competing, incompatible messages. In the case of Burundi, at least until the July 1996 coup, the various interpretations and definitions of the country's problem produced a fragmented and inconsistent international response. Lobbying to validate and promote their own solutions, private agents took part in every debate, pushing for one cause after the next—establishing a democratic or power-sharing system, averting the threat of genocide, spurring economic development, and so forth—in the process identifying many aspects of Burundi's situation without ever being able to grasp the full picture. Jumping on every new convincing idea, financial backers had a tendency to simultaneously allocate funds for projects that each focused on a different aspect of the problem. Taking center stage in the debate, humanitarian and human rights problems led the international community to focus on the short term. Mediation initiatives and conflict resolution projects were sponsored, but they tended to address only one aspect of Burundi's situation and betrayed a lack of vision in the search for comprehensive solutions. They were born of the confused desire to do something and the belief that the sum of these efforts would, as a whole, be able to reduce the level of violence.

After Melchior Ndadaye's murder in October 1993 and the failure of the Burundi election process, international agents were taken aback and, out of conservatism, diagnosed the situation as being a power-sharing problem. They then tried to restore the remnants of democracy and the state by supporting the moderates, as opposed to the "extremists"—namely, the Hutu rebel forces and the Tutsi militias. From early 1996 until the coup, this position was reinforced by a succession of short, official visits by representatives of the United States, the European Union, and the United Nations. In 1995, however, as the Hutu rebels were gaining military strength, a concurrent diagnosis began to circulate among the mediators, especially the private mediators. According to this new view, it was absurd to marginalize the "rebels" and imperative to include them in multilateral negotiations.[7] Once again in the case of Burundi, diplomacy thus became "pyromaniac":[8] while the official effort was geared toward saving the government—whose elements were one by one becoming more radical, thus substantially weakening it—various parallel mediations were calling for the inclusion in the negotiations of Nyangoma. Most officials, realizing only after the coup that their democratization tactics and their attempts to promote power sharing had failed, discreetly joined the secret negotiations, initiated by Sant'Egidio, between Nyangoma and Buyoya's new government.

The Burundians were clearly able to profit from this confusion, with agents manipulating the different negotiators in order to gain maximum legitimacy. Excluded from the various political arrangements and mediations from 1994 to 1996, Nyangoma was able to create an image for himself as a critical player in the negotiations, thanks to the mediation process in Rome. Claiming deep commitment to democratic principles, FRODEBU gained the support of certain international parliamentary organizations and of those seeking to save what was left of the electoral process. Opposing FRODEBU and playing on Northern guilt about the Rwandan genocide, the Union for National Progress (Union pour le progrès national, UPRONA), along with members of the military, sought to gain international endorsement by denouncing what they claimed was a Hutu plot to exterminate all Tutsis.

In the end, it appears that every political tendency in Burundi has found a temporary ally among the international negotiators, who, in turn, have become part of the problem. Through their various international negotiators, Burundians have discovered the potential power of the media and of international public opinion, and have become obsessed with manipulating both. At the same time, Burundians have intensified division among the various international agents by underlining and exploiting their different agendas. For instance, discussions surrounding the UN secretary-general's proposition to send a multinational force to Burundi has thrown a harsh light on the various international interests and positions. Another example is Synergies Africa's role in the internal negotiations between the government and the National Assembly in 1997 and 1998—a role that the regional mediators saw as more competitive with than complementary to the Arusha process. Not only did the internal negotiation process seem to build some trust but it was also seen as giving the conflicting parties an undesirable degree of leeway and an excuse to exit the Arusha process.

* * *

The sheer amount of analysis devoted to, and strategies devised for, Burundi has scrambled the roles of private agents and state diplomatic officials. To end escalation of the conflict, action must be taken to address the underlying reasons why both sides resort to violence. Impressed by the example of the South African reconciliation, Burundian politicians certainly had moved closer to one another during the many trips they made to South Africa; but on their return home, they found themselves alone, with no support and faced with two communities whose acute paranoia left them no alternative but to eradicate their enemy. Breaking the vicious cycle of fear requires the restoration of state authority, instituting an effective separation of powers, demobilizing and reforming the army, as well as creating a police force and an effective judicial system. To implement these reforms will require a commitment that outstrips the capabilities of private agents. Violence can be deterred only when all parties feel the potential threat of a coercive power. For this reason, parallel diplomacy can help to initiate a negotiation or facilitate a political process, but it cannot be a substitute for state diplomacy when it comes to obtaining concessions from warring factions. President Carter used his good offices to bring heads of states together in Cairo and in Tunis, but he lacked the means to ensure that the declarations were honored by their signatories. Can the Sant'Egidio–sponsored accord be taken seriously by the warring factions if no serious commitment exists on the part of the international powers to enforce a cease-fire? The political independence and the flexibility enjoyed by agents of parallel diplomacy are their strengths but also their Achilles' heel.

In this context, having private agents become de facto representatives of the international response presents the grave danger of eroding the responsibility of states to intervene. Unlike that of multinational organizations, the source of private agents' legitimacy is neither international law nor an official mandate given by governments and their peoples. Private actors tend to operate in a judicial haze and answer only to their financial backers. For states, the recent upsurge in private conflict prevention and resolution activities is welcome because it reduces the costs of intervention that states would otherwise have to undertake. By selling off or subcontracting the diplomatic function, states avoid the domestic political risks associated with, say, the dispatch of a peacekeeping force.

The Great Lakes crisis has helped to partly transform a humanitarian "market" into a mediation, conflict resolution, and conflict prevention "market." For the sake of attracting the attention of financial backers, and thus of ensuring institutional survival, several organizations desperately want to be seen at the forefront of the conflict resolution and prevention "industry" in the Great Lakes. It seems, however, that this switch from one to another has not fundamentally changed the methods and results of the international response. Capitalizing on the legacy of the "without borders" philosophy, agents of parallel diplomacy are, for the most part, the inventors and players of a new kind of intervention by Northern countries in Southern countries. It is still a case of agents from Western civil society crossing over borders, no longer to save people, but this time to teach them to make peace and reach a Western-style consensus. Although the "French doctors" had been the standard bearers of a nationalism that celebrated the grandeur of French generosity toward the South, as Ghassan Salamé explained in *Appels d'Empire*,[9] the field of conflict resolution until now has been dominated by Anglo-Saxon influence and marked by the rationale of democratic systems. Its operating concepts and its lexicon are mostly inspired by theories developed by Americans. All these methods aimed at conflict resolution by means of dialogue are based on the precept that it is legitimate to include the authors of a violence perceived as obscene and primal in a rational process leading to a consensus. In reality, keeping the mediation process alive gives the international order an image of safety. It maintains the illusion that the conflicting parties can in fact settle their differences, and can do so according to a prescribed (and highly idealized) process of conflict management. No protagonist in Burundi seems to want to end the search for an accord; it is a comfortable situation since it offends no one but does not necessarily require the factions to make significant compromises involving their fundamental interests. This cult of consensus, this frenzied activism, spares us from confronting the violence of conflict of interests, as expressed in the Great Lakes conflicts.

It also hides the fact that a host of uncoordinated projects cannot be a substitute for coherent and long-term policies. It is certainly not an answer to the problem of war, nor can it absolve us from thinking up a code of responsibility and international conduct. One of the lessons of the Great Lakes is that, when faced with the factions' strong will to pursue their war strategies—as is the case in Burundi, Rwanda, and Congo—a divided international community seeking quick antidotes to violence, even if relatively mobilized, cannot solve the problem. Every project does diversify and enrich relations between the international community and the victim populations, creating sympathy for the victims' plight; but every project also gives victim populations false hopes and hides the fact that their suffering is in competition with an array of other tragedies fighting for foreign attention and prioritized according to cynical agendas.

In conclusion, NGOs that are specialized in mediation and conflict resolution have the potential to play a positive role that official actors seem incapable of playing—but only if that role is undertaken within the framework of a coherent and coordinated official strategy. As seen in Burundi, NGOs are particularly effective in the prenegotiation phase by helping to spur dialogue between the protagonists. They can also alert public opinion to official policies and impose norms of action. However, their sheer number, their sometime diverging institutional agendas, and their various definitions of the problem risk fragmenting and therefore hindering the international response.

Given that the post–Cold War context tends to encourage nonstate interventionism in conflict situations, international players have at least the responsibility to evaluate the comparative advantages of the different agents of intervention, to understand the eminently political nature of this action and its impact on conflict, and to develop a code of conduct and accountability to regulate these activities.

**Table 1.** Conflict Resolution in Burundi (1995–98): Nongovernmental, Governmental, and Multilateral Organizations and Projects

| Organization | Organization Type | Project(s) |
|---|---|---|
| Accord | South African NGO based in Durban, South Africa | Seminar for Burundians in South Africa |
| African Development Foundation | American government agency | Support to NGOs |
| African Dialogue Center for Prevention, Management and Resolution of Conflicts | NGO based in Arusha, Tanzania | Support for Julius Nyerere mediation |
| African-American Institute | NGO based in New York | Conference on the role of the army in Bujumbura; Burundi Policy Forum sponsor |
| Africare | NGO based in Washington | Training seminar for local NGOs |
| Amnesty International | International NGO based in London | Investigation on human rights violations and weapons flow into the region |
| Carter Center | NGO based in Atlanta, Georgia | Sponsor of the Cairo and Tunis regional head-of-state summits |
| Catholic Relief Services | Humanitarian agency of the U.S. Catholic Bishops Conference | Humanitarian aid; reconciliation project with Burundian bishops |
| Center for Preventive Action, Council on Foreign Relations | NGO based in New York | Cosponsor of the Burundi Policy Forum |
| Centre canadien d'études et de coopération internationale (Canadian Center for International Study and Cooperation) | NGO based in Montreal | Democratization support |
| Community of Sant'Egidio | Catholic community based in Rome | Mediation |

| Organization | Organization Type | Project(s) |
|---|---|---|
| Human Rights Watch | NGO based in New York | Investigation on human rights violations and weapons flows into the region |
| International Alert | NGO based in London | Training for conflict resolution techniques; mediation; exchange with veterans of the South African peace process; support group for the UN secretary-general's special envoy; support for the Committee of the Apostles of Peace (CAP) |
| International Center for Conflict Resolution | NGO based in Cape Town | Mediation |
| International Commission of Inquiry | Commission appointed by the United Nations | Inquiry on President Ndadaye's assassination and the massacres that followed |
| International Committee of the Red Cross | NGO based in Geneva | Humanitarian aid; information campaign on international humanitarian law |
| International Crisis Group | NGO formerly based in London, now in Brussels | Political analysis and lobbying for a more proactive international role in Central Africa |
| Mennonite Central Committee | Protestant group based in Pennsylvania | Reconciliation project in rural areas |
| National Democratic Institute for International Affairs | Institute based in Washington, D.C.; financed by the U.S. Democratic Party | Support of the electoral process and national debate; election monitoring |

| Organization | Organization Type | Project(s) |
| --- | --- | --- |
| International Commission of Inquiry on Human Rights Violations in Burundi since October 21, 1993 | Coalition: Human Rights Watch, FIDH, NCOS, LDGL, CNCD, OMCT | Inquiry on President Ndadaye's assassination and the massacres that followed |
| Bureau of the UN Secretary-General's Special Representative | International organization | Preventive diplomacy, general coordination of efforts |
| Organization of African Unity | Regional organization based in Addis Ababa, Ethiopia | Military observation mission |
| Parliamentarians for Global Action | International NGO based in New York | Cooperation with Burundi Parliament members; support for Parliament and the democratic process |
| Radio Agatashya / Fondation Hirondelle | NGO based in Lausanne, Switzerland | Radio broadcasts on reconciliation |
| Radio Umwizero | EU regional organization based in Brussels | Radio broadcasts on reconciliation, from eastern Zaire |
| Refugees International | NGO based in Washington, D.C. | Reconciliation and reintegration of displaced people; lobbying for a military intervention in the region |

| Organization | Organization Type | Project(s) |
|---|---|---|
| Reporters sans frontières (Reporters without Borders) | NGO based in Paris | Defense of freedom of the press |
| Search for Common Ground | NGO based in Washington, D.C. | Cosponsors of the Burundi Policy Forum; opening of Studio Ijambo, offering objective information and journalist training; opening of a center for women; support for the mediation of a South African parliamentarian |
| Swedish Agency for International Development Cooperation | International NGO based in Stockholm | Training; support for Parliament; mediation |
| Synergies Africa | NGO based in Geneva, Switzerland | Regional consulting with NGOs and heads of states; support to official mediations; dialogue initiatives |
| United Methodist Church | Religious group based in Nairobi | Dialogue initiatives |
| UNESCO | UN agency based in Paris | Campaigns on human rights and for refugees; human rights monitoring; repatriation negotiations |
| Nordic Africa Institute | Institute based in Uppsala, Sweden | Dialogue initiatives in 1994 |

| Organization | Organization Type | Project(s) |
|---|---|---|
| U.S. Catholic Conference | Association of American Bishops based in Washington, D.C. | Support for the Episcopalian Conference |
| World Vision | Protestant NGO based in Washington, D.C. | Humanitarian aid; reconciliation project with the Burundi Episcopalian Conference |

*Source:* Barnett R. Rubin, ed., *Cases and Strategies for Preventive Action* (New York, Twentieth Century Fund, 1998).

*Note:* This table is based partly on a listing of organizations at the Burundi Policy Forum in Washington (now the Great Lakes Policy Forum). It does not list the following: humanitarian aid organizations whose programs do not include an explicit dimension of conflict management, such as the United Nations High Commissioner for Refugees (UNHCR), United Nations Department for Humanitarian Affairs (UNDHA), World Food Program (WFP), International Rescue Committee, CARE, Médecins sans frontières, Médecins du monde, Action contre la faim, OXFAM, Christian Aid, Concern, Action Aid, Initiative humanitaire africaine, Danchurchaid, Terre des hommes, FOCSIV, Handicap International, Pharmaciens sans frontières, GTZ (Deutsche Gesellschaft für Technische Zusammenarbeit), Equilibre, Belgian Red Cross, International Medical Corps, and UNICEF; financial backers, such as USAID and the European Community Humanitarian Office (ECHO), that supported many of the activities mentioned in the table; development organizations, such as the United Nations Development Program (UNDP), General Direction VIII (DG VIII) of the European Commission, and the World Bank; monitoring and lobbying organizations that sponsored conferences in Burundi and published regular bulletins or reports and recommendations, such as Eurostep (Brussels), Concertation chrétienne pour l'Afrique centrale (Brussels), and so on; and government diplomacy, such as the nomination of special envoys, high-level missions, and delegations of the Security Council and the UN secretary-general. In January 1995, the secretary-general's special representative estimated that since his nomination in November 1993, seventy delegations had been sent to Burundi.

**NOTES**

1. The term "track-two diplomacy" refers to efforts to improve communication between the parties to a conflict through informal, unofficial interaction outside the government power structure. "Parallel diplomacy," which is a translation of a French term, means more or less the same as track-two diplomacy—namely, nonstate diplomacy that occurs simultaneously with, but is not coordinated with, state diplomacy.

2. See Andrea Riccardi, *Sant'Edigio, Rome, and the World* (Paris: Beauchesne, 1996).

3. The ex-FAR and Interahamwe militias committed the genocide against the Tutsi in Rwanda in 1994.

4. In the judicial field, the technique is called alternative dispute resolution.

5. Funded by the Hewlett Foundation, the Harvard Negotiation Program was the pioneer of this type of program.

6. Some FRODEBU cadres rapidly went into exile after the onslaught of the war and especially after the 1996 coup, while others stayed in Burundi. From the start of the Arusha negotiation process, serious rifts appeared between the "outsiders" and the "insiders," the exiled group being wholly against any cooperation with the Buyoya government, while the FRODEBU members, having remained inside Burundi, were inclined to seek reconciliation.

7. The rebels were called *terroristes genocidaires* by Tutsi public opinion.

8. See Ahmedou Ould-Abdallah, *La Diplomatie pyromane* (Paris: Calmann-Levy, 1996).

9. Ghassan J. Salamé, *Appels d'Empire* (Paris: Fayard, 1996), chap. 4.

# Background to Chapter 8

## The Multilevel Peace Process in Tajikistan

The Central Asian nation of Tajikistan gained independence from the Soviet Union in 1991, but was quickly faced with civil war. Various democratic, nationalist, and Islamic forces competed for power, and the Commonwealth of Independent States sent a peacekeeping force to Tajikistan. A nonofficial dialogue (known as the Inter-Tajik Dialogue) began in 1993 with the aim of facilitating a public peace process. Eventually part of a multilevel peace process, the dialogue provided a forum for individuals from all points on the political spectrum to discuss the conflict and present ideas for negotiations and postconflict peacebuilding. The Inter-Tajik Dialogue helped pave the way in 1994 for official negotiations mediated by the United Nations. A comprehensive accord for national reconciliation was reached in 1997, and the Inter-Tajik Dialogue continued its work into the postconflict phase.

### MAJOR ACTORS

- Government of Tajikistan
- United Tajik Opposition (UTO)
- Dartmouth Conference Regional Conflicts Task Force
- Inter-Tajik Dialogue (ITD): composed of Tajiks close to the government and opposition, and from the society at large

- United Nations
- Russia and the Commonwealth of Independent States (CIS)
- United States

## IMPORTANT DATES

- 1991: Tajikistan achieves independence from the Soviet Union
- November 1991: First presidential election is held
- March 1992: Coalition government forms, including democratic, nationalist, and Islamic opposition
- 1992: Civil war begins in Tajikistan
- November 1992: Supreme Soviet forms new government under Emomali Rakhmanov
- March 1993: "Public peace process" facilitates first contact between progovernment and opposition citizens
- December 1993: Opposition leaders produce a common platform
- March 1994: ITD produces first joint memorandum, "A Negotiation Process for Tajikistan"
- April 1994: Official peace process begins with UN-mediated negotiations
- November 1994: Rakhmanov is elected president under new constitution
- Summer 1995: Rakhmanov and UTO sign an agreement approving creation of a Consultative Forum of the Peoples of Tajikistan
- June 1997: Comprehensive peace agreement is reached and a National Reconciliation Commission is formed to oversee implementation of the peace agreement through a transitional period

## KEY AGREEMENTS REACHED

- General Agreement on Peace and Reconciliation, including creation of the National Reconciliation Commission
- Creation of the Consultative Forum of the Peoples of Tajikistan (not yet convened as of early 1999)

## PRINCIPAL OUTCOMES

- Nonofficial dialogue provided an impetus for formal negotiations, leading to a peace agreement
- NGOs for citizenship and civil society were formed to assist in the reintegration of society

# 8

# The Multilevel Peace Process in Tajikistan

HAROLD H. SAUNDERS

The multilevel peace process in Tajikistan has embraced peacemaking and now postconflict peacebuilding at three levels of the body politic. At each level, a different kind of leadership in the peace process has been at work. Participants have found that the conceptual framework of the multilevel peace process makes it possible to build on the potential complementarities of work on multiple tracks, drawing into the peace process the energies and the resources of whole human beings interacting across levels in the whole body politic. The concept of the multilevel peace process enhances efforts to avoid the potential dilution of authority when multiple peacemaking efforts are at work by providing a division of labor, establishing ground rules for their interaction, and recognizing their complementarities.

First, at the level of citizens in influential positions outside government, the "public peace process"—a sustained nonofficial dialogue—in Tajikistan began in March 1993 under the auspices of a six-person American-Russian team from the Dartmouth Conference Regional Conflicts Task Force. After the familiar central authority in Tajikistan was suddenly removed by the dissolution of the Soviet Union, the newly independent country gradually slid into an internal struggle to fill the power vacuum and in 1992 into a vicious civil war. A small group of Tajikistanis at the second and third levels of their organizations from different regions and factions in the civil war sat down in a Moscow conference room for the first time in March 1993, barely able to look at one another. There was no other contact between the government and its opposition at that time. Since then, the Inter-Tajik Dialogue within the Framework of the Dartmouth Conference, as participants came to call themselves, had held twenty-five meetings and produced thirteen joint memoranda by the end of July 1999.

The official peace process began thirteen months later, in April 1994 as a UN-mediated negotiation. The public peace process through its first six meetings had by March 1994 played a role in paving the way for the official process, as I will describe later. When the official talks began, three participants in the Inter-Tajik Dialogue were present as members of the government and opposition negotiating teams. Beginning in December 1996, the Inter-Tajik Negotiations—the official peace process—produced a series of agreements that were incorporated in the comprehensive peace agreement of June 1997. Those negotiations took place between the two principal combatants in the civil war—the government and the United Tajik Opposition, formed in December 1993 with two Inter-Tajik Dialogue members as signatories of its joint platform. The peace agreement established a National Reconciliation Commission, with four subcommissions to oversee implementation of the peace accords through a transitional period. Four participants in the Inter-Tajik Dialogue were members of the commission. One chaired one of the subcommissions, a second was deputy chair of another, and a fifth was an adviser to a third.

As the Inter-Tajik Dialogue proceeded, two other participants established a position in what we in the West would call the "civil society"—the third level of the multilevel peace process—by launching their own nongovernmental organizations (NGOs) to work in the fields of what we would call citizenship education and civil society. Their work recognized well in advance of a peace agreement that the real unification of Tajikistan and the establishment of genuine peace would take place only as the people themselves found common public interests and work across regional and other divides that had been widened during the civil strife. Also in that period, one member of the American-Russian management team held meetings with international NGOs in Washington to lay out a "Framework for an NGO Strategy in Tajikistan." The purpose of this effort was to encourage even those organizations engaged in straightforward humanitarian work to recognize that their prescribed tasks of sustaining or rebuilding a society torn apart by civil war could include an additional dimension of helping the people of Tajikistan develop new interactions and build new institutions that would eventually constitute a civil structure of peace.

The concept of the multilevel peace process creates a framework within which participants in sustained dialogue can design a peace process to work at each level and in each phase will build on work at other levels and in previous phases. This is a case of a concept becoming a powerful tool in its own right simply because recognition of the larger framework by participants in the peace process saves specific actions from being ad hoc actions taken in isolation from others. Recognition of complementarities among actions takes advantage of the synergy that lies in collaborative efforts and avoids destructive rivalries among levels.[1]

At each level in the multilevel peace process, so-called third-party intervention has taken a different form. Because that name alone is not fully descriptive, I want to make two points:

First, the focus of this volume is "diplomatic or nonofficial assisted negotiation by more than one party." Many deep-rooted human conflicts in their early stages are not ready for formal mediation or negotiation. Other tools such as sustained dialogue are essential in changing relationships to pave the way for more formal peacemaking efforts. In those early stages at the level of citizens outside government when there is no negotiation, initial efforts cannot be seen as assisting negotiation, although that may be one outcome of work in this period. The focus in this period is on changing relationships. Later, since many political processes on the way to peace do include negotiation as an important element, it may be equally true that negotiations in the official peace process that produce a peace agreement help create conditions for crucial processes of postconflict peacebuilding by citizens in the civil society. Important as peace agreements are, they do not by themselves make peace; only people can create peaceful relationships over the long term. So it is important to note that the work in the multilevel peace process goes well beyond assisting negotiation and that the leaders in the multilevel peace process—both participants and third parties—may be different kinds of people at each level.

Second, as Christopher Mitchell writes in another United States Institute of Peace publication,[2] the most fruitful way to understand mediation itself is to recognize the many functions that must be performed in the course of mediation. This complex of activities includes, for example, the roles of instigator, communicator, persuader, organizer, precipitator, legitimizer, convener, moderator, manager, funder, teacher, and idea formulator. In other words, it may be fruitful to think of mediation as itself a political process in which different actors with different capacities perform different functions at different times.

This chapter addresses the focus of the volume with these thoughts about the actors in the multilevel peace process in mind. I cannot confine myself simply to the tasks of formal mediation and negotiation.

## THE TAJIKISTAN CONFLICT

The people of Tajikistan—the poorest of the former Soviet republics— were unprepared for the independence that befell them suddenly in 1991. The end of tight Soviet control turned loose a complex of internal forces vying to gain power to protect their own interests. The post-Soviet government could not maintain control. The people of this fragmented country— formed and held together as a republic only under Soviet rule—had little sense of national identity.

Foremost among those forces was a strong clan-based regionalism—the primary focus of identity. Challenging the traditional communist-style government were democratic, nationalist, and Islamic movements that had begun to grow as the political system in Moscow relaxed after 1985. Also part of the mix were ethnic minorities, the largest being Uzbek. Playing into the forces from outside were Pakistani, Saudi, and Iranian support for the Islamic movement; eventual Russian military involvement to protect the southern "security border" of the Commonwealth of Independent States; and the concern of Uzbekistan and other Central Asian countries over a possible fundamentalist Islamic republic next door.

Regional division was traditionally pronounced along north-south lines. The northern area—called the Leninabad region—contained about 40 percent of Tajikistan's people and was the primary industrial and agricultural area. During the Soviet period, it supplied leadership for the Communist Party and government apparatus. The one southern region that made common cause with Leninabad was the Kulyab. It was the challenge of the other southern regions—Gorno Badakhshan, Garm, and Kurgan-Tyube— to Leninabad's monopoly that nourished the democratic, nationalist, and Islamic opposition in 1990 and 1991. In a pragmatic alliance, those forces challenged the established power unsuccessfully in the presidential election of November 1991, but forced themselves into a coalition government in May 1992 and gained control of the government in September.

That new government proved unable to reassert law and order and to stem economic deterioration; Leninabad, Kulyab, and some Uzbeks refused to recognize it. People in Kulyab faced strangulation as Islamists in Kurgan-Tyube and Garm—Kulyab's traditional food sources—cut off supplies. They formed and supported financially with personal savings the only effective fighting units (the Popular Front), which gradually gained control of critical parts of the country with the unofficial help of Uzbekistan and the Russian military. They forced thousands of perceived adversaries out of the country.

In November 1992, the Supreme Soviet met in Khojand, the renamed capital of the Leninabad region, and formed a new government under Emomali Rakhmanov from the Kulyab. In a power shift that reduced the Leninabad region to second place, the new government came increasingly under Kulyabi control. Rakhmanov became president under a new constitution and election in November 1994.[3] By that time, the Inter-Tajik Dialogue was already twenty months and nine meetings old, having begun in March 1993—just past the peak of internal fighting with one of seven Tajikistanis having fled their homes

## THE INTER-TAJIK DIALOGUE: THE PERIOD BEFORE NEGOTIATION

A nonofficial dialogue can help pave the way for mediation or negotiation. When the Inter-Tajik Dialogue began in March 1993, there were no other contacts between the government and the opposition, which was ideologically diverse and geographically dispersed. That remained the case for the following thirteen months. During that time, the dialogue met six times. After each meeting, participants briefed a few top leaders in the government of Tajikistan, the opposition leadership, the U.S. government, and the United Nations. The Dartmouth Conference Regional Conflicts Task Force, which formed the dialogue, was a subgroup of the Dartmouth Conference—the longest, continuous bilateral dialogue between Soviet and U.S. citizens during the Cold War, having begun in 1960 and continuing through 1990 in a series of eighteen plenary sessions.[4] In 1981, the plenary established two task forces to work between plenary meetings—one on arms control, the other on Soviet-U.S. interactions in regional conflicts. When the Soviet Union dissolved, the Regional Conflicts Task Force made three decisions: (1) to continue as a task force focusing on the new Russian-U.S. relationship, (2) to conceptualize the experience and process of dialogue that we had learned in more than twenty meetings over a decade, and (3) to apply that process of dialogue to one of the conflicts that had broken out in the territory of the former Soviet Union.

In the mid-1980s, I wrote a book conceptualizing the official Arab-Israeli peace process in which I had participated intensively in the 1970s, flying on the Kissinger shuttles after the 1973 Arab-Israeli war and helping to draft the Camp David accords and the Egyptian-Israeli peace treaty.[5] By the late 1980s, I had begun to conceptualize the many nonofficial dialogues that I had participated in after leaving the government in 1981 as a progression of stages leading from the first efforts to establish contact through a deepening and changing of relationships to joint design of actions to change relationships in the larger body politic. My Russian cochair of the Regional Conflicts Task Force and I laid out a five-stage process of sustained dialogue in a joint article published in the spring of 1993.[6] The task force decided to apply our five-stage process of sustained dialogue to the civil war in Tajikistan.

The task force chose Tajikistan for three reasons: First, given the position of Tajikistan on the southern security border of the Commonwealth of Independent States and its proximity to the disruptive conflict in Afghanistan as well as the interests of Tajikistan's Central Asian neighbors, Iran, Turkey, Russia, and the United States in the area, the strategic significance of the fragmentation of Tajikistan was apparent. Second, while the international community was paying significant attention to the internal conflict in Georgia and the war between Armenia and Azerbaijan over Nagorno-Karabakh, very few organizations at the end of 1992 were paying attention to the conflict in Tajikistan except for humanitarian reasons. Third, two Russian members of the Regional Conflicts Task Force had extensive professional contacts in Tajikistan. The task force decided to try to establish a dialogue with individuals from the factions in Tajikistan and asked three Russian and three U.S. members to oversee the project.[7]

In early 1993, two Russian members of the team talked with more than one hundred individuals in Tajikistan about the possibility of a nonofficial dialogue. In addition to talking with potential participants, they briefed key leaders in the government. Out of that group, they chose ten to come to the first meeting in Moscow in March. They had at least the acquiescence of one senior government official.

In retrospect, their selection of participants had two consequences. The obvious one was choosing a group to meet in nonofficial dialogue, but the commitment of participants to the Inter-Tajik Dialogue over time and their involvement at all levels of the social and political life of Tajikistan produced an amazingly sound and durable group. The second consequence was ultimately revealed in the capacities of the dialogue members to help design, develop, and sustain a multilevel peace process for Tajikistan. As I described it in grant proposals for funding the dialogue, the strategy of the management team was *not* to mediate a peace agreement but to create a group within the conflict with the capacity to develop its own peace process.

In the third meeting of the dialogue in August 1993—the first meeting at which the whole group lodged and worked under one roof—one of the participants said: "What we really have to work on is starting a negotiation between the government and the opposition on creating conditions for the refugees to return home." Although the group could not go further at that meeting than simply agreeing on a purpose, that sentence set the stage for its focus over the next three meetings and seven months.

In the fourth meeting in October, participants spent the entire time talking about the obstacles to beginning negotiations and ways of overcoming them. A principal obstacle, they felt, was the geographic dispersion, ideological diversity, and lack of organization of the opposition. "If we wanted to invite you to negotiation," said one progovernment participant in frustration, "whom would we invite? Who would represent the opposition? Where would we send the invitations? How would we deal with people with blood on their hands?"

Although it is impossible to establish an exact cause-and-effect linkage, the fact is that a group of opposition leaders met in December in Tehran, produced a common platform, and created a coordination center in Moscow for opposition forces. Not only were two participants in the dialogue signatories of the platform, but four became members of the steering group in the coordinating center.

When the dialogue held its fifth meeting the first week in January 1994, the progovernment participants ruthlessly quizzed the opposition members who reported on the joint platform. At the end of the meeting, they said, "We will report this to the government. It seems to us that the basis for negotiation may exist." Meanwhile, an emissary of the UN secretary-general had been making efforts to begin a negotiation. A month later, the government agreed to join a UN-mediated negotiation.

Despite the sequence of events just recounted, it is not possible to claim that the dialogue itself was responsible for the government's decision to negotiate, but a senior official who participated in that decision later said that the work of the dialogue was significant, if for no other reason than it made it impossible to argue within the government that it was not possible to talk seriously with the opposition. UN and U.S. officials attest to the significant role of the dialogue in paving the way for negotiation.

In its last meeting before the beginning of the official peace process—the sixth meeting, which took place in March 1994—the dialogue produced the first of fourteen joint memoranda written during the next nineteen meetings. It was titled "A Negotiation Process for Tajikistan." Participants made two important judgments during that meeting.

First, participants learned the importance of structuring the agenda for a negotiation in such a way as not to block negotiation at the outset. The pro-opposition group in the dialogue started out stating that the sharing of power between the government and the opposition—that is, the creation of a coalition government—should be the first item on the agenda. In the course of the meeting, it became apparent that the government would regard that as an immediate threat and would go no further in the negotiations, whereas creating conditions for return of the refugees and other such subjects would permit negotiations to begin on subjects where more common purpose existed.

Second, participants saw the structuring of the negotiations themselves as a way of beginning a political process that could establish conditions for the unification of the country. They recommended that the negotiating teams establish four working groups on key subjects—reintegration of refugees, disarming illegal armed elements, establishing a constitution and political system, and economic recovery. Each working group would be authorized to bring together different elements of government and society to deal with those problems.

The process of dealing with those problems was itself to create an experience in breaking down the bureaucratic, regional, national, social, and other barriers to unification that had long existed and had been exacerbated during the civil strife. Although that structure was only partially adopted during the negotiations, it foreshadowed the structure of the National Reconciliation Commission and its four subcommissions, which was agreed to in the peace agreement of June 1997.

By the time the official peace process began in April 1994, dialogue participants and the management team had met six times over thirteen months, demonstrating an unusual commitment to an intense dialogue process. The intensity also reflected a level of funding that is unusual for this kind of nonofficial process.[8]

## The Dialogue during the Negotiations

Once negotiations have begun, nonofficial dialogue can focus on the political processes that will be essential to implementing and sustaining the outcome of the negotiations. Sometimes the official and public processes touch, as mechanisms and processes for the long term provide ways of solving problems or breaking an impasse in the negotiation. But the distinction that avoids destructive interaction remains clear: that citizens outside government can normally claim no authority to negotiate while negotiators normally exhibit little capacity to change human relationships in the larger body politic through their agreements alone.

When the negotiations began in April 1994, participants in the dialogue redefined the objectives of the dialogue. Especially because three participants were included as members of the two negotiating teams, the question arose whether the dialogue should continue alongside the negotiations. The quick answer was, "We played a role in starting the negotiations; now we must play a role in assuring their success." The group stated that it would not try to second-guess the negotiators because, as citizens outside government, they had no authority to negotiate. They would therefore try to think ahead of the negotiations and, particularly, they would focus now on "creating a political process of national reconciliation in Tajikistan." In other words, they would give special attention to steps in the larger body politic that would contribute to creating political processes that would support implementation of decisions made in the negotiations. This was the first redefinition of the dialogue's objectives.

As it happened, the full Russian-U.S. organizing team visited Tajikistan shortly after that meeting. During that visit, the U.S. co-moderator assured the foreign minister of Tajikistan that the dialogue would not try to play the role of negotiator—that participants in the dialogue recognized that leadership in the official peace process was in the hands of the UN mediator. He assured the foreign minister that the dialogue would focus on longer-term problems, would not seek to negotiate agreements of any kind, and would think particularly about what could be done in the body politic to support the outcome of negotiations. This was an important step in establishing unilateral restraint through these simple ground rules for dividing labor between the official and public peace processes.

Beginning in June and with particular intensity in September, the group focused on obstacles to national reconciliation and ways of overcoming them. Its hope of using a planned referendum on the constitution as a way of deepening dialogue among Tajikistanis on what kind of country they wanted to build was frustrated by the government's acceleration of the timetable in such a way as to prevent widespread public dialogue and participation of opposition elements in the referendum on a new constitution and in parliamentary elections. Much of the fall and winter of 1994–95 was spent by participants simply discussing among themselves the elections that were judged by international organizations not to have conformed to international standards. When the elections were over, the opposition participants in the dialogue made a significant decision during the eleventh meeting in March 1995. Rather than seek to overthrow the results of the elections, they developed the formulation that they would regard the period ahead as a transitional period for the development of a more inclusive political process in Tajikistan. That concept of a transitional period also found its way into the final peace accord.

Since their eighth meeting in June 1994, participants had been discussing possible ways of sharing power in Tajikistan among the regions, political movements, and nationalities. They regarded the absence of a concept of power sharing as a major obstacle in the formal negotiations. The contest over power was the obvious cause of an impasse in the negotiations as the negotiating teams left Alma Aty in May 1995 without agreement on a mechanism for overseeing a political process of national reconciliation. Still adhering to their commitment not to become a second track in the official peace process, participants in the dialogue wrote a joint memorandum laying out three options for creating a mechanism to oversee a process of national reconciliation—their primary focus. The opposition had proposed a Council for National Reconciliation to be established as a supragovernmental body. To reduce the government's sense of threat, the dialogue in its memo proposed as one option creating such a body *under* the authority of the negotiating teams, thus foreshadowing the creation of the National Reconciliation Commission after the peace accords in June 1997 to implement the provisions of those accords by broadening participation in the political process. Another option proposed was the creation of a Consultative Forum of the Peoples of Tajikistan to permit a diverse group of Tajikistanis to come together to talk about the future of the country, addressing such questions as creating a political culture of genuine power sharing.

During the summer of 1995, the president of Tajikistan and the leader of the United Tajik Opposition signed an agreement on the creation of a Consultative Forum of the Peoples of Tajikistan. That agreement was handwritten by a participant in the dialogue and signed by the two leaders. Throughout the following year, participants in the dialogue spelled out in detail how a consultative forum might function and produced several joint memoranda urging early formation of the forum. The forum was included in the 1997 peace agreement, but convening the forum is still an unimplemented decision. "It was a good idea in 1995, but it is not timely in 1998," said one participant in dialogue 21. "Both sides now fear reopening the agreement that has been reached." The point is that the participants in the dialogue were able to offer options for breaking a logjam without violating their commitment not to attempt negotiation because they were suggesting options for reaching across levels in the multilevel peace process.

Meanwhile, two participants in the dialogue started their own NGOs. One was a foundation for plumbing the thousand-year-old Tajik tradition for roots of democratic practice and for creating an educational institution to train participants in the market economy. The other was the Tajikistan Center for Civic Education, which in the first half of 1997 conducted a

series of dialogue-seminars on the subject of regionalism, which participants regard as one of the most significant obstacles to the unification of
Tajikistan.

It was in the seventeenth meeting of the dialogue in October 1996 that
participants coined the phrase "multilevel peace process." One participant
had become a member of a joint commission set up by the negotiating
teams to negotiate and oversee local cease-fires. He came to the dialogue
fresh from an intense experience in working out a cease-fire in an area
where fighting had cut the major road between east and west in this moun-
tainous country. The lives of the negotiators had been threatened at one
point, so the account of the experience was a vivid one. When he finished
his story, another participant in the dialogue observed: "One reason why
cease-fires have not held is that they have been negotiated at the highest
level without reference to those with the guns and with local interests at
stake in the fighting. What we really need is a multilevel peace process
through which people at the grass roots can be connected with the Inter-
Tajik Negotiations through working groups." One participant's experience
dramatized for the group the need for a peace process that operated at all
levels of the body politic.

During that period, while both the official and public peace processes
were continuous and active, informal communication between them took
place in two ways: First, the presence of dialogue participants as delegates
in the negotiation assured direct informal communication between the two
groups. We have had numerous affirmations that the discussions in the
dialogue and its joint memoranda were well known to members of both
negotiating teams and to the UN mediator. Second, the U.S. co-moderator
shared his analytical memoranda written after each meeting and joint memoranda produced by participants with the United Nations, both in New York
and in the field, and with the State Department. On several occasions during that period, UN officials acknowledged the Inter-Tajik Dialogue in
public comments as "one of the most important nonofficial groups comple-
menting UN negotiations active today." The other factor that was important in the relationship between these two levels of the peace process was
the self-imposed constraint defined by the Inter-Tajik Dialogue—the ground
rules deliberately separating its work from the work of the negotiations so
as to avoid confusion.

When the peace accord was signed in June 1997, the National Reconciliation Commission it created at least reflected the design laid down in
the Inter-Tajik Dialogue's first joint memorandum. The idea of a consultative forum remained in the agreement and the concept of a transitional

period to be used as a time for government and opposition to learn to work together was a central feature. As noted earlier, five participants were active in the commission and its subcommissions.

The obstacles to each group's work during this period were symptomatic of their particular responsibilities. The official peace process was frequently the context for a struggle over power between the government and the United Tajik Opposition. The public peace process suffered from uncertainty about the impact of its work. Even though there are such direct links as those cited earlier between the public and official peace processes, it is not possible to demonstrate with certainty in a complex political process exactly how ideas moved from the shadows of the dialogue room into the public arena. Moreover, in a society still dominated by a restrictive government intent on staying in power, it was difficult for citizens to launch political initiatives. As the NGOs started by dialogue participants became solidly established, it was equally difficult to describe their exact impact, and they were also still working under the eyes of a highly suspicious government.

Whatever the exact impact of the political philosophy that emerged from the dialogue's deliberations, a coherent body of thought did emerge in the nine joint memoranda written in the first twenty meetings. They were published in Tajiki, Russian, and English at the end of 1997.[9] Together, they constitute a distinct approach to the future of the country. Although they deal with practical matters, their conceptual content demonstrates an important difference from the documents produced by negotiators—another implicit division of labor between two levels of the peace process. How deeply embedded in Tajikistani political thinking and practice they will become remains to be seen, but those "ideas in the air" are one medium of interaction between the dialogue and those at other levels of the peace process. Four central themes were developed through the ten joint memoranda written through the twenty-first meeting.

*First:* The dialogue called attention to the need to focus on the larger political processes of peacebuilding—not just on issues being negotiated. From the very first memo "on the Negotiation Process for Tajikistan," the dialogue has called for "a mechanism to plan political processes for national reconciliation and formation" (March 4, 1994):

- The initial idea was that the negotiating teams would "create, coordinate and oversee four working groups which would design processes, plans and timetables for dealing with Tajikistan's main problems with the larger purpose of creating a unified and democratic Tajikistan." Those working groups would not just address practical problems but would use those problems as vehicles for bringing citizens together.

- In June 1995, the dialogue transferred that concept and that structure to its proposal to create a coordinating Council for National Reconciliation under the authority of the negotiating teams to "implement decisions from the negotiations through four commissions." Those commissions were to engage citizens in solving problems. In June 1997, the peace agreement created the National Reconciliation Commission with four subcommissions. The dialogue does not know exactly what influence it had on that decision. What remains on the active agenda is the philosophy behind the dialogue's recommending this mechanism: asking the commission "to develop broad participation in the functioning of the political system and the affairs of the civil society on the basis of ensuring equal participation in power among all regions, political parties and movements, and national communities" (June 22, 1995).

*Second:* Once negotiations began, the dialogue deepened its attention to the obstacles to designing a political process of national reconciliation. It recognized as critical the capacity to build working relationships and to share power across regional, ideological, and other boundaries.

- As early as June 1994 in a meeting in Washington, D.C., at the United States Institute of Peace, participants identified as one important question how to design a political system that would represent the interests of different regions, political parties and movements, and nationalities in Tajikistan.
- The memo from the dialogue's meeting in Dushanbe in May 1996 stated starkly: "Participants believe that the primary obstacle to peace in Tajikistan is the absence of an adequate understanding on sharing power among the regions, political parties and movements, and nationalities in Tajikistan."
- In later meetings, the dialogue discussed the sharp difference between (a) simply dividing power by allocating government positions among parties and (b) creating a political culture of working together cooperatively in the interest of the whole people of Tajikistan rather than in the interest of only one group—that is, genuine power sharing.

*Third:* In October 1996, after negotiation of an important local ceasefire, the dialogue, as mentioned above, crystallized the concept of the multilevel peace process to capture the need to draw the people of Tajikistan at all levels into the political processes of making peace and building a unified country.

- "It is necessary to broaden public participation in the efforts to achieve peace by developing a multilevel peace process in order to assure the widest popular involvement in achieving and implementing a nation-wide peace agreement."

*Fourth:* The dialogue focused on citizen mechanisms for involving them-selves. Since the summer of 1995, the dialogue repeatedly recommended creation of a Consultative Forum of the Peoples of Tajikistan as one space where citizens outside government could come together in dialogue about the future of their country.

- To quote the memo of October 1996: "Participants believe that one of the main obstacles to peace is lack of a common vision about what kind of country the Tajikistani people want their country to be." They saw the consultative forum as a space for that discussion, but in its absence, the Inter-Tajik Dialogue has provided that space.
- Participants also recognized the need for an even broader dialogue: "As a mechanism to stimulate civil society, dialogue participants encouraged the citizens of Tajikistan to strengthen and develop a growing network of citizen associations and nongovernmental organizations" (October 1996). In the memo from dialogue 21, they urged those citizen organizations to hold deliberations on proposed changes in the constitution and in the electoral laws as a way of engaging citizens in the political process (February 1998).

With this distinctive picture of the dialogue's role in the multilevel peace process and with the channel of communication to the official peace process, participants showed no interest in working at cross-purposes with the negotiations. Similarly, the complimentary reference to the dialogue by UN officials demonstrated that they felt no threat.

## THE DIALOGUE IN THE POST-ACCORD PHASE

In their twentieth meeting in October 1997—the first after the signing of the June 1997 peace agreement—the dialogue wrote a joint memorandum commending the National Reconciliation Commission for its energetic work, but offering a "perspective" on the process of national reconciliation. One of the dialogue's observations was that the peace agreement had not established a subcommission on economic recovery, and it urged creation of a roundtable in connection with one of the subcommissions in order to begin that work.

The dialogue recognized that this economic work not only would be essential to the reintegration of refugees and the integration of former military men into the economy, but it also could become an informal instrument for bringing into the political life of the country the roughly one-third of the people of Tajikistan who had not been included in the peace agreement because they had not been active combatants in the civil war. During the last six months of negotiation, the negotiating teams had grappled with the question of whether and how to include in the opposition component of the National Reconciliation Commission those groups that were in opposition but had not taken up arms. The most important single concentration was in the Leninabad region in the northwestern part of the country—Tajikistan's most economically developed and active region. They saw the creation of an informal advisory roundtable under one of the sub-commissions as a way of beginning to draw people from that portion of the opposition into the work of national reconciliation without reopening the hard-negotiated peace agreement.

In addition, although the dialogue addressed its memorandum primarily to the government and the National Reconciliation Commission, it made the point in several ways that the work of national reconciliation could not proceed until it found a variety of ways of enlisting the people of the communities of Tajikistan in its work. Its memo from the twenty-first meeting specifically urged (1) the National Reconciliation Commission to organize an "all-nation dialogue" around the proposed constitutional and legislative changes that would define the new political system and (2) citizen associations and NGOs also to convene their own meetings as a way of broadening citizens' experience in holding their own dialogues.

The dialogue thus set its sights again on the larger social and political processes of postconflict peacebuilding, not on the specific issues that the official National Reconciliation Commission had to resolve. Although participants addressed recommendations and ideas to those in the official peace process, they in no way undercut the work of official bodies in dealing with practical problems. That work would necessarily include, in the view of participants, the creation of associations of people in Tajikistan who were able in their common interests to reach across the gulfs that had divided them during the civil conflict.

It remains difficult at this point to know exactly how participants in the dialogue will respond to this new challenge. The dialogue's relationships with the official peace process and, presumably, with the official political institutions that will evolve seem likely to remain firmly established. Developing a more integrated society, polity, and economy in the period ahead will pose challenges that are more difficult to respond to. In a short-term sense, leaders of an incumbent government that regards itself responsible for managing the official peace process may see citizen activism as threatening, but this is a playing out of politics and not an interaction of mediating actors.

## LESSONS LEARNED AND CONCLUDING REFLECTIONS

It is possible to establish complementarity rather than working at cross-purposes as the norm in a situation in which a peace process is working at several levels. The keys are mutual understanding of what is possible and not possible at each level and forthright communication of limits that each party will respect. It helps when those in leading positions at each level are experienced, recognize their limits as well as their obligations, and put ego behind solving the problems at hand.

It is important to work within a conceptual framework—in this case, the multilevel peace process—that provides a diagnostic tool for clarifying what is best done at each level, where the capacities to perform certain tasks are, and the stage of development of the peace process. Experience in that context now begins to produce certain simple observations:

- Nonofficial dialogue may play a key role in paving the way to formal mediation and negotiation and may be the only player on the field at that early stage. At the beginning, the subject is the overall relationship between parties in conflict, not issues for negotiation. After exploratory talks, a dialogue group may identify the first steps along the road to ending violence and negotiating peace.
- In the Tajik case, briefing top authorities in the conflicting parties on the insights from a dialogue was essential in giving them an opportunity to assess the possibilities for fruitful negotiation and to weigh their options without taking risks they did not want to take.
- In the Tajik case, a decision to negotiate seems to have been precipitated by a combination of a UN emissary offering mediation and a report from the dialogue that a substantive basis for negotiation seemed to exist.
- It is possible for some participants in a nonofficial dialogue also to participate as delegates in the official peace process. Although it made the dialogue more difficult on a few occasions when a negotiating round was imminent, that infrequent disadvantage was outweighed by introduction into the dialogue of an authoritative account of the real issues and by creation of an accurate channel of communication directly from the public to the official peace process.
- The Tajik experience made clear the difference between setting broad directions and developing formulae for solving problems, on the one hand, and negotiating detailed agreements, on the other. It also demonstrated that a nonofficial group can respect that distinction and make use of it.
- A nonofficial dialogue group can define key problems that NGOs can work on—for example, helping citizens experience a political culture that encourages building bridges across natural divisions in a country,

such as regionalism and an inadequate understanding of power sharing. An NGO founded by someone within the dialogue as a base can find ways to address those problems.

- Tajik participants in the dialogue understand the need to accompany a peace agreement and formal implementation with efforts to build the sinews of civil society to knit a country together. That insight can be developed in dialogue. The greatest remaining challenge is how to share the experience, capacity, and perspective of the dialogue more broadly in the society.

The Inter-Tajik Dialogue has certainly established itself as an ongoing participant in that part of the multilevel peace process controlled by citizens outside government. It did not transgress the line separating it from the official mediation, but it has engaged in what might be regarded as a larger political process in which citizens helped pave the way for negotiation, assisted it while it was in progress, and now are assisting in creating a political environment for the implementation of agreements reached in the official peace process.

Because the principle of complementarity rather than the practice of competition was explicitly established, it is accurate to say that neither the official nor the public peace process was negatively affected by the actions of the other. Indeed, each seemed to gain strength from the interaction between the two.

The important experience of the two NGOs in the civil society demonstrates that yet another kind of leadership has emerged in the multilevel peace process—the leadership of citizens who have accepted as individuals a responsibility for creating conditions among citizens outside government for a political process of national reconciliation. Whereas the Inter-Tajik Dialogue has functioned as a group to produce ideas and perspectives while leaving actions to individuals in their own walks of life—including those in the negotiation—the NGOs that have sprung up are themselves actors as groups on the political scene.

In sum, I find myself most often describing the Inter-Tajik Dialogue as a "mind at work in the middle of a country making itself." When asked what the most important political institution in traditional Tajik culture has been, the answer from dialogue participants has invariably been: "In every village there is a council of elders." Participants in the dialogue have often spoken of the possible Consultative Forum of the Peoples of Tajikistan as a "national council of elders." That has the potential of becoming a leader in mediating functions in an evolving body politic, but it is still a speculation. If it came into being, it like the Inter-Tajik Dialogue would have the opportunity to avoid clashes with official bodies by defining its arena and methods of work in nonconfrontational ways.

Starting in 1995, the university-based participants in the dialogue asked the management team to help them develop modules in university-level courses in conflict resolution and building civil society. That work has proceeded through several workshops and the translation into Russian of a substantial reader—a portable library of Western material on those subjects.[10] Although it is difficult in the current political atmosphere to win approval by the Ministry of Education for creation of new academic programs, portions of courses in political science are being devoted to the subject. Since the reader is built around the concept of the multilevel peace process, the philosophy developed in the Inter-Tajik Dialogue is in this way beginning to be cemented into the educational structure of the country.

In short, the concept of the multilevel peace process and the experience of the Inter-Tajik Dialogue seemed to provide at least tentative evidence that multiple leaders at different levels in a multilevel peace process can strengthen that process if (1) they are conscious of the potential interaction across levels of the process and (2) they are careful to recognize what must be done at each level and what is not possible at each level. Far from diluting overall responsibility, the concept of the multilevel peace process provides an opportunity to enhance responsibility for the process by creating a consciousness of what is going on in building a whole body politic.

## NOTES

1. The concept of the multilevel peace process and the practice of sustained dialogue are developed in Harold H. Saunders, *A Public Peace Process: Sustained Dialogue to Transform Racial and Ethnic Conflicts* (New York: St. Martin's Press, 1999), especially the introduction and chap. 1. A full account of the Inter-Tajik Dialogue is found in chap. 7.

2. Christopher Mitchell, "The Process and Stages of Mediation," in *Making War and Waging Peace: Foreign Intervention in Africa*, ed. David R. Smock (Washington, D.C.: United States Institute of Peace Press, 1993), especially 139–160.

3. This analysis of the conflict draws heavily from Irina Zviagelskaya, *The Tajik Conflict* (Moscow: Russian Center for Strategic Research and International Studies; and Reading, U.K.: Ithaca Press, 1997).

4. The task force first met in August 1982 in Suzdal, USSR, under cochairmen Yevgeny Primakov—who later became prime minister of Russia—and Harold H. Saunders. Primakov was succeeded by Gennady I. Chufrin in early 1989.

5. Harold H. Saunders, *The Other Walls: The Arab-Israeli Peace Process in a Global Perspective* (first published in Washington, D.C.: American Enterprise Institute, 1985; rev. ed., Princeton, N.J.: Princeton University Press, 1991).

6. Gennady I. Chufrin and Harold H. Saunders, "A Public Peace Process," *Negotiation Journal* 9, no. 2 (April 1993): 155–177.

7. The Russian cochair of the task force is Gennady I. Chufrin, corresponding member of the Russian Academy of Sciences, then deputy director of the Institute of Oriental Studies and now director of a project on Russian relations with Asia initiated by the Stockholm International Peace Research Institute; Vitaly Naumkin, a senior scholar at the same institute and president of the new Russian Center for Strategic Research and International Studies; and Irina Zviagelskaya, also a senior scholar at the institute and vice president of the center. The Americans were Harold H. Saunders, cochair of the task force and director of international affairs at the Kettering Foundation; Randa Slim, then program officer at the Kettering Foundation; and Thomas Gouttierre, dean of International Studies at the University of Nebraska at Omaha, who had been a Peace Corps volunteer and then Fulbright director in Afghanistan. Naumkin and Zviagelskaya undertook responsibility for interviewing and selecting participants for the Inter-Tajik Dialogue.

8. The Inter-Tajik Dialogue has been funded by the Charles Stewart Mott Foundation and by the William and Flora Hewlett Foundation. The Charles F. Kettering Foundation has provided in-kind support.

9. Gennady I. Chufrin, Ashurboi Imamov, and Harold H. Saunders, eds., *Memoranda and Appeals of the Inter-Tajik Dialogue within the Framework of the Dartmouth Conference (1993–1997)* (Moscow: Center for Strategic Research and International Studies, 1997).

10. The preparation and translation of the reader and part of the costs of the major workshop were funded by the United States Institute of Peace.

# Part III

## Ending Violent Conflict

The Road to Settlement

# Background to Chapter 9

# The Road to Madrid

The slow pace of the decades-long Arab-Israeli peace process quickened with the end of the Cold War and the victory of the U.S.-led coalition in the Gulf War. The United States alternately applied pressure and engaged in confidence-building measures in order to establish a dialogue between Israel and the Palestinians, on the one hand, and between Israel and the Arab states, on the other. Steadfast U.S. diplomacy and a growing acceptance of American neutrality in the region finally brought the relevant actors on board. All sides were offered compromise propositions but were also threatened with being publicly blamed should their inflexibility derail the peace process. These tactics ultimately led to a peace conference in Madrid, cosponsored by the United States and the Soviet Union, that facilitated the Oslo peace process and subsequent negotiations.

## MAJOR ACTORS

- Palestine Liberation Organization (PLO): led by Yasir Arafat
- Israel: led by Prime Minister Yitzhak Shamir
- Syria: led by President Hafez Assad
- United States: represented by Secretary of State James Baker
- Saudi Arabia: led by King Fahd
- Jordan: led by King Hussein
- Egypt: led by President Hosni Mubarak
- United Nations: observer at the Madrid international conference
- Gulf Cooperation Council (GCC): a coalition of Saudi Arabia, Kuwait, Qatar, Bahrain, United Arab Emirates, and Oman

- Spain: host of the Madrid Conference
- Hamas: a rival group to the PLO for Palestinian leadership

**IMPORTANT DATES**

- March 8, 1991: Baker visits King Fahd
- March 13, 1991: Baker meets with President Assad
- April 1991: Baker engages in shuttle diplomacy between Syria, Jordan, Saudi Arabia, and Israel
- May 11, 1991: Baker returns to the Middle East for a second round of shuttle diplomacy
- September 1991: Baker returns for a third round of shuttle diplomacy
- October 12, 1991: Baker returns for a fourth round of shuttle diplomacy
- October 19, 1991: Baker and Soviet foreign minister Boris Pankin issue invitations to the international peace conference

**KEY AGREEMENTS REACHED**

- All the relevant actors agreed to attend the Madrid Conference and to meet and talk with one another

**PRINCIPAL OUTCOMES**

- The long-standing taboo on direct talks between Palestinians and Israelis was broken
- A two-track approach to negotiations with parallel reciprocal confidence-building measures was able to foster the beginning of a peace process

# 9

# The Road to Madrid

JAMES A. BAKER III

From day one of my tenure as secretary of state, the last thing I wanted to do was to touch the Middle East peace process. With what appeared to be fundamental and historic opportunities in East-West relations, I frankly saw the Arab-Israeli dispute as a pitfall to be avoided. I was reinforced in this regard by my consultations with former presidents and secretaries of state, all of whom discussed the Middle East in the cautionary tones of those who had been burned by their own involvement.

But I also understood that the Middle East was a region vital to American interests and a perpetual tinderbox whose crises had invariably demanded the attention of my predecessors. The peace process was also a fixture of domestic politics because of our special strategic relationship with Israel and the political power of the American Jewish community.

And so, while American diplomacy concentrated on relations with the Soviet Union throughout 1989, we also sought to manage those relations by pursuing what might be described as a moderately activist policy in the Middle East. It was unsuccessful and I will spare the details, other than to say that the experience left me rather cynical about the Mideast quagmire and, moreover, chagrined that I had not followed my original instincts to steer a wide berth. At the same time, I also learned some valuable lessons that would help refine my strategy for future efforts toward Middle East peace.

## A New Dynamic

As I flew from Taif, Saudi Arabia, to Kuwait City on the afternoon of March 9, 1991—less than three weeks after the end of Desert Storm—the scene out my window was almost apocalyptic: the normally brilliant desert sky had been transformed into an eerie darkness by billowing clouds of sulfurous smoke, a product of more than six hundred oil-well fires ignited by retreating Iraqi forces. For all the devastation spread out beneath our flight path, however, I had come to believe that the invasion of Kuwait and its liberation by an American-led coalition had established a dramatic new reality in the region, and a dramatic new opportunity to press for peace in the Middle East.

Iraq's defeat in the Gulf War had a dramatic effect on the region's balance of power. By reversing Saddam Hussein's aggression against Kuwait, the United States and its allies dealt a punishing blow to the forces of radicalism and rejectionism. The destruction of Saddam's offensive capability enhanced Israel's security and strengthened the hand of moderate Arab states, such as Egypt and Saudi Arabia. In liberating Kuwait, and promptly withdrawing from Iraq as we had promised, the United States had earned the respect and gratitude of all the Gulf Arab states. Additionally, the Soviet Union, long a force for trouble in the area, was now a partner of American diplomacy—and no longer a source of patronage for Arab rejectionists. American credibility in the region and internationally was higher than at any time since the end of World War II. I believed it was a historic opportunity.

Ultimately, both Arabs and Israelis chose to respond to these unprecedented opportunities for different but compelling reasons. Each of them faced powerful new realities.

The Palestine Liberation Organization (PLO) confronted the loss of its longtime patron, the Soviet Union. Moreover, the termination of support by Gulf Arabs (brought about by the PLO's disastrous support for Saddam Hussein) undermined its financial foundations. This development had a political parallel in the emergence of Hamas as a rival claimant to Palestinian leadership. In short, in the wake of the Gulf War, the PLO stood close to collapse.

Jordan's circumstances were also very difficult. Rising radicalism in the Parliament, broad economic distress, and the lingering problem of 350,000

Palestinian refugees combined to give Jordan, too, special incentives for peace.

The Israeli government faced new facts as well. The struggle between Israeli security forces and Palestinians in the West Bank and Gaza seemed as intractable as ever. Radical Islamic fundamentalism in the occupied territories and throughout the region constituted an ominous and growing threat to Israel. Perhaps most important of all, there was—and, I believe, there remains—a desire on the part of most Israelis to put the political, economic, and psychological rigors of being a nation permanently at war behind them.

Nor should we forget that the realities changed for Syria and Lebanon. Like the PLO, Syria faced the end of Soviet patronage—a consideration that weighed heavily in its decision to join the coalition against Iraq and in its new openness to American diplomatic initiatives. Lebanon's case was perhaps most acute. Politically fractured and economically ruined, Lebanon needed peace—and badly. So Lebanon was eager to see Syria say yes to the peace process.

And, as a practical matter, the United States would have been properly criticized if we had stayed on the sidelines following Desert Storm. In putting together and maintaining the diplomatic and military coalition against Iraq, I had repeatedly pledged that the United States would address the larger issue of peace between Arabs and Israelis after the crisis had been resolved. In large measure, this promise had enabled us to thwart Iraqi efforts to link the invasion of Kuwait with the Arab-Israeli dispute.

## THE TWO-TRACK CONCEPT

I had learned several important lessons from my previous experience with the peace process. It was now obvious to me, for example, that any new American initiative would fail if it merely resurrected the diplomatic status quo. A fresh attempt simply to create a dialogue between the Israelis and the Palestinians, as we had done in 1989, would prove both shortsighted and fruitless.

I also had a better grasp on how to deal with Israeli prime minister Yitzhak Shamir. He was enormously ambivalent. He wished to be a peacemaker, but he was also a settler, whose policies in the West Bank made peace more difficult. I concluded that the only way to deal with this was to put him in a position in which he could no longer say no to new initiatives.

Indeed, that was our strategy not only with respect to Israel but to the Arab states as well. The strategic moment made the United States a credible neutral broker in the Middle East, and we looked for ways to take advantage of that reality. We also sought ways to use our unique credibility in the region to exert leverage on each of the parties to pursue peace. Although there were in fact new realities that augured well for peace, no one in the Middle East wanted to blink first. So it was our job as mediator both to push and to pull the region toward peace.

One of our strongest points of leverage, with respect to all parties, was the threat to, as I found myself saying all too often, lay the dead cat on their doorstep. No one wanted to accept blame for scuttling the process. Some days this felt like the only leverage I had.

The best way to take advantage of the moment, I concluded, was to devise a means of breaking the taboo on direct talks, which had existed since the very creation of Israel in 1948. The Egyptian-Israeli peace treaty of 1979 had not really altered this grim barrier to progress. Other than Egypt, Arab governments simply would not deal directly with Israelis. It was maddeningly simple: you can't make peace if you won't talk.

In consultation with my senior advisers, I decided that we would try a two-track approach. The United States would attempt to restart a process leading to an Israeli-Palestinian dialogue—although we recognized that the question of Palestinian representation would ultimately be the most difficult issue of all to resolve. Simultaneously, however, we would propose and pursue a second track—direct talks between Israel and her Arab state neighbors in the form of a regional conference on the Middle East cosponsored by the United States and the Soviet Union, where all parties would be represented.

This format was a calculated exercise in creative ambiguity. The Arabs could claim that it was the international conference they had long sought. Similarly, the Israelis could contend that it was nothing more than the face-to-face discussions they had said they wanted for twenty-five years. They could argue that it was no different from the 1973 Geneva talks in which they had participated, and not the larger international conference sponsored by the United Nations that they had consistently opposed.

For the second track to have any chance of success, I would have to persuade both sides that the other side had undergone a significant change in attitude. For this reason, I decided to propose what came to be known as the concept of parallel reciprocity. I would ask Israel and her Arab neighbors to consider certain confidence-building measures as a means of demonstrating that both sides were now willing to break new ground in a quest for peace. I knew that each side would need something from the other for purposes of political cover. Moreover, neither side would be willing to move first. Parallel reciprocal steps, I believed, were the logical solution to this impasse.

Parallel reciprocal steps also had the positive effect of further underscoring the role of the United States as a neutral broker. We made it abundantly clear that we were prepared to press Arabs and Israelis alike to make concessions designed to create momentum for peace. Over time, we believed that consistent, credible, and visible pressure on both sides could actually enhance our already unique credibility.

## TESTING THE WATERS

Because I believed that Shamir was the most immediate hurdle, it was important to demonstrate first that the Gulf War had caused a dramatic change in Arab attitudes. For that reason, I decided that Saudi Arabia should be the first stop on a ten-day, seven-country itinerary, beginning on March 8, 1991. In all my talks, I made the case that the United States was prepared to be what President Bush had called a catalyst for peace—but not unless all the parties were willing to take risks. After explaining the two-track concept in detail, I pressed each of my interlocutors to support it, and asked whether they would consider taking conciliatory steps if their counterparts were willing to do likewise.

In my private talks with King Fahd, for instance, I outlined my idea of a two-track approach and listed a variety of confidence-building measures that both Saudi Arabia and Israel might consider. I suggested that the Saudis could drop the economic boycott of Israel, reject the 1975 UN resolution equating Zionism with racism, end the formal state of belligerency with Israel, meet with Israeli officials at a low level, or quietly exchange intelligence information on terrorist activities. In turn, I was prepared to urge Shamir to respond in kind by, among other things, halting the deportation and administrative detention of Palestinians in the occupied territories and withdrawing the Israeli army from certain towns in the West Bank and the Gaza Strip.

This is an example of how we creatively used our leverage in different ways at each different stop.

As my meetings progressed, it became apparent that the moderate Arab states, in particular the Saudis, seemed interested in exerting a greater leadership role on regional security issues and the peace process. A meeting in Cairo with Egyptian president Hosni Mubarak confirmed my expectation that he would be fully cooperative. He stressed repeatedly the importance of his relationship with President Bush and, in my presence, even telephoned Syrian president Hafez Assad to vouch for the credibility of the administration. From early on, Mubarak leaned very far forward for peace. There would have been no Madrid Conference if not for his courage.

From Cairo, I went to Tel Aviv. I urged Shamir to take advantage of what I called new opportunities and attitudes in the region, particularly on the part of Saudi Arabia. For the first time, I said, King Fahd was willing to exert leadership for peace. As I had done in my meetings with Arab leaders, I enumerated for Shamir my list of confidence-building measures that both sides should ponder. I urged him to consider less oppressive policies in the occupied territories, to declare a willingness to meet Palestinians without new elections, and to think about withdrawing from southern Lebanon within six to twelve months, if during that period we could see to it that there were no terrorist attacks against northern Israel. It was also important, I said, to consider a commitment to begin negotiations about the Golan Heights with Syria.

Shamir was more interested in talking about what the Arabs should do. At a minimum, he insisted, they should suspend the economic boycott and recognize Israel's right to exist. Nevertheless, he made several particularly interesting comments. He accepted my contention that the concept of autonomy for residents of the territories was a loaded term for the Palestinians. We need to find more effective terminology, he said at one point. He reacted favorably to my suggestion that self-government was perhaps a more useful semantic formulation. I was also encouraged by his insistence that the United States should do everything possible to keep King Hussein in power despite his support for Saddam Hussein during the war. A stable Jordan, he said, was crucial to long-term prospects for peace.

The idea of a conference had some appeal for Shamir, who said he would consider a regional conference with Egypt, Jordan, Saudi Arabia, Syria, and Lebanon. But he opposed a conference with Soviet cosponsorship. I sensed, however, that his opposition would crumble if the Soviets resumed diplomatic relations with Israel. He demonstrated a flexibility of spirit that I found both encouraging and surprising.

Despite the unhappiness of the Israeli government, I also met with a delegation of ten Palestinians, including Faisal Husseini and Hanan Ashrawi, while in Israel. My purpose was to reinforce President Bush's belief that legitimate Palestinian rights must be included in an enduring peace. But I also wanted to exert leverage where possible. I reminded them that the Palestine Liberation Organization's support of Iraq in the Persian Gulf War had not been helpful to the Palestinian cause. You've got more to gain or lose than anyone else in this process, I reminded them. If you stick to your old bottom lines, we won't get anywhere.

Shamir told me that Israel was serious about peace, but that there was nobody with whom to talk. The Palestinians I had met were unacceptable to him. We know all about them, and they're PLO, he said. I pointed out, without any success, that while many of them had ties to Yasir Arafat, none were PLO officials. It was apparent that Shamir would resist most of these Palestinians as part of an official delegation to any talks.

Shamir also produced a letter from his files that President Ford had sent then prime minister Yitzhak Rabin in 1975, reaffirming U.S. support for Israel. He asked me to read the letter with particular emphasis on its final paragraph, which pledged that in formulating future policy with respect to the terms of a peace settlement, the United States would give great weight to Israel's position that any peace agreement with Syria must be predicated on Israel remaining on the Golan Heights.

On its face, Shamir seemed to be asserting that Israel would not withdraw from the Golan under any circumstances. I concluded, however, that Shamir was signaling at least some degree of flexibility. Otherwise, I don't think he would have raised the subject with me. What if there were American troops up there? I asked him. He paused for a moment, as if he were startled by the notion. Then it would be different, he said. We would return to this topic later.

I was rapidly coming to the conclusion that Syria was the key to significant progress. Assad had long been the most intransigent of the Arab leaders. His engagement would signal, in the most dramatic fashion, that our efforts were legitimate in Arab eyes. I hoped that the collective weight of the other Arab states would have an impact on him. This was another aspect of parallel reciprocal steps. By prodding the parties to make separate gestures, I hoped to create a cumulative momentum for peace that would eventually be impossible to resist.

My first two meetings with Assad during the Gulf crisis had persuaded me that, at the very least, he was prepared to reconsider his traditional rigidity toward making peace with Israel. Our meeting on March 13, 1991, lasted seven hours. Having been briefed in advance by Mubarak on the details of my proposal, he had already digested them. He said it was his desire to make something happen. Assad supported the two-track approach, but was less enthusiastic about parallel confidence-building measures. He agreed that Israel should take such steps, but was cool to the idea that Arab states should do likewise. At every other stop in the region, the concept of parallel reciprocity had been embraced. Nevertheless, I concluded that Assad was genuine when he said that he had never before seen an American commitment of such credibility and was prepared to respond with a seriousness of his own.

I returned to Washington on March 17, satisfied that the environment had indeed been transformed in the region as a result of the war. As I flew home, three realities became clear to me. First, concrete Arab concessions would be necessary to bring Shamir along, but I believed both to be possible. Second, cutting the Gordian knot of Palestinian representation would be even more difficult than I had anticipated. And finally, there would be no effective progress without Syria's participation.

## REVERTING TO FORM

Within two weeks of my return to Washington, I had begun to fear that my guarded optimism was misplaced. At every echelon of American government, up to and including President Bush, we pressed all the parties to go beyond their platitudes, with concrete steps. None had been forthcoming.

It was apparent that unless I broke my promise to myself to avoid shuttle diplomacy, the window of opportunity created by Desert Storm would slam shut out of inertia. The lesson of course was that even when the goal is lofty, the means to that end must sometimes be less than elegant. While appealing to high purpose, I would also have to cajole and coerce and, again, use leverage in every instance possible. If I didn't, peace would be the loser, but American credibility and prestige would also suffer. Having started this process, I was now determined to try to save it from a premature demise.

As always, the tortured road to peace ran through Jerusalem, and I arrived there again on April 9. I had three core questions: Would Israel attend a regional conference with the Arabs and the Palestinians? Would they agree that the basis for any such meeting would be a comprehensive settlement based on United Nations Resolution 242? And would Israel attend if Palestinians from the territories were present?

I was relieved to learn that Shamir had moved a little. He had dropped his previous opposition to Soviet cosponsorship; Israel was now prepared, he said, to attend a regional conference, but not under UN auspices, as the Arabs had insisted for years. He also agreed to participation by Palestinians from the territories, subject to some difficult conditions including a requirement that the Palestinians be part of a joint delegation with Jordan— to diminish the PLO's impact.

Shamir was uncomfortable about the basis for the conference, however. UN Resolution 242 was premised on the exchange of territory for peace, which he had vowed he would never do. He wanted to insert the phrase as agreed at Camp David into the 242 formula, since Israel's position was that Menachem Begin had already met the requirement to exchange land for peace by returning the Sinai as required by the 1978 peace accord hammered out with Anwar Sadat under President Carter's auspices at Camp David. I told him this was merely a matter of semantics. Both sides could interpret the formula however they wished, but the Arabs would never agree as a basis for a meeting to any language limiting or modifying Resolution 242 as passed by the Security Council.

My second meeting with Palestinians from the territories was notably more upbeat than our first encounter in March. I was struck by the almost total absence of polemics and the ritual mention of the PLO, and it was clear they wanted to be part of the process. They agreed to the three preconditions Shamir had laid down as the price of meeting with them in a regional conference: thus they agreed to support a two-track process between Israel and both Arabs and Palestinians, phased negotiations, and peace with Israel.

By the next day, Shamir had decided to drop his language about Camp David, and said he would consider my proposal to allow a representative of the European Community to attend as an observer. Shamir didn't trust the Europeans, believing them overwhelmingly Arabist, but I felt strongly that some sort of gesture was necessary, if only to keep them from complicating the process. But Shamir also put a new request on the table. In our first meeting, he'd demanded a U.S. pledge that the Palestinians would never mention the PLO. Now he wanted a letter from the Palestinians attending the conference formally disavowing the PLO and attesting they weren't representing Yasir Arafat. I said I would tell the Arabs that publicly trumpeting a PLO connection would scuttle the process, something I firmly believed. I also told him that if he insisted on this letter, the process was dead and I would be sure to say exactly what caused the effort to fail.

I flew to Damascus on April 11, 1991, to see Assad. Since I knew that Assad would be the toughest Arab domino to topple, I deliberately sought very little from him at the outset. Again, I hoped that forward movement from other Arab states would help to compel Assad to move himself. But he would not be asked now to end the state of belligerency or recognize Israel. I asked that he refrain from criticizing any Palestinians willing to talk with Israel, and to work on the PLO to keep its profile low. Most of all, I wanted Assad's agreement to attend the regional conference.

He was willing to attend, he said, but only if four conditions were met. He insisted on describing it as an international conference. He wanted assurances that the cosponsors would guarantee all results. The conference must be continuous to guarantee impetus to the negotiations. And, to ensure that the conference had what he repeatedly called international legitimacy and moral authority, it must be under the aegis of the United Nations.

To varying degrees, three of his particulars posed problems for Israel, but I believed that compromises could be fashioned that Shamir might ultimately accept. In fact, Assad and I reached a middle ground on the spot on what to call the conference. He rejected out of hand the Israeli preference for a regional conference, saying it would belittle the significance of the conference. I reminded Assad that nothing could prevent him from calling it an international conference—or, I knew, Israel from calling it a regional conference. Assad finally suggested that it should be called a peace conference, and I readily agreed.

His fourth requirement concerning UN sponsorship, however, was a dagger aimed at the heart of peace. The United Nations had always been perceived, with no small justification, by Israel as a mortal enemy held at bay only by the American veto in the Security Council. The 1975 resolution equating Zionism with racism had cemented this view. I knew Shamir would never attend any conference under UN auspices, and I warned Assad that it was a deal breaker. However, I replied, the United States had no problem with a UN presence; in fact, I told Assad, I was willing to press Shamir to agree to allow a UN observer to attend.

I felt Assad's objections were primarily a cosmetic smoke screen, designed to deflect a dialogue from ever developing. I tried to appeal to Assad's practical side by pointing out that, by persisting, he would hand Israel a chance to refuse to attend and blame it on Damascus.

My disappointment with Assad coincided with irritation over an unwelcome leak from Israel, erroneously claiming that I'd agreed to exclude East Jerusalemites from any Palestinian delegation. I wrote a letter to Shamir asking for restraint on what was publicly said about sensitive issues.

Shamir's reply was even more disappointing, emphasizing, in my view, symbols over substance. Shamir argued that it made no sense to call it a peace conference, since the regional meeting would not be the forum for peace negotiations. He also wrote that Israel would never accept a Palestinian from East Jerusalem on any delegation, because it puts East Jerusalem on the agenda.

I returned to Israel days later. In another meeting with Shamir, I told him that I'd taken pains to structure a process tailored to Israel's concerns and that it was now time to begin considering compromises by Israel. I asked for enough procedural flexibility to allow the process to go forward. Shamir and his aides ignored my plea, constantly raising procedural roadblocks and debating points, reservations, and new concerns. The haggling seemed to me a calculated exercise in obfuscation designed to delay and, if possible, avoid hard choices. If you can't help me, I finally said, I'll go home.

After meeting with the Palestinians again, I decided to stop in Jordan, which I had been avoiding because of our displeasure with its support of

Iraq. But we understood there would be no peace process without Jordan's participation, and we were willing to let bygones be bygones if Jordan enlisted actively in the peace initiative. In particular, King Hussein would be crucial in persuading the Palestinians to come to the table. We also knew the United States had considerable leverage to exert, with Jordan's economy in the dumps and King Hussein desperate to rebuild his tattered ties to both Washington and his former patrons in Riyadh.

The king clearly understood that he needed to play on our terms. In short order, he endorsed the conference and declared (somewhat improbably, I felt at the time) that Jordan would attend even if Syria didn't. He also agreed to Shamir's idea of a Jordanian-Palestinian delegation in principle and endorsed my compromise of UN observer status. He pledged to tell the PLO to keep a low profile and to encourage the Palestinians to remain committed to the process. I asked him to say something to the press about breaking old taboos, which he did.

I then flew to Jeddah, where I found the Saudis returning to form. Prince Saud told me it would not be appropriate for his country to attend a peace conference. I was stunned. King Fahd's evasions, while more polite, were reminiscent of the classic Saudi preference for avoiding risks. I asked him to issue a mild statement in support of peace that I could use to put Shamir on the defensive. He demurred, not wishing to inflame Arab public opinion. We're your partners, I reminded the king. We were there for you. How can we be partners in war but not in peace? In the end, the king pledged to lean on the Syrians, the PLO, and even their erstwhile brother, King Hussein. The Saudis later issued a mild statement endorsing the U.S. initiative and supporting the idea of a conference. But the king would have to be further encouraged to produce anything of genuine effect.

On April 23, I met President Assad again in Damascus. Assad was unyielding on two demands that I knew would never be accepted by Shamir. He insisted on full participation of the United Nations, with all members of the Security Council present, as well as a continuous conference, one constantly in session. I told Assad that in response to his previous insistence that the conference cosponsors guarantee all its results, I was prepared to explore the concept of a formal American pledge guaranteeing the security of the Israeli-Syrian border along the Golan Heights. I made clear that such a commitment could be offered only after Israel and Syria had negotiated a full and complete peace, and that it would be a waste of time for me to explore this idea with President Bush unless Assad were willing to drop his two objections to the conference modalities. This position on my part was pure negotiating tactic, as I had already discussed this idea with the president.

Assad continued to spar, surfacing peripheral demands that I knew were utterly unrealistic. Before leaving I told Assad that I had a hard time understanding how or why he would forgo the chance—even if it were just a chance—to produce Israeli withdrawal from the Golan for procedural conditions that have no effect and ensure no results. I told him that if he backed off the two modalities, I would return. If not, I didn't expect to see him for a long time. The truth is, I guessed Assad would move, that he was simply waiting to see what happened in my next meeting with Shamir. But I wanted him to understand the ball was in his court.

Unfortunately, when I next met Shamir, it was apparent the Israelis were becoming more rigid, not less. Not only were they adamant on their procedural objections, they were raising new potential roadblocks. I knew this was a standard tactic, but I could barely contain my frustration. I argued that one UN observer was merely a symbol, which cost Israel nothing. I can't accept the United Nations, Shamir said.

I'm going to leave this dead cat on his doorstep, I vowed to Dennis Ross, my director of Policy Planning and one of my inner circle of advisers. Let's not rush to judgment, he counseled. He pointed out in a memo to me that Shamir and I had worked out the formula on the most difficult issue of all: East Jerusalem. The United States had agreed that East Jerusalem residents would not be included on the Palestinian side of the joint delegation. In turn, Israel had pledged not to challenge any Palestinian member on the Jordanian side of the delegation (holding a Jordanian passport) even if the member happened to have been born or raised in East Jerusalem. It remained to be seen, however, if this crucial compromise would be accepted by the Palestinians.

## New Optimism and Assad's Double-Cross

On May 3, 1991, Ed Djerejian, the very able U.S. ambassador to Syria, called me to report that Assad had capitulated on the two sticking points from our previous meeting and evidently was prepared to have Syria attend the conference. I was elated. I now had dramatic new leverage with which to challenge all the other parties, especially Israel and the Saudis, to demonstrate similar flexibility.

Dennis Ross paid a visit to the elegant Virginia home of Prince Bandar, the Saudi ambassador to the United States—who proved himself time and again to be one of the most progressive of King Fahd's advisers. Ross proposed that the Saudis send a representative of the Gulf Cooperation Council (GCC) to attend the conference as an observer. It was an ingenious way to overcome congenital Saudi caution. Sending a representative of the six-member GCC would give King Fahd some protective cover with his more militant subjects. Conversely, since Saudi Arabia was the dominant force on the council, I could argue to the Israelis that the Saudis were in fact participating in the process.

Bandar liked the idea, and three days later the Saudis announced that a GCC observer would attend the opening session of the peace conference. Even more important, the Saudis would attend the multilaterals. It was a stunning development—the Custodian of the Two Holy Mosques had agreed that Saudi Arabia would join others in the same room with Israel. Saudi participation now would increase the pressure on Israel to say yes.

The following day, on May 11, 1991, I left on my fourth trip to the region since the end of the Gulf War. In the fifteen days since leaving Israel, my spirits had done an abrupt turnaround. I had the sense that a tangible momentum for peace was finally beginning to gather force. Our strategy of creating cumulative pressure on each party to act was beginning to pay dividends.

My optimism was short-lived. As I arrived in Damascus, I was greeted by Foreign Minister Farouk Shara. He advised me that Assad had changed his mind on one key point. The United States would need to agree that the conference could be reconvened without the approval of all the parties. The next morning, Djerejian brought more bad news. Shara had advised him that Assad had also reneged on his second commitment and was now insisting that the United Nations attend the conference as a full participant.

In our meeting, Assad confirmed that he was now spurning the compromises he'd previously accepted. He went out of his way to obfuscate the facts of what had been discussed, in effect calling me a liar. I produced the transcript of our prior meeting, which was unambiguous. Assad was too smart to have misunderstood what had happened, but he was obviously trying to mitigate his own conduct by suggesting that I had agreed that the United States would guarantee a return of the Golan rather than those borders that Israel and Syria might agree upon in negotiation. He accused me of reneging on my word. I slammed my portfolio and left, but not before saying that I was disappointed. Because of your insistence, I told Assad, there will be no peace negotiations.

On my flight to Cairo, I gave a background briefing to reporters and unloaded on Assad while speaking under the protective cloak of a senior administration official. I wanted to suggest to the world that Assad might not be up to the challenges required of great leaders, and apparently I succeeded. Two weeks later in Lisbon, Shara approached Dennis Ross, whom he believed had been the source, and pleaded with him never to give such a harsh backgrounder again.

On May 14, I flew to Amman for my second meeting with King Hussein. I reminded him that his participation was critical, regardless of Assad's decision. I pressed him for a commitment, but he said he would need to consult further. He was willing to put together a joint delegation to a peace conference, but only if the Palestinians asked him. I reiterated that Israel privately understood that any Palestinian delegation would have the tacit acquiescence of the PLO, but a visible PLO role was unacceptable. The king told me that this would be no problem and agreed to use his private channels to assure the Israelis that there would be no surprises with the delegation.

My meeting with three Palestinian leaders in Jerusalem was less than satisfactory, as the officials reverted to form, dusting off their old argument that Jerusalem must be addressed before peace talks could begin. And they insisted that the formation of a Palestinian delegation was a matter for Palestinians only—a position that was unfortunately reiterated to the press afterward. They seemed to be most interested in arguing. I pointed out that we could talk forever, but while we did Israel would continue to settle what Palestinians claimed as their land.

The next day, I met with Shamir for the fifth time in as many weeks. I told him that I was still unhappy that he wasn't willing to show any flexibility on the remaining two issues in dispute: UN observer status and reconvening the conference. I also told him I was disappointed that Israel and Syria appeared to be in the same boat, both obstructing based on modalities.

The following morning, on May 16, Shamir still refused to budge on the UN observer. But he declared the multilateral talks that would follow the conference would be considered by Israel as a reconvening of the process. It wasn't much, but in tandem with a twelve-point memorandum of understanding on principles and modalities our staffs had hammered out overnight, at least there was something new I could market with Hussein and Assad.

I then returned to Washington and reviewed the entire situation with the president and National Security Adviser Brent Scowcroft. We agreed that an intensive round of telephone diplomacy involving the president should be followed by some action-forcing event. For some time, we had been considering bringing matters to a head by having the president issue conference invitations to all the parties. I wasn't sure, however, if the time for brinksmanship was quite at hand. We decided instead on an interim step. On May 31, the president sent letters to Shamir, Assad, Mubarak,

King Hussein, and King Fahd, urging that they all demonstrate new flexibility so that a peace conference could be held.

Six days later, Shamir responded with a very tough letter, rejecting any compromise on the United Nations or the reconvening issues. I'd expected his reply to be more nuanced, and his strong tone rekindled my suspicion that Shamir simply was not serious about proceeding. I felt we were left with only one last tactical stratagem—persuading Assad somehow to compromise, thereby thrusting Shamir onto the defensive.

## BREAKTHROUGH FOR PEACE

On the afternoon of July 14, Ed Djerejian called me in my office at the State Department. He indicated that Assad's response to President Bush was an unqualified acceptance of our proposal for a peace conference. I couldn't quite believe there wasn't some loophole. But I telephoned the president and briefed the press. Later, when I read the fine print, it was clear there was no catch: Syria would sit down across the table from Israel, thereby abandoning a policy position it had held since the beginning of its conflicts with Israel.

The coincidental intervention of the London G-7 summit delayed my arrival in Damascus to nail down Assad's unconditional acceptance and to pay him the appropriate diplomatic tribute. But more important, the summit also provided a fortuitous vehicle to reinforce our strategy for the peace process by underscoring the need for reciprocal Arab and Israeli gestures. Responding unanimously to a proposal by President Bush, the G-7 leaders called for an end to both the Arab economic boycott of Israel and new Israeli settlements in the occupied territories. The Israelis were not happy, but American credibility as an honest broker was enhanced with the Arabs, which was our intent.

Once I got to Damascus, it was apparent that Assad had but one thing on his mind—to confirm his acceptance of President Bush's proposals. He signaled his intention by having an uncharacteristically short encounter— a mere 150 minutes. I told Assad that his letter had galvanized the G-7 meeting and was directly responsible for securing the resolution calling for the end of Israeli settlements as well as the Arab boycott. I cannot overstate the dramatic, profound effect your letter had around the world, I said. You are now seen to have chosen peace.

I left for Cairo in an optimistic mood. I wanted Mubarak to issue a statement linking Arab willingness to suspend the boycott to a suspension of settlement activity. This statement would convey a psychological impact beyond measure by demonstrating a clear, unmistakable change in Arab attitudes toward the Jewish State. Tactically, Israel would also be thrust into the uncomfortable position of spurning something of genuine value—lifting the boycott—by adhering to its settlement policy. As always, Mubarak was stalwart in his support and issued the statement in the press conference following our meeting.

The next day, I flew to Jeddah. I can't leave Saudi Arabia with no result, I told King Fahd. With a little editing, he agreed to issue a statement supporting Mubarak's initiative. The king's endorsement was largely the handiwork of Bandar, who had come up with the idea in the first place, and argued that it would have more impact for Mubarak to propose it and the king to ratify, instead of vice versa. While Saudi foreign minister Saud may have felt more comfortable submerged in the mainstream of Arab consensus, he had promised me that I wouldn't leave Jeddah empty-handed, and he delivered. I also asked Fahd to press King Hussein and the Palestinians to form a joint delegation and to keep the PLO invisible. He agreed to all these requests.

Frankly, I was still worried about King Hussein. Even as he was asking the United States to repair his ties with Saudi Arabia, he released a white paper to justify Jordan's support of Saddam Hussein in the Gulf War. But it was quickly obvious to me on my arrival in Amman on July 21 that the courage shown by Mubarak and King Fahd had stiffened his own resolve. In three hours of talks, the king committed to come to the conference and endorsed the reciprocal gestures proposal for ending both the Arab boycott and the new settlements. He also assured me that he was now working seriously on the joint delegation.

As I'd always known, the Palestinians would be the last Arab holdouts. In early July, I'd met in my office in Washington with Husseini and Ashrawi, to press the wisdom of a joint delegation with Jordan. By then, Israel had privately agreed that Palestinians from outside the territories—so-called Diaspora Palestinians—could participate in eventual talks about the permanent status of the territories. Husseini and Ashrawi, however, were still insisting on some official PLO representation at the peace conference. I told them this simply would never happen.

When I saw them again in Jerusalem on July 21, they were still adamant. I told them the train was moving and they'd better not miss it. I asked them to make a distinction between symbols and substance. Once you and Israel engage, I predicted, there will be no turning back. But we can't get there unless we crack the representation issue. And the price of getting there, I told them, was little more than a fig leaf. The Israelis would accept a Palestinian from a prominent Jerusalem family now residing in

Jordan, but only on the Jordanian side of the joint delegation. On behalf of the president, I offered them several assurances for future negotiations, including that the current exclusion of Palestinian East Jerusalemites wouldn't set a precedent for the future.

The absence of East Jerusalemites on the delegation will be seen by Palestinians as a funeral for East Jerusalem, Husseini replied. I responded that while the Shamir government was vulnerable politically on the peace issue, it could easily mobilize great strength on the issue of Jerusalem. As a practical matter, the status of Jerusalem must wait for later. If you highlight it first, I warned, there will be no peace process, and that would be a pity first and foremost for you, because Palestinians will suffer more than anyone from its absence.

Before calling it a day, I met alone with Shamir later that evening. He couldn't really believe Assad's acquiescence and had a blizzard of questions. As the reality sunk in, however, he knew that the ball was squarely in his court and that he couldn't say no to a regional conference. At the end of the meeting, I felt I had reassured him sufficiently. But he said he needed more time to reach a decision.

Before leaving Jerusalem, I'd passed word that I was prepared to return—but only if Shamir agreed to the conference in advance of my arrival. The Israelis conveyed a message to me in Moscow, where I had gone on other business, that Shamir had accepted. Their cable, however, stopped just short of an unqualified acceptance. I telephoned Shamir and thanked him for his positive response, but told him firmly I wasn't coming back unless he told me yes at that moment.

Shamir protested that they still had concerns to discuss. Among other items, he asked me to help repeal the Zionism-is-racism resolution at the United Nations. After consulting with the president, I called Shamir back early the next morning and pledged the United States to a serious effort to repeal the Zionism resolution. I also assured him the United States would not allow the United Nations to create a competing process to the conference. But I firmly rejected his request for two years of automatic vetoes in the Security Council on any measure Israel opposed. And I told him I wouldn't come to Jerusalem to negotiate on these items. In a soft voice, Shamir said, "We have accepted." I then informed him I would be delighted to visit with him in Jerusalem the next day. I arrived with a present from Gorbachev I knew would cheer the Israelis: the USSR would resume diplomatic relations with Israel before the conference started.

Now, at long last, the onus resided on the uncertain shoulders of only one party—the Palestinians. They remained preoccupied with the representation issue and unwilling to accept any compromises. They wanted the United States to change long-standing policy opposing an independent Palestinian state. I offered them a letter of assurances that I thought would meet their concerns: a reiteration of our support for their legitimate political rights, not including a separate independent Palestinian state, but not excluding self-determination in the context of a confederation with Jordan.

I tried to convince them that they hadn't surrendered their claims relating to East Jerusalem in advance of negotiations, and that the question of East Jerusalem would be on the agenda at some point. If that's not good enough, I said, then I must tell you that your position is that symbols are more important than substance—and, unfortunately, that position has helped to create and sustain the Palestinian tragedy. For God's sake, don't let Israel hide behind symbols.

I made essentially the same arguments with King Hussein later that day in Amman. I asked him to use his private Israeli channel to give Shamir the names proposed for the Palestinian part of the joint delegation. He assured me he would do so. The king, I concluded, was at last fully on board.

## THE END GAME

During my discussions with Shamir in May, I'd committed the United States to providing a side letter elaborating American commitments and understandings. Not surprisingly, the Israelis promptly leaked this to the press. In rapid order, Syria, Jordan, and the Palestinians all demanded their own "letters of assurances." As a matter of balance, there was no choice but to oblige them. This proved to be an exasperating exercise in trying to weave through an enormous minefield. Inevitably, terminology that reassured one would offend another.

This process came to a head when I met with Assad on September 20. He claimed that the assurances given to Israel "destroy the progress we think we've made." Out of the blue, he flung down a new procedural roadblock. "I was really surprised," he said, "that there are to be multilateral committees to work to discuss regional issues while our lands are still occupied." I was frankly shocked that he was prepared to hold the work of these committees (on issues like water rights, refugees, and economic development) hostage to an issue that could take decades to resolve. I knew another trip to the region couldn't be avoided.

On the evening of Saturday, October 12, I left Washington for the Middle East, my fourth visit in as many months. The president had decided that invitations to the conference should be issued the following Friday. Increasingly, I was being nickel-and-dimed at every turn. Only the stark reality of a public invitation would silence those still maneuvering to delay or abort the process.

The trip was preceded by three weeks of intensive diplomacy designed to narrow the differences with the parties over the letters of assurances. In New York, Syrian foreign minister Shara handed me a draft that bore faint resemblance to the version I'd left in Damascus. Worse, it contained several points that represented significant change in American policy on critical issues. I told him that he was not negotiating in good faith, and that I would tell him what American policy was, and not vice versa.

On October 15, I visited Assad again, in hopes of bridging our remaining differences. Assad laid out fourteen changes he wanted in the letter; the most important of which involved the multilaterals. I offered new language designed to finesse our disagreements and was willing to give more ground if need be. The next morning, we reconvened and Assad's perpetual sparring over language I considered extraneous finally snapped something within me. "If you don't like what we're doing, and you think you can get the Golan back in any other way, then go ahead and get it back." Assad and I made eye contact. He seemed to sense that we'd reached a certain unhealthy threshold. Assad uttered the words: "We agree on the letter of assurances." I left as quickly as possible. Inexplicably, Assad hadn't even raised the subject of multilaterals.

I met later that evening with the Palestinians in Jerusalem. At long last, progress was being made on names for the delegation. Then, unexpectedly, they reopened the subject of Jerusalem, asking for another impossible concession. "How many times have we done this?" I exploded. "The souk never closes. I've had it. Have a nice life," I said, and left the room. The Palestinians asked Dennis Ross to retrieve me. He told them I would never come back unless they dropped their new demand. They agreed on the spot. The next morning, on October 18, I met with ten Palestinians in East Jerusalem, in a bow to their courage. Instead of the required fourteen names, they gave me seven, assuring me the rest would be forthcoming shortly. I saluted their courage and determination.

Invitations to the conference were issued the following day jointly by Soviet foreign minister Boris Pankin and me, giving each party five days to respond. That night, I ate dinner with Dennis Ross; Margaret Tutwiler, my chief spokesman; and Ambassador Bill Brown, the U.S. envoy to Israel. We were all utterly drained. We didn't have formal acceptances from the parties, but, for all intents and purposes, it was finally over.

En route to Madrid the next morning to thank the Spaniards for agreeing to host the conference at the last minute (predictably, even the site was a subject of great debate and consternation among the parties), I got word that the Palestinians had produced the final seven names, all of which were acceptable to Israel. The Palestinians had one final request: they wanted us to announce that they'd been the first to respond to the invitation. I had to chuckle. As the Scriptures remind us, the last will be the first and the first will be the last.

## Conclusion

The evening before Assad finally relented, I cabled President Bush that I'd had another hard day "on the Middle East roller coaster, and I don't intend to ride it much longer." In the end it had been worth it, as we were able to break perhaps the greatest taboo in the Arab-Israeli dispute: the unwillingness of the parties to even meet and talk with each other.

But the road to Madrid was very much like a roller-coaster ride, and the story of how the conference came to fruition is, in many ways, a classic tale of behind-the-scenes diplomacy: replete with grand strategy, petty bickering, high purpose, and power politics. It is a rich tale of determination, false starts, personal and political courage, blind alleys, perseverance, misjudgments, lost tempers, procedural roadblocks, scores of creative compromises, and negotiations in both good faith and bad.

In my judgment, there were four essential factors that allowed our determined diplomacy to succeed: (1) the defeat of Iraq coupled with the collapse of communism created a new geostrategic dynamic in support of peace; (2) American leadership in the defeat of Iraq, combined with a willingness to act as a neutral broker and tell difficult truths to both sides, gave us an unprecedented credibility in the region; (3) the tactical decision to pursue a two-track approach and parallel reciprocal confidence-building measures gave both sides political cover to modify long-standing policy; and (4) the looming specter of my dead cat on their doorstep prodded all parties forward.

A couple of points deserve further elaboration. The United States, of course, has always had its own interests in the Middle East. But as the world's leading body our interests are always complex and broad ranging enough that we, unlike the countries that inhabit the region, have an overriding interest in a comprehensive regional peace that benefits all parties.

And, related to that, the United States was (and remains) the only potential third-party mediator in the world that could reasonably claim this goal. The Arabs would have gone along with United Nations or European

Union mediation, but these were nonstarters for Israel. The United Nations had no credibility with Israel owing to the Zionism-is-racism resolution and Israel likewise saw the Europeans as Arabist. The Soviet Union, as an empire on the verge of collapse, was in no position to mediate for a whole host of reasons—not the least of which was that its guiding ideology was morally bankrupt and by now discredited around the globe.

So it was only the United States that could demonstrably act as a neutral broker with an overriding interest in an equitable peace. And it is important to remember that it was perhaps only through our role in the Gulf War that the United States won its credibility with Arab states. The leadership role taken by the United States in the ejection of Iraq from Kuwait and, importantly, the restriction of the Gulf War to that end and that end alone gave the United States the credibility it needed to push for a comprehensive regional peace.

In the end, the willingness of the United States to act as a neutral broker was a requisite aspect of building the Road to Madrid. Our diplomatic efforts bolstered the peace process by offering psychological sustenance, credibility, and catalytic creativity.

Ultimately, however, it was the courage and determination of the parties themselves to give peace a chance that somehow prevailed over years of enmity and chaos. And, like a phoenix, the Middle East peace process was reborn in Madrid out of the ashes of the collapse of communism and of Saddam's ill-conceived invasion of Kuwait.

## Background for Chapter 10

## Peacemaking in Southern Africa: The Namibia-Angola Settlement of 1988

In 1968, the United Nations changed the name of Southwest Africa to Namibia, and in 1971 the International Court of Justice ruled South Africa's presence there illegal. Meanwhile, Portugal's retreat from its African colonial empire in 1974–75 and Soviet-backed Cuban intervention in Angola left much of Southern Africa in turmoil. The South Africans maintained their control of Namibia, dating from the lapsed mandate of the League of Nations, and used the territory for their own regional strategy and involvement in Angola's civil war. Within this context, and against the background of the Cold War, the United States forged a diplomatic initiative linking Namibian independence to Cuban withdrawal from Angola. This broad plan focused on first achieving regional political settlements, and then resolving crises in individual states. The multiparty character of the mediation was designed to neutralize the obstruction of competing parties and states, and add reach, credibility, and access to international and regional efforts. Cuba's acquiescence to this formula in 1988 led to a bilateral agreement between itself and Angola and a trilateral agreement with the South Africans that established a basis for a peaceful transition to independence in Namibia, the cessation of hostilities between South Africa and Angola, and a timetable for Cuban withdrawal from Angola.

## MAJOR ACTORS

- SWAPO (South West Africa People's Organization)
- MPLA (Popular Movement for the Liberation of Angola): the government of Angola, led by President José Eduardo dos Santos
- UNITA (National Union for the Total Independence of Angola): the primary Angolan armed opposition, led by Jonas Savimbi
- Cuba
- South Africa
- Western Contact Group: the United States, the United Kingdom, Canada, West Germany, and France
- Frontline states (FLS): Tanzania, Zambia, Zimbabwe, Mozambique, Botswana, and Angola
- UNAVEM (United Nations Angola Verification Mission)
- UNTAG (United Nations Transition Assistance Group)

## IMPORTANT DATES

- 1978: Adoption of UN Security Council Resolution 435 as a basis for Namibia's transition to independence
- 1981: Contact Group relaunches Namibia negotiations on basis of Resolution 435 linked to Cuban withdrawal from Angola
- 1984: Angola (with tacit Cuban blessing) agrees to timetable for partial Cuban withdrawal from Angola linked to implementation by South Africa of Resolution 435
- 1985: UNITA and South Africa defeat Angolan offensive; the United States adopts limited sanctions against Pretoria in response to Pretoria's apartheid policies
- 1986: United States initiates clandestine support to UNITA; Congress adopts comprehensive sanctions against South Africa
- April 1987: U.S. and Angolan negotiators resume official meetings
- January 1988: Cubans join negotiations
- Late April 1988: The first of many U.S.-Soviet consultations takes place on eve of first round of face-to-face Angola-Cuba–South Africa talks under U.S. mediation
- Mid-July 1988: New York Principles call for total Cuban withdrawal and implementation of Resolution 435
- Mid-November 1988: Agreement reached in Geneva on a timetable for total Cuban withdrawal
- December 13, 1988: Brazzaville Protocol agreed upon, establishing mechanism for implementation of Namibia-Angola accords

- December 22, 1988: Angola, Cuba, and South Africa sign agreements at UN Headquarters
- April 1989: Implementation of Resolution 435 begins amid cross-border SWAPO infiltrations
- November 1989: SWAPO wins decisive victory in UN-administered elections
- March 21, 1990: Namibia achieves independence
- 1991: Completion of withdrawal of Cuban troops from Angola

## KEY AGREEMENTS REACHED

- UN verification plan
- U.S.-proposed joint commission to oversee implementation of signed agreements
- Brazzaville Protocol
- Total Cuban withdrawal agreement between Angola and Cuba and incorporated within trilateral Angola-Cuba–South Africa agreement linking Cuban withdrawal to implementation of Resolution 435 in Namibia

## PRINCIPAL OUTCOMES

- Namibian independence achieved, with treaties signed by Angola, Cuba, and South Africa
- Cuban forces withdrawn from Angola
- South African withdrawal from Angola and Namibia
- Violence and polarized confrontation replaced by political settlement and reconciliation

# 10

# Peacemaking in Southern Africa
## The Namibia-Angola Settlement of 1988

CHESTER A. CROCKER

### Introduction to the Southern African Negotiations of 1981–88

The decisions of a newly elected U.S. administration in early 1981 set the stage for an eight-year, Southern African diplomatic marathon. The United States would play multiple roles as alliance leader, pivot of a five-nation "Contact Group," directly intervening superpower, third-party mediator and facilitator of indirect communication between warring sides, source of proposals and compromises, and host-convener of face-to-face meetings. The diplomatic effort went through periods of greater or lesser activity, as Washington stayed with its broad strategic goals while adapting tactics in accordance with prevailing conditions and obstacles, and especially with changing internal political currents within the parties and changing military balances between them. The phases of this prolonged negotiation through the date of settlement are summarized in table 1 (pages 219–221).

By the time the Angolans, Cubans, and South Africans gathered in Geneva in mid-November 1988, they knew one another and their American mediators quite well. Everyone involved had years of experience under their belts, and the negotiating machinery appeared to be up to the task. The full resources of Washington's worldwide diplomatic reach had been deployed to get us this far, as we had mobilized all relevant relationships in the drive for settlement. Some of them were visible, for example, the presence in Geneva of Soviet and UN "observers"; most were not, but that made them no less important. Each of the parties knew exactly what the trade-offs were and what cards could be played. Closure on the remaining issue— agreeing on a precise timetable for the withdrawal of 50,000 Cuban troops from Angola, defined in reference to benchmarks in the United Nations' plan for Namibia's transition to independence—required nearly four days of nonstop maneuver as graphs, charts, and numerous illustrative examples were tabled to help resolve a mathematical-political equation that had become a metaphor for the entire conflict. After final calls to their capitals, delegation heads closed on a twenty-seven-month timetable that would remove 66 percent of the 50,000-plus Cuban force during the first and crucial year of the settlement, the period in which Namibia would achieve its freedom from South African control. Champagne toasts at the end of this negotiating round signaled that final agreement was near.

Five more weeks were required to complete the drafting of a penultimate protocol, to negotiate a UN verification plan, to agree on the terms of reference for a U.S.-proposed joint commission to oversee implementation of the agreements by the signatory parties with U.S. and Soviet observers, and, in consultation with the UN secretary-general, to set a new date for implementation of the settlement package to start on April 1, 1989. Two more rounds of tripartite meetings in Brazzaville, Republic of Congo, completed the process, producing the Brazzaville Protocol of December 13. Ten days later the parties signed their agreements in a ceremony at UN Headquarters chaired by U.S. secretary of state George P. Shultz and UN secretary-general Javier Pérez de Cuéllar.

The treaties signed by Angola, Cuba, and South Africa at the headquarters of the United Nations in New York on December 22, 1988, brought about the independence of Namibia (March 21, 1990), thus ending the colonial era in Africa. They also produced far broader results. South Africa's armed forces returned home after twenty-five years of war beyond the republic's own borders. With the completion of the withdrawal of Cuban troops from Angola in 1991, the countries of Southern Africa became free of foreign troops for the first time since the Napoleonic Wars. The agreements changed the geopolitical equation between the then South African government and its armed opponents, principally in the African National

Congress, making possible both internal change and transformed relations between Pretoria and its neighbors. Doctrines and policies based on violence and polarized confrontation were superseded by moves toward political settlement and reconciliation. Further, the treaties signaled the end of Cuba's experiment in African military intervention and Moscow's accelerating reappraisal of its African interests and policies.

The 1988 settlement is of interest at several levels.

- It represents the successful implementation of a U.S. diplomatic initiative engaging not only the three signatory parties but also a wide range of indirect parties, all of them operating within the ambit of an American strategy and associated diplomatic effort. The U.S. strategy was ambitious, requiring patience and political will as well as a readiness to use muscle when appropriate and to live with the burdens of temporary unpopularity.
- The negotiations illustrate the possibility of effective interaction between great powers and the United Nations. Namibia had long been a UN problem. The implementation of Security Council Resolution 435 (1978) as the basis for Namibia's transition to independence demonstrated the unique acceptability of UN instruments and implementing agencies in highly polarized settings.
- At the same time, the case underscores the sharp distinction between the roles of the United Nations and of its leading members, suggesting that they will continue to be dependent on each other whenever there is complex and arduous diplomatic business to be done.
- It also illustrates a wide array of possibilities available for mobilizing and deploying diplomatic leverage through coalitions and informal working groups designed for a specific purpose.
- The Southern African case sheds light on some of the most challenging issues in the fields of mediation and conflict resolution. It illustrates the different kinds of roles parties may play in a "complex" or multiparty mediation process. As in so many cases of negotiation and mediation, leverage and timing were critical variables.
- The case illustrates how the initial lack of "ripeness" obliged the mediator to concentrate on how to ripen the conflict. This, in turn, required the mediator to generate and develop leverage from within the structure of the conflict and from all the relevant diplomatic relationships surrounding the conflict.
- And it required continuous attention to the possibility of exploiting the dynamics of the military balance between the parties so as to improve

U.S. timing and make ourselves more relevant to their needs. At the most basic level, the United States needed to understand the parties and strengthen their perception of stalemate so that we could become the best answer to the quagmire in which they found themselves.

## THE U.S. DECISION TO ENGAGE: 1981

By 1975, when the United States decided to apply a global strategy to Africa, negative dynamics were already firmly established: Portugal's sudden departure from its African empire left behind one of the messiest and most irresponsible acts of decolonization in the post-1945 period; nationalist military insurgencies directed against colonial or local white authorities erupted in Angola, Mozambique, Namibia, and Rhodesia (Zimbabwe); the Soviets made the unprecedented decision to project their military power into Africa by supporting local insurgencies and through Cuban proxies sent to Angola and Ethiopia; and an increasingly isolated, bellicose, and militarily self-sufficient South Africa involved itself in the turmoil beyond its borders.

For the next six years, from 1975 to 1981, the Ford and Carter administrations sought to acquire the capacity for leadership in promoting negotiated solutions and peaceful change in Southern Africa. This necessitated a regionwide vision that embraced the Zimbabwean and Namibian conflicts as well as the imperative to end apartheid in South Africa.

By 1981, when the Reagan administration entered office, Washington had established effective working relations with the British on Africa and close working ties of its own with the African frontline states (Angola, Botswana, Mozambique, Tanzania, Zambia, and Zimbabwe) and, to a lesser extent, with the wary South Africans, still deeply scarred by the Western failure to respond to the 1975 Soviet-Cuban intervention in Angola. Washington had played a key supporting role for the British in the protracted negotiations leading to the Lancaster House settlement and the independence of Zimbabwe in 1980. At the same time, the U.S. administration had taken the lead in forming the "Contact Group" with Great Britain, Canada, the Federal Republic of Germany, and France and, with these allies, shaping a set of proposals for Namibian independence. These proposals, endorsed by UN Security Council Resolution 435 in September 1978, established a set of complex arrangements for the territory's transition to independence under South African administrative control with simultaneous UN monitoring and supervision. The next two and a half years were taken up with efforts to gain South African agreement to the implementation of Resolution 435.

Despite the progress made in the 1970s, the Southern African peace process was in trouble at the beginning of the Reagan administration in

January 1981. The South Africans, disillusioned with the Angola fiasco and with results of Western diplomacy in Zimbabwe after the victory of Robert Mugabe's Zimbabwe African National Union in the April 1980 election, were increasingly put off by the long history of the United Nations' pro–South West Africa People's Organization (SWAPO) activities and pronouncements regarding Namibia. They began to perceive a pattern in these events. The South African stance on Namibia became increasingly truculent and uncooperative, and Pretoria stepped up its bellicose statements toward its neighbors. On the ground, South African military elements were augmenting clandestine activity in a number of adjacent states, including Angola and Mozambique. Meanwhile, the African frontline states and SWAPO began to view Pretoria's stalling on Namibia as a test of Western diplomatic manhood. By early 1981, they had resisted Pretoria's provocations to abandon the Western-led peace process on Namibia and were headed instead toward calling for UN mandatory sanctions to penalize South Africa for its failure to implement the Namibia decolonization plan. The Western nations wanted neither sanctions nor a rupture with the Africans. The Contact Group mediation was caught between increasingly polarized parties that showed every sign of hardening their positions.

Faced with this regional legacy, the incoming Reagan team saw three options: (1) to continue with the Namibia-only approach, recognizing its limited prospects but judging that the continuing process could buy time and avoid trouble with our Contact Group allies and African partners; (2) to downgrade Southern African diplomacy and pull in our horns, thus avoiding the domestic grief visited on previous administrations over African issues; or (3) to restructure the negotiations fundamentally to incorporate the Angolan factor. Western diplomacy before 1981 had carefully avoided addressing the principal negative factor that had prompted Western concern in the mid-1970s: the Soviet-Cuban fait accompli in Angola.

There were reasons why Angola had played no role in Western-led regional diplomacy after 1976. The West had a weak hand—both physically and diplomatically—after the Angola events of 1975–76. Western efforts to address the question of Cuban troops in Angola, it was argued, would have undercut Angola's cooperation in Namibian diplomacy and led to accusations that the West was more concerned about the communist presence in Angola than about colonialism and racism in South African–ruled Namibia. To many observers in Africa, Europe, and the United States, such reasoning made good diplomatic sense. By 1981, ignoring the Cuban role in Angola had become the politically—and diplomatically—correct posture. Any Western nation that publicly raised the issue could expect to face stern admonishment and diplomatic isolation orchestrated by the nonaligned and communist groups in the United Nations and other international fora.

But ignoring the Cuban issue did not make for sound strategy. The issue of foreign intervention in Angola (both Cuban and South African) had always been uppermost in the thinking of decision makers in both Luanda and Pretoria. Even before 1981, Angolan leaders had recognized the connection between Namibian and Angolan events when they stated that Cubans could leave Angola *after* Namibia's independence under Resolution 435. Namibia, in other words, was viewed in terms of its impact on Angolan internal and external security: the departure of the South Africans would transform the picture. On the other side, there was a host of reasons why a narrowly defined Namibia settlement was unattractive to Pretoria. It offered no strategic "compensation" for the significant step of decolonizing Namibia and accepting the altered geopolitical situation that would go with it. On the contrary, the UN plan would inevitably be viewed as a strategic withdrawal and a political setback, especially if one factored in the prospect of a probable SWAPO victory in Namibian elections. If the Cuban presence remained next door in Angola, it would only compound the negative imagery surrounding Resolution 435 in the eyes of both the South Africans and a number of Namibian groups that were opposed to the plan.

During the Contact Group negotiations before 1981, South African officials made no secret of their interest in the issue of Cuban troops in Angola. The Carter administration had tied the establishment of diplomatic relations with Luanda to Cuban troop withdrawal, but despite prolonged internal debate over how to handle the Soviet-Cuban factor in Africa, the administration never went beyond that to create a specific link between Namibia and Angola. As a result, some of the most basic security concerns of both Pretoria and Luanda were never explicitly addressed. In a sense, diplomatic niceties had been governing Western policy at the expense of strategic realities.

The decision of the Reagan administration to link the inherited Namibia negotiating framework with Angola thus represented both continuity and change in Southern African policy. The linkage strategy, by incorporating the Cuban issue, offered two major pluses: a far better chance to nail Pretoria down to a firm commitment on Resolution 435 and an appropriate U.S. response to the Soviet extension of the Brezhnev doctrine to the Third World, including Africa. If properly orchestrated, the new U.S. approach would undermine the rationale behind Moscow's heavily militarized African diplomacy and place pressure on Soviet-Cuban-African relations—and on the Angolan regime itself if it became an obstacle to Namibia's independence. At the same time, such an approach had the potential to force decisions in Pretoria: to choose either cooperation or confrontation with the West, and either blind exploitation of its regional hegemony or successful use of that power to solve problems and achieve workable compromises.

Under this strategy, Washington would be asking more than a dozen governments and two isolated guerrilla movements to adapt to and cooperate with a fundamentally restructured negotiation. The new U.S. strategy sought to promote a broadened agenda that recognized the relationship between regional and internal conflict. It looked beyond the region's sharp military and political polarization toward an overarching but seldom voiced "common interest" in reduced violence. A skeptic would have been forgiven for wondering, in 1981, why and how all of this would work. The new strategy appeared ambitious; it would require a substantial investment of diplomatic capital, and it contained very real risks of triggering our own diplomatic isolation.

Scholars of conflict resolution speak of "ripe moments" for external diplomatic intervention.[1] Measured by such standards, the wars in Southern Africa were not ripe for resolution in 1981. Although U.S. diplomats had hopes for early progress on the basis of the new negotiating structure, we gradually came to appreciate the nature of the obstacles confronting us. There was no consensus within the South African leadership about either the need for or the desirability of a Namibia settlement, even along the lines of our linkage-based approach. Few of their senior officials believed we could bring about a Cuban withdrawal from Angola. On the Angolan and Cuban (and Soviet) sides, our new approach represented a challenge to the regime and to the external alliance that sustained it. The Angolans viewed us with both respect and fear; they would explore our diplomacy and test our capacity to deliver the other side. Their allies, in the background, would do what they could to discredit and block us.

But the absence of ripeness does not tell the mediator to do nothing and look the other way; it can point to obstacles and suggest ways of dealing with them in order to ripen the conflict. Washington decided, in its own interest, to mount a regional strategic initiative that would alter the negotiating framework, expand the range of parties and potential trade-offs, and shape a possible alternative to the parties' unilateral options.

Moreover, the Reagan administration was not simply seeking a settlement in Southern Africa; it sought a settlement consistent with Western interests in a region free of South African military destabilization and Soviet-Cuban military adventurism, a region where conflicts could be resolved politically rather than being acted out militarily. In that sense, it viewed the Southern African negotiations, which had started back in 1975–76, as akin to the Middle East peace process. As Harold Saunders has pointed out, there are occasions when the pursuit of negotiated solutions is in itself a strategy not only for regional conflict resolution but also for conflict management and for the prenegotiation phase of peacemaking until conflict arenas become ripe.[2] The prenegotiation phase is when most of the action occurs, when the basic dies are cast, when the core concepts and principles are defined and legitimized, and when much of the hardest work of the peacemakers actually takes place.

## WHY U.S. DIPLOMACY SUCCEEDED: KEY FACTORS

Eight years of diplomacy conducted against the backdrop of regional war, internal change, and external political dynamics cannot be readily "explained" in terms of causes or replicable hypotheses. Nonetheless, the key factors can be identified. They are discussed here in terms of (a) the acquisition of the credibility and diplomatic leverage needed to gain entry and maintain control of the negotiating process; (b) the link between U.S. diplomacy and the regional military power equation; (c) the value of securing UN legitimacy; (d) the importance of timing and deadlines; and (e) the strengths of the negotiating mechanism we adopted and the contributions made by other external actors, including the Western Allies, various African states, and the Soviets.

### Credibility and Diplomatic Leverage

During the launch of the new initiative and the first three stages (through March 1985 [see table 1]), Washington needed to acquire the credibility to launch a highly complex diplomacy aimed at solving both the Namibia problem and the Cuban issue in Angola. Credibility meant, in the first instance, demonstrating a *balanced commitment* to the pursuit of both parts of the linkage-based settlement. To "carry water on both shoulders" required communicating authoritatively to each side the existence of shared interests without losing the confidence of the other. Maintaining U.S. credibility through the regional turbulence of the 1980s was a severe challenge. On the one hand, the parties all favored U.S. involvement because they believed in the centrality of the U.S. government (for very different reasons) as an external actor. Closer ties with Washington were high priorities for both Luanda and Pretoria (and, later, Havana), an incentive for them to cooperate or at least go through the motions of cooperating. For eight years, Washington carefully resisted requests for bilateral "quids" (or side payments)

Table 1. From Linkage to Leverage: How the Process Worked

| Stage I: April–October 1981 |
| --- |

- Internal Contact Group discussion of Cuban troop–Namibia linkage and intensive consultations with South Africa and frontline states (FLS) and SWAPO.
- Contact Group tables proposals and launches first mission related to Namibia issues (Resolution 435).

| Stage II: November 1981–September 1982 |
| --- |

- Contact Group concludes phased negotiation of all "outstanding issues" related to Resolution 435.
- FLS, SWAPO, South Africa, and Namibian internal parties reach agreement on constitutional principles for constituent assembly.
- FLS, SWAPO, South Africa, and Namibian internal parties reach agreement on necessity of United Nations Transition Assistance Group (UNTAG) to monitor SWAPO bases in Angola and Zambia.
- Contact Group resolves South African misgivings about UNTAG and "UN impartiality" with "informal understandings."

| Stage III: January 1982–March 1985 |
| --- |

- Nearly twenty rounds of direct U.S.-Angolan talks on Cuban troop withdrawal (CTW) aimed at establishing U.S. credibility and legitimacy of linkage.
- Linkage accepted by Angola and forces in Southern Angola disengage (1984). Washington tables first negotiating document calling for two-year, front-loaded schedule of CTW to be implemented in tandem with Resolution 435.

| Stage IV: March 1985–April 1987 |
| --- |

- South Africa delays pullout from Angola, and Angola does not act against SWAPO violations.
- Angolan offensive against National Union for the Total Independence of Angola (UNITA) defeated by UNITA–South African counteraction (1985).
- Reagan administration adopts limited sanctions against Pretoria (1985).
- South Africa conditionally accepts March 1985 U.S. proposal, creating leverage to obtain further bids from Angola on CTW timing (fall 1985).
- United States resumes tangible support to UNITA (1986).
- Angola ignores South African offer of "date certain" for Resolution 435 linked to agreement on CTW (1986).
- U.S. Congress initiates further sanctions against South Africa and new sanctions against Angola and South African–controlled Namibia (1986–87).
- Structure of Namibia-Angola negotiation maintained despite mounting frictions and suspicion of U.S. motives in Pretoria and Luanda.

## Stage V: April 1987–April 1988

- U.S.–Popular Movement for the Liberation of Angola (MPLA) discussions resume (April 1987).

- United States presses Angola to reciprocate South African partial acceptance of March 1985 proposal, and Angola presses United States to offer up bilateral carrots such as an end to U.S. aid to UNITA as "quid" for new MPLA proposal.

- Angola and Cuba approve new CTW timetable, two years instead of three for removal of "southern" Cuba contingent, retaining earlier northern residual for indefinite period. Castro signals that Cuba wishes to enter talks directly.

- UNITA and South Africa smash Soviet-supported Angolan offensive, inflicting huge losses.

- United States and Angola discuss conditions for Cuban participation.

- South Africa seeks detailed information about U.S.–MPLA talks.

- Castro sends 15,000 more troops to shore up MPLA defenses and seek political leverage.

- Cuba joins Angola in negotiations and categorically accepts principle of total Cuban withdrawal (January 1988).

- Both sides move to reengage in diplomacy (March 1988).

- United States decides parties nearly ready for face-to-face talks, with U.S. mediation (April 1988).

## Stage VI: May 1988–December 1988

- First of twelve rounds of face-to-face trilateral discussion with Cuban participation begin in May.

- Scramble for position on ground and for political advantage in talks; direct Cuban–South African Defense Force (SADF) clash at Calueque (June 1988).

- Psychological turning point as parties agree to accept all tabled proposals as "basis for discussion" (Cairo talks, June 1988).

- United States assists in hammering out New York Principles, first agreed document of negotiation, calling for total Cuban withdrawal and implementation of Resolution 435 (mid-July 1988, New York).

- Military commanders of the Angolan, Cuban, and South African armies discuss for first time how to disentangle forces.

- Agreement that linkage specifics between Namibian independence and total Cuban withdrawal would be reflected in a separate bilateral Angolan-Cuban agreement to be signed on same day as tripartite Angola-Cuba–South Africa agreement (early August 1988, Geneva).

- Geneva Protocol spells out specifics and timing of disengagement of military forces in Angola including security measures affecting SWAPO deployments and a Cuban pledge not to attack UNITA's core areas.
- Pretoria proposes CTW timetable of seven months (Geneva).
- Angola and Cuba reiterate their March 1988 CTW timetable of four years.
- Four intensive rounds of negotiation in Brazzaville and New York fail to break logjam on a compromise CTW timetable; self-imposed November 1 deadline lapses (September–October 1988).
- Delegation heads close on front-loaded twenty-seven-month timetable removing 66 percent of the 50,000-strong Cuban force in the first year (November 1988).
- Penultimate Brazzaville meeting to negotiate UN verification plan and to agree on U.S.-proposed joint commission to oversee implementation of agreements and to set new date for implementation of package on April 1, 1989.
- Two rounds of tripartite meetings to complete Brazzaville Protocol on December 13.
- Parties sign agreements on December 22, 1988.

to advance the peace talks in Southern Africa, but it did nothing to dissuade the parties from believing that their cooperation could improve the climate for bilateral ties.

On the other hand, when the parties clearly were playing double games or pursuing unilateral agendas of their own—as happened on and off through much of the period—Washington had to respond with its own maneuvers. The severe ideological and racial polarization of the region's politics—as well as the sheer ambition of what we sought to accomplish—meant that the parties instinctively resisted the notion of possible common interests, even if they were attracted by parts of the agenda we placed before them. The flip side of these attractions was the hard choices we also placed on the table—for example, for the Angolans and the Cubans, a concrete timetable for Cuban withdrawal and, for the South Africans, their rigorously monitored adherence to Resolution 435, their departure from Namibia, and the end of military involvement in Angola. At times, the parties' distaste for our agenda and their strange common interest in the "status quo" of continued fighting were sufficient to drive them tactically to unite in opposition to our third-party proposals. It was necessary to counter such tactics by pulling back and letting events take their course for a while, or, alternatively, by persuading others (a European ally, a UN official, a well-placed African intermediary) to deliver some cold, hard truths about the consequences to the parties of such obstructionism.

The new U.S. initiative got off the ground in 1981–82 because it offered each of the key parties fresh openings to explore and shape both the Namibian and Angolan tracks of the linkage-based settlement concept. Each would have new ways to seek the high ground and discredit the other side or the mediator. At first glance, it appears obvious why Pretoria was quick to accept the new linkage concept: this was the "compensation" that would give "balance" to a Namibia settlement, and the South Africans probably doubted we could pull it off in any event, letting them off the hook. However, it was precisely this element of inducement toward the party that was being asked to take the biggest step (withdrawing from Namibia) that made it work. South Africa, after all, held many cards as the de facto administering power in full control of Namibia and as the regional hegemon of Southern Africa. Our approach gave us the leverage to obtain binding, cabinet-level assurances from the South Africans, assurances we never let them forget over the ensuing years. Linkage, in this sense, was an example of the "flypaper" principle in diplomacy: offer a powerful party something irresistible in order to nail down its adherence to strategic concepts capable of underpinning an overall settlement.

As a fresh initiative, the linkage concept also enabled us to obtain Angola's readiness to enter into bilateral talks with Washington in early 1982 in full knowledge that the U.S. agenda was to obtain Cuban troop withdrawal in the context of a Namibian settlement, a principle that Angola categorically rejected at the time. It would be nearly four years before the Angolan leadership authoritatively committed itself to a lopsided version of a linkage-based settlement. But U.S. communication with Luanda (the MPLA government headed by President José Eduardo dos Santos) was ironically reinforced by Angolan knowledge of our sometimes difficult but constructive exchanges with the South Africans and by our openly acknowledged exchanges with opposition leader Jonas Savimbi of UNITA, the MPLA's principal antagonist. The issue was not "trust" or "neutrality": it was our presumed leverage with the other side and, hence, our indispensability in any settlement effort, and the opportunity to deal outside the communist camp with the global adversary of one's patrons (Moscow and Havana).

Another early example of diplomatic leverage is the debate in mid-1981 between the Americans and their Contact Group allies on how to launch this new U.S.-shaped process. Washington needed allies to acquire credibility: isolation from allies—especially those in the Contact Group that had launched Resolution 435 in 1978 (Great Britain, Canada, France, and West Germany)—could be fatal to the new initiative. For their part, the allies needed a continuing Namibian diplomatic process to avert a showdown at the United Nations and with the African states, and they needed

U.S. leadership to make the whole thing credible in Pretoria. Each side got what it needed most—Washington obtained allied help internationally and with the African states, providing the momentum for completion of stages I and II (see table 1), and the allies retained both the visuals and the substance of a continuing diplomatic process.

From then on, despite public rejections of linkage by most African and "nonaligned" states, the Soviet bloc, and even some members of the Contact Group, the Cuban issue was legitimized as the one remaining issue to be resolved. This was confirmed by UN secretary-general Pérez de Cuéllar after an August 1983 visit to the region: in a report to the Security Council, he stuck with the politically correct position by dissociating himself from the link even while clearly identifying it as South Africa's last condition for implementing Resolution 435. For their part, the Contact Group allies managed to avoid responsibility for the link, thus freeing themselves to vote and speak out for the unconditional implementation of the United Nations' Namibia plan. They also obtained U.S. leadership of a visible, if controversial, process *in* Southern Africa that offered them diplomatic cover. By the time France wearied of this arrangement and suspended its participation in the Contact Group in 1983, it had served its purpose for all concerned. Washington, with quiet help from London, would continue on, having become the indispensable pivot of the region's diplomacy.

Diplomatic leverage of another sort was illustrated after mid-1987 when Castro made a private but authoritative bid to join the peace talks as an acknowledged party. His motives may have included not only the hope of extricating Cuba with honor from a failed enterprise, but also gaining some respectability in American eyes as a serious and responsible party with whom business could be done. But the United States gained at least as much from the Cuban gambit: the ability to extract a price for agreeing to Cuban participation (Washington obtained the commitment to total Cuban troop withdrawal); the ability to play on all three dimensions of the Angolan-Cuban-Soviet triangle for the first time; the acquisition of a competent and highly professional negotiating party that would have an incentive to obtain prompt and coherent action from its often opaque Angolan ally; and the presence at the table of the one party that might be capable of convincing Pretoria that, under certain conditions, the Cubans were prepared to leave Southern Africa.

### The Regional Power Equation

As in any negotiation between warring parties, the military balance and the parties' shifting perceptions of their military options played a central role in Southern Africa. What made the Namibia-Angola case especially complex was the simultaneous unfolding of three distinct armed conflicts: the bush war of the South African Defense Force (SADF) against SWAPO across the northern Namibian border; the sporadic clash between the SADF and the Cuban-supported Popular Movement for the Liberation of Angola (MPLA) troops as the SADF entered Angola to help the National Union for the Total Independence of Angola (UNITA) or to strike at SWAPO camps; and the continuous UNITA-MPLA civil war waged across the vast Angolan countryside. The U.S.-designed settlement aimed at resolving the first two conflicts and achieving the withdrawal of foreign forces from both Namibia and Angola. The third conflict was beyond the immediate reach of U.S. diplomacy: no external party had the standing or legitimacy to force its mediation on the Angolan parties, still less to create yet another linkage of the external to the internal Angolan issues. In the geopolitical and regional circumstances of the 1980s, any attempt by Washington to add this linkage would have blown up the negotiations.

Yet in practice, the MPLA-UNITA struggle was high on the list of priorities for all parties, as well as for the U.S. mediating team, which openly declared its support for political reconciliation. Each party calculated its moves on the first two conflicts in terms of their potential impact on the third conflict, Angola's civil war. Logically, a resolution of *that* war would greatly simplify the resolution of the others—termination of the civil war would simultaneously remove a major rationale for both Cuban and South African involvement in Angola's affairs. In reality, however, there was no practical way to terminate the civil war with thousands of foreign troops still engaged on Angolan soil. It would be necessary to approach the problem the other way around: resolution of the external issues would create more favorable conditions in which Angolan brothers could find each other and make peace. Getting this sequence right—regional political settlements first, followed by taking up the internal crises of individual states—was the key to peace in Southern Africa.

Peacemaking would depend on the existence or creation of perceived stalemates in all three wars. Washington would have to persuade each party that its position—or that of its Angolan ally—was strong enough to run the risk of a settlement. American officials operated throughout the eight-year period on the premise that peace would flow from a perceived stalemate, not from military preponderance or capitulation by one side or another. More important, they operated on the understanding that outright victory was beyond anyone's reach in these conflicts.

The Angolan and Namibian conflicts imposed real financial burdens on the regional parties—and, depending on Angola's ability to earn top dollar for its oil, on the Cubans and the Soviets as well. Those burdens would only grow if the parties persisted in pursuing unilateral, coercive options. The conflicts could not be "won" by anyone, but they could expand in scope, both geographically and technologically. Because of their centrality to the negotiation, it is worth exploring the conflicts more fully.

Both Cubans and South Africans had hypothetical escalatory options. The logical stalemate would come unstuck if Havana and Luanda expanded the conflict south into Namibia in response to SADF intervention in Angola. This would, however, never become feasible militarily or politically without open-ended Soviet backing: it would cost the Angolans the "high ground" they enjoyed as perceived victims of SADF aggression; it would expose the communist allies to very high costs as the SADF acquired the advantages of a defensive strategy in territory (Namibia) it had mastered; and it might be the one way of giving South Africa the Western military support it sorely missed.

Pretoria had escalatory options in Angola—to expand its pressure against SWAPO and in support of UNITA—but such action was most unlikely to drive the Soviets and Cubans out; it could, and did, lead to *more* Soviet military aid and *more* Cuban troops, not less. Over time, new military stalemates would emerge inside Angola at a higher level of cost and technology. Despite its sophisticated arms industries and undisputed status as regional superpower, South Africa faced a scenario of constraints including the international arms embargo and the absence of military allies. Escalation would run the risk, sooner or later, that the SADF would be sucked into its own Angolan quagmire where it could be matched and bled.[3]

Expanded UNITA operations in large areas of Angola, backed by increased SADF logistic help, by 1984 led to significantly increased Soviet arms deliveries to Luanda and a gradual increase in the number of Cuban troops. Luanda's logistically complex, dry-season offensives against UNITA obliged *it* to mount a conventional defense, diverting resources away from its primary guerrilla strategy. These offensives, however, also set up ideal targets for UNITA counteraction and for SADF air and artillery strikes.

U.S. strategists did not control these military equations. At best, we could endeavor to understand them and share our analysis with the parties in a tactical effort to avoid costly and time-consuming diversions. Washington, however, did have the option of supporting the repeal of the Clark Amendment[4] and providing arms to UNITA. This course was favorably considered in 1981, but the effort failed in Congress. The initial purpose in seeking the repeal had been to acquire the *option* of aiding UNITA. Such a move could have been useful in efforts to dilute Pretoria's influence with UNITA and to bolster U.S. diplomatic pressure on the MPLA. When Congress finally acted to repeal the amendment in 1985, there was an entirely different context: Soviet military aid to Luanda had expanded dramatically and a major MPLA offensive was in preparation. Washington quickly exercised the option to channel support to UNITA to bolster its morale and its independence from South Africa and to signal Luanda that the U.S. administration was tiring of its dilatory tactics. The move was also a means of informing Moscow and Havana that the United States had the means to raise the price of its escalating arms relationship to Angola.

In the view of those charged with the conduct of African policy, the decision to extend the Reagan doctrine to Angola in 1986 did not represent a change of strategy. Rather, it represented a decision to bolster U.S. diplomacy and adapt it to changing conditions on the ground. It proved to be a good investment. American aid to UNITA did not turn the tide of battle, but it raised the price of battle for Angolan and Cuban pilots and enhanced UNITA's overall battle effectiveness as well as its morale and international standing. The MPLA leadership used the U.S. action in a short-lived effort to discredit U.S. mediation, but it was quietly exploring a return to the table within six months. U.S. and Angolan negotiators resumed official meetings in April 1987, barely a year after Luanda had announced that Washington had forfeited its mediating role. Some of the MPLA's African and Western supporters purported to see the U.S. decision as destroying U.S. credibility. But Luanda, Havana, and Moscow all saw the move, more accurately, as reinforcing a strategic stalemate. That, indeed, was our goal and an illustration of the use of marginal *military* leverage in support of a primarily diplomatic strategy.

## The Asset of UN Legitimacy

Washington's decision in 1981 to retain the UN plan as the basis and pivot for a regional settlement provided indispensable leverage at the launch phase. Without it, American diplomats would have lacked the leverage to obtain improvements in the plan itself or to get the Cuban troop withdrawal issue on the agenda. Namibia's unique history as de jure UN territory under de facto South African control made this approach necessary even if Washington had wished to start from scratch. Building on the UN plan also dramatically reduced Pretoria's otherwise unlimited room for maneuver.

At subsequent stages, U.S. negotiators gained credibility in Soviet, Cuban, and Angolan eyes when they proposed to frame a package of agreements to be blessed and endorsed by the Security Council. Such an approach not only was "correct" from their perspective; it also contained a suggestion that final agreements would have a form of international "guarantee" in the event of South African violations. At an earlier stage, U.S. officials had succeeded in persuading Pretoria that UN procedures could have an advantage for South Africa as well: UN action acknowledging the Cuban issue would give it international standing comparable to the almost scriptural status of Resolution 435. This explained Pretoria's interest in welcoming the UN secretary-general, not traditionally its favorite foreign visitor, in the summer of 1983. His report to the Security Council spoke in pejorative terms of the Cuban linkage as "extraneous" and "outside the mandate" of his office.[5] But it shed a brilliant spotlight on the issue and also made clear that South Africa was prepared to implement the UN plan for Namibia if it could be resolved. Thus, Pérez de Cuéllar skillfully maintained his (and UN) "purity" on the Cuban linkage even while dramatizing its importance, a splendid finesse that served both his interests and ours.

All parties could play this game. The Angolan-Cuban decision in late 1988 to propose UN verification of the Cuban timetable was aimed consciously at persuading Pretoria of their seriousness. The Angolans and the Cubans did so less because of the United Nations' capability to conduct such verification than because the move would further legitimize Cuba as an integral and central element of the overall package of agreements. The United Nations Angola Verification Mission (UNAVEM), like the earlier extension of United Nations Transition Assistance Group (UNTAG) mission to include monitoring of SWAPO in Angola, strengthened the mediator's hand in persuading Pretoria that it would get a balanced agreement focused on monitoring the performance of all parties.

## Timing and Deadlines

Mediators dream about controlling the pace of negotiation and possessing enforceable deadlines, but Southern Africa's wars were deeply rooted, dating back to the 1960s. The ebb and flow of events was primarily regional in origin, not external. Washington did not possess the means to enforce its will. None of the parties (except after 1986, UNITA) depended on Washington for anything essential except the chance for reduced ostracism and isolation.

The revised structure of the Namibia-Angola process significantly aggravated the problem of timing and deadlines. Because there were two objectives—Namibian independence and Cuban withdrawal from Angola—the process could ripen only when both parts were in rough alignment and both sides saw the chance for a win-win outcome on both tracks. Critics on the right missed this central point when they claimed that U.S. negotiators were not sufficiently tough with the marxist parties; South Africa, also, had to be ready to compromise. Critics on the left claimed to perceive U.S. collusion in permitting Pretoria to get away with its failure to implement Resolution 435; this totally overlooked the fact that Angola and its allies had not bitten the bullet on Cuban withdrawal, the essential parallel condition. U.S. mediators had plenty of critics on both flanks during the 1980s— in Congress, within the administration itself, and from media and public sources. At times, managing and balancing these pressures consumed more energy and capital than the actual negotiation we were conducting.

Applying time pressure on the parties in these circumstances was a difficult art. Washington attempted it in 1982 and again in 1984, only to drive the parties toward separate talks in which they discussed a separate, partial "détente" that would lower the violence but avoid the basic issues. (The South Africans and the MPLA discussed cooperation in the border areas to reduce SWAPO violence and SADF actions, but the Cubans would have remained and Namibia would have continued under Pretoria's control.) In March 1985, Washington attempted to force the pace by tabling a compromise proposal. The South Africans were urged to take quick action to restore their rapidly fading image in the United States and to undercut Soviet-Cuban pressures on the MPLA to play for time. The Angolans were informed of the need for quick action to strengthen the peace faction in Pretoria and to prevent the South Africans from abandoning the negotiating track altogether. But domestic politics were not ripe in any of the key nations, including our own.

During the summer of 1985, U.S. diplomats sought to convert the mounting domestic American sentiment against *both* the apartheid regime and Soviet-aligned Angolans into leverage on them to move forward in the talks. Thus, we used the growing antiapartheid fervor at home and the upward spiral of township violence as the basis for imposing limited sanctions on South Africa, warning Pretoria of the urgency of constructive action. Shortly thereafter, in response to this move by the administration, Pretoria delivered a positive reply to our compromise Namibia-Angola proposals. These developments bought us some maneuvering room in managing the South African issue at home, but they were less successful in wedging the Angolans toward reciprocal movement. With the MPLA regime, we tried to use the growing public enthusiasm for supporting the Angolan "freedom fighters" of UNITA to squeeze the MPLA, warning that Luanda should not misread antiapartheid sentiment in the United States as pro-MPLA. We stated openly that the United States was on the verge of deciding to provide military aid to UNITA, reflecting frustration with Luanda's apparent preference for military over political solutions to its problems. In the end, however, the Angolans chose to misread the situation and were badly distracted by their ongoing, disastrous offensive against UNITA.

These developments in the fall of 1985 demonstrate the extreme complexity facing U.S. mediators: ground was shifting under our feet at home and events on the ground were changing the calculations of both parties. There was negative feedback in all our negotiating loops. The South Africans probably calculated that their forward step was a safe tactical move because Luanda was most unlikely to reciprocate. And the Angolans lived up to this expectation, assuming correctly that Pretoria would get little international credit for grabbing the high ground in the talks. Each side let the other off the hook, leaving the mediator temporarily adrift. The use of timing and deadlines is severely hampered by instability within and between the parties in a three-sided negotiating process.

An interesting example of the use of timing and deadlines occurred during the Moscow summit of May 1988. Earlier that month in London, the Cubans had proposed with a rhetorical flourish that September 29—the tenth anniversary of Resolution 435—be accepted as the target date for implementation of a settlement. In Moscow, the United States decided to test the still uncertain Soviet support for an early agreement by proposing U.S.-Soviet endorsement of the Cuban idea. Taken aback, the Soviets went along with contained enthusiasm, but a signal was sent from the summit that the two superpowers had added impetus to the process. In Havana, the Cubans' distaste for being pushed by the superpowers was matched by delight at this gesture of U.S. respect for their own proposal. The other parties were not amused. By mid-1988, the parties were setting—and missing—their own deadlines.

At the very end of the negotiations, a real deadline suddenly emerged: the U.S. election and change of administration. It is impossible to know what would have happened if Bush had lost. One week after his victory, the logjam on the Cuban timetable was broken, but in early December, American diplomats then ran into a set of final hurdles on verification and the scenario for establishing implementation dates. Openly advertising the fact that a new administration would likely mean a change of personnel and a basic policy review, the U.S. mediators pressed the Angolans, Cubans, and South Africans not to waste years of effort. The agreements were signed ten days later.

## The Negotiating Mechanism

Viewed from the perspective of the American negotiating team that I led, we were at the center of a multiparty mediation effort. Acting alone, our direct mediatory clout, even as a superpower, was finite. To pull the Angolans (and their allies) and the South Africans into a settlement would require all the diplomatic resources we could mobilize. To be sure, we were living in a competitive, Cold War environment and we did not advertise our need for help or spell out the consequences of not getting it. But in practice, we worked diligently to build a steadily expanding coalition of parties that could add reach, credibility, and access to our own efforts. The unspoken but evident purpose here was to borrow leverage and broaden the international and regional bases of the diplomacy in order to neutralize the forces of gridlock and obstructionism arrayed against us.

Initially, the Contact Group formed the core of the mediator's coalition. Within it, individual allies could play distinct roles. The second part of the initial core was the African frontline states (Botswana, Mozambique, Tanzania, Zambia, and Zimbabwe, in addition to Angola, a member of this group). Both groups had helped create the pre-1981, Namibia-only diplomacy; keeping them mobilized was one of the earliest decisions of the Reagan team. It was important, however, to broaden the diplomacy beyond these countries to give us greater strategic reach: with francophone Africa (Angola's neighbors to the north and the east, and UNITA's allies); with Portugal, Angola's former colonial power, a land that perfectly mirrored Angola's own divisions; with members of the UN and OAU secretariats; and with a range of other states actively interested in or linked to Southern Africa (Algeria, Brazil, Egypt, India, Israel, the Netherlands, Morocco, Sweden, Tunisia, and Yugoslavia, among others).

Conceived in this manner, the U.S.-led mediation by an ad hoc coalition can be viewed as a series of concentric circles expanding outward from the core, with each circle less involved and, typically, less committed to U.S. strategic goals and less predictable in the use to which it might put information and tactical gambits we might share. This was a balancing act in which American diplomats had to weigh the advantages of broadening the circle with the disadvantages of losing a measure of control, autonomy, and tactical surprise. Mediators have to give in order to get (or borrow) influence. When things were progressing positively, we expanded and energized the coalition; when we bogged down, we also pulled in our horns. If there is a general lesson from this experience, it is that mediatory coalitions can add real bargaining advantage and tangible clout when the lead mediator has the initiative and some chance to gain momentum. Success, as the saying goes, has many parents. Broadening the base of a mediation may contribute directly to the creation of such momentum and success. In some cases, a degree of broadening may be essential. This is because the lead mediator gains the benefit of the partners' insights, relationships, credibility, resources, diplomatic "reach," and political "balance." Broadening, when successful, isolates the spoilers and "rejectionists" common to most conflict situations.

There is, of course, a flip side to these propositions. To make such coalitions work is complex, intricate business. The care and feeding of eager but marginally useful partners can become a distraction. Such relationships require a lead mediator capable of much conspicuous listening and consulting, letting others carry the ball occasionally, and frequently sharing credit. Would-be mediators who insist on micromanaging each detail of a multifront process and who cannot tolerate seeing partners grab the microphone should not recruit them in the first place. But this does not mean that one wants partners with a veto power who seek to take over the enterprise or make political hay at the expense of the lead mediator. When the time comes for tough choices and major strategic decisions, it must be clear who leads after all the listening and consulting are done. This is best communicated privately, but unambiguously: in effect, one says, "This train is leaving the station. Are you on it or not?" In the end, this notion of mediation-by-coalition returns to the idea of giving in order to get: the leader does not plead for partners, he offers a role in exchange for minimally acceptable conduct and support. Partners accept to play the role because their interests, status, and prestige are affected by the conflict.

The following discussion illustrates the range of activities and roles played by other nations, concluding with the Soviets and the Cubans whom we sought to engage as well, even though this stretched the limits of Cold War protocol.

### African States

During 1981–82, the frontline states were indispensable negotiating partners as the Contact Group sought to broker understandings related to Resolution 435. Dealing with the group's emissaries at head-of-state level, they provided blunt but generally constructive advice and suggestions. More important, they usually delivered SWAPO when the Contact Group demonstrated that it could deliver Pretoria. In this sense, the frontline states served as an African contact group. Their efforts helped to buffer the diplomacy from the unhelpful intervention of Soviet, Cuban, and radical nonaligned states whose motive was to create a breakdown that would discredit Western diplomacy. The masterful performance of a small group of senior officials from the frontline states during the summer of 1982 made possible the rapid completion of the outstanding Resolution 435 issues. In the ensuing years, Mozambique, Tanzania, and Zambia continued to play significant roles as advisers to the sides (and us), as conveners of meetings, and in opening and keeping open private channels.

African states also played individual roles as intermediaries and negotiating partners of the parties. To illustrate, Mozambique repeatedly opened fresh channels of communication among Luanda, Pretoria, and Washington starting in 1983. At times, Maputo was the principal channel and an invaluable source of ideas and interpretations for U.S. diplomats. Cape Verde played a parallel role throughout the 1980s. Those two ex-Portuguese colonies were Washington's best window into the thinking of MPLA and UNITA leaders, whom the Mozambicans and Cape Verdeans knew as friends and allies in the anticolonial struggle.

The Congo government in Brazzaville extended itself over eighteen months as a champion of a negotiated solution. Excellently positioned as a neighbor of Angola and long-standing friend of the MPLA regime, the Congo used its credibility to help reactivate the U.S.-Angolan talks in 1987 and then to host five tripartite meetings during 1988. By volunteering for this role before it became fashionable, the Congolese leadership earned the respect of all participants. At an earlier stage of the process, Cape Verde and Zambia also played important facilitative roles, using their goodwill and diplomatic resources to press the parties toward common ground. Egypt, Great Britain, and Switzerland also hosted important diplomatic encounters.

Another African role of major significance toward the end of the 1980s was to encourage and speak out for movement toward national reconciliation *in* Angola. Although this has proved to be a tough challenge, the groundwork laid in 1988 was essential in (a) convincing Pretoria that Africans would not ignore their responsibility to foster internal peace in Angola and (b) persuading the MPLA that acknowledging its internal problem would be both essential and "legitimate" in African eyes. Although their roles varied greatly according to which Angolan party they favored, the governments of Zaire and Congo played key roles. In addition, Cape Verde, Côte d'Ivoire, Gabon, Morocco, Mozambique, Nigeria, Zambia, and Zimbabwe worked to advance regional thinking on the problem.

### *The Western Allies*

Washington's North Atlantic Treaty Organization (NATO) allies played a comparable range of roles in the process. The Contact Group itself functioned as a close-knit team during most of 1981–82, sharing the workload and taking on individual assignments with each of the various African parties and South Africa. Like the Americans, the British, Canadians, French, and Germans also had to balance their interests at times, explaining to

Pretoria, the frontline states, and SWAPO the merits of cooperating with the new approach. U.S. diplomats gained invaluable independent assessments of what the traffic would bear and how to orchestrate the diplomacy of linkage. Allied officials helped reinforce the U.S. message by offering their African interlocutors an unvarnished analysis of Washington political realities. Allies represented in Luanda helped to fill the empty American diplomatic chair, sometimes alarming the MPLA and sometimes persuading it to take Washington more seriously than it otherwise would have.

When the Contact Group had completed its work on Resolution 435, it came under growing strains over the linkage issue. France, to no one's surprise, was the first to strike out on its own in an effort to distance itself from the controversy in international forums. The Canadians followed the French lead. Those moves helped foster a false impression of collapse or diplomatic stalemate that only aided the foes of further progress. Nonetheless, useful work was done by the group up to 1984. France's independent channel to Cuba, starting in 1982, may have begun the task of convincing Havana that the African welcome mat for Cuban troops would not be out forever. By 1984, U.S. diplomats had begun to pick up indications of Cuban interest in talks with Washington. The Germans played a parallel role in facilitating high-level dialogue between U.S. diplomats and SWAPO's leadership, a process less obstructed by Cold War baggage and conflicting agendas than U.S.-Cuban exchanges on Angola and Namibia, which remained only indirect until 1987.

For nearly seven years, the British served as Washington's principal channel to the Angolans. British diplomacy was mobilized across Africa, Europe, New York, Moscow, and in direct support of the peace process. London had early misgivings on whether U.S. diplomats understood the region, the inherent ambition of the new approach, and the low odds for success. Soon, however, there developed an outstanding pattern of cooperation, one that served important common interests. Having full relations with Luanda, London chose not to endorse linkage explicitly, but the British provided indispensable support for the overall strategy while pursuing their own interests and tactical preferences.

Unique among U.S. allies, Great Britain had credibility in both Luanda and Pretoria and knew all the players intimately. This enabled U.S. diplomats constantly to test hypotheses and information, to develop game plans for moving the process along, and to build appropriate nuance into the messages each would pass. By the late 1980s, when Pretoria's Washington links were severely strained and weakened, London had acquired special influence there. That influence was used to support South African negotiators as they returned home from each round of meetings to seek a fresh mandate for the next set of decisions. Britain also helped save the settlement in April 1989 when large-scale SWAPO violations of the agreement threatened to derail it. Of all the diplomatic factors that permitted ultimate success, the U.S.-U.K. working relationship was probably the most important.

### The Soviets and the Cubans

Soviet policy toward the Namibia-Angola peace process went through three phases over the 1980s. In the first phase, lasting up to 1986, Moscow generally did its best to obstruct Western efforts. Drawing on the habit of opposing on principle any Western proposal, the Soviets sought to poison the well during the Contact Group's work to prepare Resolution 435 back in 1978. (They backed off in response to clear support for it from the frontline states and SWAPO.) Three years later, Moscow had switched tactical horses. By 1981–82, one might have guessed that the Soviets were the most ardent champions of Resolution 435, and they became unalterably opposed to any modifications or enhancements of it. Even more shrill was their opposition to the Namibia-Angola linkage. According to Soviet official statements, the new U.S. approach was nothing less than an attempt to block Resolution 435, to force the capitulation of Angola and its departure from the socialist camp, to join forces with Pretoria in creating a pro-Western security zone, and to reverse the tide of history in Southern Africa.

Behind the scenes, Moscow and its allies worked assiduously to promote these messages and to create an echo chamber of like-minded voices in African media and diplomatic circles. Soviet thinking appears to have been known to the Angolan-Cuban drafters of a February 1982 joint communiqué, which officially endorsed a Namibia-first variety of linkage—the Angolans and the Cubans would define a schedule for Cuban withdrawal *after* Namibian independence. Despite these efforts, the process moved ahead over the ensuing months, leading Soviet officials to protest that the Contact Group sought to usurp the prerogatives of the United Nations. Moscow played a lead role in late 1982 in floating the idea of a UN Security Council debate on the Cuban linkage, a goal that was realized the following year.

During these years, U.S. and Soviet officials held a series of "informational exchanges" on Southern Africa. U.S. objectives were minimal: to avoid surprises, to probe for constructive openings and offer Moscow a chance to bid, and to explain U.S. purposes and indicate how they might serve the interests of both sides. Moscow's objectives appeared to consist mainly of making a record to share with its allies, exploring U.S. logic, acquiring tactical insights, and gaining the visual benefit of superpower consultation. As a result, the exchanges were sterile. U.S. officials were harangued with legalistic debating points. When pressed for better ideas or possible compromises, the Soviet side would simply reiterate its support for the latest Angolan positions. In practice, Moscow had decided not to negotiate directly with Washington but to talk indirectly via Luanda and Havana. Thus, while vigorously rejecting the concept of linkage, Moscow fully endorsed the interesting 1984 MPLA proposal on partial Cuban withdrawal that was explicitly tied to Resolution 435.

Washington assumed that the Soviet Union had substantial leverage with the MPLA. Thousands of Soviet and allied officials were distributed throughout the Angolan government and armed forces, in some cases running and maintaining essential services and sensitive security functions. The arms supply relationship deepened further as deliveries doubled in the first half of the 1980s and the fighting expanded in scope and technology. Given the MPLA's dependence on the Cubans and the Soviets, it was logical for U.S. officials to assume that Angolan positions and proposals had been "cleared" in Havana and Moscow, but this assumption could seldom be tested. The three governments met frequently and exuded predictable solidarity. On the other hand, Western diplomats picked up signals of Soviet anxiety about progress in the U.S.-MPLA exchanges as well as of Angolan frustration with the influence of their allies.

A second phase of Soviet policy toward the Namibia-Angola negotiations, from January 1986 to May 1988, witnessed a gradual transition away from classic obstructionism. During much of the period, U.S. officials had the impression that the Soviets were groping for new ideas in regional policy. President Mikhail Gorbachev's declarations, starting in January 1986, in favor of "political solutions" to regional conflicts represented a shift in emphasis away from the language of struggle and confrontation. It did not at this stage, however, signify reduced opposition to U.S. proposals. Still less did it signify Soviet restraint in the military supply relationship with Luanda.

Despite determined probes, the Soviets had nothing concrete to offer that would advance the process. Publicly, their statements undercut the U.S.-led process and suggested vaguely the need for the United Nations, the Organization of African Unity, and the Non-Aligned Movement to play larger roles. Privately, Soviet officials discouraged any Angolan cooperation with Washington and criticized UN Secretariat officials for undertaking quiet probes of Luanda's latest thinking on a linkage-based settlement. In April 1986, Soviet diplomats stimulated South African doubts about the continued viability of the U.S.-led process—a line of thinking that was not unwelcome to some in Pretoria who chafed increasingly under U.S. pressure and who were enchanted with the very idea of a direct line to Moscow. In March 1987, Soviet-Cuban-Angolan consultations ratified Luanda's decision to resume direct talks with Washington; but they also witnessed strong Soviet urging that Luanda mount yet another major offensive against UNITA strongholds to be in a better position for eventual negotiation. Moscow also wanted Luanda to mount its own internal political offensive and thereby preempt UNITA's demand for talks on national reconciliation.

When senior U.S. and Soviet officials met in July 1987, on the eve of the war's largest offensive and a series of fresh Angolan-Cuban political initiatives, the Soviet side declared (inaccurately) that the U.S.-led diplomacy was at a dead end. Moscow expressed interest in fresh thinking on how U.S.-Soviet cooperation could unblock the process, but it had no concrete proposals except that Washington drop linkage or consider a wholly "new mechanism" for negotiation, a mechanism vaguely described in terms of a large UN role. In a way, Moscow was seeking to complicate an already complex negotiating machinery, either by joining it directly or by inserting formalistic UN dimensions that would have paralyzed the process and subverted its purposes. Americans had no interest in this version of multiparty mediation.

Far more interesting to us was the matter of the Cuban role, which we dimly perceived to be potentially of major importance. The Soviets may or may not have known that Cuban leader Fidel Castro was soon to make his most dramatic bid yet to join the negotiation process or that he and Angolan president José Eduardo dos Santos would soon approve a new Cuban withdrawal timetable, their first significant move on the issue in over two years. What the Soviets did know was that Soviet arms and advisers were about to support the MPLA's biggest effort yet to achieve a military victory.

Four months later, the Soviet-Angolan offensive, in which Cuban forces played no role, had turned into a SADF-UNITA rout in which thousands of members of the Forces of the Angolan People's Liberation Army (FAPLA) were killed and hundreds of millions of dollars of Soviet hardware were captured or destroyed. The Angolan war had become a humiliating fiasco for Soviet arms, planning, and training. By the end of 1987, Soviet leaders were visibly groping for a coherent policy. They professed to see opportunities for a political settlement, but made no proposals, offered no support to the U.S.-led process, and declined to endorse publicly a settlement entailing both Resolution 435 and Cuban withdrawal. They spoke knowingly of Cuba's recognition that its forces would have to leave Angola, but in the same breath, they declared that Angola would not be "thrown to the wolves."

It was the Cubans, not the Soviets, who stepped in to shape what can best be described as a chaotic policy vacuum in the ranks of the communist allies. The conditions of late 1987 offered Havana a rare opportunity: the MPLA was on its knees militarily, appealing for a stronger Cuban role; Pretoria, in a characteristic burst of hubris, risked overplaying its hand as UNITA's very public ally; Washington had offered the Cubans a place at the table if they would produce proposals for total Cuban withdrawal; and Moscow, whose attention was distracted by Afghanistan and arms control, had just suffered a humiliating setback. Cuban decisions of November 1987 to March 1988 averted a complete collapse of the MPLA military position in the southeast. The arrival and southward deployment of 15,000 fresh Cubans filled the previously empty land and airspace of southwestern Angola, creating a potentially explosive, hair-trigger military balance with the SADF. At the table, the new joint Angolan-Cuban team put forward new proposals, as promised, and urged early, U.S.-chaired, face-to-face talks with Pretoria.

As late as March 1988, the Soviets continued to sidestep numerous U.S. suggestions for joint efforts and professed uncertainty on both their role and their interest in a Namibia-Angola settlement in which "the U.S. gives nothing." But starting in late April 1988, three in-depth U.S.-Soviet consultations were held within one month. Moscow had finally given its diplomats a mandate to lend guarded official and public support to a process that was already on a fast track. Low-key side meetings with Soviet officials—self-designated "observers" who kept a discreet distance from the U.S.-led tripartite (Angola-Cuba–South Africa) talks—became a regular feature of the process. At long last, the time had come for a final broadening of the mediatory coalition. To neutralize our Cuban adversary and acquire its clout, we had agreed to direct Cuban participation in the talks as a member of the Angolan negotiating team. Now, to neutralize residual Soviet obstructionism and possibly elicit valuable insights and even help, we "invited" the Soviets to become informal "observers," a term neither side wanted to define too precisely. Washington had urged that Moscow make appropriate officials available for this purpose and publicly mentioned the Soviet "observer" role. U.S.-Soviet meetings, both during and between tripartite rounds, graduated from debates about the shape of an acceptable settlement to operational discussion of how the two sides might advance those points agreed on and how current obstacles could be handled.

By August 1988, at Geneva, the basic turning point in this final phase, U.S. and Soviet officials had settled into a fairly predictable and often useful pattern of exchanges. As the parties labored toward closure on the vital Cuban timetable, Soviet officials requested—and received—detailed U.S. briefings on the mediator's priorities and game plans. Washington sought to obtain candid feedback on Angolan-Cuban thinking to elicit suggestions and thus pressure Moscow to accept a measure of responsibility for success, and to share enough sensitive detail so that the Soviets could play a confidence-building role with their allies. Equally important, the Soviets welcomed U.S. thinking on whether and how they should talk to the South Africans. American officials strongly encouraged this, and the Moscow-Pretoria dialogue blossomed. This gave the South Africans the benefit of the two superpowers' input as a reality check on Cuban and Angolan motives during the endgame.

U.S. negotiators also persuaded Moscow to drop its advocacy of the Angolan demand that Washington should cease its support for UNITA and to focus on other issues: the key problem of narrowing the gap on Cuban timetables and the need to support and legitimize the issue of national reconciliation in Angola. The latter two issues were closely interrelated. MPLA fear of UNITA was directly responsible for its insistence on Cuban timetables that had no hope of acceptance by the South Africans. The extent of Soviet influence and pressure on Luanda to bite the bullet on Angolan reconciliation may never be known. Washington, in any case, relied on African leaders to surface the issue because, by doing so, they would make it far easier for Moscow and Havana to follow suit. What *is* known is that the Cubans, not the Soviets, faced the greatest alliance burdens over the interlinked Cuban and reconciliation issues. They wanted a deal and an "honorable exit"—just as Pretoria did. Ultimately, the Cubans prevailed on their Angolan friends to accept a withdrawal schedule remarkably similar to the one tabled by U.S. mediators in March 1985—and accepted in principle by Pretoria six months later.

The Soviet role in the final phase cannot be understood solely on the basis of the public commentary offered by American and other foreign officials who were quick to salute these novel forms of Soviet behavior. In essence, both the mediation and the solution were of U.S. origin. The Angolans, Cubans, and South Africans took the big decisions. There is no evidence of Soviet arm-twisting of their marxist allies, though Moscow certainly made clear its general support for a "political solution" and its desire to be perceived as contributing toward one. Moscow, at one level, achieved a visible role and confirmed global status by "freeriding" on an

American effort. By placing their imprimatur on a regional settlement whose time was coming anyway (thanks to the parties' own decisions), the Soviets earned some international credit and acted in accordance with the new spirit of U.S.-Soviet relations. At another level, Soviet advice and tactical thinking were at times extremely helpful to harried U.S. diplomats who had to cope day and night with the antics and idiosyncracies of three un- usual negotiating parties. With rare exceptions, such as Moscow's India- Pakistan mediation in 1965, Soviet diplomats had little experience in diplomatic problem solving and mediation of this kind. But they warmed quickly to their "observer" role, conducting themselves with considerable skill and professionalism. We knew, in addition, that they enjoyed it: as one remarked to me, this was the first occasion in a thirty-year diplomatic ca- reer to abandon reflexive obstructionism and "do creative things together." We had come full circle: the mediator's coalition had expanded to include its prime adversaries.

## LESSONS AND IMPLICATIONS

There are limits to the potential of any single case study to serve as a basis for generalizations and lessons, and this case has a number of specific quali- ties that should be noted. Occurring during the final phase of the Cold War, the Southern African conflict's structure was directly affected by the age of bipolarity. The motives of all concerned parties (including, of course, the mediator) were influenced by a mix of local/regional interests and external/global ones. Mediator motives, for example, included a blend of anticommunist, antiracist/antiapartheid, and anticolonial sentiment linked to an overarching quest for regional stability. Our European and African partners also participated in order to advance their local and international objectives. The warring parties continuously calculated their actions in terms of direct, local consequences as well as the costs and benefits in external (including "Cold War") relations, often seeking to manipulate outsiders in a perfect mirror image of what outsiders were doing to them. It is, thus, legitimate to ask whether this case is limited in its implications because it is a Cold War case.

Similarly, it is an African case, occurring in a region that the world's great powers have seldom considered of primary strategic importance. Such strategic importance as Africa has enjoyed from the perspective of outsid- ers has been as a place (a) to get around, en route to other regions, (b) to exploit for resources, slaves and military manpower, prestige, and empire, or (c) from which to recruit allies and in which to pursue proxy contests and conduct "denial" strategies. It is not a place of inherent strategic interest in its own right, and in the postcolonial era big powers (with the exception of France) have seldom tried directly to control or occupy it. Hence, we may ask whether Africa's "peripheral" place in the global system—especially in the post–Cold War era—limits the usefulness of African cases that may be considered less "strategic" and different in the range and level of third-party actors who may seek to shape them.

The best answer to both questions is yes and no. While the Cold War context shaped the specificities of external influence in Southern Africa and added weight to the mediator's incentives for engagement and perseverance, it certainly was not the only aspect of the Namibia-Angola conundrum, nor did it constitute the major "obstacle" in achieving the December 1988 settlement. In fact, the Cold War context enabled American mediators eventually to mobilize help from a range of sources and to define a settlement whose attractions included the prospect of overcoming Cold War divisions and reducing superpower meddling. What about Africa's low and declining strategic position? Arguably, this factor enhances the *possibilities* for third-party engagement, the *scope of third-party influence*, and the *ease of gaining entry* to the conflict as a third party (at least it does so in the absence of determined African resistance to external involvement). But it also *weakens the external incentives to exert leadership and to play the multiple, complex, and demanding leadership roles* illustrated in the Southern African case. This last point has particular significance for the study of complex, multiparty mediation because it underscores the importance of innovative thinking on how to manage complex diplomatic undertakings, to share burdens and risks, and to mobilize coherent regional and global responses to conflict in a region that—in this post–Cold War age—appears even more conflict prone than before.

With these qualifications in mind, we turn to some generalizations flowing from the Southern African case. What generalizations can we make about the sources of leverage in an era of multiparty mediation? First, leverage comes in many forms: direct and indirect; tangible or physical and political or psychological; immediate and contingent; derived from within the conflict structure and derived from outside it as external actors add to the parties' cost-benefit calculations; leverage applied to the conflict itself and leverage linked to the solution or settlement. The variety of sources of leverage is potentially good news for practitioners of complex mediation.

In the Southern African case, we explored the phenomenon of "borrowing" leverage and credibility by expanding the support base of an initiative to include a range of friends, partners, allies, and regional or global organizations. This is a common practice today, even if we are not always conscious of why we do it. Borrowing leverage can take the form of "friends" or "contact groups" that lend political weight and endorsement to the mediation. In the African case, an effort was made to mobilize friends of each of the parties as well as of the mediation itself; the goal was to enhance the pressures/inducements on them. Leverage is also borrowed when the mediation process has the blessing of the United Nations or an appropriate regional body and when the ultimate settlement is linked to an implementing role by such bodies (or an ad hoc group of key actors)—for example, as guarantors, monitors, observers, or verifiers. This approach should be used when it adds weight to the exercise, not as an automatic reflex or, still less, as a requirement. Given the overload facing UN Headquarters in the post–Cold War period and the absence of bipolar roadblocks to mediator entry into conflict situations, the significance of obtaining UN blessing should be weighed on a case-by-case basis.

The limiting factor is the mediator's need to retain the initiative and a measure of control and assure coherence; otherwise, the parties can simply "retaliate" by conducting an ever-expanding diplomatic dance of their own, playing outsiders off against one another, and sowing division and confusion, if not actually splitting the effort in order to engage in "forum shopping." It must be remembered that for the parties themselves the conflict is a matter of life and death and is typically their number-one national or group priority. A comparable level of laserlike strategic focus and intensity is required of the core mediator. Otherwise, leverage borrowing may degenerate into mere internationalization, thus complicating the conflict.

For this reason, a case can be made that only a limited number of potential third-party actors are capable of such sustained focus and possess the means—communications, diplomatic reach, intelligence, mandate, and finance—to pull it off. This may limit the range and variety of lead roles to major states, the UN system, and, in special circumstances, an individual or group actor tightly linked to one of them. These limits should be respected unless the parties are "ready" to settle and the conflict has ripened to the point that it literally awaits a mediated conclusion.

A prime source of mediatory leverage may come from within the conflict and especially from the military balance on the ground. A conflict mired in conditions of seesaw flux but long-term stalemate (outright victory by either side unlikely) such as the one in Southern Africa enables the third party to provide persistent coaching, information sharing, and other inputs in hopes of sobering the parties up and prodding them to negotiate. But in order for a settlement to become more attractive than continued stalemate, the settlement package must address the core issues of military security into and beyond the implementation phase of the settlement process. Complex mediation cases work better when the mediators can credibly demonstrate their readiness to remain engaged as third-party friends and guarantors for as long as necessary. In cases in which there is no stalemate or a stalemate exists objectively but is not recognized by one or both parties, the third party may need to consider direct leverage to ripen the conflict: affecting the military balance by helping the weaker side, raising the price of fighting to one side or both in order to bring about stalemate, or (as in Bosnia before Dayton) by direct intervention in support of the mediation.

The use of leverage with parties to a mediation is a more subtle business than it may appear, and this may be even more of a challenge with complex mediation led by multiple or coalition actors. The reason is that the mediator's goal is not to weaken the parties with sticks—weak parties are unlikely to be able to settle; the mediator should aim at strengthening and unifying parties so that they are strong enough to make peace but not strong enough to believe victory is possible. When both parties are strong enough to take risks for peace, the mediator's leverage is maximized. In an age of complex mediation when external opinion (as reflected in media and legislative actions) naturally gravitates toward the use of crude instruments such as sanctions or foreign assistance—instruments that may bear little relationship to the core priorities of individual leaders—it may be necessary to focus greater attention on inducements for the cohesion and reassurance of negotiating partners. This includes detailed knowledge of the domestic pressures and constraints they face, and it implies a willingness to help with political support and "cover" as well as targeted assistance and training in sensitive fields such as security. Such tactical considerations underscore the importance of having a clearly defined mediation structure capable of taking and sticking to sometimes controversial decisions.

Ultimately, as Zartman has underscored,[6] leverage in any mediation derives from the parties' need for help and their perception of the need to settle, on the one hand, and from the mediator's skill and imagination in devising a persuasive formula on which to base a settlement, on the other. This reminder is a serious challenge to multiparty mediators. It may be harder for them than for traditional, single-state actors to mobilize the focus and staying power needed for ripening conflicts. Because the leadership of a multiparty mediation will frequently be collective, it may be more difficult to achieve consensus on tough measures required to ripen a conflict. Similarly, to reach agreement on a settlement formula capable of addressing the parties' real interests and fears could also place severe strains on ad hoc diplomatic coalitions, the UN system, or the regional political fabric of the concerned region.

The 1980s Southern African case illustrates the central importance of the linkage formula for resolving the Namibia-Angola conflicts. In hindsight, no single factor provided the mediator with as much leverage as (a) the sobering experience of the battlefield and (b) the power of the linkage concept. Yet at the launch phase it took months of serious cajoling and sharp exchanges at ministerial level among five Western allies to obtain even the limited consensus we achieved on the linkage concept. Thereafter, our resolving formula became gradually and inexorably established until, after some years of painful ripening, it was seized on jointly by Angolans, Cubans, and South Africans as the best way out of the corner into which they had painted themselves.

The development of creative formulas is important in conflict management. It offers opportunities to restructure the issues, rearrange the issue sequence, and even to redefine the conflict itself. It may, as in Southern Africa or the Middle East in the early 1990s, entail expanding the agenda and enlarging the number of parties so as to acquire new bases for trade-offs and new possibilities for exchange. In the post–Cold War age, when a high percentage of conflicts are internal and involve nonstate actors and identity groups, the search for resolving formulas will pose real challenges to multiparty mediators. Those struggles often revolve around the most difficult normative questions in today's transitional state system: sovereignty, secession, territorial integrity, the protection of minority rights, accountability for abuses inflicted on civilians, and the relationship between peacemaking and democratization. Devising winning formulas in such places as Sri Lanka, Kosovo, and Sudan continues to elude mediators of all sorts. But solving this question will help us develop the leverage to stop the killing.

## NOTES

Some of the discussion in this chapter is drawn from the author's "Peacemaking in Southern Africa: The Namibia-Angola Settlement of 1988," in David E. Newsom, ed., *The Diplomatic Record, 1989–90* (Boulder, Colo.: Westview Press, 1991). The author's full account of these years is found in *High Noon in Southern Africa: Making Peace in a Rough Neighborhood* (New York: W. W. Norton, 1992).

1. See the discussion in I. William Zartman, *Ripe for Resolution: Conflict and Intervention in Africa* (New York: Oxford University Press, 1989), chap. 6.

2. Harold H. Saunders, "The Pre-Negotiation Phase," in Diane B. Bendahmane and John W. McDonald, Jr., eds., *International Negotiation: Art and Science* (Washington, D.C.: Foreign Service Institute, Department of State, 1984), 47–56.

3. For an elaboration of these judgments from a 1981 perspective, see the author's "South Africa's Defense Posture: Coping with Vulnerability," *Washington Papers* 9, no. 84 (Washington, D.C.: Center for Strategic and International Studies and Sage Publications, 1981), 84–85, 89–91.

4. An amendment, introduced by Senator Dick Clark (D-Iowa), to the Defense Authorization bill prohibited all but humanitarian aid to UNITA. It was passed over a presidential veto on January 27, 1976.

5. UN secretary-general's report S/15943, published on August 29, 1983.

6. I. William Zartman and Saadia Touval, "International Mediation in the Post–Cold War Era," in Chester A. Crocker and Fen O. Hampson, with Pamela Aall, eds., *Managing Global Chaos: Sources of and Responses to International Conflict* (Washington, D.C.: United States Institute of Peace Press, 1996), 455–457.

## Background to Chapter II

## Mediating Peace in Mozambique: The Role of the Community of Sant'Egidio

Portugal's long colonial history in Mozambique ended in 1974, when power was turned over to a nationalist movement called Frelimo. In seeking to unify the country and build a national identity, in the context of the anticolonial and antiapartheid struggles, Frelimo used a socialist structure of power that provoked resentment and opposition. Renamo soon emerged as the most formidable military resistance to the Frelimo government, and a bloody and impoverishing fifteen-year civil war ensued—a conflict fed by global Cold War tensions and regional actors, especially Rhodesia and South Africa, which both supported Renamo. The Community of Sant'Egidio, a Catholic NGO, took the lead in trying to mediate a resolution to the conflict, shifting the antagonists' goal from victory to peace. Sant'Egidio sought to fuse often disparate actors, motivations, and interests into a coherent and positive peace process. Lacking much power or authority, the mediating team employed a synergistic method that focused on achieving substantive dialogue and fostering interpersonal relations. This initiative was ultimately augmented by the support of the United Nations, which successfully implemented the resulting peace accords between Frelimo and Renamo (see chapter 23).

## MAJOR ACTORS

- Frelimo (Frente da Libertação de Moçambique): the Mozambican government, led until 1985 by Samora Machel, and thereafter by Joaquim Chissano
- Renamo (Resistência Nacional de Moçambique): the opposition, led by Afonso Dhlakama
- Mediating team of Andrea Riccardi, Matteo Zuppi, Mario Raffaelli, and Jaime Gonçalves
- ONUMOZ: United Nations Operation in Mozambique
- Government of Italy

## IMPORTANT DATES

- June 1963: Three nationalist groups form Frelimo
- June 1975: Mozambique achieves independence under the Frelimo government
- 1976: Renamo emerges as a military resistance movement
- 1984: South Africa agrees to refrain from support of Renamo, but covert operations continue
- 1985: President Machel gains support of President Reagan and Pope John Paul II
- October 1986: Machel dies in plane crash, replaced by Chissano
- 1990: Joint communiqué signals beginning of peace process
- July 1990–October 1992: Negotiations take place in Rome
- October 4, 1992: Frelimo and Renamo sign peace agreement
- 1992–94: ONUMOZ oversees implementation of peace agreement

## KEY AGREEMENTS REACHED

- Declaration of cease-fire
- Recognition of political parties
- National elections to be held
- United army to be formed
- International monitors to oversee implementation of peace accords
- Regional and international involvement negotiated

## PRINCIPAL OUTCOMES

- Transformation of Renamo from a resistance movement into a political party
- Return of millions of refugees and displaced persons
- Free and fair elections held, with an 87 percent turnout

# 11

# Mediating Peace in Mozambique
## *The Role of the Community of Sant'Egidio*

ANDREA BARTOLI

## INTRODUCTION

If the negotiation process of a political conflict could be likened to a sporting event, the ideal role of a mediator would be something between that of a referee and a coach. By maintaining dialogue between opposing parties through formal language, the mediator acts as a conduit of the negotiation process. In this way the negotiator acts much like a referee who, with gestures and whistles, puts an otherwise general battle of the wills into a formal framework with a clearly understood goal: interpreting the process that leads to a conclusive outcome. In other ways, the mediator must adopt a role that more closely resembles that of a coach. Instead of merely observing the players' actions and their relation to a system of rules and regulations, the mediator takes on a more direct and influential role, advising the players and guiding them so as to optimize the natural unfolding of the process. The process itself is a failure only if it becomes a general battle of the wills and fails to incorporate and capitalize on the genuine and unique group dynamics that can contribute to a conclusive outcome. Specifically in terms of international conflict resolution, the mediation process is successful only if it is an earnest exchange among actors that reflects a larger, self-reverberating phenomenon within the greater domestic and international political arenas.

On October 4, 1992, an international agreement was signed by leaders of opposing groups in Mozambique, ending a fifteen-year-old civil war that began almost as soon as the country itself gained independence from Portugal. On one side was the Frente da Libertação de Moçambique (Frelimo), a nationalist group that had fought for and won power to self-rule from Portugal in 1974. On the other side was the Resistência Nacional de Moçambique (Renamo), a military resistance movement against the new government that had come to hold a reputation as the "Khmer Rouge of Mozambique." The agreement, signed by Frelimo's Joaquim Chissano and Renamo's Afonso Dhlakama, marked the end of the two-phase process that brought peace to Mozambique. The first phase consisted of negotiations that took place in Rome from July 10, 1990, to October 4, 1992. The second phase involved the United Nations Operation in Mozambique (ONUMOZ), the agreement for which was signed in 1992 and expired in 1994, just before Chissano was inaugurated president as the result of the country's first fair, free elections.[1]

The sporting event metaphor fails in the case of Mozambique because there were, happily, several "winners" instead of just one. The parallel, however, is particularly useful when we begin to examine the roles that various parties played throughout the peace process, especially the team of mediators who filled the shoes of "referee." The Community of Sant'Egidio was one member of this team. An improbable mediation leader, the Community of Sant'Egidio was largely responsible for an internationally recognized peace agreement implemented by the United Nations. Sant'Egidio was able to succeed as a conduit of negotiation because of the very weakness that made it such an unlikely leader—its lack of international prestige and power, which prevented it from being cast into and constricted by the formalities of more traditional efforts. Sant'Egidio helped to solve a difficult problem by introducing and, when necessary, recruiting other players into the process in order to create synergies—and, as a consequence, political latitude—that were previously absent.

This chapter will use the term "synergy" often. It describes in a wonderfully concise way the complex dynamic of gathering and fusing together individual and in some cases disparate actors, actions, motivations, and interests to contribute to a positive process. Sant'Egidio's realization of the possibility for synergy within the negotiation team was one of its most profound contributions to the peace process. Generally, powers and powerful actors must acknowledge that their influence is heavily partial and always determined by their interactions with other powers and powerful actors. Synergy is the ability to use the energy of great powers in a coherent way. It is thus important to note the distinction between "coherence" and "coordination." While coherence pertains to the process and is, in many ways, independent of any single act (coherence can emerge from chaos, and it is possible to see patterns and recognize coherence in otherwise seemingly bizarre behavior), coordination implies a rational effort by some actor to create order. Although Sant'Egidio lacked the political prestige and stature that might have given it the authority to act as a coordinator, it was able to see coherence in the actions of the actors involved in the process and to proceed appropriately. Positive contributions, it should be noted, were made not only by the mediation team but also by the different actors (negotiating parties, observers, international agencies, public opinion, etc.) who were influenced by the leadership of the mediation team. This synergic movement created the conditions for an enlargement of the political space and thus made possible the previously impossible dialogue.

How much did the Community of Sant'Egidio contribute to the peace process in Mozambique? Would peace have been possible without the mediation? Historically, it is nonsense to assume that there are no variables in each negotiation. The Community of Sant'Egidio was there as part of the process in Mozambique, both shaping it and being changed by it. The interactive nature of the process may tell us much about the possibilities of a pragmatic approach to conflict resolution. In this pragmatic approach, mediators are chosen by the forces involved, less because of their "formal" affiliation than because of their moral and political authority. Characteristic of the mediation in Mozambique was the paradox that the weaknesses of the negotiation team reduced the possibility of imposing outside solutions (through coercive diplomacy, military threat, and so forth), which forced the parties to negotiate for themselves. Because the mediation team lacked an authoritative stance, the two parties had to engage themselves in an effective, prolonged process that transformed not only positions but also the actors themselves. The paradox is that, positioned weakly, the mediation team established a strong and effective direct negotiation almost by default.

But was the negotiation successful simply because after so many years peace was due? Was the conflict ripe for solution? The very concept of "ripeness" can be used in a tautological way. The only way to say for sure that a conflict is ripe for resolution is when it happens; when a cessation of hostility comes about and discussion of its resolution is engaged in political terms and within a stable institutional environment. But what do we say about cases in which opportunities for such positive conclusions were missed? Are we to conclude that in those cases the situation was not ripe for resolution after all? In the debate over timeliness, we tend to underestimate the power of the mediation itself—the transforming power of the experience of adversaries talking with one another and with others in a setting that is conducive to constructive dialogue. Therefore, it is probably more useful to say that violent conflicts are always ripe to end. At least we should always perceive them as such, thereby helping those involved and who have the power to stop the killing share this perspective. Often the debate over ripeness neglects the fact that there is a very different perception of the same war by rich and poor, urban and rural individuals, people with power and people without. The war is experienced by these classes very differently. Women and children, we now unfortunately know very well, experience war very differently than do male soldiers. The latter are less likely to be killed than are the former. For the weakest, ripeness is always "now," for others it may be much later. Mediations are successful when they capture the peaceful will of the people, both domestically, in the country affected by the war, and internationally, in a political framework that is sustainable.

In the case of Mozambique, the negotiations were possible because both movements, Frelimo and Renamo, were ready for these changes and, in many respects, were forced to accept the will of the people expressed through other channels (especially churches and religious movements). These conditions were the product not only of internal dynamics, but also of the broad political changes that followed the fall of the Berlin Wall. It is impressive to look at southern Africa today and see the flourishing stability of an area torn by war not long ago. While international conditions were conducive to the development process in southern Africa, they were not entirely responsible for it. It is to the credit of the negotiating parties themselves that a cessation to the peace process in Mozambique was never considered and that a framework for negotiation was created on July 10, 1990. It was on this day that the two sides recognized each other as compatriots and members of the same Mozambican family, a bond that has been strong enough to nurture the process up to the negotiation and beyond.

In the field of international conflict resolution, it is not unusual for practitioners to attempt through their experience to establish effective standards in mediation techniques. However, specific conflicts are so profoundly shaped by their own conditions and particularities that it is often impossible to render general, concrete conclusions, and redefinition of the peace process must always be considered. When there is a success story, it is difficult to separately analyze the factors that contributed the most to it. Peace in Mozambique was not an obvious outcome, as the case of Angola demonstrates. If the result has been positive, it is probably because the characteristics of the Mozambique experience have to do with the ability of the political leadership to capture, express, and deliver a policy of reconciliation that was inclusive and open to structural institutional changes. This policy was also an expression of the desire for peace of the great majority of Mozambicans. Both Joaquim Chissano and Afonso Dhlakama were able to transform military confrontation into peaceful political dynamics; the importance of the local specificity of their negotiation cannot be underestimated in understanding the process that brought peace to Mozambique. Unfortunately, we have to recognize that while descriptively the notion of an engaged leadership may help in understanding the successful dynamics of the Mozambique peace process, it does not explain much in terms of the replicability of that success. However, if we assume a systematic approach to the analysis of a conflict, we may argue that a leadership committed to peace is a necessary ingredient for any successful peace process.

Much as a referee must be versed in the rules of the sport and learn from experience the many ways in which they may be applied, he or she must also be keenly alert to the unpredictable interactions that occur on the field during each game. The analysis of specific cases such as Mozambique yields understanding of a process that, although particular, may teach us lessons applicable to other situations, present and future, and enhance our overall understanding of the possibilities within the field of conflict resolution. Factors on the ground never entirely dictate a particular outcome in a deterministic fashion. However, what we can learn from an experience such as Mozambique is that shifting the goal from victory to peace helps to shape strategies that are consistent with that goal and may well prove eventually successful. This shift is not a precondition to the negotiations. It was, in the Mozambique case, somehow the product of a long process. The commitment of local leadership, the open popular support, and the consistent participation of the international community assured that the shift was irreversible. Unfortunately, in many other cases—especially Angola—the victory paradigm still seems to prevail, the leadership and the parties are still in a "victory" mode, and there is no political room for the majority of the population that supports peace as a central political goal. In these conditions, the role of the international community is limited, and should focus on the high-level diplomatic intervention aimed at restoring communication between the warring parties. Such communication is the real prerequisite for any political solution of a violent conflict.

## HISTORY OF THE CONFLICT

Located in the southern region of Africa, Mozambique is bordered in the north by Malawi, Tanzania, and Zambia; in the west by Zimbabwe; and in the southwest by South Africa and Swaziland. It is flanked to the east by a long and incredibly beautiful Indian Ocean shoreline. The country gained independence from Portugal in 1975, as a result of changes within the Portuguese government. Although Portugal had been a presence in Mozambique since 1498, the interior of Mozambique was never colonized in the totalitarian way favored by many European settlers in North America and South Africa, who transformed entire cultural, economic, political, and social landscapes of their conquered territories. Many ethnic groups have lived for centuries in what we now call Mozambique and have never been concerned with defined boundaries among modern states. Even now, many ethnic groups and tribes—the Macau and the Luma in the north, the Sena and the Ndau in the central region, and the Shangana in the south—lead their lives with scant concern for, or awareness of, national borders.

From the beginning of this century, Portuguese control of Mozambique became increasingly significant administratively, politically, and militarily. At the end of World War II, while in many other cases both colonizers and colonized contemplated redefinitions of power structures in light of diminished colonial forces, Mozambique's status was not reevaluated by the Portuguese. Portugal did not partake in the decolonization process that peaked in the 1960s and transformed Africa into a fresh and hopeful ensemble of independent states. Portugal not only denied the legitimacy of Mozambique and its demands for independence, but continued to encourage settlement of Europeans on what the Portuguese continued to deem colonial territory. Human rights abuses were widespread, and the Portuguese military confronted the nationalist forces aggressively.

In June 1963, three major groups of the nationalist forces of the independence movement formed Frelimo. The president was Eduardo Mondlane, an anthropologist with a Ph.D. from Northwestern University and an American wife. In 1974, the armed struggle against Portuguese colonial power officially started, but internal tensions within Frelimo's leadership itself dominated the first years of the movement. The unfortunate killing of Mondlane by a parcel bomb brought to power Samora Machel, a representative of the southern tribe who favored a radical policy aimed at not only challenging the Portuguese but also liberating people from traditional authorities. Under Machel's leadership and with support from China and the Soviet Union, Frelimo expanded its presence to the north of the country, closer to the logistic bases it had in Tanzania. By 1973, it had reached the central area of the country, and the Portuguese could not counteract effectively despite their superior military capabilities.

In September 1974, after a brief negotiation following a coup in Lisbon in April, Portugal relinquished power to Frelimo without obtaining the assurance of free and fair elections as a prerequisite for the transition to independence. Frelimo was presented as the sole legitimate representative of the Mozambican people, and the movement immediately launched itself upon a mission to create a socialist country. Its task was immense: to create a new state—a new nation—from an area that had been left completely deprived of functional infrastructure, capital, and human resources, and that had never before regarded itself as having a single identity or a common cultural history.

The priorities of the new government were clearly in the sectors of education, health, and institution building. To downplay Mozambican tribal, regional, racial, or religious identities, a new nationalist, socialist identity was promoted. The government was particularly harsh on traditional local authorities that had been in place since colonial times. The government nationalized much of the economy and directly controlled property and many of the country's functions. Unfortunately, the same government lacked trained and experienced personnel. Even technicians arriving from the Soviet bloc were ill prepared to cope with the task of turning the country completely around. While the Frelimo government was able to set the tone for a liberated Mozambique, it was also forced, by lack of resources and some ideological rigidity, into an impasse. The assertion of the legitimacy of a new nationalist socialist authority over the traditional authorities created dissatisfaction and tension that were promptly used by Rhodesian military intelligence to fuel resistance to the Frelimo government.

In response to Machel's decision to close the Beira corridor (Rhodesia's traditional link to the coast) and to allow bases in western Mozambique for Robert Mugabe's ZANU troops, which were fighting the Rhodesian regime, Rhodesia fostered the creation of a military resistance to the Frelimo government. Initially called the Mozambique Military Resistance (MMR), this movement was renamed Renamo. Mozambique made it a point of honor to support the fight for the independence of Rhodesia/Zimbabwe (and subsequently to support the struggle against apartheid in South Africa), but it is evident that Mozambique was badly affected by the confrontation with Rhodesia. Its involvement in the war on the side of Mugabe's forces came with a very high price; from its modest beginnings, Renamo grew into a formidable military threat to the well-being of the entire country. Supported first by Rhodesia and later by South Africa, Renamo was able to effectively force the government on the defensive.

Led by Afonso Dhlakama, Renamo exploited the discontent of the traditional authority structures. Dhlakama was himself a member of the Ndau tribe in the center of the country, and was connected with the Shona tribe, which constitutes the largest ethnic group in Zimbabwe. Renamo's aim during the entire war was to make it impossible for the Frelimo government to function properly. Almost no military confrontation between armies on the battleground was ever recorded during the war in Mozambique; Renamo preferred to attack villages and infrastructure by demolishing schools, bridges, hospitals, and roads. The war was bloody and very destructive. Many civilians were killed and many more were forced to flee from their homes. Many found refuge in neighboring countries, especially Malawi and Zimbabwe. Although South Africa agreed in the Nkomati Accord of 1984 to refrain from any further support for Renamo, the South African covert operation continued. Renamo was less well armed than the armed forces of Mozambique, but the movement—which was divided into northern, central, and southern areas—was nevertheless able to stage many attacks. The military strategy of the government focused on maintaining control of the cities and engaging with the guerrillas occasionally; despite Frelimo's efforts, it was never able to regain firm control of much of the countryside. Renamo acquired the terrible reputation as the "Khmer Rouge of Africa," a notion formally articulated in Robert Gersony's report to the U.S. State Department in 1988.[2] Vivid reports of Renamo's violence against civilians made it impossible for the U.S. government to support the movement. At that time, Renamo had neither an articulated ideology nor an organizational structure with which to promote any political platform; more a military insurgent movement, Renamo was unable to develop much of any political strategy.

The first phase of Frelimo rule had been characterized by the rigid implementation of socialist priorities. By the mid-1980s, however, Frelimo had realized the difficulty in pursuing a strict ideological policy, both internally and externally. Thus, a more pragmatic second phase emerged and Frelimo, still under the leadership of Samora Machel, found itself closer to Europe and the United States. In 1985, Machel visited Washington and Rome, winning the support of both President Ronald Reagan and Pope John Paul II.

In October 1986, Samora Machel died in a plane crash and was replaced by Joaquim Chissano as leader. Mozambique's foreign minister for many years, Chissano was a member of the Shangana tribe in the south, had studied in Paris, and spoke French, Portuguese, and English fluently. He had an aura of flexibility and pragmatism and, while he lacked some of Machel's charisma, was able to lead Mozambique to a remarkable change in just a few years.

## MOZAMBIQUE AND SANT'EGIDIO: A LONG-STANDING RAPPORT

The Community of Sant'Egidio is often asked, "How did you come to be recognized as a mediator in the Mozambique peace process?" To answer this, however, it is necessary to rephrase the question as a more general query: "How did the Community of Sant'Egidio get involved in Mozambique?" The first question pertains to the unique series of historical events that made Sant'Egidio a mediator in the peace process. The second inquires about the methods, process, and system that constructed a context for Sant'Egidio's role. Both questions are important.

The end of the Cold War and the subsequent expansion of global interactivity have augmented the pool of actors in the international arena. Local conflicts, especially extremely violent ones, now prompt into action a large and growing number of representatives of states, international organizations, and nongovernmental organizations. In the past, action was limited to traditional diplomacy that, by definition, was interested in defending the interests of a given nation state, and not necessarily in preventing wars or resolving conflicts. In the years since the end of U.S. involvement in the Vietnam War, however, the general attitude toward war, and especially toward the legitimacy of war, has changed dramatically. Today, whereas military intervention in support of a politically defined agreement is generally viewed favorably as a constructive and pragmatic (and often indispensable) step, attempts to resolve political problems through violent means are by no means as widely accepted. Therefore, there is growing interest in "solving" international conflicts that are already under way or seem likely to occur in the future. After the case of Mozambique, the international community discovered empirically that nongovernmental organizations (NGOs) can contribute positively to the solution of deadly conflict and that, under certain circumstances, they may be better placed than more traditional diplomatic actors to play the lead role in conflict resolution initiatives.

A possible, still rudimentary reading of the evolution of NGO participation, including the roles played by former heads of state such as Jimmy Carter and Julius Nyerere, is that it provides several new options for the negotiation of peace. Although outside, unofficial, neutral actors may risk being manipulated by local forces within a given conflict, NGOs can offer new possibilities for peace to those willing to find an acceptable solution to their own conflicts and prepared to respect order and protocol once the selection of a third-party mediator has been made. The Northern Ireland peace process offers a perfect example of how an outside, unofficial, neutral actor—in this case, a retired U.S. senator—can become a hero of peace in another country. This availability of actors may be crucial in creating conditions for dialogue between warring parties through a truly respectful intervention by the international community. Both the elements of and the processes that result from the selection of the mediating team should be subjects of further study.

In Mozambique, Sant'Egidio was involved in the process in spite of the fact that it was not (and, in many respects, has never become) a professional conflict resolution agency. Founded in 1968 in Rome at the initiative of a high-school student, the Community of Sant'Egidio is an international Roman Catholic association that presently involves about fifteen thousand members throughout the world. It is a fellowship of small communities sharing a spiritual life in a secular setting while serving the poor in friendship. Almost all members live active lives in the nonreligious world with their own families and professions, and are self-supporting and unpaid by the association. The headquarters is in Rome, housed in a church called Sant'Egidio, from which the group derives its name.

In the early 1970s, Sant'Egidio consisted of a few hundred members and was based only in Rome. Jaime Gonçalves, a young ordained priest from Mozambique who was practicing in Canada and continuing his graduate work in Rome, was not a member of the group but a friend who helped with many of its activities. When Mozambique became suddenly independent because of the political upheaval in Portugal, the Holy See decided to reverse its policy of appointing only white and Portuguese bishops in Mozambique. Gonçalves was one of the few considered, and became soon thereafter bishop of Beira, the second-largest city in the country.

After a few years in Mozambique as bishop, Gonçalves returned to Sant'Egidio and explained the difficulty that religious communities, especially Catholics, were facing under the new marxist regime. Perceived as being too close to the former colonial power, Catholics were marginalized and sometimes harassed, constrained in their expression of religious belief, and unable to attend regularly to their liturgical functions. Sant'Egidio offered help, thereby involving itself in the situation in Mozambique through the group's personal relationship with Gonçalves. It decided to use its political savvy to intervene in favor of Mozambique. Although the Holy

See recognizes the Community of Sant'Egidio as an organization of laypeople, Sant'Egidio does not represent the position of the Catholic Church. Sant'Egidio derives strength from its own internal resources, and has enjoyed warm approval from Pope John Paul II.

In the mid-1970s, the Italian Communist Party (PCI) was extremely influential in Italy. It also had extensive political and economic ties with Frelimo, and was interested in establishing closer contact with Catholic organizations. Sant'Egidio played to these interests and organized meetings at its headquarters between Gonçalves and Enrico Berlinguer, the PCI secretary general. Following the first encounters, Sant'Egidio established a very positive relationship with the Mozambican government. One of the strategies Sant'Egidio used to foster this relationship was to promote Mozambican culture and the knowledge of it within Italy. At the same time, Sant'Egidio assisted the Vatican and the local Catholic leadership in Mozambique in their negotiations with the government to settle the disputes of the postcolonial period.

Sant'Egidio's connection to Renamo was established much later. It was only in the late 1980s, after it was clear that a military victory was not possible, that the Frelimo government (at that point led by Chissano) was willing to explore the possibility of a dialogue with Renamo. In that framework, again through Gonçalves but this time as a representative of a larger, interdenominational group of religious leaders supporting peace, Frelimo established contact with the Renamo leadership. In 1990, after direct meetings with Afonso Dhlakama, Sant'Egidio was ready to be considered as a possible observer to the talks that both sides were trying to organize.

## AN IMPROBABLE LEADER:
## THE NEED FOR PEACE AND CREATION OF SYNERGIES

It was well before the beginning of direct talks between the government and Renamo that religious leaders started to talk about the need for peace in Mozambique. The Conference of Catholic Bishops held there strongly expressed this need for peace, publishing several documents and advocating dialogue with Renamo—even though it was illegal to do so. It was very clear from the outset of talks that the war didn't have a party of its own. There was no unified voice expressing popular support for a military solution. The prospect of mediation offered the possibility of creating a cohesive structure that would allow the expression of a deep-rooted popular desire in a policy of peace and reconciliation.

The mediation team consisted of four members: two from Sant'Egidio (Andrea Riccardi, founder of Sant'Egidio and professor of the history of

Christianity at the University of Rome, and Matteo Zuppi, priest and vicar of the parish of Santa Maria in Trastevere), a representative of the Italian government who was chosen as chairman (Mario Raffaelli, representative of the Socialist Party and undersecretary of state of foreign affairs under Giulio Andreotti), and a representative of Mozambican civil society (Mon. Gonçalves, archbishop of Beira). This mediation team was formed in an ad hoc way, and it was recognized at the very beginning as only a team of observers to encourage high-quality direct talks between the two sides. It was only after a few months that the observers were asked to act as full-fledged mediators.

Organizationally, Sant'Egidio provided physical and psychological space, using its headquarters, a former convent of Carmelite nuns, in the heart of Rome. A support team of volunteers was formed to carry out all necessary duties, from logistics to translation, accommodation to communication. These dedicated volunteers and their conscientious service helped to define the general mood of the talks in Rome, which were based strongly on the human relationships developed there. Sant'Egidio also provided office space for those who were collecting and managing information (in the form of articles, letters, memos, news reports, and so on) that was indispensable for the success of the initiative.

During the mediation process, it was agreed that the two parties should consider "the higher interests of the Mozambican nation," and that they "must set aside what divides them and focus, as a matter of priority, on what unites them, in order to establish a common working basis so that, in a spirit of mutual understanding, they can engage in a dialogue in which they discuss their different points of view."[3] The mediation team shared not only a vision and commitment to peace, but also a realistic evaluation of its own strength. Because it was not a strong international power, the team's strength relied on its ability to create synergies and on the cumulative effect of success.

Synergies were forged through direct personal relationships between representatives of different interests and organizations. The Italian ambassador to Maputo, Manfredo Incisa di Camerana, made great contributions to the process from the beginning to the very end. In addition to involving Italian political figures, Sant'Egidio from the outset kept the United States thoroughly informed of the situation. Probably the single most important American participant was Cameron Hume. As the deputy chief of mission to the Holy See for more than three years, Hume played a crucial role in making sure that the U.S. government supported the negotiation and participated constructively. This positive approach helped the whole synergic process. The United States accepted playing a role that contributed to the process without controlling it. The U.S. diplomatic decision to indirectly support the efforts of the mediation team came early in the process, thanks to the intelligent pragmatism of Herman Cohen and Jeff Davidow, at that time U.S. assistant secretary of state and deputy assistant secretary of state, respectively. President Chissano began sending signals of interest in negotiating in late 1989, and the U.S. administration, as Hume later said, accepted Chissano's request for help in ending the war.[4] Cohen was the architect of the assistance strategy that aimed to end the war through direct talks between the parties.

That the talks occurred in Rome under the auspices of an unknown NGO was not considered by Washington a reason to distrust the process. On the contrary, regular contacts were established through the American embassy to the Holy See. Such support gave essential credibility to the process and continued throughout the entire negotiations. Davidow, who was kept constantly informed of progress, directly participated in the talks in Rome in March 1991, with a long and important meeting with Dhlakama, the mediators, and other political figures. More important was the daily contribution that Americans provided by keeping the process well informed and nourished by ideas and, when necessary, diplomatic actions. In addition, the mediation involved countries of the region such as Kenya, South Africa, and Zimbabwe, as well as the United Nations and the Vatican. France, Great Britain, Portugal, and Russia entered the process later.

The role of the United Nations in the negotiations was very important. Regular communication with and visits to UN Headquarters in New York were soon established. The contacts intensified at the end of 1991, a time when, after the collapse of the Berlin Wall, a new role for the United Nations was being debated. Several UN peacekeeping operations were proposed or under way. Mozambique felt somehow in a larger pool, fortunately overcoming the difficulties created by an organization that was uncertain about its role, its mandate, and its way of operating. The mediation team decided to involve the United Nations more for its symbolic role than for its effective contribution to the process. The synergy was also reinforced by the presence of UN representatives at the final stages of the Rome negotiations from June to October 1992. Like many of the strategic decisions of the mediation team, the decision to involve the United Nations was neither clear-cut nor preplanned. Resistance was strong, and doubts about the possibility of success in Rome were substantial. They were overcome by a series of pragmatic calculations of benefits and risks with continual communication among all parties involved. The somewhat intangible involvement of the United Nations at a very early stage of the negotiations demonstrates that synergy is not a given factor: it is an approach that must be pursued consistently to produce results.

The paradox in utilizing synergies was that, in all probability, they were possible because no single powerful actor had a sufficiently compelling interest in Mozambique to force itself into the negotiations. Other countries such as Namibia and Angola had a history of attracting great international interest in their conflicts and peace processes, whereas Mozambique was, in a way, marginal on the geopolitical map of the early 1990s. No longer under the influence of a collapsing communist world, no longer a threat to a changing South Africa that was abandoning apartheid, Mozambique did not fall under the international spotlight. The Mozambique negotiations, therefore, provided the perfect opportunity to experiment in a very original way with innovative conflict resolution methods to settle a dispute that was as bloody and terrifying in its consequences as other atrocities that did attract substantial international attention.

## THE COMPLEXITIES OF MULTIPARTY MEDIATION

As a diverse, multifaceted mediation team, the group played a role that was not limited to creating synergies. On one hand, yes, the team decided to report fully and thoughtfully to the international community and especially the United States about the development of the talks so as to explain, protect, and represent the interests of both involved parties. On the other hand, the team directly nourished the negotiations with ideas, suggestions, and critical observations. The mediators worked closely with delegations from the government and Renamo, the former led by Armando Emilio Guebuza, the latter by Raul Manuel Domingos. For the mediators, the two delegations were the main channels of communication from both sides of the conflict. Direct channels with the Frelimo and the Renamo leadership were also established through visits, telephone calls, and meetings.

The time spent with the delegations in Rome over the two-year process was a precious investment that allowed personal relationships to develop among members. These interpersonal bonds became significant assets that enabled members to better cope with difficulties encountered in later stages of the process. When the possibility of a role for an ad hoc mediation team was envisaged, it was clear that the best strategy would be to create synergies and utilize Sant'Egidio's connections in Italy. As a medium-sized power with no colonial history in Mozambique but with substantial political and economic investments in its struggle for independence, Italy supported the first years of the newly independent state. This was done primarily through

Sant'Egidio's connections to the Italian Communist Party, and through cooperative projects run by the Italian Foreign Ministry that encouraged development in Mozambique.

Italy not only provided financial support, but also offered a political atmosphere that was conducive to positive negotiations. Having blended together ideologically different perspectives from Christian Democrats, communists, liberal conservatives, and neofascists, postwar Italy was a shining example of a successful democracy built on differences. Italy's constitution, which was approved by a large majority of the united antifascist forces that rebuilt the country after World War II, was a significant building block of the Italian experience. Further, Italy's proportional electoral system allowed for the first time fair representation of minority parties, encouraging the formation of coalitions of independent parties through power sharing. Even small, regionally based parties such as Union Valdotaine and Sud Tirolen Folks Partie were represented at the national level in the Italian government. For the Italians, cooperation between NGOs and governmental levels was created by the proximity of the Community of Sant'Egidio to the political and diplomatic circles in Rome.

In the United States, the possibility for collaboration between NGOs and governments was created by the theoretical work of those who were foreseeing a role for track-two diplomacy. The U.S. diplomatic services recognized the situation in Mozambique as a case in which an NGO could effectively lead a negotiation involving many states and international organizations. U.S. support was continuous, consistent, and particularly valuable in terms of technical expertise. Sant'Egidio did not have the expertise to properly address all military, legal, economic, and institutional problems emerging from the peace process. Without requesting that the United States assume a more central role, Americans, along with the Italians, provided indispensable expertise in these fields.

Another important component in the multiparty negotiation was Mozambique's civil society, which expressed itself through churches and religious communities. Although Mozambique's newly independent state was strictly Marxist-Leninist and did not favor religious groups, a new pragmatic attitude developed in the 1980s, welcoming the participation of religious leaders and communities in forming a new, more inclusive Mozambique. It is to the credit of Mozambicans that they were able to overcome more than fifteen years of serial war fueled by international actors using domestic dissatisfaction as a tool to destabilize the country. It is to the credit of Mozambicans that they achieved reconciliation after inventing and learning from a peace process that empirically proved strong enough to absorb and reflect the different interests of the Mozambican nation. It is to the credit of Mozambicans that they passed from war to peace without revenge after thousands had been killed or injured, millions had been displaced from their homes, and widespread destruction had been visited on houses, schools, and the country's infrastructure. Why the process occurred in this way is difficult to explain. And whether it can be replicated elsewhere is very hard to say; more empirical knowledge is needed. However, it is interesting to note that extremists interested in undermining it did not seriously threaten the peace process.

Although it is difficult to assess the single crucial moment at which the process established itself as successful, the key to success was the cumulative effect of a series of positive interactions among all the actors. In walking through the process step by step, Sant'Egidio members learned what was possible; indeed, each step revealed a new level of possibility. It must be understood that the process involved the mediation team for more than two years; its length, the intensity of the exchange, and the number of people involved made coordination essential to the success of the enterprise. While focusing on the final goal of a peaceful Mozambique, the mediation team (especially Matteo Zuppi and Mario Raffaelli) carefully used all problems and issues as challenges and opportunities to establish new connections. It would be reductive to think the two official meetings between the two sides were the ultimate synthesis of the mediation. The amount of less visible daily work—collecting and sharing information, decision making, analyzing, brainstorming, creative thinking to resolve crises as well as to determine long-term goals—constituted the bulk of the mediation team's labor. To compensate for its lack of experience and prestige, the team used a strategy of incremental success in which the first step, the joint communiqué signed in 1990, opened the door to further meetings and negotiations. It was a self-generating process; with each small success, the process gained greater credibility.

The team also worked to ensure that the channels of communication were established in such a way that the commitment of the delegations in Rome was binding for the two sides. Too often the lack of communication was used as an excuse to justify changes of position by these delegations. One goal was to make sure that positions were carried through and word was kept as information traveled throughout the various ranks of each party, especially in the case of Renamo. Because delivery of information about the process to the outside world was necessary, gathering and managing it within the process was essential. The sharing of information from all over the world regarding Mozambique was indispensable to gauge movement toward peace. Even data provided by the international community regarding a drought and possible famine that might plague the country were important in shaping the course of the negotiations.

Because confidentiality was also an important element of the process, information management was crucial. Many of the meetings between the two sides were kept secret, and many details of the negotiation were never publicly acknowledged. This strategy was necessary in order to minimize a disruptive and possibly inflammatory diffusion of information. For example, Frelimo had an internal, very well articulated debate in which hard-liners openly opposed compromise with Renamo. The need for confidentiality was great, especially for Chissano, who needed to ensure that his party would follow his leadership throughout the peace process. Fortunately, the lack of interest of the international press made it easier to achieve the necessary level of confidentiality.

It was very important to build trust, not only as a psychological feeling but also as a political and social dimension, and the peace process did so through a successful sequence of appropriate responses to crisis. As stated previously, although the main actors of the process were the Mozambicans themselves, the mediation team helped the process enormously. The time spent sharing information, commenting on and analyzing it, suggesting new ideas, and making recommendations was invaluable. It was a way to interpret reality through political dialogue. More than just offering the "right" answers to a specific crisis, the mediation offered a framework within which all crises could be assessed and addressed.

If a hypothesis may be made at this point about the characteristics of the success of the negotiations, one can be identified in the "emotional intelligence" of the mediation team that was willing and able to read and react to the ever-changing interpersonal dynamics. It is very well understood now that psychological processes contribute greatly to the success or the failure of a mediation, and that a conducive environment must take into account these psychological dimensions. Interpersonal relationships are central to the Sant'Egidio strategy of conflict resolution. Interaction with all the actors illustrated that the mediators were committed to the peace process rather than to their own agendas. That none of the four mediators was ever paid for his time and effort was perceived as a sign of serious commitment. By the same token, the countless hours volunteered by the many members of Sant'Egidio were an essential part of the process. The warm respect and caring attitudes expressed on the personal level helped to absorb some of the inevitable political tensions. The setting of Rome itself, with its friendly atmosphere, contributed in the same way. Although the government and the Renamo leadership did not spend two years in Rome, direct communication channels were established. Frequent messages by phone, letter, and fax, together with personal visits, were the tools used to keep these channels open and the relationship alive. The Renamo and Frelimo delegations were also treated not as a formal unified team but as a group in which personal dynamics were always playing an important role. It is noteworthy that each member of the delegations had a person from Sant'Egidio caring for him to whom he could refer with any request—and who also provided continuous feedback. It is also important to note that while the members of Sant'Egidio were able to manage the relationship between the two sides' delegations, they could not influence the dynamic internal to each party. However, the tensions that often occurred between the delegates and their leadership were more easily offset by the excellent quality of the other relationships.

## A NECESSARY REDEFINITION OF THE PROCESS

The Community of Sant'Egidio's nontraditional contributions to the peace process in Mozambique put a premium on building on the strength of states, international organizations, other NGOs, and members of the business community, which in turn facilitated a continuous redefinition of the process by the parties themselves. Although the peace talks in Mozambique were run by nonprofessional diplomats, they produced technical instruments of great sophistication that blended specific competencies in the psychological, historical, cultural, and legal realms. Because the mediators didn't have their own agenda, they were simultaneously able to make the parties themselves fully responsible for the peace process and to draw in the international community as significant but nonintrusive actors in the process.

The result was not only that the documents were signed on October 4, 1994, but also that they were as lengthy as the parties wanted them to be and embodied the experience of all the parties involved. The principles of political pluralism were clearly stated and articulated the very ideals that had guided the process for two years. The basic notion of this process was that the answer to the crisis was political and not military, and that in general the violent option is somehow deceptive, focusing energies on disruption and power control without addressing underlying issues. This was especially true in the case of Renamo. It had always defined itself as a resistance movement against Frelimo rather than a political movement for freedom that sought to govern and was able to do so. In this sense, the transformation of Renamo into a political party capable of sophisticated communication in the political arena is a great achievement of the peace process.

Although human rights were always in the background of all talks, no truth commission was established to address Renamo's prior violent activity, and no provisions were made for indicting or prosecuting war criminals. The text of the agreement represented the reality that Mozambicans wanted peace more than they wanted retributive justice. Mozambicans preferred to accept those involved in horrible war crimes into their own communities again rather than follow the Western-oriented way of dealing with the consequences of war. Very soon they started blaming the war—not Renamo or Frelimo—for the suffering that had marked the life of the country. It is interesting that this strategy—the emphasis on political agreement to assure peace rather than on justice to prosecute a few leaders singled out as the main perpetrators of war crimes—is not particularly appreciated today within the international community as a whole. Yet, at least in the case of Mozambique, it is clear that a negotiated political settlement that reduces violence will also contribute to a dramatic reduction of human rights abuses.

The peace process in Mozambique is also an example of the successful creation of conditions for an effective exit strategy for the mediators. The secret of Sant'Egidio's fruitful mediation was its ability to create a genuine political process based on dialogue between the warring factions. That multidimensional political process started in Rome when the two sides agreed to meet on neutral ground, and it has grown over the years, incorporating new actors and expanding its effectiveness while maintaining its support for

- pluralism and inclusiveness,
- political control of military forces,
- encouragement of direct personal contact,
- adherence to human rights standards, and
- acceptance of national sovereignty and borders.

The joint communiqué of 1990 emphasized the two delegations' affirmation of their "readiness to dedicate themselves fully, in a spirit of mutual respect and understanding, to the search for a working basis from economic and social conditions for building a lasting peace and normalizing the life of all Mozambican citizens."[5] This passage clearly states that the interests of the Mozambican nation will be represented not by a single party, but by many different political parties. This was probably the single most important element of the mediation: to create an institution-building process in which the "spirit of Rome" would reverberate, multiplying the effect of a participatory process based on human rights and democratic pluralism. This notion is important if we consider the implementation of the agreement signed by the government of Mozambique and the Renamo leadership. Both the demobilization of the armies followed by the formation of a unified national army and the electoral procedure that was the pinnacle of the democratic process were clearly designed by the government and Renamo—from top to grass roots, everybody was involved in a new, transforming experience. This centrality of politics kept together disparate actors such as the United States, Italy, Great Britain, Portugal, South Africa, Zimbabwe, and many others, including the United Nations. Coordination was not a function of an organizational structure, but rather the product of a new politics able to represent the interests of millions of Mozambicans. International actors were asked to abide by the possibilities created by that very political process.

Significantly, Mozambicans did not perceive the agreement in Rome as an imposed document, but as the result of an original experiment in which they were able to have a national dialogue and to reach genuine political agreement. During the two-year period following the signing, Aldo Ajello, the UN special representative, played a crucial role in keeping the international community together in its commitment to implement the agreement, facilitating discussion and negotiation between the Mozambicans themselves, and helping the process that began in Rome to continue after the negotiation was over. Whereas the greatest success of Sant'Egidio's mediation team was seeing the process beyond its first phase, the greatest success of ONUMOZ and Ajello in particular was working with the Mozambicans to invent a new politics in a democratic Mozambique, thereby preparing the way for the United Nations' departure in 1994.

Two movements of people that signified a change in Mozambique's collective experience fascinated many observers. The first was the return of millions of refugees and displaced people to their own villages. This massive return was the most powerful sign that Mozambicans on the whole were ready for peace. Even before the UN programs were ready to support their return, hundreds of thousands had left their temporary shelters on foot to go back to the homes of their families, tribes, and ancestors. The UN programs to relocate refugees and displaced people would not have been successful without this popular participation and support. On a more local level, before this migration, Renamo did not allow free movement within the areas it controlled. What is therefore remarkable is that the people who required the flexibility to return home safely somehow accurately foresaw it. The staggering economic success of Mozambique today would not have been possible if the great majority of its people had not returned to work their land.

The second movement of great significance took place during the elections. Voter turnout was very high: more than 5.4 million people voted, comprising approximately 87 percent of all Mozambicans over the age of eighteen. The elections marked the climax of the spirit of Rome infused in Mozambican political life. As Richard Synge has noted:

> The National Elections Commission (CNE), which interpreted and enforced the electoral rules, was an entirely Mozambican body and, although established belatedly, it achieved an impressive degree of impartiality under the conciliatory leadership of its chairman, Brazao Mazula. The influence of the CNE was crucial in overcoming many of the problems that arose, particularly during the elections themselves.[6]

One of the main objectives of international observers was not to repeat the experience in Angola, where a small group of international monitors was unable to confirm free and fair elections. In Mozambique, not only was international monitoring undertaken by a larger force, but also it was coupled with a significant effort on the part of the Mozambicans to self-monitor. Indeed, in a nation as large as Mozambique, with thousands of small polling stations scattered across the country, it would have been impossible to deploy international monitors to cover each one. The success of the process was based on the Mozambicans' ability to create institutions, such as the National Elections Commission, in which interests of the people were expressed. For the first time there was political reconciliation in which both the government and Renamo had to negotiate their differences using the mediation of a *super partes* Mozambican. The election results gave Chissano 53.3 percent of the vote and Dhlakama 33.7 percent. The high level of voter participation and the peaceful conduct of the elections exemplify politically and symbolically the passage from war to peace.

Elections are not a solution per se; however, as they did in Mozambique, they can provide a powerful symbolic moment in which to unify the country within a peaceful political framework. In 1994, after sixteen years of civil war and of fighting first against Rhodesia and later against apartheid in South Africa, Mozambique was finally able to enjoy peace and independence simultaneously. It is now under a new phase of development made possible primarily by Mozambicans committed to maintaining both peace and independence.

## LESSONS LEARNED

1. Involve all parties that have influence in a conflict, because peace can come only from those who have the power to continue the conflict. If one or the other side cannot win victory by military means, then the only way to solve a conflict is to persuade the armed factions that have

the power to find a political solution. Inclusion does not necessarily mean that all the parties must participate in all the talks all the time. Bilateral negotiation as well as ongoing communication by third parties is an essential component of success. To be included in a conversation does not necessarily mean that all participants speak at the same time.

2. Do so within a logical framework. The decision whether or not to include a party must be taken in light of that party's strength and influence. A proliferation of many unrepresentative actors may undermine the credibility of the overall process. In the Mozambique case, the self-evident criterion for inclusion was that a party possess an army. This is why political parties that did not have an army, and therefore did not have an active role in the conflict, were involved in a second phase and were not actively present in the talks in Rome.

3. Make sure that all parties articulate their positions to the mediators, without seeking immediate full disclosure. What is crucial is their participation in the discourse, even if their participation is only through a third party. In this regard, it is acceptable to discuss peace during war, as in the Mozambique case, because of the transforming power of dialogue. The leadership of all the parties involved in the process must recognize that one or more parties may well have reservations about the possibility of reaching an agreement, but they must also recognize that such reservations should not preclude participation in a common discourse. While there are a number of objective indicators of participation (e.g., presence/absence at meetings, response/nonresponse to requests, compliance/noncompliance with agreements, and so on), their interpretation is always critical. The same gesture, the same decision, the same action in a different context may mean different things, refer to a different set of circumstances, and have very different consequences. This is why during the Mozambique peace process that the best assessment of the willingness of the parties to participate in the process was the result of an interpersonal evaluation continuously updated with direct contacts and double checks.

4. Understand the process. Trust and political will are rare commodities, especially the will for peace and particularly in countries torn by long wars. A strong and unswerving will for peace and a readiness to compromise principles for which groups are fighting cannot be expected, nor can subsequent mutual trust in the short term. This kind of willingness to cooperate must be developed through interpersonal relations as well as through institution building. The negotiation process

may be, as in the Mozambique case, the very laboratory of a new political life in a pacified country.

5. Involve the international community, but do not assume it will bring a solution per se. There is no magic in the international community that will enable it to resolve a conflict that is by nature local. Refrain from unprepared intervention and invest more in local negotiation.

6. Respect local cultural identities and languages; allow negotiations to be held in a safe and conducive environment; and pay attention to the personal needs of actors involved. Do not underestimate the power of interpersonal connection.

7. Do not follow a preconceived set of rules and procedures. Instead, be prepared to invent new and creative ways of encouraging and structuring dialogue.

8. Emphasize negotiation as a political process that may better serve the interests of the parties than military confrontation.

9. Strive for appropriateness. The process is self-promoting only if at early stages the answer to the problem is appropriate. Too often mediators rely on the authority derived from their own "official" role (within, say, the United Nations or a national government) and the power it supposedly gives them. But the real power for the mediator or, as in the case of Mozambique, the mediating team comes from the belief by all parties involved that the process is fair, is preferable to military confrontation, and is going to deliver results. Mediators should rely more on their effectiveness than on their role.

10. Be faithful to the process. No solution can be expected in the short term, and it is important to persevere with the process, to have patience, and to remain convinced that the process will eventually bear fruit. The process requires long-term commitment and a willingness to cope with unforeseen obstacles. Whereas political life is often brief, especially in a developing country, a peace process must be conceptualized as a long-term process extending beyond the usual turnover of personnel in governments and in international organizations.

11. Create political institutions based on the agreement. Identify rules and formal procedures to structure the political process that emerged during the negotiations. Peace is not only the agreement on paper, but also the result of a dynamic interaction between warring parties over time, no longer in a military fashion but in a political one. The careful design of institutions in which all interested parties can meet in fruitful mediation is an essential component of the process; unless the spirit of

dialogue and compromise is somehow embedded in a procedural form (e.g., commissions and councils), it will not live on after the mediation. Although institutions per se do not prevent war from occurring again, they certainly can create conditions for lasting peace.

12. Let civil society participate in the peace process. In Mozambique, churches played a crucial role in channeling and expressing civil society's position at a time of hardship, as well as in providing the political space in which civil society could express itself. Grass-roots participation in the international network of religious organizations (such as Sant'Egidio) was also important in maintaining awareness and focusing support on the situation. Labor unions and other interests groups also played a role, even if a somewhat less relevant one, given the characteristics of Mozambican society. A few years of Marxist-Leninist policy left behind a "civil society" that was often organized in support of the government. In that sense, civil society played a role in making sure that the leadership's choice for peace was carefully shared with the country through the stricture of the party (Frelimo) and of the parallel organizations.

The Community of Sant'Egidio contributed some important skills and other ingredients to the mediation process. Among them was the readiness of Sant'Egidio members to listen without preconditions, basing understanding on direct communication with the parties involved. Also important was the willingness of the mediation team to play according to rules traditionally assigned to track-one diplomacy. This may have been the result of Sant'Egidio's strong presence in Rome. Also important was Sant'Egidio's willingness to explore and experiment with innovative solutions. The whole process was in itself innovative, and though it is not advisable to seek change for the sake of it, the flexibility to adapt to the particular conditions of a specific peace process is a determinant of success. At the same time, Sant'Egidio's long-standing volunteer commitment to Mozambique and its people guaranteed impartiality in and loyalty to the process.

We live in a time in which ingenuity can achieve remarkable, indeed almost unimaginable, results. Mozambique is an example of this, for those who started addressing the religious freedom issue there in the 1970s were university students who had no recognized power. It was their friendship with the Mozambicans that encouraged the students to use their creative energy to serve the cause of religious freedom. They continued to do so faithfully for more than twenty years. That they were able to play such a crucial role in international mediation was a result of this commitment and of the ability to rise to unexpected challenges. The experience created a new setting for dialogue, a much less formal and impersonal setting than the traditional diplomatic one, and certainly less bureaucratic than those of many international organizations.

The effectiveness of this nontraditional contribution is parallel to the need for it in today's world. On at least five occasions after the signature of the agreement for peace in Mozambique, leaders from Albania, Algeria, Guatemala, Kosovo, and Burundi came to Sant'Egidio to engage in dialogue and sign agreements. In the post–Cold War world, local and international leaders may find it helpful to use a setting that has a remarkable track record, yet is free from the overwhelmingly rigid atmosphere of state-sponsored discussions. But Sant'Egidio and organizations like it can work well only when the parties themselves are willing to talk; they do not have and should not need the power to impose solutions on unwilling parties. Although this attitude may disappoint those who advocate force to solve conflict, the most effective approach to conflict resolution is a self-selecting process that allows parties to come to the table only when they are really ready to do so. The Mozambique case demonstrates once more that mediation is not merely the official time spent at the formal table, but the whole process of arriving at it. It involves bringing people face to face and helping them realize that, despite their differences, they are both committed to an experience that, for all involved, unfolds as a constant adventure driven by the desire to achieve peace. Unfortunately, new uncertainty for the very political process that brought peace to the country is now emerging, especially in the organization of new elections. Although a new war seems impossible, the transformation of Mozambique into a full-fledged democracy, stable in its own institutional framework, has still to be completed. Certainly a major contribution to this transformation process started in Rome where, with the help of many actors, Mozambicans decided to talk directly among themselves. Challenges are not necessarily bad news: they must be overcome and may become positive steps toward the strengthening of a stable, sustainable peace. It is exactly in this change of attitude—from seeing challenge as a threat to seeing it as a way to succeed—that the way to peace is often found. Mozambique seems to be a good example that this change can occur, even after a long and bloody war.

## NOTES

I would like to thank Emily Marino—writer, editor, and collaborator—to whom I owe a great deal for this article and for the launching of the International Conflict Resolution Program at SIPA-Columbia University.

1. Richard Synge, *Mozambique: UN Peacekeeping in Action, 1992–94* (Washington, D.C.: United States Institute of Peace Press, 1997), 140.

2. Robert Gersony, *Summary of Mozambican Refugee Accounts of Principally Conflict-Related Experience in Mozambique: Report Submitted to Ambassador Jonathan Moore, Director, Bureau for Refugee Programs; Dr. Chester A. Crocker, Assistant Secretary of African Affairs* (Washington, D.C.: Department of State, 1988).

3. General Peace Agreement, Joint Communiqué, July 10, 1990. The text of the agreement is available in United Nations Department of Public Information, *The United Nations and Mozambique: 1992–1995* (New York: United Nations, 1995), 124.

4. Cameron Hume, *Ending Mozambique's War: The Role of Mediation and Good Offices* (Washington, D.C.: United States Institute of Peace Press, 1994), 31.

5. General Peace Agreement, Joint Communiqué, July 10, 1990.

6. Synge, *Mozambique*, 116.

## BIBLIOGRAPHY

Abrahamson, H., and A. Nilsson. *Mozambique: The Troubled Transition from Socialist Construction to Free Market Capitalism*. London: Zed Books, 1995.

Africa Watch. *Conspicuous Destruction: War, Famine, and the Reform Process in Mozambique*. New York: Human Rights Watch, 1992.

Alden, C., and M. Simpson. "Mozambique: A Delicate Peace." *Journal of Modern African Studies* 31, no. 1 (1993).

Andersson, H. *Mozambique: A War against the People*. London: Macmillan, 1992.

Bowen, L. "Beyond Reform: Adjustment and Political Power in Contemporary Mozambique." *Journal of Modern African Studies* 30, no. 2 (1992).

Catholic Institute for International Relations, ed. *The Road to Peace in Mozambique, 1982-1992*. London: Catholic Institute for International Relations, 1994.

Chincongo, M. *The State, Violence, and Development: The Political Economy of War in Mozambique, 1975-1992*. Aldershot, Vt.: Avebury, 1996.

Department of Information, United Nations. *The United Nations and Mozambique, 1992-1995*. New York: United Nations, 1995.

Finnegan, William. *A Complicated War: The Harrowing of Mozambique*. Berkeley: University of California Press, 1992.

Hoile, D. *Mozambique: A Nation in Crisis*. London: Claridge Press, 1989.

———. *Mozambique, Resistance and Freedom: A Case for Reassessment*. London: Mozambique Institute, 1994.

Hume, Cameron. *Ending Mozambique's War: The Role of Mediation and Good Offices*. Washington, D.C.: United States Institute of Peace Press, 1994.

Magaia, Lina. *Dumba Nengue: Run for Your Life—Peasant Tales of Tragedy in Mozambique*. Trenton, N.J.: Africa World Press, 1988.

Mondlane, Eduardo. *The Struggle for Mozambique*. New York: Penguin, 1996.

Morozzo della Rocca, Roberto. *Mozambico, dalla guerra alla pace: Storia di una mediazione insolita*. Milan: Edizioni San Paolo, 1994.

Newitt, Malyn. *A History of Mozambique*. Bloomington: Indiana University Press, 1995.

Ohlson, Thomas, and Stephen John Stedman. *The New Is Not Yet Born: Conflict Resolution in Southern Africa.* Washington, D.C.: Brookings Institution, 1994.

Rich, Paul, ed. *The Dynamics of Change in Southern Africa.* New York: St. Martin's Press, 1994.

Synge, Richard. *Mozambique: UN Peacekeeping in Action, 1992–1994.* Washington, D.C.: United States Institute of Peace Press, 1997.

United Nations Department of Public Information. *The United Nations and Mozambique: 1992-1995.* New York: United Nations, 1995.

United States Institute of Peace. *A Conference Report: Discussions from Dialogues on Conflict Resolution: Bridging Theory and Practice, July 13-15, 1992.* Washington, D.C.: United States Institute of Peace Press, 1992.

Venancio, M. "Mediation by the Roman Catholic Church in Mozambique, 1988–1991." In *Mediation in Southern Africa.* London: Macmillan, 1993.

Vines, Alex. *Angola and Mozambique: The Aftermath of Conflict.* Washington, D.C.: Research Institute for the Study of Conflict and Terrorism, 1995.

Vines, Alex, and K. Wilson. "The Churches and the Peace Process in Mozambique." In *The Christian Churches and Africa's Democratization,* ed. P. Gifford. Leiden: Brill, 1995.

Zartman, I. William. *Elusive Peace: Negotiating an End to Civil Wars.* Washington, D.C.: Brookings Institution, 1994.

## Background to Chapter 12

## Bringing Peace to Cambodia

Cambodia suffered long and intensively from the violence that accompanied superpower intervention in the Vietnam War in the 1970s, a profound communist revolution in the late 1970s in which more than a million people were killed in a kind of "auto-genocide," and a protracted struggle for regional influence in Indochina between Vietnam and China. During the 1980s, the United Nations, ASEAN, and France made initial efforts toward mediating a settlement among Cambodia's warring political factions, which were supported by several outside powers, but it was only with the end of the Cold War in 1991 and a secret deal between Vietnam and China to reconcile their differences that a negotiated end to hostilities came to fruition.

The United States took a lead role in constructing a UN peace process through conference diplomacy sponsored by the United Nations and through informal dialogue. In the fall of 1991, a comprehensive settlement was agreed upon that satisfied the international rivals if not the domestic combatants. In implementing the peace plan, the United Nations assumed control of state operations in Cambodia for a two-year period, and a power-sharing government was formed after internationally supervised elections in 1993. Although internal power struggles resurfaced after the elections, the UN settlement succeeded in ending foreign intervention in Cambodia's affairs, and it created conditions in which the genocidal Khmer Rouge revolutionary movement turned in on itself in a final spasm of self-destructive violence. By 1998, Cambodia had a successful second round of elections and gained a degree of normalcy that was recognized by its acceptance into ASEAN.

## MAJOR ACTORS

- People's Republic of Kampuchea (PRK), later the State of Cambodia (SOC): led by Hun Sen and his Cambodian People's Party (CPP)
- National United Front for an Independent, Neutral, Peaceful, and Cooperative Cambodia (FUNCINPEC): led by Prince (later King) Sihanouk, with influence from his son, Prince Ranariddh
- Khmer People's National Liberation Front (KPNLF): led by Son Sann
- Party of Democratic Kampuchea (PDK, also known as the Khmer Rouge): led by Pol Pot
- Vietnam, with its foreign minister, Nguyen Co Thach, playing an active role in the diplomacy of a peace settlement
- The five permanent members (the "Perm Five") of the UN Security Council: China, France, the Soviet Union/Russian Federation, the United Kingdom, and the United States
- The Association of Southeast Asian Nations (ASEAN), with Indonesia's foreign minister, Ali Alatas, playing a lead role in the diplomacy of the settlement process
- Various regional states: especially Australia, Japan, and Thailand
- UNTAC, the United Nations Transitional Authority for Cambodia

## IMPORTANT DATES

- 1975: Pol Pot's Khmer Rouge topples the U.S.-backed Khmer Republic, led by Lon Nol, in the wake of the Vietnam War
- 1978: Vietnam invades Cambodia, overthrows the Khmer Rouge regime, and installs a surrogate regime led by Heng Samrin and Hun Sen
- 1988-89: Jakarta Informal Meetings (JIM I and II), organized by Indonesia, advance diplomacy on a Cambodia settlement
- August 1989: Paris Peace Conference on Cambodia, cochaired by France and Indonesia
- January–August 1990: UN Security Council Perm Five consultations produce a framework agreement
- 1990–91: Secret Sino-Vietnamese negotiations on normalizing relations
- October 23, 1991: Comprehensive Peace Agreement on Cambodia reached at reconvened Paris Conference

- March 1992: UN implementation force—UNTAC—arrives in Cambodia to oversee transition to elections and administer the government
- May 1993: Free and fair elections won by Prince Sihanouk's party, FUNCINPEC

### KEY ELEMENTS OF THE UN PEACE PLAN FOR CAMBODIA

- Cease-fire among the four Cambodian (Khmer) factions, with cantonization and eventual demobilization of their militaries and an end to foreign assistance
- Khmer refugees in camps along the Thai-Cambodian border repatriated; Vietnamese forces in Cambodia return home under UN verification
- Cambodia to become a constitutional monarchy, with a new government formed on the basis of UN-supervised elections
- The United Nations to implement the peace agreement through UNTAC and oversee civil and military functions during the transition to elections and the formation of a new Cambodian government

### PRINCIPAL OUTCOMES

- Cambodia achieved a degree of domestic political stability, a return to economic growth, and the withdrawal of foreign interference in its domestic affairs
- The United States normalized diplomatic relations with Cambodia and, later, Vietnam, and ended trade embargoes
- Indochina gained stability through the withdrawal of major power intervention, affirmation of the integrity of its three separate states (Vietnam, Laos, and Cambodia), and integration of the three states into ASEAN

# 12

# Bringing Peace to Cambodia

RICHARD H. SOLOMON

## INTRODUCTION

The years 1990–93 marked the phasing out of more than a century of great power interventions in Indochina and the first fully cooperative effort of the UN Security Council at the end of the Cold War to construct and implement a peace process.[1] The focus of this activity was Cambodia, a country ravaged for more than two decades by the Vietnam War and internal revolution. The United States played a leading, catalytic role in moving the five permanent members of the Security Council in 1990 to design a political process that would bring peace to Cambodia. Its efforts succeeded because the situation was ripe for settlement given the combined effects of a military stalemate among the Khmer factions, prior work on a Cambodian settlement during the preceding decade by a number of interested parties, and the desire of the major powers to normalize their bilateral relations and disengage from Indochina's travails.

These circumstances were reinforced by the efforts of several regional states—especially Indonesia, Thailand, Australia, and Japan—to eliminate foreign intervention from Indochina and stabilize Southeast Asia in an era of accelerating economic growth. Ultimately success came, however, when the two major protagonists in Indochina's conflicts of the 1980s and 1990s—China and Vietnam—made a secret, bilateral deal to reconcile their differences and support the UN peace plan for Cambodia.

The work of constructing a peace process, in toto, spanned more than a decade and involved multiple players—primarily the United Nations, the Association of Southeast Asian Nations (ASEAN), and individual countries such as Australia, France, Indonesia, Japan, Thailand, and the United States. The history of this effort can be divided into five rather distinct phases.

The first phase covered most of the decade of the 1980s and, as mentioned, involved the partially successful prenegotiation efforts of the United Nations and ASEAN.[2] These initiatives helped define the issues relevant to a settlement and saw the first attempts to bring the four major Cambodian political factions to a bargaining table.[3] As these efforts proceeded, the factions sustained their military confrontation, supported by outside backers—the Chinese and the Thai supporting Pol Pot's Khmer Rouge; the United States and several ASEAN countries supporting Prince Sihanouk and Son Sann; and Vietnam and Moscow supporting Hun Sen's Cambodian People's Party (CPP) and its government, the People's Republic of Kampuchea (PRK)—a designation changed in 1989 to the State of Cambodia (SOC).

The second phase, from the spring of 1989 through August of that year, centered on a French-Indonesian-organized peace conference convened at Paris during the month of August. The third phase began in the fall of 1989, following suspension of the Paris Conference, and centered around the U.S. initiative to construct a UN peace process through the work of the five permanent members of the Security Council (popularly referred to as the P-5 or Perm Five). It concluded when the Perm Five reached consensus on a framework for the peace process at the end of August 1990.

The fourth phase, which began with UN publication of the Perm Five framework agreement on August 28, 1990, ran through the fall of 1991 and involved broadening international backing for the Perm Five framework agreement and, most significantly, gaining the cooperation of the four Khmer political factions. The fifth phase was the period of implementation of the United Nations' settlement plan. It began in early 1992 with the arrival in Cambodia of UN troops under the supervision of the secretary-general's special representative, Yasushi Akashi; ran through the elections of May 1993; and concluded with the establishment of a new government and withdrawal of the UN presence from Cambodia in September of that year. U.S. involvement in this five-phase process was most active in the second and third phases—during the first session of the Paris Conference and the subsequent Perm Five negotiations that produced the framework agreement.

The story of the Cambodian peace process is significant beyond itself in that it provides larger lessons about collective international mediation efforts. These include insights into (1) peacemaking at a time of major change in the international political system; (2) the importance of a broader strategic objective on the part of some of the parties (in this case, the desire of China, the Soviet Union, and the United States to disengage from Indochina) in providing positive incentives for the mediation; (3) the importance of domestic political pressures in shaping the U.S. government's negotiating approach (especially pressure from the U.S. Congress) that constrained and shaped the mediation strategies and tactics of the Bush administration; (4) the role of political "ripeness" and timing in the mediation effort; and (5) the importance of leadership—how and when it is expressed—in maintaining cohesion among the participants in a complex mediation. This chapter will examine some of these lessons.

## BACKGROUND

There is no little irony in the fact that the United States was probably the most effective of the major powers to play a catalytic role in the UN aspect of the Cambodian settlement, given the history of our involvement in the Vietnam War. But in the early 1990s, the United States was seen by most of the other players as the most "neutral" and capable member of the Security Council to help structure a settlement. The Soviets/Russians and the Chinese were still sparring over influence in Indochina through their surrogates—the Hun Sen government in Phnom Penh and Pol Pot's Khmer Rouge guerrillas in Cambodia's jungles—although Moscow's influence was declining rapidly as its resources and political outreach contracted. The French, while a prime mover at one stage in the diplomatic maneuvering, were seen as a player with an agenda—seeking to restore their colonial-era influence in both Vietnam and Cambodia. And the British, although skillful in the world of UN diplomacy, lacked the will and the resources to be a major influence in Southeast Asia.

The ASEAN countries, led by Indonesia, had laid the basis for a settlement by hosting a series of prenegotiation encounters—the Jakarta Informal Meetings (dubbed the JIM meetings) of 1988–89; and in the spring of 1989 Indonesia joined forces with France to sponsor an international conference in Paris dedicated to achieving a comprehensive settlement of the Cambodian conflict. This effort foundered on unresolved differences between China and Vietnam and their surrogates among the Cambodian political factions, but the conference played a major role in building an international consensus on the elements of a peace process. Paris put a settlement within reach.

In the early fall of 1989, the Bush administration, at once impelled and constrained by domestic political cross pressures, initiated a consultation effort with the five permanent members of the UN Security Council intended to build on the decade-long series of UN- and ASEAN-sponsored diplomatic efforts and on the Paris Conference accomplishments. This initiative, and a structured process of normalizing U.S.-Vietnam relations that grew from it, ultimately succeeded because Vietnam, increasingly isolated by the rapidly failing Soviet Union and under unrelenting pressure from China, abandoned its objective of establishing a hegemonic position over the other states of Indochina—Laos and Cambodia.

Two years later, in the fall of 1991, after an intense series of diplomatic encounters, a U.S.-brokered Security Council framework agreement for a Cambodia peace process was accepted by all the participants of the Paris Conference and formally adopted by the United Nations General Assembly. And in early 1992 the first contingents of UNTAC—the United Nations Transitional Authority for Cambodia—arrived in Phnom Penh to implement the peace plan.

The U.S. mediation effort was facilitated by the United Nations. Although the United Nations was, and remains, the object of political attack in the United States, it was a relatively neutral and competent international vehicle for both constructing and implementing a settlement process. The United Nations was not, however, a prime mover in the politics of the settlement, but a screen behind which China, the Soviet Union, and Vietnam privately resolved their differences over the future of Indochina. Based on a series of secret bilateral meetings between senior leaders in Hanoi and Beijing beginning in the fall of 1990 and running through the summer of 1991, the Chinese induced the Vietnamese to accept the UN peace plan for Cambodia as part of a broader normalization of bilateral relations. The UN plan was subsequently formalized by all international participants in the Paris Conference and by the United Nations and was put into effect in early 1992. The United Nations verified the withdrawal of all Vietnamese troops from Cambodia, UNTAC restored a semblance of civil government in 1992, and in the spring of 1993 the United Nations administered a remarkably successful popular election in Cambodia that established a political structure legitimated by Khmer public opinion. Cambodia was now on its own to run its affairs largely independent of outside influence.

As this process advanced, the United States and Vietnam resumed efforts to normalize relations after the war years and Hanoi's late 1978 invasion of Cambodia. With a focus on supporting the UN settlement plan for Cambodia and accounting for America's missing-in-action (MIA) in Vietnam and Laos, the United States developed in 1991 a "road map" to normalization with Vietnam that was largely fulfilled with the establishment of diplomatic relations in July 1995. The United States thus moved beyond its Cold War–era involvement in the strategic and domestic complexities of Indochina to confront the uncertainties and conflicts of the post–Cold War world. For the first time in more than a century, Indochina was unburdened of the interventions of the major world powers.

This chapter will focus on the U.S. role as one among several players in constructing a peace process for Cambodia, placing the Bush administration's diplomacy in the complex historical and political context of Indochina, the last years of the Cold War, and American domestic politics. It details the evolution of a multilayered settlement process during the years 1989–92 and assesses the outcome of the Cambodian settlement five years after the UN-supervised elections of 1993.

## INDOCHINA: TRAPPED BETWEEN MAJOR POWERS

Any effort to understand the Cambodia peace process must take account of the complex and multifaceted history of Indochina, for virtually all the players in the politics of the early 1990s were burdened with baggage packed with rivalries and conflicts decades if not millennia in the making. The very name "Indochina" designates a region at the geographical boundary between China and the Indian subcontinent, an interstitial zone in world affairs long subject to complex international cross pressures. India and China each had imprinted their marks on the culture and politics of Indochina in assertions of national power going back millennia.

Of more immediate relevance to this assessment, the colonial era saw the French bring European influence to Vietnam and Cambodia in the 1800s; and it was Paris that placed a teenage Prince Norodom Sihanouk on the Cambodian throne in 1941 (in the face of an imminent Japanese invasion of Indochina). Following World War II and France's defeat at the hands of the Vietnamese communists in 1954, Paris was again seeking to regain some of its global outreach by playing a leading role in international diplomacy and reestablishing a presence in Cambodia. Japan, while cautious in its political assertiveness in Asia following the defeat of its imperial ambitions in World War II, was looking to gain greater regional stature in an era of "geoeconomics." Some officials in the Japanese Foreign Ministry, seeking to translate their country's economic power into political influence, even looked anew to a time of "Asia for Asians."[4]

Indochina in the 1970s had become a cockpit of the global rivalry between the Soviet Union and China that developed after the breakdown of their alliance in 1960. Although the two communist giants had supported the Vietnamese in the 1960s during their war against the Americans, by 1974 Beijing had turned against Hanoi to resist the regional expansion of the victorious Vietnamese, whom the Chinese saw as a surrogate of the Soviet Union in its effort to encircle and contain China's influence in Asia.[5] After Vietnam's invasion of Cambodia in late 1978, the Chinese launched a limited border war on the Sino-Vietnamese frontier and supported an insurgency against Vietnam's client regime in Phnom Penh—a regime that was supported by the Soviets as well.

As has been the case with so much of Indochina's complex history, the influence of outside powers was amplified by regional rivalries and internal political factionalism. The three states of Indochina—Cambodia, Laos, and Vietnam—along with neighboring Burma and Thailand have a long and complicated record of interventions and shifting dominations going back centuries. Cambodia's contemporary politics reflects this history in an intense burden of distrust and hostility toward the Vietnamese. Fear of Vietnamese "colonialism," in the form of Hanoi's invasion of Cambodia in 1978 and subsequent military occupation, and the presence in the country of several hundred thousand Vietnamese settlers, constituted one of the key political issues at play in the peace process of the early 1990s.

America's post–World War II involvement in Indochina had grown slowly after the Vietnamese defeat of the French at Dien Bien Phu in 1954—in reaction to the Sino-Soviet alliance of 1950, which projected the Cold War throughout Asia. Seeking to prevent states allied to the major communist powers such as North Vietnam and North Korea, or indigenous communist parties in countries like Indonesia, from spreading the influence of Moscow and revolutionary China, the United States took on the costly and ultimately unsuccessful task of thwarting revolutionary nationalism in Vietnam and Cambodia. After Hanoi's successful military reunification of the country in 1975, the United States—having normalized relations with China in 1972 in an effort to make common cause against the expansionist Soviet Union and its allies—came to work alongside China by supporting anti-Vietnamese Khmer resistance forces based in Thailand. Both Washington and Beijing, along with the ASEAN countries, were determined to prevent Hanoi from consolidating its client government in Phnom Penh led by a former Khmer Rouge commander, Hun Sen.

## FROM WAR TO DIPLOMACY

The 1950s, 1960s, and 1970s were a time of military efforts—by the French, the Americans, the Chinese, and the Vietnamese—to shape the future of Indochina. The 1980s saw efforts slowly shift toward diplomacy. Early in the decade international concern focused on Vietnam's 1978 invasion of Cambodia and Hanoi's attempt to gain international recognition of its client government in Phnom Penh led by Hun Sen. In the summer of 1980 the Japanese sponsored a small conference in Tokyo designed to build pressure on Vietnam to withdraw its troops from Cambodia; and in July 1981 the United Nations convened an International Conference on Kampuchea (Cambodia) in New York.[6] The UN session, chaired by Foreign Minister Willibald Pahr of Austria, was attended by ninety-one countries—but not by the Soviet Union or Vietnam. It sought to attain a comprehensive settlement of the Cambodian situation based on the withdrawal of Vietnam's military forces, disarmament of the contending Khmer factions, and the establishment of an interim administration pending national elections for a new Cambodian government.

These issues—a comprehensive (as opposed to a partial) settlement plan under some form of international supervision, withdrawal of Vietnam's troops, disarmament of the Khmer factions, and the establishment of a legitimate government through elections—were to be the essential elements of diplomatic maneuvering over Cambodia for the ensuing decade. Only the ability of the Vietnamese, and their Soviet backers, to sustain a friendly government in Phnom Penh was to be the critical variable in the otherwise constant diplomatic equation.

The remainder of the 1980s saw fruitless political and military maneuvering among the contending Khmer parties, with the UN secretary-general's special representative for Cambodia, Rafeeuddin Ahmed, and the ASEAN states, led by Indonesia's foreign minister, Ali Alatas, trying without success to establish the basis for a political settlement. Of special importance in these efforts were two "informal" meetings in Jakarta—the JIM meetings—held in 1988 and early 1989 that succeeded to the point of getting the four Khmer factional leaders together, along with representatives of the other Indochina states and the ASEAN countries. JIMs I and II put on the agenda the issue of some form of international control mechanism to supervise a settlement, but a political process failed to take hold as the Khmer factions continued to test their strength through military action on the ground.

Two other factors began to change the diplomatic equation by the mid-1980s. Public revulsion at the horrendous violence perpetrated by Pol Pot's Khmer Rouge (Red Khmer)[7] during its reign of revolutionary terror between 1975 and 1978, weakened international support for the anti-Vietnamese coalition of Khmer parties that included the Khmer Rouge—formally termed the Coalition Government of Democratic Kampuchea (CGDK)—especially in the United States.[8] And the ascension to power in Moscow of Mikhail Gorbachev in 1985 led to a fundamental shift in Soviet foreign policy, away from the expansionist initiatives of the Khrushchev and Brezhnev eras and toward normalization of relations with the United States and China.

In July 1986 General Secretary Gorbachev announced the withdrawal of some Soviet troops from Afghanistan and Mongolia—a clear signal of his interest in improving relations with China. The Soviet leadership continued to express support for Vietnam—in part by deferring to Hanoi's regional objectives by speaking of Vietnam, Laos, and Cambodia as if they were a single political entity. But behind the scenes Gorbachev and his foreign minister, Eduard Shevardnadze, were making clear to the Vietnamese that the era of Soviet support for Vietnam in its confrontation with China, including subsidization of the Vietnamese occupation of Cambodia, was fast coming to an end. On April 5, 1989, one month before Gorbachev traveled to Beijing to complete the normalization of Sino-Soviet relations, Vietnam announced that it would withdraw all its forces from Cambodia by the end of September of that year—unilaterally if necessary, under some form of international verification if possible.[9]

## CONSTRUCTING A PEACE PROCESS FOR CAMBODIA

I had been publicly nominated as assistant secretary of state for East Asian and Pacific Affairs on March 24, 1989, ten days before the Vietnamese announced their intention to fully withdraw their military forces from Cambodia by the end of September. Not long thereafter, I received my first official invitation—from France's ambassador to Washington, Emmanuel "Bobby" de Margerie—to a breakfast in honor of my soon-to-be French counterpart, Claude Martin, director of the Quai d'Orsay's Asia-Oceania Division. Martin was coming to Washington specifically to gain U.S. support for the conference on Cambodia that France and Indonesia were planning for August.

The Bush administration, in its first months, had reaffirmed with China its opposition to Vietnam's occupation of Cambodia and its support for the noncommunist resistance. While the Bush administration's attitude toward the Khmer Rouge was decidedly unfriendly, it did sustain the Reagan administration's policy of supporting the Sihanouk–Son Sann–Khmer Rouge coalition government (the CGDK) as the legitimate incumbent in Cambodia's UN seat—as a way of blocking recognition of the Vietnamese-installed government of Hun Sen. It also reconsidered the issue of providing assistance—both lethal and humanitarian—to the noncommunist resistance forces of Prince Sihanouk and Son Sann, leader of the Khmer People's National Liberation Front (KPNLF).[10] The rationale for such assistance—which had been first proposed in Congress in 1985 by the chairman of the House of Representatives' Foreign Affairs Subcommittee on Asian and Pacific Affairs, Stephen J. Solarz, and his Republican colleague Jim Leach—was to strengthen the noncommunist elements in the resistance vis-à-vis the Chinese-backed Khmer Rouge and to give them more credibility in any negotiation involving the Hun Sen government in Phnom Penh.[11]

The Bush administration was not inclined to take the lead on Indochina issues, however. My official instructions were to support the French and the Indonesians as they prepared for the August conference in Paris. Claude Martin and I had a cordial first encounter at the French embassy; we were to become active collaborators in the months to follow.

The evolution of major power cooperation on a Cambodia settlement was complicated in early June 1989 by the violent events at Tiananmen Square in China's capital, Beijing. Eight days before my confirmation hearings in the U.S. Senate, Chinese troops fired on unarmed pro-democracy demonstrators who had been protesting official corruption for several months. The violence was broadcast live and worldwide by CNN. Overnight our official dealings with China became a domestic political liability. In an effort to sustain a policy dialogue with the Chinese leadership—now publicly denigrated as "the butchers of Beijing"—President Bush dispatched a secret mission to China in early July that, when revealed at the end of the year, ignited a domestic firestorm of criticism of our dealings with the Chinese.

Ironically, Tiananmen and the worldwide criticism of the Chinese leadership that it evoked heightened Chinese sensitivities about their continuing support for the ruthless Khmer Rouge, and probably increased Beijing's interest in a political settlement of the Cambodia conflict in a way that would distance China from Pol Pot and his movement. But China's strategic objective remained consonant with that of the United States: to prevent Vietnam from establishing hegemony over all of Indochina.[12]

This contradictory mix of public criticism of China and private diplomatic cooperation made for complex relations between the State Department and the American public and Congress. In the months following Tiananmen we collaborated diplomatically with the Chinese in an effort to replace the Hun Sen government with a UN-backed transitional authority headed by Prince Sihanouk committed to establishing a democratic government in Cambodia, yet we were attacked in Congress and in public for supporting China's strategy of undermining Vietnam's client government in Phnom Penh by building up a resistance coalition that included the dreaded Khmer Rouge.

Our diplomatic objective, in fact, was a settlement process that would lead the Chinese to terminate their military assistance to Pol Pot and to control the Khmer Rouge with a substantial UN presence in Cambodia. In terms of domestic American politics, however, it was not clear that the administration could accommodate Beijing's political requirements of including the Khmer Rouge in a transitional Cambodian leadership or give Khmer Rouge leaders the opportunity to run for office in the UN-supervised elections. For the Bush administration, squaring this circle was to be the most politically contentious and risk-laden aspect of constructing a peace process.

## PROGRESS AT PARIS

The American delegation to the Paris Conference on Cambodia departed Washington on July 28, 1989, under the leadership of Secretary of State James A. Baker III. On the plane to Paris, Baker briefed the press on U.S. objectives in supporting the French-Indonesian initiative. He said that the administration's goal, in support of ASEAN and the CGDK, was to achieve a comprehensive settlement with five elements: immediate cease-fire and eventual end to all foreign military assistance to the Khmer factions; formation of an interim administration headed by Prince Sihanouk; establishment of a process leading to an internationally supervised election of a new constitutional government; voluntary return to Cambodia of the substantial Khmer refugee population in Thailand; and an international control mechanism for implementing a settlement process, "which we think ought to be a United Nations monitoring force."

In Paris, the Vietnamese delegation, headed by Nguyen Co Thach, senior diplomat and foreign minister, pressed for a partial settlement with the argument that including the Pol Pot faction in a political process risked legitimating and returning to power genocidal murderers. Thach sought to strengthen the rationale for his position by asserting that only the Hun Sen government, intact, had the power to prevent the Khmer Rouge from fighting its way back to power. This argument found little resonance among the conference participants, who generally supported the view that the best way to constrain the Khmer Rouge was to give it some stake in a political process subject to international supervision. This rationale, however, did elicit certain support in the United States and in a few other countries—substantially complicating the administration's task of building domestic political backing for a UN settlement plan that involved a limited and constrained form of inclusion of the Khmer Rouge.

After Baker and most of the other ministers departed the Paris opening, the conference broke into five technical working groups: one to work out the mandate for an international control mechanism to oversee a settlement process (chaired by Canada and India); a second to guarantee Cambodia's sovereignty while committing all parties to the settlement to support its implementation (headed by Laos and Malaysia); a third, chaired by Australia and Japan, to consider the issues of repatriating the more than three hundred fifty thousand Khmer refugees in Thailand and reconstructing the country. The fourth group, an ad hoc committee composed of the four Cambodian political factions, was chaired by France and Indonesia. Its mandate was to focus on the most difficult issue of constructing an interim Khmer political authority, involving the four factions under Prince Sihanouk's leadership, which would oversee internationally supervised elections during the transition to a new government. A fifth working group, termed the "coordinating committee" and also cochaired by France and Indonesia, took responsibility for drafting a final conference document for consideration at a concluding ministerial session.[13]

These groups labored on at the Kleber Conference Center through much of August, enjoying elegant French cuisine and making significant progress on all the assigned issues except the key "internal" matter of a power-sharing arrangement among the Khmer factions. Hun Sen's delegation, backed by the Vietnamese, resisted any arrangement that would include Pol Pot's Khmer Rouge or weaken the standing of the State of Cambodia government in Phnom Penh. The Khmer Rouge delegates, on the other hand, resisted characterization of Khmer Rouge policies and practices during their rule in the 1970s as constituting a "genocide." They stressed the need for a four-party coalition governing authority under Prince Sihanouk's leadership as the only way to restore Cambodia's sovereignty after a decade of "colonial" rule by Vietnam's surrogate regime under Hun Sen—a situation that they said would be sustained after the withdrawal of Vietnam's troops because of the presence of more than a million ethnic Vietnamese "settlers" in the country. By August 20 it was clear to the French that their conference was headed for a deadlock on the "internal" issue of a power-sharing arrangement among the fractious Khmer.

French foreign minister Roland Dumas, who along with Indonesia's Ali Alatas chaired the concluding session, challenged the delegates to muster the political will to resolve five major issues crystallized by the conference: the role of the United Nations, if any, in a settlement; how to organize and control a cease-fire of the Khmer combatants; how to deal with the issue of Pol Pot's genocide—its past and possible resumption; the matter of the Vietnamese "foreign settlers" in Cambodia; and how to create a process of national reconciliation among the four Khmer factions. Rather than declare failure, the French and Indonesian organizers "suspended" the monthlong session. "It is not yet possible to achieve a comprehensive settlement," noted the final conference communiqué. The cochairs urged all the conference participants to intensify their efforts to reach a settlement, declaring that they would begin consultations within six months with a view to reconvening the conference in Paris.

In fact, efforts were already under way to pursue other routes to a settlement. Prime Minister Chatichai Choonhavan of Thailand was preparing to initiate from Bangkok an effort at "shuttle diplomacy" between the four Khmer factions designed, as a first step, to achieve a cease-fire.[14] (Chatichai's effort, as it unfolded, was to split his government and fail in its purpose.) Prince Sihanouk, alienated by French pressures to side with Hun Sen, was also looking for a solution based on regional diplomacy. Rather than return to the Paris Conference, the prince was talking to the Thai about a new round of talks based in either Bangkok or Phuket involving the UN Security Council's five permanent members, the six ASEAN states, Laos, Vietnam, and the four Khmer factions. As well, Indonesian foreign minister Alatas, leader of ASEAN's initiatives on Cambodia, the Japanese, and the Australians were each beginning to conceptualize their own follow-on diplomatic efforts. Meanwhile, on the ground in Cambodia, the Khmer Rouge and Hun Sen's State of Cambodia were launching new tests of military strength.

## THE UNITED STATES INITIATES A UN-CENTERED EFFORT

After I returned from Paris at the end of August, I instructed the experts in our delegation to prepare a strategy for building on the results of the Paris Conference through a UN-centered initiative. The Paris Conference had had an ambiguous outcome regarding a role for the United Nations in a settlement process; some proposed it, a few opposed it. The idea of a settlement with significant UN involvement had been floating around for some time. In April 1989, U.S. congressman Stephen J. Solarz had had a long discussion with Sihanouk's son, Prince Norodom Ranariddh, at the

FUNCINPEC refugee camp—"Site B"—along the Thai-Cambodian border about approaches to achieving an end to his country's travail. Solarz had raised the possibility of establishing a UN trusteeship over Cambodia as a way of working around the inability of the Khmer factions to establish a process of national reconciliation.[15]

By the time the General Assembly convened for its annual session at the end of September, we had prepared the secretary of state to launch his second key intervention in the increasingly roiled waters of Cambodian peace diplomacy. On September 29, 1989, Secretary Baker informed the ministers that in view of the "suspension" of the Paris Conference, he believed the time had come for the UN Security Council to "lay its hands" on the Cambodia issue so as to prevent "the dialogue of diplomacy from being replaced by the dialogue of the battlefield." The next three months saw planning advance within the State Department for a Cambodian peace process premised on "an enhanced role for the United Nations."

The policy judgments that shaped the U.S. role in the ensuing diplomacy are important to detail, for they became the focus of intense domestic political attack and some international challenge (as will be described later). Based on the experience of the Paris Conference and the previous decade of diplomacy, we had come to the conclusion that the most promising approach to achieving the goals expressed by Secretary of State Baker was through a major role for the United Nations in a transition to elections—in controlling or dismantling the factional military forces, administering the institutions of civil authority, organizing elections, and dealing with reconstruction issues such as the repatriation of Khmer refugees in Thailand, promoting economic development, and protecting the human rights of the population.

The United Nations, moreover, was viewed as an institution that would "internationalize" the diplomacy of a settlement. The Bush administration was well aware of the lingering burden of the Vietnam War in American politics and was determined to avoid a settlement process that would seem to make Cambodia—again—an American problem. As well, the United Nations could muster international financial resources in support of a settlement, at a time when U.S. post–Cold War foreign affairs budgets were contracting. We also believed that the leadership of Prince Sihanouk—however "mercurial"—was essential to constructing such a settlement.[16]

There was, however, an alternative approach—one advocated primarily by the Vietnamese and the Hun Sen regime—that asserted that such a UN role was a fundamental violation of Cambodia's sovereignty and that preservation of the government and military capabilities of the State of

Cambodia was the only way to prevent the Khmer Rouge from fighting its way back to power. This perspective, or elements of it, found some international support, and it had a number of passionate proponents in the United States.

Our critique of the Vietnamese–Hun Sen approach was based on the judgment that to build a settlement around Hun Sen and his political-governmental structure would only have further polarized Cambodia's politics and sustained the fighting. It would have failed to draw on Prince Sihanouk's symbolic authority (as we had every reason to believe he could not be induced to switch sides and ally himself with Hun Sen) as the one Khmer leader with true legitimacy and national standing. And it would have played to the political and military strengths of the Khmer Rouge at a time when no one was interested in or capable of mounting effective military operations against their border strongholds. China and Thailand, we assumed, would not tolerate consolidation of a Vietnamese surrogate regime in Phnom Penh. They would continue to give political support and armaments to the Khmer Rouge, and the fighting would continue—playing out the conflict in a way that would magnify the strengths of the Khmer Rouge as seasoned guerrilla fighters.

The best alternative, we believed, was to create a relatively neutral, internationally supervised political environment in Phnom Penh and to tolerate the Khmer Rouge's inclusion *in a limited and controlled way* in a UN-managed settlement process. This approach would control the hated Pol Pot regime through a UN peacekeeping presence and subject the regime's political legitimacy to the test of Cambodian public opinion. We could not imagine that the Khmer Rouge would prevail in a reasonably fair political contest; and by drawing on the authority and resources of the United Nations, we would enable—or pressure—China and Thailand to end their support of the Khmer Rouge.

Although this policy was hardly risk free as a way of constraining and undermining the Pol Pot regime, it seemed to the Bush administration a far better bet than the certainty of backing Hun Sen in what would be an ongoing military conflict with the Khmer Rouge, who would have continuing Chinese and Thai support. These contrasting perspectives shaped the politics—both international and domestic—of the Cambodian peace process for the next two years.[17]

In October 1989 I met in New York with Thai officials, in part to assess the state of their efforts to broker a cease-fire among the Khmer factions; and in late November I traveled to Australia and was told by Foreign Minister Gareth Evans on November 23 that he was about to announce in the

Australian Senate a major initiative on Cambodia also centered on the United Nations. And at the turn of the year, Secretary Baker sent letters of invitation to all his counterparts on the Security Council urging them to join in an effort to see whether the UN Security Council's Perm Five could agree on the outlines of a settlement plan.

As events were to unfold in 1990, reaching agreement among the Perm Five was easy relative to the complex processes of maintaining support from other interested international parties—especially Japan and Thailand—and, above all, developing domestic political backing for a UN-centered initiative.

## BUILDING A SECURITY COUNCIL CONSENSUS

The first of six Perm Five meetings convened in Paris on January 16–17, 1990, at the Hotel de Crillon.[18] After several hours of reviewing the results of the previous summer's Paris Conference, the U.S. delegation retired to the American embassy on Place de la Concorde with British counterparts in an effort to draft a set of basic principles by which to structure the work of the five.

To our surprise, the second day's plenary discussion revealed unanimous support for sixteen propositions we had drafted the previous evening.[19] (Only the noncontroversial addition of one point—that the Perm Five would support responsible efforts by regional parties to achieve a comprehensive settlement—capped the list.) The meeting established the agenda for what would be the next seven months of work. Beginning with the proposition that a military outcome was unacceptable, the Perm Five agreed that a political settlement required an "enhanced United Nations role." The document reaffirmed that the settlement had to be comprehensive; that the withdrawal of Vietnam's military forces from Cambodia had to be subject to UN verification; that the Khmer refugees in Thailand should return home in conditions of security; that the human rights of the population should be protected (which in this instance meant protection against a return to the violent rule of the Khmer Rouge); and that the United Nations should substantially manage a "free and fair" electoral process that would form a new government. Recognizing that such a UN-managed transition to election of a new government was a substantial invasion of Cambodia's sovereignty, the five looked to the formation of an ill-defined political body, tentatively called a Supreme National Council, as the "repository" of Cambodia's sovereignty during the transition to a new, popularly elected government.

Publication of the outline elicited relief from many quarters, for it had not been clear following suspension of the Paris Conference that there was any life left in the international effort to bring peace to Cambodia. Yet the January document did little more than identify the critical issues that had to be explored in detail in designing an operational plan for a settlement. How would security in the country be maintained in conditions where the Khmer political factions continued to test their strength on the battlefield? Would the United Nations even enter the country in the absence of a cease-fire among the factional armies, and what would happen to those armies? How to repatriate the hundreds of thousands of Khmer refugees who had been encamped in Thailand on Cambodia's western border for more than a decade? How to protect the human rights of a population that for more than a decade had been ravaged by genocidal violence, social revolution, and warfare? Who would run the government pending elections? And who would pay the substantial costs of the UN settlement process? To advance consideration of these issues, the Perm Five scheduled a second round of consultations for New York on February 11, 1990.

The second session was shaped by three intersecting layers of politics and diplomacy and shifts in the military balance. In Cambodia, the resistance forces of Sihanouk, Son Sann, and the Khmer Rouge were gaining some ground from Hun Sen's troops, putting significant pressure on Hun Sen and the Vietnamese for some form of settlement that would weaken outside support for the resistance coalition. Despite the military action, the possibility of a political settlement involving a major UN role seemed real enough that Secretary-General Javier Pérez de Cuéllar and his special representative for Cambodia, Rafeeuddin Ahmed, briefed the U.S. delegation before the second Perm Five meeting on the full range of issues that would have to be addressed if the United Nations were to manage a settlement process. Perm Five discussion of the settlement issues, in turn, was shaped by persisting differences between China (representing the interests of the Khmer Rouge as well as its own) on the one hand, and the Soviet Union (speaking for the Vietnamese and Hun Sen) on the other hand, about the balance of influence that would likely emerge from a political settlement.

The February meeting, and those of March, May, and July, elaborated on three core aspects of a settlement: how to end the fighting and control the factions' military units; how to account for Cambodia's sovereignty during the transition to election of a new government; and how to administer the country. The five readily agreed that to stabilize a cease-fire, the contending military forces should be put under UN control in cantonments where they would be disarmed and eventually reorganized into a new national army under the authority of the Cambodian government that would emerge from the elections. (Getting the Khmer factions to agree to this process, or some variant of it, however, would be the focus of another year of diplomacy and political maneuvering.)

The issue of how to constitute the Supreme National Council embodied the highly contentious issue of whether to include in a settlement *at all* the feared Khmer Rouge—in the process giving it a measure of legitimacy and an opportunity to regain power though the UN-managed political process. The Chinese made clear that they would not support a UN settlement from which the Khmer Rouge was fully excluded. For the Bush administration, this was the central political issue that was likely to undermine congressional support for a UN—or any other—settlement plan. The issue was ultimately resolved for the Perm Five at the July session by agreeing that the Supreme National Council should be composed of "*individuals* representing the full range of Cambodian public opinion" (italics mine), and by depriving the body of any operational authority.

By thus eliding the membership issue, and by creating a mechanism of only symbolic weight, we avoided recognizing the Khmer Rouge *as an organization*, even though Khieu Samphan, the Khmer Rouge's foreign minister, as an individual would represent the forces of Pol Pot as one of the guardians of Cambodia's sovereign rights. This arrangement, we estimated, gave the Chinese sufficient political leverage to "deliver" their hated client to the settlement; yet it so constrained the Khmer Rouge within the UN-managed process that it would substantially diminish their chances of regaining power.

The question of how to administer the country during the transition to elections reflected the same issues of sovereignty and political control that burdened discussion of the Supreme National Council; yet it had the immediate reality of how to deal with the existing governmental structure of Hun Sen's State of Cambodia. At the March meeting the Perm Five agreed that the United Nations should form a "transitional authority" as the vehicle for international supervision of the settlement process, but the scope of this international authority was a matter of substantial contention. The Chinese initially pressed for complete dismantlement of Hun Sen's government, while the Soviets called for a minimal UN oversight role in both the transitional administration and the election process. By July, however, the Chinese—for reasons not evident at the time—had decided to support the UN settlement process. This enabled the Perm Five to reach agreement that UNTAC should be mandated to assume "supervision or control of the existing administrative structures."

The British and U.S. delegations pressed the issue of protecting the human rights of the Khmer people as an oblique approach to dealing with the threat of Pol Pot's return. The Soviets, mirroring Thach's use of the "geno-cide" issue, initially pressed for explicit reference to the need for measures to control Pol Pot. By the March meeting, however, they dropped their use of the term "genocide"—which would invariably elicit a counter from the Chinese—and agreed to the indirect formulation developed at the Paris Conference of the need to "undertake effective measures to ensure that the policies and practices of the past shall never be allowed to return." These included agreement at the May meeting that the United Nations should formally monitor and protect the human rights of the Cambodian people as part of the settlement process.

The matter of controlling the factional military forces was to be the most contentious of the settlement issues—and it was not resolved until the eve of final agreement on the settlement plan in August 1991. The initial Perm Five discussions were divided along predictable lines, with the Soviets supporting the Vietnamese in their determination that Hun Sen's forces should remain intact. Only gradually did agreement develop on a program of ending foreign military assistance to the factional armies, plac-ing them in cantonments and disarming and retraining the troops. There was no agreement on the size of a UN peacekeeping presence, and whether it should just monitor the departure of the Vietnamese forces and supervise the return of the refugees or play a major role in disarming and reorganiz-ing the factions. (Ultimately, the United Nations deployed an international peacekeeping force of 16,000—supported by 5,000 civilian administrative personnel—for eighteen months.)

It was at this point of substantial progress in the Perm Five discussions that Secretary Baker made his third critical intervention affecting the dy-namic of the mediation effort. During the fall of 1989 and into the spring of 1990, domestic political pressure had been building in the United States against *any* agreement that would seem to legitimate the Khmer Rouge by including its leadership in a settlement plan—much less increase the party's chance of returning to power by some combination of military and political maneuvering. As I will detail later, I faced unrelenting criticism on this issue in congressional hearings, and even certain American mass media outlets were trying to make the case that the administration's Cambodia activities were strengthening, indirectly if not directly, covertly if not openly, Pol Pot's military forces.

In early July a bipartisan group of sixty-six senators led by Democrat George Mitchell of Maine and Republican John Danforth of Missouri sent Secretary Baker a letter urging the administration to withdraw its support for the Sihanouk–Khmer Rouge political coalition, the CGDK, still occupying Cambodia's seat at the United Nations. The letter debunked the notion that a political settlement would lead to China withdrawing its support for the Khmer Rouge ("China is the problem, not the solution in Cambodia . . .") and urged that U.S. policy "should be based, first and foremost, upon preventing the return to power of the Khmer Rouge." Although not explicitly calling for a settlement based on support for Hun Sen's State of Cambodia, the senators asserted that it was "counterproductive for the United States to decline all contact with the Hun Sen regime." They called for easing restrictions on humanitarian and development aid for (Hun Sen's) Cambodia. The implicit warning behind this letter was that if the administration did not shift its approach to a Cambodian settlement away from Sihanouk's coalition, Congress would cut off all financial support for the noncommunist resistance.[20]

The sum of these pressures impelled an adjustment in our Cambodia policy. The alternative was to have Congress impose a set of restrictions or conditions that would tie the administration's hands as a negotiating party, likely producing a collapse of the delicately balanced house of cards that we were constructing through the Perm Five consultations. We were in a race between the growth of domestic political forces determined to oppose any deal involving the Khmer Rouge, no matter what the alternative, and the conclusion of a Perm Five–Security Council consensus on a UN-centered process. In a manner not anticipated at the time, the secretary of state took an initiative that helped precipitate a successful endgame of the Perm Five consultations.

On July 18, as we were concluding the fifth Perm Five session in Paris, Secretary Baker was meeting in the same city with his Soviet counterpart, Foreign Minister Eduard Shevardnadze. Emerging from the ministerial discussions, the secretary announced to the press that the United States was withdrawing its support for the CGDK—Prince Sihanouk's diplomatic coalition with the Khmer Rouge—as the legitimate incumbent in Cambodia's UN seat. Baker added that, in the search for peace in Cambodia, the United States would initiate consultations with the Vietnamese government and was even considering contacts with Hun Sen.

I had presaged this development with the Chinese a few days earlier by showing them the letter from the sixty-six senators to the secretary of state as evidence of the intense domestic political pressures on our policy; and the secretary had informed Shevardnadze of this shift in our position just minutes before meeting with the press. In its effect, this defensive tactical move was a political bombshell for all those involved in the negotiations. It implied that the United States had switched sides and was now tilting toward

Vietnam in the search for peace in Cambodia, and that the administration was closely coordinating policy with the Soviet Union.

The Chinese responded to the secretary's announcement by publicly expressing strong "disappointment" with the development. Privately they told us that the shift had caused "confusion" in their leadership about our policies. (Yet behind the scenes, and largely unknown to us at the time, Beijing was in the process of shifting its own policy toward Vietnam.) The concern of the Chinese, as with the even sharper public criticism of the move from Indonesian foreign minister Alatas, was that by thus opening toward Hanoi we would stiffen the resistance of the Vietnamese and Hun Sen to the nearly fully formed UN settlement process.

In fact, as events were to confirm, the secretary of state's move put China under heightened pressure to come to closure in the Perm Five consultations so as to keep the Khmer Rouge on track to a political (as opposed to a military) settlement. And we had given the Vietnamese, increasingly isolated as the communist world began to collapse in Eastern Europe and then in the Soviet Union, an opening to improve relations with the United States—which we told them was contingent upon their support for a UN-managed settlement.[21]

The sixth Perm Five session convened in New York five weeks after the Baker announcement, and the final elements of a consensus settlement framework quickly fell into place. The United Nations, through UNTAC, would take control of Cambodia's key governmental functions during the transition to elections. The refugees on Thailand's border with Cambodia would be repatriated under UN supervision, and the United Nations would verify the departure of all Vietnamese forces from the country. Cambodia's sovereignty would be "embodied" in a Supreme National Council composed of individuals, but the body would have no operational authority pending UN-supervised elections. The Khmer military forces would be placed in cantonments and disarmed pending their reorganization into a new national army. And the international community would take measures through the United Nations to safeguard the human rights of the Cambodian people.

On August 28, the five permanent members of the Security Council publicly announced their agreement on this framework for a UN-centered, comprehensive political settlement of the Cambodia conflict. Reaching this point reflected the significant degree of international consensus on the elements of a settlement process that had emerged over a decade of diplomacy, especially through the JIM and Paris Conference efforts. It also was an expression of the degree to which great power relations were changing as the Cold War approached its end. Yet getting this far had required complex, multilayered diplomacy affecting the interests of a number of states that were not permanent members of the Security Council—and it was to continue to do so. Following through on the Perm Five framework agreement was to take more than an additional year of intense diplomacy to bring the four Khmer factions to accept it. And concurrent with the UN-centered effort, other interested countries were exploring alternative paths to a settlement.

## HERDING CATS

The complexity of the Cambodia mediation effort reflected the diverse national interests of more than a dozen states involved in the diplomacy, as well as the separate interests of the four Khmer political factions and a number of individual political figures from various countries who played leadership roles. The desire of different mediators to assume leading positions, and to take credit for any successes, fosters a competitive and self-interested aspect to the diplomacy of peacemaking that can undermine the coherence of efforts needed to achieve success.

One of the remarkable aspects of the ultimately successful Cambodia settlement was that it substantially reconciled such diverse if not divergent interests. Yet reaching consensus on the UN plan required more than two years of intense diplomacy, even though the basic elements of a settlement had been defined at the Paris Conference in the summer of 1989.

Once the Paris Conference had been "suspended," it was not clear that such a consensus would "congeal." Beginning in the fall of 1989, a number of divergent efforts were initiated that tried to build on the political momentum established in Paris. We have already reviewed the efforts of the five permanent members of the UN Security Council that began in the fall of 1989. Concurrent with this activity, Australia, Indonesia, Japan, and Thailand also initiated efforts to create a settlement either on a regional basis or through the United Nations. And behind the scenes China, the Soviet Union, and Vietnam were pursuing bilateral diplomacy designed to deal with their political/military confrontations that were only partly related to the Cambodia conflict.

These varied activities created a certain air of confusion, if not competition, as different political leaders advanced alternative approaches to reaching a settlement. What is remarkable about the diplomacy of 1990–91 is that ultimately these varied efforts became mutually reinforcing. Yet for diplomats operating in an atmosphere of uncertainty and rivalry, the challenge was to build consensus with apparently competitive governments—a process that at times had the character of herding cats. The ultimately successful outcome, in retrospect, reflected the political weight of the UN Security Council and the consensus of the five major powers that either subsumed or overrode these other efforts. Moreover, the Chinese, Soviet, and Vietnamese agreement, reached in the summer of 1991, to support the Perm Five plan put ineluctable pressure on the most recalcitrant of the Khmer parties—Hun Sen's Cambodian People's Party and Pol Pot's Khmer Rouge—to go along with the UN settlement process.

\* \* \*

As noted at the outset, the Bush administration's early approach to the diplomacy of a Cambodia settlement had been to let ASEAN and France take the lead. With success in building the Perm Five framework agreement, however, the United States acquired a certain measure of paternity and vested interest in the semiformed UN settlement plan. As of the early fall of 1990, we entered a period of nearly a year's effort to broaden support for the framework agreement within the international community and to encourage the countries supporting the various Khmer factions to "deliver" their surrogates to the UN-centered process. This proved to be a challenging but by no means impossible task, for as the Perm Five effort advanced it acquired a momentum and authority that proved difficult for those governments with other ideas and other interests either to resist or to subvert. My instructions from Under Secretary of State Robert Kimmit were to work along with these other initiatives, but also to protect our investment in the advancing Security Council effort.

One alternative approach was promoted by the government of Chatichai Choonhavan in Thailand. Prime Minister Chatichai had been voted into office in mid-1988 to form the first civilian Thai government in a decade. Early in his tenure he had promoted a policy of transforming Indochina "from a battlefield into a marketplace." In this effort he had the support of two trusted civilian special advisers—his son, Kraisak Choonhavan, and Kraisak's colleague, Pansak Vinyaratin. The two were an irrepressible duo who came to be dubbed, with some affection, the "Bobsy twins" of Cambodia diplomacy as with enthusiasm they embarked on a diplomatic effort centered around trying to form a Cambodian government based on a Hun Sen–Sihanouk coalition.

In late April 1989 the Thai government hosted a "seminar" of senior officials from all the Indochina states to build support for their plan, which they promoted with the vision of transforming all of Southeast Asia into a "Golden Peninsula."[22] Their approach, however enticing, was to succumb to four fatal flaws: It implicitly pitted capitalist Thailand allied to the United States against socialist Vietnam allied to the Soviet Union, and the Vietnamese were not (yet) prepared to cede leadership in the region to a long-time strategic and ideological rival. It would require Sihanouk to abandon his CGDK allies and side with Hun Sen, and Thailand to break with the ASEAN consensus on Cambodia policy. It also required domestic political support, when in fact the policy was splitting the Chatichai administration from the Thai military (which was determined to resist Vietnamese influence in Cambodia through support for the Khmer Rouge) and from the Foreign Ministry, which was committed to sustaining close relations with ASEAN and the United States.

After suspension of the Paris Conference, however, Chatichai saw an opening for a diplomatic initiative. On September 11, he announced that he would try to broker a cease-fire among the Khmer factions before the Vietnamese withdrew their troops at the end of the month.[23] His objective required a kind of shuttle diplomacy from Bangkok involving the factions, as well as a direct appeal to the Chinese for support—in order to get Sihanouk to move away from his coalition with the Khmer Rouge. This effort fizzled as the factions resisted a cease-fire. The Khmer Rouge took a major battlefield initiative in late October that led to its capture of the gem-mining town of Pailin—only a few miles from Thailand's eastern border with Cambodia.[24]

Chatichai's activist advisers were not deterred by this setback. In the spring of 1990 they responded to an approach from the director of the First Southeast Asia Division of the Japanese Foreign Ministry, Masaharu Kohno, who asked them to join forces in a further effort to entice Prince Sihanouk into a coalition with Hun Sen—in part with the appeal of Japanese economic support for Cambodia's reconstruction. They also calculated, with some justification, that the growing success of the Khmer Rouge on the battlefield might now interest Sihanouk in "tilting" toward Hun Sen—perhaps as a way of getting the Chinese to impose constraints on their brutal Khmer client. As well, the Thai advisers (and we ourselves) were not sure at this point that the Perm Five consultations, still in midcourse, would succeed in reaching a consensus. They pressed ahead for a regional settlement.

To work with the Thai, I agreed to their proposal that I meet secretly with the prime minister's advisers to coordinate policy before a Hun Sen–Sihanouk summit meeting that they were planning with the Japanese for early June.[25] The objective of the advisers was to gain American support for their regional approach; mine was to convince them of the value of the Perm Five process and to keep lines open to an initiative by two allied governments. The Bush administration's risk in agreeing to the secret meeting—in the ever-conspiratorial world of Asian politics—was that as word of the encounter leaked out we would sow distrust or confusion among our ASEAN colleagues, or even weaken the growing Perm Five consensus. Despite these liabilities, I traveled unannounced to Rome in late May for a day of talks with Pansak Vinyaratin. We each made our case, and on June 4 Prince Sihanouk met with Hun Sen in Tokyo at the Japanese-hosted summit.

The Thai-Japanese effort initially seemed to succeed, for the Tokyo summit ended with the announcement of a cease-fire among the factions and an agreement of the two delegations (Sihanouk and Hun Sen) to join a reconvened Paris Conference to finalize a settlement on a "two governments" basis. Yet key issues remained unresolved. Kraisak Choonhavan, who came to Washington with his father in mid-June for a meeting with President Bush shortly after the Tokyo summit, informed me that Hun Sen had not accepted an "enhanced role" for the United Nations in a settlement. He also said that Sihanouk had left Tokyo unclear about how he would deal with the Khmer Rouge—which had boycotted the Tokyo session—in the subsequent "two governments" negotiation that the French, Japanese, and Thai were planning for Paris. "Let Sihanouk figure out how to deal with the KR [Khmer Rouge]," Kraisak told me dismissively.

During his Washington visit, Prime Minister Chatichai informed President Bush that he foresaw the cease-fire leading to elections monitored by some (unspecified) form of international control mechanism and the formation of a coalition government along the Thai model of a constitutional monarchy. Under such an arrangement Sihanouk would be largely a symbolic figure, with political and administrative power in the hands of a prime minister—Hun Sen. Chatichai seemed confident that China would deliver the Khmer Rouge to such an arrangement.

Within two months, however, the Thai-Japanese initiative collapsed. Following the Tokyo summit, Sihanouk returned to his residence in Beijing and apparently encountered intense pressure from the Khmer Rouge and the Chinese to repudiate the Tokyo agreement. He did so publicly on September 4 (just a week after publication of the Perm Five framework agreement), calling instead for an interim administration of Cambodia structured with equal representation from all four Khmer factions. At the turn of the year Chatichai's government was deposed by the Thai military on charges of corruption. The activist advisers, Kraisak and Pansak, were now out of the Cambodia negotiations; and the successor military government in Bangkok returned to support the ASEAN consensus on Cambodia and the now-advancing UN settlement process.

So, too, did the Japanese, although the Foreign Ministry continued to chafe at Japan's peripheral role in the negotiations. As one Japanese official confided to me, "We want to be in the huddle, not on the sidelines, especially if you expect us to pay for a major share of the settlement and Cambodia's reconstruction." The core issue behind Japan's second-rank status in the diplomacy was not U.S. resistance to Japan's playing a frontline role, but the fact that Japan was not a permanent member of the UN Security Council. We made assiduous efforts to brief our Japanese counterparts before and after each Perm Five session—they would send special delegations to either Paris or New York for prompt and direct readouts—as we did as well with the ASEAN countries and Australia. But this consultative approach was insufficient for governments with serious interests in the outcome of the process, especially those facing considerable domestic political pressure to be significant players, to be doing something about the issue.

The need to be doing something, to play a role in shaping the settlement, applied as much as anyone to the Australians. The Hawke government, with its activist and articulate foreign minister, Senator Gareth Evans, in the lead, was trying to shape Australia's Asian environment in anticipation of the end of the Cold War. And like the Bush administration, the Hawke government was under considerable pressure, from Parliament, to shape a Cambodian settlement in a way that would prevent the Khmer Rouge from regaining power. The Australians play their politics much like they play rugby—with rough-and-tumble scrums and a good deal of open-field running. This was much the style of our relationship with the government in Canberra as the Cambodia negotiations advanced.[26]

As noted earlier, in the fall of 1989—as we were laying the groundwork for the secretary of state to launch the Perm Five effort—Senator Evans's ministry was preparing what came to be called the "Red Book," a comprehensive assessment of the elements of a UN-administered settlement of the Cambodian conflict.[27] In late December Evans dispatched his deputy, Michael Costello, on a tour of Asia to gain support for the Australian plan. Costello visited China and the relevant countries in Southeast Asia and met with the Khmer factions—including the Khmer Rouge. This effort proceeded in parallel with the beginnings of the Perm Five consultations in Paris and New York and—following publication of the first and second Perm Five joint communiqués expressing support for an "enhanced UN role" in a settlement—led to a new JIM meeting in Jakarta at the end of February.

Foreign Ministers Alatas of Indonesia and Evans of Australia succeeded in getting the four factions together, along with Vietnam's Thach and representatives of other regional states, in an effort to build support for the "enhanced UN" approach. While the Khmer factions verbally agreed to have the United Nations deploy a peacekeeping force and administer elections, the meeting collapsed when Thach raised the same issue of "genocide" that had deadlocked the Paris Conference. As well, Thach and Hun Sen opposed the establishment of a Supreme National Council headed by Sihanouk as the governing authority in the transition to elections (vice administration by Hun Sen's State of Cambodia).[28] Thach and Hun Sen were to continue to block progress toward a consensus among the Khmer factions for more than a year—even as Thach tried to cultivate a positive relationship with the United States.

The Australian initiative, which had codified much of the discussion of the Paris Conference, was unsuccessful, but it was important to demonstrating that there was substantial international support for a major UN role in the settlement. And as the Perm Five consensus grew, the Evans effort naturally merged with it. Behind Canberra's support for the UN-centered process, however, domestic Australian political tensions persisted over the question of the role of the Khmer Rouge in a settlement. This was the same issue that was polarizing U.S. domestic politics: a UN transitional authority for the Cambodian settlement that included an essentially powerless Supreme National Council involving individuals representing the Khmer Rouge versus the alternative of a settlement built around Hun Sen and his State of Cambodia.

Prior to initiation of the Perm Five process, Australia's ambassador to Bangkok, Richard Butler, had publicly attacked the Paris-ASEAN notion of a comprehensive settlement, instead supporting the position of Chatichai and his advisers that a more limited settlement should be constructed around Hun Sen. Butler was criticized by his government in Canberra for publicly challenging the ASEAN position, but other pro–Hun Sen forces in Australia continued to press for a settlement that would exclude the Khmer Rouge and preserve the integrity of the State of Cambodia.[29]

These pressures were evident in U.S.-Australian relations in the spring of 1990 as the Perm Five pressed ahead to design a Supreme National Council composed of Cambodian leaders that would somehow involve the Khmer Rouge. One night I received a call at home from Michael Costello, ostensibly to review our respective positions on the evolving UN settlement mechanism, and was startled when Costello warned me not to support a Supreme National Council that would include the Khmer Rouge and weaken the State of Cambodia. "We'll remember who brought back the Khmer Rouge," he threatened, "and one day there will be an accounting."

Costello's threat reflected the deepening political controversy around the evolving UN settlement plan. We felt such political pressures most intensely and immediately in our day-to-day efforts to build support in the United States for the Perm Five plan.

## DOMESTIC POLITICAL FURY

One of the distinguishing characteristics of U.S. foreign policy in the twentieth century has been the tension between the imperatives of realpolitik or balance-of-power politics on the one hand, and moral or human rights concerns on the other hand.[30] Since World War II and the Nazi holocaust, no issue has embodied these tensions more than that of mass political violence. Even though the United States, in practice, has at best a sluggish record in responding to situations of mass political murder—as most recently in Rwanda, Bosnia, and Kosovo—or in supporting the development of an international legal regime to cope with the aftermath of gross violations of human rights, genocide is a powerful symbol in our domestic foreign policy debates. This was certainly the case in managing the politics of a Cambodian settlement, where public revulsion at the Khmer Rouge's systematic murder of between 1 and 2 million Cambodians between 1975 and 1978 dominated much of the U.S. public's consideration of the settlement process.

This aspect of our domestic political debate was given immediacy and political force by the American public's outrage at the Chinese government's violent suppression of peaceful demonstrators at Tiananmen in early June of 1989—just as we were preparing for the Paris Conference. The Bush administration, headed by a president who had developed close relations with the Chinese from his days as chief of the U.S. Liaison Office in Beijing, came under persistent domestic political attack for what were characterized as insufficient efforts to censure the Chinese, for seeking to maintain the U.S.-China relationship, for "coddling dictators." During the Cambodia negotiations, the administration was criticized for working with the Chinese to counter Vietnamese influence in Indochina—at the cost of ignoring the threat of the Khmer Rouge. This public attack had potency in the context of our domestic political cycle, given the approaching 1990 midterm elections and, two years further down the road, the 1992 presidential contest.

As the Vietnamese moved to withdraw their forces from Cambodia in 1988 and 1989, informed American observers urged the Bush administration to pressure the Chinese to cut off arms shipments to the Khmer Rouge (which we had been doing—repeatedly—through diplomatic channels)[31] and to prevent the inclusion of the Khmer Rouge in any governing authority in Cambodia.[32] A few public figures went so far as to say that the Khmer Rouge danger was so great that the United States should break with Sihanouk and support Hun Sen, or at least press for a Hun Sen–Sihanouk coalition. Hun Sen's government, asserted a former director of the CIA, "is clearly preferable . . . to another Khmer Rouge government."[33]

This was an appealing position that might well have gained the administration's support after the Vietnamese withdrew their forces from Cambodia, but as a political strategy it had one fundamental deficiency: Sihanouk was dependent on Chinese support; and the Chinese would not back away from the Khmer Rouge as long as they saw Vietnam as a stalking-horse for Moscow's effort to encircle them and as long as the Vietnamese were determined to preserve their influence in Cambodia. Hence, as detailed earlier, we calculated that it was fruitless to press Sihanouk to break with his Khmer coalition partners, and the Chinese, in the absence of a comprehensive settlement. And for the United States to side with the Hun Sen government on its own would only have polarized Cambodian politics in circumstances in which the United States was unprepared to involve itself in an open-ended guerrilla war against the Khmer Rouge. But the moral imperative of opposing genocidal murderers trapped the administration in an unsustainable political position at home: as long as we supported Sihanouk, we seemed to be supporting—or at least not actively opposing—the Khmer Rouge.

This moral and political dilemma was dramatically exposed during my first congressional testimony on Cambodia policy on September 14, 1989— a little more than two weeks after suspension of the Paris Conference. In three hours of intense and emotional review of the outcome of the conference, the Bush administration was roundly criticized by representatives from both sides of the political aisle for going along with the Sihanouk-ASEAN position that the transitional authority in Cambodia should be a quadripartite governing body including the Khmer Rouge.

Our counterargument—that this approach was advocated by our allies in the region as the best way to move the conflict from the battlefield to the ballot box—gained few supporters. Republican congressman Jim Leach of Iowa, noting that by our own admission the administration had not taken the lead at Paris, urged that we at least take the moral high ground and distance the United States as far as possible from the Khmer Rouge and its Chinese supporters. Democratic congressman Chester Atkins of Massachusetts—from the state's Fifth Congressional District, which contains a sizable Khmer community—said he was "angry as hell" because the U.S.

delegation, according to his information, had remained silent on the issue of preventing genocide (which was not the case). Atkins implied that the administration should withdraw its support from Sihanouk and the noncommunist resistance and "take a fresh and more reasoned assessment of the successes of the Hun Sen government."[34]

To accommodate this criticism, of course, would have required accepting the Vietnamese–Hun Sen position as it had been put forward at Paris. But to do so would have meant abandoning prospects for constructing a political process that would break Chinese military support for the Khmer Rouge, controlling it with a UN peacekeeping force, and creating a new Cambodian government through internationally supervised elections.

Fortunately, the alternative of a UN-managed settlement, which we were in the process of designing, was a way to break out of this political trap. More important, it was the best way to deal with the real-world threat of the Khmer Rouge. The contentious congressional hearing in early September gave us every incentive to abandon our relatively passive diplomatic posture and take the initiative in a way that would give us greater influence in shaping the terms of a peace process. In the absence of any congressional (or administration) interest in a *unilateral* American effort to bring peace to Cambodia, which very likely would have required deploying U.S. forces to control the Khmer Rouge, the United Nations—through the Security Council—seemed to provide the best alternative to a workable way to attain our policy objectives, as Secretary Baker had expressed them on the way to the Paris Conference.

## THE PROVOCATIVE ROLE OF THE MEDIA

Our public debate, however, did not define the issue in these terms. Successive American administrations—under Presidents Carter, Reagan, and Bush—had encouraged the formation and growth of a noncommunist resistance as an alternative to a settlement that would be a choice between two communist factions—Pol Pot's "Democratic Kampuchea" or Hun Sen's "State of Cambodia." But this approach was weakened by Prince Sihanouk's anti–Hun Sen *political* coalition with the Khmer Rouge. In late April 1990 this situation was given national television prominence by ABC News, which aired a special program, "From the Killing Fields," hosted by anchorman Peter Jennings.[35] The program was constructed to expose the "fact" that American aid to Sihanouk was strengthening the Khmer Rouge and that the prince's forces and the Khmer Rouge were conducting joint military operations against Hun Sen's forces. Jennings sought to make his case around a provocative statement by Sihanouk that implied the United States was supporting Pol Pot's fighters because they were the most effective counter to Vietnam's occupying force in Cambodia. Jennings also took out of context a statement of mine that obliquely implied that U.S. aid for the noncommunist Khmer was getting to Pol Pot's forces—something that we had no evidence was occurring.

Fortunately Jennings's opening material in this special program was followed by a live discussion session that included informed and credible observers of the Cambodian scene such as Congressman Solarz, former assistant secretary of state Richard Holbrooke, and our ambassador to the United Nations, Thomas Pickering. Both Solarz and Pickering debunked the premise of the Jennings program. And although the objective of the program—to expose a presumed secret program of U.S. military assistance that was strengthening the Khmer Rouge—died, the issue persisted in the form of public and congressional attacks on Sihanouk's political coalition with the Khmer Rouge and on the administration's policy of supporting Sihanouk.[36]

A year later, on April 10, 1991—the eve of one of my last presentations before Congress—ABC News broadcast another provocative story on the Jennings nightly news program based on film purporting to show Sihanouk's military forces conducting a joint attack with the Khmer Rouge. Such evidence, if true, would be grounds for cutting off all American aid to Sihanouk and Son Sann. Fortunately, the evening broadcast was aired fifteen hours before my scheduled congressional testimony. Because of the time difference between Washington and Bangkok, we were able to confirm overnight from U.S. embassy sources that the filmed "evidence" was in fact a staged encounter between Sihanouk and Khmer Rouge units that ABC News had purchased from a freelance photographer operating out of Thailand. During my testimony the next day before the House Subcommittee on Asian and Pacific Affairs, I was able to undermine the credibility of the "evidence." But the timing of the ABC broadcast revealed the close coordination that had developed between congressional opponents of the administration's policy and at least one national news organization.[37]

This same congressional session included one of the last attacks on a key premise of our policy: that the UN settlement plan, whatever its limitations, was the best vehicle for preventing the Khmer Rouge from regaining power. House Chairman Solarz took the unusual step of inviting Congressman Atkins to testify at the hearing. Atkins, in an impassioned prepared presentation, asserted that the UN peace process made the United States party to a settlement that would legitimate the Khmer Rouge and help it regain power. He denigrated Sihanouk for working with the Chinese and their unholy agent, the Khmer Rouge, and urged an end to a policy of "isolating, punishing, and condemning" the Phnom Penh regime, which he asserted "has the only army protecting the Cambodian people from the Khmer Rouge." He urged "the immediate cessation of all aid to the noncommunist resistance," implied that the UN plan should be modified to exclude Khmer Rouge participation in the Supreme National Council, and called for the United States to increase its humanitarian aid to Hun Sen's government and support an international tribunal to bring to justice Pol Pot, Son Sen, and the other top Khmer Rouge leaders.

Chairman Solarz's response to Atkins's critique was a withering cross-examination of his congressional colleague that exposed the fact that there was no credible alternative to the UN plan for pursuing the objective of preventing the Khmer Rouge from regaining power. Solarz observed that Atkins's assessment of circumstances in Cambodia was "fundamentally incompatible with the realities of the situation." He noted that the Perm Five had abandoned the Paris Conference concept of a quadripartite transitional governing body composed of all the Khmer factions in favor of a UN-administered transition, with Cambodia's sovereignty represented in the essentially powerless Supreme National Council. Solarz asserted that the UN peace process would in fact undermine the Khmer Rouge by cutting off its support from China and Thailand, controlling it within an international peacekeeping operation, and exposing its lack of public support through supervised elections. Solarz's cross-examination also made evident that Atkins was unprepared to support the kinds of U.S. actions that, in the absence of the UN plan, would be needed to counter the Khmer Rouge: deployment of U.S. military forces to Cambodia or, at minimum, military assistance to Hun Sen's forces; a major aid program; and diplomatic recognition of the State of Cambodia.

The Solarz-Atkins exchange was mirrored by Senate attacks on the matter of possible battlefield cooperation between Prince Sihanouk's forces and the Khmer Rouge. These concerns sustained congressional pressure on the administration's policy for another six months, until the UN peace plan was formally ratified at the second session of the Paris Conference on Cambodia on October 23, 1991. The agreement finally enabled the noncommunist resistance to disassociate itself from the Khmer Rouge, which was now boxed in by the settlement process.[38] During the final Paris ministerial meeting, at which foreign minister Khieu Samphan signed the UN peace plan, Secretary Baker confronted the Khmer Rouge delegation and expressed American support for international efforts to ensure protection of the human rights of the Cambodian people and "bring to justice those responsible for the mass murders of the 1970s. . . ."[39]

## BUILDING CONSENSUS FOR THE UN SETTLEMENT PLAN IN CAMBODIA AND THE REGION

Building an *international* consensus for the UN plan, once published by the Perm Five in their framework agreement of August 1990, was relatively easy. The difficult part was getting the four Khmer factions to shift their conflict, as Secretary of State Baker liked to put it, "from the battlefield to the ballot box." In advancing this "internal" aspect of the UN plan, the United States played a secondary role, working through continuing Perm Five monitoring of negotiations with the four Khmer factions, which were managed largely by the cochairs of the Paris Conference, with Indonesian foreign minister Alatas in the lead. Between early September 1990 and September 1991, there were more than nine meetings involving the Khmer factions that intertwined the Perm Five consultations, the JIM process, and the Paris Conference leadership in an effort to define in operational terms how the Perm Five framework of August 1990 would be implemented.

Behind these consultations, indeed driving them, the major powers who had been supporting the Khmer combatants as an extension of their own rivalries—primarily China, the Soviet Union, and Vietnam—were conducting their own bilateral diplomacy. Sino-Soviet relations, as noted earlier, had taken a major turn for the better in the late 1980s with Moscow reducing its troop deployments along the Sino-Soviet frontier. In May 1989 Gorbachev traveled to Beijing to normalize relations, and this summit was followed by a series of ministerial and subministerial encounters that progressively reduced Moscow's support for both Vietnam and Cambodia and brought Soviet diplomacy regarding Indochina into line with the Perm Five process.[40]

The diplomatic activity involving the factions accelerated in early 1990, when the Indonesians, along with the French and the Australians, convened an informal meeting in Jakarta in late February in an effort to salvage the progress of the Paris Conference. The Khmer initially seemed to accept the idea of an enhanced UN role in a settlement, but provocative interventions by Vietnamese foreign minister Thach kept the discussion polarized. As the meeting collapsed, Gareth Evans expressed frustration at the squabbling factions, and Alatas, angered at Thach's disruptive proposals, concluded that the meeting had undercut any momentum remaining in the peace process.[41] Thach continued to play the spoiler role until a major leadership shake-up and policy realignment in Vietnam led senior political leaders to "retire" the veteran diplomat in June 1991, sixteen months later, when Sino-Vietnamese relations were well on the way to full normalization.

Despite the continuing resistance of Hun Sen and the Vietnamese to a settlement, the Perm Five consensus put all the Khmer factions under heightened pressure to accede to a UN-managed political process. In early September 1990, just two weeks after publication of the Perm Five framework agreement, Alatas convened another session in Jakarta, and the factions agreed to form a twelve-member Supreme National Council (SNC).[42] Sihanouk absented himself from the meeting, however, in order to gain leverage for his claim to be the thirteenth member and chairman of the SNC. The prince and Hun Sen continued to spar over the structure of the body for ten months, finally agreeing in early June 1991 to an arrangement with Sihanouk as president and Hun Sen as vice president.

Subsequent meetings of the SNC with representatives of the Perm Five, the JIM countries, and the Paris Conference were held in late September, November, and December 1990. The meetings narrowed disagreements over such operational aspects of the peace process as the mandate of the UN transitional authority, the UN role in repatriating the Khmer refugees along the Thai border, controlling the military forces, and designing the structure of an electoral system (a one- versus two-stage process, and voting on the basis of either a proportional system or territorial constituencies). Yet the interchanges never came to closure, with Hun Sen and the Vietnamese continuing to resist UNTAC arrangements that would weaken the authority and structure of the State of Cambodia.

The endgame of Sino-Vietnamese diplomacy affecting the Cambodia settlement came in the period July through September 1991, with the negotiations conducted by Xu Dunxin and his new Vietnamese counterpart, Nguyen Dy Nien, who replaced the intensely anti-Chinese Thach. As this activity advanced in the late summer of 1991, rumors began to circulate in the press and diplomatic channels that Beijing and Hanoi were cooking up a "Red solution" to the Cambodian conflict, one that would largely exclude the United Nations from a settlement in favor of a power-sharing arrangement between the Pol Pot and Hun Sen factions of the Khmer communist movement.[43]

In fact, Beijing remained committed to the Perm Five process. The Chinese hosted an SNC meeting in Beijing in mid-July that saw the creation of an SNC secretariat and the formation of a new Cambodian UN delegation—in anticipation of the fall meeting of the General Assembly. The delegation was headed by Prince Sihanouk and included representatives of the other political factions. A month later a full-dress SNC meeting was held in Pattaya, Thailand, with the Perm Five, the ASEAN states, Laos, and Vietnam in attendance. The meeting produced agreement on the core "power" issue of the disposition of the military forces. Despite Sihanouk's public appeal that the factional armies be completely dismantled and reorganized,[44] consensus was reached on a formula of 70 percent disarmament, 30 percent cantonment under the supervision of a UN peacekeeping force, and an end to all foreign military assistance.[45] Hun Sen also agreed to drop any reference to the Khmer Rouge's genocide in the section of the agreement dealing with human rights in the interest of removing a major stumbling block to final agreement.[46]

The August Pattaya meeting was significant because it revealed that final agreement among all the parties to the peace process was all but accomplished. The progress had been made possible, in substantial measure, because of Perm Five collaboration in support of a settlement. The Soviets and the Chinese, after three decades of bitter feuding and confrontation, were now working together, and the United States was able to coordinate policy on Indochina with both former adversaries. The Cold War was coming to an end.

An almost poignant example of the altered relations among the major powers was the Perm Five session at Pattaya on August 29.[47] In a discussion of national commitments to the economic reconstruction of Cambodia, Soviet representative Igor Rogachev bemoaned that he could not make an aid commitment on behalf of his government because "I'm not sure I have a country to represent." A coup against Gorbachev had split the Soviet leadership ten days earlier and the Baltic republics, Ukraine, and Byelorussia were voting for independence from Moscow. Dissolution of the Soviet Union was just four months away.[48]

A final SNC meeting was convened by the Perm Five in New York in late September, on the eve of the Forty-sixth UN General Assembly. The last major issue—the structure of the election process—was finally resolved in favor of a system of proportional representation that would give each faction a share of seats in the new national assembly according to its share of the total popular vote.[49] Four days later, Sihanouk called on President Bush, also in New York for the General Assembly session, to describe the all but complete peace process that, counting from the time of the Paris Conference in August 1989, had taken just over two years to construct. A month later, on October 23, the second session of the Paris Conference on Cambodia ratified the agreement.

In retrospect, it is clear that the parallel and mutually reinforcing reconciliations of 1991 between Beijing and Moscow, and Beijing and Hanoi, made possible the fundamental political deals that enabled the Perm Five's peace plan for Cambodia to fall into place. Although the content of this bilateral diplomacy remains largely unknown to outside observers, subsequent developments make it evident that a major issue for all the communist parties was the ending of more than three decades of Sino-Soviet hostility and military confrontation. For the Chinese, this meant that Moscow was no longer trying to "encircle" China. For the Vietnamese, this meant the end of Moscow's diplomatic and military support and assistance programs, which had seen them through the war with the Americans in the 1960s and 1970s and their confrontation with the Chinese in the late 1970s and 1980s. Thus isolated, Hanoi had no recourse but to give up on Ho Chi Minh's dream of an Indochina Federation—of Vietnam as the hegemon over Laos and Cambodia—and normalize relations with China on Beijing's terms.

Once the Vietnamese had come to terms with the Chinese, Hun Sen was under irresistible pressure from both Hanoi and Moscow to accept compromises that would make the peace process work. And the Chinese were concurrently pressing the Khmer Rouge to compromise in the interest of the settlement. At the final SNC meetings there was no longer the impasse between "genocide" and "colonialism" but concentration on the core "power" issues of the military dispositions and the electoral system. Under the pressure of the major powers, Cambodia's factions moved their unresolved and probably irreconcilable differences, however reluctantly, from the killing fields to the UN-managed political process.

## CONCLUSION: THE UNITED STATES AS AN INTERNATIONAL MEDIATOR

What lessons can we learn from the Cambodia settlement about successful international mediation in support of a peace process? Three broad themes stand out in this reconstruction of the negotiations of 1989–91: the issue of "ripeness," of whether the political environment is favorable to building support for a settlement; the importance of leadership in constructing a consensus; and the element of serendipity, of unexpected developments that influence the balance of factors in support of, or in opposition to, a settlement.

### Are Circumstances "Ripe" for a Settlement?[50]

*A helmsman must learn to ride with the tide,*
*or else he will be swamped by the waves.*
*—Premier Zhou Enlai of China, to Henry Kissinger, 1971*

It took more than a decade to construct a peace process for Cambodia, and the efforts of the United Nations and individual countries in the 1980s occurred in circumstances that were not favorable to successful diplomacy.

Late in the decade, however, as the Soviet Union began to withdraw its support for Vietnam and the Hun Sen government in Phnom Penh, circumstances began to change. The Paris Conference of August 1989 also took place before political forces in support of a settlement had fully "ripened," yet the diplomacy at the Kleber Conference Center, in combination with the prior efforts of Indonesia in the JIM process, contributed to building a broad international consensus in support of what evolved into the UN settlement plan. There was thus substantial "prenegotiation" that created a multilayered regional and international coalition in support of a settlement.

The one element in the coalition that never fully "ripened" was the core of the conflict—the rivalries among the Khmer political factions. The international community essentially imposed a political settlement on Hun Sen and the Khmer Rouge. Only Prince Sihanouk and Son Sann gained from the process. The subsequent deterioration in Cambodia's politics following the successful elections of 1993 underlines the fact that without broad *internal* support for the terms of a settlement, the investment of the international community in a peace agreement can easily be lost without effective mid- to long-term follow-through. There are almost never rapid and costless solutions to long-standing, bitter conflicts such as the one that ravaged Cambodia. If the international community seeks only a quick exit from such a conflict, it is unlikely to create a stable peace.

In the case of Cambodia, once the UN-mandated elections came to a successful conclusion in 1993, the international coalition that had created the peace process began to dissipate as the major powers turned to more pressing and higher-priority concerns. One of the prices of peace building in the post–Cold War world is sustained international action in support of a conflict resolution process. The costs of such action are usually far less than a return to warfare, yet mustering the international political will for such follow-through is a major challenge.

### The Importance of Leadership

The United States was one of several countries that took the risks of leadership in bringing peace to Cambodia. Indonesia and France, at different times in the decade-long effort, made major contributions as well. The United States was an important catalyzer of the diplomatic process in the year from September 1989 through August 1990 as it structured the Perm Five negotiations that produced a framework agreement for a UN-managed peace process. The U.S. effort drew strength from the JIM meetings and the Paris Conference. It was facilitated by the various mechanisms of the United Nations, which provided neutral ground for the Security Council consultations and political backing through votes of the Security Council and the General Assembly in support of the settlement plan. And the plan was implemented with remarkable effectiveness through the office of the UN secretary-general.

The United Nations thus gave effect to the international consensus for a Cambodian settlement. Yet it was the political weight and initiative of the United States in pressing for a UN-managed peace process that prevented dissipation of the Paris and JIM-centered diplomacy. It also preempted a settlement worked out bilaterally between the Chinese and the Vietnamese-Soviets—the feared "Red solution." U.S. leadership, and the United Nations, gave China, the Soviet Union, and Vietnam a relatively neutral process by which to back away from decades of confrontation.

The particular challenge for the Bush administration—as for any U.S. government taking a significant initiative in international diplomacy—was to build and sustain domestic political support, especially in Congress. Internal political considerations impelled the administration to take the lead in promoting a settlement of the Cambodia conflict, yet congressional "symbolic politics" surrounding the peace process—the concern to prevent another genocide, and the political imperative of being *seen* to be doing so—were in constant tension with the mechanics of constructing a realistic settlement process that would control the Khmer Rouge.

At several points in the two-year period between the fall of 1989 and the signing of the peace plan in Paris in October 1991, congressional opposition might have undercut the administration's diplomacy by cutting off assistance to Prince Sihanouk and Son Sann. When the political issues in a settlement are highly divisive and when the uncertainties of politics (the diplomatic counterpart to the "fog of war") allow for profound differences in judgment, much of the business of international diplomacy in fact becomes management of domestic political byplay.

In that effort, senior administration leadership of the diplomacy—by the president and the secretary of state—becomes critical to the work of designated negotiators, whether they be a presidential special representative or an assistant secretary of state. Such support entails incurring the significant political risk that a negotiation might not succeed—as well as the risks and costs of inaction, of *not* taking the lead. Support from congressional leaders is also critical to building bipartisan executive-legislative support. In the case of the Cambodia settlement and the associated process of normalizing relations with Vietnam, the support of Congressman Stephen Solarz and a number of senatorial Vietnam War veterans was critical in preventing a fundamental split between Congress and the administration.

## Serendipity

In the conduct of diplomacy, political factors, policy agendas, and events influencing the evolution of a negotiation are often incalculable, unknown, or unanticipated. The real world is full of surprises, and leaders facing unpromising or uncertain circumstances may well seek to drag out a negotiation in hopes that some unexpected development will enhance prospects for success. Evaluating the "correlation of forces" influencing a political process is a major leadership skill; playing for time in hopes of the intervention of some unexpected or hoped-for development is the instinct of a risk taker.

In the politics of the Cambodia settlement, serendipity played an important role in the ultimate success of the negotiations of 1989–91. The unexpected factor, only vaguely anticipated at the time of the first Paris Conference, was the collapse of the Soviet Union, which brought with it pressures on Vietnam to accept the UN settlement plan and to normalize relations with China. Had Moscow not been forced by its own economic and political straits to withdraw support from Vietnam and the Hun Sen government, it is doubtful that the Perm Five process would have come to closure. And had the Vietnamese leadership not fundamentally shifted its policies in mid-1991, it is equally doubtful that Hanoi would have acceded to Beijing's terms for normalization, which included support for the UN settlement in Cambodia.

Yet such fortuitous developments *did* occur, helping to bring to fruition the collective efforts of the international community to bring peace to Cambodia.

### Notes

1. This chapter is an abbreviated version of the author's book-length study, *Exiting Indochina: U.S. Leadership of the UN Settlement Process for Cambodia, and Normalization of Relations with Vietnam,* to be published by the United States Institute of Peace Press in 2000.

In preparing this retrospective history and assessment, the author had significant research support from James Rae. He also received over the years helpful inputs from a number of colleagues regarding the history of the Indochina conflicts and the Cambodia negotiating effort: Morton Abramowitz, Elizabeth Becker, Nayan Chanda, Richard Childress, Gareth Evans, Karl Jackson, Stanley Karnow, Robert Kimmit, Masaharu Kohno, Robert Manning, Claude Martin, Steve Pieczenik, Kenneth Quinn, Brent Scowcroft, Sichan Siv, Stephen Solarz, and Paul Wolfowitz. He alone is responsible for the interpretations developed in this retrospective assessment, as well as for any errors of fact.

It should be stressed that this interpretation is from an American perspective, with the objective of assessing how the United States can play an effective role in multilateral international efforts to mediate settlements of violent conflicts. The history of the events reviewed in this assessment is so complex that other observers, particularly those from other countries involved in the Cambodia peace process, would almost certainly give a different weight to the roles that various countries played in the process, and perhaps have a different interpretation of various events—à la *Rashomon*.

2. See Harold Saunders, "We Need a Larger Theory of Negotiation: The Importance of Pre-negotiating Phases," in *Negotiation Theory and Practice*, ed. J. William Breslin and Jeffrey Z. Rubin (Cambridge, Mass.: Harvard Law School, Program on Negotiation, 1991), 57–70.

3. The four political factions were Prince Sihanouk's United National Front for an Independent, Neutral, Peaceful, and Cooperative Cambodia (FUNCINPEC); Son Sann's Khmer People's National Liberation Front (KPNLF); Pol Pot's Party of Democratic Kampuchea (PDK), generally referred to as the Khmer Rouge; and Hun Sen's Cambodian People's Party (the CPP, prior to 1989 known as the Kampuchean People's Revolutionary Party, the KPRP).

4. See Yoichi Funabashi, "The Asianization of Asia," *Foreign Affairs* (November-December 1993): 75–85.

5. As late as 1989, Deng Xiaoping told President Bush that Moscow's relationships with Vietnam and Cambodia were of concern because they represented a continuation of Soviet efforts to "encircle" China going back to the Khrushchev and Brezhnev eras. See George Bush and Brent Scowcroft, *A World Transformed* (New York: Alfred A. Knopf, 1998), 94–96.

6. The early name for Cambodia was Kambuja, pronounced *Cambodia* by Westerners but *Kampuchea* by the Khmer. Throughout this document we will use the name Cambodia, except in official designations that use Kampuchea. Khmer is the designation of ethnic Cambodians; we will use both terms—Khmer and Cambodian—in this account as appropriate.

7. The Pol Pot faction of the Cambodian communist movement is commonly referred to as the Khmer Rouge. The movement established a state termed Democratic Kampuchea (DK) after its successful insurgency against the U.S.-supported Lon Nol government of the Republic of Cambodia in 1975. After the Vietnamese drove the Pol Pot government out of Phnom Penh in late 1978, the movement renamed itself the Party of Democratic Kampuchea (PDK), and in 1982 it allied itself with the noncommunist forces of Prince Sihanouk and Son Sann under the name of the Coalition Government of Democratic Kampuchea (CGDK).

8. Specialists in Southeast Asian affairs were generally aware of Khmer Rouge violence, which had been first reported in diplomatic channels by a U.S. Foreign Service officer, Kenneth Quinn, as early as 1974. (Quinn was to play a central role in subsequent negotiations in the early 1990s regarding the Cambodia settlement and normalization of relations with Vietnam.) The genocidal violence of the Khmer Rouge in power was documented by Elizabeth Becker in *When the War Was Over: Cambodia and the Khmer Rouge Revolution* (New York: Public Affairs, Perseus Books, 1998); and Nayan Chanda in *Brother Enemy: The War after the War* (New York: Collier Books, 1986). The 1984 film *The Killing Fields* made the Khmer Rouge revolution a matter of wide public awareness in the United States.

9. The Vietnamese had announced troop withdrawals in previous years, but these "withdrawals" were assessed to be annual rotational reassignments. In May 1988 Hanoi announced

it would withdraw 50,000 troops by the end of the year and place the remaining Vietnamese troops under the command of the Hun Sen government. The April 1989 announcement was the first in which Vietnam said it would withdraw *all* its troops from Cambodia.

10. The issue of U.S. assistance to the noncommunists in the resistance was to become one of the most controversial domestic political issues in developing a settlement plan. Both the Reagan and Bush administrations provided nonlethal humanitarian assistance to FUNCINPEC and the KPNLF and their military forces on a covert basis. They considered but rejected proposals to provide lethal military equipment, which was supplied by China and several ASEAN states. In the spring of 1991, under congressional pressure, the Bush administration began several overt humanitarian assistance and economic development–oriented aid programs that included support for programs in the Hun Sen–controlled areas of the country.

11. See *Congressional Record*, 99th Cong., 1st sess., 1985 (July 9), vol. 131, no. 90, sec. 206–207. Neither the Reagan and Bush administrations nor the 99th Congress, 1st session, advocated the supply of lethal assistance to the noncommunist resistance, in part because they did not seek a military solution to the conflict and in part because they calculated that military aid would re-create some of the international and domestic political dynamic of the Vietnam War period.

12. There is a long history of efforts by Ho Chi Minh to establish an Indochinese Communist Party as the vehicle for uniting the three states of Indochina under Vietnamese leadership. See MacAlister Brown, "The Indochina Federation Idea: Learning from History," in *Postwar Indochina: Old Enemies and New Allies*, ed. Joseph J. Zasloff (Washington, D.C.: Foreign Service Institute, Department of State, 1988).

13. The work of the Paris Conference, and the subsequent UN settlement agreement, are described and assessed in detail in Steven R. Ratner, "The Cambodia Settlement Agreements," *American Journal of International Law* 87, no. 1 (January 1993): 1-41. Ratner was an attorney-adviser in the Office of the Legal Adviser, U.S. Department of State. He participated in both the Paris Conference and the UN–Perm Five negotiations as a member of the U.S. delegation.

14. See Steven Erlanger, "Thai Leader Trying to Break Cambodian Impasse," *New York Times*, September 11, 1989.

15. See Becker, *When the War Was Over*, 393.

16. The matter of Sihanouk's role in a settlement process was an issue of some contention. Some American observers of the Cambodian scene, and several congressmen, believed that Sihanouk's past association with the Khmer Rouge compromised his credibility as a political leader. Others felt that his well-deserved reputation for "mercurial" political maneuvering—which included periods of anti-Americanism—made him an unpromising partner in a settlement process. We concluded that the prince's standing as a nationalist and the political legitimacy that he could bring to a settlement were valuable assets that might facilitate reconciliation in an otherwise polarized Khmer political environment. The trick was to use Sihanouk's standing among the Khmer without having him dominate the process of constructing a political settlement, which might never come to closure as he maneuvered—without a political organization or military forces—to establish himself as the senior authority and "balancer" among the contending Khmer factions. We believed the UN Security

Council could provide the structure and create the process that would contain the prince's maneuverings while drawing on his authority as the unifying "cement" of a political settlement.

17. Congressman Stephen J. Solarz laid out these policy perspectives in a lucid *Foreign Affairs* article. See Solarz, "Cambodia and the International Community," *Foreign Affairs* 69, no. 2 (spring 1990): 99-115, esp. 109–110. As is detailed later, Solarz's advocacy in Congress on behalf of the Bush administration's Cambodia policy, which had been substantially influenced by his prior actions on the issue, became an essential element in building domestic political support for the administration's efforts.

18. The second meeting was in New York on February 11–13; the third in Paris on March 12–13; the fourth in New York on May 25–26; in fifth in Paris on July 16–17; and the final in New York on August 27–28.

19. See "Text of the UN Declaration on the Conflict in Cambodia," *New York Times,* January 17, 1990.

20. This situation was a reprise of the congressional cutoff of support for the Lon Nol government in 1973—an action that in some measure accelerated the Khmer Rouge's coming to power. See Henry A. Kissinger, *Years of Upheaval* (Boston: Little, Brown, 1982), 349–369.

21. During the Reagan administration, low-key contacts had been maintained with the Vietnamese in the interest of resolving POW-MIA issues. These contacts stressed the need for Vietnam to withdraw from Cambodia, as well as to resolve several hundred "last known alive discrepancy cases," as a basis for normalizing relations. See Richard T. Childress and Stephen J. Solarz, "Vietnam: Detours on the Road to Normalization," in *Reversing Relations with Former Adversaries: U.S. Foreign Policy after the Cold War,* ed. C. Richard Nelson and Kenneth Weisbrode (Gainesville: University of Florida Press, 1998).

The Bush administration held its first formal bilateral consultation with the Vietnamese in New York on August 6, 1990, three weeks after the Baker announcement. Deputy Assistant Secretary of State Kenneth Quinn represented the United States; Vietnam's permanent representative to the United Nations, Trinh Xuan Lang, represented Hanoi. The subject of discussion was the Cambodia peace process.

22. See Steven Erlanger, "Thailand Seeks to Shape a 'Golden Peninsula,'" *New York Times,* April 30, 1989.

23. See Steven Erlanger, "Thai Leader Trying to Break Cambodian Impasse," *New York Times,* September 11, 1989.

24. See Rodney Tasker, "Another Year Zero?" *Far Eastern Economic Review,* November 9, 1989.

25. See Nayan Chanda, "Japan's Quiet Entrance on the Diplomatic Stage," *Christian Science Monitor,* June 13, 1990.

26. During the period 1989–92 the government in Canberra took a number of diplomatic initiatives involving U.S. interests—initially without prior consultation. In 1989 the Australians joined with the Japanese to launch a regional economic cooperation organization that eventually became the Asia-Pacific Economic Cooperation (APEC) initiative. In its first articulation, APEC did not include the United States, a curious omission given the importance of economic relations with the United States to both countries. The Evans

Cambodia initiative, premised on a UN role in the settlement, was launched with little prior consultation with the United Nations or the members of the Security Council. And in 1992 Senator Evans floated the idea of a Conference on Security and Cooperation in Asia (CSCA)—in parallel with a similarly named organization in Europe. Again, the initiative was taken without prior consultation with the United States, another counterproductive approach given the relevance of the U.S. military presence in East Asia to Australia's security interests. Yet domestic political forces require many governments to demonstrate that they are "out in front" and doing the right thing on issues important to the nation's interests.

27. See Gareth Evans, *Cooperating for Peace: The Global Agenda for the 1990s and Beyond* (St. Leonards, Australia: Allen and Unwin, 1993), 107–108.

28. See Hamish McDonald, "Entrenched Positions," *Far Eastern Economic Review*, March 15, 1990, 13.

29. Tasker, "Another Year Zero?" 12–13.

30. See Henry A. Kissinger, *Diplomacy* (New York: Simon and Schuster, 1994), esp. chap. 2.

31. Although the Carter administration tolerated, if not encouraged, Chinese support for the Khmer Rouge as a point of pressure on the Vietnamese after their invasion of Cambodia, Secretary of State George Shultz, during the Reagan administration, began urging the Chinese to switch their support to the noncommunist resistance, a position that was maintained in the Bush administration.

32. See, for example, Frederick Z. Brown and Paul H. Kreisberg, "Speaking Out against the Khmer Rouge," *Christian Science Monitor*, June 2, 1988.

33. Jeremy J. Stone and William E. Colby, "Block the Khmer Rouge," *New York Times*, April 28, 1989.

34. All quotations and summary assessments of congressional testimony cited in this study are drawn from the *Congressional Record* or records of the appropriate committee hearings of the appropriate dates.

35. See Robert Koehler, "A Tougher Peter Jennings Probes Cambodia Quandary," *Los Angeles Times*, April 26, 1990.

36. See, for example, my testimony before the Senate Foreign Relations Subcommittee on Asian and Pacific Affairs on July 20, 1990.

37. The matter of possible battlefield cooperation between the Khmer Rouge and military units of the noncommunist resistance had been a matter of intense concern and attention within the administration for several months. A detailed review of intelligence reporting from the field indicated the possibility of occasional, sporadic coordination of tactical military actions by Khmer Rouge and Sihanouk units, but no systematic cooperation based on senior-level policy guidance.

38. Sihanouk formally declared the dissolution of the CGDK on February 3, 1990.

39. The United States was the only country, following the UNTAC settlement, to unilaterally take steps to bring the Khmer Rouge to justice. In April 1992 Senator Chuck Robb of Virginia introduced legislation that directed the State Department to establish an Office of Cambodian Genocide Investigation that would collect information on the Khmer Rouge's violent rule of the late 1970s. Such information would be the basis for eventual establishment

of a national or international criminal tribunal that would prosecute the Khmer Rouge leadership for crimes against humanity and genocide. Such an office was established, and it collected material on the Khmer Rouge, in part with the assistance of the Cambodian government established after the UN-supervised elections of 1993. As of the spring of 1999 the issue of establishing a tribunal to bring surviving Khmer Rouge leaders to account was still a contentious political matter, with Hun Sen resisting the idea of an international tribunal and the international community questioning the ability of Cambodia's domestic judicial system to bring the remaining Khmer Rouge leaders to justice.

**40.** This Soviet diplomacy was conducted by Moscow's representative in the Perm Five negotiations, Deputy Foreign Minister Igor Rogachev. In late 1989 and early 1990 Rogachev was active in the region, holding talks with Hun Sen, the Vietnamese, and the Chinese. Moscow's clients were under increasing pressure to support a UN-managed settlement. In April 1990 Premier Li Peng of China visited Moscow, at which time Gorbachev announced more Soviet troop reductions in the Far East and major cutbacks in Soviet aid to Vietnam and the State of Cambodia. By the end of 1990 the Soviets were selling combat aircraft to China—an indication of how far the improvement in Sino-Soviet relations under Gorbachev had progressed. And in May 1991 China's senior leaders traveled to Moscow to sign a major agreement settling long-standing territorial disputes along the Sino-Soviet frontier. In August the Cambodia deal was essentially done.

**41.** See Steven Erlanger, "Peace Talks on Cambodia Break Down," *New York Times,* March 1, 1990.

**42.** See Steven Erlanger, "Ending Talks, All Cambodian Parties Commit Themselves to UN Peace Plan," *New York Times,* September 10, 1990.

**43.** See Michael Richardson, "Asians Fear Deal on Cambodia as China-Vietnam Ties Warm," *International Herald Tribune,* August 7, 1991.

**44.** Kulachada Chaipipat and Yindee Lertcharoenchok, "Sihanouk Calls for Armies to Be Disbanded," *The Nation* (Bangkok), August 24, 1991.

**45.** Press rumors indicated that this formula for resolving the military issue had been worked out behind the scenes by the Chinese representative, Xu Dunxin, and his Vietnamese counterpart, Nguyen Dy Nien. Rodney Tasker, "What Killing Fields?" *Far Eastern Economic Review,* September 12, 1991, 15.

**46.** "Khmers Agree on Dropping All References to Genocide," *Bangkok Post,* August 30, 1991.

**47.** Perhaps the most bizarre scene in this diplomatic endgame was the celebratory banquet at Pattaya. Sihanouk was in a ebullient mood, for the international community was about to give him back his country. The prince, long famous for his musical interests, led the dinner orchestra in renditions of his many original Khmer and French love songs. In elation, Sihanouk approached me and directed that I sing a song in celebration of the Perm Five's contribution to the peace process. Having little musical talent I resisted, saying I would perform only in the company of my Perm Five colleagues. I couldn't think of an appropriate song that might conceivably be known by all five members of this unlikely diplomatic quintet, but it suddenly occurred to me that the first anniversary of the Perm Five framework agreement was at hand and that Sihanouk's sixty-ninth birthday was only weeks away. I implored my British, Chinese, French, and Russian counterparts to join me on the stage for a collective rendition of "Happy Birthday." For me the celebratory mood was chilled, however, by the ghoulish sight of Khmer Rouge delegates Khieu Samphan and Son Sen laughing at the diplomatic revelers in the crowded banquet room.

**48.** See Bush and Scowcroft, *A World Transformed*, 518–561.

**49.** Paul Lewis, "Cambodians Reach Accord on Elections," *New York Times*, 21 September 1991. Hun Sen resisted the proportional system in favor of a territorial constituency-based system—which would have played to the strengths of his political organization throughout the country. This compromise was to be the basis of a major challenge by Hun Sen to the outcome of the May 1993 election.

**50.** The concept of political "ripeness" has been developed by Professor I. William Zartman. See his *Elusive Peace: Negotiating an End to Civil Wars* (Washington, D.C.: Brookings Institution, 1995), esp. 18; also, Louis Kriesberg, "Timing and the Initiation of De-escalation Moves," in *Negotiation Theory and Practice*, ed. J. William Breslin and Jeffrey Z. Rubin (Cambridge, Mass.: Harvard University Law School, Program on Negotiation, 1991), 223–231.

### BIBLIOGRAPHY

Azimi, Nassrine, comp. *The United Nations Transitional Authority in Cambodia (UNTAC): Debriefing and Lessons*. London: Kluwer Law International, 1995.

Becker, Elizabeth. *America's Vietnam War: A Narrative History*. New York: Clarion Books, 1992.

———. *When the War Was Over: Cambodia and the Khmer Rouge Revolution*. New York: Public Affairs, Perseus Books, 1998.

Brzezinski, Zbigniew. *Power and Principle: Memoirs of the National Security Adviser, 1977–1981*. New York: Farrar, Straus, Giroux, 1983.

Bush, George, and Brent Scowcroft. *A World Transformed*. New York: Alfred A. Knopf, 1998.

*Cambodia: An Australian Peace Proposal, Working Papers Prepared for the Informal Meeting on Cambodia, Jakarta, 26–28 February 1990*. Canberra, Commonwealth of Australia, Department of Foreign Affairs and Trade, 1990.

Chanda, Nayan. *Brother Enemy: The War after the War*. New York: Collier Books, 1986.

Crowley, Monica. *Nixon in Winter*. New York: Random House, 1998.

Doyle, Michael W. *UN Peacekeeping in Cambodia: UNTAC's Civil Mandate*. London and Boulder, Colo.: Lynne Rienner Publishers and International Peace Academy, 1995.

Evans, Gareth. *Cooperating for Peace: The Global Agenda for the 1990s and Beyond*. St. Leonards, Australia: Allen and Unwin, 1993.

Childress, Richard T., and Stephen J. Solarz. "Vietnam: Detours on the Road to Normalization." In *Reversing Relations with Former Adversaries: U.S. Foreign Policy after the Cold War*, ed. C. Richard Nelson and Kenneth Weisbrode. Gainesville: University of Florida Press, 1998.

Findlay, Trevor. *Cambodia: The Legacy and Lessons of UNTAC*, SIPRI Research Report No. 9. Oxford: Oxford University Press, 1995.

Gorbachev, Mikhail S. *Memoirs*. New York: Doubleday, 1995.

———. *A Time for Peace*. New York: Richardson and Steinman, 1985.

Hampson, Fen Osler. *Nurturing Peace: Why Peace Settlements Succeed or Fail.* Washington, D.C.: United States Institute of Peace Press, 1996.

Hiebert, Murray. *Cambodia: Perspectives on the Impasse.* Washington, D.C.: Center for International Policy, February-March, 1986.

Kamm, Henry. *Cambodia: Report from a Stricken Land.* New York: Arcade Publishing, 1998.

Karnow, Stanley. *Vietnam: A History.* New York: Penguin Books, 1997.

Kissinger, Henry A. *Years of Upheaval.* Boston: Little, Brown, 1982.

Macchiarola, Frank J., and Robert B. Oxnam. *The China Challenge: American Policies in East Asia.* New York: Proceedings of the Academy of Political Science/Asia Society, vol. 38, no. 2, 1991.

Peou, Sorpong. *Conflict Neutralization in the Cambodia War: From Battlefield to Ballot-Box.* Kuala Lumpur, Malaysia: Oxford University Press, 1997.

Ratner, Steven R. "The Cambodia Settlement Agreements." *American Journal of International Law* 87, no. 1 (January 1993): 1–41.

Shawcross, William. *Cambodia's New Deal.* Washington, D.C.: Carnegie Endowment for International Peace, 1994.

Shevardnadze, Eduard. *The Future Belongs to Freedom.* New York: Macmillan, 1991.

Shultz, George P. *Turmoil and Triumph: My Years as Secretary of State.* New York: Charles Scribner's Sons, 1993.

Solarz, Stephen J. "Cambodia and the International Community." *Foreign Affairs* 69, no. 2 (spring 1990): 99–115.

Sutter, Robert G. "America and the Cambodian Peace Agreement." In *The Diplomatic Record, 1991–1992,* ed. Hans Binnendijk and Mary Locke, 197–214. Boulder, Colo.: Westview Press, 1993.

## Background to Chapter 13

## The Road to Sarajevo

Fighting erupted in the multiethnic and multireligious province of Bosnia-Herzegovina shortly after the 1991 breakup of Yugoslavia. Various European and American mediation efforts failed to resolve the conflict, and the ferocity of the war spiraled out of control. A renewed American attempt, backed by the threat and eventual use of NATO air strikes, led to a cease-fire, an end to the siege of Sarajevo, and a partition of Bosnia. These partial, interim agreements provided a basis for the 1995 Dayton Peace Accords, which sought to foster stability in a multiethnic Bosnia by mutual recognition among the states of Bosnia, Croatia, and Yugoslavia; by the demobilization of forces; and by the formation of a Serb and a Muslim-Croat entity within a Bosnian Federation (see chapter 21).

### MAJOR ACTORS
- Serbia: led by President Slobodan Milosevic
- Bosnian Serbs
- Bosnian Croats
- Bosnian Muslims
- United States: represented by Assistant Secretary of State for European and Canadian Affairs Richard Holbrooke
- NATO
- United Nations
- European Union

325

**IMPORTANT DATES**

- October 1991: The Bosnian Parliament votes for independence; Bosnian Serbs vote to remain part of a Serbian-dominated Yugoslavia
- March 1992: Bosnian voters overwhelmingly approve independence, but Bosnian Serbs boycott the referendum
- April 1992: The European Union and the United States recognize Bosnia's independence; war begins in Bosnia
- October 1992: The United Nations establishes a "no-fly zone" over Bosnia
- Early 1993: Lord David Owen, the EU mediator, and Cyrus Vance unsuccessfully try to mediate in Bosnia-Herzegovina
- March 1994: A U.S.-mediated effort achieves the Washington Agreement, creating the Muslim-Croat federation in Bosnia; fighting stops between Bosnian Muslims and Croatians
- Spring 1994: France, Germany, Russia, the United Kingdom, and the United States establish the five-nation Contact Group
- July 1995: Serbs massacre thousands in two Muslim "safe havens" in eastern Bosnia
- August 1995: Holbrooke and his team begin negotiations, meet with Slobodan Milosevic
- August 28, 1995: Serbs shell Sarajevo; NATO responds with two-week bombing campaign against Bosnian Serb targets as Croat and Bosnian government forces take back territory from Serbs
- September 8, 1995: Agreement signed in Geneva dividing Bosnian territory between Bosnian Serbs and Bosnian government
- September 14, 1995: Agreement ends the siege of Sarajevo
- September 26, 1995: Agreement signed in New York
- October 12, 1995: General cease-fire takes effect
- November 1–21, 1995: Comprehensive peace agreement negotiated at Dayton, Ohio

**KEY AGREEMENTS REACHED**

- Cease-fire
- End to the siege of Sarajevo
- Partition of Bosnia

**PRINCIPAL OUTCOMES**

- Formation of a single Bosnian state consisting of two entities, one Serb, one Muslim-Croat
- Demonstrated a basis for the eventual end of the war by introducing force with diplomacy

# 13

# The Road to Sarajevo

RICHARD HOLBROOKE

The first time I saw Sarajevo, I placed my feet for a moment in the footprints that had been pressed into the concrete sidewalk on the spot where Gavrilo Princip stood when he fired the bullets that killed Archduke Franz Ferdinand and triggered the First World War. This was in the summer of 1960. I was hitchhiking across Yugoslavia with a friend, and I was nineteen years old. A guide appeared, and offered to translate the words engraved in Serbian on the wall above the footprints. I can still recall my astonishment: it was my first encounter with the different meanings that history can hold for different people. "Here, in this historic place," the plaque read, "Gavrilo Princip was the initiator of liberty . . . the 28th of June, 1914."

"Initiator of liberty"? What was this all about? How could anyone regard the assassination as heroic? Every high-school student knew that the Archduke's murder had started Europe's slide into world wars, communism, and fascism.

That first brush with extreme nationalism came back to me vividly when Yugoslavia fell apart, in the early nineteen-nineties. By the time I saw Sarajevo again, thirty-two years later, Bosnia-Herzegovina had become the site of a vast failure on the part of the Western powers to stop the destruction of the Muslim people by their Serb neighbors in a vicious war that had given the language an appalling new phrase: "ethnic cleansing."

In 1992, with Bosnia on the brink of collapse, I made two trips to the region as a private citizen for the International Rescue Committee. On the second trip, in December, I returned to Sarajevo, traveling across Serb lines in a Danish armored personnel carrier. No longer a dazzling mixture of Muslim, Catholic, and Eastern Orthodox cultures, the city had turned into a desperate hellhole, with no heat and little water—a place where children gathered twigs for firewood and people piled shattered buses into makeshift barriers against the constant threat of snipers.

Sarajevo was then under heavy mortar and artillery attack by the Serbs, and the trip was far more dangerous than I had realized when I started out. After finally reaching the city, I ran into an old friend—John F. Burns, of the *New York Times*—and asked if we could visit Princip's footprints in the pavement. Impossible, he said with a laugh: they had been destroyed by the Bosnian Muslims and Croats. But the spirit of the fanatical Serbian nationalism that had lain behind those footprints and the inscription on the wall was still alive—murderously so.

I had spent a year as Ambassador to Germany when, in the summer of 1994, President Clinton and Secretary of State Warren Christopher asked me to return to Washington to become Assistant Secretary of State for European and Canadian Affairs. Deputy Secretary of State Strobe Talbott made it clear that difficulties with our situation in Bosnia had led to the reassignment.

The first ten months that I spent in Washington were filled with more disasters on the Bosnia front. The Bosnian Serbs continued to ignore international mediation efforts and to defy the United Nations. In the summer of 1995, the worst war crimes committed in Europe since the Holocaust—the massacre of thousands of people whom the Serbs had rounded up—took place at two Muslim enclaves in eastern Bosnia that had been designated UN "safe areas," Srebrenica and Zepa, while UN peacekeepers stood by helplessly.

With Bosnia apparently poised for the last act of a terrible drama, President Clinton instructed his foreign-policy team to make a concerted peace initiative. By the end of August, military action—in the form of massive NATO air strikes—would finally be added to the mixture, greatly aiding the diplomatic efforts. But at the beginning of the month, when Anthony Lake, the National Security Adviser, and Peter Tarnoff, the Undersecretary of State for Political Affairs, launched the American diplomatic offensive with a trip to the major European capitals, the Administration had not yet made airpower part of its strategy.

I met Lake at the American Embassy in London on August 14 for what the bureaucrats call a "handoff" meeting: he would brief me on his talks with our allies and the Russians, and I would proceed to the Balkans with a small interagency team to begin negotiations that we hoped would end the war.

Our meeting was quietly emotional. Tony Lake and I had entered the foreign service together in 1962, had served in Vietnam and Washington in five Administrations, and had been linked through close personal and professional ties ever since. "This is the kind of thing we dreamed of doing together in Vietnam," Tony began, in a low, intense voice. We discussed the American peace initiative, which was not a detailed plan but, rather, a starting point for our negotiating efforts. Then Tony headed back to Washington, and our team boarded a small military jet for the Balkans.

* * *

The Mt. Igman route to Sarajevo, a narrow, winding dirt track originally created for farmers and shepherds, had often been described as the most dangerous road in Europe. Since the Sarajevo airport had been closed by Serb artillery, the Igman road was the only way to reach Bosnia's capital without crossing Serb checkpoints, where hostages had been taken and people killed. Still, parts of the route lay directly in the line of fire of Serb machine gunners, who often shot at vehicles as a reminder that, if they wanted to, they could cut Sarajevo off entirely from the outside world. The roadbed itself had little foundation and no reinforcement along the sides; in several places it was virtually impossible for two vehicles to pass each other. All in all, it was a road to avoid. But our negotiating team had to get to Sarajevo, because we wanted to begin our mission by consulting with the main victims of the war. Our plan was to go by helicopter from the Croatian coastal city of Split to a UN landing zone high on Mt. Igman, then transfer to armored vehicles for the two-hour drive to Sarajevo.

On August 15, we made our first attempt to reach Sarajevo. Because we were unable to find a break in the heavy clouds over the landing site, our helicopter circled for two extremely unpleasant hours before returning us, frustrated and tired, to Split. With darkness approaching, we decided to fly to Zagreb, the capital of Croatia, where, the following day, we met with the Croatian President, Franjo Tudjman. Then, after a few hours, we flew on to Belgrade for talks with the most important protagonist in this phase of the drama, Slobodan Milosevic, the President of Serbia. This was to be my first encounter with the man who, in my view, bore the heaviest responsibility for the war in Bosnia, and I approached it nervously. Over the past months, my deputy, Robert C. Frasure, who carried the additional title of the President's special envoy for Bosnia, had spent many hours with Milosevic in unproductive talks.

Our first meeting with the Serbian leader, on August 17, lasted five hours and produced no indication that he had changed any of his positions. Milosevic was smart, tricky, and evasive; we thought he was playing games—verbal jousting devoid of serious content. I felt dissatisfied with the exchange, and thought that perhaps I had not been blunt enough, so I asked for another meeting. Early the next morning, Frasure, Nelson Drew of the National Security Council staff, and I were ushered for a second time into the spacious meeting room in the Presidential Palace in Belgrade. As was true of so many official chambers in communist and former communist countries, from Beijing to Bratislava, the architects had tried to make up for a lack of charm with drab gigantism. Milosevic seated himself in an armchair a few feet from my place at the end of the sofa, where Bob and Nelson also sat. His Foreign Minister, Milan Milutinovic, faced us from another soft chair, and Goran Milinovic, Milosevic's loyal aide, sat nearby, taking notes. It was a room whose every detail I came to know well during the next seven months.

Milosevic had a penetrating gaze. His small eyes were highly focussed, and his face, which was oddly cherubic, was not without a sort of brutal charm. He was a forceful presence with a quick and retentive mind. Because of his success in stirring up Serb fanaticism, he was widely regarded as an extreme nationalist, but in fact he had no deep commitment to nationalism: he had merely exploited it to gain power. This was in sharp distinction to the motives of his sometime allies—the genuinely racist Bosnian Serb leaders, who rained mortar and artillery rounds down upon Sarajevo. Still, we held Milosevic accountable for the aggression. As the most powerful Serb in the former Yugoslavia, he had used his authority to promote war against the Croats and the Muslims in the hope of uniting the Serbs in all parts of the region under a single flag.

That morning, it was obvious that nothing had changed. Thinking of the difficulties we faced in trying to reach Sarajevo, I said, "Mr. President, it's demeaning to the United States that our peace mission, sent by our President, must travel to Sarajevo over the most dangerous road in Europe. You claim to want peace. Will you arrange for us to fly directly to Sarajevo without any interference from the Bosnian Serbs?"

In his excellent English, Milosevic said, "You're right. I'll try," and turned to his aide. When Milinovic had left the room, Milosevic said, "I'm sending a message to General Mladic." We noted with fascination this evidence of a direct link between Milosevic and Ratko Mladic, the commander of the Bosnian Serb forces in Bosnia, whom the International War Crimes Tribunal had indicted as a war criminal. Twenty minutes later, Milinovic returned and handed a note to his boss. "Mladic says the airport is too dangerous," Milosevic said. "He cannot guarantee that you won't be shot down by Muslims or Croats."

I smiled at this transparent sophistry. Everyone knew, I said, that the only danger at the Sarajevo airport came from the Serb gunners who ringed the hills around it.

But Milosevic was not finished. "Mladic says you can fly to Kiseljak and go in by road from there," he added. "You will be completely safe."

I knew that route. It was safer only in terms of terrain. But it ran through Bosnian Serb territory—what Bob Frasure called "Indian country." That was the road I had travelled in 1992, huddled in the forward seat of the Danish armored personnel carrier (APC) and trying to appear inconspicuous under a UN helmet. We had been stopped half a dozen times by Serbs, who had waved machine guns around while checking our I.D. cards. Two weeks later, on that very road, the Serbs had killed a Bosnian Muslim deputy prime minister during a search of a French APC.

I told Milosevic this story and said, "We can use that road only if you give us your personal guarantee that we won't be stopped by any Bosnian Serbs."

"I can't guarantee that," Milosevic said, "but I'll ask Mladic."

"That's out of the question, Mr. President," I said. "We will never accept any guarantees from Mladic."

Bob Frasure leaned over to me and whispered, "We have no choice except Igman."

That afternoon, we flew to Split. On the bus to the hotel, Frasure and Joseph Kruzel, a Deputy Assistant Secretary of Defense, improvised a reggae-rap song. Its refrain went something like "Goin' up Mt. Igman, mon, tryin' to make da peace, mon." It wasn't much to listen to, they admitted, as they danced in the aisle.

\* \* \*

My teammates were four men who represented different parts of the national-security bureaucracy. Each brought his own strength and style to the diplomatic effort. Bob Frasure, who had been the first American ambassador to Estonia, was a fifty-three-year-old, craggy, cynical professional diplomat who loved his work while grumbling about it continually.

At the end of 1994, as the situation in Bosnia continued to deteriorate, Secretary of State Warren Christopher, who greatly admired Frasure's unusual combination of cool detachment and fierce loyalty, added to his responsibilities by naming him chief Bosnia negotiator. Bob had enormous energy as well as a keen strategic sense. His reports of negotiating with Milosevic over lengthy dinners of lamb and plum brandy were widely read for their conciseness and humor. He had a gift for metaphor: "We're trying to sit still on a rockslide," he would mutter—or, after things had changed slightly for the better, "the ledge we're clinging to just got a couple of inches wider." Bob's greatest joy was to retreat to his farm in the Shenandoah Valley. By the summer of 1995, he was visibly worn out, and we'd agreed that after this trip he would return to Washington to act as our primary backstop.

Joe Kruzel, fifty, had a steel-trap mind notable for combining theoretical and practical ability. He often wore his eyeglasses on the lower part of his nose and peered over them in a manner that evoked his academic background. He was equally proud of having spent his undergraduate days at the United States Air Force Academy and of having received a Ph.D. from Harvard. Like Frasure, Kruzel had a highly developed sense of irony and a biting wit, which found expression in word games. In Split, Joe stayed up well past midnight rewriting our presentation for Sarajevo. Reading his paper the next morning, I saw that he had slipped in a joke, perhaps to see if I was paying attention: "We will need a mini–Marshall Plan (you know Minnie Marshall—George's sister)."

Lieutenant General Wesley Clark, representing the Joint Chiefs of Staff, held a complicated position on our team. A West Pointer, a Rhodes Scholar from Arkansas, and a decorated Vietnam veteran, he had been one of the fastest-rising officers in the U.S. Army. He had a personal relationship—it was not clear how close—to another former Rhodes Scholar from Arkansas, who was now Commander-in-Chief. At fifty, with three stars on his shoulders, Clark was at a critical point in his career: either this assignment would lead him to a fourth star—every general's dream—or he would have to retire. Being part of a negotiating team was hazardous duty, because it could put him in career-endangering situations with senior officers. Clark's boyish demeanor and charm masked an extraordinary intensity. Great things were expected of him, and he expected them of himself. (In the end, he got his star.)

Samuel Nelson Drew, a forty-seven-year-old Air Force colonel who had recently joined the staff of the National Security Council, was a short, solid man with a serious air about him. Out of uniform, he had none of the aura of a military officer; at bottom, he was an impressive intellectual who happened to specialize in military intelligence. For the previous four years, at NATO headquarters, he had worked primarily on Bosnia, but this was his first trip to the region.

* * *

August 19, 1995. The helicopter taking us to Split had room for only six passengers. Counting my assistant, Rosemarie Pauli-Gikas, and General Clark's aide, Lieutenant Colonel Daniel Gerstein, we were seven, so Rosemarie offered her seat to Gerstein, saying she would wait for us to return to Split. We landed in a soccer field on Mt. Igman, where two vehicles were waiting for us. One was a French armored personnel carrier, a large, heavy vehicle, painted in UN white. The other was a United States Army Humvee, a relatively new replacement for the ancient and storied jeep.

General Clark said to me, over the roar of the helicopter, "Have you ever been in one of our new Humvees? You ought to see how much better it is than what you were used to in Vietnam." I told him that I was looking forward to the experience, then walked with Frasure, Kruzel, Drew, and Gerstein to the APC. Kruzel and I speculated about what the attitude of the Pentagon and NATO would be toward American military involvement in Bosnia if such a thing became necessary. "They won't like it," he said, laughing. "It would disrupt their training schedule."

Waiting at the APC was an American who introduced himself as Pete Hargreaves. As a member of the security detail in our Embassy in Sarajevo, he would accompany my colleagues in the APC. The back doors of the vehicle swung open, and Frasure, Kruzel, Gerstein, Drew, and Hargreaves climbed in. "Think hard about how we make the presentation," I said to Frasure. He gave a sardonic laugh, and the doors closed.

The Humvee was heavily armored, and the windows, which did not open, were almost two inches thick. Even so, Wes Clark insisted we buckle our seat belts and put on flak jackets and helmets. As it turned out, our colleagues in the APC did not take the same precautions.

The first section of the road wound through seemingly peaceful woods. We passed French construction units and tanks from a new and powerful Rapid Reaction Force, which President Jacques Chirac had created to show the Serbs that at least one European nation would not be pushed around. After a while, we reached the steep incline above Sarajevo. The road hugged the mountainside, presenting a nearly vertical wall on our left and a sharp drop on our right. We were approaching an area in which we would be directly exposed to Serb machine gunners, but in such a well-armored car I felt safe. It was nine-thirty in the morning.

As we rounded a corner, an approaching French convoy pulled over against the inside wall to let us by. We started to pass it on the outside, moving slowly but steadily. As we passed the last vehicle, a soldier began yelling. I got out, and understood him to be saying that a vehicle behind us had gone off the road. Behind us was—nothing.

Wes Clark and I ran back about fifty yards to a place where the edge of the road seemed to have broken off. Below, we saw nothing except some fallen trees. We could hear voices in the woods, and we realized that somewhere down there lay the APC, with our colleagues. In our heavy flak jackets and helmets, we jumped the road edge and started down the steep incline. Suddenly, two enormous explosions went off below us, and then small-arms fire broke out. We heard soldiers yelling in French, "Mines! Get back on the road!" We scrambled back, pulling ourselves up by tree roots, and regrouped.

As we stood there, a French corporal came up and explained that the APC was farther down the mountain than we'd imagined. It had fallen below the next turn in the road. At that moment, we realized just how horrible the situation was.

Wes and I started running. We rounded the hairpin turn and continued for a kilometre. Finally, we reached a group of French vehicles, clustered at the spot where the APC had *bounced over* the road and tumbled down the mountain. The trees had been flattened as if a plow had leveled them. The French soldiers were trying to deal with the situation. In addition to the five Americans, three of their own men were missing.

It started to rain. The shooting died down. We established a scratchy radio contact with the Embassy in Sarajevo, but because we did not know exactly what had happened I asked Sarajevo not to report anything to Washington just yet. It was only about four in the morning there, and at that hour there was nothing Washington could do.

I stayed on the road to help the French while Wes searched for our comrades. We anchored a rope around a tree stump so he could descend. After a while, I heard Wes yelling through his walkie-talkie that he needed a fire extinguisher. I looked around, in vain.

A French jeep arrived, and I spotted a figure sitting upright in the back seat. Covered in blood and bandages, he was unrecognizable. I asked him who he was. "Hargreaves," he replied. "Your security officer, sir." He said that he wanted to lie down. Two French soldiers helped me ease Hargreaves out of the jeep and onto a cot by the roadside. I got down on my knees and asked him what had happened.

He was having difficulty speaking, but said he should have saved people; it was his fault; he thought his back was broken. "Frasure!" I almost shouted. "Where is Ambassador Frasure?"

"He's dead."

In my years as a civilian in Vietnam, I had been exposed to combat and seen its consequences, but this was much closer—much more personal.

"Joe Kruzel," I said. "What about Kruzel?"

"Don't know. Think he made it."

"Nelson Drew?"

"Gone. Didn't make it." Hargreaves started to cry. "I tried . . ."

"It's not your fault," I said. "There was nothing you could have done." Even though he was badly injured and in shock, his first thoughts—typical of a highly responsible security officer—were of those in his charge.

Wes Clark struggled up the hillside. "It's the worst thing you've ever seen down there," he said. The APC had caught fire after the live ammunition it was carrying exploded. Bosnian soldiers had reached the scene first, and had taken two of the Americans, tentatively identified as Kruzel and Gerstein, to the nearest field hospital. Clark had seen the remains of two other men inside the APC. He was all but certain that they were Bob Frasure and Nelson Drew.

Another jeep arrived, and out of it stepped a tall, thin French officer. This was General Jean-René Bachelet, the French commander of UN forces in Sarajevo. Behind him were three American security officers from our Embassy in Sarajevo. They reported that journalists had picked up our frantic radio communications and had begun to broadcast a garbled version of the accident around the world. Leaving Clark in charge, I climbed into Bachelet's jeep and headed for Sarajevo.

\* \* \*

The American Embassy in Sarajevo occupied a villa next to the United Nations military headquarters. The American in charge, a young United States Information Agency officer named John Menzies, who was then awaiting final Senate confirmation to become the Ambassador to Bosnia, had already alerted Washington to the tragedy. Now, shortly after 2 P.M. in Sarajevo, the State Department Operations Center set up a conference call with Tony Lake; his deputy, Sandy Berger; Strobe Talbott; and the Chairman of the Joint Chiefs of Staff, General John Shalikashvili. I reported that Bob Frasure and Nelson Drew had apparently died inside the APC, and that Joe Kruzel had survived the crash and was on his way to a field hospital. We did not know where Colonel Gerstein was.

The response was grim.

I suggested that the people designated to tell the news to Mrs. Frasure and Mrs. Drew not confirm their husbands' deaths yet but prepare them for the worst. Finally, I asked that someone call my wife, Kati, whom I had married three months earlier, and tell her the news, so that she would not hear an inaccurate report when she woke up.

Wes Clark arrived from the site of the accident. We called General Shalikashvili again to discuss arrangements for bringing the dead and the injured home. As I was talking to him, Menzies came into the room. "Kruzel is dead," he said. "Didn't make it to the hospital. Massive head injuries."

The thought of Joe—sardonic, wise Joe—dying on the way to the field hospital was too much. After asking Shalikashvili to tell the others in Washington, I turned the telephone over to Clark.

A short time later, President Clinton called—from Jackson Hole, Wyoming, where he was taking a three-week-long vacation. I did not realize then that it was his forty-ninth birthday. With Strobe Talbott listening in, the President spoke of how terrible the loss was, both personally and for the nation. Then he asked what effect I thought the tragedy would have on the negotiations, and whether we would be able to continue the mission. I said that after bringing our colleagues home we would be ready to resume.

"That's fine," the President said. "Come home as soon as you can, but make it clear that our commitment to the peace effort will continue."

Talking to the press from Jackson Hole a few minutes later, he said of the dead diplomats that they would have wanted to "press ahead, and that is what we intend to do."

We found Gerstein alive, in a makeshift French hospital in a basement in Sarajevo, banged up but otherwise in surprisingly good shape. He told us how the APC had started to slide over the edge; how no one had had time to speak; how he had grabbed a metal pole above his head and pressed his face hard against the outer walls of the vehicle as it tumbled—he estimated twenty or thirty times—four hundred metres down the mountain; how it had come to a stop, and how he had climbed out through the hatch on top; then, hearing Pete Hargreaves moaning, he had gone back in to help Pete out.

He told us that he and Hargreaves had pulled Kruzel out through the hatch as the ammunition started to go off, just before the APC exploded. (These were the explosions that the French had mistaken for mines.)

We wanted to leave Sarajevo that evening, but the only way to do so was by air. This time, with dark irony, the permission to use the airfield which had been denied by the Bosnian Serbs—the very authorization that would have prevented the accident—materialized, having been arranged swiftly by the French with Mladic.

By six o'clock, the light had begun to fade and the weather was deteriorating. At the airfield, we stood at attention in a light drizzle while a French honor guard escorted three unvarnished wooden coffins, each one draped in an American flag, onto a helicopter. The rain intensified, and the clouds seemed to descend upon us, obscuring the mountains that ringed the airfield. I turned to Wes Clark and said, "We've had enough for one day. Let's try again tomorrow." That night we slept, fitfully, on Army cots in the Ambassador's office, in a city still under siege.

The following morning, Sunday, August 20, we set out once again by convoy for the airport. The coffins were placed on a French helicopter and the injured men were carried on stretchers to a British helicopter. Suddenly—irrationally—I began to feel scared. As I started toward the British chopper, Clark stopped me. "We should go with the coffins all the way," he said. He was right, of course, and we boarded the French chopper. With my knees pressed against one of the coffins, I tried to read a John le Carré novel, *The Secret Pilgrim*, but couldn't focus on the words.

After an overnight stay at the Ramstein Air Base in Germany, we landed at Andrews Air Force Base shortly after noon on August 21. There, we walked into a silent crowd of colleagues, friends, and family—Warren Christopher, William Perry, Strobe Talbott, Tony Lake, Madeleine Albright, Peter Tarnoff, Sandy Berger, and my wife, Kati, among others—who were sitting behind a velvet rope. Under a blazing sun, Christopher, Perry, and Lake spoke movingly of the tragedy.

The families of Bob, Joe, and Nelson had chosen Arlington National Cemetery for the burials. The first of the funerals, held on August 22, was for Bob Frasure, and it was made particularly heartwrenching by the eloquent anguish of his sixteen-year-old daughter, Sarah, who spoke from the altar above her father's casket. "Now I will never wake to hear him making pancakes on a Sunday morning," she said in a breaking voice. "One question I will always ask myself is 'Why?'"

Putting a flower on Bob's casket, I said goodbye, and turned back toward Washington.

\* \* \*

A week later, things in Bosnia had changed drastically. In an action that combined brutality and stupidity, the Bosnian Serbs had slammed a mortar shell into the marketplace in Sarajevo on August 28, killing thirty-seven people and wounding more than eighty others. The attack angered President Clinton, and he told the United Nations and our NATO allies that we would wait no longer; it was time to "hit the Bosnian Serbs hard." His determination led to the start of the massive NATO air campaign. Consulted before the bombing, I told Talbott that our team unanimously favored a strong military response. Since I had long favored air strikes against the Bosnian Serbs, my position was no surprise to Washington. But coming from negotiators, who would normally oppose military action during delicate talks, it now carried weight.

Over the next eight weeks, we were engaged in talks of extraordinary intensity. We were able to shift gears quickly and show up within a few hours anywhere in Europe thanks to our "eighth member"—a military jet provided by Secretary of Defense Perry. However, shuttle diplomacy, no matter how dramatic or productive, has its limits. In the end, an all-out push for peace would require that the three Balkan presidents gather in a single place, preferably in the United States. We decided to delay such a high-risk event in order to give the Croat-Muslim offensive time to gain more ground against the Bosnian Serbs. Meanwhile, we would continue to try to narrow the differences between the sides through partial, interim agreements.

We announced two such agreements at meetings of the foreign ministers of the three countries—the first in Geneva, on September 8, and the second in New York, on September 26. These accords established a single Bosnian state consisting of two entities, one Serb and the other Muslim-Croat. We knew that the agreements were anything but airtight, and we made sure that our announcements spelled out their weaknesses and limitations. This continued to be our approach to public statements: never overstate the achievement; always assume the worst about the behavior of the parties; and repeatedly portray the glass as half empty rather than half full.

After Geneva, we returned home. We had been in the field for thirteen days, visiting eleven countries, and we felt that the momentum had finally begun to shift toward peace. Yet the fighting throughout Bosnia was very heavy, Sarajevo was still under siege, and NATO air strikes and missiles were pounding the Bosnian Serbs.

We had been back in Washington just three days when, with the fighting intensifying in western Bosnia, Christopher asked us to return immediately to Belgrade. We announced that we were dedicating our mission to the memory of Bob Frasure, Joe Kruzel, and Nelson Drew; then, the following day, we left—exhausted—for what turned out to be the most dramatic meeting of the shuttle.

*   *   *

The reconstituted team was of high calibre. It consisted of Christopher Hill, the State Department officer responsible for the Balkans, who was passionate and argumentative; Brigadier General Donald Kerrick, an un-flappable intelligence officer who represented the National Security Council; James Pardew, the head of the Pentagon's Balkan Task Force, who brought valuable skepticism to every unexamined assumption; and Roberts Owen, a distinguished Washington lawyer. He had been added to the team at the suggestion of Warren Christopher, who felt that we lacked the legal expertise that would be essential if the negotiations became technical. With Wes Clark, Rosemarie Pauli-Gikas, and me as holdovers, this superb team would remain intact throughout the negotiations.

As we flew to Belgrade, two issues became particularly worrisome. The first concerned the question of how long the Allied bombing would continue. Most NATO military planners wanted to end the air strikes as soon as possible. They were pleased with their accuracy and effectiveness but concerned that prolonged bombing would draw us into the conflict too deeply. The military feared what they called "the slippery slope" or "mission creep"—two phrases that evoked past disasters. When they talked about Bosnia, they often thought of Vietnam or Somalia.

Shortly before we returned to the region, U.S. Admiral Leighton Smith, the commander of the bombing campaign, told us that his pilots were running out of the targets that had been authorized by NATO. He said that in a few days he would be able to keep the bombing going only by attacking targets that had already been hit—or, as he put it, in his best, salty-old-seadog style, by "cleaning up a few stray cats and dogs."

These conversations profoundly affected our strategy for the next meeting with Milosevic. Returning to old targets was potentially more risky than the initial strikes, since the Serbs could have moved surface-to-air missiles to more effective sites as they learned to "decode" NATO's targeting strategy. In addition, we were under increasing pressure from our European allies to stop the bombing.

The second issue was what to do in the event that Milosevic asked us to meet with the leaders of the Bosnian Serbs—their so-called President, Radovan Karadzic, and General Mladic. Although both Karadzic and Mladic had met in the past with Western mediators, including former President Jimmy Carter, those contacts had led nowhere. Warren Christopher and I had concluded that we should negotiate only with Milosevic, holding him accountable for the actions of the Bosnian Serbs. Both Karadzic and Mladic had recently been indicted as war criminals. The question was: Should we meet with them?

I was influenced by the examples of Raoul Wallenberg and Folke Bernadotte, two legendary Swedes who had negotiated, respectively, with Adolf Eichmann and Heinrich Himmler in 1944 and 1945. Wallenberg and Bernadotte had dealt directly with these Nazi murderers in order to save lives; their decisions had resulted in the rescue of tens of thousands of Jews. As we descended toward the military airport in Belgrade, everyone agreed that we should meet with Karadzic and Mladic if it would help the negotiations.

\* \* \*

Two hours after landing, on September 13, we met Milosevic at a hunting lodge outside Belgrade. I was struck by a change in his tone. The bombing was obviously having an effect. Milosevic was in a rush to see it ended. Not for the first time, we knew that our chances for a viable peace would improve if the bombing continued, at least for a while. But we didn't know how much time was left.

Milosevic loved to keep people off balance with sudden changes of position or mood. On September 13, after we had talked for nearly an hour, he sprang a surprise. "Karadzic and Mladic are in another villa about two hundred meters away," he said. "Why don't we ask them to join us?"

"Mr. President," I said, wanting to slow things down, "we're ready to meet with them under two conditions. First, they must be part of your delegation; you must lead the discussions, you must control them. Second, they must not give us a lot of historical bullshit, as they have done with others. They must be ready for serious discussions."

"They will agree," Milosevic said.

Minutes later, two Mercedes sedans pulled up in the driveway. Two men stepped out. As they approached through the trees in the light of the early September evening, we saw their unmistakable silhouettes: Karadzic tall, with a shock of wild hair, and wearing a suit; Mladic short, with a burly frame, dressed in combat fatigues and walking as though he were wading through a muddy field.

I said to Milosevic, "We'll take a walk while you explain the ground rules. Then we'll return." We waited in the woods behind the villa, until an aide came to tell us that the President and his guests were ready.

I did not shake hands, although Karadzic and Mladic tried to get me to. Some of my team did, others did not; the choice was theirs. We all sat down at a long table on the patio facing one another. Immediately, Karadzic, speaking partly in English and partly in Serbian, started calling the bombing unfair. He said that he was ready to see an end to hostilities, but it became clear that he was referring to arrangements that would lock in the existing division of the country and result in its partition, with the Serbs controlling much more than the 49 percent of the land already agreed to in a previous plan. The other Bosnian Serbs sat silent. Glancing at Mladic, I found myself thinking that if Hollywood wanted to cast a war criminal, it could hardly do better than this. The general said nothing: he simply glowered as he engaged each of us, one by one, in a staring contest.

Karadzic, by contrast, was on his best behavior. He showed no sign of the sinister qualities that had led even so judicious an observer as Warren Zimmermann, the last American Ambassador to Yugoslavia, to label him the Himmler of his generation. He revealed his true nature only once, when he launched into a self-pitying diatribe against NATO and the Muslims, whom he wildly accused of mortaring their own marketplace on August 28 in order to lure NATO into the war. After a few minutes of this, I turned to Milosevic, ignoring Karadzic. "Mr. President," I said, "you assured us that this would not happen. If it continues, we are prepared to leave immediately."

Karadzic responded heatedly. "If we can't get anything done here, I will call President Carter," he said. "I am in regular contact with him." Karadzic started to rise, as if to go to a telephone. We knew, of course, that he had asked the former president to get involved again before the bombing started. We had asked Carter to stay out of the process, and, as far as we knew, he had done so.

For the first time, I spoke directly to Karadzic. "Let me tell you something," I said, my voice rising. "President Carter appointed me Assistant Secretary of State for East Asia. I worked for him for four years. Like most Americans, I have great admiration for him. But he is now a private citizen. We work only for President Clinton. We take orders only from President Clinton. That is all there is to it."

Karadzic sat back. Milosevic spoke quietly to him, and Karadzic then proposed that the Americans present an agreement that would end the bombing and stop the fighting around Sarajevo. I agreed, and asked Clark, Owen, Hill, and Pardew to draft a document that would end the siege of Sarajevo.

For the next half hour, as the team hunched over pads of paper, Milosevic and I walked around the garden. "Those guys," he said, meaning the Bosnian Serbs, "are so cut off they think Carter can still make American policy."

We watched from a distance as Wes Clark, standing between the Bosnian Serbs, began to read his draft out loud, pausing for translation. The booming voice of the interpreter drifted toward us. "We better join them right away," Milosevic said. "They are getting into trouble."

Although everyone else was standing, Milosevic pulled up a chair and sat down. I did the same to establish a rough equality. Above us, Karadzic, clearly angry, was saying that our draft proposal was unacceptable. Suddenly, Mladic erupted. Pushing himself to the center of the group, he began an emotional diatribe: the United States could never destroy the spirit of the Serb people; the bombing was a criminal act; and so on. Then a memorable line: "No one can give away a metre of our sacred Serb soil!" This was the real Mladic—the one who could unleash his troops on murderous rampages. I stood up and faced Milosevic, deliberately turning my back on Mladic and Karadzic. "Mr. President," I said, "this behavior is clearly not consistent with our agreement. If your 'friends'"—I said the word with all the sarcasm I could muster—"do not wish to have a serious discussion, we will leave now."

Milosevic paused, perhaps to gauge whether I was bluffing. Then he spoke sharply to his associates. As the Serbs began to argue, I motioned for my colleagues to withdraw to the other end of the patio, and we waited there, listening to the sounds of an acrimonious debate.

It was over in less than ten minutes.

\*　\*　\*

Our draft document required that the Bosnian Serbs "cease all offensive operations" in the Sarajevo area and remove all heavy weapons from that area within a week. They were to open two land routes out of Sarajevo to unimpeded humanitarian road traffic, which was broadly defined to include the transport of such items as glass, shoes, and radios. The Sarajevo airport was to be reopened within twenty-four hours. In return, NATO would cease the bombing for seventy-two hours, reserving the right to resume it if there was no compliance.

I called Washington from an adjoining room to alert the State Department to report what was going on. Afterward, Milosevic said that I had insulted Mladic by not shaking his hand. This, he said, would not make subsequent negotiations easier. "So be it," I replied. "We are expecting you to make this process work."

It was past midnight before the text was close to final form. The Bosnian Serbs had objected to nearly every word, but we obtained what we wanted: after four years, a lifting of the siege of Sarajevo. For our part, we would "recommend" to NATO that the bombing be suspended.

There was still one important procedural matter to resolve. The Serbs demanded that I sign the document. I refused, explaining that we had no formal authority concerning the activities of NATO or the United Nations. The only document we would accept was one whose only signators were the Bosnian Serbs, with Milosevic as a witness. It was an unusual structure

for such an agreement—one, as far as we knew, without diplomatic precedent. The Bosnian Serbs protested vigorously, but after another lengthy
argument they agreed to our format.

\*   \*   \*

At 2:15 A.M. on September 14, after more than ten hours of negotiations,
the Bosnian Serbs signed the document, one by one: first, Karadzic, who
signed without hesitating; then Nikola Koljevic, the "Vice-President of
Republika Srpska," a diminutive Shakespeare scholar who had taught in
Michigan, and who had spent much of the evening quoting the Bard and
trying to buttonhole me about his commitment to eternal Serb-American
friendship; then Momcilo Krajisnik, the hard-line speaker of the Bosnian
Serb parliament. Mladic was the last to sign. He sat slumped on a couch,
away from the rest of his colleagues. A Milosevic aide carried the paper to
him. He grabbed the pen, scrawled his name on the document without
looking at it, and sank back into the sofa. He seemed utterly spent, and, in
fact, he checked into a hospital the following day for what was described as
a kidney-stone problem. I was beginning to get a sense of these men: they
were headstrong, given to grandiose statements and theater, but they were
essentially bullies. Only force, or its credible threat, worked with them.

We got up to leave, carrying the precious original with us. Karadzic
grabbed my hand. "We are ready for peace," he said, in English. "Why did
you bomb us?"

"You know the answer to that," I said.

Two days later, we finally flew into Sarajevo. Coming into the city from
the airport, past overturned buses and shattered buildings, we drove through
streets crowded with pedestrians for the first time in months. By the time
we reached the Presidential offices, several hundred people had gathered
across the street. As we got out of our cars, they applauded. The siege of
Sarajevo was over.

**NOTE**

This article first appeared in the *New Yorker*, October 21–28, 1996, 88–104. Copyright ©
1996 by Richard Holbrooke.

# Background to Chapter 14

## Ending Violent Conflict in El Salvador

Violence in El Salvador escalated into military confrontation with the merging of five insurgent groups into the Frente Farabundo Martí para la Liberación Nacional (FMLN) and the launching of its "final offensive" in 1981. Cold War antagonisms helped to fuel the civil war and inhibited the United Nations and the Organization of American States from playing a mediating role. Regional peacemaking efforts achieved little, and eventually gave way to a concerted single-party mediation under the auspices of the UN secretary-general after a military offensive by the FMLN in November 1989 revealed the conflict to be a stalemate. The protracted mediation process took a relatively independent course, despite the misgivings of the United States and the mutual distrust of the participants. The mediator's impartiality and the backing of the UN Security Council, which gave him legitimacy, eventually fostered a series of agreements between the two parties that ended the civil war, addressed its root causes, and went a long way toward reintegrating Salvadoran society.

### MAJOR ACTORS

- Government of El Salvador: led by President Alfredo Cristiani
- Frente Farabundo Martí para la Liberación Nacional (FMLN): coalition of armed insurgent groups
- Alvaro de Soto: personal representative of the UN secretary-general; mediator of the negotiations
- United Nations: led by Secretary-General Javier Pérez de Cuéllar

- Organization of American States (OAS): led by Secretary-General João Clemente Baena Soares
- Contadora Group: Colombia, Mexico, Panama, and Venezuela
- Support Group: Argentina, Brazil, Peru, and Uruguay
- Friends of the Secretary-General: Colombia, Mexico, Spain, and Venezuela
- United States
- Soviet Union
- Cuba

## IMPORTANT DATES

- 1981: "Final offensive" of the FMLN
- 1984: President Napoleón Duarte proposes peace talks
- November 1986: UN-OAS joint diplomatic initiative to negotiate peace in El Salvador
- August 1987: Esquipulas Declaration is adopted
- June 1, 1989: President Cristiani proposes dialogue with the FMLN
- September 1, 1989: Alvaro de Soto appointed UN secretary-general's personal representative for Central American "peace process"
- November 11, 1989: The FMLN launches its largest offensive of the war
- January 31, 1990: Pérez de Cuéllar agrees to assist El Salvador negotiations; de Soto begins shuttling
- April 4, 1990: Geneva Agreement formulates basic rules and framework for the negotiations
- May 21, 1990: Caracas Agreement sets general agenda and timetable for the negotiations
- July 26, 1990: San José Agreement on human rights is reached
- April 27, 1991: Mexico agreements on constitutional reforms, legal matters, and a truth commission are reached
- September 25, 1991: New York agreement on a National Commission for the Consolidation of Peace and on the Compressed Agenda is reached
- December 31, 1991: New York Act I finalizes the substantive peace accords
- January 13, 1992: New York Act II completes the remaining items and implementation calendar
- January 16, 1992: Peace agreement signed at Chapultepec Castle in Mexico City

## KEY AGREEMENTS REACHED

- Cease-fire
- Demobilization of troops
- Military reform, including dismantling of paramilitary bodies
- Creation of national civil police
- Creation of national human rights oversight mechanism
- Electoral and judicial reform
- Formation of a truth commission

## PRINCIPAL OUTCOMES

- Civil war was ended, coupled with the removal of overbearing miltary power and the opening of unprecedented political space
- The FMLN became a political party and participated in the 1994 elections

# 14

# Ending Violent Conflict in El Salvador

ALVARO DE SOTO

## INTRODUCTION

In the 1990–91 negotiations to end the conflict in El Salvador there were many players, but only one mediator.[1] As I will explain later, a key innovation was the use of a "friends of the secretary-general" mechanism, possibly giving the impression that the mediation was somehow a collective effort. The fact is that one of the keys to the success of the effort was precisely that, except for one episode of aborted diplomatic hijacking, there was never any question about the unity and integrity of the third-party mediation and who was in charge of it.

In early 1989, United Nations Secretary-General Javier Pérez de Cuéllar had received the backing of the Security Council, and the legitimacy that derived from it, to accede to the request of the warring parties that he assist them in solving the conflict, which is said to have resulted in seventy-five thousand deaths.[2] He kept the council informed in general terms about his efforts as they unfolded, but he neither sought nor was issued any guidance

349

or instructions on the exercise of his good offices. The Security Council, a body of fifteen members, resisted isolated attempts to have it interfere in the conduct of the mediation, quite properly leaving it in the hands of the secretary-general and his representative. Did the collective source of his support make the UN-led mediation a multiparty endeavor? I think not. The Security Council sometimes lays down principles and parameters for negotiation, such as, for example, those that guide the secretary-general in the Cyprus talks. But it rarely involves itself in the nuts and bolts, which as a practical matter must be the domain of the secretary-general acting somewhat as the United Nations' agent. The Security Council, when it comes to conflict resolution by negotiation, is board rather than manager, certainly not micromanager.[3]

I represented Pérez de Cuéllar in the El Salvador peace negotiations, and no one but my staff and me sat with the representatives of the government and the Frente Farabundo Martí para la Liberación Nacional (FMLN) at the negotiating table or attended the countless separate meetings with them or with their leaders. Because of acute distrust between the parties that ruled out direct give-and-take, we wrote much of what they signed as agreements, unassisted by anyone outside the employ of the UN Secretariat. Given all these circumstances, I believe I am safe in asserting that the UN-led role cannot properly be described as multiparty mediation in the sense used in other chapters of this book.

Given the limited space available for these personal notes, I will not attempt a comprehensive, linear narration of the negotiation nor bore the reader with one more potted summary of the El Salvador peace accords. The milestones are well known: the Geneva Agreement of April 4, 1990, containing the basic rules and framework for the negotiation; the Caracas Agreement of May 21, 1990, on the general agenda and timetable for the comprehensive negotiating process; the San José Agreement of July 26, 1990, on human rights; the Mexico agreements of April 27, 1991, on constitutional reforms and other legal matters and on the Commission on the Truth; the New York agreement of September 25, 1991, on the creation of the National Commission for the Consolidation of Peace and on the Compressed Agenda; New York Act I of December 31, 1991, finalizing the substantive peace accords; New York Act II of January 13, 1992, completing all remaining items, including the calendar of implementation of all agreements; and the Peace Agreement signed on January 16, 1992, at Chapultepec Castle, in Mexico City.[4]

It is not possible here to do justice both to the substance of those accords and to the dynamics of mediation, which are the theme of this book.

Mediation being the theme, I will dispense with a substantive discussion of the smooth cease-fire; the punctually dismantled assault battalions; the disbanded paramilitaries; the orderly demobilization of the FMLN; the reformed and purged army, now under civilian control, removed from politics and confined to external defense; the pioneering civilian police; the new ombudsman; the reformed judiciary and electoral system; the reintegration programs; the far-reaching, cathartic report of the Commission on the Truth; the functioning democracy that has ensued—the "negotiated revolution."[5] For the texts of the accords and an acceptable general narration of the milestones of the negotiation, if not for the more colorful details, I will rely on UN publications.[6] I will refer to the accords and to the narrative of the negotiation only insofar as they are strictly germane to the subject at hand.[7]

The goal of the government in the negotiation was to end the armed confrontation and to demobilize the FMLN. The Salvadoran armed forces were, from the government's perspective, merely responding to FMLN aggression: the state was defending not only the rule of law but also itself. The FMLN leadership insisted that it had only resorted to arms when all peaceful efforts to address substantive political grievances—inequitable land distribution and economic marginalization; stifling restraints on democracy; massive violations of human rights and impunity—had failed, and state repression had become unbearable. The original goal of the revolutionary movement was to take power. However, by 1989, and particularly after the November offensive of that year, it sought to use the battlefield to force consideration of political issues and thus achieve changes in society and in the institutions of state. It would not cease its military pressure until these ends were achieved. When the United Nations accepted to take on the mediation, therefore, the stage was set for a wartime negotiation. Its purpose would be to agree on changes necessary to satisfy not only the FMLN itself, but also significant sectors of society who felt that their aspirations were represented by the insurgents. In his remarkable address at the signing of the peace accords at Chapultepec Castle, in Mexico City, on January 16, 1992, President Alfredo Cristiani accepted candidly that when he had assumed the presidency in 1989, there did not exist in El Salvador a democracy capable of accommodating discussion of grievances such as those voiced by the FMLN. Vestigial Cold War rhetoric of the 1980s about an epic struggle against communism notwithstanding, the peace negotiation in El Salvador turned out to be about the building of democracy.

I have written earlier about the sustainability of the El Salvador peace accords.[8] In late 1996, the General Assembly asked for an evaluation of the implementation of the peace accords in light of the stated goals of the negotiation. In his report, the secretary-general noted the deficiencies in the implementation of some of the accords, but concluded:

> Five years after the conclusion of the negotiations in far-ranging and ambitious peace agreements, an extraordinary transformation has taken place in El Salvador. The peace process has generated, in a slow but steady manner, conditions that provide the basis for the gradual consolidation of democracy within the country.[9]

## WHY THE UNITED NATIONS, AND HOW

### Prior Attempts at Mediation

During the years preceding Alfredo Cristiani's presidency, none of the moves toward peace had ever led to anything approaching a negotiation in earnest, let alone a third-party mediation. Into this category fall the 1984 initiative of President Napoleón Duarte that led to the talks at La Palma and those at the papal nuncio's residence in 1987. The mediatory efforts of the Catholic Church in El Salvador were mostly of a humanitarian character, until the church-sponsored initiative to promote dialogue at a national level in 1988.

Javier Pérez de Cuéllar took office in 1982 as UN secretary-general. His being a Latin American did not at first alter the fact that the United Nations was, for all intents and purposes, off-limits as either forum or agent for addressing problems of peace and security in Latin America—the United States' "backyard." The Reagan administration was in power in Washington. Jeane Kirkpatrick was the U.S. permanent representative to the United Nations. The United States made no secret of its distaste for any hint of a UN role in Central America. Nicaragua tried to bring to the Security Council its complaints about the cross-border attacks against it by the Contras and other sabotage activities by U.S. agents. The council gave it precious little comfort. U.S. allies in Central America were wary of the Security Council as a diplomatic instrument, sharing the U.S. perception that, for these purposes, it was hopelessly tainted by the permanent membership of the Soviet Union and therefore by and large unreliable. Intervention by the Organization of American States (OAS) was similarly discouraged. Nicaragua's suspicion of the OAS as a U.S.-dominated body did not stop Nicaragua from occasionally airing its grievances there, but the United States at the time did not encourage attempts at negotiated solution of the Central American conflicts by anyone. The United Nations and the OAS therefore canceled each other out and were mostly out of the picture until late 1986.

Into this diplomatic vacuum leaped the Contadora Group, founded by the foreign ministers of Colombia, Mexico, Panama, and Venezuela on the island of that name off Panama on January 9, 1983, offering to the Central American governments their diplomacy and sometimes considerably more. For several years they ploughed an unpromising field, showing more ambition than success. Indeed excessive ambition may have been their Achilles' heel: rather than addressing the separate components of the crisis piecemeal, each according to its specificity, they went for a comprehensive approach, trying to establish rules to be applied across the board concerning cross-border military activity, limitation of armaments, democratization, and economic and social development. The four foreign ministers treated their Central American brethren initially with studied deference, to the point where another important flaw in their approach consisted of the absence of any clear mechanism for bringing into the peace effort the insurgent or irregular groups that were pitted against the established authorities. Their deference may have reflected concerns about potential or actual insurgencies in their own territories. In due course, they became frustrated with the exercise, and by late 1985 the Central Americans had grown weary of being treated, in their view, somewhat impatiently, if not downright patronizingly, by their more powerful colleagues.

In 1983, pursuant to repeated Nicaraguan pinpricks, the United States had consented to the adoption by the Security Council of a resolution that tepidly endorsed the efforts of the Contadora Group and asked to be kept informed. The secretary-general, for whom some members of the council had tried to provide a role, was grudgingly conceded a bit part as the conveyor of Contadora's reports. By and large, however, the Contadora Group did not bring the secretary-general into its confidence or inform him systematically of its efforts. No actual negotiation, let alone mediation by the Contadora Group, between the government of El Salvador and the FMLN took place.

In January 1986, at a low point in prospects for a diplomatic solution, I proposed to Pérez de Cuéllar a scheme for the United Nations to insinuate itself into a diplomatic role. In order to show that they were not mutually exclusive and could even work together, he—the first Latin American secretary-general of the United Nations—and João Clemente Baena Soares, his colleague the secretary-general of the OAS, would join hands to gently remind the Central American countries and the Contadora Group of the services that the two organizations could provide, separately or together. Pérez de Cuéllar was not enthusiastic about the idea, and it took several months before he allowed me to take it up with Baena Soares. He finally came around in late August, when I broached the subject at Mount Sinai Hospital, where he lay following quadruple coronary bypass surgery.

Baena Soares was also cautious when I flew to Washington to visit him in early September. It was only in November, after I bearded him repeatedly through his principal aide, Harry Beleván, a Peruvian diplomat like myself, that he agreed to come to New York to further discuss the idea with Pérez de Cuéllar and me. My UN colleague Francesc Vendrell drafted a non-paper in the format of an à la carte menu spelling out available UN and OAS services, which included good offices. Baena agreed to it with few changes. That very day we called in the Central American and subsequently the Contadora Group ambassadors (strengthened, by this time, with the addition of a "support group" composed of Argentina, Brazil, Peru, and Uruguay) and presented them with the joint paper. The Central Americans expressed somewhat nonplussed thanks. The Contadora Group was less enthusiastic: one ambassador even asked Pérez de Cuéllar, rather pointedly and certainly rhetorically, whether he had a mandate to take such an initiative.

The November 1986 joint initiative was not appreciated by the United States, as was politely made clear to Pérez de Cuéllar by the U.S. permanent representative to the United Nations, General Vernon Walters, and to Baena Soares by Walters's colleague at the OAS. It nevertheless became our entry point to the Central American peace efforts. The two secretaries-general toured Central America with the Contadora and Support Group foreign ministers in January 1987, at the invitation of the ministers. That in turn led, for the first time, to the presence of both the United Nations and the OAS at the Central American summit, in August 1987, when the Esquipulas Declaration was adopted by the presidents of the five countries of the region (Costa Rica, El Salvador, Guatemala, Honduras, and Nicaragua), and the two organizations were assigned a role in international verification of the implementation of their undertakings.[10] These undertakings were to prevent the use of their territories to destabilize their neighbors, and to take steps toward democratization and national reconciliation. This opened the way for the establishment, in December 1989, of the United Nations Observer Mission in Central America (ONUCA), the first UN peacekeeping operation ever in Latin America, with unarmed, uniformed observers patrolling the borders. It also made possible the monitoring by the United Nations (and the OAS, separately) of the turning-point elections in Nicaragua, the first such operation by the United Nations in an independent state. Thus by 1989, with the fissures in the Cold War turning to cracks and with the Bush administration in power in Washington, and with a manifest desire in Central America to shed the shackles of ideological warfare, the United Nations found itself positioned to play a role that had seemed unthinkable but a few years earlier.

In his inaugural speech on June 1, 1989, Cristiani proposed the initiation of dialogue with the FMLN. The church helped arrange a meeting between government and FMLN representatives in Mexico in September, at which the principal agreement was to meet again the following month in San José, Costa Rica, and, at the insistence of the FMLN, to invite representatives of the United Nations and the Organization of American States to be present as "witnesses."

I attended the October meeting, where two members of the Salvadoran bishopric sat at the head of the table accompanied by the deputy papal nuncio in San Salvador. It was readily apparent that the role of the church was confined to procedural facilitation rather than anything resembling mediation or good offices, which implies a substantive role. The meeting—held in a nunnery—cannot fairly be described as anything but a calamitous failure, and certainly nothing that can remotely be labeled as negotiation occurred. The parties mostly hurled rhetoric at each other and at the nearby press, and as if things were not bad enough, they quite openly taped the proceedings, thus quashing any possibility of a free exchange that might lead to serious give-and-take. Despite these fatal flaws, the parties agreed to gather again one month later in Caracas. However, the FMLN, on the pretext of the brutal murders of noncombatant political and other leaders in the interval, canceled their participation. Three weeks later, on November 11, the real reason came out when they launched the largest offensive of the war, penetrating the main cities including the capital.

The General Assembly of the Organization of American States was meeting in Washington, D.C., when the offensive was launched, and Baena Soares was invited to El Salvador by the government in order to preempt a Nicaraguan proposal that the OAS should give him a mediating role. The government discouraged any effort by him to mediate or enter into contact with the FMLN, and he was forced to make a somewhat undignified exit after a military incident that trapped him in his hotel.

The government and the FMLN did not resume contacts until they were brought together in late March 1990 under UN auspices.

### November 1989: The Watershed

The November 1989 offensive left many dead, including six Jesuit priests murdered by order of senior army chiefs.[11] The silver lining was that the offensive was, almost literally, the defining moment—the point at which it became possible to seriously envisage a negotiation. The FMLN had been reviewing its long-term prospects and strategy since 1988, adjusting its sights in light of the evolving climate. Its leaders were coming to the view that time was not entirely on their side, though this was unrelated either to the support they continued to enjoy inside and outside El Salvador, or to their well-stocked arsenals, which had been recently improved by the acquisition of surface-to-air missiles. However, the offensive showed the FMLN leaders that they could not spark a popular uprising, even in the poor districts (where they were bombed by the Salvadoran air force). The offensive also showed the government, and elites in general, that the armed forces could not defend them, let alone crush the insurgents (the FMLN for an agonizing few days captured the residential districts of the wealthy, mostly treating them attentively, then melting away). However inchoate at first, the elements of a military deadlock began to appear. Neither side could defeat the other. As the dust settled, the notion that the conflict could not be solved by military means, and that its persistence was causing pain that could no longer be endured, began to take shape. The offensive codified the existence of a *mutually hurting stalemate.* The conflict was *ripe* for a negotiated solution.[12]

At this juncture, with the effective withdrawal from the scene, long since, of the Contadora Group as a diplomatic agent, and the eclipse of Baena Soares following his San Salvador misadventure, the United Nations was the only would-be mediator left standing. Within a matter of weeks, we were approached, first by the FMLN, then by the government.

We had had discreet contacts with the FMLN ever since Fidel Castro arranged for a quiet, unscheduled encounter with two prominent guerrilla commanders in Havana during an official visit by Pérez de Cuéllar to Cuba in 1985. Pérez de Cuéllar stayed only for a few minutes; Vendrell and I heard them out. Vendrell maintained contacts with the FMLN over the years, mostly on the margins of nonaligned conferences. He became my deputy following my appointment on September 1, 1989, as the secretary-general's personal representative for the Central American peace process. Late in November 1989, while the FMLN's offensive was still in full swing in El Salvador, the FMLN's political-diplomatic commission formally asked to see me in Mexico, where it had offices. I insisted on the commission's coming to UN Headquarters, but one of its two representatives could not get a U.S. visa, so I arranged for a semiclandestine meeting under an indirect UN umbrella, the headquarters of the International Civil Aviation Organization in Montreal. This took place on December 8.

The FMLN representatives had yet to be fully convinced about UN involvement. They did not perceive the USSR as an unconditional ally, and this led them to apprehension about the U.S.-dominated Security Council that they saw emerging. A recent event gave the FMLN pause: the UN secretary-general's decision to allow the deployment of South African police to restore order following a large South West African People's Organization infiltration at the start of the implementation of the Namibia independence plan, before the arrival of UN military and police personnel— a decision that the FMLN wrongly thought had been imposed by the United States. If the secretary-general could thus be pushed around by the United States in faraway Africa, the FMLN reasoned, how could he withstand U.S. pressure concerning an issue so close to home? Vendrell and I disabused the representatives about the Namibia events, and explained that if the secretary-general undertook to mediate between the government of El Salvador and the FMLN, he would be strictly impartial, and that the role of the Security Council in negotiations conducted by the secretary-general was minimal. I assured them that Pérez de Cuéllar was particularly adept at keeping the Security Council in the picture only as much as was necessary to maintain its support, but not enough to allow it a margin for micromanaging the process. The Security Council's role, in any case, would not be under Chapter VII of the UN Charter, which provides for coercive measures. Even in the aftermath of a solution to the conflict, were the United Nations called on to play a role in monitoring a separation of forces and a cease-fire—a peacekeeping role—it would be under Chapter VI, and it would require the cooperation, if not the consent, of both parties, including the FMLN.

The FMLN representatives remained skeptical. To overcome their concern, they advocated the creation by the secretary-general of a grouping of states whose declared role would be to assist and advise him, but whose true purpose would be to counterbalance the weight of the Security Council. I resisted this idea, which to me sounded too close to a collectivization of the negotiating effort. It was reminiscent of the Contadora Group, at whose meetings I had witnessed several foreign ministers, some of them individually highly talented, even brilliant, spending hours discussing tactics and ending up with compromises that soaked up all creativity and sense of direction. It is inherent in good mediation that there should be one agent unquestionably and unequivocally in charge. If there are several mediators, parties in conflict might be tempted to play one off against the other. I made no commitment except to be strictly impartial.

The approach of the Cristiani government was indirect, the channel the Summit of Central American Presidents held in Costa Rica on December

11 and 12, 1989. President Oscar Arias, the host, was leaving office early in 1990, and he was genuinely concerned that none of the other regional leaders could assume the role he had taken on with such missionary zeal of pursuing the peace process. He thought the prodding would have to come from outside the region, and the time was ripe for the United Nations to don his peacemaker's mantle. I had prepared identical letters to the five presidents in anticipation of the summit and had Pérez de Cuéllar sign them before I went to Montreal, delaying their dispatch until after my meeting with the FMLN. The letter emphasized two points: the need for a visible and viable mechanism for bringing guerrilla groups into the effort to solve the conflicts in the region—missing in the Esquipulas scheme and the Contadora approach—and the need to commit to the effort powers from outside the region without whose cooperation, or at least lack of obstruction, success might prove elusive. Pérez de Cuéllar offered to assist in both efforts.

Arias called me at home on December 11, during a break in the talks, saying that his colleagues had turned their attention to Pérez de Cuéllar's letter. We discussed ways of responding in the summit communiqué. The following day, in their joint statement, the presidents asked the secretary-general to "do everything within his power to take the necessary steps to ensure the resumption of the dialogue between the government of El Salvador and the FMLN, thereby facilitating [the] successful conclusion [of the conflict]." They furthermore asked the secretary-general to establish "the necessary connections" to involve states with interests in the region more directly in the peace efforts. The statement, a direct response to Pérez de Cuéllar's overture, overcame in two strokes the structural flaws of the Contadora and Esquipulas approaches. Cristiani's concurrence with the communiqué bringing the United Nations directly into the picture spoke for itself. In early January he announced his intention to travel to New York to call on Pérez de Cuéllar personally.

On January 23, the FMLN wrote to Pérez de Cuéllar formally requesting him to bring together the two sides to the conflict "with the purpose of formally initiating a serious negotiation with the mediation or good offices of the secretary-general." Such a mediation should have "a new and different focus and methodology" (from that followed at their September and October gatherings under the auspices of the church). As Pérez de Cuéllar's guest for lunch on January 31, 1990, Cristiani, accompanied by his minister for defense, General Humberto Larios, handed the secretary-general a letter confirming his request to help bring the parties together. During the table conversation, he expressed no reservations about a UN role going beyond mere matchmaking. The following day, on February 1, I flew to

Mexico to meet the FMLN and begin to lay down conditions for the initiation of a serious negotiation.

## The Ground Rules

I shuttled for eight weeks between Mexico City, where I met, seriatim, all five members of the FMLN general command (who carefully sized me up), and San Salvador, where I saw President Cristiani, in order to work out the framework and the basic rules for the negotiations. It was intrinsically difficult to agree since, not surprisingly, their differences on fine points of procedure masked deeply rooted divergences on strategy and substance.

Shuttling was unavoidable because, in the wake of the offensive, neither side was ready to meet face to face with its adversary, and because Cristiani had chosen not to be represented by truly plenipotentiary negotiators, but rather insisted on personally agreeing to specific language—while at the same time assuring me that his "dialogue commission," as he called it, was fully empowered to negotiate. (This commission was composed of two government ministers, a ranking member of the armed forces who, however, was not in the High Command, and private citizens. The individual talent and good will of some of them notwithstanding, none were political figures carrying any weight in El Salvador.) I had my own exigencies; I was determined to avoid the pitfalls that had doomed the Contadora Group effort as well as the efforts of the church, at least in part for lack of clearly agreed ground rules, and was therefore convinced that the investment of time and effort in this exercise would be amply justified over time.

My suspicion that I would need to play a proactive role was quickly confirmed. I knew that I would have to resort to the single negotiating text technique, in which I had been steeped during my long association with the Law of the Sea Conference, where I had been the Group of 77's coordinator and negotiator. This technique consists of consulting with the parties on each issue and subsequently submitting a text to them, as far as possible simultaneously, and then discussing it with each of them separately and revising it in light of their reactions so as to narrow down differences, repeating the exercise as many times as necessary. It was painstaking and time consuming but unavoidable in circumstances in which any proposal presented by one side was automatically rejected by the other. We succeeded in saving some time through the genius of my legal adviser, Pedro Nikken, a distinguished Venezuelan jurist, who churned out formulas on his laptop computer, sitting next to me at the head of the negotiating table, and discussing them with me, on the spot, while the negotiators droned on—surely a first in peace negotiations (the laptop, not the droning). The peace accords were largely negotiated through this technique: except for the final details of the Geneva Agreement, the fairly straightforward drafting of the human rights agreement, and the final wrap-up deal concerning constitutional reforms at dawn on April 27, 1991, no give-and-take ever took place between the negotiators sitting face to face. Indeed, most of the time at the misnamed direct negotiating rounds was devoted to my shuttling between the same parties under the same roof.

The main issue dividing the parties on procedure was stated by them at the outset, in the late January letters from Cristiani and the FMLN. The government wanted to stick to the format laid down in Mexico the previous September that gave the third party—the church at the time—a minimal role. The FMLN wanted to depart radically from that format so as to give the United Nations a mediating role, with the emphasis on separate dealings between the mediator and each of the parties. They were extremely skeptical about direct negotiations, without the presence of an intermediary, in which, they said, the government could stonewall and get away with it. They argued that by ensuring an authoritative, third-party participation and presence throughout the negotiation, the seriousness of the parties could be independently guaranteed. Thus, in a sense, they wanted the United Nations to keep the parties honest. The government favored open-ended negotiating sessions between representatives of the parties with only short breaks. The FMLN negotiators insisted on breaks of several weeks between sessions so as to consult their constituents, who were either in the field or under deep cover in the cities in El Salvador.

It took the better part of the eight-week shuttle to persuade the parties to accept a compromise between the two positions, which was to combine and alternate the two. The secretary-general was entrusted with the responsibility of ensuring that the process would be "continuous and uninterrupted." This was meant to enhance our authority by allowing us to exercise our discretion on which method—shuttling or direct talks—was to be used at each stage to ensure that they indeed remained "continuous and uninterrupted." The FMLN leaders suspected that decisions would be taken by Cristiani himself, in consultation with leaders of the armed forces, and with nudging by the United States. They inferred from this that Cristiani would not have the capacity to empower a team of negotiators to engage in real give-and-take in face-to-face talks away from San Salvador. Although the details could be worked out in direct talks, the political heavy lifting would have to be done in separate dealings of the secretary-general's representative with the parties. Cristiani nevertheless continued to insist that even though he remained at the disposal of the secretary-general himself, and he would accept to see me in San Salvador whenever I so requested, his representatives had the necessary instructions and authority to negotiate on his behalf, and that he would expect negotiations to take place primarily in direct talks. He barred his own direct, personal participation in face-to-face talks as well as any meetings in El Salvador. As a result, during the two-year mediation I made more than thirty trips to see Cristiani in El Salvador, sometimes in the middle of a negotiating session in some nearby capital.

The methodological preferences embraced by the parties did not remain static over the course of the negotiation. There was much tactical wavering and shifting of roles as each saw it in its interest to seek direct contacts or discourage them, and to press for an increased or diminished UN role. In practice, my powers in scheduling the pace and the venue of meetings and shuttling turned out to be considerably less than dictatorial, and in fact such decisions were taken after arduous and time-consuming wrangling on venues, dates, and duration in which Cristiani was sometimes personally involved. As Woody Allen might have said, half of mediation is making sure that the negotiators show up.

At my insistence, the parties specifically empowered me to consult with Salvadoran political and social organizations, as well as with states from outside the region in a position to lend assistance to the UN effort. This was broadly written to leave the choice entirely at UN discretion. Despite the FMLN request at Montreal, there was no reference to the creation of any groupings of states, let alone to any specific countries. I had in mind a mechanism somewhat different from what they envisaged, as I will later describe. I was left at liberty to carry out these consultations as I deemed fit, without the parties having any say in the matter.

As it turned out, the final details concerning the rules and the framework governing the negotiation had to be worked out in a face-to-face meeting that I persuaded the parties to hold, in strict privacy. Getting the FMLN to agree to this meeting took quite a bit of cajoling. We gathered in Mexico City on March 27, 1990, and ironed out remaining differences in a few hours. The representatives initialed the text, but I insisted that the agreement required proper solemnity (and hence, visible political commitment), for which purpose it had to be signed in public, in the presence of the secretary-general, and at a UN venue. I managed to waylay Pérez de Cuéllar for a few hours in Geneva on a trip between two European capitals. The signing of what became known as the Geneva Agreement took place in the United Nations' Palais des Nations on April 4, 1990.

## The Agenda and the Calendar

The following month, the negotiating teams were sequestered, according to my specifications, on the campus of a Venezuelan think tank in the hills above Caracas. The issue at hand was the substantive agenda for the talks. On this subject, all that had been agreed on at Geneva was: "The purpose of the process [of negotiation] shall be to end the armed conflict by political means as speedily as possible, promote the democratization of the country, guarantee unrestricted respect for human rights and reunify Salvadorian society."

Although this terse description of the fourfold goal of the negotiation was not insubstantial, a more specific, itemized agenda needed to be fleshed out. Before I could persuade the negotiators to get down to business we had to sit through a lengthy exchange of historical recitations and political analysis (which, while educational, was distracting from the perspective of a mediator in a hurry). The FMLN insisted that the first issue that needed to be addressed was that of the armed forces. They were highly doctrinaire on this point, arguing that the issue was so insidiously pervasive that it would be pointless to address anything else until there was agreement about what to do with the military. Therefore, this had to be the first item on the agenda. The next should be the question of human rights, followed by the judicial system, the electoral system, constitutional reform, economic and social issues, and verification by the United Nations.

The FMLN's handling of economic and social questions as the last substantive issue was particularly revealing, given that the root cause of much of the unrest that had led to the insurgency was grinding poverty and marginalization in a densely populated country with an acute shortage of land. Confronting brutal armed forces repression was a pressing need, but the military apparatus was at its origin and ultimately only a tool for keeping discontent about the root causes under control. The FMLN, whether because of factional divergences, lack of expertise, or a sober appraisal of political realities, left the examination of these root causes for a late stage; it was only in the last six months of the negotiation that the FMLN began to articulate its ideas, studiously refraining from any revolutionary proposal. It did not try to tamper with the economic model that Cristiani's administration was promoting, which included economic stabilization and structural reform. Instead, it substantially lowered its sights, and the economic and social question metamorphosed at the eleventh hour into a hastily crafted arrangement on reintegration of combatants and their supporters.

The government, at this stage, still approached the exercise more as a dialogue than a negotiation, and it was thus able to rationalize its willingness to discuss almost anything. Therefore, it did not object to any of the items proposed by the FMLN for inclusion on the agenda, or to the order in which they were to be considered, though a measure of deft drafting was required to make sure that the headings would be neutral in formulation. The only serious controversy was over the nomenclature of the armed forces item: the FMLN would have liked to discuss the *future* of the armed forces (which it proposed to abolish), whereas the government wanted to restrict discussion to *restructuring* or, better, *modernization*—which it claimed was already under way.

More difficult than settling on the agenda was agreeing to a two-stage approach to the negotiation. This was implicit in the Geneva Agreement, but needed to be spelled out and clarified in the agenda. The government surprised me by agreeing to the FMLN's proposal that the initial objective would be to reach political agreements on the seven agenda items *before* a cease-fire would be negotiated. Even though the government's overriding goal—perhaps its sole one—was to stop the fighting and dismantle the FMLN, it was willing to wait until the FMLN obtained the political agreements it pursued before the government's own goal was even addressed. Only once a cease-fire was in place would the negotiation move to the second stage, which was described as the "establishment of the necessary guarantees and conditions for reintegrating the members of the FMLN, within a framework of full legality, into the civil, institutional and political life of the country." Under this general heading, which implied the demobilization of the FMLN without actually saying so (FMLN combatants had their pride; they had not been defeated), the same items as those addressed in the first stage were enumerated, with the addition of "reintegration of FMLN members" as the second to last question—before "UN verification."

I hoped that if the pace of the negotiation was sufficiently intense, the agenda could be dealt with in a matter of a few months, and feared that the government might find it difficult to sustain support for continuing to negotiate if the ambitious agenda as a precondition for reaching a cease-fire did not include some notion of duration of the process. I therefore proposed that a target date should be set for the conclusion of the first stage. With some misgivings, the FMLN agreed to "the middle of September of 1990" as that date. Obviously it was not meant to be more than a psychological device to egg negotiations on; it would have defied common sense to set a date certain for the conclusion of negotiations, which depended on two sides agreeing on mutually acceptable terms. The FMLN would never have agreed to setting a deadline. Additionally, an estimated duration for the second stage was mentioned—two to six months. Thus was the Caracas Agreement structured, in one week, until then the longest cohabitation between government and FMLN negotiators since the beginning of the war.

Key aspects of the Caracas Agreement proved later to be the source of problems for one or both of the parties. For the FMLN, the issue of the target date blew entirely out of proportion largely because, owing to a mis-reading of the Caracas Agreement, the target date was translated into English as "deadline." Bernard Aronson, assistant secretary of state for Inter-American Affairs, not famous for his mastery of the language of Cervantes and therefore presumably working from the English translation, took to browbeating me (rather than the FMLN, with which the United States would have no direct contact at the time) about the FMLN's failure to come to a cease-fire, notwithstanding the lack of synchronized, verifiable agreement, accompanied by a timetable for implementation, on all but one of the seven issues on the agenda as required in the Caracas Agreement.

Another major problem was the two-stage format. It surfaced when discussion concerning the cease-fire regime began in earnest in 1991. The cease-fire was to involve the separation of combatants in zones to be specified, under UN supervision, while the list of items encompassed under the "establishment of guarantees and conditions for reintegrating the members of FMLN" was negotiated. So far, so good. However, by mid-1991, with the negotiation in a deep rut, it became clear that my original estimate of how long it would take to negotiate political agreements had been rather optimistic.

The prospect of a longer-lasting negotiation cast the parties' assumptions on the cease-fire regime into an entirely new light. There was no disagreement between them that, during the cease-fire, neither of the two sides could be left at a military disadvantage, since there was no certainty on when, or indeed whether, the remaining negotiations would lead to a final settlement. There, however, the common ground ended. For the FMLN, maintaining military capability entailed not only combatants retaining their weapons, but also ensuring supply lines, continuing recruitment and training of new fighters, and the ability to carry out maneuvers. All of this would occur in sizable swatches of Salvadoran territory, and of course for an indefinite period of time—awaiting the uncertain, far from foregone conclusion of an extremely difficult and complex negotiation, in an atmosphere that did not yet lend itself to distension and democratic discourse. The government, not surprisingly, would hear nothing of such arrangements, which they described as an "armed peace," inadmissible under the constitution in force.

With the spectacular Mexico agreements on constitutional reform and the creation of the Commission on the Truth, in April 1991, the negotiation had yielded as much as it could do within the two-stage negotiating scheme; the fact that the FMLN felt compelled to maintain full military capability and preparedness during a cease-fire, given that it was impossible to ensure the outcome of continuing negotiations, placed agreement on cease-fire terms beyond reach. Although the Mexico agreements were a crucial watershed, providing as they did the legal basis without which it would not have been possible to attain the peace accords, the job was far from complete: the details of armed forces reform needed to be spelled out, including appropriate legislation; there was as yet no agreement on the purge of the armed forces; the conception of the new civilian police had to be carefully worked out; the reintegration programs had yet to be proposed, let alone negotiated.

By midyear it became necessary to rethink the entire negotiating scheme, with a view to compressing the two stages into a single one, eliminating the cease-fire in the middle and the uncertain "armed peace" in the second phase. In May the FMLN had tentatively suggested such a reappraisal, but Cristiani, not yet realizing that it was an objective need rather than a concession to the FMLN, was still unconvinced. The FMLN withdrew its proposal, but I revived it in July. It was not until September that it proved possible to untie this Gordian knot—as we described it at the time—by summoning Cristiani and the full FMLN command to UN Headquarters to meet with Pérez de Cuéllar. The knot was indeed untied, and the negotiation resurrected, after ten days of intensive talks held mostly in my UN conference room. Special precautions had to be taken to ensure that during their movements in the building, Cristiani and the FMLN would not bump into each other.

## MANAGING THE PLAYERS

### The Friends

My insistence that the secretary-general and I have the right to consult with governments that in our judgment could usefully assist in our efforts was first a precautionary measure: I did not want to expose us to criticism later by one or the other party for consulting with the United States, the Soviet Union, or Cuba about those efforts, as I was convinced would be necessary in order to obtain and retain their support or, at least, to contain any failure on their part to cooperate with us. On the other hand, it was the basis for enlisting the advice and diplomatic assistance of those governments that came to be known as the "friends of the secretary-general." While I consulted with a wider number of governments than is publicly known, the core "friends" were Colombia, Mexico, Spain, and Venezuela, all but

Spain members of the original Contadora Group. Seven years have elapsed since the final peace agreements were signed at Chapultepec Castle on January 16, 1992, a decent interval following which I may now reveal that the "friends" mechanism also had the purpose of preempting rival initiatives that might confuse the negotiation. I pay tribute to the friends, especially to the ambassadors of Colombia, Mexico, Spain, and Venezuela to the United Nations, for their solidarity, support, and intellectual contribution. They were fully caught up in the mystique of the effort. They had a profound awareness of what was at stake. To say that they did not participate in the mediation *per se* in no way diminishes their contribution to ending the ten-year conflict in El Salvador.

In late 1988, shortly after his election, President-elect Carlos Salinas de Gortari sent outgoing Foreign Minister Bernardo Sepulveda to inform Pérez de Cuéllar that his administration would discontinue the leading role his predecessor had played in the Contadora effort, and to ask the secretary-general to take up the relay. Without Mexico's dynamic leadership and world-class diplomacy, it was difficult to imagine that the Contadora Group could resuscitate, quite apart from the lack of objective conditions to do so after the Central Americans had decided to—literally—take matters in their own hands via the 1987 Esquipulas Declaration. Salinas's passing of the baton codified the earlier demise of the Contadora Group.

Colombia was beset by its own internal turmoil and could not aspire to fill the vacuum left by Mexico. Indeed, in the same spirit as Salinas's passing of the baton, the Colombian ambassador in the Security Council led the 1989 effort to give the secretary-general a mandate that produced Resolution 637 (described by some observers as the repeal of the Monroe Doctrine, which had marked off the Americas as a U.S. zone of influence barred to nonregional powers). Colombia's internal predicament never clouded its assessment of, or approach to, the conflict in El Salvador and the peace negotiation.

Venezuela was a case apart, with the return of the boundlessly talented, hyperactive Carlos Andrés Pérez to the presidency in early 1989. In a region where he enjoyed myriad friendships, he could be counted on to use the not inconsiderable resources at his disposal to make his weight felt, as he had done a decade earlier in supporting the overthrow of Somoza by the Sandinistas. He had been extremely helpful to us in Nicaragua—a full Venezuelan army battalion was dispatched with amazing alacrity, wearing UN colors, to disarm the Contras in Nicaragua in 1990. Apart from the facilities that Venezuela generously laid on for negotiations on Venezuelan territory, Pérez characteristically rolled up his sleeves, picked up the phone, and played a helpful role, particularly during the cliffhanger negotiations on constitutional reforms in April 1991. But it would have been out of character for him to resign himself to a purely backstage or supporting role. I made more than one trip to Caracas for the sole purpose of keeping him personally briefed, and spent a considerable amount of time with him on the telephone, sometimes at ungodly hours.

Spain, a newcomer to the Central American peace effort, had gained great currency in the region by building bridges to Europe through its membership in the European Union and by the capacity of its leaders, many nurtured in clandestinity and exile, to fathom the thinking of repressed Latin American opposition and insurgent movements. Credit goes to Felipe González personally for his intellectual input to untying the Gordian knot in September 1991 by getting us to think about institutional arrangements for early involvement of the FMLN in the transition to the postwar. His was the idea that led to the creation of the National Commission for the Consolidation of Peace, a critical instrument in its time.

Constant briefing of the "friends" had multiple purposes, the first being to intimate that we were in the lead, doing our job, and had the situation in hand, the second to make clear that we would tell them when we needed them, and when we did so we would spell out exactly what it was we wanted them to do. This was done on several occasions, with appreciable effect, to the point that the parties, in a curious reversal of roles, took to lobbying the friends so that they would bring influence to bear on the secretary-general. The friends had been chosen deliberately among countries that did not have a strategic stake in the outcome of the conflict. The unity of the negotiating effort had to be preserved lest the parties to the negotiation be permitted to play the would-be mediators off against one another. Individual forays can only undermine that unity. "The more the merrier" doesn't apply to mediation. However, in managing the friends mechanism, we sought to ensure looseness and informality as well as confidentiality. By dealing with the friends individually I sought to enrich and deepen the intimacy of their commitment and, I devoutly believe, prevented the integrity of the effort from escaping our management. I believed that if the friends mechanism were to become a formal one, identified as such on appointments agendas and in official documents and press notices, the components of that mechanism would be tempted to acquire a life and personality of their own, separate from that of the mediator. Even against their own better judgment, or perhaps pressed by their capitals, they would want to become more active. Even the confidentiality of the effort might become compromised, and if that occurred, the whole enterprise might be imperiled.

We were not so naive as to believe that such arrangements could be strictly adhered to in anything but laboratory conditions. But they served us well for at least the first eighteen months of the negotiation, during which I invested many precious hours, when I was in New York, talking individually to each of the four ambassadors—Fernando Cepeda of Colombia, Jorge Montaño of Mexico, Juan Antonio Yañez of Spain, and Diego Arria of Venezuela—and sincerely seeking out their views and their estimate of the degree of support that we could hope to continue enjoying. I would insult the intelligence of these ambassadors—friends, to this day—if I said that they were unaware of what I was doing or why I was doing it. I am convinced that everyone knew what their role was, and my only breach in writing this now consists of making explicit what was understood by all concerned. The solidarity, even complicity, that developed between us survived not only an attempted hijacking of the negotiation but also the transition to the formalization of the friends as a group, which occurred during the first Ibero-American Summit, in Guadalajara, Mexico, in July 1991.

## A Thwarted Hijacking Strengthens the Friends

The euphoria produced by the agreement on constitutional reforms in April 1991 and their adoption by the Legislative Assembly, largely unaltered, within three days, barely in time to meet the constitutional deadline, did not last, and we soon ran up against the barrier earlier described—the Gordian knot. We were not yet out of the woods. At this low point, President Pérez, perhaps misled by overeager and underinformed advice (though not from his able and distinguished foreign minister, Reinaldo Figueredo), quietly summoned key negotiators of the government and the FMLN to Caracas in early July, submitted to each separately, deus ex machina, a barebones proposal, and attempted to bring them together to negotiate on that basis. Had I been asked about the initiative I could have told him that it was a nonstarter on the substance (and, incidentally, poorly conceived in form and technique). Of course there was no chance of my being consulted, since the whole idea was to do it behind my back. I only saw the proposal later, after the demise of the initiative following the FMLN's refusal to consider the proposal or to meet with the government representatives under any but UN auspices. It was difficult for the FMLN to turn down a summons from President Pérez, even if they were unaware of its purpose; it was another thing to accept a proposal that seriously compromised its interests.

Ten days later, everyone gathered in Guadalajara for the first Ibero-American Summit. Pérez de Cuéllar met with the four presidential friends, including a suitably chastised Carlos Andrés Pérez, and the incident was closed, leaving the process and the "friends" mechanism curiously strengthened, with the secretary-general's authority reaffirmed. The dynamics of relations between the friends, and their involvement in the UN-led effort, were critical in defusing a potentially negotiation-breaking episode. The other three friends, who had loyally adhered to the rules of the game, taken by surprise, had rallied behind the secretary-general.

This incident demonstrates that a somewhat Panglossian scheme that requires leaders and other senior officials of sovereign states to subsume their protagonism under that of the secretary-general, while desirable and achievable, is difficult to sustain over the long term. If a government is spending diplomatic capital in assisting a peacemaking effort, it is unrealistic to ask it to do so indefinitely. Pressure to be in the picture increases as results begin to appear. In their messages to their national legislatures, in their campaigns for reelection, or in their speeches before the UN General Assembly, not unreasonably, leaders will be tempted to take credit for the role they are playing in support of a noble cause, particularly if it is bearing fruit.

I began to meet with the friends jointly for the remaining five months of the negotiation. Meeting them jointly had clear advantages. It saved time and facilitated the coordination of the diplomatic action that I asked them to undertake. I frequently provided them with talking points for démarches to be conducted with the parties (or others, including particularly the United States). These were tailored according to the comparative advantage of each, or prompted by visits to capitals of representatives of the parties or other encounters. The FMLN and Cristiani had increased the frequency of their visits to the capitals of the friends, where they usually discovered that the leaders had been duly prepped. By then we were a solidly knit group—not without difficulties and even some passing friction, but by and large well attuned. The photos taken at the initialing of the accords, around midnight on December 31, 1991, with the four ambassadors standing above Pérez de Cuéllar and me, bear testimony to our complicitous relationship, which was to continue through the years of implementation of the agreements.

## Cuba, the Soviet Union, and the United States

Days after the Central American presidents' December 1989 appeal to the secretary-general to help in Salvadoran peace efforts and, specifically, to draw in countries from outside the region who could assist him, Pérez de Cuéllar called in the ambassadors of Cuba, the United States, and the USSR one at a time. He sounded them about a mechanism to involve the three in bringing about a negotiated settlement to the Salvadoran conflict. He argued for a loose framework rather than a structured formula. Their reactions varied, but none quarreled with the notion of supporting an effort by the secretary-general, which was in keeping with Security Council Resolution 637. The United States, however, objected to involving Cuba, citing its repudiation of the Esquipulas Declaration adopted by the Central American presidents in 1987—which the United States had itself been less than enthusiastic about at the time. Cuba had objected to Esquipulas II for the same reason that the FMLN resisted it: there was no role in it for the insurgents.

These were, as we chose to interpret them, details we could gloss over lightly. It sufficed to have the blessing of the Central Americans, including El Salvador, for involvement of outside actors at the secretary-general's discretion, and the well-publicized meetings with the three ambassadors allowed us to say that we had engaged them in supporting the effort under way. We had ample cover for continuing contacts with the three governments, and a semblance of a commitment of support, each on its own terms. The combination of the Security Council mandate, the request from the Central American presidents, and the secretary-general's extended hand to the three influential outside powers made it unseemly for any of them to deny him their support or raise obstacles to his actions—at least overtly. The seeming U.S. veto of Cuba was irrelevant since we were not attempting to formally create a consultative or other body in which they would be obliged to recognize each other's role or sit at the same table. All three shared an overriding political goal, albeit in varying degrees and conditions, which was to see an end to the war, and none of them had any clear means available to achieve it except through the UN-led process.

Dealing with the Soviet Union was the least of my problems. With the waning of the Cold War, the Soviets were by and large only too happy to accommodate by making the right public and, presumably, private noises. My U.S. interlocutors seemed to set a considerable store by these pronouncements, and Aronson spent quite a bit of time and effort in ensuring that the USSR was backing the effort to end the war. He appeared to attach great importance to the assurances he received from his Soviet counterparts that they were "leaning" on the FMLN and expected it to fall into line, and professed surprise and indignation when the FMLN did not do so more or less automatically.

I am inclined to believe that the FMLN leaders, not oblivious to my sheepdoglike movements, were on the whole right when they told me that we were barking at the wrong flock: the FMLN, as Schafik Handal, one of the five commanders and the secretary-general of the Communist Party, simply put it, was not susceptible to pressure from the USSR. The Soviets had no leverage to exert over the guerrillas, to whom they provided no direct assistance. Whatever indirect leverage they might still have through Cuba lasted only as long as the USSR itself. Pérez de Cuéllar dutifully kept the USSR briefed about El Salvador in his meetings with Soviet leaders, including Gorbachev and Shevardnadze. I had long meetings with senior officials of the Foreign Ministry in Moscow and New York on the subject.

Dealing with Cuba was more difficult given the history of Cuban clandestine involvement in Latin America, acute U.S. sensitivities, and its effect on Washington's analysis of events. However, notwithstanding U.S. objections to involving Cuba in the mechanism bruited by Pérez de Cuéllar, the United States never raised any objection to my frequent contacts with Cuban officials and my trips to the island, and I sense that they understood and appreciated that this was useful. They accepted that my purpose was to make sure that I could count on Cuba bringing to bear a positive influence on the FMLN, but they also tried to use my channels to Havana to obtain commitments from Cuba for the cessation of supplies of weapons to the FMLN. The Cubans assured me, and through me the United States, that they did not provide military assistance to the FMLN, while insisting on their right to do so if requested. The FMLN leaders had chosen, of their own accord, to seek a negotiated solution to the conflict in El Salvador, they said, and Cuba respected and supported that decision. The Cubans followed progress at some remove. During their 1990–91 membership in the Security Council, which spanned the life of the negotiations, they were most constructive.

On one occasion, the El Salvador government tried to induce the Security Council to take a position on the peace talks that was in contradiction with the rules agreed between the parties. The Soviets and the Cubans and other members of the council asked me whether the initiative had the support of the secretary-general and whether he felt it would help him in his efforts. My answer to both questions was no. The initiative did not prosper.

The key nonregional player was the United States, and relations with the USSR and Cuba must be seen largely through that prism. Not surprisingly, the United States was also the most difficult non-Salvadoran player. The starting point, we were later told by a cordially indiscreet U.S. diplomat, was that, until the advent to Washington of the Bush administration, standing policy was simply to keep the United Nations out of the region as a political actor.

President Bush changed that, but he did so as a by-product of what was first and foremost domestic fence-mending. The primary purpose was to make peace with Congress. This has in effect been confirmed by James Baker,[13] who undertook the move to stop aid for the Contras as one of his first initiatives on taking office in 1989 as Bush's secretary of state, cutting a masterfully engineered deal with congressional opponents of that aid. He was a veteran of Reagan's White House; he knew better than anyone how the previous administration's policy had weighed it down. No matter what the motives were, however, the change that Bush and Baker wrought in U.S. foreign policy signaled a historic turnabout in its relations with the region—as well as with the United Nations.

However, old habits are difficult to break, and relations between the United Nations and the United States during the El Salvador negotiations traveled a rocky road. There were moments when it seemed as if the bumping and the lurching would knock our Land Rover into a muddy ditch. Notwithstanding Bush's vocal support for the secretary-general's and my efforts, there seemed to exist, at certain levels, a reluctance to accept the consequences of the mediation having been entrusted to a genuinely impartial good officer, and the corollary that he could not unilaterally move the goalposts.

I have referred to the target date for attaining a cease-fire, interpreted as a deadline by the United States and, in its wake, the Salvadoran government. A factor in this was that the negotiation was not entirely self-contained. It was being played out in Mexico, Caracas, San José, or wherever else the talks were being held, but the audience was frequently the Democratic-controlled Congress. The administration had put before Congress legislation allowing for continuing military aid to the Salvadoran armed forces. The November 1989 murder of the Jesuits, suspected (and later confirmed) to have been committed on orders of senior members of the armed forces, had strengthened those Democrats who sought to stop that aid. It therefore became a side goal of the FMLN to score political points in the U.S. Congress—while knowing that this would not have an immediate impact on the battlefield since it would not impede aid already in the pipeline. A decision to deny or substantially cut the aid, even without practical consequences, would send a strong political message and heap political pressure on a beleaguered, weakly motivated Salvadoran army and further put it on the defensive at the negotiating table. In fact, the relentless pressure from Congress to investigate the murder of the Jesuit priests and to deny aid to the presumed perpetrators was crucial in obtaining concessions at the negotiating table that might otherwise have remained out of reach: the

army leadership had to yield in the negotiation if it was to continue impeding the investigation to escape the murder charges. Attempting to thwart
the aid cutoff, the U.S. administration and the Salvadoran government seized
on the elusive goal of a mid-September cease-fire—the deadline that
wasn't—and blamed the FMLN for not having met it. They pounced on
me to put pressure on the FMLN to cease fire, presumably unilaterally, and
to publicly denounce the FMLN for noncompliance and thereby weaken
the case for suspension of military aid. This I obviously could not do, and
was roundly castigated for not doing. I was even accused of "tilting" toward
the FMLN.

## On the High Wire

Following the July 1990 human rights agreement, despite many meetings,
much shuttling, and some futile procedural tinkering, nine months were to
go by without any new substantive agreements. This was not entirely surprising in light of the priority accorded by the parties to the armed forces
question, the sole item under consideration, which was far and away the
most difficult on the agenda. The negotiators had set themselves a high
hurdle. Another factor coming into play was that legislative and local elections were scheduled for March 1991, and the FMLN was reluctant to
allow the governing party to reap the political benefit of achievements at
the negotiating table. Pressure began to increase from both the Salvadoran
government and the United States, who urged me to move things along by
submitting a proposal on the armed forces to the parties.

In all cases previously—the framework agreement, the agenda and the
calendar, human rights—I had submitted drafts only at the request of both
parties. Even though a text on the armed forces was well advanced, the
FMLN had made clear that it was not ready for me to present a paper to
the parties on this subject. I did not feel that I could simply spring it on
them without seriously jeopardizing my continued usefulness. The FMLN
had requested UN mediation based on clear understandings regarding how
we would conduct ourselves, particularly under pressure. I went about persuading FMLN leaders that it was in the interest of the process that I
should submit a working paper. This proved extremely difficult. The realization that some of their most cherished, but unrealistic proposals—a front-
loaded, ad hominem purge of the armed forces, for example—were not
going to receive encouragement from me may have had a bearing on their
thinking. In the meantime, while FMLN leaders agonized among themselves about my ideas for an independent review of the army officer corps
as a substitute for wholesale prearranged dismissals—a process rather than

a deal—the representatives of the two sides, at the table, continued to listen to my painstaking oral recapitulations of the state of discussions, without anything that could be described as negotiation taking place. The notes of the endless sessions of those months are nothing short of mind numbing in their repetitiveness. I finally persuaded the FMLN to agree that I should present my working paper on the armed forces, which stood ready, on October 31, 1990.

In November 1990, one year after its 1989 offensive, the FMLN launched another strong, coordinated attack on a number of military objectives. Although there was nothing in the Geneva Agreement, which in effect enshrined wartime negotiations, to bar the FMLN from such action, Pérez de Cuéllar made a public statement of concern. We were obviously treading water, notwithstanding my efforts to present a sober but upbeat front. In January, a U.S. army helicopter was downed in El Salvador and members of its crew were executed by FMLN fighters. My failure to deliver was beginning to fray my relations with Washington.

I felt the need to explain publicly what the United Nations was up to in El Salvador. The groundbreaking nature of our engagement in the Salvadoran conflict raised many questions. I prepared an op-ed article for the *Wall Street Journal* that, I hoped, would reach a wide readership, particularly in circles not usually interested in the United Nations' work. My purpose was to break simplistic characterizations by describing what was at stake in the negotiations and, in the process, explain why they were taking so long: "The goal of this effort is not merely to stop the fighting, but to establish conditions that will ensure that once fighting stops, it will not resume . . . because the root causes of the war are being addressed. . . . It follows that a cease-fire is not likely to come about without agreement on profound changes in El Salvador. . . . There is no such thing as instant peace in a conflict of this nature. The Salvadoran people cannot settle for a slapdash job." The article appeared on January 11, 1991, in the Friday "Americas" column.[14]

I obviously hit a nerve, for on February 1, an article datelined in Washington appeared prominently in the *New York Times*.[15] It was largely based on statements attributed to unnamed "Administration officials." The main thrust seemed to be that the mediator "did not appear to have a clear strategy of where to take the talks nor how to end the war," a curious statement in light of my *Wall Street Journal* article, which, if anything, laid out a rather ambitious strategy based entirely on the agenda agreed by the parties. The anonymous sources resurrected the old canard about my "accepting the guerrillas' plea to suspend a previous *deadline* [italics mine] of Sept. 15 to reach a cease-fire." By doing that, I had "played into the hands of rebel hardliners who want to continue the war."

I refused to meet with U.S. envoys until a satisfactory disavowal was obtained from the State Department spokesman, which took several days. Secretary Baker wrote to Pérez de Cuéllar reiterating U.S. backing for his and my efforts. I can't fathom to this day what the anonymous sources sought to obtain by their strange behavior. By undermining the mediator, they risked putting a drag on the negotiations whose sluggishness they purported to decry. Perhaps what they wanted was to have me replaced. Obviously such a publication did little to raise my standing in the more recalcitrant circles in San Salvador. Reports of dissatisfaction with my performance emanating from the Department of State not only undermined me; they had the additional, presumably unwitting effect of weakening Cristiani's own standing vis-à-vis the rejectionists in his party and government. Mutterings about the need for my replacement or for the secretary-general to move me aside and take over personally began to be heard at about this time. They were punctuated by the constant drumbeat of demands for pressure-cooker, open-ended negotiating sessions that, as experience demonstrated, would have been of little usefulness until the proper conditions existed, particularly since the government delegation was not composed of decision makers. My critics did not understand that—as Pedro Nikken so aptly put it—fruit does not ripen by being thrown against the wall.

Fortunately for the process, I was not left out on a limb. Pérez de Cuéllar, with whom I had worked closely since his years as ambassador to the United Nations, had the rare virtue of knowing how and to what degree to delegate, and the courage to do so. The latitude he gave me to conduct this negotiation was a remarkable and humbling gesture of trust, but it also entailed a heavy attribution of responsibility. In essence, he left me in charge of the mediation, knowing from our long years of collaboration that I had a clear notion of what it meant to represent him. He frequently told me that it was up to me to determine when he should involve himself personally. He was thus able to maintain a healthy distance from details and intricacies. He knew that excessive intervention could undermine me and expose him, and was therefore conservative about intervening. He never offered me direct guidance, deferring instead to my proposals and initiatives. During the two rounds in New York, for instance, much of the work fell to me and my colleagues; but it required his personal invitation and drawing power to bring the principals to New York and he therefore lent his name to it; it sufficed amply.

I suffered from some of the drawbacks of being the sole channel between untrusting parties. One basic rule for a good mediator is to convey to party A the position of party B as it truly is rather than as party A would like it to be. This may seem obvious, but in practice many a mediator falls prey to the temptation to tell an interlocutor what he would like to hear. It is inherent in human nature to wish to please. In mediation it can and almost always will be counterproductive. A corollary of this basic rule is for the mediator to avoid giving the impression to party A that a position he is taking may make a positive impact on party B when the mediator knows that it doesn't stand a chance of doing so. Predictably, my slavish adherence to these rules did not always endear me to the parties. For the Salvadoran government it was particularly galling to be dealt with on an equal, impartial plane by the mediator, except on protocol matters, and it was sometimes difficult for them to live with the fact that the FMLN couldn't simply be ordered around. This was reflected, at moments of exasperation, in appeals to the secretary-general to "exercise his authority" over the FMLN that seemed to overlook the fact that the FMLN was a military insurgency with at least enough power to have earned its place at the negotiating table, whatever else one might think of it, and for which the negotiation and the UN role in it had resulted from choice rather than imposition.

Cristiani's refusal to speak directly to anyone from the FMLN, on arguable legal grounds, had its pitfalls: his representatives, in my experience, could not always be relied on to convey or explain faithfully the FMLN's views. By default, I was the principal intermediary between the FMLN and Cristiani, as was the case with the State Department. U.S. officials refused to speak with authoritative guerrilla representatives and, like Cristiani, they fell prey to the classic blurring of message and messenger. I sometimes felt that Cristiani was dealing with me as if I were one of the "Comanches"—Salvadoran elite parlance for the FMLN. Little did he know that one powerful FMLN leader, an intelligent man, was convinced that I was in the employ of the CIA.

Tension with my interlocutors in the State Department heightened late in the April 1991 negotiations on constitutional reform, when a delegation of Salvadoran legislators turned up uninvited at our meeting place in Mexico City with only a few hours' advance notice—at least to me —and advised us that two days later they would submit to the Legislative Assembly a set of constitutional amendments. Any changes in their proposals—which I was not shown—would have to be agreed by consensus among the four parties who had signed them.

I had since mid-1990 tried to persuade a reluctant Cristiani to broaden his political base of support by including high-level opposition representatives in the negotiation. I was convinced that this would help him to sell the concessions he would have to make in the negotiation with the possible bonus of enhancing the quality of his negotiating team. But I had long since given up this effort, and was kept in the dark about the legislators' belated, inopportune initiative, which Assistant Secretary Aronson later told me he had strongly encouraged. After the legislators' departure, I perused their proposals. They fell substantially short of what was needed to solve the fundamental problem of the role of the armed forces in society and government, and indeed of what at that precise moment was within reach at the negotiating table. Among other relics, the proposals would have left largely intact the power of the armed forces to intervene in matters of internal public order, even though the government had already accepted the creation of a new police body under civilian authority that would obviously be incompatible with the armed forces retaining such powers. Furthermore, the proposals would have left untouched the constitutional role of the armed forces as defender of constitution and laws, which was the basis for their acting in effect as the ultimate arbiter of the political life of the country.

Not surprisingly, the FMLN rejected the proposals brought by the legislators, but not before I was severely criticized by U.S. representatives meeting Pérez de Cuéllar back in New York for treating the legislators as "interlopers" and failing to take their proposals on board. Discrepancies between Washington and the secretary-general concerning his efforts in the negotiations have subsequently been dismissed as "occasional tactical differences."[16] The April 1991 episode would appear to reveal a more substantive discrepancy, with some in Washington prepared to settle for a greater army role in Salvadoran life and politics than the negotiators in Mexico. A number of the supposedly rebuffed legislators, celebrating the thorough job that had been done on the armed forces chapter of the constitution—ignoring their last-minute proposals—were later to tell me that those who had prodded them into this foray had been somewhat economical in their description of the state of play in the negotiation.

I have earlier mentioned the confusion—if that is the word—that arose in respect to the target set in Caracas in May 1990 of reaching political agreements on all agenda items leading to a cease-fire by mid-September. A recurring theme then, which has cropped up since, is the desirability of "creative" use of deadlines to accelerate agreement by exposing parties who do not meet them to potential blame.[17] It is evident that a real deadline can be parlayed into a catalytic agent, and there is no doubt that this was very important in the negotiations on constitutional reform, as was as the imminent expiration of Pérez de Cuéllar's term in office at the end of the year. Failure to agree on the first would have been a major, perhaps irreparable setback. The FMLN's use of red herrings—insistence on a temporary relaxing of the constitutional amendment procedures to circumvent the deadline; calling into question the permanent character of the armed forces—helped pry substantive reforms within the deadline. It is hard to predict what might have happened had the negotiations spilled into the administration of Pérez de Cuéllar's successor (beyond the two weeks that they indeed spilled). I am inclined to think that pressure from Congress on the Jesuit murder investigation, which the army leadership feared above all else, was as important a factor, if not more so, in overcoming the government's sometimes maddening indecisiveness and securing army reforms, than the deadline itself.

Where I disagree is that it is desirable for an impartial mediator to conjure up and attempt to impose deadlines artificially. In order to threaten the FMLN with penalties for not ceasing fire in September 1990, I would have had to assume either stupidity or laboratory-pure naïveté on their part. Building into the Caracas Agreement the notion of a target date had been my idea, not a proposal of the government, but I could not honestly pressure the FMLN to do something that it had manifestly agreed to do only if certain conditions were met without calling my credibility into question. A similar case existed when the FMLN spoke of the possibility of an "accelerated negotiating scheme" in April 1991, which could have led to a cease-fire by May 30 if certain conditions were met in connection with constitutional reforms. The FMLN was offering a shortcut deal, but the government was not prepared to meet the conditions to close that deal. Would it have been realistic to demand, as I was pressed to do, that the FMLN hand over a cease-fire without the quid pro quo?

Let us for a moment leave aside the bedrock fact that there was no commitment by the FMLN, or anything remotely resembling it, to cease fire until certain conditions were met, in September 1990 and May 1991. Let us also suspend disbelief as long as necessary to imagine that the FMLN would have docilely capitulated and indeed ceased fire in mid-September 1990, without having secured agreements on anything but the establishment of a human rights monitoring mechanism, without reforming or creating institutions to underpin the national capacity to promote and protect those rights. Would these reforms have been achieved later on, absent military pressure? Would it have been wise to leave the task midway, at a promising stage in May 1991, without having cleared the obstacles whose removal later required the personal presence of Cristiani in New York on two occasions? Apart from the shabby spectacle of a mediator advocating a breach of the rules he has painstakingly persuaded the warring parties to agree to, I suspect that the list of achievements of the negotiation at the beginning of this chapter would have been substantially shorter if a deal had been closed in May 1991, and the Salvadoran people ill served as a result.

Moreover, there can be a downside even to real deadlines. No one can doubt that the imminence of the departure from office of Pérez de Cuéllar at midnight on December 31, 1991, coupled with a private signal from Pérez de Cuéllar's successor to Cristiani that the priority accorded to the El Salvador negotiation would plummet after January 1, 1992, galvanized the negotiation. There was a significant casualty, however, which consisted of the inadequacy of the provisions for the reintegration of combatants into society, for which the FMLN may share some of the blame, but for which I admit responsibility as the mediator. The FMLN almost deliberately let slip this question, but we could have done a better job of marshaling expertise to ensure that the agreement reached was not seriously flawed—so much so that it had to be renegotiated and expanded on in a supplementary agreement in October 1992.[18]

A better-forged agreement on reintegration questions—and more assiduous government compliance—might well have lessened the postwar crime wave that bedevils El Salvador to this day. Many combatants demobilized in bitter disappointment that their leaders had settled for much less than the revolutionary goals set in some of their manifestos on the age-old agrarian question; the discovery later of large FMLN arms caches may be related to this and other flaws in the agreements. Quick fixes have a way of coming back to haunt the fixed as well as the fixers.

Indeed, from the El Salvador experience we have drawn the lesson that planning carefully for the implementation of peace agreements so as to ensure their durability, including proper handover to successor international and national institutions and arrangements, should be an essential component of the negotiation itself. This in turn requires the closest possible working relationship between the mediator of a peace agreement and whoever is likely to be responsible for overseeing its implementation. In addition, there is a crying need, particularly as a negotiation draws to a close, to make sure that all international actors will collaborate toward the single overriding goal of ensuring that once the guns fall silent, they will not be fired again. There can be no one better placed than the mediator, if he is worth his salt, to indicate what needs to be done to make sure this is the case. This requires close sharing of information and coordination of postconflict policy that is sometimes difficult to reconcile with the confidentiality that must be the leitmotiv of a good-offices mediation effort. That, however, might and indeed has been the subject of separate writings.[19]

U.S. ambassador to the United Nations Thomas Pickering, assisted by his able deputy Alexander Watson, was imaginative and energetic in helping us to homeport in the closing months of 1991. They belied the widespread feeling that the United States "just doesn't get it" about Latin America. But earlier there seemed to be a genuine unwillingness among others in the administration to accept that the consequences of misunderstanding the problem could be grave indeed, and not just over the long term. They seemed unable to fully grasp the substance, the structure, the texture, and the dynamics of relations between the parties on the ground and at the negotiating table, or the fact that the FMLN had only two concessions to make, to stop fighting and to disarm, whereas the government had to agree to a lot of reforms in exchange. This led to an equation that on the face of it was not neatly balanced. Leaving aside some of their more outlandish posturing, and without condoning their sometimes egregious use of violence, the FMLN leaders, in their denunciation of what was wrong in El Salvador, were often right, and many in the political mainstream were privately grateful that someone had dared raise his voice (if not his guns) to correct the evident wrongs in the country. The government at no point tried to put forward a vision of what it wanted for the nation. Throughout the negotiations, the government was in a reactive mode and allowed the FMLN, as *demandeur,* to set the agenda—both technically at the negotiating table and on the Salvadoran political scene. This was perhaps inevitable, since it was not the government that wanted to change things. The agreements, which largely satisfied the FMLN's essential demands, won ample support and even put the government, on the defensive throughout the negotiation, in a position in which it could say that everything in them was wholly agreeable. At Chapultepec, Cristiani rose to the occasion, and El Salvador is today a country transformed by negotiation.

## CODA: LESSONS LEARNED

The following is a decalogue of sweeping generalizations, as un-Salvadorcentric as it is possible to make them. One or two of them may seem obvious, but, to paraphrase Jacques Lacan, this does not mean they are not important.

1. *Unity and integrity of mediation.* The worst enemy of mediation is the appearance of confusion as to who is mediating. Mediators can easily

be played off one against the other. Negotiations of a multidisciplinary character—a common feature in complex internal conflict—stand the best chance of success if they are unequivocally controlled by a single, clearly identified mediator. Second-guessing a mediator is a dangerous game for it can undermine the mediation itself.

2. *Inclusivity: dealing with the devil.* Peace is made between enemies. Leaving a warring party out of a negotiation is a recipe for failure. Direct negotiation between warring parties may be desirable if circumstances including personal dynamics are propitious and a government can bring itself to face rebels. However, direct negotiation is not indispensable and indeed may be counterproductive, leading to exacerbation of hostility and delays, if circumstances are not propitious. Indirect arrangements can be better suited to wartime negotiations, as in proximity talks where the parties don't see each other but deal through a third party. The essential condition is that parties be confident that they are dealing seriously with those with whom a deal must be struck.

3. *Elimination of preconditions: wartime negotiations.* Especially in internal conflict, it is rarely useful to expect that parties will cease armed pressure in advance of negotiated arrangements. It will almost always be in the interest of one of the parties to keep up armed pressure. Respect for humanitarian rules of combat should be pressed for, but insistence on additional military concessions outside the context of a negotiation usually stems from a misunderstanding of the dynamics of conflict and negotiation. Demanding a cease-fire or laying down of weapons as a condition for negotiating in an internal setting is more often than not merely a political posture, and may mask a determination to continue fighting. It follows that abandoning such a condition is a signal that serious negotiation may be in the offing.

4. *Continuing the war by other means.* Exclusionary policies frequently trigger civil insurgency. Social groups in many cases take to arms to achieve participation in a political process from which they are barred. In a sense, in such a scenario the goal sought is better governance. This makes it possible, in the negotiation, to attempt to put in place a process to solve an issue rather than negotiate the solution itself. For example, the FMLN wanted the dismissal of a large number of army officers identified by name, but was persuaded to accept that an impartial panel should make recommendations that the president agreed, sight unseen, to carry out within his powers as commander in chief. The FMLN also agreed not to press for negotiation of economic reforms, agreeing that the economic policy should be left to a government elected in a free and fair process with ample, internationally verified participation.

5. *Friends of the mediator.* This is a useful device to marshal diplomatic efforts inter alia by inhibiting would-be rival mediators and spoilers. It must be preceded by prior clarification of the cardinal rule, which is a commitment to work only—or at least principally—at the behest of whoever is responsible for the mediating effort. It should become part of the accepted ethos that striking out on one's own, however well intentioned, is bad form.

6. *Collective mediation.* Understood as mediation conducted by a group of equal mediators, collective mediation usually doesn't work. Indeed, it may well be a contradiction in terms, like one hand clapping.

7. *Deadlines.* Real deadlines—those that are not in the power of the mediator or the parties to move, such as constitutionally established terms—can and should be grasped and manipulated by a mediator to prod a negotiation along and pry concessions from recalcitrant parties. Let the mediator beware, however, of conjuring up deadlines not anchored in reality. Calls to settle by a given date "or else" frequently put the mediator's credibility at risk and devalue the coin. The full story behind George Mitchell's notification to the parties in the Northern Ireland negotiations that he would withdraw at a date certain, which seems on the surface to be a contradiction of this assertion, has yet to be told.

8. *Impartial mediators versus mediators with a stake in the outcome.* The key is the desire of the parties to work with a given mediator. The United States can hardly be deemed a disinterested player in the Middle East peace process. However, both the Israelis and the Palestinians clearly prefer to deal with the United States. The choice of the parties cannot be second-guessed by outsiders. A mediator with a stake in the outcome of the negotiation who stumbles, however, runs a greater risk of criticism, ridicule, or opprobrium should his efforts fail.

9. *Beware of quick fixes.* Intrastate conflict, the prevailing variety after the Cold War, is by and large more deeply rooted than interstate war, particularly if ethnic or other identity factors are involved. Unless the outcome is a breakup of the state, the warring parties must continue to live with each other within the same borders. Solutions to such conflicts need to go equally deeply, addressing root causes, providing avenues for reintegration of combatants and, especially, creating, reforming, or strengthening institutions so that subsequent disputes may be solved by peaceful means. There is frequently a need also to reckon with the past through appropriate mechanisms. This places an additional, heavy burden on the mediator to ensure—sometimes counter to public opin-

ion, which demands a swift end to the bloodshed whatever the cost—that the warring parties are aware of the need to address root causes. Unfinished business following hastily achieved settlements can lead to the resurgence of conflict or to long-term, onerous international supervision or enforcement to prevent a recurrence of fighting.

10. *Diplomacy backed by (outside) force.* The threat of use of force may assist in defusing crises or midwifing interim accords, but deep-rooted conflict of an internal character is almost impossible to solve except by settlements freely arrived at by the parties concerned. On his return from his mission to Baghdad in February 1998, Secretary-General Kofi Annan stated to the Security Council that "if diplomacy is to succeed, it must be backed both by force and by fairness." He has himself emphasized, however, that this statement must be read contextually, not as a one-size-fits-all generalization. Dag Hammarskjöld's words in this regard are worth recalling:

> The Secretariat [of the United Nations] too has to negotiate, not only in its own interest, but for the cause of peace and a peaceful development of our world. The weight we carry is not determined by physical force or the number of people who form the constituency. It is based solely on trust in our impartiality, our experience and knowledge, our maturity of judgment. Those qualities are our weapons, in no way secret weapons, but as difficult to forge as guns and bombs.[20]

## NOTES

The views expressed here are entirely those of the author and should not be attributed in any manner to the United Nations. I am grateful to Blanca Antonini, Ilana Bet-El, Graciana del Castillo, Maria Rosa Fort Brescia, Freda Mackay, Annika Savill, Shashi Tharoor, Francesc Vendrell, and Teresa Whitfield for their advice and to Melanie Redondo for her unflagging assistance and unfailing expertise.

1. The terms "mediator" and "mediation" in this chapter are used somewhat loosely, since they do not appear in the rules agreed by the parties that refer to the secretary-general's "good-offices" role. The government was not prepared at the outset to concede to the secretary-general and his representative the rights that are normally accorded to a mediator, which include the presentation of proposals as such. As the negotiation progressed, especially following the breakthrough agreements of April 1991, my submission of "working papers" was not only accepted but encouraged by both sides.

2. United Nations Security Council Resolution 637 of July 27, 1989 (S/RES/637).

3. I addressed this precise point in a letter to the editor of *Foreign Affairs*, in response to an article that argued that the United Nations cannot mediate. *Foreign Affairs* 74, no. 1 (January-February 1995): 185–186.

**4.** United Nations Department for Public Information, *The United Nations and El Salvador, 1990–1995* (New York: United Nations, 1995).

**5.** Terry Lynn Karl gave currency to this coinage in her article, "El Salvador's Negotiated Revolution," *Foreign Affairs* 71, no. 2 (spring 1992): 147–164. It appeared in print previously, attributed to me, in James LeMoyne, "Out of the Jungle: In El Salvador, Rebels with a New Cause," *New York Times Magazine,* February 9, 1992, 24–67.

**6.** Periodic reports were submitted by the secretary-general to the Security Council and the General Assembly from 1990 to 1997. A narrative and a compilation of the documentation appear in the United Nations Department for Public Information, *The United Nations and El Salvador, 1990–1995.*

**7.** Pérez de Cuéllar's version of the El Salvador negotiations in his 1997 memoirs contains many errors and oddities, as well as discrepancies with respect to my own record. I was interviewed in the early stages of the preparation of the book, but I was not given the opportunity to read it before it appeared in print. In the foreword the author explains that his book was—in effect—put together and largely drafted by James S. Sutterlin, a member of his Executive Office, who played no role in the negotiations and, indeed, was no longer with the United Nations at that time. This author-drafter duality, added to the distance of both from the negotiations, may explain the shortcomings.

**8.** Alvaro de Soto and Graciana del Castillo, "Implementation of Comprehensive Peace Agreements: Staying the Course in El Salvador," *Global Governance* 1, no. 2 (May-August 1995): 189–204.

**9.** United Nations General Assembly, "Assessment of the Peace Process in El Salvador: Report by the Secretary-General," A/51/917 (July 1, 1997), 16.

**10.** The Esquipulas Declaration, as it became known, was signed in Guatemala City on August 7, 1987 by the five Central American presidents. It is also sometimes referred to as "Esquipulas II." Its formal name was "Procedure for the Establishment of a Firm and Lasting Peace in Central America." It was touted as a peace plan for Central America by the Central Americans.

**11.** For an analytical study of this event and its significance, see Teresa Whitfield, *Paying the Price: Ignacio Ellacuría and the Murdered Jesuits of El Salvador* (Philadelphia: Temple University Press, 1994).

**12.** The concept of "ripeness" illustrates the conditions that render a conflict more susceptible to negotiated settlement. It was developed by I. William Zartman, *Ripe for Resolution: Conflict and Intervention in Africa* (Oxford: Oxford University Press, 1989).

**13.** James A. Baker III, *The Politics of Diplomacy: Revolution, War, and Peace, 1989-1992* (New York: G. P. Putnam's Sons, 1995).

**14.** Alvaro de Soto, "UN Negotiations Not among Casualties of War in El Salvador," *Wall Street Journal,* January 11, 1991, A11.

**15.** Clifford Krauss, "U.N. Aide Assailed in Salvadoran Talks," *New York Times,* February 1, 1991, A3

**16.** Joseph G. Sullivan, "How Peace Came to El Salvador," *Orbis* (winter 1994): 83–98.

**17.** Ibid.

18. This agreement is included in United Nations Department for Public Information, *The United Nations and El Salvador, 1990–1995*.

19. See Alvaro de Soto and Graciana del Castillo, "Implementation of Comprehensive Peace Agreements"; and, by the same authors, "Obstacles to Peacebuilding," *Foreign Policy*, no. 94 (spring 1994): 69–83. See also Graciana del Castillo, "Post-Conflict Peace-Building: A Challenge for the United Nations," *CEPAL REVIEW*, no. 55 (April 1995): 27–38; and "Arms-for-Land Deal: Lessons from El Salvador," in *Multidimensional Peacekeeping: Lessons from Cambodia and El Salvador*, ed. Michael Doyle and Ian Johnstone (Cambridge: Cambridge University Press, 1996).

20. *The Servant of Peace: A Selection of the Speeches and Statements of Dag Hammarskjöld*, ed. Wilder Foote (London: The Bodley Head, 1962).

# Background to Chapter 15

## Haiti: Canada's Role in the OAS

In 1990, four years after the fall of the corrupt, despotic, and long-lived Duvalier regime, Haiti staged successful democratic elections. However, the newly elected populist president, Jean-Bertrand Aristide, was soon ousted by a military coup. Haiti thus became a test case for the Organization of American States (OAS), which had recently adopted the Santiago Declaration that committed the organization to counter any threat to democracy in a member state. The OAS initiated a diplomatic effort to restore Aristide and reconstitute Haitian democracy, an effort that later expanded to involve the United Nations and a number of interested states. Although a new member of the OAS, Canada assumed a facilitative role both within the OAS and among the international community at large in promoting strong action against the military regime in Port-au-Prince. After a number of abortive efforts to evict the military from power by negotiation and persuasion, a combination of intense diplomatic pressure and the imminent dispatch of a U.S. invasion force succeeded in returning Aristide, restoring democracy, and creating a more stable political environment.

### MAJOR ACTORS

- Jean-Bertrand Aristide: President of Haiti
- Haitian military: led by Colonel Raoul Cedras
- Organization of American States (OAS): led by Secretary-General João Clemente Baena Soares
- United Nations Mission in Haiti (UNMIH)

387

- Multinational Force (MNF): a nineteen-nation intervention force
- United States
- Canada

## IMPORTANT DATES

- 1986: Fall of Duvalier regime
- December 16, 1990: Aristide elected president
- September 30, 1991: Cedras overthrows Aristide
- October 1991: Aristide appeals for international support at the United Nations; OAS begins a voluntary trade embargo on Haiti
- Early 1993: UN Security Council adopts an international arms and fuel embargo on Haiti
- July 4, 1993: Negotiations held at Governors Island, New York
- October 11, 1993: USS *Harlan County* unsuccessfully attempts to dock at Port-au-Prince
- October 16, 1993: Haiti's justice minister is assassinated; UN reimposes sanctions and subsequently authorizes a naval blockade
- July 31, 1994: UN Resolution 940 authorizes all necessary means to remove Haitian regime
- September 16, 1994: President Clinton dispatches Jimmy Carter, Colin Powell, and Sam Nunn to negotiate the peaceful landing of MNF troops
- October 15, 1994: Cedras departs and Aristide returns

## KEY AGREEMENTS REACHED

- Direct deployment of UN personnel to modernize Haitian military
- Creation of new and independent police force
- Parliamentary ratification of a new prime minister chosen by President Aristide
- Amnesty for leaders of the military coup

## PRINCIPAL OUTCOMES

- Resignation of Cedras, return of Aristide
- Peaceful military takeover of Haiti by a multinational force
- Human rights abuses significantly reduced and political repression ended; economic hardship, however, continues
- Political and diplomatic ties with the OAS strengthened

# 15

# Haiti
## *Canada's Role in the OAS*

BARBARA MCDOUGALL

**A**lthough one of the smallest countries in the Western Hemisphere, and still its poorest, Haiti gleaned a remarkable degree of world attention at the start of the 1990s. It was early in the era when, for the first time in history, human suffering played itself out live on international television twenty-four hours a day. In democratic nations, a sense of cynicism and déjà vu had not yet taken over the public mind-set, and the response to these newly visible horrors was a demand that something be done. Political views, though more cautious, were not out of line with the public mood. Given that the Cold War was retreating into history, various bodies politic around the world were more optimistic than they had ever been concerning the capacity of the international community to settle disputes within and between sovereign states.

It was in this context that a collaborative effort was mounted by the international community to restore to power the ousted Haitian president, Jean-Bertrand Aristide, following a military coup. That effort was initiated and in its early stages led by the Organization of American States, comprising all of the countries of the Western Hemisphere.[1]

389

Recent academic attention to multiparty mediation within the field of international relations is a welcome development. Considerable time has passed since Canadian philosopher Marshall McLuhan first defined the global village, but the global institutional framework for conducting international mediation is still relatively primitive. There is no reason to expect that relationships between and among nations will be anything but more intense in the foreseeable future, and demands for multiparty efforts to resolve conflicts will no doubt multiply. Even keeping in mind that theories of multiparty approaches sometimes bear little resemblance to actual human behavior at the negotiating table, pertinent study of this evolving form of problem solving is essential to make it a more effective tool in international affairs.

Haiti is instructive for purposes of this study because it marked the first time the Organization of American States mobilized itself to intervene on behalf of a member state whose democracy had been overturned. It is useful to examine the mediation processes put in place by an organization with no precedents, no institutional experience, and only modest resources to deal with an intervention of this nature.

## THE EVENTS

Haiti is a French-speaking nation founded in the early nineteenth century by slaves rebelling against their harsh colonial masters. Its own leaders turned out to be no better. For close to a hundred ninety years the vast majority of the population was held illiterate in unspeakable poverty. As a result, superstition and voodoo are seen as legitimate and taken more than seriously by most Haitians. Although French is the country's official language, the everyday language of choice is Creole, a partially French patois that is virtually unintelligible to outsiders.

Throughout much of the twentieth century a coalition of military elites and a wealthy business class ensured political "stability" by supporting antidemocratic leaders: strongmen who ruthlessly put down any rudimentary effort to improve the life of the country's poor politically or economically. The last and most notorious of these were the Duvaliers, *père et fils,* widely known as "Papa Doc" and "Baby Doc." Jean-Claude Duvalier, or Baby Doc, having succeeded to the Haitian presidency on his father's death, proved to be incompetent as well as ruthless, and in 1986, following a period of considerable turmoil, went to his reward: a life of luxury, not to say outright decadence, in the south of France.

After his departure, Haiti endured a succession of military-backed governments that had violently disrupted efforts to put in place democratic elections. Despite the oppression, a surprisingly widespread and resilient popular movement sought to create a strong civil society and a democratic government. Coincidentally, many of the other member countries of the Organization of American States (OAS) were themselves turning away from military and other kinds of dictatorship. Thus, the leading countries of the OAS were looking for ways to assist Haiti along the same path. The OAS passed several resolutions offering cooperation with Haiti in the building of democracy, and even money, in the form of an inter-American fund for a democratically elected regime.

In 1990, a shaky interim government in Haiti appealed to the OAS and to the United Nations for assistance in assuring a truly democratic election. With some difficulty, the two organizations convinced the military to stand aside, and under the scrutiny of international observers, on December 16, 1990, in a reasonable facsimile of a clean election, Jean-Bertrand Aristide won an overwhelming majority. He was sworn in as president on February 17, 1991.

Aristide was a Catholic who had left Haiti for Montreal, Canada, where he completed a master's degree in theology. He returned to his own country in 1982 to be ordained as a priest by the Salesian Order, from which he was subsequently expelled, allegedly for his political activity. He was a populist, charismatic and unpredictable, who was reputed to have eliminated his enemies by "necklacing," a grotesque local method of execution by which a rubber tire is forced around an individual's neck and set alight. These allegations were contained in what were believed to be Central Intelligence Agency (CIA) documents circulating in a small circle of diplomats and OAS foreign ministers.[2] They were never proved, but Aristide's public speeches did contain phrases that could easily have been taken as incitements to his followers to deal with their opponents in the time-honored Haitian way.

Aristide may have been the choice for president of the overwhelming majority of the Haitian people, including the small but dedicated group of middle-class professionals, but he was certainly not the choice of the Haitian military and wealthy elites, or of the U.S. Department of Defense and the CIA, both of which took a strong interest in the stability of this tiny island country for their own strategic reasons.

The new president made sporadic attempts to reform the country's economic structure and to generate activity in an economy that was chronically devastated. His efforts were well meaning but largely superficial and, without the participation of the country's educated business leadership, were doomed to failure. The country's primitive democracy was also shaky: with very few exceptions, institution building was well beyond the grasp of those elected along with Aristide, and was only a limited part of the mandate international donor countries gave themselves in Haiti, along with modest humanitarian assistance. It quickly became clear that the new president and his undisciplined followers were a threat to the interests of the country's traditional and still powerful elites, whom Aristide never attempted to cultivate. Aristide's rhetoric in public was often inflammatory, and it was only a matter of time before the wealthy and military classes reasserted their traditional authority.

On September 30, 1991, nine months after his triumphant election and seven months after assuming office, Jean-Bertrand Aristide and his fledgling government were ousted in a short but bloody military coup. Colonel Raoul Cedras, who became head of the new de facto Haitian military regime, exiled Aristide to Caracas, Venezuela.

The countries of the OAS, particularly the new Latin democracies, were clearly agitated by this turn of events. Only three months before, the foreign ministers of the OAS had met in Santiago, Chile, marking the first time that thirty-four of the thirty-five member countries were meeting as democracies.[3] It also marked the first time that Canada had taken its seat as a member of the OAS, as part of a Canadian government strategy to build stronger relationships with its Latin neighbors and to play an active role in hemispheric events. In a burst of collegial democratic commitment, the meeting developed and signed the Santiago Declaration, which committed the OAS to take action to counter any threat to democracy in its member states. Haiti became the test of the declaration almost before the ink was dry.

For the next few weeks, events moved quickly. Aristide was urged to take advantage of the declaration and formally seek support from his OAS colleagues. He did so, and two meetings of the OAS followed in quick succession: permanent representatives of OAS member countries came together immediately at OAS headquarters in Washington, D.C., and on October 2, 1991, foreign ministers formally met with Aristide in a media-packed session in the same locale. The Ministerial Council, as it is called, wallowed in considerable press attention and prodemocratic rhetoric. President Aristide made a speech calling for action to be taken against the de facto government.

## THE MEDIATION

The OAS settled down to determining its role in this unprecedented situation, but difficulties arose almost immediately. Because the organization is made up of thirty-four active members, the required commonality of purpose among sovereign states with different histories and interests was hard to come by. Like many other regional organizations, the OAS operates on consensus, which means, essentially, unanimity.[4] It also does not have the means to impose binding measures on its members: all actions falling out of OAS resolutions are voluntary. Hence, aside from the usual preamble condemning the antidemocratic actions of the de facto government, the following was the strongest call to action that could be agreed upon:

> I (3) To declare that no government that may result from this illegal situation will be accepted, and consequently that no representative of such government will be accepted.

> I (4) To urge the member states to proceed immediately to freeze the assets of the Haitian State and to impose a trade embargo on Haiti, except for humanitarian aid. All humanitarian assistance must be channeled through international agencies or non-governmental organizations.[5]

While the call to action was weak, the resolution was ringing and sincere in its intent, calling unequivocally for the restoration of democracy and the return to power of the legitimate president.

Following a formal request from President Aristide, the Washington meeting hastily undertook a mission to pressure the de factos to conform, armed with nothing more at this early stage than moral suasion. The secretary-general of the OAS, João Clemente Baena Soares, and foreign ministers from Argentina, Bolivia, Canada, Costa Rica, Jamaica, Trinidad, and Venezuela left directly from Washington for Port-au-Prince, in an aircraft provided by the Canadian military, to confront the generals. The United States was represented by a senior official of the State Department. Most members of the group had misgivings concerning lack of leverage, and unrealistic hopes that this lack would be less transparent to the military leaders than it was to us. To the extent that there was a negotiating strategy, it was cobbled together during the flight.

The objective of the mission was to reconstitute democracy in Haiti at a time when there was considerable confusion in the country and when, it was believed, the new hierarchy was weak and precarious. It was agreed that we would remain adamant in our objective, and, with no fallback position, we would more or less hope for the best. The attention being paid to the country went well beyond the Western Hemisphere, and the pressure of worldwide condemnation was felt to be a factor in the mission's favor. Colonel (soon to be General) Cedras was a virtual unknown, and the hierarchy of the Haitian military was a backward one. The army was unruly and poorly trained, and had never participated in any kind of confrontation except against its own people. It was, however, sizable in proportion to the population and had nothing to be ashamed of when it came to equipment.

The meeting took place over three days in what passed for the VIP lounge in the dilapidated Port-au-Prince Airport. Our first discussions were with General Cedras and his fellow officers, led on the OAS side by Carlos Itturaldi, the Bolivian foreign minister who currently held the rotating presidency of the OAS, and Secretary-General Baena Soares, a Brazilian. One of the first hurdles was the language barrier. The officers spoke no English and would frequently lapse from French into Creole, sometimes to obscure deliberately the point they were making, or in response to a question they did not want to answer. An interpreter was provided, but was of questionable trustworthiness. The atmosphere was tense, and nearby outbursts of gunfire from the streets regularly interrupted the discussion. The de facto leaders were adamant on two points: first, it was Aristide who had violated the constitution, not they; and second, they were prepared to negotiate new elections but under no circumstances would Aristide be allowed to return as president. Probing by various members of the mission, few of whom spoke French, identified almost no points on which to base a confidence-building strategy.

In a private caucus session, frustrated members of the OAS mission decided to meet with leaders representing other interests in Haiti to identify those who could help build a coalition in support of Aristide's return. After protracted negotiations with General Cedras, the mission identified, through the recommendation of the American ambassador, a number of local leaders. The Canadian ambassador, a francophone and well liked in the Haitian community, was actively helpful, but had only recently returned from home medical leave.

We met with, among others, representatives of the business community, the church, political parties, the Constitutional Court, and the police, and were only just able to avoid a meeting with the head of the voodoo religion. To a person, they proclaimed that Aristide's actions as president had been unconstitutional and that the country could not move forward until after new elections. The head of the new human rights commission, appointed by Aristide, could be described only as equivocal. He was more critical of Aristide's alleged incitements to necklacing than of the military's bloody overthrow of constitutional government and its misdeeds that followed. And Bernie Aronson, who was Secretary of State James Baker's personal representative on the mission, startled everyone by assailing René Préval,

Aristide's deposed prime minister, for the president's alleged incitements to violence.

The mission retreated to Washington with little progress to report. However, even the generals had agreed that Haiti needed a new prime minister, and the mission determined that Aristide, in absentia, should appoint one who could be made acceptable to all sides and could become an instrument for the reconstitution of democratic authority.

This option was presented to President Aristide, who, completely convinced of his popularity with the Haitian people, was proving, through a series of private meetings with the members of the ad hoc mission, to be a difficult ally. His first objective on the return to power he took for granted was to remove the leaders of the coup from the military and punish them. A series of choices he put forward for prime minister during a protracted period of negotiations was unrealistic at best. Over time, observers came to harbor the suspicion that the deposed leader rather enjoyed living in exile, in more than reasonable comfort, courtesy of the Venezuelan people. This hardly helped the negotiating environment.

While events had moved briskly in October 1991, it was clear that the OAS, if it hoped to succeed in its objective, would have to settle in for the long haul. It was agreed that a civilian mission, made up of prominent and experienced politicians and diplomats, be appointed to work with the secretary-general in a continuation of the effort to achieve a diplomatic solution. This mission received its mandate and got under way in November 1991, and continued a pattern of periodic shuttle diplomacy throughout the crisis.

It was also clear that with its charter restrictions—the need for consensus and the restriction against moving beyond voluntary actions—the OAS could accomplish only so much on its own, and the effort would have to be broadened to engage more actively the United Nations. The advantage to UN intervention was that Security Council decisions are binding on all member countries, so that sanctions, for example, could begin to bite. However, the UN bureaucracy can be officious and heavy-handed, and administrative jealousies on the OAS side, while perhaps understandable, did nothing to advance the partnership. Nevertheless, a superb diplomat, Dante Caputo, a former foreign minister of Argentina, became the personal representative of both the secretaries-general: João Clemente Baena Soares of the OAS and Boutros Boutros-Ghali of the United Nations. Cooperation between the two organizations did not come easily. Baena Soares, understandably, was reluctant to give over authority and leadership to another body. The United Nations, on its side, had as always a large agenda. Of the Security Council members, only France and the United States among the Permanent Five had an interest in Haiti, and it was hardly at the top of their priorities. Canada, whose two-year term as a rotating member of the Security Council had unfortunately just ended, led the way in insisting on UN engagement, with the help and encouragement of Venezuela, but it was nearly a full year before it could be said that the United Nations was ready to take action.

Finally, after eighteen months of unproductive voluntary sanctions and continued human rights abuses, the UN Security Council unanimously adopted a resolution (UNSCR 841) imposing a mandatory international arms and fuel embargo.

The threat of mandatory sanctions prompted Cedras finally to participate in serious negotiations at Governors Island in New York harbor on July 4, 1993. The resulting Governors Island Agreement (GIA) included:

- parliamentary ratification of a new prime minister chosen by President Aristide, a demand on which President Aristide was firm, and firmly supported by both the OAS and later the United Nations;
- the creation of a new police force independent of the military;
- an amnesty for leaders of the military coup—the most contentious point between President Aristide and the de factos from the earliest days of the OAS intervention;
- the resignation of General Cedras;
- the direct deployment to Haiti of UN personnel to assist in modernizing the army;
- the return of President Aristide on October 30, 1993; and
- the suspension of sanctions following the ratification of the new prime minister, which was seen as the step that would jump-start the process.

Although a new prime minister was subsequently appointed, and sanctions lifted, it will come as no surprise that neither Aristide nor the de factos made much effort to implement the remainder of their GIA commitments. Nevertheless, the United Nations proceeded with its own obligations by approving the deployment of military and police personnel to what was called the United Nations Mission in Haiti (UNMIH).

But on October 11, 1993, on the arrival in Port-au-Prince harbor of the first sizable deployment of UNMIH troops on board the USS *Harlan County,* a violent dockside demonstration of "attachés," or de facto henchmen, took place with the attachés screaming, "We are going to turn this into another Somalia!"

This was a direct reference to the eighteen U.S. soldiers who had been killed just the week before in UN operations in Somalia. Fearing a public outcry if more American deaths occurred in nonessential tasks in support of UN operations, Washington promptly withdrew the *Harlan County*. Canadian personnel were also withdrawn, as were UN-OAS mission staff shortly thereafter. On October 16, the same day Haiti's justice minister and a critic of the de factos was assassinated, the United Nations reimposed sanctions followed by a naval blockade.

As the sanctions began to take their toll, international attention was soon drawn to the plight of Haitian boat people. The new Clinton administration's continued policy of forced repatriation was severely criticized by Aristide, the congressional Black Caucus in the United States, and Randall Robinson, a leading African American activist, who launched a well-publicized hunger strike in opposition to the U.S. government's repatriation policy.[6]

By the summer of 1994, the White House was facing increased pressure over the new issue of the Haitian refugees. Violence continued unabated in Haiti. On July 31, following intense lobbying at the United Nations, the Security Council adopted Resolution 940 authorizing the use "of all necessary means to facilitate the departure from Haiti of the military leadership"; the United States recruited nineteen countries to join a multinational force (MNF) that, on September 15, President Clinton signaled was ready for invasion.

However, in a final effort to avert bloodshed, the president dispatched to Haiti former U.S. president Jimmy Carter, recently retired chairman of the Joint Chiefs of Staff, General Colin Powell, and chairman of the Armed Services Committee, Senator Sam Nunn, to negotiate a peaceful landing of MNF troops.

The negotiations were reported to be difficult. However, the moment it was confirmed to Cedras and his colleagues that the Eighty-second Airborne Regiment was about to depart from Fort Bragg, North Carolina, for Haiti, the de factos capitulated. Operation Uphold Democracy—the military takeover of Haiti involving over twenty thousand MNF troops—unfolded smoothly. Cedras and other military leaders quit the country, and on October 15, 1994, President Aristide returned to an emotional welcome in Haiti.

Since that time, Haiti's political development has remained fragile, and its leadership dubious. Sadly, it would be a mistake to assume that the restoration of democracy has brought with it a dramatic improvement in the everyday lives of Haitians. On balance, the multinational effort to return Aristide to power can be viewed as a modest success. The systematic political oppression that marred the modern history of Haiti was broken. Human rights violations are no longer a daily reality, and the Haitian people themselves are now more assertive of their rights.

But they are not more hopeful for their future. Sanctions had devastated an already impoverished economy, and although long-term prospects are difficult to predict, regrettably, even five years later, Haiti shows few signs of progress.

## Analysis

A personal anecdote: in September 1991 I attended the United Nations to make the annual speech on behalf of Canada to the General Assembly. This is the time of year, as the General Assembly opens, when foreign ministers and heads of government from around the world gather to make their ritual speeches, and the exercise can be one of endurance for those imprisoned in their diplomatic seats.

But just ahead of me was President Aristide, the newly elected president of Haiti, who was to my knowledge the only head of government in the history of the United Nations to actually have a gallery. The public seats above the assembly were packed with Haitians who laughed and cheered and egged their leader on. Aristide gave a lengthy and fiery political speech in French, English, and the Creole that confounded even the long-suffering UN interpreters, reinforcing the enthusiasm of his followers. It was a remarkable experience to witness such an event, which demonstrated both how important Aristide was to the Haitian people, and how vocal the Haitian diaspora could be—a lesson, as it turned out, for later.

It was immediately after his New York triumph, when Aristide returned home to Port-au-Prince, that he was deposed, and the scenario I have described began to unfold. Given the commitment to act in defense of democracy in the hemisphere as laid out in the Santiago Declaration so recently passed, the Organization of American States was obligated to intervene in the crisis in Haiti with all the legal means at its disposal. In hindsight, it is easy to see how limited those means were, and even at the time the representatives of most countries recognized the handicap under which we operated. It was critical, if there was any hope at all for success, that action be taken quickly. The need for decisiveness precluded any detailed planning, or even investigation into what might, in the end, motivate General Cedras and his military collaborators to accede to diplomatic pressure. For a mediator, or multiple mediators in the case of multilateral interventions, it is useful to have the measure of the adversarial parties, but whereas the OAS participants came to understand the motivations of President Aristide all too well, little was known of the military leaders, and, with the exception of the general, that remained the case virtually throughout.

During the first days of the crisis and particularly during the ministerial mission that is the primary focus of this analysis, it was enough that the member countries of the OAS shared a common aversion to malodorous military regimes. But once this initial mission ended in frustration and further action was called for, differences in approach among thirty-four countries with different interests and histories were revealed in the failure to move ahead decisively and consensually.

As per its October resolution, the OAS launched its voluntary trade embargo, which predictably proved in the months ahead to be ineffective. Those countries that did support the embargo were slow to implement it, and some had legal impediments to overcome. Mexico, more sensitive than most to issues of sovereignty because of its long history of territorial disputes with the United States, was reluctant to take decisive action and had a following among a number of other countries. These views were more likely to be expressed in in-camera meetings: publicly, Mexico supported the declared OAS position. The Chilean government wanted to be actively engaged, and was tremendously helpful behind the scenes but, because of the continuing Pinochet influence early in its own democratic development, was not in a position to step to the forefront. Among the Latin American partners, Argentina and Venezuela were dedicated and consistent advocates for a strong response, particularly Venezuela, which is geographically close to Haiti.

As a new and welcome member of the OAS, Canada enjoyed excellent relations with other member countries—relations that were not hampered or influenced by previous OAS baggage. Canada was probably the most aggressive advocate of strong action against the de factos. Because Haiti is a French-speaking country, Canada has political ties through la Francophonie.[7] Canada's francophone radio and television networks are an important component of Haiti's cultural life and, in addition to President Aristide himself, many prominent Haitians are educated in Quebec and retain strong ties to the large Haitian community in Montreal. As usual, all politics are domestic, and the Canadian Haitian community is an important block of votes in Canadian elections. Still, even with Canada, there were frustrating delays in implementing the modest OAS action plan, because the country had at the time no legal authority to freeze Haitian assets, an important component of the agreement. Although legislation was brought forward, the delay was costly in terms of overall impact because many Haitians held property and assets in Canada.

Nevertheless, Canada remained steadfast in its commitment to democracy in Haiti and, it is probably fair to say, was the country most responsible for ensuring that Haiti's plight did not fall off the international agenda. Prime Minister Brian Mulroney and President Carlos Andrés Pérez of

Venezuela formed an immediate personal alliance in defense of Haiti following the coup and worked together to shore up international support. More important, action at the Canadian foreign minister level was reinforced by the prime minister's strong interventions with President George Bush. The prime minister and the president were staunch friends and allies on a variety of files, and spoke often, both officially and informally. Haiti was of genuine concern to the prime minister, and his frequent exhortations, like water on stone, had their impact on President Bush. This was highly useful, given what seemed to be inexplicable confusion in the U.S. position.

As the crisis in Haiti progressed, it gradually became apparent that within the United States there was disagreement on an appropriate response. The resulting inconsistencies were confusing to other OAS members and counterproductive to dealing with President Aristide and the de factos. The State Department, it turned out, had a genuine interest in supporting democracy in the hemisphere, although it had no particular strategic objective for a country as poor and weak as Haiti. Also, the State Department was mindful of Latin countries' resentment of its domination of the political agenda of the hemisphere, and extreme sensitivity to matters of sovereignty. However, it supported, and was prepared to implement, the OAS resolution, although happy to let others take the lead.

The Defense Department and the CIA, on the other hand, were deeply distrustful of the populist and unpredictable President Aristide, and reputedly were providing behind-the-scenes encouragement to the Haitian military. Although difficult to confirm, such a stance helps to explain why the military in such an impoverished country was able to sustain itself so long in the face of damning world opinion, and particularly helps to understand some of the more puzzling aspects of the ad hoc ministerial mission in October 1991.

One of the inexplicable events of that mission was the failure of the French ambassador to meet with OAS ministers. Given the ties of language and culture between France and Haiti, the ad hoc group had identified the French ambassador in Port-au-Prince as one who could provide both insight and diplomatic assistance to the mission. Despite repeated requests placed through the U.S. ambassador who arranged the meetings with local civilian groups, the French ambassador failed to appear.[8] We were later told by other diplomats that the U.S. ambassador had manipulated the meeting agenda to exclude the French. It also made no sense at the time that, considering President Aristide's capacity to build almost fanatical loyalty within his eclectic coalition of followers, and considering that he had only recently been elected with a large majority, no one could be found to speak to the mission on his behalf. Fear of the military was seen at the time as the deterrent, but once again it later emerged that the agenda had been stacked. And finally, given the volatility in the country, it was puzzling that the de factos felt secure enough that they believed it was unnecessary for them to move even slightly from their original position.

There were, of course, other factors at work that made the outcome of the mission problematic. Language barriers hampered the ability to communicate; the absence of effective carrots and sticks hampered the ability to negotiate. It was thrust home during meeting after meeting over the three days, with military and civilian alike, that the practice of democracy was incomprehensible to even educated Haitians. And those who had lived for long periods in other democracies had simply suspended their belief that democracy was within the capacity of their own country. As well, the perceived need to act urgently, despite the absence of a well-thought-out strategy with an assigned role for each individual in the mediating party, meant that the questions, sometimes probing, must have been confusing to the Haitians on the other side of the table.

The civilian mission established the following month by Secretary-General Baena Soares following ministerial instruction faced fewer frustrations: interpreters were made available, planning and research were more comprehensive. Still, the parties remained virtually at a stalemate until mandatory UN sanctions brought about the Governors Island Agreement. And democracy returned to Haiti only under threat of force, following abandonment of the Haitian military's position by its reputed allies, the CIA and the Defense Department.

## CONCLUSION

Mediation involving multiple parties is difficult in part because of the need in most multilateral organizations to operate by consensus among diverse interests. In the case of Haiti, although some negotiation had to be undertaken with President Aristide, there were essentially two parties at the table: the de facto government in Port-au-Prince and the OAS, which did its best to merge the interests and positions of thirty-four countries. Negotiation on this scale was also new to the OAS. Under the best of circumstances, obtaining multiparty agreement is slow, but with under-the-counter support for the adversaries from within the United States,[9] the de facto regime had more time to become entrenched.

Of course, this is the dilemma faced by all international organizations in dealing with crises. The need to achieve consensus often precludes the possibility of rapid response, leaving the aggressor more time to consolidate. However, precipitate action without consensus can invite early, and potentially disastrous, failure; while action taken in the long run with consensus can be a mighty force. This is certainly one of the lessons from the Haiti experience.

If the OAS intervention in Haiti was in any sense a success, a positive factor was the considerable interaction among leading members of the OAS at both political and diplomatic levels. This interaction is an essential element in multiparty mediation. Because the ability to bring escalating pressure to bear is another important element in a successful mediation, the absence of enforcement measures or mandatory measures of any kind was a distinct disadvantage of the Haiti discussions during the OAS phase. The inadequacy of such measures was extremely frustrating. Freezing assets abroad is effective only if every country with a stable banking system acts in concert. Canceling air and landing rights is realistic only if there is no possibility of egress overland. Full-blown sanctions are the bluntest of instruments: their impact on the poor is always more devastating than on a well-to-do leadership. Military intervention is, of course, the ultimate enforcement, but is problematic in an age when most countries are opposed to using ground troops if there is a danger of major casualties. In the end, of course, military action became the instrument by which the crisis was ultimately ended. But military action would not have been politically acceptable without the prelude of strenuous diplomatic efforts.

Another positive factor was the sustained political and hence media attention from OAS countries, which curtailed the proclivity of the military regime to violate human rights at will, although it certainly did not eliminate them. Media attention to a mediation process takes on a life of its own and may or may not be helpful, but in the environment enveloping Haiti, although inconvenient to the mediators at times, it probably contributed to their ability to sustain political interest in the crisis and hence see it through to a conclusion.

In the end, leadership—patient leadership, particularly in a multiparty effort—is the single element most critical to the success of international mediation. It's fair to say that the ability of Canada to play a leadership role based on its considerable experience in a variety of multilateral organizations was a significant factor in sustaining international political pressure on the Haitian de factos.[10] It is worth pointing out that France, after the false start in Port-au-Prince, became an important player. France's participation was useful in generating interest in the European Economic Community and was critical to ensuring success at the UN Security Council, where France is a permanent member. Canada's influence on France was helpful, and Canada's ability to minimize frictions between France and the United States—always potentially problematic—relieved bilateral tensions.

In the end, of course, leadership rightly passed to the United States. Internal pressure, notably from the Black Caucus, made diplomatic intervention with the White House less critical, but OAS and UN cooperation with the United States during the military intervention ensured that the multilateral commitment to Haiti was never abandoned.

Finally, multiparty mediation cannot be expected to progress in a straight line. Other pressing priorities divert political attention, other crises suddenly arise, resources are scarce, other diplomatic avenues open up. In this context, the transition of institutional leadership from the OAS to the United Nations and ultimately to the United States does not detract from the vital role each institution played. It is not atypical in multiparty mediation for authority to shift as appropriate, although strenuous diplomatic effort and leadership is usually necessary to ensure that each institution plays its part in an appropriate and timely way. Positive change came out of the initial OAS efforts, and multiparty negotiation is now embedded in OAS processes and values.

**NOTES**

For information used in this article, I am deeply indebted to the following: Ann Marie Blackman of the OAS's Unit for the Promotion of Democracy (telephone interview, February 1999); Stanley Gooch, the Canadian head of mission in Mexico (telephone interview, January 1999); David Malone's book, *Decision-Making in the UN Security Council: The Case of Haiti* (Oxford: Clarendon Press, 1998); and Lisa Marcus's study, "The Ongoing Struggle for Democracy in Haiti" (M.A. thesis, York University, Toronto, January 1999).

1. Cuba, for obvious reasons, is a nonparticipant and is not relevant to this discussion.

2. There are several references in this article to the presence in Haiti at the time of the Central Intelligence Agency. As of this writing, some eight years later, the CIA presence is difficult to corroborate; one knowledgeable diplomat confirmed the references in this article but did not wish to be identified.

3. The thirty-fifth member, Cuba, was (and remains) an inactive member.

4. Later, and in part because of the difficulty in achieving consensus on Haiti, the practice at the OAS was changed to consensus minus two.

5. Organization of American States, Ad Hoc Meeting of Foreign Ministers, Resolution 2/91, 2 October 1991.

6. The role of the Black Caucus was crucial in pressuring President Clinton to take further action.

7. La Francophonie is an organization of French-speaking countries that bears a modest resemblance to the British Commonwealth.

**8.** The complete breakdown in Haiti's telecommunications system following the coup meant that the visiting mission, essentially trapped in the airport, was dependent on the goodwill of interlocutors who could move around the highly charged capital more freely.

**9.** Minor undercover support was also given to the de factos by some other regimes.

**10.** At last count, Canada belonged to more multilateral organizations than any other country, and is an active player in most of them.

## Background to Chapter 16

## The Ecuador-Peru Peace Process

The border dispute between Peru and Ecuador, the oldest such conflict in the Western Hemisphere, had persisted despite a 1942 treaty designed to end it and "guaranteed" by the United States, Argentina, Brazil, and Chile. A renewal of fighting in 1995 prompted a new peace process that culminated in a comprehensive settlement signed in 1998. The peace process was based on close cooperation between the governments of the two parties and the four guarantors. Although coordination among the participants (and within the U.S. government) was often difficult, the autonomy of the guarantors reinforced the two sides' trust in the process and helped them develop a mutually acceptable agreement.

### MAJOR ACTORS

- The parties: Ecuador and Peru
- The guarantors: Argentina, Brazil, Chile, and the United States
- MOMEP: Military Observer Mission, Ecuador-Peru

### IMPORTANT DATES

- 1809–30: Ecuador and Peru become independent with conflicting territorial claims
- 1830–1938: Reason and force both fail to produce an agreed-upon boundary
- 1941: Border incidents escalate into war

- January 29, 1942: Rio Protocol provides for "Peace, Friendship and Boundaries"
- 1942–48: Ecuador and Peru demarcate 90 percent of the border
- 1948–94: Ecuador stops demarcation; armed clashes occur in 1981 and 1991
- January 1995: Sustained fighting breaks out in the remote, undemarcated Cenepa valley
- February 17, 1995: Declaration of Itamaraty calls for cease-fire and talks
- March–October 1995: MOMEP separates combatants
- January 1996: With guarantor witnesses, foreign ministers of Ecuador and Peru discuss the border for the first time since 1942
- November 1997: The guarantors propose talks on navigation, integration, and security as well as the border
- January 19, 1998: Ecuador and Peru agree to seek a comprehensive settlement by May 30; positions on the border remain far apart
- August 10, 1998: Jamil Mahuad becomes president of Ecuador in the midst of renewed military tensions
- October 8, 1998: Mahuad and Peruvian president Alberto Fujimori ask the guarantor presidents to propose a border solution
- October 16, 1998: The congresses of Ecuador and Peru vote to accept a guarantor finding
- October 23, 1998: The guarantor presidents declare that Peru is sovereign over the Cenepa but must grant Tiwinza to Ecuador as private property
- October 26, 1998: A comprehensive settlement is signed in Brasília

**KEY AGREEMENTS REACHED**

- Declaration of Peace of Itamaraty, authorizing a military observer mission to separate forces and committing the parties to enter direct talks
- Comprehensive multipart settlement, establishing agreed-upon borders, promoting navigation, trade, border integration, and security, and enclosing the 1995 combat zone within contiguous ecological preserves.

**PRINCIPAL OUTCOME**

- A peaceful, forward-looking settlement to a bitter historical conflict

# 16

# The Ecuador-Peru Peace Process

LUIGI R. EINAUDI

The comprehensive settlement signed on October 26, 1998, by the presidents of Ecuador and Peru in the presence of five other presidents from South America, the king and queen of Spain, and representatives of the president of the United States and of Pope John Paul II broke historical stereotypes and created major opportunities for future inter-American cooperation.

Two aspects of the settlement are particularly noteworthy for students of conflict resolution:

- First, the settlement was constructed by developing modern interests that offset traditional disagreements. The settlement promotes the economies of both countries and advances common interests in regional integration, trade, navigation, security, the environment, and Indian affairs.
- Second, the settlement was made possible by the active participation of third parties—the outside states known as the guarantors of the Rio Protocol of 1942—which acted to stop a sudden spasm of sustained

combat in early 1995 and then persevered diplomatically until the parties reached a settlement.

This chapter discusses the period from the renewal of fighting in 1995 to the signing of the comprehensive settlement almost four years later. Drawn from a larger work in progress, it sketches the background of the conflict and briefly summarizes the evolving positions of the parties and the details of the settlement. In keeping with this volume's concentration on multi-party mediation, the primary focus here is on the role of the guarantors.

In response to the warfare of early 1995, the guarantors monitored an uneasy military stalemate while organizing a diplomatic effort to reach a definitive settlement. This chapter discusses guidelines used to lay the foundations for settlement and the interaction that took place to resolve the few points on which the parties were unable to reach agreement by themselves.

## BACKGROUND

In the struggle for control over South America's vast and largely unknown Amazon interior that followed the end of the Spanish empire, Ecuador and Peru disputed sovereignty over some three hundred fifty thousand square kilometers—an area the size of France or Spain, in fact an area larger than New England plus New York, New Jersey, Delaware, and Maryland combined.[1] The century following independence saw little settlement but much military and diplomatic activity. The king of Spain and the president of the United States attempted to act as arbiters. No agreed boundary emerged.

Each incident, each failure was magnified in the telling, until the layers of mutual distrust almost made it seem as if each country were writing its history as an "anti-history" of its neighbor.[2]

In 1941, a clash in the populated coastal area escalated, the vastly weaker Ecuadoran army collapsed, and Peru occupied southern Ecuador. The foreign ministers of Peru and Ecuador met in Rio de Janeiro under the auspices of Brazilian foreign minister Oswaldo Aranha. On January 29, 1942, they signed the Protocol of Peace, Friendship and Boundaries between Peru and Ecuador, commonly referred to as the Rio Protocol, after the city where it was negotiated. Ratified a month later by the congresses of both Ecuador and Peru, the treaty was also signed by representatives of Argentina, Brazil, Chile, and the United States. Ever since, those four countries have been collectively known as the treaty's "guarantors."

Though conceived as a comprehensive framework for peace, the protocol's key provisions were those that established the common land boundary in accordance with named points and specified natural features (Article VIII).

The treaty also committed the guarantors to help settle disagreements "until the definitive demarcation of frontiers between Peru and Ecuador has been completed" (Articles V, VII, and IX).

Over the next six years, a Mixed Ecuadoran-Peruvian Demarcation Commission worked with the assistance of guarantor experts to fix the boundary on the ground. Progress was rapid in the settled coastal area, slower in the unsettled and less-known eastern interior. The United States lost two Army Air Force planes and fourteen crew members while helping to map the fog-shrouded mountain jungles of the eastern territories.[3] In 1943 and 1945, arbitration by Brazilian military geographer Braz Dias de Aguiar helped resolve Peruvian-Ecuadoran differences.

In 1948, with markers formally in place along more than 90 percent of the border, Ecuador took the position that a December 1946 U.S. Army Air Force aerial survey should be interpreted to mean that there were two watersheds where the framers of the protocol had believed only one existed. Asserting that this "new geographic reality" made the protocol *"inejecutable"* (impossible to implement), Ecuador withdrew from the Mixed Commission, halting demarcation.

Opinion in Ecuador was responsive to arguments that the protocol had been imposed by force and deprived Ecuador of as much as half its national territory. In fact, during negotiation of the protocol, the guarantors had insisted on a line respecting the territorial status quo ante. Peru withdrew from El Oro province, occupied during the 1941 war, and the Rio Protocol line ultimately displaced no civilian populations. Even changes in frontier outposts were minimal. But Ecuador's nineteenth-century claims merged with national pride into a mythology of Amazonian greatness denied. Maps depicting Ecuador's territory reaching as far as Iquitos, others actually traversing Brazil to the Atlantic mouth of the Amazon, were displayed in schools and public buildings. Opposition to the protocol became unchallengeable political correctness.[4]

In 1960, Ecuador declared that the "geographic error" made the protocol invalid as well as unworkable. The guarantors rejected the thesis of nullity: under international law, boundary treaties cannot be renounced by a single party. Peru responded by denying that any problem existed. It used its superior military force to enforce the disputed frontier as if it had been fully demarcated where Peru's experts (and unofficially most guarantor experts) believed it should go, along the Cordillera del Condor and the watershed between the Cenepa and Coangos Rivers. Ecuadoran military patrols crossing that line were asked to withdraw when detected, and generally did so, accepting the reason of force if not of the protocol.

Despite occasional skirmishes between armed patrols, the issue disappeared even from the back pages. Clashes in 1981 and again in 1991 sparked momentary interest, which quickly evaporated once forces were separated.[5]

## THE 1995 CRISIS

By January 1995, when sustained combat broke out in the upper valley of the Cenepa, technology and economics had drastically altered realities both on the ground and regionally. Instead of machetes and turn-of-the-century Mausers, the two militaries were engaging with jets and rockets. Casualties, almost all military,[6] were running into the hundreds. Both countries mobilized air forces, armored units, and navies. Escalation to more heavily populated areas was feared. A war between Ecuador and Peru would be the nail in the coffin of the hemispheric hopes raised by the Summit of the Americas in Miami just a month earlier but already buffeted by the Mexican peso crisis.

The guarantors reacted with unaccustomed speed and vigor. Reassuming the role of coordinator it had played in 1942 and since, Brazil called for an immediate cease-fire and asked the two parties to meet immediately with the guarantors. After an inconclusive first round in Rio, Assistant Secretary Alec Watson asked if I would agree to represent the United States in a continuing guarantor effort. I answered with two questions of my own. Was our objective just to stop the shooting? Watson answered that everyone wanted to go for a permanent fix if one could be found. My second question was whether anyone would object if my first call was to General Barry McCaffrey, then the commander in chief of the U.S. Southern Command? A permanent fix would be unthinkable without military support. Again, I got the answer I needed. I was to seek full interagency support and speak for the United States, not just for the State Department. Three days later, I was in the capital of Brazil, helping to negotiate the framework for a cease-fire.

### The Declaration of Itamaraty

After a frustrating month during which hostilities continued and even worsened, Ecuador and Peru reached agreement with the guarantors on February 17, 1995. In the Declaration of Peace of Itamaraty, the parties accepted a guarantor offer of a military observer mission and authorized it to monitor an immediate separation of forces and to recommend an area to be demilitarized. Because the guarantors were not prepared to accept an open-ended military commitment, the declaration set a ninety-day limit for the observers, allowing for renewals by common agreement.

This time, however, the guarantors were no longer ready to define success as the absence of hostilities. Paragraph 6 of the Declaration of Itamaraty committed the parties to enter into direct talks to seek a peaceful solution to all remaining disagreements as soon as the military crisis was overcome. To bridge Ecuador's insistence that there were major (if undefined) problems and Peru's equally adamant view that all that needed to be done was to put in appropriate border markers, the disagreements were identified only as the *"impases subsistentes"* (residual impasses). Paragraph 4 stipulated that geographic references involved in the separation of forces and the demilitarization would have no further applications, implicitly negating their potential use in any claims that might arise in discussions of demarcation.

The guarantors' newfound determination found vital legal support in a unilateral move by Ecuador. For the first time since 1960, Ecuador had moved to accept the validity of the Rio Protocol. On February 17, when the Declaration of Itamaraty was signed, Ecuadoran president Sixto Durán Ballén made a radio address to his nation. Confirming statements he had made in January, Durán Ballén said that "this Protocol, taking into account the history and the basic geographic realities discovered afterwards, must be the basis for a definitive and just settlement of the territorial problem that divides our two countries."[7]

## The Guarantors Separate the Combatants

When the guarantor military observers finally reached the conflict area in March,[8] thousands of heavily armed soldiers from the two sides were still dangerously intermingled in the upper Cenepa valley. Instead of frontlines, the Military Observer Mission, Ecuador-Peru (MOMEP) found small units—tired and hungry but armed to the teeth—intermingled in front, behind, above, and below each other in seventy square kilometers of heavily mined and uniquely inhospitable triple-canopy mountain jungle. To devise a scheme to separate the contending forces without bringing them into contact severely tested the professionalism of the military observers from the United States, Brazil, Argentina, and Chile. It was a minor miracle that MOMEP not only drew up such a plan, but succeeded in directing its execution by early May without casualties either to the parties or to the observers themselves.[9]

By October 1995, MOMEP had organized the withdrawal of more than 5,000 troops from the areas where conflict had occurred and monitored the demobilization of an additional 140,000 troops on both sides. Peru and Ecuador had complied with the military obligations they had assumed in the Declaration of Itamaraty and in the MOMEP terms of reference (which among other things required Ecuador and Peru to pay all costs incurred by the observers). At this point, the guarantor senior officials made an unusual request. The guarantors would agree to a third ninety-day renewal for MOMEP, but only if the parties began to assume greater responsibility for the observation. Ecuador and Peru agreed. The officers they contributed to the observer force transformed MOMEP into a six-nation enterprise in which former combatants worked side by side with third-party observers.[10]

## Diplomacy Takes Center Stage

In 1996, the foreign ministers of Ecuador and Peru discussed border matters face to face, meeting successively in Lima, Quito, Buenos Aires, and Santiago. Their encounters were the first ministerial meetings about the border in more than fifty years—the first, in fact, since the Rio Protocol was signed in 1942. By the time the fourth meeting concluded, in October 1996 in Santiago, the ministers had agreed on what to discuss and how. For the first time, Peru had accepted that problems affecting the implementation of the Rio Protocol did exist and should be discussed. For the first time since 1960, Ecuador not only had accepted the validity of the protocol, but also had begun to define specifically what problems it saw in its implementation.[11] That Ecuador included sovereign access to the Amazon as an impasse produced strong negative reactions in Peru, where some even accused Foreign Minister Francisco Tudela of agreeing to negotiate away Peru's sovereignty.

Further progress was temporarily blocked by unexpected events in both countries. In Ecuador, President Abdalá Bucaram was removed by Congress. In Peru, Foreign Minister Tudela was among the hostages taken by terrorists at the Japanese ambassador's residence in Lima. The formal presentation of the disputed points finally took place in Brasília between April and September 1997. The presentations were disappointingly marked by formalism and maximalist stances. Both sides laid out their positions as though they were negotiating for guarantor support rather than attempting to deal with each other. It would not be an exaggeration to say that Peru's position remained that the solution was to drive in border markers where Peru had always said they should go, while Ecuador challenged the protocol's workability in the area of the Cordillera del Condor while also asserting a right to sovereign access to the Amazon. Most simply put, Peru reaffirmed its claim to every millimeter of the territory it had always claimed, while Ecuador sought to document rights to major parts of that very same territory.

Had things been left there, the negotiations would have ended virtually without starting. But neither the guarantors nor the parties themselves could allow a stalemate to harden. All sides were painfully aware that in the long run the alternative to settlement was war.

## A Settlement Begins to Take Shape

In November 1997, the Brazilian foreign minister proposed in the name of the guarantors that, having identified the issues, the parties change their focus to consider four broad categories of action that, if effectively developed, could address their differences and thus form the basis of a comprehensive settlement. These four courses of action were the conclusion of a treaty of commerce and navigation, the fixing of the land frontier, the development of a border integration regime, and mutual security understandings.

The Rio Protocol stipulates in Article VI that Ecuador is to enjoy free and untaxed navigation on the Amazon and its northern tributaries. However, a treaty to that effect had never been negotiated. As the Itamaraty process evolved, debate and preparation inside Ecuador seemed to have produced greater clarity and realism than in the past. If Ecuador could obtain rights of Amazon navigation and commercial use that were substantial and permanent, even if not sovereign, perhaps it would become easier to define the land border in compliance with the Rio Protocol and its complementary instruments.

Border integration and security matters were also of great potential benefit to both countries, particularly to the border populations who for generations had borne the brunt of uncertainty and conflict. Measures to these ends were not explicitly called for in the protocol. Moreover, Ecuador's challenges to the protocol had led Peru to oppose any and all discussions not directly related to setting the boundary as diversionary maneuvers to evade application of the provisions for demarcation. Peru's decision to accept the guarantor proposal thus moved the Itamaraty process toward what some saw as a "protocol plus" mode that could lead to a settlement.

The new approach added practical and highly positive considerations of security, usufruct, and binational development to the traditional and highly conflictive preoccupations that had until then dominated the agenda. On January 19, 1998, this modern vision was front and center in Rio de Janeiro. Ecuador and Peru agreed to a Work Plan that called for the creation of four commissions to prepare a comprehensive settlement.

## LEGAL BASIS OF THE GUARANTOR ROLE

The four negotiating commissions convened on February 17, 1998, the third anniversary of the Declaration of Itamaraty, which had been negotiated under guarantor auspices, and from which the peace process took its name. Driving home the critical role played by the guarantors, the four commissions each met in one of the four guarantor capitals under the auspices of the respective guarantor special envoy.[12] Guarantor initiatives had in fact been essential to progress from the start. In 1995, it was the guarantors who found a way to separate the combatants. In 1996, every time the ministers met, the guarantor special envoys were present to act as witnesses and facilitators.

The guarantor role is defined in the Rio Protocol only as acting to *help* or *assist* the parties. However, this assistance is not limited in time. As noted previously, the protocol commits the guarantors to help settle disagreements "until the definitive demarcation of frontiers between Peru and Ecuador has been completed" (Article IX). In addition, guarantor efforts are directed both to specific issues, from military observation (Article III) and the fixing of the land border (Article IX), and to the broadest of issues, such as the settlement of "any doubt or disagreement which may arise in the execution of this protocol" (Article VII).

That these provisions did not in themselves require intense activism had become evident in the half century since the protocol's signing. But with unprecedented military and economic risks made obvious by the 1995 conflict,[13] they provided ample authority and coherence for a serious six-country effort to resolve the Western Hemisphere's oldest and most bitter dispute.

As agreed in the Declaration of Itamaraty, once the military confrontation had been contained, the focus shifted to the underlying issues. Immediately the practical scope of the guarantor role took center stage. At the very first meeting of the Peruvian and Ecuadoran foreign ministers, in Lima in January 1996, the guarantor senior officials stressed their autonomy from the parties. In a joint statement read by their Brazilian coordinator, they announced their readiness to make their own evaluations, recommendations, and public declarations on the peace process. Anticipating an issue that was to become central to the success of the peace process, they also began to assert a role when the parties could not reach agreement. If asked by the parties, the guarantors said, they would be willing to make suggestions or recommendations that the parties could, if they wished, agree in advance to treat as binding.

At the next ministerial meeting, in Quito in February 1996, the guarantors were forced to invent a fresh technique to prevent a new stalemate. The parties were ready to exchange papers defining their respective understandings of the *impases subsistentes*. This was to be the first practical step in carrying out the commitment in Paragraph 6 of the Declaration of Itamaraty to hold talks on the underlying issues. It was also to be the first such concrete exchange since Ecuador had declared the protocol unworkable almost fifty years before. But Paragraph 6 also specified that the talks were to take place *after* the military measures specified in Paragraphs 1–5 had been completed. Ecuador's foreign minister argued that Peru had not complied fully with the demobilization provisions. To forestall the developing stalemate, the guarantors offered to hold in trust in sealed envelopes the definitions from each of the parties. Only after MOMEP had certified that certain force levels and demobilization actions affecting the conflict areas had actually taken place, would they complete the exchange by delivering them to the other party.[14]

In Buenos Aires in June, the guarantors sharpened their Lima position. Reaffirming that they would "participate actively and autonomously in the discussions," they agreed with Peru and Ecuador that "the Parties, if they so agree, will make recourse to the Guarantors obligatory whenever they have not reached an agreement regarding a particular point, within the terms of the Article VII of the Rio Protocol of 1942."[15]

The Santiago Accord of October 29, 1996, completed the shift from procedural to direct substantive talks. In it, the guarantors agreed to create a special "Support Commission" made up of senior guarantor diplomats.[16] The Support Commission was in effect a diplomatic equivalent of MOMEP, ensuring that the negotiations would be kept on an even keel without vetoes or interruptions.

The parties started out needing the guarantors for rather different reasons. Peru's objective was primarily to have the guarantors enforce the Rio Protocol. Ecuador, in contrast, sought to use the guarantors as buffers against Peru's greater military power, while asking them to support an outcome that would prove "equitable" or "just" rather than one that merely enforced the protocol's obligations as interpreted by Peru. Wide as these differences were, another disturbing reality also became evident in the initial phases of talks: little communication and no agreement were proving possible between the parties without the guarantors being present. Because the four guarantor states were powerful and successful countries, this automatically put pressure on the parties at least to appear to be working toward a settlement. In fact, major forces in both countries wanted to settle, and both knew they would need help in doing so.

## MAKING THE PROCESS WORK

Assistant Secretary Watson had said that my ability to be patient was a key reason he wanted me to take on this assignment. As events unfolded, it became clear that, apart from the capacity to make decisions and the ability to listen (the latter not unrelated to patience), patience was *the* critical attribute for the guarantor special envoys. Patience in dealing with the parties. Patience in dealing with each other. And patience in dealing with their own governments.

But patience is not a strategy. Through trial and error, in the crucible of difficult experiences, I developed five guidelines to follow in pushing for closure.

**First, and above all, maintain unity.** Close and continuing coordination was vital on two levels, first within the U.S. government and then between the United States and the three other guarantor powers.

In Washington, I quickly realized that it was an illusion to think that being a "special envoy" gave me any special authority. Rather, it was more like an admission pass to a circus with competing ringmasters. Having served most of 1994 as the acting deputy director of the secretary of state's Policy Planning Staff, I was unusually well placed to relate effectively to different bureaus and offices within the State Department. In addition, a quarter century of coordinating activities in Washington, including several years as executive secretary of the old State Department–National Security Council (NSC) Inter-Agency Group, had given me considerable experience in dealing with the foreign affairs community in the executive branch and to some extent in the Congress.

Even so, I spent as much time with U.S. officials, agencies, and problems as with the parties and the guarantors combined. In part, this was because the need to station U.S. soldiers in a faraway jungle automatically put Peru-Ecuador onto the active screen of the NSC and the intelligence community as well as the Defense Department. But to an even greater extent, the need for extensive internal coordination simply reflected the many faces of the foreign affairs community in an age of bureaucratic differentiation and democratic empowerment.[17]

What in Washington were perceived to be "big decisions"—that is, decisions affecting major U.S. interests, like the stationing of troops abroad—came under the purview of the Inter-Agency Group chaired by the NSC. But this group—which typically met in the White House Situation Room—was convened rarely and at too high a level to provide regular information exchange and coordination. Accordingly, to stay in touch with the disparate entities whose support I felt I needed (or who themselves felt they had a right to be heard), I instituted an informal Inter-Agency Working Group. Although members of the NSC staff often participated, "informal" and "working" made clear that this was not the formal Inter-Agency Group chaired by the NSC. Attendance at the working group meetings, which I convened about once a month, included representatives from a dozen offices in the State Department and as many more from other agencies.[18]

Despite such gargantuan efforts, coordination still sometimes broke down.[19] The potential fault lines were many. In Washington, they included disagreements over matters of interpretation or prospects, personnel turnover, competing personal and bureaucratic interests, lack of resources, changing and conflicting priorities, even complications caused by congressional reporting requirements. In the field, such problems were compounded both by distance from Washington and by differences in perspectives or circumstances among our embassies in Quito, Lima, and the various guarantor capitals.

Coordination among the guarantors was also time consuming. State Department officials had been merciless in characterizing past guarantor efforts as "cumbersome, . . . reluctant to take decisions," and with "a distinct tendency to play favorites."[20] It was little wonder my colleagues in the State Department thought I would need all the patience gleaned from my previous experience as ambassador to the Organization of American States. And it was certainly true that having four countries involved in the guarantor effort naturally entailed a host of potential frictions. These included differing national interests and perspectives, such as U.S. activism compared with Latin caution, or the intrusion of bureaucratic or domestic politics. There were also occasions when the parties sought to divide the guarantors. Even when there were no ulterior motives, the parties' individual consultations with individual guarantors could produce contradictory information or imply policy differences when there were none.

But if these problems underscore the importance of forging unity (and of being patient), the difficulties should not be exaggerated. In the renewed guarantor effort after 1995, Brazil was from the start the undisputed coordinator. The four special envoys rapidly developed good personal chemistry and exchanged telephone calls and faxes to supplement contacts through their respective embassies. In a matter of months, they had also developed a practical definition of what constituted a "guarantor meeting." Unless all four envoys were present, there was no meeting and no guarantor statement could issue from it. More than once other senior officials, including foreign ministers, saw this as an implicit challenge to their own authority, but this simple mechanism proved very effective in maintaining coherence and informed decisions.[21]

So long as unity was maintained, there were advantages to having more than one interlocutor. Having advocates of different views and interests within the ranks of the guarantors created balance. The existence of different perspectives was also reassuring to the parties, increasing confidence that their views would be represented in the debates among the guarantors and not dismissed arrogantly without a hearing.

Having a common line enabled the guarantors to use their own bilateral channels to make clear to the parties the importance of their reaching a settlement. So persistent was this message in bilateral channels that I more than once received complaints from one or another of the parties that we had so stereotyped them that they would be unable to achieve other national objectives unless they first reached a settlement. Finally, guarantor unity was also very helpful in dealing with the Organization of American States, the United Nations, and the Vatican—other third parties with an interest in the outcome but not directly involved in the negotiations. So long as the guarantors were united in saying that they were making progress, these other potential intermediaries, conscious that they lacked the unique legal standing of the guarantors, could act as a supporting cast instead of feeling driven to take initiatives of their own that would in all likelihood only have muddied the waters.

Coordination with the parties deserves a further word. Frustrating as trying to organize the United States and guarantor communities could become, these problems paled in comparison with the substantive and institutional difficulties of the parties. For Peru and Ecuador, the issue was literally one of war and peace compounded by all the complications of civil-military intrigue. Never easy under the best of circumstances in any country, civil-military coordination in Ecuador and Peru had the additional burden of traditional concepts of political and military activities as belonging to separate spheres. As each was therefore to be kept from being tainted by the other, any coordination would have to take place in the respective national security councils or higher.

But the parties' difficulties were not just internal. They also had to deal with each other. And Peru and Ecuador for a long time simply refused to talk to each other.[22] Their failure to communicate was borne of fear, distrust, frustration, a sense of futility. Sometimes, of course, silence was helpful to the peace process. But silence added to the pressure on the guarantors. As each side considered the other hopelessly unreasonable or prejudiced, each looked to the guarantors to speak for them, and somehow miraculously introduce or induce the necessary elements of reason or flexibility in the other party.

With each party so distrusting the other that it would automatically dismiss anything it might put forward, an observer from outer space might have been forgiven for concluding that one of the key functions of the guarantors was to force the objective evaluation of possible courses of action simply by confusing their origin. There were times, even years into the process, when the only communication between the parties took place through the guarantors. Indeed, there were times when direct communication between the parties would only have made things worse.

**Second, ensure military support for diplomacy.** The creation of MOMEP, so necessary to separate the combatants and then to monitor the demilitarized zone (DMZ), gave the guarantor military a place at the table. This complicated coordination and introduced major complexities. But it also created an essential additional channel to the two parties, in both of which military commanders were influential. Communication among the six countries could now take place at the level of military institutions as well as among diplomats. This was a critical element at times of high military tension as late as August 1998, just two months before the settlement.

In the field, the military observers were frequently isolated from the guarantor diplomats and targeted for influence by the parties. The eternal complaint that "the diplomats aren't doing anything" was heard regularly, not infrequently on military lips. In Washington, there were interminable debates over rules of engagement, reimbursement (even after Peru and Ecuador agreed to pay MOMEP costs), NSC-State-Defense debates over "exit strategies," and other matters of abstruse doctrine. Behind these debates was unease at the exposure of U.S. military personnel to risks in a mission about which the American public knew little. Officials understood U.S. participation in MOMEP as using the military to support peace, but the desire to withdraw U.S. forces to avoid antagonizing the Congress was always in the back of decisionmakers' minds.[23]

Despite these many debates, the strategic implications for the two countries and the hemisphere arising from changing military technologies and firepower were not as readily appreciated as the challenges of logistics in difficult geographic conditions. The major exception was concern that purchases of Russian MiGs might set off a regional arms race.

But there were also major successes. My call to General McCaffrey in January 1995 had led to constant close cooperation and mutual support. For more than two years I was in daily telephone communication with U.S. Southern Command, often with McCaffrey personally. The command's deputy director of plans, Colonel Leon Rios, accompanied me on my every trip to Peru, Ecuador, Brazil, Argentina, and Chile. For security and flexibility, Southern Command also furnished our little team a C-21 aircraft and a communicator. The Washington contingent would pick up (and leave) the C-21 in Panama, enabling a full debrief with McCaffrey and his staff at the beginning and the end of each trip to the field.

This intimate cooperation was crucial to the effectiveness of our military observers during MOMEP's difficult start-up times. And after the DMZ was functioning, our close coordination facilitated intelligence collection and exchange. And it greatly helped our diplomacy as well. Many diplomatic as well as military initiatives originated in this unique State-Defense partnership, which also enabled us to present a united military-diplomatic front to the parties and to the other guarantors.[24]

With little tradition of civil-military teamwork among the other guarantors (the Latin tradition being one of separate *fueros* or institutional autonomy), I was the only special envoy who regularly traveled with military officers as part of my team. Yet in May–June 1995, when the area to be demilitarized was defined in arduous negotiations in Brasília, guarantor diplomats and military officers worked effectively together and with the general officers from Ecuador and Peru who acted as liaisons to MOMEP. There were other times when the guarantor diplomats found it desirable to treat military complaints from the parties as technical matters separate from high policy. Compartmentalizing some military matters was an effective way to prevent their becoming politicized or affecting diplomatic questions. In truth, of course, this too required coordination between guarantor diplomats and their military observers who needed support for their service in difficult and remote conditions on the ground.

**Third, remember the parties must lead.** One of the least appreciated aspects of interstate disputes involving sovereignty is that *nothing can be done without the parties themselves*. The guarantor role is defined in the protocol as acting to *help* or *assist* the parties, not as leading an enforcement operation under Chapter VII of the UN Charter. Nor are these provisions to be dismissed as purely formulaic respect for the sovereign equality of states required in treaty language. In practice as well as law, no settlement would have been possible without political sensitivity to nationalist opinion in both countries. Moreover, it is just common sense to realize that without committed political engagement by the parties themselves, no settlement is likely to be implemented for very long.

Disputes over sovereignty are often so entwined with history and national psychology that those involved perceive them as different from all others—or at least sufficiently unique to inoculate them against formulaic solutions imposed from the outside. Unless both of the states involved have governments willing to assume responsibility, resolution of the conflict is impossible.

As the peace process between Peru and Ecuador unfolded, the commitment of the parties was in fact demonstrated repeatedly. How to stop the shooting was handled by the vice ministers working with the guarantor special envoys and MOMEP. As the diplomatic issues came to the fore, vice ministers yielded to ministers who in turn yielded to national negotiating delegations once substantive legal and geographic issues were tabled. Finally, after the elements of a comprehensive settlement had been identified, the two presidents took over. Without the courage and vision of Jamil Mahuad and Alberto Fujimori there could have been no settlement.

When in 1998 Alberto Fujimori and Jamil Mahuad led, the guarantor presidents had the good sense to follow. Occasionally they shared the lead. The willingness to be responsive is not automatic, and the guarantors clearly deserve much credit for the peace. But the guarantor envoys and their superiors never forgot that no matter what they themselves did, no matter what responsibilities they accepted, it was the parties who had to lead the way.

**Fourth, use the law.** The authority of the guarantors flowed to an important extent from their relative power and unity. Nonetheless, the legitimacy of their actions and recommendations derived from the Rio Protocol, and subsequently from the Declaration of Itamaraty and the MOMEP Terms of Reference. In Ecuador, the association of the Rio Protocol with accusations of imposition and claims of *inejecutabilidad* was offset by the positive association of the Declaration of Itamaraty and MOMEP with the peace process and the prevention of an escalating war against a stronger Peru. In Peru, Ecuador's past avoidance of implementation of the Rio Protocol produced great skepticism about Ecuador's intentions. But for both parties, the existence of a legal framework to be applied was a fundamental source of legitimacy and coherence for the peace process, militarily as well as diplomatically.

In both 1995 and 1996, MOMEP successfully requested the parties to alter troop dispositions it concluded were contrary to formal agreements. In 1997, applying the latest technology to reduce technical barriers to implementation of the law, the United States provided to both parties the first-ever set of cloud-free images of the area where the workability of the Rio Protocol had been challenged. In 1998, the commission formed to recommend the setting of the land border referred disagreements between the parties to two "technical-juridical" panels nominated by the guarantors. The most controversial of these panels was headed by a justice of the Brazilian Supreme Court.[25]

**Finally, keep sights high.** With so much history and bloodshed over territories whose symbolic value is far greater than their material worth, the best approach to creating new common ground was to focus everyone's attention on the future. This was not easy. When fears of an immediate hot war declined in late 1995 as MOMEP stabilized the military situation by monitoring the DMZ, the reassertion of vested interests, nationalism, and deeply rooted prejudices all caused interest in reaching a comprehensive settlement to decline as well. Peace would bring pain. Why bother to make peace? A Peruvian negotiator observed in a down moment, "The least Ecuador can accept is more than the most Peru can give." The guarantor initiative of November 1997 sought to alter this negative dynamic by building development, integration, and modernization into the settlement. And to sustain momentum, the guarantors always sought agreement on some next step before adjournment of any meetings.

The Summit of the Americas scheduled for April 1998 in Santiago, one of the guarantor capitals, provided a natural target date for completion of an accord. For months, I attempted to use the upcoming summit as an action-forcing event to mobilize both domestic and international support for a comprehensive settlement. Unfortunately, my efforts to mesh the summit and the peace process often looked to my fellow guarantors like typical American impatience. To many Peruvians, they seemed unwanted pressure, while many Ecuadorans were reminded of 1942, when the hemisphere had seemed more eager to unite against the Axis than to give Ecuador a full hearing.

But another factor was already helping to ensure that sights were kept high. The approach of the millennium was working for peace. How could a conflict born in colonial times and largely shaped in the nineteenth century be allowed to hold Peru and Ecuador back as the rest of the world entered the twenty-first century?

## RIPENESS, SOVEREIGNTY, AND THIRD PARTIES

The inauguration August 10, 1998, of Jamil Mahuad as president of Ecuador created a coincidence rare in the history of the conflict. With Mahuad in Ecuador joining Alberto Fujimori in Peru, both countries suddenly had strong, legitimate presidents.

The situation was clearly ripe for leadership. Military tensions were so high that it almost seemed as though some in both countries were out to scuttle any settlement. At the same time, opinion polls showed enormous majorities in both Peru and Ecuador were hungry for a lasting peace. After nearly four years of unprecedented military and political effort, the guarantors had helped men and women of goodwill in both countries to build the foundations of a modern settlement.

Yet ripeness, Professor Zartman reminds us, is not self-enacting or self-enforcing.[26] Few issues are more intractable than disputes involving sovereignty. And the dispute between Ecuador and Peru touched the national self-image of both countries.

In 1996, after Peru changed its diplomatic posture and accepted that real problems existed with Ecuador, the necessary next step was to allow each side to define what it thought the problems were. When Ecuador defined one of its *impases subsistentes* as a claim to sovereign access to the Amazon, this was read in the Peruvian press through such emotional and historical lenses that many Peruvians, blinded to the reality that without definitions no settlement would be possible, cried treason and blamed everyone from Peru's diplomats to the guarantor officials.[27]

In 1998, some Ecuadorans reacted with comparable anger to the prospect that the land frontier might be set along the Coangos-Cenepa watershed, where Peru had long sustained it belonged. Agreements on border integration (connecting oil pipelines, electricity grids, and irrigation projects of enormous benefit to populations reeling under the devastation of El Niño), navigation and commerce (guaranteeing Ecuador free and perpetual if not sovereign access to the Amazon), and new understandings on security (designed to end risks and fears of war and the costly drain of an armed peace) were being read through such emotional and historical lenses that some were led to argue that all the benefits meant less than a few square kilometers of unusable tropical jungle.

Leaders in both countries understood that changes in military technology have enormously raised the risks and costs of conflict even among forces armed only with conventional weapons. They understood as well that economic growth and development have increased the potential of integration and thus the material benefits of peace. Even so, the true costs of conflict were hidden for many by the passions of history and war. When all is said and done, this was the most tragic aspect of the Ecuador-Peru dispute— and the one that did the greatest damage to both countries. For decades, even centuries, lives were lost, stunted, and embittered by the conflict and the sacrifices it exacted. There were the necessary (but otherwise unnecessary!) expenditures for military preparedness and deterrence—all the more painful for countries afflicted by social division and numbing poverty.

But it was the indirect costs of forgone development that were in many ways the greatest tragedy. At the very moment that military technology was escalating the dangers and the costs of battle, the potential for conflict was denying the two nations, particularly southern Ecuador and northern Peru, the benefits of integration and development that are elsewhere driving

South America's political and economic resurgence. Freed from this historic burden, Ecuador and Peru could work together in ways that would immensely benefit their citizens and strengthen the weight of South America in world affairs.

Alberto Fujimori did not attend Jamil Mahuad's inauguration because military tensions near the undemarcated border were too high for such a gesture. Yet in the next two months, Presidents Mahuad and Fujimori met alone at the Paraguayan inauguration, at the Rio Group Summit in Panama, and in Brasília as guests of President Cardoso. Every step of the way, they insisted that they needed and wanted a "global and definitive peace." With the help of mutually compatible aides,[28] they reviewed together the cumulative work of the previous three years. At every meeting, the two presidents insisted they were reducing the number of disagreements but that they had yet to find a way to resolve all of them. And as they worked, so did the guarantor senior officials, developing an option for environmental preserves in the area so bitterly fought over in 1995.

Indeed, the 1995 combat had left a legacy that was a potential dealbreaker. Never more than a few huts and trenches, it was a spot lost in the virtually inaccessible mountain valley of the Cenepa River and hidden under triple-canopy jungle in the heart of the demilitarized zone. Typically, the parties could agree neither on its precise location nor even on the spelling of its name. For Ecuadorans, "Tiwintza" symbolized national dignity. For Peruvians, "Tiwinza" symbolized Ecuadoran aggression. Ecuador claimed it had successfully defended Tiwintza against Peruvian attacks. Peru claimed it had recaptured Tiwinza, preserving Peru's sovereign rights. Both sides had watered its soil with the blood of their soldiers. Neither could conceive of yielding it to the other.

Yet a comprehensive settlement that ended the risk of war and provided important benefits to both countries was clearly at hand. The procedures had all been followed. The issues had all been defined. Ancient disagreements and emerging opportunities had been exhaustively studied, even largely decided. Even the time consumed had helped, for it removed potential grounds for further delay. The persistence of the guarantors had strengthened the hand of the parties of peace. Even before the two presidents began their review, the commissions established under the January 19, 1998, Work Plan had agreed on perpetual navigation rights on the Amazon for Ecuador and identified major development projects for the border. But agreement on the boundary had remained elusive despite the advisory opinions of guarantor jurists and geographers.

By October 8, back in Brazil with President Cardoso, the two presidents realized they could not reach agreement by themselves. Some problems, particularly Tiwintza, had become so freighted with emotional and historical baggage that neither president felt he could make the concession the other needed. So, falling back on the procedural agreement reached in 1996 in Buenos Aires by two since-departed foreign ministers ("the Parties . . . will make recourse to the Guarantors obligatory whenever they have not reached an agreement regarding a particular point"), they asked the guarantor presidents to resolve the few remaining points between them. Then they visited Washington, Buenos Aires, and Santiago to convey their request personally to Presidents Clinton, Menem, and Frei.

To their enormous credit, the guarantor presidents accepted the challenge. Instead of merely "keeping the ball in the air," they accepted the shared responsibility of making decisions knowing that they would be criticized. But they asked that the congresses of Ecuador and Peru both accept in advance that they would be bound by the guarantor decision. By similar votes of approximately three to one, both congresses did so, and the hemisphere's oldest and most violent dispute was virtually over.

On October 23, 1998, the guarantor presidents made their finding. First, they recorded with satisfaction that the parties had agreed on drafts for a "Treaty of Commerce and Navigation," for "Navigation in Sectors Cut by Geodesic Lines and the Napo River," for a "Broad Agreement of Border Integration," and for the creation of a "Binational Commission on Confidence-Building Measures and Security," as well as an "Agreement for the Establishment of Measures to Assure the Efficient Functioning of the Zarumilla Canal." Then they stated that to conclude the fixing of the common land boundary and complete the comprehensive and definitive settlement, Peru was to be sovereign over the Cenepa valley but must grant one square kilometer around Tiwintza to Ecuador as private property in perpetuity. Finally, all the major points of the 1995 conflict, including Tiwintza, were to be enclosed in 54.4 square kilometers of adjacent ecological reserves freely transitable by members of native communities and coordinated with the help of private nonprofit organizations.

When the comprehensive settlement[29] was signed October 26, 1998, the parties and the guarantors had together achieved what many thought was impossible.[30] "Today we have opened the door to the future," said Presidents Mahuad and Fujimori, whose foresight had been matched only by their courage.[31]

## NOTES

1. The geographical comparisons are from George McCutchen McBride, *Ecuador-Peru Boundary Settlement: Report to the Secretary of State by the United States Technical Advisor*

(Washington, D.C., 1949). McBride, one of the most distinguished academic geographers of his generation, served from May 1942 to September 1948. His admirable account (now declassified, but published so far only in Spanish translation) was transmitted to Dean Acheson on July 19, 1949, and includes a chapter on the dispute's colonial and precolonial origins as well as detailed accounts of the geography, the demarcation, and the difficulties encountered.

2. The phrase is that of the Peruvian José Carlos Mariátegui, who attributed to such mistrust the lack of significant regional cooperation in the decades after Bolívar.

3. The difficulties of operating in this remote region were again confirmed in 1981, when a U.S. military helicopter with a crew of three disappeared without a trace.

4. The former president of Ecuador, Osvaldo Hurtado, attempted to counter these and other dangerous distortions by pointing out Ecuador's failure to settle or defend the territories in question, even formally ceding substantial tracts to Peru in the late nineteenth and early twentieth centuries. See his *Julio Tobar Donoso víctima expiatoria* (Quito: Fundación Ecuatoriana de Estudios Sociales, 1994).

5. The best single overview of the history, much of it written from U.S. Department of State records, is William Krieg, *Ecuadorean-Peruvian Rivalry in the Upper Amazon* (2d ed., enlarged to include the 1991 Paquisha incident), a study prepared for the Department of State under its External Research Program in 1986. Félix Denegri Luna, *Perú y Ecuador: Apuntes para la historia de una frontera* (Lima: P.U.C., 1996), is illuminating.

6. Though some indigenous populations were displaced by the fighting, many had previously simply stopped visiting certain places, like Cueva de los Tayos, when they became military outposts.

7. The full text of the president's radio address is printed in Foreign Minister Galo Leoro Franco's *Informe a la nación*, vol. 2, *1994–1995* (Quito: Ministerio de Relaciones Exteriores), 375–378.

8. The delay was caused partly by the logistical problems of pulling together the necessary ten officers (plus support personnel) from each of the four guarantors and transporting them to Patuca, Ecuador, the remote base from which the 100-member force would principally operate. Perhaps more significantly, the delay was also caused by difficulties in negotiating the rules of engagement to be followed. How were the observers to be armed? What would be their internal chain of command? What authority would they have? After extensive risk assessments and endless debates (most of which of course had to be referred back to the guarantor capitals), it was determined that each observer would carry personal arms, that a Brazilian general would act as coordinator of four contingents under national control, and that the parties would provide specified logistical support.

9. Colonel Glenn R. Weidner, the able original commander of the U.S. contingent in MOMEP, gives an eye-witness account with maps in "Operation Safe Border: The Ecuador-Peru Crisis," *Joint Force Quarterly* (spring 1996): 52–58.

10. Inclusion of observers from the parties was novel and did occasionally bring complications. Both sides tended to use the information obtained as grist for psychological warfare activities against each other. To ensure autonomy of MOMEP operations, transportation and communications remained exclusively in guarantor hands. In November 1997, Brazil replaced the United States as the major logistical support for MOMEP, providing the needed

pilots and helicopters. In September 1995 and again in August 1998, MOMEP monitored further separations of forces north and south of the demilitarized zone.

**11.** Ecuador's concerns are well documented in Julio Tobar Donoso and Alfredo Luna Tobar, *Derecho territorial ecuatoriano*, the fourth edition of which was published by the Foreign Ministry of Ecuador in 1994. What Ecuador had *not* done prior to February–March 1996 was to turn these concerns into specifically defined issues and national positions that could be addressed in the course of negotiations.

**12.** To underscore the U.S. commitment, Secretary of State Madeleine Albright attended the Washington opening of the commission charged with developing a comprehensive agreement on border integration. The other commissions dealt with the drafting of a treaty of commerce and navigation (Buenos Aires), fixing the common land boundary (Brasília), and mutual confidence and security measures (Santiago).

**13.** Gabriel Marcella provides the best account of military factors in his *War and Peace on the Amazon: Strategic Implications for the United States and Latin America of the 1995 Ecuador-Peru War* (Carlisle, Pa.: Strategic Studies Institute, U.S. Army War College, 1995).

**14.** The delay proved to be only about two weeks, and the exchange of impasses took place in Brasília on March 6, 1996.

**15.** Press release, Buenos Aires, June 19, 1996.

**16.** The U.S. representative on the Support Commission was Ted Wilkinson, who had followed the process from the start from his position as political counselor in our embassy in Brasília. The other guarantors gave similar attention to their commissioners, all of whom had ambassadorial rank.

**17.** When I retired for personal reasons from the State Department in July 1997, I agreed to stay on as special envoy only after then Assistant Secretary Jeffrey Davidow agreed to appoint David Randolph, a senior Foreign Service officer who had just served as political counselor at our embassy in Quito, to a new position as full-time coordinator for Ecuador-Peru matters within the U.S. government. Even as a full-time official, I had needed full-time help in coordination. In 1996–97, Foreign Service Officer Lynn Sicade provided much support, making some notable contributions along the way.

**18.** To say that representatives normally came from the NSC, the State Department, the Defense Department, the Arms Control and Disarmament Agency, the Central Intelligence Agency, and the Agency for International Development is to understate the complexity. State Department participants from the Bureau of Inter-American Affairs typically came from the Offices of Andean Affairs, Policy Planning, and Brazilian and Southern Cone Affairs as well as the Office of the Assistant Secretary. Other State Department participants came from the Office of the Legal Advisor, the Bureau of Political-Military Affairs, and the Bureau of Intelligence and Research, which was often represented by the Office of the Geographer as well as by intelligence analysts. Aside from U.S. Southern Command in Panama, which was often represented by its Washington liaison office, Defense Department entities with contributions to make included the Office of the Secretary of Defense for International Security Affairs, the Joint Chiefs of Staff, and the Defense Intelligence Agency. Finally, other government entities played important roles at particular points in the process. One critical example was the National Imagery and Mapping Agency (NIMA), whose

Panama office developed maps for MOMEP as well as the first cloud-free imagery of the disputed areas.

**19.** Readers should know, however, that I always received unstinting support and encouragement from the three who led the State Department's Bureau of Inter-American Affairs during the peace process—Alec Watson, Jeff Davidow, and Peter Romero—as well as from Jim Dobbins at the NSC and Mack McLerty at the White House.

**20.** Krieg, *Ecuadorean-Peruvian Rivalry in the Upper Amazon*, 142 ff.

**21.** The high rank of the guarantor special envoys (or *altos funcionarios*) helped enormously as did their continuity. As a senior adviser to the secretary of state, I was well placed, but was not in the actual U.S. chain of command. Fortunately my fellow envoys all held positions roughly equivalent to the undersecretary for Political Affairs, the third-ranking official in the State Department. As the only guarantor representative who did not change after Itamaraty, I developed a unique familiarity with the parties and the issues, but even that was very relative, as the other guarantors changed only once (Brazil went from Fernando Reis to Ivan Cannabrava, Argentina from Juan Manuel Uranga to Alfredo Chiaradia, and Chile from Fabio Vio to Juan Martabit).

**22.** Except, all too often, through the press. Often manipulated for internal consumption, press reports were influenced by psychological warfare by the respective military intelligence services. In an effort to at least contain the damage, the guarantors formally requested the parties to agree on a moratorium on the details of the negotiations.

**23.** As things turned out, these fears proved unwarranted. The generally cautious American Overseas Interests Act of 1995, adopted on June 8, 1995, by a vote of 222 to 192, explicitly "applauds the earnest work of the United States government as a guarantor of the Rio Protocol" (Section 3225G, H.R. 1561). Similar bipartisan support was evident in 1997 when House International Relations Committee Chairman Benjamin Gilman (R-New York) and the committee's ranking minority member, Lee Hamilton (D-Indiana), wrote to the presidents of Peru and Ecuador in support of the peace process, as did Senate Foreign Relations Committee Chairman Jesse Helms (R-North Carolina). Congressional awareness owed much to the staff work of Michele Manatt and Roger Noriega, the first a Democrat in the State Department, the second a Republican on Capitol Hill.

**24.** Ironically, one of the worst breakdowns in internal U.S. coordination was due to this unique partnership. In February 1996, a representative of another agency whom I had included on my team to the Quito foreign ministers meeting misconstrued how well we were working in preparing new terms of reference for the guarantor observers and concluded that we were seeking to expand MOMEP at a time the NSC and some in the Department of Defense were eager to have it end. His misinterpretation of our objectives and of the situation on the ground (I am convinced he thought we were running virtually a rogue operation) robbed the military observers of needed momentum and flexibility at a critical moment.

**25.** The justice was Nelson Jobim. The U.S. representative to the panel was Professor Clarence W. Minkel of the University of Tennessee and dean of American geographers concerned with Latin America. He was ably assisted by John Gates of the National Imagery and Mapping Agency.

**26.** I. William Zartman, informal remarks at a United States Institute of Peace seminar, September 17, 1998, Washington, D.C.

**27.** One columnist went so far as to accuse me of being "an anesthetist come to prepare Peru for a new territorial amputation," a reference to Peru's nineteenth-century territorial losses to Chile and Colombia.

**28.** Enormous credit must go to Foreign Ministers Fernando de Trazegnies of Peru and José Ayala Lasso of Ecuador and their teams. Peru's ambassador to Washington, Ricardo Luna, and Ecuador's chief negotiator, Edgar Terán, sustained everyone in the darkest months of 1996 and 1997. Enrique Iglesias, president of the Inter-American Development Bank, was a constant source of encouragement and support. Private citizens who made critical contributions included Ecuador's Ivonne A-Baki (who became Mahuad's ambassador to Washington) and Harvard professor Roger Fisher, principal author of *Getting to Yes* (2d ed., New York: Houghton Mifflin, 1992).

**29.** The full texts of all the agreements and maps are published (alongside commentaries from a Peruvian perspective) in a special edition of *El Sol* (Lima) printed on November 8, 1998, entitled *Llegó la paz* (Peace has arrived).

**30.** Not least among the doubts overturned by the successful settlement was the widespread belief that the armed forces of the two countries would block any agreement out of institutional self-interest.

**31.** "Shaping a Common Future," *Brasília Speeches*, October 26, 1998 (Lima, Peru: PromPeru, December 1998).

## Background to Chapter 17

## The Good Friday Agreement in Northern Ireland

The long-standing conflict between Protestant and Catholics in Northern Ireland escalated in the late 1960s into widespread and sustained violence as loyalist and nationalist paramilitary groups began battling one another and British troops. Throughout the 1970s and 1980s, violence and intimidation paralleled and undermined repeated attempts to negotiate a solution. Then, in the mid-1990s, a renewed peace process focusing on internal negotiations and bolstered by international support began to gain momentum. An international body was appointed to explore the thorny issue of disarmament ("decommissioning"); this team was subsequently asked to chair negotiations. The mediation team insisted that participants adhere to democratic and nonviolent methods, and oversaw a three-strand approach to negotiations that involved the Northern Ireland parties and the governments of the United Kingdom and Ireland. Nothing would be agreed upon until everything was agreed upon, and all decisions would require the approval of a majority of the electorate. The final agreement, reached on Good Friday in 1998, provides a blueprint for peace, though its success depends on finding answers to such unresolved issues as decommissioning.

### MAJOR ACTORS

- Unionist/loyalist political parties: among them, the Ulster Unionist Party, the Democratic Unionist Party, the United Kingdom Unionist Party, the Progressive Unionist Party, and the Ulster Democratic Party

- Unionist/loyalist paramilitary groups: among them, the Ulster Volunteer Force and the Ulster Defence Association
- Nationalist/republican political parties: among them, the Social Democratic and Labour Party and Sinn Féin
- Nationalist/republican paramilitary groups: among them the Irish Republican Army and the Irish National Liberation Army
- Nonaligned political parties: among them, the Alliance Party, the Northern Ireland Women's Coalition, and the Labour Party
- United Kingdom government
- Republic of Ireland government
- Mediation team: George Mitchell (United States), Harri Holkeri (Finland), John de Chastelain (Canada)

## IMPORTANT DATES

- 1968: The "troubles" (civil violence and unrest) begin
- 1972: Direct rule of Northern Ireland from Westminster instituted
- 1973: Sunningdale Agreement reached
- 1985: Anglo-Irish Agreement reached
- 1991: Multiparty talks in Belfast begin
- November 1992: Talks suspended
- 1993: Downing Street Declaration issued
- August 1994: IRA cease-fire begins
- October 1994: Loyalist cease-fire begins
- 1995: Frameworks Document signed
- December 1995: International Body begins work
- February 9, 1996: IRA breaks its cease-fire with a bomb in London
- 1997: Labour Party wins British elections, Fianna Fail wins Irish elections
- July 20, 1997: Second IRA cease-fire begins; some unionist parties quit talks
- April 10, 1998: Good Friday Agreement reached in Belfast

## KEY POINTS OF THE GOOD FRIDAY AGREEMENT

- Mechanism established linking Belfast, Dublin, London, Edinburgh, and Cardiff
- Mechanism established linking London and Dublin governments
- Instituted review of such issues as policing, prisoners, and human rights
- Called for the complete decommissioning of all paramilitary arms
- A power-sharing executive to be established
- Mandated north-south bodies to be created
- An elected assembly to be established

- The Irish Constitution to be amended and the Government of Ireland Act to be abolished

### PRINCIPAL OUTCOMES

- The agreement was overwhelmingly endorsed in referenda held in Northern Ireland and Ireland
- Elections to the local assembly were successfully held
- As of November 1998, north-south bodies have not been set up and the decommissioning of weapons has not begun

# 17

# The Good Friday Agreement in Northern Ireland

JOHN DE CHASTELAIN

**F**or nearly thirty years, starting at the end of the 1960s, Northern Ireland endured almost continuous violence. The Good Friday Agreement of April 10, 1998, was the culmination of a series of efforts to address the problems that caused that violence. Although the Agreement was only the most recent in a number of attempts to find a permanent end to the "troubles," it embodied in one complex and conditional document an accord acceptable to each of the differing traditions and backgrounds within Northern Ireland. Not a settlement in itself, the Good Friday Agreement presented a blueprint for a future of democratic government free from the threat of violence. A true settlement will be reached only after each aspect of the Agreement is implemented to the satisfaction of the majority in Northern Ireland, including a majority within both unionist and nationalist traditions.

The aim of this chapter is to review the period between the start of the work of the International Body in December 1995 and the attainment of the Good Friday Agreement of April 10, 1998. The chapter is written from the personal perspective of the author, who was a member of the international team involved in both the decommissioning review and the chairing of various aspects of the political process, as well as the chairman of the decommissioning body still engaged in working to achieve its mandate. (A glossary of names and terms appears at the end of this chapter.)

## BACKGROUND

Serious attempts to resolve the political problems in Northern Ireland began almost as soon as violence escalated dramatically in the early 1970s. The Sunningdale Agreement of 1973 brought the British and Irish governments together with a proposal that gave nationalists and Dublin a voice in the affairs of Northern Ireland. Contested by extreme elements within the unionist community, it was followed by the Anglo-Irish Agreement of 1985, which gave the Irish government a formal consultative role in Northern Ireland for the first time, and by the Downing Street Declaration of 1993 and the Frameworks Document of 1995. The last two underscored the principle of consent: the acceptance by Dublin and London that the future of Northern Ireland lay in the hands of the majority of its people and not in Westminster or in the Dáil Eireann.

Two attempts to resolve the political future of the province took place in the form of multiparty talks in Belfast in 1991 and in Belfast, London, and Dublin in 1992. These talks involved the four main constitutional parties—the Ulster Unionist Party (UUP), the Democratic Unionist Party (DUP), the Social Democratic and Labour Party (SDLP), and the Alliance Party. The aim of the talks was to address the totality of relationships within Northern Ireland (referred to as Strand One), the relationships between north and south (Strand Two), and the relationships between London and Dublin (Strand Three).

In 1991 the British government chaired the talks, as they were then confined to Strand One only. In 1992, with the Irish government joining them, the talks were extended to include Strands Two and Three. As the Strand Two talks involved the participation of both governments as well as the parties, a neutral observer, the former governor general of Australia, Sir Ninian Stephen, was invited to chair them. Negotiations were suspended in November 1992 without reaching agreement, but some progress had been made and the participants were able to agree that most, if not all, of the elements of a political settlement had been discussed.

### Cease-Fires

In 1994, after more than thirty-two hundred deaths and thousands injured, and the wearisome prospect of continued violence and destruction, moves to bring an end to the conflict led to an Irish Republican Army (IRA) cease-fire in August and to loyalist cease-fires in October. The IRA's cease-fire was seen by many as a response to the Downing Street Declaration of eight months earlier. John Hume of the SDLP, Gerry Adams of Sinn Féin, and the taoiseach (the Irish prime minister), Albert Reynolds, put forward a common view that since nearly thirty years of violence had not achieved the republican goal of a united Ireland, it was time to allow a political approach to try to do so. The loyalist cease-fires were a reaction to the IRA's decision. Loyalists too accepted to seek their goal—confirmation of Northern Ireland as an integral and unchangeable part of the United Kingdom—by political means alone.

More than a year later the process of political negotiation on the future of Northern Ireland had still not begun. In the Downing Street Declaration the two governments made clear that in the circumstances of "a permanent end to the use of, or support for, paramilitary violence . . . democratically mandated parties which establish a commitment to exclusively peaceful methods and which have shown they abide by the democratic process, are free to participate fully in democratic politics and to join in dialogue in due course between the Governments and the political parties on the way ahead." This declaration remained the base criteria for participation in negotiations, with many politicians and citizens arguing that an irrevocable commitment to exclusively peaceful means could be fully demonstrated only through the decommissioning of paramilitary weapons. They believed that retention of weapons was incompatible with a permanent end to the use of, or support for, paramilitary violence.

Many unionists therefore agreed that Sinn Féin should not be invited to the negotiating table until the IRA decommissioned its arsenal. The British government, whose position was expressed by Northern Ireland Secretary of State Sir Patrick Mayhew in March 1995, wanted evidence of all paramilitary groups' willingness to disarm progressively, to accept an agreed practical understanding on the modalities of decommissioning, and to actually decommission some arms to test the practical arrangements and to demonstrate good faith.

The IRA's view was that the cease-fires were declared without precondition. IRA leaders pointed out they had not been defeated. They would not have declared a cease-fire if they had known decommissioning was a prerequisite for Sinn Féin's involvement in inclusive negotiations.

By the fall of 1995 the cease-fires appeared to be increasingly vulnerable—this at the very time President Clinton planned a visit to Belfast and Dublin. The United States was providing crucial political encouragement to both traditions and continuing support to help create an economic foundation for a lasting settlement. President Clinton's visit to Ireland was planned to underscore his personal involvement and his commitment to the peace process.

## Twin-Track Process

Given their concern over the cease-fires, Prime Minister John Major and the Taoiseach, John Bruton, called for a twin-track process that would address the issue of decommissioning and pave the way for a process of political negotiations. In November 1995, they committed to the establishment of an International Body that would address decommissioning over a two-month period, and to the initiation by the end of February 1996 of a political process to begin later the same year.

While the process involved the two governments and the representatives of ten political parties elected for the purpose, it involved no third parties directly (other than the independent chairmen). Other parties played important supporting roles: Countries of the European Union gave financial support and political encouragement in the pursuit of peace. South Africa offered advice and a venue for informal discussion based on its own history of conflict resolution. And the United States provided support to help rebuild the economy and political encouragement to both traditions.

But these states had no direct involvement in the process. As agreed by London and Dublin, the people of Northern Ireland would decide the future of Northern Ireland. The involvement of chairmen drawn from outside was simply an acknowledgment of the need once again to have neutral individuals oversee the talks involving the two governments and the parties.

## THE INTERNATIONAL BODY

### Composition and Role

On November 28, 1995, the British and Irish governments issued a communiqué announcing the establishment of an International Body to "identify and advise on a suitable and acceptable method for full and verifiable decommissioning; and—report whether there is a clear commitment on the part of those in possession of such arms to work constructively to achieve that." It comprised three individuals drawn from the United States, from a Scandinavian country, and from a country of the Commonwealth. Senator George Mitchell, recently retired from the United States Senate, was invited to chair the body. He was a man of impeccable reputation, known for his skill as a jurist, politician, and mediator. Since his retirement from the Senate at the end of 1994, he had spent much time on the island of Ireland advising the United States on economic issues. He had an intimate knowledge of the people, north and south, and of the history and nature of the conflict. He was known and respected by leaders in Dublin, London, and Belfast.

Harri Holkeri had recently been prime minister of Finland. Retired from active political life, he was a member of the Board of Governors of the Central Bank of Finland and involved in numerous Finnish and international enterprises. He was known for his intellect, political acumen, patience, and negotiating skills. A leader and a man of firm principle, he was also a swift study of personality and a team player.

Given that the mandate of the International Body was to deal with the issue of paramilitary weapons, it was considered helpful to have one member with a military background. At the time, I was about to retire as Canada's chief of Defence Staff and was invited to be the third member of the group.

Senator Mitchell called the group together for the first time in New York on December 9, 1995. The intention was to introduce ourselves and to formulate a plan of action to meet the two-month mandate. As chief of staff of the body, Senator Mitchell engaged Martha Pope, former sergeant at arms of the United States Senate who, like Mitchell himself, was much aware of the situation in Ireland and Northern Ireland and knew the main players involved in the political process. Each member had an assistant provided by the foreign affairs department of their respective countries: David Pozorski from the United States, Timo Kantola from Finland, and David Angell from Canada.

During the New York meeting the body agreed on a plan of four days of interviews in Belfast and Dublin in December, to be followed by a further period of two weeks there in January. The second period was to include the time necessary to write the report due to be delivered to both governments by January 15. Senator Mitchell had been in Belfast and Dublin when President Clinton visited in November, and he had already met with Prime Ministers Major and Bruton after the announcement of the body had been made public. By the time of our meeting in New York he had formulated the outline of a plan to address the body's mandate. During the meeting he sought Holkeri's and my input. Mitchell and I had met briefly in 1993, when he was Senate majority leader and I was Canadian ambassador to the United States, but it was the first time either of us had met Harri Holkeri. The personal chemistry was instantly good. We agreed on the outline without hesitation. This cooperative spirit characterized the rest of our work together.

## Mandate and Research

The mandate of the International Body was twofold: to report on the willingness of the parties to engage in decommissioning, and to suggest how that could be accomplished. The problem with decommissioning had been one of timing—the requirement that it take place before negotiations or as a result of them—but that was not an issue we were asked to address. Nonetheless, it was clear we would have to comment on it somehow in our report.

During his dealings on Ireland, Mitchell had become aware that the central issue dividing the two traditions on any approach to negotiation was the lack of trust. Decommissioning was but one symptom of that mistrust, albeit a powerful one. His plan was that we should get the views of as many as possible in Northern Ireland, London, and Dublin, and then write our report so that it responded to the specific questions of the mandate. But we would couch it in such a way that it laid a solid basis for confidence building, on which the next phase of the process—the political negotiations—could be founded.

Meetings with the prime ministers in London and Dublin, and then with Secretary of State Sir Patrick Mayhew in Belfast and Foreign Minister Dick Spring in Dublin, were our first priority. We then chose to meet with each of the Northern Ireland political parties, or at least with those that agreed to meet us. For the second round in January, we planned to meet with the same parties again, as well as with any individuals and groups we felt could be helpful.

Of the political parties, we met with two unionist parties—the UUP and the United Kingdom Unionist Party (UKUP); with two nationalist parties—the SDLP and Sinn Féin; and with two loyalist parties—the Progressive Unionist Party (PUP) and the Ulster Democratic Party (UDP). We also met with the Alliance Party. Particularly interesting were the meetings with the loyalist parties and the forceful declaration by each of the need for peace. Some of their spokesmen were men with paramilitary backgrounds who had served time in prison. They were eloquent in their determination that a future of peace had to be found. It was one of them who introduced the Body to a statement heard many times subsequently: "What is needed in Northern Ireland is not a decommissioning of arms but a decommissioning of mindsets."

During the process of information gathering, results were not always encouraging. Traditional positions were firmly entrenched and their validity was constantly reiterated. On one occasion we scheduled an hour-long evening meeting with a political party, to be followed by a working dinner with a senior politician. The meeting was difficult and ran longer than scheduled. Late in getting to the hotel for dinner, we apologized to the senior politician, who was already waiting, for the delay. He could see our meeting had not gone well. After listening to our dispirited assessment of where we were, he suggested we list the number of positive things we had encountered so far. We listed five. He asked for the number of negative things and we listed four. "There you are, you're winning," he said. We sat down to dinner in a better frame of mind, but reassurance was not always so simple.

By the end of our tour in December we had a fair idea of the scope of the issue and the attitude of the parties. In January, we were able to confirm and clarify those conclusions and to seek further pertinent detail from the governments and security forces. Meetings with the general officer commanding in Belfast and the chief constable of the Royal Ulster Constabulary (RUC) helped us understand the technical dimension of the mandate. Similar meetings with the Garda Siochana and the Defence Force in Dublin were likewise useful. Meetings with church leaders helped us understand the divide between the traditions, and the work the churches were doing to overcome it. But it also became clear that the people of Northern Ireland were just as interested in what we were doing as were the politicians, the security forces, and the church. After nearly thirty years of conflict the people had enjoyed a year and a half of respite and they did not relish losing it.

With the concurrence of the governments, we decided to delay our report by a week and arranged to meet individuals and groups who had asked to see us and whom we felt we should hear. These included organizations such as Families Against Intimidation and Terror and the Pat Finucane Society, both groups opposed to violence and terrorism. We met with groups representing families seeking information on the location of relatives abducted by paramilitary groups and believed killed. We met with those seeking an end to the use of the baton-round by security forces in Northern Ireland, those wishing to see a reduction in the number of legally held arms in the province, and those seeking change in the makeup of the RUC and its method of operation. And we met with groups that worked to bridge the gulf between the communities at the social level. We toured their operations on the Falls and Shankill Roads and we spoke to citizens gathered there to meet us.

### The Report

By January 19 we had finished collecting information and moved to London to write our report, away from the requests for media interviews and other distractions. On the willingness of paramilitary groups to engage in decommissioning, the answer was straightforward. They would not do so prior to negotiations. It was not that they could not; they would not. That was also the conclusion of many of the parties and individuals we spoke to or who provided written submissions. Again, it seemed clear that mistrust was the problem. If mistrust could be overcome, and a commitment given to purely democratic means of negotiation, then we might have the stimulus to get the parties to the table without decommissioning.

We drafted six principles of democracy and nonviolence that we felt, if adopted, might get the talks started. As confidence grew during the talks, we believed, a beginning of decommissioning during them "could help create the atmosphere needed for further steps in a progressive pattern of mounting trust and confidence."[1]

Thus we suggested that participants in all-party negotiations should affirm their total and absolute commitment: "To democratic and exclusively peaceful means of resolving political issues; to the total disarmament of all paramilitary organisations; to agree that such disarmament must be verifiable to the satisfaction of an independent commission; to renounce for themselves, and to oppose any effort by others, to use force, or threaten to use force, to influence the course or the outcome of all-party negotiations; to agree to abide by the terms of any agreement reached in all-party negotiations and to resort to democratic and exclusively peaceful methods in trying to alter any aspect of that outcome with which they may disagree; and to urge that 'punishment' killings and beatings stop and to take effective steps to prevent such actions."[2]

Putting these six principles—later to be dubbed "The Mitchell Principles"—in our report was not strictly within our remit. But since the aim of our work was clearly intended to help the democratic process move forward, including helping to create the climate in which decommissioning could occur, we felt their inclusion was warranted.

The second issue we were asked to address was "to identify and advise on a suitable and acceptable method for full and verifiable decommissioning."[3] Our discussions with security forces and with those associated with, or close to, paramilitary groups were helpful to us in reaching conclusions. Thus we suggested four methods: the transfer of armaments; the provision of information leading to their discovery; the depositing of armaments for collection; or their destruction by the paramilitary groups themselves. But we believed that if any of the methods were to be acceptable and believable, the process would have to require guarantees. It should suggest neither victory nor defeat; it should take place to the satisfaction of an independent commission; it should result in the complete destruction of armaments in a manner that contributed to public safety; it should be fully verifiable; it should not expose individuals to prosecution; and it should be mutual.

With the two questions answered, our report was ostensibly complete. We felt that the six principles could provide the confidence necessary for the political parties to begin negotiations. We believed that stipulating the need for avoiding the impression of surrender and prohibiting forensic testing of arms handed in voluntarily could help convince paramilitary groups to begin decommissioning. But our meetings with individuals and other groups convinced us there was a third constituency whose confidence in the overall process needed to be bolstered: the people.

## Confidence-Building Measures

Accordingly we included at the end of the report a section entitled "Further Confidence Building." In it we incorporated some of the concerns expressed to us verbally or in writing that we felt particularly worthy of mention. Introducing them we noted: "We make no recommendations on them since they are outside our remit, but we believe it appropriate to comment on some since success in the peace process cannot be achieved solely by reference to the decommissioning of arms."[4] Items in this section included the need to review paramilitary activities such as surveillance and targeting; the provision of information on the missing and the exiled; action on prisoners and on emergency legislation; the need to review the holding of legally held arms "as the threat reduces"; more balanced representation in the police force; the need for increased emphasis on economic and social development; and the utility of an elected body to enhance the process of building confidence.

The latter comment was a sensitive one. The elected body at Stormont was removed in 1972 at the height of the troubles and replaced by direct rule from Westminster. That situation prevailed. The concept of an elected body in which unionists would still have a majority—even one without full powers to rule—was unattractive to nationalists. Nonetheless, the November 28 Joint Communiqué creating the International Body had questioned "whether and how an elected body could play a part" in the peace process. We felt it timely to include reference to that in our report.

Although the report was only twenty-two pages long, in double-spaced type, we spent three and a half days writing it and revising it over and over again. It was clear that every phrase would receive close scrutiny from all who had a special interest in it. We knew how eloquent the people were and the store they placed on meaning and nuance. We wanted it clear that what we wrote was what we meant. We also felt it important to emphasize that the report reflected our unanimity.

## Mandate Completed

On January 22, 1996, we delivered the report simultaneously to London and Dublin and the next day held a press conference in Belfast to answer questions on it. Then the International Body disbanded and we returned to our respective homes.

The report was received with varying degrees of enthusiasm or dismay, unsurprising given the contentious nature of the issues and the bitterness of the conflict it was intended to help resolve. Unionists were disappointed their demand for decommissioning before negotiations had not been supported. Nationalists were disappointed by the emphasis the British government placed on the suggestion of an elected body.

On February 9, little more than two weeks after the report was delivered, the IRA bombed Canary Wharf in London and their cease-fire ended.

## THE INDEPENDENT CHAIRMEN

### The Political Track

Despite the shock of the abrupt end to the IRA cease-fire, Prime Ministers Major and Bruton persisted with the promised political track of the talks. A communiqué on February 28 put in place the mechanism for elections in May to a Forum, from which the participants to the talks would be drawn. An election in Northern Ireland was the responsibility of the British government. In announcing one in the communiqué, John Major said he had taken "account of the differing positions of the parties and the view of the International Body" and believed "an elective process would offer a viable and speedy route to all-party negotiations."[5]

For his part, the taoiseach agreed and indicated that "the Irish Government would support any proposal of that kind which, it was satisfied, was broadly acceptable to those parties, had an appropriate mandate, and was within the three strand structure."[6]

Elsewhere in the communiqué the two governments undertook to consult widely with the Northern Ireland parties during March, and attempt to reach agreement on "proposals for a broadly acceptable elective process leading directly and without preconditions to all-party negotiations on 10 June."[7] In stipulating there would be no preconditions, the two governments accepted that decommissioning by a paramilitary group would not be a requirement before the party associated with it could be admitted to the negotiations. But by insisting that parties to the negotiations be ones "exclusively committed to peaceful methods to secure a comprehensive negotiated settlement," they signaled the exclusion of Sinn Féin until the IRA cease-fire had been reestablished. To underline the point, the prime ministers stipulated that "all participants would need to make clear at the beginning of the discussions their total and absolute commitment to the principles of democracy and non-violence set out in the report of the International Body."[8]

## Ground Rules

Following some consultation with the parties, the governments drew up a series of Ground Rules for Substantive All-Party Negotiations, which confirmed June 10 as the date for the start of the negotiations and which indicated their intentions with regard to structure, agenda, participation, format, and conduct. Here it was foreseen that Strand One would involve the Northern Ireland parties only and would be chaired by the British government, while the Irish government would be kept informed of progress. Strand Two would involve the parties and both governments and would be chaired by an independent chairperson. And Strand Three would be negotiated between the two governments, with the parties being kept informed and involved through a process of regular meetings designed specifically for that purpose.

On the contentious issue of reaching agreement, the governments suggested that "nothing will be agreed in any strand until everything is agreed in the negotiations as a whole," although it was foreseen that "on the basis of consensus among the participants" discussion could proceed on the assumption of contingent agreement.[9] The Ground Rules also foresaw the talks taking place in Belfast, with the Strand Two negotiations able to move between Belfast, Dublin, and London.

## The Forum

The elections to the Forum were held on May 30. A particular effort was made to ensure the presence in it of the smaller political parties representing special interests. Election in the eighteen constituencies was by a party list system and allowed for a top-up whereby the top ten parties received two additional seats to bring the Forum strength to 110. This top-up operated on a regional basis by accumulating the votes cast for each party in the various constituencies, and it allowed parties that might not otherwise have received seats to be included in the negotiations. Among these were the two loyalist parties: the PUP, with links to two paramilitary groups (the Ulster Volunteer Force [UVF] and the Red Hand Commando [RHC]), and the UDP, also with links to two paramilitary groups (the Ulster Defence Association [UDA] and the Ulster Freedom Fighters [UFF]).

The Forum's mandate was to promote dialogue and understanding, and it would have a life span of two years. It would meet weekly while negotiations in the talks process were under way, and it would provide the parties' representatives in the talks. The larger parties—Alliance, DUP, Sinn Féin, SDLP, UKUP, and UUP—each received three seats in the talks, although Sinn Féin was to be excluded as long as there was no IRA cease-fire. The Labour Party (not affiliated with the British Labour Party), the Northern Ireland Women's Coalition (NIWC), and the two loyalist parties each received two. Where decisions were to be taken in the talks, the parties voting strengths were weighted according to the overall vote they obtained in the May elections. Each of the parties would be allowed three unelected members to attend the talks in a supporting capacity, but they would not be seated at the table and would have no right to speak or vote.

## Framework of the Negotiations

In early June, the governments produced three internally circulated documents to provide the basis for the beginning of the negotiations: Scenario for the Opening Session, Procedural Guidelines for the Conduct of Substantive All-Party Negotiations, and Draft Agenda for Substantive All-Party Negotiations. The Scenario document committed both governments to "work with all the participants to implement all aspects" of the Report of the International Body. This undertaking included the requirement for leaders of the negotiating teams to make clear their party's commitment to the six principles of democracy and nonviolence (the Mitchell Principles) as well as to the report's proposals on decommissioning. The Ground Rules provided that the negotiations would start with an Opening Session of the Plenary Committee and that there would be a Business Committee to deal with procedural issues. The Scenario document confirmed those provisions and suggested that, in addition to the committees negotiating the three strands, a subcommittee on decommissioning be formed to address that issue.

Finally the Scenario document invited the three members of the International Body, George Mitchell, Harri Holkeri, and me, to chair those aspects of the negotiations that required independent chairmen (the Plenary Committee, Strand Two, the Business Committee, and the decommissioning subcommittee). Senator Mitchell would chair the Plenary Committee and the other positions would be approved as the negotiations proceeded.

We arrived in Belfast on the weekend of June 8 and 9, and the Office of the Independent Chairmen came into being. The time before the planned opening of negotiations on Monday, June 10, was spent in meetings with Patrick Mayhew and Dick Spring and with their principal colleagues, Michael Ancram and Sean O h'Uiginn. We also met with representatives of some of the parties to the talks. From the latter it was clear that the governments' preparations and plans for the negotiations were not approved by all the parties. It began to seem likely that the opening ceremonies on Monday afternoon, at which the two prime ministers would make introductory statements, and Mayhew and Spring would then invite the chairmen to take their seats and start the proceedings, might not go as scripted.

## Beginning of the Talks

A delegation representing unionist parties met with us at the hotel on Monday morning. Its purpose was to express a number of concerns. The first was that some unionists objected to the presence of outside representatives in what was purely a domestic matter. The delegation wished us to be aware of that before the meeting, to make sure we realized no offense was intended toward us personally. Another concern was that certain parties would take part in political negotiations without their associated paramilitary groups having started to decommission. But the delegation's strongest criticism was that the various documents agreed on by London, the Northern Ireland Office, and Dublin about the structure and conduct of the talks were being presented as a fait accompli. The unionists had a particular concern that in the governments' proposed opening Agenda, the subject of agreeing on an agenda for the substantive negotiations in three strands was placed ahead of the discussion on decommissioning. Having reluctantly accepted that talks could begin without decommissioning under way, the unionists thought that any suggestion that its importance was being downgraded was a bridge too far.

Thus, when we moved that afternoon to Stormont for the opening ceremonies, in rooms set aside for the talks in the Castle Buildings, we were ready for the unexpected.

## Seating the Chairmen

The two prime ministers made their introductory remarks in the large main conference room, flanked by colleagues from their respective countries seated on one side of a hollow square of tables around which the nine parties were ranged. The independent chairmen and their staff remained in an adjacent room, waiting for an announcement that the Plenary Committee was called into formal session, with Senator Mitchell in the chair assisted by Holkeri and me.

The warnings given us earlier proved correct. Twenty-four hours later we were still not seated, and it seemed unlikely we would be. But at midnight on Tuesday we were informed that a compromise had been found and we were led to our seats. The proposal that was then tabled was accepted by all the participants except the DUP and the UKUP, who left. Under the compromise, instead of the planned formal session of the Plenary Committee—organized and controlled under the rules proposed by the governments' Ground Rules, Scenario, Procedural Guidelines, and Draft Agenda documents—an informal session would convene under the interim chairmanship of Mitchell and his colleagues, and would continue in that format until Rules of Procedure, the final decision on the chairmanship, and an agenda for the remainder of the Opening Plenary had been agreed upon by the participants.

Mitchell took the chair and accepted, individually, the formal adoption of the six principles by the two governments and the seven remaining parties (the Alliance Party, Labour Party, NIWC, PUP, SDLP, UDP, and UUP). He then adjourned the session. When it reconvened later in the day, the leaders of the DUP and the UKUP separately returned for long enough to declare their acceptance of the six principles and then left again. But they returned later in the week and the informal session of the Plenary Committee—now with the chairmen, the two governments, and nine of the ten parties participating—began the task of agreeing on the Rules of Procedure by which the negotiations themselves would be structured and executed. Sinn Féin was still excluded in the absence of an IRA cease-fire, a circumstance underlined by an IRA bomb that devastated the center of Manchester the following weekend.

### Rules of Procedure and Approval of the Chairmen

Approving the Rules of Procedure, the chairmanship, and the agenda for the remainder of the opening session was to take nearly two months. In the interim, the nature of the challenges lying ahead were made clear.

The first problem was determining what constituted agreement, in the absence of rules defining it. It was accepted that for the purpose of the informal session, all decisions required unanimity. A second difficulty was the belief held by a number of parties that the documents produced by the two governments to establish the talks, particularly the Ground Rules, needed review and amendment. But the governments had not reached agreement on these documents without considerable discussion and, in some cases, compromise. Having them reopened, and subjected to possible disagreement by the parties, was potentially destabilizing. Whatever might be proposed as an alternative would require the eventual approval of both governments, as well as of the parties. But it was clear that until a sense of ownership of the process was felt by the parties, progress toward substantive negotiations was unlikely.

A further difficulty was the precise nature of the role the governments themselves would play in the process. On the one hand they were participants, the same as the nine parties. But both governments had the final say on who could and could not be part of the process, both governments paid its costs, and both governments would steer the final disposition of any recommendations for constitutional change that could—and most likely would—come out of the negotiations. In the event, the chairman's handling of the procedures dealt with the issue. By calling for the same input from government representatives during negotiations as he did from the parties, while leaving to the governments the resolution of issues that were clearly their responsibility alone, he solved the problem.

From the outset George Mitchell's personal approach to chairing the negotiations was made clear. It included calling on all participants to extend to the others the same courtesies they expected to receive themselves; it allowed participants the maximum leeway in making their point, without interruption, and subject only to time limits imposed by the participants; it included being firm in dealing with breaches of protocol; and it included obtaining the views of the majority on each next step in the talks. The objective manner in which he handled his role, and the wise way in which he proposed solutions to contentious issues, quickly impressed all the participants, including those with earlier reservations about outside involvement. Harri Holkeri followed the same practice when he stood in for Mitchell during his absence.

The talks proceeded in a format of three days of negotiations a week, with a fourth set aside for parties to deal with internal business. Fridays were reserved for meetings of the Forum. All the while, incidents of violence were a constant reminder of the need for progress. The cease-fires of the UVF and the UDA remained intact, owing in no small measure to the constant efforts of the PUP and the UDP, but dissident groups as well as the IRA continued with their "armed struggle." A republican group, the Continuity IRA, detonated a bomb at the Killyhevlin Hotel near Enniskillen in July, causing extensive damage but injuring no one. Another republican group, the Irish National Liberation Army (INLA), engaged in attacks and feuding leading to deaths, and a dissident loyalist group, the Loyalist Volunteer Force (LVF), was likewise active, particularly surrounding the marching dispute at Drumcree.

The marching season reached its climax in July, when loyalist Orders celebrated the 1690 Battle of the Boyne and the related political and religious struggles in seventeenth-century Ireland. It produced, annually, the most vivid demonstration of the clash between traditions. The Orange

Order's wish to march down a traditional route to their church service at Drumcree—down the Garvaghy Road, in an area now occupied predominantly by nationalists—led to confrontation in 1995. In 1996, the confrontation was worse, with loyalists initially denied the march and subsequently allowed it, over the objections of nationalists. The decision was perceived by these to be a backdown by the RUC in the face of loyalist pressure. After weeks of violent confrontation, the flying in of additional troops, carjackings, and the destruction of property all across Northern Ireland, the parties saw how close the province had come to a serious breakdown in law and order. It was against this background that they made a final effort to reach some form of agreement before breaking for the summer.

**Agreement on the Rules**

On July 29, when only a handful of issues were left outstanding on the Rules of Procedure, the first vote taken in the informal session of the Plenary Committee agreed, unanimously, the rule of sufficient consensus. The rest of the rules were then passed, when necessary by sufficient consensus. As it eventually emerged, sufficient consensus required four elements: the positive support of the parties representing a majority of the electorate by reference to the elections of May 30, 1996; the positive support of the parties representing a majority of each of the nationalist and unionist communities, respectively, by reference to the May 30 elections; the positive support of a majority of the parties participating in the negotiations; and the positive support of both governments. All four elements were subject to the caveat that the Irish government's agreement was not required in Strand One and the parties' agreement was not required in Strand Three.

By applying the principles of consensus, agreement was then also reached on two other issues: the approval of the chairmen and the setting up of the Business Committee. Attempts to approve an agenda for the remainder of the Opening Plenary failed. But participants broke for the summer with the positive announcement that agreement had been reached on three issues, and with the parties invited to make proposals on the agenda, to be addressed when the talks reconvened after August.

**Agenda for the Remainder of the Opening Plenary**

When the talks resumed in September, the Plenary Committee was no longer an informal body. The Rules of Procedure had been agreed. One rule called for parties to be removed from the talks if it could be demonstrated they had betrayed the principles of democracy and nonviolence. The rule stated: "If during the negotiations, a formal representation is made to the Independent Chairmen that a participant is no longer entitled to participate on the grounds that they have demonstrably dishonoured the principles of democracy and nonviolence as set forth in the Report of 22 January 1996 of the International Body, this will be circulated by the Chairmen to all participants and will be subject to appropriate action by the Governments, having due regard to the views of the participants."[10] Based on this rule, some of the parties began the new session by laying charges against others for actions that occurred in July surrounding the events at Drumcree. The resumption of the talks was preoccupied with this procedure. No parties were removed, but the precedent for such action was established.

Meanwhile, changes had occurred in the chairmen's staff. Given the pace of work and its attendant public relations aspects, as well as his heavy commitments elsewhere, George Mitchell had seconded Kelly Currie, a young New York lawyer, to be his personal assistant. Holkeri's assistant on the International Body, Timo Kantola, had returned to the arms talks in Geneva and was replaced by Marcus Laurent, a diplomat from Helsinki. My assistant, David Angell, was reassigned to the Canadian permanent delegation at the United Nations in New York, and was replaced by Clifford Garrard from the Canadian High Commission in London. The three chairmen, Martha Pope, and David Pozorski continued as before.

Agreement on an agenda for the remainder of the Opening Plenary was reached by the middle of October. It too involved compromise. Nationalist concern that substantive issues be addressed early was met by the decision to make the first item on the agenda the requirement for parties to circulate proposals on the Comprehensive Agenda for the substantive negotiations in the strands. That Comprehensive Agenda would not be adopted until the second item had been addressed. The second item was consideration of the International Body's proposal on decommissioning. Unionist concerns were thus met. The third item was the adoption of the Comprehensive Agenda. The fourth was the launching of the negotiations and the agreed mechanisms on decommissioning. The final item was the concluding remarks by the chairman. George Mitchell promised that no more than fifteen seconds would be needed to deal with it. But it was to take nearly a year to deal with the first four.

## Lack of a Timetable

Although a timetable for the work of the International Body had been set at two months, none was established for the political negotiations. The Forum was elected for a period of two years, and it was from the Forum's membership that participants in the talks process were drawn. To some, that meant negotiations had to be completed by the end of May 1998. To others, there was no time limit.

Shortly after the talks started in June, a delegation from South Africa led by Rolf Meyer and Cyril Ramaphosa visited Belfast. Meyer was the secretary-general of the National Party and Ramaphosa the secretary-general of the African National Congress. They were among the principal instigators of the South African peace process as well as its principal negotiators. They held a two-day seminar on that process in Belfast, including meetings with representatives of the governments, the talks participants, and Sinn Féin. I spent an hour with Meyer, and he listed eight key lessons he had drawn from their negotiations. These were to build trust; to ensure the negotiators believed they owned the process; to make progress but to be patient; to set a timetable and stick to it; to refuse to go back on decisions once these had been agreed; to leave the negotiations to subordinates and the final decision to leaders; to keep the requirement for decommissioning to the fore, but the decision on its implementation to the right moment; and not to be deterred if parties left the table, or if violence occurred, given that these measures might simply be aimed at derailing the process.

Meyer said he recognized that the situations in South Africa and Northern Ireland were different, but he expressed surprise that a timetable and a deadline for the negotiations had not been set. The fact that this was indeed a problem became more and more evident to the participants and to the public as the days passed. By mid-October the talks had been under way for four months and agreement had still not been reached on how the substantive negotiations—the reason for which the talks had been instigated—should be addressed. The public was growing nervous about the lack of progress and by the fact that participants were engaged in "talks about talks" and not the real issues.

## Paramilitary Violence

Alarm was also caused by the increasing pace of paramilitary activity. In September, an IRA bomb factory was raided by police in London and one IRA member was killed and four were arrested. In October, the IRA exploded a bomb in Thiepval Barracks outside Lisburn, the headquarters of the British army in Northern Ireland. One soldier was killed and more than twenty soldiers and civilians were injured. The same month in the republic, the Garda Siochana uncovered a cache of mortars in Dundalk in October, a follow-up to the large cache of weapons it had found in Clonaslee,

County Laois, some weeks earlier. A suspected IRA offshoot called "Direct Action Against Drugs" killed an alleged drug dealer in Belfast in September, and a 250-pound bomb planted in Belfast's downtown College Street later the same month by the dissident republican group, the Continuity IRA, was defused by security forces before it exploded. So-called punishment beatings continued, seemingly unaffected by the peace process, with thirty-eight attacks being carried out by loyalists and more than sixty by republicans in the first three months of the talks.

Elsewhere confrontations took different guises. Still angry over the march of loyalists down the Garvaghy Road, Catholics imposed sanctions on Protestant-owned shops and businesses in surrounding towns. Annoyed by the RUC's refusal to allow an Apprentice Boys march in Dunloy in County Antrim, loyalists mounted a picket outside a Catholic church in nearby Harryville, subjecting churchgoers to a gauntlet of abuse as they arrived for Saturday evening Mass and requiring the presence of RUC officers to protect them. The picket would remain in place for months. In a separate instance, an off-duty RUC constable was kicked to death as he left a public house. The apparent motive was anger over the refusal to allow loyalist marches in Dunloy.

## Difference of Views

Public concern over the future of the talks in light of these events was not helped by the fact that when the Christmas break arrived, the participants were still deadlocked on the second agenda item: decommissioning. The first item had been quickly resolved with each of the parties submitting proposals on the Comprehensive Agenda for the substantive negotiations in the strands. In these, there was surprising congruence of opinion. On decommissioning there was not. Each of the parties was asked to make proposals on the issue and each did so, several at some length. But the divergence of views was clear.

The Nationalists felt that decommissioning was not the priority; getting into substantive negotiations was. Decommissioning was desirable in the long term, but the nationalists did not wish to raise a high hurdle for Sinn Féin's entry into the talks. They felt that at this stage decommissioning should be handed to a subcommittee of the Plenary Committee. This subcommittee would be subjected to the checks and balances of elected members, whereas a separate decommissioning body would not. They proposed that by dealing with decommissioning in this way, approval of the agenda for the substantive negotiations could be wound up by Christmas and the strand talks themselves started at the beginning of the new year. They also felt that confidence-building measures should be addressed in the same context as decommissioning, and preferably by the same subcommittee.

The overall unionist position was that decommissioning had to be thrashed out conclusively, before any other progress could be made. The unionists had, with reluctance, accepted that talks should start with the participation of those parties associated with armed paramilitary groups engaged in a cease-fire, even if the latter had not started to decommission. The PUP and the UDP were cases in point. The UUP had accepted, with some skepticism, the International Body's suggestion that some decommissioning during the talks might help the process move forward; but they were conscious that no such activity had taken place, even four to five months into the talks. They were particularly keen to specify a strict decommissioning regime as a condition for Sinn Féin's eventual admission to the talks.

Their position was broadly encapsulated in a statement made by a UUP member at a party meeting in mid-November. He said the party's four prerequisites for Sinn Féin's entry into the negotiations included a complete and permanent end to IRA violence; the handover of a significant amount of guns and of the explosive Semtex; the completion of the Plenary Committee discussions on decommissioning before Sinn Féin's admission; and the handling of decommissioning in a manner independent of the political negotiations. Unionists too acknowledged that confidence-building measures needed to be addressed, but not by the same group charged with decommissioning.

The two governments stood by the February 1996 requirement for an unequivocal restoration of the IRA cease-fire as a condition for Sinn Féin's participation in the negotiations. This position was supported by the SDLP as well as by the loyalist parties, Alliance, Labour, and the NIWC. Both governments wished to see the decommissioning issue addressed and resolved to the satisfaction of the participants during the negotiations, alongside progress in the strand negotiations on key political issues.

### End-of-Year Impasse

By mid-December, it was clear there would not be agreement on decommissioning and it was agreed the talks should be stood down for Christmas. It was also agreed that during the break the participants would review their proposals on decommissioning, in light of the previous discussions, to see if they could identify areas of potential compromise. The chairmen would likewise review the parties' papers to see if they could find areas of convergence. The talks would then resume in bilateral fashion in mid-January to see whether a basis for compromise had emerged. The full Plenary Session would resume at the end of the month.

Some commentators believed the talks were ending on a defeatist note and would not survive long into the new year. Pessimism was increased by a republican attempt on the life of a senior DUP member during a visit to his child in hospital, and by a retaliatory car bomb attack by loyalists against a senior republican. Both attacks failed in their objectives, but concern that tit-for-tat retaliation would cause the cease-fires to break down was heightened days later, when a large IRA bomb was defused outside Belfast Castle. The public response was to call on the parties to get back to the table and produce results.

The talks reconvened in bilateral mode with the parties meeting each other, both separately and in groups, and with each meeting with the chairmen. No compromise was reached and by mid-February it was proposed that the chairmen adopt a mediating role. They would meet with parties, or groups of parties, and go through their proposals line by line. This format was followed over a period of weeks, but the will to compromise remained elusive. A limiting factor was the imminence of general elections in the United Kingdom in May and in Ireland in June, with council elections in Northern Ireland also scheduled for May. Parties with particular concerns were reluctant to make compromises just before going to the polls. On March 5, the talks were adjourned to June 3. Then the results of the British and the council elections would be known, and a new attempt could be made to resolve the agenda item on decommissioning.

## The 1997 General and Council Elections

The elections themselves would have no effect on who would represent the parties in the negotiations: those elected to the Forum and assigned to the talks would remain. But they would have dramatic consequences for each of the two governments and more modest ones at the council level. In May, the Conservative Party of John Major, with a slim majority going into the election, was replaced by the Labour Party of Tony Blair, with a massive majority. In the Northern Ireland council elections, the ranking of parties remained much the same, but the UUP's percentage dropped against the unionist share of the vote, and Sinn Féin's increased at the expense of the SDLP. In June, the Fine Gael party of John Bruton was defeated by the Fianna Fáil party of Bertie Ahern. A result of the proportional representation system used in Irish elections, Bruton's coalition had held only a slender majority. It was probable that any coalition Ahern could put together would likewise have a slim lead.

There were two important results for the peace process. Both new prime ministers declared that successful completion of the talks was a major priority for each, and both agreed there had to be a swift end to the discussion of procedural issues. They made it clear they wanted substantive issues addressed as soon as possible and the talks completed within a year. Further, in an innovative and significant gesture, Tony Blair pledged his government to begin the devolution of some powers in both Scotland and Wales at the same time as self-rule was reinstated in Northern Ireland. While of no particular interest to nationalists, this decision gave unionists the satisfaction of seeing that devolved government in Belfast would not give the impression of weakening links with the United Kingdom; rather it would put Northern Ireland, Scotland, and Wales in a parallel position with Westminster.

The Plenary Committee reconvened on June 3, with the new foreign secretary, Marjorie (Mo) Mowlam, leading the British delegation, accompanied by her political affairs minister, Paul Murphy. Mowlam had been shadow secretary in the Labour cabinet for some years and was well aware of the state of play in the talks. June 3 was also three days before the Irish election and three weeks before the taoiseach's domestic negotiations revealed the exact nature of the Fianna Fáil coalition. But there was no delay in reopening discussions. Dick Spring's outgoing Irish delegation understood the urgency of keeping the process going, especially as only two months remained before the summer break and with a hiatus likely during the major marching week in mid-July. To ensure continuity, he kept the incoming government informed and involved in the whole process. Thus, when the new team members, led by Foreign Minister Ray Burke (and subsequently by his successor, David Andrews) took their seats, they were already fully abreast of the situation.

Another notable change had taken place in the Irish delegation during the summer. Sean O h'Uiginn, who had been a key figure in developing the Irish approach to the talks from the very beginning, was appointed ambassador of Ireland to the United States. He was replaced by the incumbent ambassador, Dermot Gallagher, who was as familiar as O h'Uiginn with all the developments to date.

## IRA Cease-Fire

When the talks resumed, Sinn Féin was still not at the table. The IRA murder of two policemen in Lurgan in mid-June made it seem unlikely they would get there soon. But as the weeks passed, rumors increased that an IRA cease-fire could be imminent. If that occurred, and after a period to determine that it was genuine and met the two governments' February 1996 stipulation concerning an unequivocal restoration, Sinn Féin could be admitted to the talks. The DUP and the UKUP let it be known that if that happened, without the decommissioning of IRA weapons having first begun, they would leave.

The period of June and July was almost exclusively preoccupied with a review of the participants' papers on decommissioning as well as the preparation, and ultimately the discussion, of a joint British-Irish paper on the same topic. Interrupted by a period of confrontation and violence surrounding the march at Drumcree, this review took place. In a series of Plenary Committee meetings held between July 16 and 23, the decommissioning papers produced by the parties and by the governments were debated but then denied consensus. On July 20 the IRA declared a new and "unequivocal" cease-fire. On the 23, the DUP and the UKUP left the talks, predicting that the cease-fire was a tactical ploy, and that Sinn Féin would nonetheless be admitted when discussions resumed in September.

## Decommissioning Legislation

While no progress was being made in getting agreement on decommissioning, legislative action had been taken by both governments to enable the process to begin. The Decommissioning Act 1997 (Ireland) and The Northern Ireland Decommissioning Act 1997 (United Kingdom) set in place in each jurisdiction the appropriate measures and technical requirements necessary for the process to start. In August, the two governments completed an agreement establishing an Independent International Commission on Decommissioning, which would come into operation when the talks moved into the substantive negotiations phase. The governments also announced that this body would maintain the representation from Canada, Finland, and the United States. Commissioners-designate were named from Finland and the United States each, but the governments held back on naming the third and on announcing who the chairman would be.

When the Plenary Committee reconvened in early September it was not initially clear that the UUP and the loyalist parties would rejoin. Like the other parties, they were prepared to meet with the governments and the chairmen in bilateral session for the moment, but the decision on whether they would remain in the talks would be discussed at a UUP Executive meeting scheduled for September 13. It seemed likely the loyalists' decision might depend on what the UUP decided. The UUP Executive opened the way for the party to remain involved if its delegates felt progress could be made, and they decided to do so, initially if only to make the case for

Sinn Féin's expulsion from the talks. But they were not present for the Plenary session in which Sinn Féin sat down at the table and subscribed to the Mitchell Principles.

## Governments' Procedural Motion

In recognition of the urgency that both governments had placed on getting into substantive negotiations, a joint government paper in the form of a Procedural Motion was tabled at the September 19 Plenary session. It was based on the joint paper on decommissioning proposed in July, and it suggested a way in which the Opening Plenary agenda could be agreed, with the decommissioning item being solved by handing the task to the Independent Commission approved the previous month. A Liaison Sub-Committee on Decommissioning made up of the participants would be established, to which the commission would report. There would also be a Liaison Sub-Committee on Confidence-Building Measures established to address a number of concerns identified by the parties. After days of negotiation, numerous bilaterals and much debate in the Plenary Committee, the Procedural Motion was approved. The way was now open for the substantive negotiations in the three strands to begin.

The Procedural Motion established George Mitchell, Harri Holkeri, and me as cochairmen of the Strand Two negotiations, and me as chairman of the decommissioning body. Mitchell would continue to chair the Plenary Committee and the Strand Two negotiations. Harri Holkeri would continue to be the alternate chair for both, and would chair the liaison subcommittees. I would continue as chairman of the Business Committee and assist Holkeri with Strand Two meetings when Mitchell was unavailable. Much of my attention, and that of my assistant, Clifford Garrard, would now be on decommissioning.

## The Decommissioning Commission

The two other commissioners arrived in Belfast in September and spent the time being briefed there and in Dublin. Retired Brigadier Tauno Nieminen, recently employed with the International Commission on the Former Yugoslavia, and his diplomat assistant, Aaro Suonio, were appointed from Finland. Ambassador Donald Johnson, recently U.S. ambassador in Mongolia and more recently head of the Organization for Security and Cooperation in Europe (OSCE) mission in Moldova, was joined by a former State Department official, Andrew Sens, as his assistant.

The first two tasks in the commission's four-part mandate was to consult widely and then to make recommendations to the governments on the methods of decommissioning it thought would be appropriate. These would then be put into regulations in both jurisdictions by the respective government. Dividing its resources between permanent offices in Belfast and Dublin, the commission began the consultation process immediately in both cities, meeting with government officials, politicians, and the security forces. The third part of the mandate was to "undertake any tasks it might be given by those regulations to facilitate decommissioning." The fourth was to report on progress. Reporting would be to the two governments and to the Liaison Sub-Committee on Decommissioning.

**Substantive Negotiations**

The Business Committee met for its first formal session on September 30 in a small room set aside for that purpose. The size of the room proved to be important. In order to be able to seat two members from each of the two governments and each of the eight parties, the lines of tables forming a hollow rectangle had to be placed close to each other. Instead of looking at other delegates across the large space of the Plenary Committee chamber, participants in the Business Committee were eyeball to eyeball. The committee's role dealt with scheduling and with unresolved procedural issues, not contentious subjects within themselves; even so, from the outset the atmosphere was cordial and workmanlike. The rhetoric and the point scoring that had characterized so many of the Plenary Committee sessions were absent. It was a lesson soon carried over into the running of the Strand One and Strand Two negotiations, which also sought to meet in more close-up circumstances. In the later stages of negotiations a subgroup of the Plenary Committee was struck, smaller than the main one, to meet in the more productive atmosphere of close-up discussion.

While there was relief that substantive negotiations on important issues had begun, there were difficulties of cross strand coordination. Important issues affecting the form of government to be set up in Northern Ireland (Strand One) could not be finalized until decisions were made on how north-south relationships would be constructed (Strand Two). The period before Christmas was spent in trying to establish lines of agreement in both areas. In the new year the governments attempted to inject momentum into the process. They tabled a Heads of Agreement paper that reinforced commitments each had made to the principle of consent and the potential for constitutional change outlined previously in the Frameworks Document of 1995.

This paper became the basis for discussion in the Strand Two talks held in London toward the end of January, but discussion there elicited opposition from both nationalist and unionist camps. Sinn Féin characterized the paper as the British government "playing the Orange Card," and one UUP delegate tore up a copy of the Frameworks Document on camera to demonstrate his party's concern with it. More acceptable to most parties was a portion of the paper dealing with Strand Three issues. Here both governments proposed an Intergovernmental Council that would bring London and Dublin together with representatives of Belfast, Edinburgh, and Cardiff to discuss issues of mutual concern. Standing governmental machinery would have London and Dublin discussing nondevolved issues of mutual interest, with the participation of Northern Ireland ministers when appropriate.

The governments' paper was not the only focus of attention at the Strand Two talks in London. Around Christmas, Billy Wright, the leader of the LVF who had played such a prominent role in the protests surrounding Drumcree in 1996 and who was serving a sentence in the Maze prison, was murdered by INLA prisoners. This act set off a spate of sectarian murders in and around Belfast over the following weeks in which a number of Catholics were murdered by loyalists. The chief constable announced his belief that the UFF was responsible for three of the deaths, and talks participants then announced their intention to cite the UDP for expulsion from the negotiations. Although not admitting UFF involvement in the murders, UDP leader Gary McMichael nonetheless led his party from the talks. In leaving, he pledged his continued belief in the validity of the process and promised to be back.

In the following month, a meeting of Strand Two in Dublin was totally preoccupied with a censure motion against Sinn Féin for the claimed IRA murder of a UDA man in Dunmurry. Sinn Féin pointed out that it was not the IRA and should not be expelled; but the decision was made that Sinn Féin must go. In the event, both the UDP and Sinn Féin would be absent for only a month.

### Easter Deadline

The governments had said they wished to see the talks end by May, and Senator Mitchell refined that further by calling for them to be over by Easter. His reasoning was that unless that happened, the Easter break would unfocus attention and a decision by May would be impossible. There was another reason. There was fear among the participants that the process might not survive another marching season, particularly another Drumcree. The disastrous happenings of Drumcree 1996 had caused a reappraisal in 1997, and that had limited some of the confrontations that year, though not nationalist bitterness over the decision to allow the Orange Order to march down the Garvaghy Road once again.

If agreement could be reached by Easter, that would allow the necessary time to prepare for referendums in both jurisdictions in May. Depending on the results, an election of an assembly could be called in June to put in place the appropriate structures and organizations before the new marching season began. That might limit problems that occurred in previous years.

## Opposing Views

But at the beginning of March there seemed little reason to believe agreement would be reached by Easter. There had been no final agreement on Strand One, and Strand Two was far from resolved. For nationalists, the overriding issue was their insistence that north-south bodies and power sharing must underwrite any move to reinstitute a Northern Ireland Assembly. Unionists insisted there should be such an assembly, drawing its powers from Westminster and underpinning the continued existence of the province as part of the union. They also insisted on the total disarmament of all paramilitary groups within a specified period.

From opposing points of view, both nationalists and unionists wished to see constitutional change. Unionists wished to see the abandonment of Articles 2 and 3 of the Irish Constitution—which laid claim to Northern Ireland—but no change to the constitutional guarantees concerning the union. Nationalists wished to see abandonment of the Government of Ireland Act 1920—which had initiated partition—but no change to the declaration calling for a united Ireland. The Frameworks Document of 1995 essentially promised both changes, the reason it had attracted such hostility before from extremes on both sides.

All parties agreed that confidence-building measures must be an integral part of any accord. Unionists expected to see the decommissioning of illegal weapons within a fixed time frame. Nationalists wanted the removal of the British army and its installations, and a complete review of the RUC. Loyalists and nationalists both wanted to see a speedy release of paramilitary prisoners, whom they regarded as political prisoners. All parties agreed on the need for human rights legislation, a review of the criminal justice system, and the need for the responsible paramilitary groups to identify the location of the "disappeared" and the return of exiles.

The British government had already moved on some confidence-building measures, establishing a Parades Commission to rule on contentious parades, and an international judicial commission to reexamine the events of the 1972 "Bloody Sunday" killings in Derry/Londonderry. Mo Mowlam had already visited the Maze prison to urge prisoners there to continue their support for the cease-fires, demonstrating official recognition of the political linkage of their crimes. But while it was clear there would be no agreement without the inclusion of confidence-building measures, it was equally clear there would be no agreement without resolution of the main issues.

**Decommissioning Schemes**

On the main issue of decommissioning, the Independent Commission continued to work along a parallel track to put in place the means to implement the third part of their mandate, the facilitation of actual decommissioning. By focusing on practical issues, and avoiding the question of when it would occur, the commission was able to secure consensus—including the tacit or active approval of the paramilitary groups engaged in cease-fires—for two possible "schemes." These were based on two of the four methods first proposed by the International Body. One involved the destruction of weapons by those in possession of them, with verification provided by the commission. Another involved the provision of information leading to the discovery of arms by the commission for subsequent destruction. In each case, complete destruction, including disposal of the residue, was intended. There was to be no recycling of decommissioned weapons, nor were they to be assigned to memorials or museums.

The commission's proposals were approved in March by the Liaison Sub-Committee on Decommissioning, and the governments committed to enact regulations in each jurisdiction before the end of June, to allow the schemes to be put into effect.

**The Last Phase**

With two weeks left before Easter, and insisting (with the agreement of the participants) that the timetable be kept, George Mitchell made a proposal to the Plenary Committee to accelerate progress. The chairmen would draw together the parties' proposals on Strand One and Strand Two, and, together with the governments' paper on Strand Three and a paper on confidence-building measures, produce an outline draft Agreement for circulation and debate. The draft would be produced during the week and distributed on Friday. Saturday and Sunday would be used by the parties to consider the draft and to meet separately with the chairmen to give them their views. The chairmen would work on areas of disagreement, and then produce a reworked draft for circulation on Monday. There would then be three days of debate, with a final vote being taken on Thursday, April 9, the day before Good Friday. The Plenary Committee approved the proposal.

But drafting problems and an unanticipated government decision delayed the distribution of the draft until Monday, losing three days of consultation and redrafting. That turned out to be the least of the difficulties. If Sinn Féin found the Heads of Agreement paper too "Orange," the unionist and nonaligned parties found the draft Strand Two paper too "Green." One prominent unionist said he "wouldn't touch it with a barge-pole." In a bid to save the timetable, Tony Blair and Bertie Ahern moved to Belfast to lead the discussions. For three days a process of shuttle negotiation took place, often through the night, in which the two prime ministers, Mo Mowlam, and David Andrews played a key role in trying to narrow the differences on the few, but crucial, remaining areas of disagreement.

As dawn broke on Good Friday, and to everyone's surprise, it seemed there might be agreement. A time was set for a final meeting of the Plenary Committee to approve it. Soon afterward concerns were raised within the UUP that threatened to dash hopes, but by late afternoon UUP leader David Trimble telephoned George Mitchell to say he was ready to go ahead. Mitchell called the meeting immediately and the Good Friday Agreement was approved.

Right after the ratification ceremony, and once the two prime ministers had left, the chairmen gave a press conference on the steps of the Castle Buildings. Then the Office of the Independent Chairmen disbanded. George Mitchell and Harri Holkeri returned to their respective countries, and I turned my attention exclusively to decommissioning.

## Reaction to the Good Friday Agreement

Surprise at the achievement of the Good Friday Agreement was matched by the euphoria it produced. After thirty years of violence and nearly two years of negotiation, it seemed possible that a new era free from violence and discord might be achieved. None of the parties was wholly happy with the result. In all cases they had accepted less than what they wanted. Had it been otherwise, there would not have been an agreement. But everyone got much of what they wanted. The nationalists had been guaranteed inclusive government with a power-sharing Executive and mandated north-south bodies. Unless these were put in place the Agreement would self-destruct. Unionists wanted an elected assembly and they would have it. They also wanted a time limit on the complete decommissioning of all paramilitary weapons, and that was set for a date two years from the time of the referendums. All had wanted confidence-building measures enacted and these were built into the Agreement. Underlying the whole was a reaffirmation of the principle of consent: there would be no change to the constitutional situation of Northern Ireland without the consent of a majority in Northern Ireland. The Government of Ireland Act would be abolished and Articles 2 and 3 of the Irish Constitution would be amended.

David Trimble's acceptance of the Good Friday Agreement was endorsed by a meeting of his party within days, as was Gerry Adams's by the majority of republicans. While a "No" campaign was vigorously conducted by the two parties that had left the negotiations, 71 percent of those who voted in Northern Ireland, and 95 percent of those who voted in Ireland, supported it in the referendums of May 22. The percentages for and against the Agreement were broadly reflected in the election results on June 15, when, out of 108 assembly seats, the two parties against the Agreement, the DUP and the UKUP, captured 20 and 5 seats, respectively.

The element within the UUP that was against the Agreement, and that had so indicated to David Trimble on the morning of Good Friday, was reflected in the three UUP members who were elected as independent anti-agreement unionists, as well as by others who remained in the party but declared themselves far from satisfied by the terms of the Agreement. This was a situation with the potential to cause difficulty in the future, as agreement in the assembly calls for a majority of both unionists and nationalists, either through consensus or a weighted majority.

## CONCLUSION

In the six months between approval of the Agreement and the writing of this chapter (late November 1998), the strengths and weaknesses of the Agreement have become clear. The overwhelming strength is its acceptance by the vast majority of people north and south, and the fact that events long believed impossible have taken place. Unionist parties that pledged never to sit in the same room with Sinn Féin, beyond the level of local councils, are doing so. Sinn Féin, without betraying its goal of achieving a united Ireland, has accepted to sit in an assembly that recognizes a border, and to seek its ends through the democratic process. A weakness of the Good Friday Agreement lies in the nature of some of the compromises, which, though essential to reaching consensus, nonetheless left some details unclear.

There is no doubt that serious difficulties lie ahead in putting together the new government of Northern Ireland. Optimists make light of the problems and pessimists make much of them. Both have reason to be concerned, but both might remember that the parties have been mandated by the people to make the Agreement work. If unionists and nationalists have moments of despair, they might reflect that more good things exist in the Agreement for each of them than bad—which is why they agreed to it on April 10.

That, surely, is reason enough to want to move forward. And that, surely, is worth compromise and effort.

## Assessment

It is too early to draw conclusive lessons why this move to reach agreement succeeded when others did not. First, it is premature to say that a settlement has been reached, though the Good Friday Agreement was historic in getting a measure of accord between the traditions and the two governments after such a long period of conflict. Some have characterized it as the most significant development in Anglo-Irish and internal Northern Ireland relations since 1920. Much work remains before there is truly a settlement, and as this chapter is written, north-south bodies have still not been set up and decommissioning has still not started.

On the other hand, previous attempts at mediation over the years, whether purely internal, orchestrated by the two governments, or involving outside participation, were unable to produce the results achieved on Good Friday.

Several factors may have been significant. The first was that people north and south were fatigued by thirty years of conflict. Paramilitary groups saw their efforts no nearer achieving success, while many of their members had been killed and many sent to prison for lengthy terms. There was a yearning for peace in Northern Ireland, born of weariness and desperation, that was ready for exploitation by the governments, the parties, and the people.

Second, internationalization of the process underlined the significance of this attempt to produce a solution. Coupled with the investment made in the negotiations by the two governments and the parties, it gave a suggestion of "now or never." As President Clinton noted in Belfast four months after the Agreement, if what had been achieved on Good Friday was not seized upon and made to work, it might be the last chance to do so in his lifetime and in the lifetime of those who had sat around the table.

The third factor was that lessons learned elsewhere, though not applied at once, were nonetheless brought into play. The parties were eventually given the means to realize they owned the process. A timetable and a deadline were not fixed until late; but they were fixed eventually, and then adhered to, despite strong temptations to do otherwise. Continued violence and departures from the talks were condemned or lamented, but they were not allowed to destroy the process. The subject of decommissioning was predominant during the talks, but the decision to implement it was not permitted to hold the process to ransom. And finally, when needed, the prime ministers were called in to make the vital decisions the negotiators had been unable to make.

The close cooperation throughout between the British and Irish governments was critical in arriving at a successful outcome to the talks. Close cooperation between the two had become a fact with the Anglo-Irish Agreement of 1985, and it was evident in the several agreements, declarations, and communiqués signed by both governments in the intervening period. But in 1998, under the direction of Mo Mowlam and David Andrews, respectively, and in the final weeks with the direct personal involvement of the British prime minister, Tony Blair, and the taoiseach, Bertie Ahern, the two governments, acting throughout in concert, ensured the outcome was comprehensive and balanced across the full range of issues to be addressed.

But perhaps the most important reason agreement was reached on April 10 was the determination of those who took part in the negotiations. They understood the significance of the people's wish that this time a solution must be found. They were obliged to judge the degree to which they had to represent their constituents' views unfailingly, or when they should take risks to find a compromise.

At the ratification ceremony, the prime ministers thanked the chairmen and staff for their involvement and the role they played in helping the parties reach agreement. That was a gracious act and not undeserved. But the real credit goes to those who took the necessary risks, and to the people who supported them in doing so. Further risk taking and continued popular support will be needed if the Good Friday Agreement is to be turned into a lasting settlement.

### NOTES

1. Report of the International Body, Belfast, January 22, 1996, paragraph 35. The various documents agreed by the governments to direct the talks—including the Communiqués, Ground Rules, Scenario, Procedural Guidelines, and Draft Agenda documents—were not published. They were circulated among the participants. The same is true of the Rules of Procedure, once these had been agreed. The Report of the International Body was not published, but it was reproduced and circulated widely. It is on the Internet in the section of the *Irish Times* website (www.ireland.com/special/peace) that deals with the peace process. The same is true of the Good Friday Agreement. The pertinent legislation (Decommissioning Acts, Anglo-Irish Agreement, Downing Street Declaration, and Frameworks Document) was published by the respective governments and is presumably available through them. The same may be true of the governments' joint communiqués and the documents they prepared to direct the talks.

2. Ibid., para. 20.

3. Communiqué of the British and Irish Governments, 28 November 1995, para. 7.

4. Report of the International Body, para. 51.

5. Joint Communiqué of the British and Irish Governments, February 28, 1996, para. 7.

6. Ibid., para. 9.
7. Ibid., para. 10a.
8. Ibid., para. 12.
9. Ground Rules for Substantive All-Party Negotiations, April 16, 1996, para. 23.
10. Rules of Procedure, July 29, 1996, para. 29.

## GLOSSARY

| | | |
|---|---|---|
| Alliance Party | | nonaligned political party |
| Continuity IRA | CIRA | republican paramilitary group |
| Dáil | | Irish parliament |
| Democratic Unionist Party | DUP | second-largest unionist party |
| Fianna Fáil | | Irish political party |
| Fine Gael | | Irish political party |
| Garda Siochana | | Irish police force |
| Irish National Liberation Army | INLA | republican paramilitary group |
| Irish Republican Army | IRA | republican paramilitary group |
| Labour Party | | nonaligned political party |
| loyalist | | wishes to keep Northern Ireland in the United Kingdom |
| Loyalist Volunteer Force | LVF | loyalist paramilitary group |
| nationalist | | seeks a united Ireland |
| Northern Ireland Women's Coalition | NIWC | nonaligned political party |
| Progressive Unionist Party | PUP | loyalist party with links to UVF and RHC |
| Red Hand Commando | RHC | loyalist paramilitary group |
| republican | | seeks a united Ireland |
| Royal Ulster Constabulary | RUC | Northern Ireland police force |
| Sinn Féin | | republican political party |
| Social Democratic and Labour Party | SDLP | nationalist political party |
| Strand One | | talks dealing with northern issues |
| Strand Two | | talks dealing with north-south issues |
| Strand Three | | talks dealing with London-Dublin issues |
| Taioseach | | Irish prime minister |
| Ulster Defence Association | UDA | loyalist paramilitary group |
| Ulster Democratic Party | UDP | loyalist party with links to UDA and UFF |
| Ulster Freedom Fighters | UFF | loyalist paramilitary group |
| Ulster Volunteer Force | UVF | loyalist paramilitary group |
| unionist | | wishes to keep Northern Ireland in the United Kingdom |

| | | |
|---|---|---|
| United Kingdom | | England, Scotland, Wales, and Northern Ireland |
| United Kingdom Unionist Party | UKUP | unionist political party |
| Ulster Unionist Party | UUP | largest unionist political party |

# Background to Chapter 18

## Multiparty Mediation in Northern Ireland

A history of communal factionalism and a persistent culture of intimidation prevented the emergence of a negotiating middle in the Northern Ireland conflict. With the unionists and nationalists locked in a stalemate, and with their respective communities accustomed to a certain level of violence, there were very few opportunities to find a resolution to the protracted conflict. However, the end of the Cold War, improved Anglo-Irish relations, a new administration in the United States, and a growing emphasis worldwide on negotiated peace created a ripe moment in Northern Ireland. Faced with a hurting stalemate, and with the British, Irish, and U.S. governments working hard to foster a peace process, the republicans were persuaded to begin negotiating in earnest through a range of behind-the-scenes activities, including track-two diplomatic efforts and workshops. These workshops promoted the official mediation by creating a safe, neutral, and supportive environment to focus on issues of content and process. This complementary track borrowed from the South African experience, examined human rights, and created a collegial atmosphere among the second-tier political leadership it attracted. As such, it contributed to the process of negotiation that yielded a mutually acceptable agreement to end the violence and begin political and social renewal.

### MAJOR ACTORS
- Ulster Unionist Party (UUP)
- Socialist Democratic and Labour Party (SDLP)

- Sinn Féin
- Alliance
- Democratic Unionist Party (DUP)
- Progressive Unionist Party (PUP)
- Ulster Democratic Party (UDP)
- Northern Ireland Women's Coalition (NIWC)
- Government of the United Kingdom
- Government of the Republic of Ireland
- Government of the United States
- European Union

## IMPORTANT DATES

- 1920: Partition of Ireland
- 1968: The "troubles" begin in Northern Ireland
- 1972: Imposition of direct rule from Great Britain
- 1974: Collapse of power sharing
- November 15, 1985: Anglo-Irish Agreement signed
- 1988: Meetings between the SDLP and Sinn Féin
- 1990: A series of eight workshops begins that will continue through 1998
- 1993: Hume and Adams issue statement seeking a negotiated settlement
- December 15, 1993: Downing Street Declaration issued
- 1994: Clinton administration grants Adams a visa to visit the United States
- August 1994: IRA declares a cease-fire
- October 1994: Combined Loyalist Military Command (CLMC) declares a cease-fire
- October 7, 1997: Formal talks begin in Belfast
- April 10, 1998: Belfast Agreement (the Good Friday Agreement) reached

## KEY POINTS OF THE GOOD FRIDAY AGREEMENT

- A power-sharing executive to be established
- Mandated north-south bodies to be created
- An elected assembly to be established
- A schedule agreed for decommissioning of arms

## PRINCIPAL OUTCOMES OF THE MEDIATION

- The workshops helped to improve political skills and build personal relationships among second-tier political leaders
- Formation of a Northern Ireland Centre in Europe (NICE) to promote cross-communal cooperation

# 18

# Multiparty Mediation in Northern Ireland

PAUL ARTHUR

*There is nothing more difficult to take in hand, more perilous to conduct, or more uncertain in its success, than to take the lead in the introduction of a new order of things.*

—Machiavelli

"Success breeds many children": when "the Agreement" reached in multiparty negotiation was signed in Belfast on April 10, 1998, there was no shortage of those who sought the mantle of progenitors. It is not difficult to identify some of the key players in the negotiations—the British and Irish governments, the Northern Ireland parties that had stayed with the talks, the Clinton administration, and the European Union—but that is to ignore the dynamics, the nuances, the complexity of the process.[1]

The purpose of this chapter is to examine those elements, looking at Northern Ireland as a particular case study of a violent conflict that has been brought to a conclusion—at least in the interim—through a complex mediation. We will be emphasizing the temporal component, that is, the role of mediation during the life cycle of a conflict; the distinction between the more passive activity of facilitation and the potential proactive role of mediation—indeed the distance between facilitation, negotiation, and implementation; and the significance of "circum-negotiation." The Northern Ireland case study will also touch on the potential range of interventions raised by changes in the international system and norms, and the question of how one imposes coherence in multiparty mediation exercises. The problem of coherence (or the lack thereof) suggests that drawing a further distinction between "ad-hocry" and more cumulative efforts may actually be less important than analyzing such exogenous factors as the "hurting stalemate" and the effectiveness of particular mediations.

Above all, the major message derived from this interim resolution is the significance of *process*. The Northern Ireland conflict has had a life cycle of thirty years—at least. Most commentators acknowledge the huge importance that history and "memory" have played in sustaining the conflict. From its inception in 1920–21 the conflict produced a political culture that had avoided the very essence of political activity—the ability and desire to negotiate. Here was a classic case of a zero-sum game. Not only was there no agreement on who the major players were—obviously the two communities in Northern Ireland (but did the *Irish* government as well as the British government have a role to play and what was to be the significance of the international community?)—but more fundamentally there wasn't even agreement on the nature of the problem. Mediation is about seeking solutions to problems, but first the problem has to be defined and agreed upon. That becomes a particularly difficult exercise in the middle of an incipient civil war. Political violence imposes its own unpredictable dynamic.

Hence the emphasis on process and the temporal component. Although it would be foolish to lay down an iron law on when is the precise moment for a successful mediation to begin, this chapter will lay some emphasis on the concepts of the "ripe moment" and the "hurting stalemate" as guidelines in the activity of complex mediation. But the chapter carries its own health warning. It can be no more than a tentative (and partial) introduction to the relationship between official and unofficial diplomacy in *one* particular conflict. Even the most mundane terms we use can change their meaning over time. One example will suffice. The word "center" is employed here with two distinct meanings. *Historically* it alludes to the asymmetric Anglo-Irish relationship over several centuries whereby the "center" (the British government) appeared to have total control over the Celtic periphery, including the island of Ireland. *Contemporaneously* the center refers to efforts to build up a working coalition within Northern Ireland to ensure that the Agreement will endure.

## THE CONTEXT

Nomenclature is important in the Anglo-Irish conflict. One of the more esoteric debates in recent times centered on finding a less prosaic title for the April 10 document than "the Agreement." To describe it as the Anglo-Irish Agreement was to hark back to November 15, 1985, when an agreement of the same name was imposed on an extremely reluctant unionist population (as well as Irish republicans) by the British and Irish governments. In fact, there was much political activity over the following decade to remove that very agreement. To cite it specifically in geographical terms—as in the "Belfast (or Stormont) Agreement"—might have implied that the status quo ante had been reimposed. Hence the prosaic—although the Agreement was to become more popularly known as the Good Friday Agreement, itself entirely appropriate for a population noted for its religiosity and for a conflict that had been defined (somewhat inaccurately) in terms of religion. It was appropriate, too, in that Good Friday held a very special place in the Christian calendar, being the day of the ultimate sacrifice that led to redemption. The popular title implies transcendence.

To begin with the Good Friday Agreement is to begin toward the end of the process. This chapter will be concerned with the journey rather than the destination. It will pay obeisance, too, to the topography encountered along the way—the collapse of the Berlin Wall; the end of communism as an aggressive ideology in geopolitics; South Africa's removal from pariah status and the dismantling of apartheid; the Oslo Accord. Although all of these are inherently interesting in that they freed republican and loyalist paramilitaries to reassess their old modes of thinking and to learn from peace processes elsewhere, our concern with them lies in what they tell us about the current status of the mediation process (multiparty or not) in the cycle of a conflict.

One of the subliminal messages will be that conventional diplomacy may have less to offer than heretofore imagined. The United States Advisory Commission on Public Diplomacy, for example, has commented on the effects of the information revolution at a time when the number of societies in transition is unprecedented and where the globalization of issues "is blurring the separation of foreign affairs and domestic politics." This calls for the practice of a new kind of diplomacy where "policies and negotiated agreements will succeed only if they have the support of publics at home and abroad." The commission borrowed from Joseph Nye's concept of "soft power"—the "ability to set the agenda in ways that shape the preferences of others," which "strengthens American diplomacy through attraction rather than coercion."[2] Soft power was invoked in Northern Ireland in ways that worked outside the parameters of formal, conventional diplomacy. It appealed beyond the paramilitary and political elite levels to the wider public at a crucial phase of the process—somewhere between negotiation and implementation—when that public was invited to slough off its historic fatalism and to become proactive in the search for peace. It was a further indication of the demotic nature of Northern Ireland's political culture whereby political leaders had been unduly influenced by their more extreme supporters to follow an intransigent agenda. The Agreement produced an inversionary effect in that the demos ceased being fatalistic and began to urge their politicians to work for peace.

We shall see that the role of American diplomacy was paramount in securing the Good Friday Agreement, but we must not separate American diplomacy from the other elements at work. They include, for example, the role of the European Union (EU) and of what might be considered a semi-autonomous Eminent Person's Group (EPG) composed of former senator George Mitchell (United States), General John de Chastelain (Canada), and former prime minister Harri Holkeri (Finland). The work of international and national nongovernmental organizations (NGOs) must also be emphasized. It is worth noting that one of the first decisions made after the signing of the Agreement was the creation of a new Police Commission to begin work on a fundamental review of the Royal Ulster Constabulary. It was to be headed by the former governor of Hong Kong, Chris Patten, and was composed of a seven-member commission drawn from Canada, Ireland, the United Kingdom, and the United States. The Police Commission is another example of the role that external actors, particularly NGOs, can play in depoliticizing extremely contentious issues and an acknowledgement that they can be an enormous asset in assisting countries making the transition out of conflict: "In many ways they can do things better than government. They foster a flexible style that encourages innovation. . . . They offer the world a winning combination of . . . professional skills, a wealth of experience, fresh perspectives, and enormous good will."[3]

To add to this list we should keep in mind the Commonwealth as a putative agent of preventive diplomacy and soft power. Next to the United Nations it is the world's largest multilateral organization comprising more than a quarter of the world's total population with members from every major regional bloc and economic zone. Like the United Nations, it is an example of the successful pursuit of unity in diversity, displaying cooperation between diverse countries that encompass many races, religions, traditions, cultures, and language groups. In these circumstances it is not altogether surprising that divisive pluralism—the "existence in societies of groups having distinctive ethnic origins, cultural forms and religious affiliations [which become] the sources for disunity, destabilization and conflict with negative effects on the political process"[4]—exists within the Commonwealth.

The Commonwealth may be illustrative in the case of Northern Ireland for two reasons. First, its extensive comparative experience in dealing with diverse cases ranging from South Africa to Sierra Leone to Bangladesh— it has monitored elections in thirteen Commonwealth countries since the Harare Declaration of 1991—adds another dimension to conflict resolution. Second, the Commonwealth may have a particular resonance and role to play in the Irish peace process because when the Republic of Ireland was created in 1949—formerly it had been known as Eire—it broke away from the (British) Commonwealth. Since then the latter has changed in character and composition. Although it accepts Queen Elizabeth as (symbolic) Head of the Commonwealth, a majority of its countries are republics and it is no longer controlled from London. This unusual arrangement allows the Commonwealth two benefits in an Irish context: republicans may no longer fear it as a uniquely British-dominated entity and unionists can point to its symbolic relationship to Her Majesty. That could be enough to suggest that it may have a role to play in implementing the Agreement.

The Commonwealth's experience is similar to that of the recent history of the United Nations. As of January 28, 1997, there were twenty-five special/personal representatives or envoys of the UN secretary-general, all but four of whom were engaged in conflict prevention and peacemaking activities: eight in Africa, three in Asia, five in Europe (the Balkans, Cyprus, and Georgia), two in Latin America/Caribbean, two in the Middle East, plus one envoy who serves as the secretary-general's special "trouble-shooter." But as Cyrus R. Vance and David A. Hamburg point out:

> Information about the role of special representatives and personal envoys is sparse because these missions typically are undertaken without publicity by practitioners of "quiet diplomacy" who tend not to reveal what they do and how they do it. Scholarly research and policy-relevant information has been meager; the subject remains, in the words of one UN expert, "an academic mystery."[5]

This chapter will attempt to unravel some of that mystery through analyzing the Anglo-Irish case. In global terms it is worth noting that from 1985 to 1989 there were, on average, five declared man-made emergencies each year. That number jumped to twenty in 1990, peaked at twenty-six in 1994, and decreased to twenty-four in 1995. The United Nations was involved in many of these conflicts, through diverse forms of intervention from peace-keeping and enforcement to humanitarian and diplomatic intervention, some of which were kept quiet.

It may be that the United Nations is seeking a larger role for special envoys in a world in which "the traditional norms of nonintervention in the internal affairs of member states continue to weaken." As sovereign boundaries diminish in the context of increasing globalization, there is greater incentive for intervention. It was no accident (as we shall see later) that two of the earliest track-two initiatives in Northern Ireland were concerned with anticipating the impact of the Single European Act—with its promise to create a Europe without borders—on a troubled peripheral region of the European Union. The former Norwegian prime minister, Gro Harlem Bruntland, addressed this issue in a speech delivered at the Fifty-first Session of the UN General Assembly: "Preventing conflict and human suffering must not be hampered by the traditional norm of what is essentially within states' domestic jurisdiction. . . . A lot could be achieved if the UN were better able to send experienced diplomats and support missions to conflict-ridden areas." In the same speech she went a step further in suggesting that Norway was prepared to make an extra contribution to establish a Fund for Preventive Action at the United Nations that would facilitate immediate deployment of first-class expertise for proactive diplomacy. All of this has to be set within the context that "nearly all of today's wars occur not among but within countries. Inevitably, the UN is being drawn into redefining sovereignty and accountability with regard to how governments deal with domestic demands for greater self-determination."[6] The same trends have been noted by Sir Brian Urquhart when he spoke of a "historical shift in two fundamental aspects of the United Nations":

> The first is that the United Nations was originally a bureaucratic and diplomatic organization that has increasingly become involved in complex emergencies. Secondly, the United Nations was set up to deal with problems of conflicts *between* states, but is increasingly required to deal with problems *within* states, often involving nongovernmental groups. In this transitional period the job of the secretary-general is particularly demanding.[7]

We can see an indirect relationship between this shift in the international political climate and the conduct of Anglo-Irish relations. When the conflict erupted in the late 1960s the Irish government tried to internationalize the issue by seeking an emergency debate at the United Nations. Besides a perfunctory debate at the Security Council, the matter received little or no attention: it was a cathartic moment whereby the United Nations fulfilled its unofficial mandate as "sacred drama." In any case (and in anticipation of preemptive action by the Irish government at the United Nations), the British and Northern Ireland prime ministers had issued a communiqué on August 19, 1969—known as the Downing Street Declaration—which said, inter alia, that the Northern Ireland conflict was purely one of domestic jurisdiction in which there could be no international interference. A similarly named declaration—this time signed by the British prime minister and his counterpart from the *Republic of Ireland*—of December 15, 1993, was much less parochial in its content and paid obeisance to the role of the international community. The difference in tone and style in the second Downing Street Declaration reflected the historical shift that Urquhart described and the frustrations of two leaders who were intent once and for all on finding a solution to a problem that had bedeviled Anglo-Irish relations for so long.

All of this suggests that mediation in the Northern Ireland conflict is multidimensional and complex. But it could have significance for other mediations in that it stresses the impact of the changing world order. In 1969, Northern Ireland appeared to be hermetically sealed from the rest of the world. "The troubles" (as they were euphemistically called) were considered to be solely a matter of domestic jurisdiction. This was a problem for the British government alone: no one—not the United Nations and certainly not the Irish government—had any political role to play. That position stood throughout the 1970s. Particular governments made anti-British statements from time to time and the Council of Europe produced a bland report in 1976, but the case remained that this was a British issue. Admittedly, Irish constitutional nationalism through the leadership of John Hume began to broaden the scope of interest by appealing to Irish Americans and ultimately to the U.S. administration. And from 1980 the British and Irish governments began to work much more harmoniously.

The cumulative effect of these interventions was to internationalize the problem and to broaden its parameters. It is in this context that we can understand Urquhart's comments about the "historical shift . . . of the United Nations." It provides another point of leverage in trying to unlock the problem. Similarly, since the signing of the Good Friday Agreement, a low-level debate has begun within political circles in the Republic of Ireland about the merits of rejoining the Commonwealth. That debate can enhance the possibilities of successful implementation.

All of this leaves us with a paradox: the increase in the number of actors at the negotiation stage can impose a lack of coherence *as well as* additional points of leverage. This paradox highlights the significance of the facilitation component. We shall see that it is here that track-two exercises can have a particularly valuable role to play. They can act as midwives to the formal negotiations.

## Constraints on Mediation

Efforts to mediate the Anglo-Irish conflict have been hampered by an intimidatory culture; factionalism within the different communities; and the problems of memory. These features of Northern Ireland society add attitudinal and structural constraints on the process of mediation. For example, one explanation for the delay in seeking a solution lay in a political culture denoted for its sense of victimhood and fatalism. The former has been described as a political economy of helplessness with Northern Ireland as "a victim-bonded society in which memories of past injustice and humiliation are firmly entrenched in both communities."[8] In such circumstances, the desire to seek a solution was low on the list of priorities in both communities until the 1990s.

Unionists had been satisfied with the status quo until the civil rights campaign challenged some of that complacency after 1968; the prorogation of the devolved parliament and government with the imposition of direct rule in 1972 further dented the unionists' self-confidence. However, they believed that, as in earlier crises, they would overcome. Unionism had long practiced the politics of procrastination. As early as the seventeenth century, Protestants had indulged in "public banding" by refusing to place trust in their British overlords and relied instead on local arrangements.[9] Such a practice enabled them to withstand London's attempt to impose home rule in Ireland after 1912. It was to succeed again in 1974 when a Conservative government attempted a consociational solution for Northern Ireland. Even after the Anglo-Irish Agreement was signed in 1985, unionist parties believed that it would simply be a matter of time (and sustained extraparliamentary activity) before that policy would be reversed. The painful realization that that was not to happen helps to explain the more engaged atmosphere of the 1990s when mediation efforts began in earnest.

Nationalist attitudes and actions were slightly less complex. The Catholic community believed that it was a persecuted minority denied its birthright with the partition of Ireland in 1920 and the victim of systematic discrimination thereafter. It fell back on a combination of fatalism and of manifest destiny—God had made Ireland an island, a natural geographical and political entity, and some day it would be reunited. Unity would be achieved either through physical force (the Irish Republican Army [IRA] response) or demographic change—"the revenge of the cradle." In any case, and notwithstanding the collapse of power sharing in 1974, Catholic self-confidence had grown with the imposition of direct rule in 1972. Over time Catholics realized that the peculiar territorial politics of the United Kingdom was in a state of flux. J. G. Bulpitt has described it as a "dual polity": "a structure of territorial politics in which Centre and periphery had relatively little to do with each other," and in which "until recently the Centre sought not to govern the United Kingdom but to manage it."[10] Once the center was forced to intervene in Northern Ireland the nature of the game changed.

The historic center-periphery relationship had enabled unionists to rule Northern Ireland in the manner they saw fit. The center had operated a policy of "let sleeping dogs lie." It had withdrawn from Ireland (militarily and psychologically) when it imposed partition in 1920–21. When it was forced to intervene in 1972, it had to begin to rectify the misrule of the previous half century. That meant challenging unionist hegemony and learning anew the nature of the problem. Now there was a new asymmetry in which the Protestant community perceived itself as a beleaguered minority. The result was that the center was not in a position to act as a mediator or neutral arbiter because it was viewed as being hostile to the majority community. In the longer term a new definition of "center" had to be established; that is, it had to shift from rule from London to the creation of a "negotiating middle" or "strong center" whereby Northern Ireland's political parties created their own devolved government working in tandem with London and Dublin. The Agreement provided the framework to enable this to happen.

The violence that erupted in the late 1960s was implicit in an intimidatory culture emphasizing territoriality and vigilance and a memory of past oppressions. Violent acts were undertaken that were "so natural as to be beyond comment" given the sad, turbulent history of Ireland. The republican sense of victimhood, accentuated by Protestant mob violence (sometimes) with police complicity, was enough to relaunch the IRA in 1969: "All that was needed was to exploit the existing reality."[11]

Part of that reality was that both communities had been practicing (and finessing) violence for a very long time. In his comparative analysis, Frank Wright comments that in place of what "metropolitans call peace," Northern Ireland enjoyed at best "a tranquillity of communal deterrence."[12] This view is complemented by John Darby's analysis of political violence in the north of Ireland since 1800 that depicts a polity in which "the power of intimidation springs from its essentially defensive nature. Local minorities were driven by violence and fear to move to other communities in which they could become part of a majority. They were often willing to encourage the expulsion of ethnic opponents from their new community." The picture is not totally bleak in that Darby's study indicates that "Northern Ireland's conflict is remarkable for the limitations on its violence rather than for the violence itself."[13] That condition produced a paradox and a further constraint on mediation. Violence neither reached genocidal levels nor was it sustained enough to induce compromise. An unfortunate side effect was that "there has been no resolution because the violence has not been intolerable. By whatever calculus communities compute their interests, the price of compromise is still thought to be greater than the cost of violence."[14] That was to change in the 1990s and was an indicator of the effects of the "hurting stalemate."

Additional aspects of Northern Ireland's society lend themselves to protracted conflict. The demotic culture shunned visionary leadership. Power tended to emanate from the "bottom up" with elites paying close attention to the will of the demos. The Protestant tradition of public banding in which Protestants have traditionally chosen their own local defenses over the state security apparatus underscores this suspicion of leadership. They remain suspicious of the intention of the center, particularly the British government, a position reinforced by the cooperative trend in Anglo-Irish relations since the mid-1980s. Further features of the Protestant community in this regard are its denominational differences that have ensured that no one church can speak on behalf of the whole community; its democratic ethos; and its suspicion of centralized authority in contrast to the hierarchical and authoritarian nature of Catholicism.[15] This led to an unusual amount of local autonomy and an inordinate amount of influence for extrapolitical organizations such as the deeply conservative Orange Order, which acted as a denominational and social emollient among the different Protestant faiths. The extensive representation (twelve MPs, fifty-two Northern Ireland MPs in Stormont, and several hundred local councilors in the period from 1921 to 1972) provided the structural terms of a "face-to-face" democracy, buttressing the demotic tendency in Northern Ireland.

On the other hand, if the "bottom" is prepared to take risks for peace, it has the capacity to produce political realignment. This was the case in Northern Ireland when the fringe loyalist parties began to take part in the electoral process independent of the mainstream unionist parties, thereby pressuring the latter to become more actively engaged in inclusive dialogue. Sinn Féin too began to make political inroads with its commitment to the peace process, through its campaign for the Forum elections of May 1996.

In this sense, the loyalist and republican parties acted as "transcenders," who "connect what violence has severed."[16] Finally, factionalism has mirrored Northern Ireland's demotic culture. Both communities suffer crippling internal splits: at times the *intra*-ethnic seems as intense as the *inter*-ethnic. Consequently, the leadership of each community wages war on two fronts. As Cynthia Enloe asserts, ethnic conflict

> can be irreconcilable and thus most harmful to nation-building when each of the chief contestants is politically underdeveloped. Fraught with internal dissent and suspicion, each community is incapable of presenting leaders who can negotiate and institutions that can accurately represent the community's views.[17]

These difficulties have become more evident in the multiparty peace talks, in which, for example, unionism was represented by five different political parties: the Ulster Unionist Party (UUP), the Democratic Unionist Party (DUP), the United Kingdom Unionist Party (UKUP), the Progressive Unionist Party (PUP), and the Ulster Democratic Party (UDP). The PUP and the UDP, representing loyalist paramilitarism, had been encouraging dialogue in the period preceding the official negotiations, and were fully committed to the peace process. On the other hand, the DUP and the UKUP saw the peace process as an attempt to "break the Union" and left the peace talks in the summer of 1997 in anticipation of Sinn Féin's inclusion in the fall. This left the UUP in the awkward position of proceeding into negotiations with Sinn Féin without the support of significant sections of unionist opinion. Caught between progress and the inevitable backlash from the more right-wing elements both within and outside the party, the UUP was often seen to hesitate, to procrastinate, and to waver, slowing the dynamics of the process.

The unionist community has been pulled in these multiple directions since the late 1960s. Interdenominational divisions within Protestantism ensured that the community did not possess the kind of communal solidarity that the Catholic community enjoyed. Perhaps even more important, the Protestant community cleaved around attitudes toward the constitutional status of Northern Ireland. These divisions have been noted in the literature: Richard Rose distinguished between the terms "ultra" and "allegiant";[18] Owen Dudley Edwards between "fearful" and "confident" Protestants;[19] Paul Bew et al. between "populist" and "antipopulist" Unionists;[20] and finally Jennifer Todd refers to the "Ulster British" and the "Ulster Loyalist" traditions.[21] Sarah Nelson explained that in a community that was "historically dominant, well organized and successful in so many walks of life," this was new territory. The larger community of Ulster's defenders was now "uncertain," possessing "a singular lack of confidence in its own efficacy and power."[22] As John Whyte noted, it "is because Protestants distrust Protestants, not just because Protestants distrust Catholics, that the Ulster conflict is so intense."[23]

Though nationalism's divisions were fewer, they were perhaps more profound. Nationalism has been divided into "constitutional" and "physical force" traditions since the mid-1800s, distinctions revived and accentuated in the escalating violence of the 1960s. Whereas in the past constitutionalism may have dallied with the physical force tradition, the extensive violence of the Provisional IRA after 1970 made any contact with them politically taboo. In the late 1980s, in an effort to persuade republicans to abandon the armed struggle and enter the democratic process, John Hume of the Social Democratic and Labour Party (SDLP) began a series of secretive dialogues with Sinn Féin leader Gerry Adams that were highly criticized by mainstream opinion when the effort was made public. The SDLP took advantage of Sinn Féin's moral(e) weakness in the aftermath of the Enniskillen bombing of 1987 and began to stress alternate means to violence. The dialogues resulted in the Hume-Adams statement of 1993. This statement encouraged the British and Irish governments to enter discussions with all parties to the conflict on the basis of relationships within Northern Ireland, between Northern Ireland and the Republic of Ireland, and between the Republic of Ireland and the United Kingdom. It rehearsed many of the issues that appeared in the Joint Declaration and the Frameworks Document, which had been endorsed by the British and Irish governments and had preceded the Good Friday Agreement. The evolving consensus within the nationalist/republican tradition was one aspect of the preplay leading into the multiparty negotiations.

Perhaps a more insidious effect of factionalism in Northern Ireland was the extent to which fear of the extreme forced political leaders to take intransigent positions. As Ian Budge and Cornelius O'Leary argue, politicians tended to perceive their constituents as more extreme than they really were and hence, the elite took on complementarily extreme positions in order to gain reelection. The consequence was circular: electors assumed conditions were worse than they imagined and politicians matched these perceptions with ever more intransigent positions:

> Certainly, a majority of Unionist adherents and councillors—seconded by the press—wished in 1966 to make conciliatory moves towards the Catholics. . . . But moderate councillors were discouraged and conservatives strengthened by an overestimate of intransigence among the population: while the resultant failure of the moderate leaders to act strongly reinforced popular impressions of Unionist intransigence and immobility.[24]

In the absence of moderation or incentives for such, protracted conflict was inevitable.

Memory was a further obstacle to mediation since (in some societies) "there is no other memory than the memory of wounds."[25] Hence, in the Northern Ireland context, we begin a cycle of what John Mack calls "the egoism of victimization":

> The egoism of victimization is the incapacity of an ethno-national group, as a direct result of its own historical traumas, to empathize with the suffering of another group . . . ethno national groups that have been traumatized by repeated sufferings at the hands of other groups seem to have little capacity to grieve for the hurts of other peoples, or to take responsibility for the new victims created by their own warlike actions. Victims kill victims through unendingly repeated cycles that are transmitted from one generation to another, bolstered by stories and myths of atrocities committed by the other people, and by heroic acts committed in defense of the nation and its values by one's own.[26]

Memory serves this cycle as it gives "the unofficial sense of history"[27] and allows history to be used in an applied sense to avoid the despotism of fact and re-create new "realities." For example, when modern Sinn Féin and the IRA were resurrected in 1969, they claimed to be the direct descendants of those who led the Easter Rising in 1916; they in turn claimed to be the descendants of the United Irishmen of 1798, who rebelled against the British in 1798 under the banner of nonsectarian republicanism. The thirty years of "long war" since the 1960s was fueled by the characteristic Irish time frame that inclined "Irishmen to a repetitive view of history and that such a view inclines them—perhaps in defensive wariness and from fear of failure—to prize the moral as against the actual, and the bearing of witness as against success."[28]

### Complex Mediation

> Sustained conflicts are social systems which tend to remain stuck in states of "cold war"—low-level contention and friction that is neither all-out war nor a durable peace. . . . Resolution of such conflicts (when and if it occurs) comes about through some combination of: (1) changes in the balance of driving and restraining forces in the system; and (2) the actions of facilitating channel factors to overcome residual barriers.[29]

This section will be concerned with the factors that induced the attitudinal change that led to the Good Friday Agreement. We should not assume that the Agreement in itself guarantees peace; a "peace agreement is merely one element of a larger peace process, an element that may create some new opportunities but hardly alters all aspects of the conflict."[30] We will concentrate on the flow of the driving and restraining forces in the system by attempting to define what we mean by the "negotiating middle" or "strong center" and by considering the role of facilitating channel factors.

Where there is intense and protracted communal conflict, moderates will often attempt to build relationships with moderates on the other side of the divide, to bridge the gap, and to develop a "centering" dynamic.[31] This "negotiating middle" or "strong center" is required for peace processes to take hold. According to Adrian Guelke, the center is an alliance fused around the mutual recognition that settlement must be achieved, "come what may." In the case of South Africa, "the prospect of a settlement seemed poor up to September 1992, when de Klerk and Mandela got together and signed a Record of Understanding, to the absolute fury of Chief Buthelezi."[32] The substance of the Record of Understanding was relatively unimportant, but the document "symbolized the determination of the two parties, the ANC and the National Party, to reach agreement. . . . It stemmed from their mutual recognition that unless there was a settlement, the country faced disaster." The strong center created by this pact "proved unshakeable, despite the backdrop of very high levels of political violence."[33] In the Middle East as well, "an initial commitment to agreement, with the details following later," lay the groundwork for progress between the Rabin government and the PLO.[34] This pact formed a somewhat weaker strong center than in the South African case.[35]

In contrast, Northern Ireland lacked a strong center until the 1990s. Earlier attempts at internal settlement based on accommodation between the "constitutional" parties—consociationalism in 1974, round-table discussions in 1979–80, rolling devolution in 1982–86—all had failed. The violent "margins" continued to demonstrate that they could not be ignored. In the Northern Ireland context, the center was assumed to be the UUP and the SDLP. The problem was that the strength of the center was compromised by the weakness of its members; elements outside the two groups could exercise a veto over the process through the use of violence. These significant players had to be brought into play. Hence, new techniques of mediation had to be employed.

As we have seen, one such effort was John Hume's dialogue with Gerry Adams. Despite strong criticism for these contacts, Hume argued that this kind of dialogue was necessary to end IRA violence. The SDLP leader made his first bid in March 1988 shortly after the republican movement was reeling from the public relations disaster of the Enniskillen bomb in

November 1987, which killed eleven Protestants commemorating their fallen dead of two world wars. These first series of meetings lasted until September 1988 but ended without agreement. The symbolism and the significance of these meetings should not be underestimated. For the first time Sinn Féin had removed itself from the interstices of a sect to engage in a dialogue with political opponents who desired the same *end*—Irish unity—but disapproved fundamentally with the *means* (political violence). Talks recommenced in 1993 and produced three joint statements (which have not been published), underscoring the common cause of the two parties and encouraging the Irish and British governments to begin multiparty talks. In the meantime there had been secret meetings between a senior Sinn Féin representative and an emissary of the British government in which certain assurances were given to republicans to encourage them to renounce violence and to enter into political dialogue.[36]

Key players in the Irish American diaspora had also played their part in bringing the IRA into the fold. Paramount in this process was the decision of the Clinton administration to grant Gerry Adams a visa to attend a conference in New York, sponsored by the National Committee on Foreign Policy in 1994. Subsequent visas, the privilege of raising funds in the United States, invitations to the White House and Capitol Hill, and the continued support of the Clinton administration reinforced the call to Sinn Féin to engage in the process of political dialogue. Intense pressure from Irish Americans, particularly Irish American business leaders whose success in lobbying Congress over Irish immigration issues in the late 1980s and early 1990s gave them greater self-confidence in political dealings, encouraged the Clinton administration to deal with Sinn Féin. The development of a united front in Irish America between the "tree-tops" led by senior Democratic Party politicians such as Senators Kennedy and Moynihan and the "grass-roots" represented by Northern Aid (or NORAID), the Congressional Ad-Hoc Committee, and the Irish National Caucus also fueled the deconstruction of the "external support system" within U.K. politics that had isolated Sinn Féin.[37] In these circumstances it was not too difficult to persuade loyalist paramilitaries to follow the lead of the IRA's declaration of a cessation of violence in August 1994. The Combined Loyalist Military Command (CLMC) followed suit on October 13, 1994. After all, they perceived themselves to be counterterrorists dedicated to fighting IRA violence. Once the latter ceased there was no reason for loyalist violence.

All of these political developments suggest that there may be an optimum moment to engage the conflicting parties in mediation and negotiation.

The momentum of events and dialogues after 1990 illustrate that a "hurting stalemate" had created the "ripe moment" for intervention. Kirsten E. Schulze maintains that the latter is "composed of a structural element, a party element, and a potential alternative outcome—that is, a mutually hurting stalemate, the presence of valid spokespersons, and a formula for a way out." Schulze places this in terms of the dynamics of the conflict when she considers the ripe moment as a process rather than a specific point in time: "While the 'ripe moment' deals with the shift, theories on possible settlement are dealing with the end product. This leaves the highly important interim phase inadequately studied."[38] Northern Ireland may well be at that interim phase stage; and it may be prudent to recognize that a "peace agreement" may only be the beginning of a process:

> One thing that is imperative is to establish realistic expectations about how much and how quickly a weak and tentative peace agreement can alter the basic nature of a long and profoundly bitter conflict. It is also important for the leaders on both sides to recognize that the game has changed, that the behaviour necessary to get to a provisional agreement is not always the behaviour appropriate for the postagreement period: needs and priorities change, interests must be redefined or revisioned, and a joint learning process must be institutionalized and accelerated.[39]

## TRACK-TWO INITIATIVES

Track-two exercises can be especially relevant in terms of the joint learning process and in inducing behavioral transformation. In contrast to official diplomacy, track-two exercises tend to be less focused and more modest. They belong to the world of the quotidian. A deviant political culture does not respond well to exercises in reconciliation, as the Northern Ireland case study demonstrates.[40]

Since 1990 I have been involved in eight unofficial track-two workshops on Northern Ireland.[41] Two of the workshops complemented each other: those at the Airlie House Conference Center in Virginia (January 28 to February 2, 1990) and the Center for Defense and International Studies at the University of Social Sciences, Grenoble, France (August 27–30, 1990). Both had been organized by the same teams from the Centre for the Study of Conflict, University of Ulster, and the Center for Conflict Analysis and Resolution, George Mason University. Both involved the same set of politicians (although they were allowed to add to their numbers for the Grenoble workshop), and both resulted in a single product that made, and continues to make, a significant impact on the political process in Northern Ireland.

Two workshops—Des Moines and Strasbourg—complemented each other insofar as they were concerned with a Bill of Rights and a human rights culture. Three—South Africa and Harvard twice—were more reflective in that the participants learned from experts and activists about conflict resolution elsewhere. Belfast was the only workshop that was totally public and that involved large numbers of people.

Track-two diplomacy, "increasingly the diplomacy of choice for problems beyond the reach of official efforts,"[42] is most succinctly defined as

> unofficial, informal interaction between representatives of adversary groups or nations which aims to develop strategies and create an environment which could contribute to the resolution of their conflict. It must be understood that track two diplomacy is in no way a substitute for official 'track one' government-to-government or leader-to-leader contact. Rather, track two activity is designed to assist official leaders by compensating for the constraints imposed upon them by the psychologically understandable need for leaders to be, or at least *be seen* to be, strong, wary and indomitable in the face of the enemy. . . . Track two diplomacy, then, is conceived of as several levels of process designed to assist official leadership in the task of resolving, or in the first instance managing, conflict by exploring possible solutions, out of public view and without the requirement to formally negotiate or bargain for advantage. Track two diplomacy on its more focused level seeks political formulae or scenarios which might satisfy the basic security and esteem needs of all parties to a dispute. On its more general level, it seeks to promote an environment in a political community, through the education of public opinion, that would make it safer for public opinion to take risks for peace.[43]

All except the Belfast workshop were held outside Northern Ireland. That allowed for valuable distance away from media distortion and peer group pressure. In addition, the distance allowed for the creation of a safe, neutral, and supportive environment in which each delegation started on equal footing. None of these factors can be ignored. That the workshops took place in scholarly settings was advantageous because journalists were inclined to dismiss them as being merely "academic" and not newsworthy. It was up to the delegations to decide whether they wanted to issue press communiqués before or after each event, although it must be stressed that the politicians did so as individuals rather than as representatives of their respective parties. Some, for example, issued deliberately bland statements to satisfy their absent party colleagues, among other reasons.

All the workshops addressed transitional, rather than final-status, issues because they were concerned with building up a culture of trust among politicians who, for the most part, occupied second-tier positions within their parties. Virginia and Strasbourg had as their theme "Northern Ireland in Europe: 1992." Des Moines was billed as a seminar on the feasibility of a Bill of Rights for Northern Ireland; Strasbourg as a seminar on

"Constitutional Protection of Human Rights: Comparative Experiences."
The South Africa workshop gave Northern Ireland politicians an opportunity to hear about the challenges of the transition in South Africa from a
politically very diverse group. The Kennedy School of Government at
Harvard billed its case study method as "Managing Change in a Diverse
Society." In that respect, location and format were more challenging intel-
lectually and encouraged reflection.

The opportunity to meet at the margins of the formal workshops was a
vital component. Participants were housed in comfortable surroundings all
under the same roof and all along the same corridor. (Harvard was an exception to this arrangement, but even there, accommodation consisted of
executive-style apartments with adjacent space to hold informal meetings.)
A common meeting place was established, and it was the practice to eat
together. This was not compulsory; a high degree of leisure time was built
into most exercises. The South African trip included an overnight stay at a
game park; at Harvard, participants attended a baseball game and a reception in a Boston art gallery and went on a one-day trip to Martha's Vineyard.

These workshops took place against a backdrop of continuous tension
in which politicians had often adopted adversarial positions. The absence
of the media—a policy that participants had fully endorsed—meant that
there was no need to strike poses. A parallel can be drawn with the Oslo
process:

> Our quiet meetings proved to have several advantages. The news media which
> focus on what divides rather than what unites were not involved. There was
> no time-consuming diplomatic protocol to be followed and no speeches to
> the gallery. The participants in the official and public negotiations appeared
> to spend 100 per cent of their time blaming one another, whereas the nego-
> tiators in Norway spent at least 90 per cent of their time awake, meals
> included, in real negotiations. The many mutual provocations and acts of
> violence in the field did not derail the efforts of the secret negotiators as
> they did the official channel in Washington.[44]

Of course the parallel is not precise. Oslo was about negotiation; the Northern Ireland workshops were more modest. But the absence of the media
and the opportunity to build on a collegial spirit should not be underestimated. The workshop settings tended to be formal and formidable. They
enabled participants to hone their political skills. Leisure time allowed
for building personal relationships and trust. However, two examples
stand out.

I have a vivid recollection of a conversation between a nationalist and a
unionist in a Strasbourg restaurant in December 1993 when the former

explained his concept of an "agreed Ireland" and gave a graphic description of the physical and emotional damage visited on him and on his family by his alleged allies in the republican movement. The sheer emotion of the occasion impacted on both men and on those who had had the privilege of listening in on this dialogue. At a less dramatic level, the opportunity for private conversations over a meal or in hotel bedrooms increased the sense of collegiality and assisted the formal workshop sessions occurring in civilized fashion.

The Harvard workshop provides a negative example. It was the first occasion in which Sinn Féin was in the same company as the UUP. The other unionist parties with parliamentary representation, the Democratic Unionist Party and the United Kingdom Unionist Party, did not participate. That put some pressure on the UUP representatives since they could not afford to consort with Sinn Féin. So they found themselves in the same workshop as Sinn Féin, but they would not socialize outside. They would not share the same dining tables nor would they sit for the group photograph. Although one can understand the electoral imperative that forced them into this situation, the consequence was that they were made to look foolish. Indeed, at the second Harvard workshop, not only did DUP members participate, but along with the UUP they agreed to a group photograph, although they too did not socialize with Sinn Féin members. It was one small indication that they recognized that the nature of the game had changed and that the Agreement had created a new dynamic.

## The Workshop Teams

Two further general points need some elaboration. One concerns the quality of the workshop teams and the other the standing of third parties. Ideally, politicians need to be tolerant, respected, and representative. All of this is relative and may be dictated to some extent by the relationship between the third party and individual politicians. Tolerance simply means a willingness to listen to and work with others. Since the politicians were willing to participate, ipso facto they were tolerant. Because some workshops reflected rising tension on the ground in Northern Ireland, dialogue could be robust at times, but generally it was pursued in a civilized and inquiring manner. In a divided society, a respected politician who has the capacity to transcend that division is a very rare bird: in that context "respected" means within one's own community. These politicians need not necessarily hold elective positions—indeed, it may be an advantage to target emerging talent. Two criteria were adapted in the eight workshops under discussion: either the delegates were potentially part of their respective negotiating teams or they were perceived as emerging leaders. The result was that the workshops were dominated by the secondary leaderships.

The question of representation in the workshops is more problematic and may have some relationship to the role of a third party. My standing with individual politicians was crucial. Besides a sustained effort to involve the same cadre of politicians throughout, the selection of politicians tended to be self-fulfilling. Initially, I approached politicians with whom I had some previous relationship either through interviewing them for academic projects or some other involvement. They were people with whom I had established a degree of mutual trust and respect. In every instance, I called on the same cadre of politicians, and if leading members were not available they would nominate like-minded individuals. Thus, over a period of six years a small group of politicians became versed in a process of shared learning.

It might be objected that there was a certain arbitrariness to the selection of participants. In the beginning this was the case. It was my judgment that two of the party leaders would have considered the type of exercise in which we were involved to be foreign to their way of doing business. But I made a conscious effort to identify those who might make a political impact in the longer term and who represented a newer generation. Total consistency was impossible in any case because much depends on the vagaries of timing. Each workshop had its own preplay and could take a few years to plan. Once a date had been set, we came up against parliamentary and personal timetables. More important, however, was that parties had accepted that this type of exercise complemented track-one efforts.

It is impossible to measure how representative these delegations were. There had been no female representation before the Strasbourg workshop in December 1993. Indeed, the issue did not properly surface until the formation of the Northern Ireland Women's Coalition to contest elections in June 1996. In recent workshops an attempt has been made to establish a more equitable gender balance. Generally, the process cannot be totally representative in that it cannot contain those who spurn "the gentle art of reperceiving." Instead of an idealized form of representation, my colleagues and I sought to concentrate on those who had leadership qualities to move some of their own intransigent colleagues.

## Notable Successes?

The workshops in Virginia and Strasbourg may be considered successes, at least tentatively. They had a beginning, a middle, and an end; they were designed to complement each other; and they produced a product. The theme, "Northern Ireland in Europe: 1992," had been chosen for a number of reasons. One was the introduction of the Single European Act,[45] which was going to change the nature of politics with the reduction in boundaries across Europe. The act had the potential for either positive or negative impact on regions such as Northern Ireland. So the topic had practical content: How does Northern Ireland prepare itself for the Single European Act? It also had symbolic content in that it was concerned with questions of sovereignty and subsidiarity. Traditionally, the unionist parties were seen as antithetical to the European vision, whereas the Social Democratic and Labour Party was very pro-European. Despite this symbolic input, the topic was perceived as being noncontentious enough to enable the politicians to use the workshops to cover any issue they desired.

Discussion at the workshops focused on the implications of the Single European Act and specifically on how it might affect the relationships among the various Northern Ireland parties and other interested parties elsewhere. The theme of the Single European Act had been chosen by the organizers because it was believed that, while some thought had been devoted to the economic implications of the act, there had been little anticipatory thinking on the likely political and social consequences of "a Europe without boundaries." It was hoped that the Virginia workshop might allow some shared agreement to develop about the nature of the opportunities and problems the new Europe was likely to present to the people of Northern Ireland.

Another theme that emerged was a strong feeling that Northern Ireland's interests were not well represented in the European Community in spite of the efforts of its Members of European Parliament (MEPs). Hence it was suggested that a Northern Ireland input in Brussels could take the form of a Northern Ireland Centre in Europe (NICE), and a tentative draft proposal for exploring the possibilities of establishing such a center was drawn up. Following the Airlie House workshop in Virginia, the three Northern Ireland MEPs were apprised of the deliberations and agreed in principle to support the establishment of NICE. On March 16, 1990, the Northern Ireland participants met at a neutral and secluded venue in Belfast and requested a study of the feasibility of NICE.

With a grant I had received from the Ireland Funds, I commissioned a retired civil servant to conduct a feasibility study. His study was considered by the Northern Ireland participants in Belfast on July 6, 1990, and was judged to form a firm basis for progress. It was decided to hold a second workshop to expedite the business of establishing NICE. In the meantime, I had learned that sections of the business community were proceeding with a similar model that was to be launched by the secretary of state for Northern Ireland in September. I conveyed this information at the outset of the second workshop, in Grenoble. This information angered some participants who were aware that their standing in the community was low because it was perceived that they did not cooperate across the sectarian divide. Here was an example of practical cooperation that looked like it was not going to be recognized by the general electorate. They conveyed that anger to the British government's Northern Ireland Office immediately and had the proposed launch of the business community's model postponed. This was a rare example of track one clashing with track two.

Participants used their visit to Grenoble to study firsthand how other European regions were preparing for the impact of the Single European Act. At the Rhone-Alps Regional Office in Lyon, they questioned local officials who were concerned about their region's relationship with the wider world and, especially, the axis of development the region had cultivated with Bad-Wurtemburg (Germany), Catalonia (Spain), and Lombardy (Italy).

As a result of the workshop, the feasibility study was amended and it was agreed that it would be published to engender public debate about "Northern Ireland in Europe: 1992." That debate led eventually to the establishment of NICE in a partnership between the political parties and the business community. The feasibility report acted as the catalyst for NICE. Funding was to be derived from a combination of public and private sources, and it was recognized that the project could succeed only if it had a broad base of support from political, economic, and institutional interests in Northern Ireland.

Besides being a successful proactive exercise, NICE was important for two further reasons. It served as a useful reminder of how third parties can be facilitators, and it gave political participants the space to explore the more pressing demands arising from the conflict. The NICE project was serviced throughout by academics from both sides of the Atlantic, some of whom had considerable experience in this type of exercise. It might be said that the Northern Ireland academics provided the linkage to, and integrity of, the conflict, whereas other academics provided most of the technical expertise. The combination of Northern Ireland and outside academics produced a level playing field in which both sides to the conflict knew that they could call on the existing support system even though they were not always in agreement with that support.[46]

The very first workshop in Virginia, for example, was opened with a mildly provocative philosophical paper from a distinguished practitioner in conflict resolution who had some experience of Northern Ireland at the early stages of the conflict. In other words, he was au fait with the nature of the problem, sufficiently distanced from the action, and sufficiently skillful in drawing the politicians into dialogue.

In addition, participants in Virginia were able to call on academic expertise ranging from knowledge of the evolution of the European Union to academics who had organized workshops concerned with the conflicts in Cyprus and the south Atlantic. A similar support system existed in Grenoble.

These workshops also produced what one participant described as "shared learning." That meant not only that participants were able to take advantage of the technical expertise, but also that they had a better understanding of their political adversaries.[47] Discussions went well beyond the European question. Even on that level, many of the myths about the European Union were exposed, and the notion that 1992 would "open up the possibility of manipulative politics" (according to one unionist participant), whereby the Single European Act would be utilized to force Northern Ireland into a closer relationship with the Republic of Ireland, was fully rehearsed.

One of the participants' primary concerns was that it might not be clear to their constituents back home that there was a distance between analysis and negotiation, and they wished to ensure that that distance was maintained. They used the cover of Virginia and Grenoble to tease out a formula that would allow them to reenter the political dialogue without an apparent loss of face. The phraseology they produced was remarkably close to the formulation devised by the two governments at a later stage to keep the process in existence. Similarly, the SDLP participants used the workshops to talk down some of the unionist fears about the Irish dimension and the Anglo-Irish Agreement of 1985. These shared understandings enabled the bilateral and multilateral track-one exercises to proceed more smoothly than might have been expected, a fact confirmed by my interviewees.

### The Impetus of South Africa

The visit to South Africa in 1994 was not so much for a single workshop but for a series of consultations with all the necessary parties inside South Africa. Northern Ireland participants learned from the firsthand experience of those who were involved in the South African negotiation process. The consultations were sponsored by the Institute for Democracy in South Africa (IDASA) and designed to provide key players in Northern Ireland with an opportunity to reflect on their own process in light of the South

African experience: "In IDASA we have seen the value of such exposure programmes for our own process and a similar value might be expected for the participants." On the question of participation, IDASA accepted that it might have to "exclude some sections of opinion who will have to be drawn into the process at a later stage. South Africa has lessons for how the various groups were negotiated into the settlement at various times as well."[48] That last comment was shorthand for the exclusion of Sinn Féin because, as the link person to Northern Ireland, I was pressured (slightly) by South Africans to have Sinn Féin included. The South Africa workshop occurred before the IRA cease-fire, and because it was clear that unionists would not participate if Sinn Féin attended, nothing came of the suggestion.

Like the NICE project, the 1994 South Africa exercise delivered a palpable product, but it should be examined in conjunction with the subsequent 1997 South African visit (with which I was not involved). The latter was the first fully inclusive process in that it contained high-powered delegations from all points of the political spectrum including Sinn Féin and the fringe loyalist parties (it also was graced with a visit from President Mandela). It indicated too how useful shared learning could be when participants were learning from another conflict. South Africa had moved beyond its pariah status in the international community and had illustrated that "intractable" problems need not necessarily be intractable. It was a shining example of what could be achieved if the will was there.

Representatives such as Sinn Féin's Martin McGuinness and others involved in the official multiparty talks made frequent references to their South African experience. At the formal opening of substantive talks in Belfast on October 7, 1997, the Alliance leader, Lord Alderdice, said that the "message Northern politicians learned from the recent examination of the South African experience was that if deadlines were not met 'you never achieve the outcome you want to achieve.'"[49] It was an Alliance participant who made the point in interview that workshops such as Des Moines were about looking at particular pieces of content whereas South Africa was looking mostly at process—how to get from point A to point B. He believed that South Africa pointed out design faults in the Northern Ireland process.

Specifically, the South African participants took away three messages: how to make use of technical committees to further the process; the need to accept the notion of "sufficient consensus" for the same reason (which has now become part of the political furniture in the multiparty talks); and a recognition that parties must not allow themselves to be left behind by the process. Individuals took away other specific ideas on matters such as policing. But most important—so I firmly believe after a series of interviews with four of the participants (there were seven interviewees in all)—the South African visit helped to make relationships more manageable and allowed the multiparty talks negotiators to use the same language and have a clearer idea of what was possible. Some used the South African experience in talks with government and in discussions within the DUP. One participant asserted that if Des Moines was "nearest to track two, then South Africa was more like track one and a half."

## CONCLUSION

Track two has the potential to make dialogue more open and brainstorming more creative.[50] Because it is not restrained by formal protocols, track two can "generate new ideas for settlement," which can eventually be fed back into political debate. The face-to-face character of unofficial contacts is also important because it allows individuals to build trust and overcome isolation. Track two can be a crucial factor in the success of track one. It need not always be so. There was, for example, no contact between government officials and the organizers of the first two workshops that led to the creation of NICE, although there may have been meetings with some of the politicians who participated. The government was unaware of the advanced stage of the NICE project, and the secretary of state, who had agreed to launch a similar (but less advanced) project from the business community, was forced to abandon the latter and deal with the politicians. The result was a minor diplomatic frisson and a salutary lesson in the pitfalls of complex mediation. In an ideal world there should be strong lines of communication between all points on the mediation chain.

Track two also assisted the formal initiative in that the modest ends of "process promotion" (and less frequently "problem solving") were not considered to be threatening either to the participants or to those in control of the official process. If the latter had any reservations about track two, they could have had the capacity to do serious damage to the workshops. The former, however, were able to build on establishing group cohesion and to have a sense of the group's strategic significance in the faltering negotiating process. The experience enabled the group to have a greater appreciation of its own capacity to make a serious contribution to the process.

It is important to remember too the role of the exogenous factors of the so-called New World Order in shaping the center and changing the pressures on the participants in the conflict to engage each other. The new system of open borders, open trade, and open minds blurred the lines of conflict and fed the decline of the Anglo-American special relationship as did the end of the Cold War, increasing globalization and interdependence, particularly the process of European integration, and the ascendance of the Commonwealth.[51] The consequences—felt, for example, in the Adams visa decision, the involvement of the Clinton administration and the European Union, the expansion in the Irish economy—were to gradually remove some of the more powerful strategic barriers to negotiation and compromise. Informal diplomacy allowed participants in the conflict to take advantage of these "momentum-building processes."[52]

With the advantage of hindsight it could be argued that the Anglo-Irish conflict had reached the state of hurting stalemate. It would be fallacious to give too much credit to our prescience. The best that can be said was that the participants shared a concern that something needed to be done, and at the very least they should explore the others' options. Track two presented the best opportunities to do so. The absence of the media, the physical location, the neutral backup support, all were as far removed as possible from the rawness of the Northern Ireland political arena. These factors illustrate Chester Crocker's observation that how "third parties can intervene most effectively depends upon (1) their own capabilities, leverage, and linkage to the conflict; (2) the conflict's status, form, and ripeness; and (3) the character of the parties to the conflict, their accessibility, and their decision-making systems."[53]

The experience of all the workshops suggest that while they may be studied discretely we should not ignore their incremental effect. In that respect, they helped a key cadre of politicians gain from the process at a technical level and learn to trust one another. At the very least, the politicians became familiar with one another in the official bilateral and multilateral meetings conducted by government. It is true that the parties entered the workshops with their separate agendas and extracted their own lessons, suggesting that they participated without very high general expectations. Yet, in some instances there were palpable products—emotional, intellectual, and institutional. Common themes emerged, and there was a commonality on how to use the process.

The process was both credible and reflective—credible in that participants became advocates for the process, and while naturally they used it to present their own positions, they also demonstrated a capacity to grow and learn. The process was reflective in that participants absorbed considerable new information, technical and otherwise. They were prepared to assert their opinions but to listen carefully to those of others. Many of them matured as a result of the process. With the passage of time, the process became more inclusive of diverse voices from Northern Ireland. Indeed, even a group dynamic had been established as early as 1990. On the last day of the Grenoble meeting, one of the politicians made the point that "contacts are now established and we don't need academics to keep them up." Nevertheless, academics were called upon on quite a few other occasions in the intervening years.

But once we move outside this tiny elite, questions have to be asked about the utility of track two. The cease-fires made it easier to make the process more inclusive; and in including the parties associated with the paramilitaries we were broadening the base in which track two had a useful role. The leaders of Sinn Féin and of the Progressive Unionist Party and the Ulster Democratic Party were very close to their respective communities.

With the obvious exception of the Adams visa, it is impossible to quantify the effect of these workshops on track-one efforts. The story of the Adams visa is a near perfect example of the symmetry of intervention and leverage. In contrast, the incremental Northern Ireland exercises did not complement directly the official mediation, though participants certainly used their unofficial experience to rehearse positions taken up at the formal level. The unionist politicians in particular realized that they were in danger of being marginalized by the intergovernmental dynamic—that gave track two an added urgency. At a more mundane level, the NICE project damaged relations between the Northern Ireland Office and participants for a brief period, while the South African visit played directly into the multilateral talks. It is important to establish that the process is meant to complement the formal negotiations rather than be a constraint. The same comments from two participants from opposing camps—that people should not get engaged in "solution-mongering" and that matters can be much more relaxed when participants realize that there is no hidden agenda— suggests that the process has a real role to play. My own experience is that no one has refused to take part because they mistrusted the purpose and motives of the exercise.

It is more difficult to be precise about how ideas emanating from the workshops can reach a wider audience. Most of my interviewees maintained that they discussed the outcome of the different workshops with a small coterie of political friends, although one said that he passed on much of his experience to the party through speeches and articles. One participant considered that the most important measurement of success is engaging party leaders in the whole process because they are the only ones who can deliver. In the light of the 1998 (Belfast) Agreement, that might be called into question. Here was an agreement that was driven by the two governments because they perceived that in a demotic culture there was a real desire for change. This was contrary to the strongly held opinions of some political leaders. The final outcome will serve as an indication of how far we have moved toward process and inclusivity; whether we have gone beyond analysis and are beginning to look at negotiation and implementation; and whether we have moved beyond confusion and are working through more realistic cognitive frameworks. It should tell us, too, whether track two in Northern Ireland needs to move into a new phase in which leaders will have to recognize that the rules of the game have changed. But always we should keep in mind that *fortuna* lurks in the political undergrowth.

## NOTES

1. Following the referendums in the Republic of Ireland and Northern Ireland, which overwhelmingly endorsed the Agreement, a survey based on thirty news reports and comments from twenty countries between May 24 and 28, 1998, conveyed certain themes. Three will suffice. The German newspaper *Handelsblat* (May 25) stressed process: "It is not the political solution that counts but the momentum created by the willingness to come to an understanding. If this momentum is set in motion it will be difficult to reverse, and it will make old enemy images obsolete." Israel's *Maariv* (May 24) set the Agreement in the context of Israel's own peace process: "This is more than the 'Oslo agreement.' . . . One thing is for certain: The Irish have taken . . . an important step towards the longed-for peace, while it is increasingly becoming more remote in this region." And Pakistan's *Dawn* (May 26) alluded to one aspect of conflict resolution: "Another important lesson to have emerged from the Irish peace exercise is that conflict resolution is made easier when some outside powers directly concerned with the political future of a territory decide to push for peace." All of these will surface in this chapter. See USIA Media Reaction@ notes1.usia.gov.28May1998.

2. United States Advisory Commission on Public Diplomacy, *A New Diplomacy for the Information Age* (Washington, D.C.: United States Advisory Commission on Public Diplomacy, 1996).

3. Ibid.

4. Chief Emeka Anyaoku, *Space in Which Hope Can Grow: The Commonwealth and Preventive Diplomacy*, INCORE Occasional Paper no. 4 (Belfast: INCORE, University of Ulster, 1996), 13.

5. Cyrus R. Vance and David A. Hamburg, *Pathfinders for Peace: A Report to the UN Secretary-General on the Role of Special Representatives and Personal Envoys* (New York: Carnegie Corporation of New York, September 1997), 21–22.

6. Ibid., 5.

7. Cited in ibid., 6.

8. Padraig O'Malley, *Biting at the Grave: The Irish Hunger Strikes and the Politics of Despair* (Belfast: Blackstaff Press, 1990), 8–9.

9. David W. Miller, *Queen's Rebels: Ulster Loyalism in Historical Perspective* (Dublin: Gill and Macmillan, 1977).

10. J. G. Bulpitt, *Territory and Power in the United Kingdom: An Interpretation* (Manchester: Manchester University Press, 1983), 238.

11. J. Bowyer Bell, "Aspects of the Dragonworld: Covert Communication and the Rebel Ecosystem," *Intelligence and Counterintelligence* 3, no. 1 (1990): 41.

12. Frank Wright, *Northern Ireland: A Comparative Analysis* (Dublin: Gill and Macmillan, 1987), xiii.

13. John Darby, *Intimidation and the Control of Conflict in Northern Ireland* (Dublin: Gill and Macmillan, 1986), viii–ix, 10.

14. Ibid., viiii.

15. See John Dunlop, *A Precarious Belonging: Presbyterians and the Conflict in Ireland* (Belfast: Blackstaff Press, 1995), 84.

16. Byron Bland, *Marching and Rising: The Rituals of Small Differences and Great Violence in Northern Ireland* (Stanford, Calif.: Center for International Security and Arms Control, Stanford University, 1996), 10–11.

17. Cynthia Enloe, *Ethnic Conflict and Political Development* (Boston: Brown, Little, 1973), 169–170.

18. Richard Rose, *Governing without Consensus: An Irish Perspective* (London: Faber and Faber, 1971).

19. Owen Dudley Edwards, *The Sins of Our Fathers: Roots of Conflict in Northern Ireland* (Dublin: Gill and Macmillan, 1970), 64 ff.

20. Paul Bew et al., *The State in Northern Ireland, 1921–72: Political Forces and Social Classes* (Manchester: Manchester University Press, 1979).

21. Jennifer Todd, "Two Traditions in Unionist Political Culture," in *Irish Political Studies* (Galway: PSAI Press, 1987), 1–26.

22. Sarah Nelson, *Ulster's Uncertain Defenders: Protestant Political, Paramilitary, and Community Groups and the Northern Ireland Conflict* (Belfast: Appletree Press, 1984), 177.

23. John Whyte, "Catholic-Protestant Relations in Countries Other than Ireland," in *Sectarianism: Roads to Reconciliation,* ed. J. B. Earley (Dundalk: Three Candles Press, 1976), 278.

24. Ian Budge and Cornelius O'Leary, *Belfast: Approach to Crisis—A Study of Belfast Politics, 1613–1970* (London: Macmillan, 1973), 355.

25. The phrase is Czeslaw Milosz's; it is used as an epigraph by Frank McGuinness to introduce his play *Carthaginians* (London: Faber and Faber, 1988).

26. John Mack, "The Psychodynamics of Victimization among National Groups in Conflict," in *The Psychodynamics of International Relationships,* ed. Vamik D. Volkan et al., vol. 1 (Lexington, Mass.: Lexington Books, 1990), 125.

27. Denis Donoghue, *Warrenpoint* (London: Jonathan Cape, 1991), 124.

28. Oliver MacDonagh, *States of Mind: A Study of Anglo-Irish Conflict, 1780–1980* (London: Allen and Unwin, 1983), 13.

29. Michael Watkins and Kirsten Lundberg, "Getting to the Table in Oslo: Driving Forces and Channel Factors," *Negotiation Journal* (April 1998): 117.

30. Robert Rothstein, *The Political Economy of Reconciliation* (Jerusalem: Truman Institute, Hebrew University, n.d.), 3.

31. Roger Fisher terms this "co-mediation." See Roger Fisher, "Negotiating Inside Out: What Are the Best Ways to Relate Internal Negotiations with External Ones?" *Negotiation Journal* 5, no. 1 (1989): 33–41.

32. Adrian Guelke, "Improving the Political Process: Peace by Analogy," in *Excerpts from the Conference Held at Queen's College, Oxford, 9–11 September 1994* (London: British-Irish Association, 1995), 16.

33. Ibid., 17.

34. Ibid. See also Watkins and Lundberg, "Getting to the Table in Oslo."

35. It would appear that the commitment to resolution by the PLO and the Rabin government did not reflect a broader consensus within mainstream society about the need for progress on this issue.

36. Sinn Féin, *Setting the Record Straight* (internal Sinn Féin paper; later published in Dublin in January 1994).

37. Bulpitt, *Territory and Power in the United Kingdom*, 59.

38. Kirsten E. Schulze, "The Northern Ireland Political Process," *Irish Political Studies* 12 (1997), 104.

39. Rothstein, *Political Economy of Reconciliation*, 3.

40. I have looked at these earlier examples in "Quiet Diplomacy and Personal Conversation: An Analysis of Track-One and Track-Two Diplomacy" (work-in-progress paper, United States Institute of Peace, Washington, D.C., May 1998), 24–27.

41. Airlie, Virginia, (January 1990); Grenoble, France (August 1990); Des Moines, Iowa (December 1991); Strasbourg, France (December 1993); South Africa (April 1994); Belfast (June 1995); Harvard University, Cambridge, Massachusetts (July 1996 and July 1998).

42. Carnegie Commission, *Preventing Deadly Conflict* (New York: Carnegie Commission on Preventing Deadly Conflict, 1997), 50.

43. Joe Montville, *Track Two Diplomacy: The Development of Non-Governmental Peace Promoting Relationships* (Dublin: Irish Peace Institute, 1986), 1.

44. Jan Egeland, "Norway as an International Peacemaker" (paper presented to the Royal Geographic Society, London, October 1994), 4–5.

45. The Single European Act was introduced by the European Commission to harmonize social, economic, and political arrangements among European Union members. It was posited on the notion of a Europe of regions. In that respect, Northern Ireland—as a peripheral and divided region—was conscious that it might fall behind other European regions.

46. A DUP participant felt that he was addressed at times by people "who didn't have an understanding of Northern Ireland [and who were sometimes] trying to push their own point of view." He accepted, however, that there was no hidden agenda involved.

47. A participant from the Alliance Party believed that the Des Moines workshop allowed him to have very useful exchanges with an Ulster Unionist, which led to a very successful working relationship; and that in South Africa he had managed to use one social meeting "to work things out" with a member of the SDLP.

**48.** IDASA press release, September 16, 1994.

**49.** Gerry Moriarty, "Divisions Stark on All-Ireland Dimension," *Irish Times*, October 8, 1997, 11.

**50.** David Smock, introduction to *Private Peacemaking: USIP-Assisted Peacemaking Projects of Nonprofit Organizations*, ed. David Smock (Washington, D.C.: United States Institute of Peace Press, 1998).

**51.** See Paul Arthur, "American Intervention in the Anglo-Irish Peace Process: Incrementalism or Interference?" *Cambridge Review of International Affairs* 11, no. 1 (summer-fall 1997): 46–64.

**52.** Watkins and Lundberg, "Getting to the Table in Oslo," 119.

**53.** Chester A. Crocker, "The Varieties of Intervention: Conditions for Success," in *Managing Global Chaos: Sources of and Responses to International Conflict*, eds. Chester A. Crocker and Fen Osler Hampson with Pamela Aall (Washington, D.C.: United States Institute of Peace Press, 1996), 187.

# PART IV

# SETTLEMENT AND IMPLEMENTATION

## Background to Chapter 19

## More and Less Than It Seemed: The Carter-Nunn-Powell Mediation in Haiti, 1994

The fall of the corrupt Duvalier regime in 1986 left Haiti in chaos but also with an opportunity to join the widening democratic community in the Americas. Haiti's first attempt at democracy, however, ended when President-elect Jean-Bertrand Aristide was overthrown in a military coup d'état in 1991. Mediation efforts by the United Nations, the OAS (see chapter 15), and others unsuccessfully sought to restore constitutional government. The UN Security Council imposed an oil and arms embargo against Haiti but proved unable to remove the coup leaders; several attempts to enforce the Governors Island Agreement failed ignominiously. Success was finally achieved by the team of Jimmy Carter, Colin Powell, and Sam Nunn, who negotiated with Haiti's military rulers even as U.S. warplanes approached the island to spearhead a military assault. It was not, however, the actual movement of troops so much as the credible threat of force that, combined with effective diplomacy, secured a resumption of constitutional government.

### Major Actors
- Jean-Bertrand Aristide: ousted president of Haiti
- General Raoul Cedras: military ruler of Haiti after ousting Aristide
- Emile Jonassaint: provisional president

505

- United States: represented by former president Jimmy Carter, Senator Sam Nunn, and Ret. General Colin Powell
- United Nations
- Organization of American States (OAS)

## Important Dates

- December 16, 1990: Aristide elected president as Haiti holds its first free and fair election
- February 7, 1991: Aristide assumes office
- September 30, 1991: Military coup topples Aristide
- October 8, 1991: OAS condemns coup, urges return of constitutional government, and recommends that member states impose economic sanctions
- July 4, 1993: Governors Island Agreement calls for a return of Aristide and landing of a contingent of UN security officials
- October 11, 1993: USS *Harlan County* aborts landing at Port-au-Prince
- July 1994: UN Security Council Resolution 940 approves use of "all necessary means" to restore Aristide to the presidency
- September 17, 1994: Carter, Nunn, and Powell arrive in Port-au-Prince
- September 18, 1994: Peace agreement signed as a U.S. force prepares to invade Haiti
- October 15, 1994: President Aristide returns to Haiti

## Key Agreements Reached

- Aristide allowed to return to Haiti and resume office of president
- U.S. troops allowed to enter Haiti unopposed
- Senior Haitian military officers resign

## Principal Outcomes

- International community determined a military coup against a democracy was a threat to peace and grounds for the legitimate use of force
- Force and diplomacy were combined to achieve desired results, although not in the way it appeared

# 19

# More and Less Than It Seemed

## The Carter-Nunn-Powell Mediation in Haiti, 1994

ROBERT A. PASTOR

*Diplomacy without power is feeble, and power without diplomacy is destructive and blind.*

—Hans Morgenthau

*[The Haitian foreign minister] tells me that the people there are doubtful as to our motives. . . . I assured him of our entirely unselfish motives and that in landing marines in Haiti we had acted on account of two reasons: first, that it was in the interest of humanity and, second, that in case we had not taken the step, in all probability some other nation would have felt called upon to do so. I further said to him that the intelligent Haitians should feel gratified that it was the United States rather than some other power whose motives might not be as unselfish as ours.*

—Secretary of State Robert Lansing to President Woodrow Wilson, August 7, 1915

507

At noon on September 17, 1994, former U.S. president Jimmy Carter, Senator Sam Nunn, and Ret. General Colin Powell arrived in Port-au-Prince, Haiti. They had instructions from the president of the United States to negotiate the Haitian military's exit from power within twenty-four hours. At the moment of deadline, the three of them stood cramped in a small, stuffy room protected by the Secret Service. As their adviser, I stood next to them, taking notes while they spoke and listened to a secure speakerphone.

At the other end of the phone was President Bill Clinton. His voice was clear and commanding but unmistakably nervous and tense, reflecting the burden of responsibility and the knowledge that an invasion was on its way—a fact not yet known to the four of us in the room or the Haitian military command in the room down the hall.

Time and the president's patience had run out. "I order you, President Carter, Senator Nunn, and General Powell to leave the country right now!" he instructed. The three negotiators responded that their principal goals had already been attained and that a complete agreement was within reach, but that they needed a little more time to resolve the additional items that the president wanted. Skeptical that an agreement was possible, the president was ready to end the talks, but after several exchanges, allowed his negotiators some more time. Five hours later, an agreement was signed that permitted the entry of U.S. troops into Haiti without loss of a single life and the peaceful return of the elected president, Jean-Bertrand Aristide, on October 15, 1994.

Frederick the Great wrote: "Diplomacy without force is like an orchestra without a score." This, of course, is the first lesson learned by students of international diplomacy. On its face, President Clinton's policy on Haiti, culminating with the dispatch of his most skillful orchestra, Carter, Nunn, and Powell with the best marching music, seemed a textbook example of the adept use of diplomacy combined with a credible threat. Alas, it was both more and less than it seemed. For nearly three years, the United States practiced diplomacy with empty threats. Then, it chose to use force without considering diplomacy. And then, in the space of three days, owing to the persistence of former president Carter and several other factors, an effective mediation was constructed. Even then, the negotiations came within a knife-edge of failing.

The mediation in Haiti was a superb case study—but not of how to combine diplomacy with force, but why it is so difficult, practically impossible, particularly for a democracy, to combine these two elements into an effective strategy. The case study is important for three other reasons, which raise pivotal questions:

- It was the first time that the international community—using the voice and vote of the United Nations Security Council—declared a military coup against a democratically elected government a threat to peace and thus grounds for the legitimate use of international force. How significant was this precedent?
- Second, the mediation team was an unusual combination of two private citizens and a senator sent by the president but with substantial autonomy. Is this model worth replicating?
- Third, this quasi-governmental mediation occurred after negotiating failures by a group of foreign ministers, an OAS envoy, a UN envoy, and presidential envoys. Why did these fail, and the Carter-Nunn-Powell mission succeed?

In this chapter, I will define the Haitian case and describe the rise and fall of the different mediation missions. Finally, I will discuss the implications of the case for conflict resolution and draw lessons for future cases.

## BACKGROUND

On December 16, 1990, Haiti held its first and only election that was judged free and fair by all its political parties and the international community.[1] A young, multilingual priest, Jean-Bertrand Aristide won two-thirds of the vote in a race for the presidency against twelve other candidates.

Aristide took office in February 1991 when democracy seemed to reach a crest in the hemisphere. In June, foreign ministers from all the states of the Americas met in Santiago, Chile, at the General Assembly of the Organization of American States (OAS) to discuss new ways to strengthen democracy in the hemisphere. All approved a resolution that called for an emergency meeting of the OAS in the event of an unconstitutional change of government to be followed by specific actions to encourage the coup plotters to return power to constitutionally elected leaders.

On September 30, 1991, the military overthrew Aristide, and Haiti, a country with almost no experience in democracy, became the hemisphere's first test of its commitment to restore it. OAS foreign ministers met in emergency session in Washington, condemned the coup in the strongest terms, called for the restoration of democracy, and sent a group of foreign ministers to Port-au-Prince to negotiate Aristide's return. This exercise in multilateral diplomacy proved to be worse than a disaster.

The foreign ministers knew little or nothing about the military leaders or even the country. The new military leaders handled the diplomats' arrival with the ineptitude that one would expect from a group that was desperate to find a purpose for its coup and eager to assert its nationalism. The generals treated the mediators with utter disrespect, and the foreign ministers returned to Washington and recommended sanctions and a trade embargo against the military regime.

Why did this mediation fail? OAS foreign ministers viewed their role more as judges than problem solvers. They judged the coup a violation of the Santiago Declaration, and they arrived in Port-au-Prince to present their conclusions and order the military to step down. It was hard to imagine a less effective approach to the military. The OAS foreign ministers then disagreed on how tight to make the embargo, and the result was that the embargo was not effective, and the international community and the Haitian military froze into an unproductive relationship.

Aristide escaped with his life largely because of the efforts of U.S. ambassador Alvin Adams, and the young president went into exile first in Venezuela, then Europe, and finally Washington. Wherever he went, Aristide marshaled international support for his return. The Caribbean states, led by Jamaican prime minister Michael Manley, realized that a diplomatic effort without a credible threat of force would not succeed. Manley approached Secretary of State James A. Baker III in December 1991 with a proposal for a multinational force, not unlike the one that intervened in Grenada in October 1983.[2]

After the invasion of Panama and especially after the triumph of Desert Storm, President George Bush did not have to prove his willingness to use force to defend U.S. interests. It made little sense to risk U.S. lives in an election year for a leader whose stability was questioned by the administration and in a place where few thought U.S. interests were directly engaged.[3] Bush demurred. The principal Haitian issue that concerned the Bush administration was refugees, but Bush solved that by returning all Haitian refugees to the island. Presidential candidate Bill Clinton criticized this policy as inconsistent with American tradition and international law, but soon after his election, intelligence reports of a new wave of refugees led Clinton to adopt the same policy. With African Americans as a core base of his political constituency, however, an antirefugee policy was unsustainable, and so Clinton pledged to restore Aristide to power.

It took eighteen months for Clinton to come to grips with the implications of that promise. In the fall of 1992, the OAS secretary-general asked Manley, who had recently resigned from his position as Jamaican prime minister because of poor health, to be a special envoy to negotiate the return of Aristide, but Manley still believed that the negotiations would be futile without a credible threat. He and I worked out an arrangement in November 1992 whereby he would ask the UN secretary-general to appoint former president Carter to be the UN envoy and jointly negotiate U.S.-Caribbean military support for an enhanced mediation effort. Manley, UN secretary-general Boutros Boutros-Ghali, Carter, and I met in Atlanta in December 1992. Carter spoke with President-elect Clinton several times, and the Venezuelan president, Carlos Andrés Pérez, a close friend of Manley's and Carter's, threw his support behind the arrangement. Everything seemed in order, but then Boutros-Ghali returned to New York and appointed a former Argentine foreign minister as his special envoy. Manley, feeling betrayed, resigned from his position as OAS special envoy. Why did this effort fail? First, Clinton was not willing to commit himself to a policy or to Carter at that time, and second, some of Boutros-Ghali's UN advisers were ideologically opposed to the idea of using an ex-president of the United States as a UN mediator. Haitians suffered from this second missed opportunity.

During the next eighteen months, the United Nations and the United States pursued a number of diplomatic options backed up by threats against the Haitian military junta. Those threats proved empty, and the Haitian military drew the obvious conclusion.

The most significant nonevent was the attempted landing of the USS *Harlan County* that was bringing 218 U.S. and Canadian military engineers on October 11, 1993, for a noncombat mission in Port-au-Prince to prepare for Aristide's return. The landing was part of an agreement reached on July 4, 1993, at Governors Island in New York.[4] The timing, however, was bad, soon after the gruesome public death of American troops in the chaos surrounding a U.S.-UN intervention in Somalia. When Haitian thugs, obviously orchestrated by the regime, threatened the ship, the Pentagon feared another Somalia and persuaded the president to withdraw it. The American bluff had been called.

The withdrawal proved so embarrassing, however, that the president seriously contemplated military intervention during the subsequent week.[5] He wisely chose not to do so then, but this event sat heavily on his mind. This incident was comparable in some ways to the embarrassment that President Bush suffered in October 1989 in Panama when the United States failed to come to the support of officers trying to overthrow General Manuel Antonio Noriega. Neither Bush nor Clinton wanted to repeat that mistake, but Noriega and Cedras drew a conclusion opposite that of the two presidents. They thought that since the president had shown weakness once, he would show it a second time.

In July 1994, U.S. leadership in the United Nations led the UN Security Council to approve Resolution 940 that called on member states "to use all necessary means to facilitate the departure from Haiti of the military leadership."[6] This was an unprecedented and historic statement by the international community; it was the first time that the United Nations legitimized the use of force in the internal affairs of a country in defense of democracy. Clinton's threats against the Haitian generals became more blunt, although they were not interpreted any differently by the generals than those that he had made before. Port-au-Prince did not take the threats seriously when Washington began to discuss possible invasion plans in the summer.[7] Although support for the possible use of military force "to restore a democratic government in Haiti" increased from roughly 36 percent in a survey of American public opinion on May 15 to 45 percent on June 26, opposition still exceeded that,[8] and it began to coalesce from different sources. Conservative Republicans viewed Aristide a leftist, if not a communist, and did not want him returned to power. Some moderates believed that the United States should employ force only when its vital interests were threatened, and they did not believe that the restoration of democracy in Haiti constituted a vital interest of the United States.

## THE CARTER CONNECTION

Although rebuffed by the Clinton administration in the winter of 1992, Jimmy Carter and Carter Center staff continued to pursue the Haiti issue. The center's involvement in Haiti had begun a year after Jean-Claude Duvalier had fled Haiti in February 1986. In the fall of 1987, just after the assassination of a leading candidate for president, leaders from various nongovernmental organizations invited Carter to Haiti. Carter invited George Price, the prime minister of Belize, to join him. Price was a member of the Council of Freely Elected Heads of Government, a group of presidents and prime ministers of the Americas, that was established at a meeting of the Carter Center in October 1986. Carter's trip stabilized the situation, but the presidential elections were aborted two months later by the military.

In the summer of 1990, the provisional president of Haiti, Ertha Pascal-Trouillot, invited Carter and the council to observe the elections scheduled in December, and the council agreed to work with the National Democratic Institute for International Affairs (NDI). Through trial and error, the Carter Center had learned that observing elections in a country with little or no experience in democracy required an active mediating role over an extended period of time—both before and after the election. As a result, Carter and his colleagues made numerous trips to Haiti between the summer of 1990 and Aristide's inauguration in February 1991. On each trip, council members worked to address all parties' complaints about the electoral process so that by the eve of the election, the council had gained the trust of all the candidates and the Haiti Election Commission, which was responsible for conducting the election. The Carter Center also worked closely with the military and with Colonel Raoul Cedras, who was the officer designated to assure public order on election day. Cedras did well then.

After the coup, Cedras became a general and the commander in chief of the army, and in July 1993, a close friend of Cedras's passed a message, inviting Carter to Haiti and indicating that "Cedras has complete confidence in President Carter's objectiveness and world perspective." However, the message arrived at a tense moment in the negotiations between the United Nations and the Haitian military, and Carter did not pursue it.

After the coup, Aristide visited the Carter Center several times and stayed in close touch with Carter and me. He also joined the Council of Freely Elected Heads of Government and worked closely with two leading council members, Carlos Andrés Pérez of Venezuela and Michael Manley of Jamaica.

Carter continued to offer ideas to President Clinton on Haiti policy, writing detailed memoranda to him in October 1993 and May 1994, but the administration did not respond to Carter's many offers to help.

Then, on August 6, less than one week after the passage of the UN Security Council resolution sanctioning an invasion of Haiti, Robert Novak conducted a CNN interview in Port-au-Prince with General Raoul Cedras. Novak asked whether he would welcome a mediation by Carter. Cedras answered positively: "I met Mr. Carter in 1990 when I was in charge of security for the election of 1990. He did good work in Haiti. I am open to dialogue with all those who come to understand the Haitian problem."

This report precipitated other speculation of a Carter trip to Haiti, and the de facto foreign minister, Cedras's brother, and others contacted me at the Carter Center to invite Carter to Haiti. On September 12, National Security Adviser Anthony Lake warned Cedras that the invasion clock would strike midnight in "minutes, not hours." After so many threats, it was obvious that Lake's watch had not been synchronized by Swiss craftsmen. The only question was whether the watch was a Timex that would keep on ticking after midnight, or whether time was really running out. When Carter returned from a trip to Africa the next day, I briefed him, and he began talks with Cedras and with President Clinton about the prospects for negotiations.

I recommended that Carter bring Senator Sam Nunn into the discussions and a senior Republican senator. Nunn suggested General Powell as an alternative. Both Nunn and Powell said that they would consider going only if President Clinton authorized the visit. Clinton then phoned Powell, and according to the latter, the president said, "Jimmy Carter is sometimes a wild card, but I took a chance on him in North Korea, and that didn't turn out too badly." The president wanted to make sure that Powell understood that if they went, the only purpose was to negotiate "how, not if, our troops would go ashore."[9]

That evening, the president addressed the American public on national television. He defined U.S. goals in Haiti, said that all diplomatic options had been tried and failed, and warned the generals to leave power. In fact, there had been no diplomatic initiatives for at least six months; the embassy had been prohibited from contacting Cedras or the provisional government. A few hours after the address, the president phoned Carter and tentatively approved the mission.

## THE TWENTY-FOUR-HOUR SOLUTION

The next afternoon, on Friday, September 16, at 5:00, President Clinton finally authorized the three of them to leave the following morning at 7:00. Carter asked me to accompany and advise the group and prepare a schedule and strategy by 4:00 A.M.—the time I had to leave the office to meet the plane at Warner Robbins Air Force Base.

The Carter-Nunn-Powell (CNP) team understood its objectives but intended to approach the Haitian military very differently than the Clinton administration preferred. This is not surprising. The administration had already moved to a war footing. The three-day countdown to an invasion had begun. In the early evening, National Security Council officials sent us "talking points," which were nothing more than insults and threats. Carter sought my views, and I told him that if the administration insisted that CNP use the paper, there was no sense going. Carter phoned the president, who was prepared to give him more flexibility.

A second clue of the administration's perspective came at 2:00 A.M. when a senior official phoned me with a report that apparently came from the U.S. embassy in Port-au-Prince. The essence of the report was that the CNP team was not invited and not welcome by the Haitian military; the plane would not be permitted to land, but if it did, the Haitians would take military action against the team. I thanked the official for the information and told him that the team would still go. I interpreted the report to mean that the U.S. embassy had no contact with the Haitian military, and that officials were not aware that Carter had informed President Clinton about the invitation.

Each member of the mediation team approached the negotiations with the benefit of a distinct but complementary background. As someone who had traveled to Haiti many times, knew Cedras, and had mediated a host of Third World conflicts, Carter not only brought the stature of a former president but also familiarity with the specific case. His skills in mediation derived from a combination of charm, empathy, mastery of detail, and a focus on the finishing line.[10] Carter's determination and courage surprised Powell.

Sam Nunn was then chairman of the Senate Armed Service Committee and the most respected individual in the Senate and, to most informed individuals, in the country on national security issues. Carter had great respect for his judgment, and Nunn brought a cool, calm wisdom to the deliberations and a keen lawyer's eye to the text of the agreement. A few days before the trip, Nunn spoke on the Senate floor against an invasion, which impressed the Haitians and gave him greater credibility when he delivered the hard message that he would support an invasion when it came.

General Colin Powell had been chairman of the Joint Chiefs of Staff under Presidents Bush and Clinton. The victor of Desert Storm, Powell was being touted in the United States as the "Eisenhower of the 1990s," but everyone in Haiti and the Caribbean knew and admired him as a son of Jamaican immigrants who had risen to the highest military office in the United States.

Together, Carter, Nunn, and Powell were skeptical if not opposed to a U.S. invasion, but they understood that the president had already decided, and that their job was to use the leverage provided by that decision to persuade the Haitian generals to leave power peacefully. From years of experience, the three also understood that they would have to listen closely to the Haitians, to put on their shoes in order to persuade the Haitians to leave office.

Soon after their arrival, Carter, Nunn, and Powell met with the former army commander in chief, General Herard Abraham, one of the shrewdest political actors in the country. It had been Aristide's decision in the summer of 1991 to replace Abraham that eventually culminated in the coup. (Aristide himself later acknowledged the mistake.) Abraham said that the delegation would have to pay respects to the provisional government and not insist that the general staff go into exile—astute comments as it turned out. Then, disregarding the objections of administration officials, the group met the foreign minister of the de facto government; he had technically invited Carter, Nunn, and Powell. He encouraged the group to think of alternatives besides war or insisting on surrender.

The next stop—at 2:00 P.M.—was the National Military Command Center for their first meeting with General Cedras, General Biamby, and the general staff. After an exchange of courtesies, Carter and his colleagues explained to the generals quietly but with great care that an invasion would occur if the negotiations failed. Up until that moment, the Haitian military did not believe that the United States would invade. There had been too many bluffs in the past. All three said they were against this invasion, but the American people would support it when it occurred. And when Powell described in extraordinarily vivid detail exactly how it would happen, any question about the willingness of Clinton to use force that remained in the minds of the Haitian generals had dissolved.

After putting the threat on the table, the three Americans put it aside, never to use it again in the negotiations. Instead, they listened and worked through a series of points that together made up the final agreement.

The general staff were coming from a very different direction than the administration had anticipated. They never raised issues related to their exile or money, which were the only issues that the administration thought they would raise. They saw themselves as representing, in effect, the ancien régime, protecting the country against a leader whose return would bring chaos.

Cedras alone spoke for the general staff. He spoke of the nation's history in fighting for its independence against Napoleon's imperial army and then resisting every form of foreign interference after that. He knew his army could not prevail against the American forces, but national pride required that they fight and resist. General Powell empathized and discussed how a new Haitian-U.S. military agreement could not only assure stability during the transition but permit a renewal and modernization of the armed forces. Senator Nunn said that he would be prepared to support such an aid program in Congress. Carter said that amnesty was possible, but he returned to the central point of the talks: UN forces would arrive in war or in peace, Aristide would return, and General Cedras would have to step down and go into exile.

The Haitians made very clear that they were not prepared to countenance exile, as it was unconstitutional to banish a Haitian, and second, they did not want a relationship with the United Nations. They were willing to consider a new relationship only with U.S. forces, but the delegation had to pay respects to the provisional government of Emile Jonassaint, which was one of several governments that the military had installed after the coup. That was the opening. Even more significant was Cedras's remark at the end of the first round of talks at 5:45 P.M. Cedras pleaded with Carter: "You cannot leave Haiti without a solution. Speak to others. We have great respect for you, but you don't have the right to leave the country knowing your mission could be a failure."

The group had dinner with political and business leaders and made clear that Aristide's return was inevitable, and that they needed to adapt to it. Marc Bazin, a former senior official of the World Bank, who had placed a far second to Aristide in the 1990 presidential election, suggested to Carter that the group meet with Cedras's family: "Cedras's wife is very strong and influential."

After the meeting, Carter, Nunn, Powell, and I retreated to Carter's suite to review Carter's draft proposal. We went through three drafts, and then returned to the National Military Command Center for a meeting that began at 10:50 P.M. and ended at 2:00 A.M. Carter put the main elements of the proposal before the military; we discussed it at some length, and the military asked for time to consider it. We agreed to meet the next morning.

At 6:00 A.M., Carter asked me to arrange a meeting with Cedras's family after our breakfast at the ambassador's. We were supposed to meet with a group of Aristide's principal supporters, but the only one who came was the mayor of Port-au-Prince, Evans Paul. It was an ominous sign that we failed to recognize at the time, believing that Aristide's other supporters were simply afraid of traveling to the ambassador's residence because of the state of fear in the city. In fact, Aristide was very upset by the entire negotiation and probably told his people not to attend.

The team then went to Cedras's home. What would have been a nice middle-class house in the United States was palatial in poor Haiti but not atypical among elite army officers. Cedras's wife was a strong, articulate woman whose father and grandfather had both been commanders in chief of the army. She told us that the entire family had made a pact the night before that they would die together in the house when the invasion occurred. It was obvious why Cedras felt he had so little room for maneuver; she was prepared for an invasion and believed the military had to fight. Carter and Nunn argued for alternatives, but the key figure was Colin Powell. We knew that she admired Powell greatly, but President Clinton had called Powell out of the breakfast to talk about the status of the talks. Finally, Powell returned and explained that the honorable path for a soldier was to reach agreement with the United States.

After this very emotional meeting, we returned to the military headquarters but only after stopping to see the provisional president, Jonassaint, who pulled Powell aside after the meeting and asked him to return to help rebuild the military just as MacArthur had done in Japan!

The High Command had worked through the night on its proposal, which took a few elements from the CNP paper, including the main one permitting U.S. forces to enter Haiti. But the proposal, presented in English, posed conditions on their arrival and operation that were clearly unacceptable. The real negotiations began. After about ninety minutes, a few minutes beyond the deadline, the Haitians accepted compromises from CNP that permitted the three to report to the president that they had achieved the principal goal—getting approval of the entry of U.S. forces and flexibility on their operations—but they needed more time to set a deadline for Aristide's return and the generals' departure.

## Four-Sided Talks

The negotiations were occurring not only between the three Americans and the Haitian military, but also between the American mediators and President Clinton and between the administration and President Aristide in Washington. And President Aristide was proving very difficult. Subsequently, Aristide's aides confided that they had hoped for an invasion to destroy the military. Aristide wanted it both ways: he wanted an invasion, but did not want to invite or endorse it, and he also did not want to see President Clinton retreat.

CNP were asked to incorporate some important issues and some minor details that took time because the military was already feeling as if it had given up more than it should have. Washington was uncertain about the proposal and when it was faxed, some officials thought the proposal was CNP's and insisted on rewriting it completely, not realizing that the proposal represented the military's rewriting of the original CNP proposal.

When the administration sent a different proposal at about 1:00 P.M., CNP were confused, but took some of the important language and tried to insert it into the existing Haitian proposal.

We did not know that the countdown for an invasion had already begun, and by 2:00 P.M. on Sunday, September 18, the U.S. invasion checklist was advanced. Later I discussed with our military officers, including General Hugh Shelton, now the chairman of the Joint Chiefs of Staff, their perceptions. Shelton was on the aircraft carrier offshore that was responsible for the first wave of troops and planes. He said that every time they checked a major item on their list, they would turn on CNN and see us walk into another meeting, and they would all scream at the television, "Get out of there!"

The tension in the president's voice grew with each conversation. Finally, at 4:00 P.M., General Philippe Biamby, who was the number two in the Haitian military forces, burst into the talks and said that he had intelligence that the 82nd Airborne was getting its parachutes and was about to depart for an invasion. He said that the negotiations were over, and he was taking General Cedras, the commander in chief, out of the room, to prepare the nation's defenses. The talks would end. He grabbed Cedras and began to leave. Carter stepped between them and made a passionate case to end the negotiations by signing the agreement. It was a very tense moment. Carter then asked me to stay with the military while he went to speak to the president. I tried some small talk, however incongruous it now sounds.

When Carter returned, he asked the foreign minister to call Emile Jonassaint for a meeting with CNP and Cedras. It was a brilliant move because Cedras could not reject the request from the civilian authorities. In the earlier meeting with Jonassaint, we had tested his interest in such an agreement and found him ready. So Carter, Nunn, and Powell took Cedras with them to the presidential palace.

I was left to finish typing the agreement on my computer, with Biamby and the others getting pumped for war. I thought to myself, "Guys, do you mind keeping it down? I'm trying to finish this agreement!" I finished typing it. I raced down the stairs.

Just to give you a sense of the mood, for that whole thirty hours, hundreds of military "attachés" were screaming at us, at high pitch, waving their machetes right outside the headquarters, as a way to intimidate us. And as you know, that kind of noise can wear you down after a while. Well, I was so flustered, I raced downstairs with the agreement and my computer under my arm, right into this crowd of thugs, and they were, fortunately, as surprised as I was, and more interested in Carter, Nunn, and Powell's car than in me.

At the presidential palace, Jonassaint asked the military, "Can you defend us against attack?" Cedras said no. Jonassaint said, "In that case, I'm signing this agreement." The minister of defense resigned. Cedras would not sign the agreement, and it was still not clear that President Clinton would authorize Carter to sign it. But at the end, the agreement was signed.

Carter, Nunn, and Powell returned to Washington, and I remained to brief the ambassador and the Joint Chiefs and to set up meetings the next day, as were required, between the U.S. military and the Haitian military that would permit the peaceful entry of U.S. forces.

The problem was that the U.S. embassy and the U.S. military didn't believe the agreement would work and had postponed, not canceled, the invasion until the next morning. I tried to explain that option wasn't chosen, but I wasn't in a position to convince them. I called Carter on Air Force One as he was flying to the White House and tried to explain the issue to him so that he could raise it with the president.

It was very hard to reach Cedras to set up this meeting. With barely ninety minutes before the troops would land, I finally persuaded Cedras's wife to arrange a meeting with him, General Jared Bates from the Joint Chiefs, Ambassador Bill Swing, and me. I told her that he needed to meet us in fifteen minutes, as 3,500 American troops were going to land at the airport with twenty helicopter gunships. During the meeting, both sides were able to discuss details for cooperation and the terms of engagement between the two forces. We then raced to the airport just as the helicopters were landing. General Shelton had the courage and the foresight to understand the situation, and despite advice he received from some of his aides, he came to town to meet with Cedras. Despite near universal skepticism, the agreement held.

## Ten Lessons

For three frustrating years, between the military overthrow of Haitian president Aristide on September 30, 1991, and his return to power on October 15, 1994, the United States and the international community wrestled with the "problem" of Haiti. An assortment of mediators-negotiators was deployed with a quiver of weapons, including international condemnation, diplomatic isolation, repeated negotiations, economic and financial sanctions, threats, and finally the use of force. All but the last mediating effort by Carter, Nunn, and Powell failed to achieve the objective.

How would one define the "case" of Haiti, and from where did all the mediation missions come? Why did the other mediations fail? Why did the Carter team succeed? What can be learned from the case that would contribute to the theory and practice of international mediation?

In the past two hundred years, until Aristide's return, Haiti experienced about seven months of democracy.[11] Yet the coup that overthrew that very fragile flower was seen as a "crisis" by the international community requiring a response. The reason had more to do with the changes in the hemisphere and the world than they did with Haiti, and the failure of the earliest mediation efforts—by the OAS and the United Nations—were due partly to the fact that the international community knew very little about Haiti and even less about the military that took power. The Bush administration and, to a slightly lesser degree, the Clinton administration saw the Haitian crisis as a refugee problem, and after "solving" that, the need to deal with the harder political challenge diminished.

To those who understood the mind-set of the Haitian military, the problem could not be solved until the international community or the United States dispatched a skillful mediator reinforced by the decision to use force in the event of failure. To reach that point took nearly three years of trial and error.

What lessons can we drawn from the entire experience?

First, the age-old adage of the need to connect diplomacy and the use of force is correct. The proper equation can change the balance of decision making in a manner that can compel leaders to recalculate their options and choose a different course than they would have in the absence of adept mediators backed by force. That equation is easy to conceptualize but very hard to execute.

Second, an effective mediation requires understanding why it is so difficult to find a practical expression to the conventional wisdom on diplomacy and force. It is not just because a state's leaders are inexperienced, although this might be the case; there are numerous structural reasons why it is so difficult to balance "power with principle," as Zbigniew Brzezinski once wrote, and the difficulties of doing that are multiplied when the task requires approval by a multinational organization like the United Nations. The answer to the question as to why it was so difficult to back up threats with force for two and a half years, and why it was so difficult to authorize serious negotiations once the president decided to use force lies embedded in the concept of the democratic peace. Democracies find it difficult to employ force unless their direct security interests are threatened, which was, of course, not the case in Haiti. And, therefore, although the president threatened force, he was reluctant to use it because he knew American lives would be lost, and the operation could fail. He was not ready to cross that threshold until "politics"—the pressure from the Black Caucus and others—compelled him to recognize that his power and prestige were at risk for failing to deliver on his repeated pledge to restore Aristide to power.

The other side of that equation is: Why, after you make that decision, can't you negotiate? Why, for a six-month period preceding the entry of U.S. troops, were there no serious talks with the military or with Jonassaint? If the answer to the first question resided in a "democratic peace," then the answer to the second can be found in the "logic of war." As a democracy moves closer toward war, its leaders demonize its adversary for an obvious reason. It's hard to persuade a nation to risk its children's lives and to murder others unless the other side is evil. The problem is that once a people are convinced that they face a heinous enemy, it is hard to entertain serious negotiations. To understand just how difficult such talks would be, imagine Israel negotiating with Hamas after the suicide bombings? Or the United States negotiating with Libya? The democratic connection is both solution and problem on this issue.

The issue, then, for policymakers is how to mobilize a populace for war while retaining the space to negotiate. This is easier to do for a dictatorship, but it's not impossible for a democracy. The president has to build a critical mass of support in the U.S. Congress and once he feels he can threaten credibly, identify the people who can best deliver the message.

That brings us to the third lesson: finding the right mediator. It should be a person or persons with experience in the country, credibility with the key actors, and a mediator's special skills. All good mediators understand that an effective negotiation requires an ability to listen to the other side *and to convince the other side that one is listening*. In the case of Haiti, President Clinton selected three mediators who understood intuitively that to accomplish anything they needed to show respect to their interlocutors. The basic lesson here is that a good mediator needs to get into the shoes of his adversary. This is more easily understood in the abstract than it is in the confines of a tropical room when there are hundreds of people screaming at you from outside. For all these reasons, as a situation becomes tense, a political actor is more likely to want to get under the skin of his adversary than to think about ways to get into his shoes.

By choosing mediators of great political stature like Carter, Nunn, and Powell, the president also takes a serious risk because they have autonomous power. No doubt, that was why Clinton contemplated that option for so long. In the end, he chose wisely, but he also paid something of a political price.

The fourth lesson is that deadlines are dangerous but unavoidable. Samuel Johnson once wrote that knowing one will die in a fortnight concentrates one's mind. Up until the critical moments of a negotiation, both sides have powerful reasons for not making the decision they are being asked to make—in Haiti, for the military to give up power, or for President Clinton to use force or to retreat. Both sides want the other to make the decision. The only way to get closure on a negotiation is to impose a deadline. That was very effective in Port-au-Prince.

The fifth lesson is that a mediator needs to purposively drive toward closure. This is one of Carter's strengths. He has a way of focusing on the principal goal and not allowing anything to divert him from achieving that, and Nunn and Powell, possessing the same strength, reinforced Carter.

The sixth lesson is that once the major goal is accomplished, the deadline can be relaxed. There is a certain dynamic in any tough negotiation. When one side makes the major concession, it often needs some time or something symbolic or real to reduce the humiliation. In the case of the Haitian talks, the military conceded the entry of U.S. troops, but at that moment, the administration insisted on other demands—for example, an October 15 deadline for the return of President Aristide—which were reasonable, though not essential, but which also needed more time to negotiate. Having achieved the principal goal, the negotiators should have received an extension of twelve hours to wrap up a satisfactory agreement.

The seventh lesson is to find a way to seal the agreement. This often requires a symbolic concession, which might come back to haunt the negotiators. To close the agreement, Carter told Cedras: "If you cannot accept the agreement, I can assure you that there is no way to stop the invasion. If you can accept the agreement, that will be an honorable decision and I can assure you that I will be at your side and will express my gratitude and admiration for your decision."

After the events, Carter was criticized for being too complimentary of Cedras, but this was part of what Carter felt was necessary to complete the agreement. Similarly, Powell told Cedras that if he stepped down, Powell would make sure that it was with full military honors. Again, that proved difficult to implement, once Aristide returned, but it was a helpful element to complete the negotiations.

The eighth lesson is that it is important to have an exit strategy. Again, this is rarely done. On the eve of the departure for Haiti, the administration still had not asked the group what they would say if the talks failed. In numerous talks with Carter over three months, I repeatedly asked this question of him. Four out of six times he agreed that he would, in effect, not only condemn the Haitian military but also endorse the U.S. invasion. But the administration never asked or sought such a commitment from him, and so it found itself in an awkward position as the deadline approached. If the three mediators announced they had reached agreement, but the administration rejected it, would Congress have accepted a war? Doubtful.

The ninth lesson derives from a critical distinction between the threat and the use of force. *The credible threat of force facilitated an agreement; the actual decision to use force came within a hair of scuttling the talks and, in the end, created a new problem for the United States.* Biamby shut down the negotiations on learning that the invasion was under way; only Carter's quick decision to change the negotiating venue from the military headquarters to the presidential palace kept the talks going. But that move created serious problems for Aristide and the administration that refused to recognize the legitimacy of the provisional government. But by then, it was clear the military would not sign, and that a fall-back option was needed.

Finally, one needs to be careful *not* to generalize. All cases have their unique and generalizable features. Haiti is uniquely isolated from the world, and the only way to move the military out of power was to alter the terms of the decision. There are other kinds of issues that can be solved by a free election, and intercommunal tensions that will take centuries to resolve. It is always useful to ask how other cases are different, not just how they are similar.[12]

* * *

The world is not a laboratory that will hold still while a social scientist changes one variable to see if that will produce a different result. But the Haiti mediation was as close to a hothouse laboratory as one is likely to find, and the outcome was on such a knife-edge that it almost went wrong several times. We know these three mediators reached an agreement. Could a different set of mediators have succeeded? Could they have failed?

There were three critical moments. The first was at deadline—on noon, on Sunday. It is hard to imagine a different set of mediators standing up to the president at that moment and insisting that they be permitted to stay. Within a few hours, Powell learned that an invasion was in process, and at a discreet moment, told the others, and so they understood the reason for the tension in the president's voice. And yet none of them dodged the bullet. All insisted that they complete their job.

The second moment occurred when General Biamby burst into the room and insisted on stopping the talks. Here again is a perfect example of the counterproductive use of force in a delicate negotiation. By shifting the venue to the presidential palace, Carter created serious problems for the administration and Aristide, but he also saved the talks.

We know what would have happened if the negotiations had failed. When I was driving to the Haitian military headquarters the Monday morning after the agreement had been signed, a senior military officer described in great detail which buildings would have been bombed, and what were the anticipated casualties. Many Haitians would have died, and some Americans as well. The healing challenge that faced Aristide was simply nothing as compared with what would have happened if there had been a violent invasion, and that would have happened if negotiations failed.

The third moment occurred the morning after. We were within two hours of an invasion. By that time, the Haitian forces were not on alert, but the prospects of some violence, either deliberately or by accident, were very high in the absence of a clear statement from the High Command. That only occurred after the meeting was arranged with the U.S. ambassador and military.

This case, in brief, offers ten valuable lessons on what can go wrong, and how to increase the chance that it goes right. Many of these lessons suggest that democracy is both the solution and part of the problem, and that we need to learn more before democracies can threaten and negotiate effectively.

**NOTES**

1. This was no coincidence, but rather the result of years of mediation among the political parties by the Carter Center–based Council of Freely Elected Heads of Government, National Democratic Institute, the United Nations, and the OAS. See the reports of the United Nations and the OAS and the Council of Freely Elected Heads of Government and National Democratic Institute for International Affairs, *The 1990 General Elections in Haiti* (Washington, D.C.: National Democratic Institute, 1991).

2. Interview with former prime minister Michael Manley, December 1992, Atlanta, Georgia.

3. See James A. Baker III, *The Politics of Diplomacy: Revolution, War, and Peace, 1989–1992* (New York: G. P. Putnam's Sons, 1995), 601–602.

4. For a good survey of the talks leading up to the agreement, see James Morrell, *The Governors Island Accord on Haiti*, International Policy Report (Washington, D.C.: Center for International Policy, September 1993).

5. Confidential interview with a senior White House official in the Clinton administration.

6. The UN resolution was reprinted in *New York Times*, August 1, 1994, A6.

7. See "Should We Invade Haiti?" *Newsweek*, July 18, 1994, 40–43.

8. Richard Morin, "Support for Sending GIs to Haiti May Be Increasing, Poll Shows," *Washington Post*, June 29, 1994, A11.

9. Colin Powell with Joseph E. Persico, *My American Journey* (New York: Random House, 1995), 597–602.

10. For the definitive work on Carter's postpresidency, see Douglas Brinkley, *The Unfinished Presidency: Jimmy Carter's Journey beyond the White House* (New York: Viking, 1998), especially chap. 21 on Haiti.

11. See Robert A. Pastor, "A Popular Democratic Revolution in a Predemocratic Society: The Case of Haiti," in *Haiti Renewed: Political and Economic Prospects*, ed. Robert I. Rotberg (Washington, D.C.: Brookings Institution, 1997).

12. Richard E. Neustadt and Ernest R. May, *Thinking in Time: The Uses of History for Decision Makers* (New York: Free Press, 1996).

## Background to Chapter 20

## The Oslo Accord: Multiparty Facilitation through the Norwegian Channel

Violence between Israelis and Palestinians has flared often since Israel achieved statehood in 1948, but the 1978 Camp David Accords initiated a turn toward negotiated settlement in the region. The 1991 Madrid process (see chapter 9) renewed attempts to resolve the ongoing conflict, and served as a precursor to the secret and informal "Norwegian channel." Norway facilitated this multiparty process, which included NGOs and government officials and eventually garnered the economic and diplomatic support of the United States. The two negotiating teams developed a mutual trust and affinity through hundreds of hours of close contact, and this led to an official (although not a face-to-face) dialogue between Israeli foreign minister Shimon Peres and PLO chairman Yasir Arafat. The two sides reached a series of groundbreaking agreements, known as the Oslo Accord. These accords, however, have yet to be fully implemented.

### MAJOR ACTORS
- Israel: led by Prime Minister Yitzhak Rabin and Foreign Minister Shimon Peres (negotiators: Uri Savir, Yair Hirschfeld, Ron Pundak, and Joel Singer)
- Palestine Liberation Organization (PLO): led by Chairman Yasir Arafat and Abu Mazen (negotiators: Abu Alá, Hassan Asfour, and Mohamed Abu Koush)

527

- Norway (facilitators: Mona Juul, Jan Egeland, and Terje Rød Larsen)
- United States (sponsor of official peace process)
- Ad Hoc Liaison Committee (AHLC): United States, European Union, Japan, Canada, Russia, Israel, and the Palestinian Authority, with Norway as chair; associated members: Egypt, Tunisia, and Jordan

## IMPORTANT DATES

- September 11, 1992: Norway offers to open communication between Israel and the PLO
- January 1993: First unofficial talks
- June 1993: Secret negotiations become official
- August 20, 1993: declaration of Principles initialed in Oslo, Norway
- September 13, 1993: Rabin and Arafat officially sign the declaration at the White House
- October 1, 1993: AHLC created to mobilize economic assistance to the Palestinians
- May 1994: Cairo Agreement forms Palestinian Authority
- August 1994: Early Empowerment Agreement gives Palestinians limited self-rule
- September 1995: Interim Agreement calls for elections and withdrawal of Israeli forces from West Bank
- February 1997: Agreement on redeployment from Hebron reached

## KEY AGREEMENTS REACHED

- Declaration of Mutual Recognition
- Palestinian self-rule to be established, with elections to be held in Gaza, Jericho, and the West Bank; Palestinian Authority to exercise responsibility for education, culture, health, social welfare, taxation, and tourism
- Palestinian Authority and Police Force to be created
- Israeli forces to be withdrawn from the West Bank
- Support to be given for development of infrastructure and security

## PRINCIPAL OUTCOMES

- The armed conflict between Israel and the PLO has been ended with mutual recognition and peaceful negotiations aiming toward a final settlement of the conflict.
- Although a plan for Palestinian self-government was agreed upon, it has yet to be fully implemented; it was agreed that discussions on the status of Jerusalem and of refugees and of the final status of the Palestinian entity and Jewish settlements in the occupied territories would be left to a later phase

# 20

# The Oslo Accord
## Multiparty Facilitation through the Norwegian Channel

JAN EGELAND

The "Norwegian channel," which led to the Oslo Accord, was a multi-party effort to seize a historic window of opportunity to bring together for the first time two old enemies: Israel and the Palestine Liberation Organization (PLO). In an informal and secret back channel, three Palestinian and four Israeli negotiators, assisted by a handful of Norwegian facilitators, soon produced remarkable joint proposals.

During eight hectic months in 1993, some fourteen rounds of secret negotiations in the Oslo area produced a mutually agreed Declaration of Principles. Initialed in Oslo at 1:30 A.M. on August 20 in the presence of only twenty negotiators and security police, the accord took Israeli, Palestinian, and world public opinion by complete surprise—not even the Israeli Mossad had detected the Norwegian back channel. A television audience of a billion people would later watch as the Oslo Accord (or "Oslo

Agreement"—both names are commonly used) was officially signed and sealed by the Rabin-Arafat handshake on the White House Lawn on September 13, 1993.

The Oslo process changed the whole political architecture of the Middle East. The two bitter enemies in the center of regional conflicts, Israel and the PLO, became each other's legitimate counterpart in peaceful negotiations seeking the end to an age-old dispute. Consequently, the local and global images of the two parties fundamentally changed. The PLO, regarded as a criminal "terrorist" organization by Israel and the United States, gained legitimacy and recognition where it counted most, in Jerusalem and Washington, D.C. Israel, regarded as a repressive "occupant" by the Arab countries and large parts of the Third World, received almost universal approval for its investment in the peace process.

The Israeli-Palestinian process is, however, still far from bringing peace to those two troubled peoples. The process fell way behind the original Oslo schedule, and mutual confidence built during the Norwegian channel became severely depleted. The counterforces were stronger than we originally expected. Terrorism has taken the lives of too many civilian Israelis and Palestinians, creating a paralyzing insecurity and derailing the talks. A new political leadership in Israel hostile to the original Oslo Accord midway in the implementation halted a process that needed gradual progress in order to avoid regression. Still, there is no alternative to the Oslo agreements. That became evident during the talks mediated by President Clinton at the Wye plantation in Maryland in October 1998.

The 1991 Madrid process of official talks between Israel and its Arab enemies had until the Oslo Accord seen little progress. The PLO, undisputedly the Palestinian political leadership, had been prevented from representing the Palestinians at those talks because of political and legal barriers primarily in Israel but also in the United States, which had initiated the Madrid talks and hosted most of the negotiations. In contrast, our confidential back channel to the ongoing formal and public Washington negotiations included from the beginning the highest levels of the PLO. The Israeli side was, owing to the political and legal barriers, in the first phase represented by two academics who had personal and organizational links to the new Israeli Labor government.

Our "third party" consisted of a few individuals from the leadership of the Norwegian Ministry of Foreign Affairs and the director of a nongovernmental think tank, the Institute for Applied Social Science (FAFO). From the government side we provided the necessary official aura and financial resources to create an attractive and serious atmosphere for negotiations. Equally important, our nongovernmental partner, a small, efficient, and flexible operator, provided an academic camouflage that gave the parties their much-needed "deniability."

The U.S. State Department was informed of and cautiously positive about the establishment of the Norwegian channel. When presented with the initialed but still secret Oslo Accord, the Clinton administration crucially decided to give its full political, diplomatic, and financial backing.

As a third party organizing and initiating the Norwegian channel, we undertook multiparty *facilitation* rather than mediation between the two enemies. The Israelis and the Palestinians turned out to be uniquely qualified for and motivated to doing the actual negotiations by themselves once we, the facilitators, had been able to organize a direct and confidential meeting place and a continuous and secret channel for communication.

The Norwegian channel also produced, in the two weeks that followed the initialing of the Oslo Accord, a Declaration of Mutual Recognition between Israel and the PLO, which was to transform the two parties from enemies into neighbors. Several rounds of negotiations in Oslo and Paris helped new, decisive elements in the peace process fall into place, ultimately leading to the Norwegian foreign minister's public shuttle diplomacy with the actual letters of recognition between Prime Minister Yitzhak Rabin and Chairman Yasir Arafat.

The five-year framework agreement on Palestinian self-government in Gaza and the West Bank was analyzed and discussed throughout the world. Palestinians and Israelis had agreed to establish the first-ever Palestinian self-rule, but agreed to disagree until a later phase of negotiations on the status of Jerusalem, the refugees, the final status of the Palestinian entity, and the Jewish settlements in the occupied territories. We, a small team of facilitators, were also thrown into the international spotlight. One question was asked countless times: How could a small country like Norway come to be at the center of such an international political drama?

### THE PRENEGOTIATIONS PHASE

A precondition for any effective third-party involvement in conflict resolution is gaining the confidence of the parties. It was Norway's close ties with Israel that made Norway so interesting to the PLO. Conversely, our direct contact with Chairman Arafat made Israel choose us as their back channel. Other countries had closer contact with the PLO than did Norway, and others had an even more unstrained relationship with Israel, but few had our trusted relationship with both.

After World War II, Norwegians, who had seen Jewish friends and neighbors rounded up during the Nazi occupation, felt a special sympathy for the Jewish people and for the state of Israel when it was established in 1948. Our Labor governments forged close ties with their Israeli counterparts. Although the Israeli occupation of the West Bank and Gaza after the 1967 Six Day War strained those ties, it did not destroy them. At the same time, sympathy for the plight of the occupied Palestinian people was growing, and through the 1970s and 1980s our Labor governments began to build relations with the PLO.

After the Gulf War in 1991, a weakened PLO was ready for peace and needed a third party through whom it could approach the Israelis. Norway came to be seen as an interesting candidate, recommended by, among others, the outgoing Swedish foreign minister, Sten Andersson, who was close to Arafat and who had helped establish an indirect channel for communication between the PLO and the U.S. State Department. Several PLO delegations came to Oslo in 1991–92 to ask Norway to facilitate direct contact with Israel at meetings with Foreign Minister Thorvald Stoltenberg and me. Our contact with Israel was also renewed and intensified. A new generation of Israeli "doves" had emerged within the Israeli Labor party, which won the elections in June 1992 with a clear mandate for peace.

Together with two personal friends, the director of FAFO, Terje Rød Larsen, and my Foreign Office assistant, Mona Juul, his wife, I got a green light from Foreign Minister Thorvald Stoltenberg to approach the two parties. On September 11, 1992, we asked my new Israeli counterpart, Deputy Minister Yossi Beilin, to facilitate direct or indirect lines of communication to the PLO.

We were able to provide the perfect camouflage for such a channel: extensive standard-of-living studies being carried out by FAFO in the West Bank and Gaza. These "studies" required frequent contact and meetings with Israeli and Palestinian counterparts. The discreet September 11 late-night meeting was held in my hotel room after an official dinner in Tel Aviv that Beilin had hosted for my delegation, which was visiting not only Israel but also Syria and Lebanon and Norwegian members of the UN peacekeeping mission UNIFIL. The meeting had been well prepared by Larsen and Juul with Beilin's old friend, Professor Yair Hirschfeld, the only other Israeli present. Beilin refused to see the PLO himself, but confirmed his interest in indirect contact, as the "Madrid set-up was bringing the peace process nowhere." It was generally recognized that the official multi-party negotiations had become too big, too public, and too much of a buffer between the real leaders who could make the real decisions regarding war or peace in the Middle East.

It was still a criminal offense under Israeli law for Israeli citizens to meet with the "terrorist" PLO when the two courageous Israeli academics, Yair Hirschfeld and his NGO colleague, Ron Pundak of the Economic Cooperation Foundation, confirmed their willingness to come to our first meeting in January 1993. Their counterpart was the minister of economy of the PLO, Abu Alá, a moderate force at PLO headquarters in Tunis whom we got to know during his visit to Oslo in February 1992. Two colleagues from the staffs of Chairman Arafat and Abu Mazen, respectively, had joined Abu Alá. A secluded country house in Sarpsborg, a hundred miles south of Oslo, was the venue for the first meetings.

The two teams were determined to break away from the tradition set by earlier Israeli-Palestinian talks and most Jewish-Arab discussions and agreed *not* to dwell on the past. I remember both sides saying during the very first meeting: "If we are to quarrel about the historic rights to these holy lands, about who was there first, or about who betrayed whom and when, we will sit here quarreling forever. We must agree to look to the future."

Abu Alá and his closest adviser, Hassan Asfour, as well as Yair Hirschfeld and Ron Pundak, were experts in the field of economics and development. Their no-nonsense, pragmatic approach soon produced results. They agreed on arrangements for self-rule, infrastructure development, and security. Importantly, they also agreed that self-rule could start up in Gaza and gradually grow to include the West Bank, an old proposal of Shimon Peres that previously had been totally rejected by the PLO. A draft common paper was drawn up following the second meeting in February. After the third session in the seclusion of the country house, the two teams agreed on a draft declaration of principles, which included many of the elements in the final, signed agreement.

We were amazed and elated. The academic contact point we had established proved to hold far greater potential than we had originally assumed. However, the paper had one major drawback: there was still no official backing from the Israeli side. Abu Alá had not failed to point out the asymmetric levels of the two delegations: high officials of the PLO "government" were sitting down with two unofficial Israeli citizens.

To mollify the Palestinians, I emphasized (when I visited the sessions in the Foreign Ministry limousine) that the Norwegian government was pleased that my counterpart, Yossi Beilin, had welcomed these talks. We were, however, more nervous than we appeared to be in front of the

Palestinians: we only had Beilin's and Hirschfeld's oral assurances that they would be in touch and in due time pass on any outcome to higher political decision makers. But, as Ron Pundak remarked in a private talk: "The other side will for some time have to live with uncertainty about whether they are negotiating with Rabin's Israel or with two monkeys."

## The Official Negotiations

It took two more months, April and May 1993, for Beilin to secure the support of Foreign Minister Shimon Peres and Prime Minister Yitzhak Rabin, who were both impressed by the constructive, businesslike, and moderate "Gaza-first" text drafted in Sarpsborg. After hundreds of telephone calls in which we kept Jerusalem and Tunis informed about the other's questions, answers, threats, and propositions, Beilin could report back that Israel had agreed to upgrade the talks to an official level.

Similar discussions took place in what the Palestinians described as the "Arafat kitchen" in Tunis. Only five Palestinian leaders participated in the "kitchen," including Chairman Arafat, Abu Mazen, and Abu Alá. For the Palestinian leadership, Israel's willingness to initiate direct talks with the PLO was a breakthrough, as it meant de facto recognition of the organization as the legitimate representative of the Palestinians. This recognition was also reflected in the provisions of the draft agreement, which stipulated that the PLO could start to govern at least parts of Palestinian territory immediately as Israeli forces withdrew.

The director general of the Israeli Foreign Ministry, Uri Savir, was sent to Oslo in May to "test the seriousness" of Abu Alá and his two colleagues, Hassan Asfour and Mohamed Abu Koush. Secrecy became even tighter. We never used hotels or other public venues for the negotiations nor the real names of our guests. We always used our VIP facilities at the Oslo airport so that our guests could avoid meeting people they might know and who might well have been surprised to see our guests in Norway. It was also important for the Palestinians to be taken swiftly through the airport because they were traveling under passports that had caused them and us embarrassing problems the first time they went through immigration.

For the official negotiations in June we used the two-hundred-year-old Heftye House belonging to Oslo municipality, which we needed, I said, for internal "Foreign Ministry seminars." As I prepared to leave the ministry and join the negotiators, our press spokesman rushed into my office with a dispatch from the Washington correspondent of Agence France Press (AFP) claiming that there was a secret Norwegian channel between Israel and the PLO. "My God, Jan, what are you up to now?" he asked. I told him to inform the Norwegian and international press that the AFP story was based on a misunderstanding, and probably referred to a large, public multilateral conference on Palestinian refugees in Oslo in May. This had actually taken place as part of the official U.S.-sponsored peace process and our elaborate smoke screen.

At the house I met Savir and Hirschfeld first. They read through the AFP report that quoted anonymous State Department sources. "I think we can deal with this, but don't tell the Palestinians since the negotiations are in a crucial phase," Savir told me. Ten minutes later I gave the same dispatch to Abu Alá, who calmly said he knew about the report through PLO intelligence and had already instructed Tunis on how to deal with it. "But don't show it to the Israelis," he said. "The negotiations are making good progress."

Rabin-Peres and Arafat–Abu Mazen were following the negotiations closely and imposed increasingly strict terms for their negotiators. Their goals were ambitious, but not mutually exclusive: the Israelis wanted maximum security for all their citizens indefinitely; the Palestinians wanted maximum self-rule, territory, and economic development immediately.

## BREAKDOWN AND BREAKTHROUGH

In July we experienced the first breakdown in the negotiations. We had rented a large country estate through a colleague of my wife some 150 miles north of Oslo and brought in the Norwegian security police to guard a session we hoped would see the final breakthrough. As talks turned official I realized that our guests, in particular the Palestinians, we thought, were running an increasing security risk from extremists who would not tolerate fraternization with the enemy. With the consent of the parties, our new foreign minister, Johan Jørgen Holst, told the head of the security police the necessary minimum about the channel. A team of eight policemen was then assigned to help us not only with security but also with the growing logistical demands as the sessions were organized more frequently, often with only a few days' notice.

We told the owners of the estate that we were bringing a group of eccentric Middle Eastern academics working round the clock to finish a book. We knew that the Israelis had received a green light from Rabin-Peres to agree to initial an agreement that would meet the Israeli demands. Terje Rød Larsen, Mona Juul, and I spent the last night on sofas, hoping that the final pieces of the puzzle would fit together in the next few hours. Instead, the two teams broke off their talks at 5:30 A.M. and asked to be taken to the airport. They had spent thirty-five of the forty-four hours at the house negotiating. When the owners of the estate awoke to prepare breakfast, we had all gone. After both teams had left Oslo to report home, we did not know whether there would be any further negotiations.

During the official negotiations in July and August, both sides engaged in brinkmanship realizing that a historic agreement might be within reach. The leaders thus instructed their negotiators to introduce a series of new and additional demands, but gave them little flexibility to accept new language from the opposing side.

In addition to Savir, Rabin had appointed Joel Singer to join the two original and unofficial Israeli negotiators, Yair Hirschfeld and Ron Pundak. Singer was a successful New York–based lawyer who had played an important role at the Camp David negotiations in the 1970s. His role was to scrutinize every word and meaning of the text and present hundreds of "clarifying" questions to Abu Alá and his two colleagues, Hassan Asfour and Mohamed Abu Koush.

The reason for the first breakdown in July was that the Israelis presented the other side with a new text, redrafted by Singer and containing numerous new elements that differed from the old Sarpsborg text. The Palestinians felt this was a violation of the "Sarpsborg spirit" of always having one joint text. Only after a long break and a "walk in the woods" taken by Abu Alá and Savir alone did the Palestinians agree to go through the new text line by line, formulating alternative Palestinian wording along the way. When the negotiators broke up they had settled dozens of smaller points, but still differed on the wording of some fundamental issues. These included any references to UN Resolutions 242 and 338 on Israel's occupation of Gaza and the West Bank, future negotiations on the permanent status, the organizing of elections in Jerusalem, and the redeployment plan for Gaza and Jericho.

This and subsequent breakdowns in the negotiations were always followed by daily contact with the parties by telephone. Larsen and Juul kept their cellular phones within reach on their twenty-four-hour watch and either called or were called by Uri Savir and Abu Alá continually to ask for or tell about developments on either side. This was an important part of our facilitation: to keep up a constant momentum by urging and begging them for new positions, clarifications, and talks. Having learned in the ministry that all phones might always be tapped I suggested that we used a primitive code. Thus we tried to avoid all references to names and countries. The prime minister level was termed "the grandfathers" (Rabin and Arafat), the foreign ministers became "the fathers" (Peres, Abu Mazen, Stoltenberg, and Holst), and the deputy ministers became "the sons" (Beilin, myself, and so forth). A typical call was: "They have already briefed their grandfather and will soon have news back. Have you informed yours?" "No, but the son sees his father today as he will talk with our grandfather tomorrow morning."

The parties agreed to a second meeting in July only a week after the first breakdown. This time the Palestinians presented the other side with a new document containing some twenty-five new elements. The Palestinian position paper included the establishment of a corridor between Gaza and Jericho, which the Israelis saw as effectively "cutting" Israel in two, and the reference to "the PLO" in all places where the text had previously referred to "the Palestinians." Predictably, the Israelis this time became angry and refused to negotiate "on this basis." The parties again broke up in frustration and the Israelis warned, "This may be the end of the channel."

We also traveled to Israel and Tunis between the sessions. In July Foreign Minister Holst had brought Juul, who was later joined by Larsen, for a previously scheduled visit to Tunis where they had several meetings with Arafat. Attending some UN meetings in Geneva, I was called by Uri Savir, who urgently wanted Juul and Larsen to come to Jerusalem as Rabin and Peres had started to doubt the intentions of Arafat and the internal clout of Abu Alá. After dozens of calls between Geneva, Oslo, Tunis, and Jerusalem, Larsen and Juul the next day flew directly from Tunis to Israel where they reported on the most recent talks with Arafat and Abu Alá. Reluctantly, Rabin agreed to continue the talks. In late July and early August, steady progress demonstrated the willingness of the leadership on both sides to run the race to its end.

As in other tough negotiations the final points of contention were lifted to the highest levels and left for the final hours before the final deadline. Shimon Peres's official visit to the Scandinavian countries in mid-August became our perceived deadline for initialing the agreement. In the early morning of August 17, Peres called Foreign Minister Holst, who was visiting in Iceland: "Can you meet me discreetly in Stockholm tonight? It is now or never." That night Holst sat for eight hours with a phone at the Swedish Haga Castle and transmitted messages from Peres next door to Arafat, who sat in his office in Tunis. At 5:00 A.M. the final wording on security for Israeli settlers and on the location and authority of the future-elected Palestinian Council were agreed on. The negotiators embraced in Tunis as well as at the Swedish castle.

On the evening of August 19, we could, finally, host our official dinner for Shimon Peres, who started his official visit to Norway on that very day. The conversation revolved around general Norwegian-Israeli ties, but those of us who knew what was to come after the dinner guests had taken their leave could think of nothing else. Just after midnight, the Norwegian Security Service escorted the Palestinian and Israeli negotiating teams through the back entrance. They brought with them the final, agreed version of the Declaration of Principles, signaling peace at last between Israel and the PLO.

The last editing of the text had been undertaken only hours before at what was the fourteenth round of secret negotiations in Norway. At 1:00 A.M. Foreign Minister Peres joined our small group as an observer when the heads of the two negotiating teams, Abu Alá and Uri Savir, initialed the historic Declaration of Principles. A greeting from Chairman Arafat was read aloud. It seemed as if the channel had lasted forever, though only eight months had elapsed since the first session in January.

## The Advantages of the Back Channel

Our secret meetings proved to have several advantages over traditional conference diplomacy. First, the news media, which tend to focus on what divides rather than on what unites, were not involved. As a former news reporter and a strong believer in free speech and open societies, I was struck by how disruptive the constant news coverage was at public peace negotiations for the Middle East. As soon as the delegates arrived in Washington or other official venues, journalists would confront them with the more hostile comments made by the opposing side, thus leading to even more aggressive responses. This was also evident during the six weeks I spent in 1993 as a deputy to the European Union and UN mediators for the former Yugoslavia, Lord Owen and Mr. Stoltenberg.

Second, there was no time-consuming diplomatic protocol to be followed and no speeches to the gallery. The parties in the official and public sessions in Washington appeared to spend almost 100 percent of their time blaming one another, whereas the negotiators in Norway spent at least 90 percent of their waking hours, meals included, in real negotiations. Even the many mutual acts of provocation and violence in the field did not hamper the efforts of the secret negotiators as those acts did the efforts of the official channel in Washington.

Third, an atmosphere of mutual trust and affinity was allowed to develop between a handful of individuals who spent hundreds of hours working, eating, quarreling, and joking together in front of Norwegian fireplaces and surrounded only by peaceful countryside. With only seven negotiators at the table the dialogue was always direct, honest, and effective. From the beginning of the official negotiations in June, all the negotiators except for one Palestinian who joined midway were the same throughout. This provided for continuity and an institutional memory within the small group.

Fourth, close cooperation with FAFO, the nongovernmental organization, enabled us to offer the parties "deniability"—the opportunity, if necessary, to deny that anything official had happened. If anything leaked out, we could explain the meetings as academic seminars or as Norwegian participation in the official peace process. The small size of our team also helped us to keep things quiet. We were prepared to keep our secret forever if the negotiations broke down. That was important, because both sides feared that if news of secret negotiations in Oslo leaked out before any agreement had been reached, there might be disastrous repercussions at home.

## IMPLEMENTING THE OSLO ACCORD

The process that culminated in the Oslo Accord and the subsequent negotiations (that led to the agreement known as "Oslo 2") has been followed by numerous crises and setbacks, but also by historical breakthroughs. Enemies of peace on both sides have repeatedly tried to derail the process, mounting terrible terrorist attacks against civilians, including women and children, in Hebron, Jerusalem, Tel Aviv, and elsewhere. Other obstacles to the peace process such as new settlements and border closures have also played their part in preventing the implementation of the Oslo Accord and Oslo 2.

The Oslo Accord or the Declaration of Principles was, as the name implies, an agreement on the principles to guide the relationship between Israelis and Palestinians for a five-year period from 1993 to 1998 and on the milestones to be passed along the way. An important element of the Oslo Accord is its gradualness. It does not try to solve all problems at once, but rather paves the way to a given destination.

The first milestone reached was the Cairo Agreement of May 1994, which established Palestinian self-rule in Gaza and Jericho. A Palestinian Authority was set up in the space of a few months, enabling almost a million Palestinians to shape their own administration. A Palestinian Police Force, initially assisted and funded by an international task force headed by Norway, was set up under difficult circumstances to promote security and stability in the self-rule areas. Through agreements on early empowerment in August 1994, the Palestinians were given responsibility for education and culture, health, social welfare, taxation, and tourism on the West Bank in addition to Gaza and Jericho.

The second milestone—the Interim Agreement or "Oslo 2"—was reached after marathon discussions that were concluded in September 1995 in Taba, Egypt. It paved the way for extended Palestinian self-rule on the West Bank and Palestinian elections in the spring of 1996, through the withdrawal of Israeli forces from towns and villages on the West Bank. The agreement was to a large extent negotiated by the Oslo team of Abu Alá and Uri Savir.

In February 1997, a new agreement was reached on redeployment from Hebron, the largest and most conflict-ridden town on the West Bank. Coordinated by Norway, a six-nation observer group is currently operating as the "Temporary International Presence in Hebron." In October 1998, another major effort by the United States and other third-party facilitators led to a new agreement regarding further redeployment from the West Bank, as already detailed in the Interim Agreement. Furthermore, the Palestinian side undertook an obligation to step up their fight against terrorism. In late summer 1999, Israeli prime mininster Barak and Palestinian president Arafat agreed to renew negotiations in a positive spirit.

## INTERNATIONAL ECONOMIC ASSISTANCE

One of the main arenas for international involvement in the peace processes has been through economic assistance. In order for peace to endure, it must make a difference in people's daily lives by providing better living conditions, employment opportunities, and a feeling of personal security. Discussing the challenge of implementation with our U.S. counterparts as the Oslo Accord had just been initialed, we agreed that the Palestinian self-rule areas should be treated as a special case in international development assistance.

An Ad Hoc Liaison Committee (AHLC) was thus set up at the International Donor's Conference in Washington on October 1, 1993, to mobilize international assistance to the Palestinians. The AHLC consists of the cosponsors of the peace process, the United States and Russia; the major donors to the Palestinians; and the two parties, Israel and the Palestinian Authority. Egypt, Jordan, and Tunisia are associated members. Norway has acted as chairman of the AHLC since 1993. At the Washington conference, $2.4 billion was raised in grants and loans. This sum has, after a slow start in 1994 and 1995, been disbursed according to plan.

Economic activities in Gaza and the West Bank have, however, suffered a number of serious setbacks during the many long and harsh border closures after terrorist attacks in Israel. In 1996 some $5 million was lost every day the borders were closed, a loss of income greater than the value of all foreign assistance in this period. Per capita income among the Palestinians has decreased in the period since 1993.

The prolonged crisis of confidence between the actors in the Middle East peace process made it evident that the understanding and trust reached between political leaders like Rabin-Peres and Arafat-Mazen did not filter down to the ordinary man and woman as we believed, perhaps naively, in 1993. Under the Oslo 2 agreement a major new effort was therefore launched to promote cooperation between Israeli and Palestinian citizens in fields such as economics, cultural affairs, and education.

It is hoped that this people-to-people exercise will help do away with some of the stereotyped images of Israelis as "occupying soldiers" and of Palestinians as "terrorists." Norway has been asked to facilitate the programs. Some one hundred bridge-building projects are already under way involving youth groups, businesspeople, academics, and local politicians.

## OTHER MULTIPARTY FACILITATION

The Oslo Accord is the most famous of a series of Norwegian efforts to assist, with varying degrees of success, in peace processes in Central America, the Balkans, the Caucasus, Burundi, Sudan, Sri Lanka, and elsewhere. In all these peace processes, Norwegian participation has operated within a multiparty effort of the United Nations, other intergovernmental organizations, or other countries. And in all peace processes, the Norwegian government has worked with or through nongovernmental organizations (NGOs).

NGOs often prove to have the best access to people and networks that can be mobilized quickly. They can operate in a very flexible manner. Decisions can be decentralized, and operations can be started more quickly. To utilize these resources the Norwegian Ministry of Foreign Affairs has established the Norwegian Emergency Preparedness System (NOREPS) and the Norwegian Resource Bank for Democracy and Human Rights (NORDEM). These are flexible standby arrangements with a number of governmental and nongovernmental organizations.

Dozens of NGOs in Norway receive government funding for development assistance and human rights activities in more than a hundred countries. Over the years, thousands of Norwegians have acquired field experience from working with these organizations as well as with the government development cooperation agency, NORAD. Fifty-five thousand Norwegians, a number that equals more than 1 percent of our population, have participated in UN or UN-mandated peacekeeping operations. These people constitute a valuable resource, which Norway is utilizing in conflict prevention on a rapid deployment basis.

Through the standby procedures of NOREPS and NORDEM, several hundred relief workers, human rights advisers, peace mediators, and observers are dispatched each year to more than thirty countries at the request of UN agencies, newly born democracies, and parties to armed conflicts.

The peace process in Guatemala was initiated in Norway in March 1990 when representatives of the government peace commission and the guerrilla movement, URNG, signed an "Oslo Agreement," which established a format and an agenda for future negotiations. Almost seven years later, in December 1996, the parties successfully came full circle when they finally signed the cease-fire agreement in Oslo, bringing a generation of civil war to an end. The able mediators of the United Nations and a "Group of Friends" (Colombia, Mexico, Norway, Spain, the United States, and Venezuela) made steady progress at the negotiating table possible, and the final peace accord was signed in Guatemala City on December 29, 1996.

Norway facilitated this peace process and hosted several rounds of negotiations through close cooperation between the Foreign Ministry and two NGOs: the Norwegian Church Aid and the Lutheran World Federation. Since 1990, we have even provided financial support to the guerrilla movement to enable its delegates to participate fully in the negotiations. At the same time we actively tried to influence the Guatemalan armed forces through an extensive military exchange program between their top generals and Norwegian military and civilian delegations. Both the financial support to the bankrupt but still militarily potent guerrillas, and the funding of the visits from the controversial Guatemalan military proved crucial for the success of the UN-led mediation. Without the efficient, locally active, and morally untouchable Norwegian Church Aid, I would not, as a responsible politician in the Norwegian government, have supported and funded these activities.

Norwegian small-state activism is in no way unique. Canada, the Netherlands, and Sweden have frequently been entrepreneurs in the settlement of conflicts and the promotion of human rights. The special "Norwegian model" is the mutually trusted partnership with many NGOs and academic institutions that, to paraphrase Mao Tse-tung, lets "a hundred flowers flourish" in a creative and multiparty effort to facilitate peace in many theaters of conflict.

## Lessons Learned

In conclusion, what are the lessons we have learned from Norwegian experience in attempting to facilitate peace on different continents and under different circumstances?

First, and most fundamental, there will be no real and lasting peace if the parties themselves—the leaders as well as the peoples—are not willing to work toward the often painful compromises that are needed to realize peace. This has been graphically illustrated by the many failures to truly implement the Oslo Accord and Oslo 2 as they have been formally adopted and signed by the two parties. There has not been less mediation or facilitation undertaken by Norway, the United States, and other third parties since 1996 than there was in the years from 1992 to 1995. The main change was that a new, democratically elected government took over policy formulation in one of the two parties. With the Netanyahu government in office, close to all multiparty efforts to further the peace process have been frustrated, because the new Israeli government is not willing to compromise as the Rabin-Peres governments were.

Second, even when conflicting parties are willing to make peace, inadequate mediation machinery and the absence of secret back channels can thwart the best of intentions. Israel and the PLO were able to effect negotiations and agreements themselves as soon as we managed to establish a link between the PLO leadership and the Israeli government in secret, without time-consuming diplomatic protocol, and in an environment of trust. International diplomacy is surprisingly underprepared in terms of providing the personnel, the expertise, and the material support necessary for effective multiparty peace facilitation. Sufficient discretionary funds ("venture capital for peace") are needed to flexibly finance meetings, travel, expertise, and logistics in an often prolonged negotiation process. It is a paradox that there seem to be more such discretionary funds available in the Norwegian humanitarian assistance budget than in the enormous U.S. foreign and security assistance budgets.

Cooperation with NGOs and academic institutions has also enhanced the ability of the Norwegian government to provide without delay the appropriate tools for a mediation process. Such tools range from experts on the separation of military forces to constitutional lawyers, and from remote country houses to executive airplanes.

Third, the ability of smaller nations to play a role as a trusted and effective third party should not be underestimated. Small countries such as Norway are perceived as having no national interests that conflict with an impartial settlement of a dispute. The national political consensus needed to undertake and fund a longer-term political, diplomatic, and economic investment in a peace program is also a characteristic of the parliaments in several smaller European countries, in particular the Nordic countries and the Netherlands.

Fourth, a third party should carefully avoid the temptation to take on a role that it lacks the resources to play convincingly. For the smaller state, the advisable role is that of *facilitator*, which is a more activist role than that of technical host for negotiations, but less ambitious and demanding than that of mediator (as performed by the United States in Dayton or by the United Nations in El Salvador and Guatemala). Norway has no stick and too small a carrot to threaten or bribe the parties to accept a controversial compromise. Neither does it have the skilled teams of mediators that inter-governmental organizations are able to muster. However, the smaller country can discreetly, flexibly, and effectively seize new opportunities presented by the post–Cold War era to actively facilitate bridges between parties and organizations that are ready to seek a compromise.

Fifth, a third party should define *realistic goals* when embarking on conflict resolution. More often than not it is advisable to seek limited humanitarian or other confidence-building agreements on the way toward the very ambitious goal of making peace. In Sri Lanka, the parties in 1995 agreed to ask Norwegian standby personnel to oversee and facilitate two cease-fire panels as the government and Tamil Tiger representatives unsuccessfully tried to agree on a format for peace talks. In the Caucasus, Norwegian-funded NGOs helped talks between the South Ossetians and the Georgians on telecommunication links and between other ethnic groups on a refugee exchange agreement. Gradually, more ambitious goals can be set. The Oslo Accord came out of a process that was started as a confidence-building meeting between Israeli academics and the PLO.

Sixth, a third party should not naively believe the stated intentions of the leaders involved. In the ten conflict resolution efforts in which I have been involved, *all* the leaders at all times claimed their goal was "to end the suffering of our peoples." In reality, there were always influential political, military, or economic warlords who had their personal and professional interests tied to continued conflict. For a general or a guerrilla leader, peace can be a very scary prospect: demobilization, early retirement, alienation, and, increasingly, investigation for possible war crimes. For the political wartime leader, peace may mean democratic elections that often bring in a new generation of leadership. Bosnia is a salient example: Mladic and Karadzic were in firm control of their respective military and political apparatus during the war. Today they are only pathetic war criminals.

Seventh, there is a need to carefully plan how a third party should treat the parties in conflict before, during, and after negotiations. In many cases it is vital to provide the parties with equal status, even though there is an indisputable asymmetric power relationship. We meticulously gave Israelis and Palestinians as well as the Guatemalan government and the URNG guerrillas the same formal status at the negotiations. We also realized that a final compromise is likelier to be closer to the original position of the stronger, not the weaker, party. In the typical internal conflicts of the 1990s, with numerous armed nongovernmental entities, a third party should, however, avoid giving any kind of violent opposition the legitimacy it often seeks through participation in formal negotiations. As an adviser to the peace process of the new Colombian government, I agree with the government's decision to undertake formal and political negotiations with the guerrillas, but not with the right-wing paramilitary groups. The latter are criminal terrorist organizations that should be met with only to discuss the laying down of arms. The random killing of fellow citizens in a society should not lead to negotiations in the presidential palace.

Finally, we must learn that no matter how hard it seems to be to reach a negotiated agreement between the parties in an armed conflict, the process of implementing any agreement will be harder. The rebuilding of societies, the integration of ex-combatants and refugees, the protection and promotion of human rights, and the establishment of democratic institutions make for an uphill marathon from day one after the signing of a peace agreement. More often than not the war will have created a climate of violence, frustration, and despair that may take a generation to change. The expectation of social and economic progress is always unrealistically high, as the economy nearly always is further depressed as peace breaks out. As seen in the Middle East and Northern Ireland, postconflict societies are also extremely vulnerable to terrorism.

Any third-party conflict resolution effort must therefore be long term, and must extend beyond the negotiating table to reach the participants in the shooting war. Norwegian development assistance and institution-building efforts have steadily grown in the Palestinian territories, in Bosnia, and in Guatemala in the years since the agreements were made.

Will the Oslo process ultimately lead to peace between Israelis and Palestinians? I still firmly believe so, even though I readily admit that peace will take more time and the process will see more uphill battles than we originally and optimistically expected. The gradualness of the Oslo process is both its strength and its weakness. Embarking on a bargaining process that attempts to settle the age-old disputes around Jerusalem and other final-status issues is the same as inviting a permanent deadlock in the talks. However, gradual implementation will unavoidably lead to countless frustrations and setbacks in an atmosphere clouded by political violence and extremism. Perhaps the biggest mistake made during the Oslo negotiations was to agree to judge the success of the peace process based on what could be achieved during a five-year period rather than over the course of a generation. It has taken many generations to build the political, social, cultural, and religious barriers in the Middle East. It will take time to overcome those barriers.

Whether Norway will facilitate peace agreements between conflicting parties again is an open question. Perhaps only one in a hundred attempts will succeed. Even so it will be worth the effort.

# Background to Chapter 21

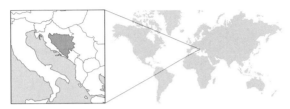

## A Bosnian Federation Memoir

The consequences of the breakup in 1991 of the former Yugoslavia were tumultuous and bloody. Fighting erupted on many fronts between many groups: Serbs battled Croats, Croats fought with Bosnian Muslims, and a lengthy and brutal war was waged between Bosnian Serb forces and the Army of Bosnia-Herzegovina. Individually and jointly, the European Union, the United States, and the United Nations made various attempts to halt the bloodshed and rebuild Bosnia. A U.S.-led effort supported by the United Nations ended the Croat-Muslim war and helped to lay the foundations for a multiethnic and democratic Bosnian Federation. Signed in March 1994, the Washington (or Federation) Agreement introduced a form of power sharing. Though fragile and unloved by the Bosnians themselves, the federation has nonetheless survived and, indeed, has taken institutional root. The Washington Agreement also eventually served as a key element in the Dayton peace accords, though resolving tensions over the role of the federation and developing a coherent approach to its role in the larger peace process proved difficult.

### Major Actors

- Yugoslavia and the Yugoslav National Army (JNA): led by President Slobodan Milosevic
- Croatia: led by President Franjo Tudjman
- Bosnian Croatians: led by President Kresimir Zubak
- Croat Defense Council (HVO): led by General Zirko Budimir

547

- Bosnian Muslims: led by President Alija Izetbegovic
- Army of Bosnia and Herzegovina (ABiH): led by General Rasim Delic
- Serb Republic Army, VRS
- North Atlantic Treaty Organization (NATO)/NATO Implementation Force (IFOR)
- Contact Group: France, Germany, Russia, the United Kingdom, and the United States
- European Union
- United Nations

## IMPORTANT DATES

- 1992: fighting breaks out between Serbs and Croats, Croats and Muslims, and Bosnian Serbs and the Bosnia Army
- March 1994: Bosnian Federation formed, Croat-Muslim war ends
- March 18, 1995: Friends of the Federation is launched
- Summer 1995: Muslim and Croatian forces take large portions of western Bosnia after NATO air strikes against Bosnian Serb targets
- December 14, 1995: Dayton peace accords signed at Paris
- 1995–96: NATO begins implementation of the Dayton agreement

## KEY AGREEMENTS REACHED

- Croat Republic of Herzeg-Bosna to be dissolved
- Refugee repatriation to begin
- Federation government, army, and payments system to be created

## PRINCIPAL OUTCOMES

- Fighting between Croats and Muslims has been halted
- The Bosnian Federation government is functional, with cantons, municipalities, a constitutional court, and an assembly
- The federation provided a temporary solution to part of the Bosnia conflagration until the Dayton peace process could take hold

# 21

# A Bosnian Federation Memoir

DANIEL SERWER

There will be many memoirs of Bosnia. This one is written from my own peculiar point of view. From October 1994 to July 1996, I was the primary U.S. State Department official responsible for the Bosnian Federation. I worried daily about how to keep the Croats and the Muslims (also known as Bosniaks) from fighting again, as they had in 1993–94. I helped them build common institutions that would contain their conflict within civil bounds. And I tried to firm up the federation even as a much weightier structure, the Dayton peace agreement, was built on top of this shaky foundation.

The pursuit of these objectives took me to Bosnia about twenty times. I met with all the key Muslim and Croat participants in the Bosnia crisis (but never with Serbs, except for those loyal to the Sarajevo government). President Alija Izetbegovic; Vice President Ejup Ganic; President Kresimir Zubak; Prime Ministers Haris Silajdzic, Hasan Muratovic, and Mehmed-beg Kapetanovic; Foreign Minister Jadranko Prlic and his deputy, Hasan Dervisbegovic; Interior Minister Avdo Hebib and his deputy, Jozo Leutar; and Defense Minister Vladimir Soljic and his deputy, Hasan Cengic—all knew me as "Mr. Federation." So, too, did the many European capitals I visited, as well as officials in Jakarta, Kuala Lumpur, and Tokyo.

I worked "alone": at most I had a secretary and one professional diplomat working with me. But it was clearly impossible to do what needed to be done without enlisting the cooperation and combined efforts of many others. This was a multiparty effort. Before Dayton, the other key players were the UN High Commissioner for Refugees (UNHCR), the civil affairs officers of the United Nations Protection Force (UNPROFOR), and the World Bank. After Dayton, they were joined by the NATO implementation force (IFOR) civil affairs and the office of the High Representative, who had overall responsibility for Dayton implementation. Throughout, I had a strong relationship with the Germans, who took a particular interest in the federation, and with the European Administration of Mostar, the south Bosnian city where the war between the Muslims and the Croats had been particularly intense.

Mine was not a role that caught the public eye outside Bosnia, but no one dealing with Bosnia at the time doubted the significance of the mission. If I failed, the Croats and the Muslims would go back to war and multiethnic democracy would die in Bosnia, consumed by the flames of nationalism on all sides and resulting in three-way partition. If I succeeded, the ramshackle barrier against war that I worked to build would impress no one. It would always be called weak, fragile, likely to collapse.

I succeeded. On my watch, the federation did not collapse but strengthened. When I departed in June 1996, the federation had a government, many of its ten cantons, and most of its municipalities, as well as a constitutional court and an active assembly. The federation has made more progress since, though it is still difficult to predict whether the relative success will last. Maybe not. Few days pass that do not bring evidence of continuing tension within the federation. But with little fanfare, the Croats and the Muslims have built up functioning common institutions and so far have managed to keep from relapsing into suicidal fratricide. Those who bemoan the continuing tensions between them should remember that the federation, for all its faults, has kept the peace for five years. I can only hope that it will continue to do so.

## SO WHAT IS THIS FEDERATION?

A short history is required to set the stage for my role, which was part mediator, part cheerleader, part nation builder.

Bosnia suffered three wars in the early 1990s. It started in 1992 with Serb attacks on Croats, an extension of the Serb attacks on Croats inside Croatia. Bosnian Croat appeals for help from Sarajevo went unheeded—the Sarajevo government had no army to speak of. It was then that the

Croats formed the Croat Defense Council (HVO), which defended Mostar from the Serbs and included among its ranks a significant number of Muslims.

With Mostar saved from Serb attacks, in the fall of 1992 Croats and Muslims started fighting each other throughout central Bosnia, including Mostar. I have heard many versions of how this second war started, and why. My own take is that issues people really cared about—language, education, religious and national symbols—were exploited by nationalist leaderships, which in a bizarre perversion of democratic principles decided they could become a majority and get their way by chasing members of the other "ethnic" group out. The fighting was most intense where the Muslims and the Croats, who in fact are all Slavs and mostly irreligious, were closest to equal in population (many considered themselves "Yugoslavs" or had intermarried, making ethnic identity ambiguous, at least for their children). The fighting was exacerbated by Croatian security goals, which included the creation of a band of Croat-dominated territory along the Herzegovinian border of Bosnia with Croatia, and by Muslim nationalists, who aimed for a Bosnia that Muslims would control. Fifty thousand Muslims and one hundred fifty thousand Croats were displaced by the Croat-Muslim war.

It was this second war that ended with the signature of what is known as the Washington (or Federation) Agreement in March 1994. A cease-fire had been negotiated earlier by the United Nations, and a cessation of hostilities agreement was reached with the help of former supreme allied commander John Galvin. The Croats wanted to end the fighting because they were losing. The HVO was not then or later an impressive fighting force, though it was good at frightening civilian populations and ethnic cleansing. The Muslims wanted to end the fighting because they could not win their war against the Serbs while fighting the Croats. There was no love lost between the Croats and the Muslims, but under intense pressure from Washington—which wanted to simplify the equation before trying to resolve the Serb/Muslim conflict—they agreed to set up the Bosnian Federation. This was on paper a set of governing institutions delicately balanced between Croats and Muslims (with little room for Serbs). On all issues of importance, both groups had to agree for action to be taken—this was not Jeffersonian democracy but a classic "power-sharing" arrangement.

The federation institutions were supposed to govern the territory controlled by the HVO and the Bosnian Army, which originally was planned to be 58 percent of the total territory of prewar Bosnia and Herzegovina. The United States, for reasons that are obscure to me, reduced this territory to 51 percent and convinced the "Contact Group" (then France, Germany, Russia, the United Kingdom, and the United States) in the spring of 1994 to endorse that number, which in any case appeared overly optimistic. At the time, the Bosnian Army and the HVO controlled only about a third of the territory, and it seemed unlikely that they would ever control much more. As part of the federation arrangements, the European Community— as the European Union was then known—took on the unenviable task of administering Mostar.

The Bosnian Federation at the time of its formation was split between areas controlled by the HVO and areas controlled by the Bosnian Army (ABiH). Checkpoints and separation zones were still in place when NATO troops arrived to implement the Dayton agreements in the winter of 1995– 96. Moreover, the Croats had set up a political counterpart to the HVO, which became known as the Croat Republic of Herzeg-Bosna, a parastate with no legal claim that nevertheless was the only civilian governing authority in areas controlled by the HVO. In areas controlled by the Bosnian Army—which included most of central Bosnia as well as the northwestern enclave of Bihao and the eastern Bosnian enclaves of Srebrenica, Zepa, and Gorazde—the writ of the internationally recognized Republic of Bosnia and Herzegovina, the Sarajevo government, nominally ruled. With the signature of the Washington Agreement in March 1994, the Croats reentered the Republic of Bosnia-Herzegovina, whose government ministries were at the same time "double-hatted" as Bosnian Federation ministries.

The third war in Bosnia is the one most of us remember from the headlines: the war that began in 1992 between the Bosnian Serbs—assisted extensively by the Yugoslav National Army (JNA)—and the Bosnian Army, which was controlled by the Muslim-dominated government in Sarajevo. This was the war that saw the siege of Sarajevo, the massacre of Srebrenica, and the NATO bombing of Serb positions. And it was this war that the Dayton agreements reached in November 1995 ended with the division— but not partition—of Bosnia into the Bosnian Federation (51 percent) and the Serb Republic (49 percent).

## A WINTER OF NEAR COLLAPSE

Richard Holbrooke, assistant secretary for Europe in the State Department, asked me to serve as special coordinator for the Bosnian Federation in October 1994. He had returned from his first official trip to Bosnia a few weeks before and believed that the federation had to be saved. It was the only good thing that we had done in Bosnia, he thought, and it was a mistake to have left its future to chance after the signing of the Washington

Agreement in March. He arranged for my appointment to be covered in Al Kamen's *Washington Post* column, which was helpful in making me at least appear to be of some importance. He suggested that I drop the "special" from my title, as it implied my job was a temporary one. I would be needed for a long time, he thought. And he suggested, in dire terms, that if I did not get busy quickly the federation would come apart, perhaps while I was still standing in his office.

The special envoy for former Yugoslavia, Charlie Thomas, was helpful. The federation would get nowhere, he believed, unless it was pushed from abroad. The United States would have to push hard. But we were all too obviously limited in means—we had recently dredged up a paltry $20 million from the U.S. Agency for International Development (AID) to support reconstruction in the federation and underlying ethnic reconciliation. Western Europe and the Islamic countries would have to provide the bulk of the assistance money, which would eventually amount to billions. Thomas passed on a thought left to him by Chuck Redman, who had negotiated the Washington Agreement: organize some sort of commission, under U.S. leadership, to push the federation ahead. This idea became what I called "Friends of the Federation," an informal group of countries that would offer assistance to the federation if the Croats and the Muslims would get on with it. I proposed, and Holbrooke accepted, launching the Friends on the first federation anniversary, March 18, 1995, at a meeting in Washington hosted by Secretary of State Warren Christopher.

Holbrooke was not satisfied. He felt a sense of urgency about the physical situation on the ground in Bosnia. The federation, he often said, had to survive physically before it could thrive politically. Most of the front between federation forces and the Serbs was relatively quiet, and in fact the military situation had not changed significantly in over a year. There were two real problems. One was Bihac, the Muslim-dominated enclave located in the Croatian "V," where the Bosnian Army overextended itself in victory late in the summer and by fall was tasting defeat. Little could be done for Bihac, where the conditions of the population were dreadful. But complete defeat was unlikely because the Croatians—who did not want a Serb victory close to their borders—could be expected to try to avoid it (which they did, by resupplying the Bosnian Army there through the winter).

Sarajevo was the second of the acute physical problems. Conditions for the general population in Sarajevo were better than those in Bihac, but that was small comfort. People were leaving the capital, and its travails were well covered by the international press. Food was not the issue, and even the water situation was by then acceptable, because of the efforts of engineers who worked for George Soros's Open Society Institute. Fuel was the problem: irregular supplies of Russian natural gas, which had to cross Serbia and Bosnian Serb–held territory before reaching Sarajevo, were insufficient. What was needed, the Bosnians told us, was an electrical cable from Bosnian government–controlled territory in central Bosnia, over Igman, through the tunnel they had secretly dug under the airport and into the city. The Bosnians had prepared the basic specifications and had started the trenchwork over Mount Igman using "civil defense" labor (required labor by civilian males not in military service). Would the U.S. government and Soros pay the few million dollars required to procure the equipment abroad and install it by the end of 1994?

The question was still unanswered when I visited Sarajevo for the first time in November 1994. I was determined not to go empty-handed. On the electrical cable, I could do no more than assure the Bosnians that it would get a fair hearing. I had, however, solidified a consensus behind a strong U.S. position on natural gas: it would go to Serbia only if sufficient supplies arrived in Sarajevo. I was also able, despite a good deal of resistance, to carry with me two draft agreements: one for economic development cooperation and one for military cooperation. They were both boilerplate, but getting our bureaucracy to clear them for delivery to the Bosnians was no small matter. It was odd indeed for the United States to propose agreements for the benefit of the Bosnian Federation, a subnational entity that existed only on paper. It was an unusually friendly and inventive State Department lawyer who managed the clearance process. I also carried to Sarajevo the idea of the Friends, which was sure to please the Bosnians.

I later made the trip to Sarajevo so many times that it is hard to remember much about the first one. But some things are unforgettable: As we stumbled out of the airplane in Sarajevo, soldiers stood pointing at the tail, saying we had been hit by small arms fire. We all gathered to take a look but were quickly shooed off the tarmac by UN Blue Berets, who warned that the shooting could still be going on. I glimpsed the airport: shattered glass, massive berms of dirt, sandbags. A movie set, but so wretched and miserable it had to be real. Our suitcases were deposited in a mud hole beyond the sandbags, and we carried them around to the front of what was left of the terminal, where no one met us. Mortars could be heard in the distance. I tried to hitch a ride in an armored personnel carrier, but the French soldiers said it was going to Mount Igman, not downtown. We waited nervously. Soon John Menzies, the cheerful newly appointed deputy chief of mission at the American embassy bounced up in a Toyota

Landcruiser, sorry he was late—no one had let the embassy know which plane we were on until almost its arrival time.

The drive into town was not the one used now and before the war. The Serbs were known to be looking for Americans, so we did not go through their checkpoints. Sierra 4, on the short route in from the airport, was notorious, not the least because a member of the Bosnian presidency had been taken from a French armored personnel carrier there earlier in the war and murdered. So we drove, until after the end of the war, through the shattered neighborhood of Dobrinha, built for the Sarajevo Winter Olympic Games. Barricades protecting the crossroads, a Bosnian Army checkpoint, little traffic, a few scurrying people, destroyed apartments, shattered glass. Then into the main street, trams no longer running, blast marks in the asphalt, more destruction, past armored personnel carriers ineffectively protecting pedestrians from snipers (there are the high-rise apartments, less than 200 meters away, from which they fire!), a U-turn at high speed and suddenly calm as we approach the rear of the Holiday Inn, protected by the building from snipers.

I would later spend many weeks in the Holiday Inn, but again some moments of that first stay are unforgettable. The embassy was still located there, a few rooms facing a side street past which gunfire crackled day and night. I was quickly installed in the room of one of the embassy officers who was away. I slept well enough until about 3:00 A.M., when the gunfire stopped. I woke up cold, put my overcoat over the many blankets already covering the bed, and lay awake for some time, waiting for the gunfire to start again. Later, I would sleep through both gunfire and lulls. The morning the Dayton agreement was signed in Paris I awakened to a clattering fusillade of antiaircraft fire smashing into the facade of the hotel, rolled over, and went back to sleep. I had learned, as did every Sarajevan, that if you could hear it, you were probably okay and should ignore it. There was certainly no point in going to the window to look out, as it increased the risk.

I met Ambassador Victor Jackovich for breakfast the next morning and learned that he grew up speaking Serbo-Croatian with his extended family in Iowa and that he would accompany me to see the prime minister. Off we went at the usual breakneck pace (thought to be too fast to allow snipers to get their aim), screeching to a halt in front of the red-brown, nineteenth-century Presidency, sedate in the midst not only of gunfire but the ravages of Sarajevo's hideous modern buildings, one more garish than the last. I later commented to a Bosnian prime minister, Hasan Muratovic, that some of the destruction was probably an aesthetic plus for the city. He agreed. The Presidency, though, was always dear to me, sitting casually on the street in modest dignity, its soldier-guards attentive but relaxed, its protocol officers friendly but proper, its shabby gold carpet bespeaking less the glory of the past than the hope for being replaced in the future, a container of lilies on the main landing trying to speak eloquently of national aspirations.

After being ushered into what I later discovered was the all-purpose reception room, we installed ourselves in the standard-issue gold-painted and red-upholstered chairs that seem so ubiquitous in European diplomatic establishments, arranged in a semicircle so that we could talk without inhibiting the camera angles. In swept the prime minister, the animated but always unhappy Haris Silajdzic, as angry with his friends as with his enemies. He trailed cameras. The press would leave after a few silent shots, he explained, and would not be allowed to talk with us afterward.

I did my points—Friends of the Federation, energy supplies for Sarajevo, agreements on military cooperation and reconstruction—and tried to appear as helpful and attentive as possible. Silajdzic complained about the Croat failure to implement agreements on border guards and federation police and asked that we help build a truck tunnel under the airport. The bullet holes in the wall were hard to miss, as was Silajdzic's peculiar charm. Eyes rolling, he would wind himself up for a denunciation of the world and its cruelty to the Bosnians, including those who would pretend to be their friends. I rejected his charges, told him we would do the best we could, and knew that in fact he had good reason to be upset. We got up after half an hour, the doors opened, and of course the press was there in full force. Silajdzic took most of the questions. CNN asked me if the prime minister didn't sound mighty gloomy about the Bosnian Federation and I gave my best State Department reply: I was sure the prime minister saw many problems, as did I, but we both looked hopefully to the future.

Silajdzic tugged at my elbow and took me off down the hallway, around a corner, and into President Alija Izetbegovic's large but sparsely furnished office. Then and later I had the sense that I was talking with someone's immigrant grandfather—halting English, tired skin, few words, a puzzled look. Izetbegovic was impressed that my plane had been hit—this made me courageous in his view. I thought not, as it seemed to me there was no courage in discovering after landing that your plane had been hit but a great deal of courage in sitting for several years in a Presidency room that you knew your enemies were targeting (and in fact hit several times). If there was courage in the room, it was among the Bosnians. But the courage did not come with statesmanship: Izetbegovic heard me out on the federation, but it was only later that I would realize how little store he set in it, and how little he was willing to do to bring the Croats back into Bosnia.

During this conversation, Ambassador Jackovich began to speak to the Bosnians in their own language. To get back into the conversation, I commented on how good his command of Serbo-Croatian was. A tense silence ensued, with everyone looking to Izetbegovic. "You mean," the president said directly but with good humor, "his excellent Bosnian," precipitating a relieved laugh all around.

As soon as we were done, the ambassador rushed us to the car and all but forcibly delivered us to the airport for a flight back to Zagreb. We should not stay another night—it appeared both sides were building up for a battle over Sarajevo, and the UNPROFOR flights might be suspended. He was right. They were suspended a few days later and did not resume again for more than a month.

Back to Zagreb we went, stayed overnight, and headed for Washington the next day, a pattern I would follow for the next eighteen months. We had seen Foreign Minister Mate Granic on the way into Sarajevo. Thoughtful and positive about the Bosnian Federation, he chose his words carefully but always somehow managed to convey that if it were up to him the federation would come alive faster than Croatian president Franjo Tudjman was permitting. Just as President Tudjman, whom we called on in the splendor of his faux Western palace, a Titoesque shrine to modernity furnished in the traditional fashion of monarchs, always gave the impression that the federation caused him heartburn, no matter how enthusiastic his words.

After I returned to Washington, my immediate task became the electrical cable into Sarajevo, the need for which Prime Minister Silajdzic had confirmed with his usual guilt-inducing flagellation. He had also wanted propane tanks to provide cooking fuel to that part of the population that lacked electrical connections, but no one ever figured out how we could safely transport trucks full of propane past the Serb gunners into the city. The Soros people undertook a technical evaluation of the underground electrical cable. The results were essentially positive, though only a small proportion of the population could be served. George Soros, who had been the first to mention the cable project to the State Department, was ready to fund half, but only if the U.S. government would take the lead with the other half.

AID dragged its many bureaucratic feet. The humanitarian-relief people said it was a development project. The development people said it was humanitarian relief. The intelligence people said the cable would be cut easily by the Serbs. The U.S. government could not make up its mind, and some suggested Soros lead the way. Weeks started to drag into months. Weather conditions would not permit the project to be completed in midwinter. I urged, pleaded, begged, first our own people and then Soros, asking them to go ahead even without the U.S. government. That, in the end, is what happened. To their credit, AID's humanitarian-relief people eventually anted up their portion as well. Later, in the spring of 1995, when the city was completely cut off by the Serbs, electricity delivered through this cable saved Sarajevo (though at the time it was said that the electricity came from diesel generators in the city, as the cable project was still regarded a secret).

Although Richard Holbrooke was pleased with this effort for the electrical cable, it did not satisfy his need at the time for some sort of public triumph. The anniversary of the Bosnian Federation in March was not soon enough, he said (I can only imagine what sorts of pressures created this sense of urgency). On a week's notice, he called a Contact Group meeting for February 18 in Munich, during the annual Wehrkunde meeting of defense ministers, with the Bosnians and the Croats to discuss the federation.

They came. Prime Minister Silajdzic led the Bosnian delegation, which included President Kresimir Zubak and Vice President Ejup Ganic of the Bosnian Federation. This was the first time I met them. Zubak, who always appeared cautious, was then firmly committed to ethnic separation in Bosnia. The exuberant Ganic had hopes for the kind of multiethnic democracy he had observed firsthand during his years teaching and doing research in the United States. Neither was surefooted politically: Zubak came from central Bosnia (near Doboj) rather than from the nationalist heartland near the Herzegovinian border with Croatia; Ganic, though known as a Muslim nationalist, came from Sandzak (in Serbia) and betrayed his birthplace, I was told, with every word he spoke. There was a big difference, however: Zubak took orders from Zagreb (though he denied it vehemently), while Ganic repeatedly ran risks by pushing the federation harder than Izetbegovic liked (all the time insisting he was acting with the president's approval).

Zubak and Ganic were not, however, big players at the Munich meeting. Silajdzic was the key Bosnian and came to the meeting with the idea of getting the Americans much more deeply involved in making the federation work. The other protagonists were Defense Minister Goyko Susak and Foreign Minister Mate Granic of Croatia. Among the Americans, Richard Holbrooke and the U.S. ambassador to Croatia, Peter Galbraith, were the key players, but several senators and the Contact Group played cameo roles.

Silajdzic arrived in Munich with a long list of action items that were required to make the federation work. Galbraith interpreted this list as an invitation for the United States to reengage with the federation, and in fact to decide many of the issues that the Bosnians themselves seemed incapable of sorting out. These ranged from tax collection to criminal justice, to payment of pensions and dissolution of the wartime Croat Republic of Herzeg-Bosna, which was supposed to have been dissolved with the formation of the Bosnian Federation. After late-night and early-morning meetings with Silajdzic and Susak, Galbraith was able to convince Holbrooke that we might convince the Bosnians—both Muslim and Croat—to accept binding arbitration by a U.S. arbitrator. I had some doubts about the wisdom of getting the United States too deeply engaged in this way and thereby removing the burden of finding solutions from the Croats and the Muslims, but Holbrooke bought the idea, pacing barefooted as we discussed Bosnia's future late into the night in his hotel room.

The formal meeting opened the next day, cameras rolling. Holbrooke had invited several U.S. senators—I believe they were Joe Lieberman, William Cohen, and Sam Nunn—to address the group. They lambasted the Croatians, who were thought to be plotting with Serbia to divide up Bosnia. Holbrooke then shooed the press from the room and asked the Croatians if they wanted to reply (without the cameras present). To his credit, Granic said unequivocally that Croatia would not try to divide up Bosnia, a reply he repeated in front of the cameras later.

The main issue at the meeting was whether the Bosnians would accept binding arbitration of any issue that either side brought to the arbitrator. Zubak resisted, knowing full well that his vision of a segregated Bosnia would not have much of a chance with an American arbitrator. The meeting had to be adjourned briefly while Susak literally took Zubak into a corner and told him what to accept. This was all done under enormous time pressure, as Holbrooke had arranged for Secretary of Defense William Perry to say a few words to the group (part of his already considerable effort to get the Pentagon to lean further forward on Bosnia). Zubak came back and agreed, and I ran off to complete the final version of the communiqué.

Thus, the United States took another step in the direction of deeper involvement in Bosnia, or at least in the one-third of Bosnia then controlled by the federation. While the Germans thought the arbitrator's job should go to them (and we eventually agreed to their appointing the affable Christian Democrat Christian Schwarz-Schilling as federation mediator), and we went through the motions of preparing a list of candidates, Secretary of State Warren Christopher quickly chose his friend Roberts Owen for the job. A former State Department legal adviser and partner at the prestigious Washington law firm Covington and Burling, Owen undertook the effort with enormous enthusiasm and intelligence.

The issues to be arbitrated were incredibly complex, involving the formation of dozens of municipal and cantonal governments. We sent out an "observer group" to gather basic data and try to resolve as many disputes as possible, drawing its staff from the American and German embassies and including a professional mediator and a Covington and Burling employee. This enabled Owen to issue during the summer of 1995 a long series of "opinions" intended to resolve many outstanding questions. Who should be the members of a municipal council? How were cantonal governments to be formed? What role would people displaced from their homes play in the postwar governing arrangements? More generally, he quietly gained respect and became one of the key players at the Dayton negotiations the next fall.

Friends of the Federation met in March 1995 in Washington, on the occasion of the first anniversary of the Washington Agreement that had established the Bosnian Federation. Secretary Christopher's staff refused to commit him to the event until the last moment, despite Holbrooke's urging. I was sent off on an around-the-world trip to encourage participation, stopping throughout Europe as well as in Jakarta, Kuala Lumpur, and Tokyo. Only the Japanese were truly negative. Our Tokyo embassy sent a cable after I left saying that the Japanese would never get seriously involved in Bosnia financially (the embassy was dead wrong, as the Japanese later paid some big bills). I got back a few days before the event and was sent off again overnight to Vienna, where U.S. ambassador Swanee Hunt—who had hosted key federation negotiations a year earlier—had organized a federation anniversary meeting.

The Friends of the Federation event itself was a disappointment: Secretary Christopher's commitment to attend came too late to encourage foreign attendees (local embassies sent representatives). There was lots of glitz, but Holbrooke decided to try for an agreement on Mostar and failed, leaving the actual meeting of the Friends sitting in a different room and accomplishing very little.

More successful was a meeting the Germans convened shortly thereafter in their official guest house at Petersberg (near Bonn), where they—working with Charlie Thomas as the American representative—persuaded the Croats and the Muslims to agree to the first in a long series of implementation timetables. The pattern established there was repeated many times: the mediators would listen to complaints from each side about the other and craft a balanced package of mutually agreed concessions. The trouble was that everything was linked to everything else, so the smallest dispute over whether something had been adequately implemented would bring the entire process to a crashing halt. Many items would appear and reappear in these implementation packages, with new dates but little progress. Overall, however, the packages crafted under German and American pressure and guidance slowly pushed the process forward. If nothing else, the Croats and the Muslims became used to dealing with each other without staring down the barrel of a gun.

## THE GENERAL AND THE DIPLOMAT

U.S. appointment of a military adviser for the Bosnian Federation was one of the other specific items announced at the Munich meeting. This, too, was part of Holbrooke's effort to get the Pentagon more involved. The Defense Department only reluctantly agreed to allow a retired general to be appointed—jointly by the State Department—to replace John Galvin, who had been instrumental in negotiating the cessation of hostilities and disengagement of forces that preceded the Washington Agreement on the federation. The Pentagon's first choice for the job backed out at the last moment, not wanting to help only one side and thinking if anything the federation was the wrong side. Much scurrying at that point turned up General John Sewall, a retired two-star and former Rhodes scholar, who was vice director of the Institute for National Strategic Studies at the National Defense University.

Sewall was enthusiastic about supporting the federation. There was not much concrete that he could do—the UN arms embargo was still in place, and both the Pentagon and the Allies were watching carefully to ensure that we did nothing to affect the military balance. But just by appearing and insisting that there be a federation military to be advised, Sewall had a positive impact on the relationship between the HVO and the ABiH. We made several trips into Sarajevo and central Bosnia together. These trips helped me to understand the causes of the Croat-Muslim conflict in terms that were not available in the diplomatic reception rooms of the Presidency in Sarajevo.

The first was in the spring of 1995, when it was still impossible to get into Sarajevo because of the siege. We flew first to Stuttgart, where the European Command's General Charles Boyd was conducting a verbal campaign against the federation—especially the Muslims—and in favor of the Serbs. My remark to this effect to his political adviser—Jacques Klein, later to be the UN transitional administrator in eastern Slavonia and deputy high representative in Sarajevo—won me a one-hour private session with the general. Had I heard anyone who was pro-Serb during my day's briefings with his intelligence folks? No, I said honestly, we had had a good and highly professional exchange of views. The general then proceeded to lecture me on how the Serbs had been blamed for too much and the Muslims for too little, a lecture he later published in large part in *Foreign Affairs* (in the September-October 1995 issue). The publication happened to coincide with the U.S. revelation in the Security Council of a mass grave in eastern Bosnia, containing several hundred Muslims murdered by Serbs.

The stop in Stuttgart served its main purpose: to cushion Boyd's opposition to our activities. We picked up two of his intelligence people to travel with us, which helped the mission look a bit weightier. I had already had some pro-federation language inserted in a UN Security Council resolution and Sewall wisely used his acquaintance with Kofi Annan to ensure us UN logistical support. We went into Bosnia (after the obligatory stop in Zagreb) by UN helicopter from Split, landing at Medjugorje, site of Bosnia-Herzegovina's most famous Catholic shrine.

We met almost immediately with Jadranko Prlic (later foreign minister of Bosnia and Herzegovina), whose bald head and glassy stare convinced many Westerners that he looked like a war criminal. His imminent indictment by the Hague Tribunal was rumored for months. Prlic in the spring of 1995 was the defense minister of the Croat Republic of Herzeg-Bosna, the parastate the Croats created during their war with the Muslims, as well as deputy defense minister of the Republic of Bosnia-Herzegovina (the Muslim-controlled government in Sarajevo). Reporters later told me that he had been in charge of the siege of Mostar, a particularly brutal effort in 1993 to chase the Muslims from the western part of the city and to destroy the eastern part. I later discussed the accusations with him. He thought himself not guilty of sins of commission, though he felt some guilt about omissions. In any event, he would go to The Hague if indicted, a declaration he later repeated in public.

During my first meeting with Prlic, the main topic was the basic defense law of the federation, which had been under discussion for more than a year between Prlic and his Muslim counterpart. Only three problems remained in the text, Prlic said, presenting us helpfully with an English translation: the name of the army (would it be called *Armija*, the name used by the Bosnian Army, or *Vojska*, the name preferred by the Croats?); the commander in chief of the army (the Croats would not accept President Izetbegovic); and how it was to be decided whether someone would serve in the Bosnian Army component of the federation forces or the Croatian Defense Council portion (the HVO), it having already been decided to preserve the two separate components. Only casually did he mention another big problem: the HVO was being paid about 300 deutsche marks per month (raised recently from 100) while the Bosnian Army was unpaid but received ample food rations. It was obviously going to be difficult to merge the two armies into a single force unless the soldiers were paid the same amounts.

The differences of course were greater than Prlic led us to believe. The fundamental problem was that the Croats were not prepared to give up a separate military force while the Muslims wanted a single army under Izetbegovic's control. I was later to spend many hours mediating this problem, resolving some aspects but not others. Only with the advent of the Equip and Train program aimed at arming and training the federation forces were the issues resolved, and even then with great difficulty.

John Sewall, our European Command (EUCOM) colleagues, and I proceeded on what was to be a tour of the federation, at peace with itself but still at war—at least its Muslim portion—with the Serbs. We drove north from Mostar, past still-contested power plants, to the gloomy Muslim town of Jablanica, where we sat down for our first talks with majors and colonels who had once fought each other but were now nominally allied in the federation. It was not sweetness and light. A Muslim major vigorously accused the HVO of continuing to hold Muslim war prisoners in Croatia and offered as proof the testimony of recent returnees. The Croats were relatively restrained in response, but took us aside afterward to explain that these were Muslim deserters who told such stories to explain their disappearance during the war. This was close to the truth, we later concluded— the prison camp turned out to be a refugee camp, out of which the Muslim returnees, who probably had deserted, simply walked. Distrust caused both sides to tape the entire conversation.

Several hours of mutual accusations later, Sewall and I were whisked into a Herzeg-Bosna–plated BMW and taken up the hill to the Bosnian Army's local guest house. Luxurious it was not, but as we later found out much more comfortable than the "hotel" where our colleagues, anxious about whether they would ever see us again, remained. Sewall and I hesitated to talk much, as we were reasonably sure of being listened to, but we took a stroll in the small village and appreciated the truly spectacular mountains facing us, which gave us some security from the Serb lines not too many kilometers away. We noted a few positive signs from this first day: the Croats and the Muslims quarreled, but they were blunt and open with each other; we were being escorted, as we had requested, by officers of both armies (something the CIA had told us was impossible); the escorts had traveled in each other's territory previously (that is, without foreigners present); and both Croats and Muslims agreed that the Serbs were the enemy, much as they might not like each other.

The next day we were off to Vitez, where I came to appreciate the profound absurdities of the war, and the peace. Our host was an HVO colonel,
whose forces still surrounded the old Muslim center of the town but were
in turn surrounded by much stronger Muslim forces outside the town. Sour-
faced but professional, he took us and our Bosnian Army escorts to the
confrontation line above Vitez, showing us the trenches separated by no
more than a hundred yards and noting carefully the minefields, which had
not been cleared. That evening I talked at length with one of the HVO
generals and the local Croat potentates about why they had gone to war
with their Muslim neighbors. The fundamental issues were surprisingly
familiar: which language (or dialect, depending on your perspective) should
be used in the schools, what should be taught there, and who was going to
decide. When I asked how the Croats, a minority on the newly formed
federation city council, would pursue their interests, the response was telling: the federation rules gave them complete equality—they were not a
minority—and nothing could be decided without their consent.

In the morning, we stopped by the Catholic church. The Croat part of
town was visibly more prosperous than the Muslim part, and much more
damage had been done to the mosque than to the church. "No," the
Franciscan priest said, he had no regular contacts with the local imam,
though they had spoken once since the fighting (the mosque was no more
than a couple of hundred yards away). Nor had he offered any assistance in
rebuilding the mosque. My military colleagues pressed the point: Why not
organize a reconciliation picnic, parading through both parts of town? The
priest looked at them with disbelief and assured them that he had no role
to play in local politics (and that he had never seen any of the HVO officers
present in church). Vatican officials later told me their frustration at not
being able to convince the Franciscans to play a more positive role.

We met General Rasim Delic, the Bosnian Army commander, for the
first time in Zenica and traveled together to Kakanj. Imposing and
unamiable, he had doubts about a civilian like me and felt more comfortable talking with General Sewall. Delic was clear and realistic about military matters and profoundly ill equipped on civilian questions. He did not
hide his distaste for the HVO, which he regarded as illegal and illegitimate,
even if unavoidable and necessary as an ally in the current situation. Nor
did he mince words about the West's failure to prevent the Serbs from getting military assistance from Belgrade, which paid the Serb Army officers—the Bosnian Army found their pay stubs in the pockets of the dead—
and provided at night lots of equipment across pontoon bridges on the Drina.

I got a chance to ask Delic a key question: What was his army's war aim?
The intelligence community and EUCOM had told me the Bosnian Army

aimed to conquer 100 percent of the territory, an aim the Croats did not share because there were no Croats in most of eastern Bosnia before the war. Delic's response was revealing: to enable all those who want to return to their homes in 100 percent of the territory of Bosnia-Herzegovina to do so. For all their mutual hostility, this was an aim the Croats and the Muslims could share.

The response did not entirely surprise me. We had already met with General Mehmed Alagic, one of the corps commanders, in Travnik. Alagic's headquarters were decorated with bucolic landscapes, in oil. We asked about the paintings. They were of his hometown near Sanski Most, he said, and he was fighting to go home. So, too, were many of his men, whom he had organized into units to fight for the recovery of their hometowns. I was to think of this response the next fall, when the Bosnian Army failed to observe the Dayton cease-fire around Sanski Most and fought on for several days, much to the dismay of some in Washington. It was Alagic, fighting to go home. The issue of repatriation of displaced people and refugees, regarded so often in America and Western Europe as a romantic desire of old women in babushkas to return home, in fact involves men with guns. The failure to fulfill their desires is still the major unresolved issue of the Bosnian war.

We flew on from Kakanj to Tuzla and from there to Tomislavgrad, passing over many villages in central Bosnia whose roofs had been blown, from the inside, during the Croat-Muslim war. My military colleagues found this fascinating, and appalling. I found myself intrigued by the lunarlike landscape above Tomislavgrad, not the least because it helped take my mind off a stomach that found the ride in fog and rain rougher than it liked. It seemed somehow fitting that people who lived in this strange place had strange habits and conducted their wars in ways that were difficult to comprehend.

By then, though, I had a pretty good idea of what had motivated the Muslims and the Croats. Their fighting was essentially over political control and in fact was most intense where control was most uncertain: in those areas where Muslims and Croats were close to equal in population. Tomislavgrad had seen no war between Muslims and Croats, because all understood that the Croats (with 85 percent or so of the population) had the upper hand there. Likewise, in Tuzla the Muslims were clearly in control, and in addition a common enemy stood close by, so Croats and Muslims did not fight each other around Tuzla. But in Novi Travnik, Bugojno, Mostar, Gornji Vakuf, Vitez, and other places in central Bosnia, they fought to establish who would be in charge, seeking (in a peculiar perversion of democratic principles) to chase out as many of their opponents as possible. It is true that the Muslims were on the whole less vicious about it, but that was because they had a majority in central Bosnia as a whole. The Croats were literally fighting to avoid being a minority, believing that there could be no worse fate for their national identity. Neither adversary appeared to have the slightest notion that a minority could thrive in a democracy, or that they were doing harm to themselves by destroying each other. One of my colleagues later told me the story of a meeting with Muslims and Croats at which the Muslims claimed that a decision had been made democratically; the Croats responded that it was not true. "They outvoted us," said that defeated side.

Our wrap-up meeting was in Mostar, where for the first time we were able to talk with HVO commander Tihomir Blaskic, later indicted for war crimes committed during the Croat-Muslim war, and on trial as of July 1999. Tall, young, and good looking, he had replaced the wartime HVO commander—Ante Roso—who gave fascist salutes to his troops. Blaskic deferred on all but strictly military questions to Vladimir Soljic, who was then defense minister of Herzeg-Bosna and later defense minister and president of the federation. Soljic delivered long historical tirades on Croatian culture, the history of Bosnia—which he doubted really existed—the difficulties of overcoming past events, and the Croats' strict adherence to NATO principles of civilian control over the military and more generally to Western culture, which they were prepared to defend against onslaughts from Islam.

Our task at this point was to deliver some sort of sensible idea about how to reconcile the HVO and the Bosnian Army and begin the process of building up a federation army. John Sewall had concluded that integration below the corps level would not be possible in the foreseeable future, but that the civilian and military command structures should be brought together and a combined defense ministry and joint staff formed. This ministry and joint staff might begin to focus not so much on military issues per se, but rather on civilian/military issues, such as war prisoners (or allegations thereof), repatriation of displaced persons, reconstruction of basic infrastructure, and elimination of checkpoints, and only gradually move on to real military command and control once the war was over. It was a modest proposal, one both sides could accept, even in their current state of continuing tension. It was to become an important step toward the Dayton accords.

Sewall and I returned to Bosnia a couple of months later to visit the newly established joint staff at Novi Travnik. It was not much: largely empty rooms in a town where an HVO officer at one end of the main street told me that the arms factory at the other end had been closed for some time, though I had just come back from a run during which I had seen dozens of Muslims headed for work in the clearly active facility. We found it difficult to get Blaskic and Delic into the same room at the same time. When we succeeded, Delic complained bitterly that Blaskic was not really in charge of the HVO, which was commanded by a Croatian army general who was calling the shots in the campaign to retake large portions of western Bosnia. Muslim officers failed to find the restaurant the Croats took us to, though we had all sat peaceably enough at the meetings during the day.

The Bosnian Federation was, however, winning the war, with the HVO and the Bosnian Army fighting in parallel—and even competing for territory—and without combining their operations. As Sewall and I headed out once again to visit the federation forces in August 1995, President Clinton launched his peace initiative. I immediately called to see whether we were still doing the right thing in supporting the federation, since the peace initiative (the details of which were secret) might not have included it. I was assured that the peace initiative did and that we were doing the right thing, but we received a call in Stuttgart a few days later. Washington was concerned that we not be seen as encouraging the federation to pursue its military success when the White House was calling for a cease-fire. Our efforts on behalf of a federation army were over until Dayton.

I suspected then, and believe now, that the federation—with Croatian support—would have taken Banja Luka within weeks if the HVO and the Bosnian Army had been allowed to fight on. Stories of stiffening Serb resistance were invented to frighten Izetbegovic, who had ample reason to wonder if his army was overextending itself. The American insistence on a cease-fire ended the fighting and saved President Clinton's peace initiative, but it also saved Serbian president Slobodan Milosevic from a vast influx of Serb refugees from Bosnia who would have threatened his hold on power. And it left Bosnia a divided country, one where war criminals are still at large and hundreds of thousands of displaced people and refugees are prevented from going home.

## Getting Ready for Peace

The Bosnian Federation was already at peace. I had felt for some time that we had to do more to support reconstruction, reconciliation, and repatriation. The essential ingredient was economic recovery: Croats and Muslims would never really be reconciled until they prospered, preferably together. The Croat-controlled portion of the country had not suffered as much as the Muslim-controlled portion. The thriving Croat wartime economy—based in part on arms smuggling and other black marketeering—threatened to cause a kind of economic partition to parallel the political partition between the Sarajevo government and the Herzeg-Bosna authorities in

Mostar. AID was already at work in Bosnia, channeling very limited resources (now increased to about $30 million) into federation projects through nongovernmental organizations (NGOs) with a clear focus on ethnic reconciliation (separate but equal projects were forbidden). But Bosnia needed much more than AID: it needed the U.S. Treasury, and it needed the World Bank and the International Monetary Fund (IMF).

The World Bank and the IMF had already begun meeting with federation officials. I first met the soft-spoken duo of Bosnian financial stability—the aging Muslim central bank governor Kasim Omicevic and the young, soccer-playing Croat finance minister Neven Tomic—on a visit they made to Washington in the early spring of 1995. Tomic, later the Croat deputy prime minister of the post-Dayton Bosnia and Herzegovina, had kept the Croat tax system as close to the Muslim one as possible during the Croat-Muslim war, when he was finance minister of Herzeg-Bosna, in anticipation of reconciliation. Omicevic also seemed committed in that direction and had the additional virtue of having refused to print money for the Sarajevo government—he would issue only local currency during the war against hard currency deposits in the bank. This policy avoided serious inflation in the Muslim-controlled areas (it was avoided in Croat-controlled areas by the use of the Croatian kuna, which closely followed the deutsche mark) and made economic reconciliation a real possibility, though the road to it turned out to be long and hard.

The IMF and the World Bank refused, however, to send people into Bosnia. I managed to convince the U.S. Treasury to do so, using initially a professor from the University of Connecticut, Robert Kravchuk. He was hesitant about entering a war zone, but after a lot of encouragement (and many difficult-to-make phone calls to arrange his appointments in Bosnia), he finally went to Mostar and caught the bug of providing support for the Bosnian Federation. Tax, budget, and other experts followed, paving the way for the much-needed international financial institutions (IFIs).

What were they trying to do? There were several big problems: the currencies used in the Croat- and Muslim-controlled areas were different, the payment system that would allow checks to be written in Mostar and cashed in Sarajevo had broken down, the federation had no revenue at all, and customs—when collected—were being deposited to the accounts of Herzeg-Bosna and the Muslim-controlled Republic of Bosnia-Herzegovina (not to the federation). The currency problem, we decided early on, was difficult, and a proposition I liked won the day until Dayton (and as it turned out for a long time afterward as well): the deutsche mark, in use throughout the federation, should be allowed to continue to circulate as its de facto currency, while the Bosnian dinar and Croatian kuna circulated in parallel. The problem, as I (and many others) saw it, was that Bosnia had joined the deutsche mark zone; no federation currency was going to be attractive enough to chase it (or the kuna) out of circulation, and no state existed that could enforce its use. The system was functioning reasonably well, and Bosnia was in fact monetarily where most of Western Europe wanted to be (in the deutsche mark zone), so why fix it?

The payment system, revenue, and customs were more intricate problems. The federation could not begin to operate without revenue, which was all going to two other governments: Herzeg-Bosna and the Republic of Bosnia and Herzegovina, the first illegitimate and the second not in control of the territory it claimed. The payments system was essential to reviving commerce within the federation, which all too obviously was still limited to the Croat-controlled areas. So our Treasury experts set out to try to reestablish a common payments system, find some revenue for the federation, prepare its first budget, and reestablish legitimate customs authorities.

It would take much longer than we anticipated, largely because of the enormous political obstacles in the way, and because Dayton interrupted the process. The political obstacles became more difficult as Dayton approached in the fall of 1995. Neither Croats nor Muslims wanted to give up anything in advance of what they expected to be the crucial deal making. The Croats held on to Herzeg-Bosna, the de facto government of the part of the country that the HVO controlled; giving it up was their ultimate bargaining chip. The Muslims held on to the Republic of Bosnia-Herzegovina, which in their view was the government of all of Bosnia-Herzegovina and had the right to represent Bosnia abroad, even if it controlled only a small portion of the country. As the second meeting of Friends of the Federation approached in September 1995 in Madrid, I was hectically trying to square this circle, getting the Croats to give up Herzeg-Bosna in favor of the federation and the Muslims to delegate authority over all but essential issues from the republic to the federation.

In Washington, the importance of what I was trying to do was clear enough. Without a strong federation, the peace process to come would be built on an infirm foundation, one that could easily collapse and leave Bosnia in three pieces: Croat, Muslim, and Serb. It was the Muslim ministate that caused the State Department, the White House, and the Pentagon to be concerned. Partition would likely lead to a greater Croatia and a greater Serbia, a process that would suggest to others (in particular the Kosovar Albanians) that national aspirations could be satisfied through the use of force, and that of course was to be avoided. But it was the "rump" Muslim state that was expected, under Iranian sponsorship, to cause chronic security problems for Europe and the United States.

The Serbs had already managed to carve out an area largely cleansed of Muslims and Croats. The creation of the federation in March 1994 suggested that Bosnia would be divided between the federation and the Serbs, on the basis of the Contact Group's already-agreed 51/49 split, though many still hoped the federation would become all of Bosnia in due course, and that possibility was purposely left open. Richard Holbrooke began discussions within the State Department as early as the spring of 1995 on how to approach a possible peace negotiation. In a brainstorming roundtable of Bosnia hands, including Roberts Owen and Lloyd Cutler from outside the department, he put forward the notion that the "map," that is, the way in which Bosnia was to be divided internally, could be left to the last, as it would be very difficult to draw. Instead, he wanted to begin with what he termed "constitutional arrangements." Both our ambassador in Zagreb, Peter Galbraith, and I objected, on grounds that this would lead to the recognition of the Serb Republic and acceptance of ethnic cleansing. Galbraith argued that the "Serb Republic" should be recognized only if it clearly met international human rights standards. We were not only overruled, but also treated thereafter as threats to Holbrooke's broader enterprise, however useful we might be in our more narrowly assigned roles. Criticism was treated as disloyalty.

The American readiness to accept Bosnia's division between the federation and the Serb Republic made the federation even more critical. Only by preserving the integrity of the federation could the collapse into three-way partition be avoided. But Holbrooke, while eager to see the federation preserved, was unwilling to put his own growing prestige behind it. After insisting that the Spanish go ahead with the Friends meeting in Madrid (they were hesitant to do so as the broader negotiation approached), he refused to attend it. I was sent off to Bosnia to prepare for the meeting, it having been made plain to me that no one in Washington would lift a finger but would be glad to place the blame on my shoulders if the federation did not get to Dayton in good shape.

It got there, and in reasonable shape, but it was not an easy road. Nor was the one I traveled in Bosnia. Ejup Ganic, the vice president of the federation, was clearly one of the keys to moving forward politically, but he had been severely injured earlier in the year in an automobile accident (and saved by Croat police, who transported him to a hospital in Split). His interim replacement, Edhem Bicakcic, was a man of serious political weight in Muslim Bosnia, but he was unwilling to move far in dealing with the

Croats. I went to Sarajevo once again, but this time decided to go see Ganic in Fojnica, where he was recuperating in an orthopedic hospital.

My trip there was the first I made overland through Serb lines, the cease-fire having taken full effect. Sarajevo for me had always been an island, a small one surrounded by sharks—not even a toe stuck out in the wrong direction. It was an adventure to climb into an armored Humvee, squat and uncomfortable, and drive up the main street, past the Muslim and Serb checkpoints. Landmines were still visible (they were put on the road at night) as we left the all but leveled Croat neighborhood of Stup and entered the Serb neighborhood of Ilidza, at one end of the airport runway—probably the place from which Serb snipers took potshots at UN aircraft landing in Sarajevo. There was clearly less destruction in these neighborhoods than in Sarajevo, but lots of obvious misery, with packages of cigarettes and gasoline in quart glass jugs and gallon plastic containers the main signs of commerce. Curiosity, anger, dismay greeted the sight of this American-flagged vehicle moving quickly through the streets and on into the countryside. We crossed Croat checkpoints, refusing to stop, and then back into Muslim-controlled territory and the pleasant mountain village of Fojnica, streets crowded with Muslim males, many of them on crutches or showing other obvious signs of war injuries. The bullet-scarred hospital looked out over a Catholic church on the hillside, still guarded by the HVO.

I asked Ganic, who was well into his recovery, what he thought the Croats and the Muslims could bring to the meeting in Madrid that would convince the Serbs that the Bosnian Federation was real and would be a serious interlocutor in Dayton. Zubak had been less than forthcoming during our discussions in Sarajevo, though he had made reference to party discussions among both Croats and Muslims that might lead in a good direction. Ganic explained that the major nationalist parties were close to agreement on a scheme that would separate the federation government from the government of Bosnia and Herzegovina. Ministers were still "double-hatted." The idea would be to appoint two separate sets of ministers, defining their distinct functions clearly, and divvying up the portfolios in both governments according to an ethnically based formula.

This would be a major step, one that would begin the inevitable process of thinning out the functions of the republic and devolving authority toward the cantons and the municipalities. Why inevitable? Because reducing the functions of the central government was clearly the only way of convincing the Serbs to remain in Bosnia (other than force of arms). It would also help with the Croats, who resented Muslim domination of the national government and, like minorities in many other situations, argued for greater local control, especially of schools. The Croats wanted Izetbegovic to become president of the federation, even if he remained president of the republic, believing that only then would real power be devolved from the republic to the federation. The Muslims, however, thought the Croats were trying to trick Izetbegovic out of the republic presidency and refused to go along.

In order to convince the Muslims to "weaken" the central government, the Croats were going to have to give up Herzeg-Bosna and allow its functions to be transferred to federation institutions. This they refused to do in Madrid, where the German Contact Group representative Michael Steiner and I spent many hours trying to convince Zubak, who refused to budge a comma from what his political party had decided the week before. Madrid was nevertheless useful, as it was a well-attended meeting (about thirty-five countries and many international organizations), at which it was made clear to the Bosnians that they had to move ahead with the federation or risk the loss of aid and a weakened position in negotiations with the Serbs. The Spanish were disappointed, though, because Holbrooke did not come and Washington ignored the event, which unveiled the important idea of separating the federation and republic governments for the first time.

## DAYTON FROM A DIFFERENT ANGLE

Dayton began not long after. I was not there for the opening. Holbrooke was continuing to ignore the federation: he wanted it there and knew the importance of it being there, but he wanted to expend none of his own physical energies or political capital on it. He soon found that the Muslims and the Croats were not ready to negotiate with the Serbs until they had sorted out some of their own problems. Holbrooke persuaded them to agree to repatriation of displaced people to four towns in central Bosnia so that he could announce something to the press, an agreement he quickly forgot about (and never wrote down). But he was not going to waste time on the federation. I received a call on the second day, asking me to come immediately, and I arrived in Dayton the next morning.

I was to continue working with Michael Steiner, and over the next ten days we fashioned with the Muslims and the Croats an agreement that foreshadowed much of what Dayton was ultimately about. Authority over all but functions essential to sovereignty and the need to interact with the rest of the world would be devolved from the central government to a separate federation government. Herzeg-Bosna would be dissolved, a federation payments system would be created, and refugees would be repatriated. I got the Muslims and the Croats to write down, sign, and transmit to Bosnia the repatriation agreement Holbrooke had announced to the press—though years of constant effort by many people have not yet led to its full implementation. The federation army would be created along the lines John Sewall proposed. We brought in the Muslim and Croat mayors of Mostar, and the Germans took the lead in getting them to agree on a unifying statute for the divided city.

The work went well in an environment that I would describe as a sleep-away camp for adults, some of whom had just finished a war. Holbrooke had chosen the air force base at Dayton in order to isolate the participants and give himself maximum control, both of them and of the press coverage. This made it appear for a few weeks a kind of Olympus, where the gods gathered and occasionally allowed a few mortals in. The reality was of course more mundane. Some of the participants seemed to watch a lot of *America's Funniest Home Videos* in the "sports bar." I spent most of my many waking hours doing a gavotte from one room to another, working out the details of the federation agreement: from Prlic's messy bedroom, to Zubak's impeccable sitting room, back to Izetbegovic's identical sitting room, to the furious Silajdzic and the amiable but unreliable Bosnian ambassador to the United Nations Mohammed Sacirbey, a few words with the Muslim lawyers (always a last-minute stumbling block), back up to see Steiner and his ever-gloomy but profoundly committed associate, Christian Clages. Every once in a while there would be a group meeting, but they were unlike so many we had all attended: short, businesslike, and largely friendly. The Dayton magic Holbrooke had hoped for was working.

I came to appreciate during those ten days as I had not before the position of the Croats. Prlic was particularly effective in convincing me that the Muslims were blocking the federation, because they were holding on to the republic in preparation for an even tougher negotiation with the Serbs. This was true. John Sewall, who came briefly to Dayton to help out with the military portion of the federation negotiations, and I went to see Izetbegovic to ask him to accept eventual amalgamation of the HVO and the Bosnian Army, under a commander in chief who would be the president of the federation. He turned us down flat, insisting on the separate existence of the Bosnian Army and his own role as commander in chief. He did not soften in response to our argument that this would leave the HVO a separate army with its own commander in chief. Nevertheless, we persuaded the Muslims to agree to give up enough of the central government authority that the Croats agreed to give up Herzeg-Bosna and turn its functions over to the federation. It seemed a big triumph at the time, though implementation has taken years.

My biggest problems at Dayton were with the American delegation. First, I was blamed for not having finished up the work on the federation before Dayton. Then, when Steiner and I began to succeed, we were resented for having success while the broader negotiation appeared to be failing. Indeed, the Federation Agreement reached after ten days at Dayton was the first real result there and, until the last moment, looked as if it might be the most significant. And there were several moments when the federation negotiations risked contradictions with the broader effort in Dayton, where the Americans were staking out a position in favor of as strong a central government as possible.

One row during the ten days or so I spent in Dayton concerned the central bank. Previous federation agreements had foreseen the formation of a federation central bank, and the federation payments system was an essential step in that direction. Holbrooke, however, had promised the Muslims that he would support the central government institutions, including a central bank (which he wrote into the Constitution that the Americans tabled at Dayton). I was convinced, as were the World Bank and the IMF, that the Serbs would not in fact implement a central bank for some time to come (no matter what they signed) and that one was essential for moving ahead with World Bank and IMF assistance. The federation bank, in this view, would be a stepping-stone, one that would eventually be expanded to include the Serbs and thereby become a central government institution in due course.

Holbrooke wanted none of this. Monetary policy and a single Bosnian currency would have to belong to the central government from the first, and the bank would begin operating within weeks. I was told to shut up about this, and to get World Bank official Christine Wallich to Dayton. I found Wallich somewhere in Germany, on her way back from Sarajevo. She somehow managed to arrive in Washington late that evening and in Dayton the next morning. An early convert to support for the federation, she repeated my line before I told her what it was: a federation central bank could be formed almost immediately and should act as a transition institution (to enable the IMF and World Bank to begin working in Bosnia) until the Serbs agreed to join. Holbrooke, told what she would say, refused to speak with her, even when we met around the quad, though she eventually managed to get in her pitch. He was unmovable. Two years later, there was still no functioning central bank in Bosnia, though eventually a rudimentary one began to operate.

The Germans caused a second row. Behind my back, Steiner began working with the Muslims and the Croats on the division of portfolios in the new federation government, which we all understood was a precondition for implementing the separation of the federation government from the republic government. Holbrooke, seeing that the text of the federation agreement was finished but not knowing about this side negotiation, consulted directly with Steiner and decided to get Secretary of State Christopher to Dayton to witness the signing of the agreement. The Croatians, realizing that this gave them enormous leverage, threatened the evening before the signing (after Christopher's presence had been announced) not to sign unless the personnel question was settled first.

Holbrooke turned on me, casting blame for this snafu (though Steiner had blindsided him as he had me). I was called at midnight to a meeting, asked to explain my having screwed up and was told, toward 1:00 A.M., to go get Steiner. I arrived at Steiner's door to find that the Germans had posted one of their military officers to protect him from being awakened, as Holbrooke had already called demanding that he come over for the meeting. Across the hall, the chief British delegate was having a loud tirade about how the Americans had cut the Europeans out of all the important negotiations. Though I was grudgingly forgiven for not physically engaging the German soldier, the next morning I woke Steiner up and began the process of getting the Croatians to back off, or the Muslims to agree to a division of the ministerial posts. Steiner was enormously pleased with himself: he was using the leverage provided by the American secretary of state's visit to get the Muslims to agree on a division of posts in the federation government, but in the end Holbrooke got the Croatians to back off their threat not to sign.

The Germans insisted that I sit on the dais with Steiner during the signing, something Holbrooke's people resented. Word of the agreement had been published the day before in the *Washington Post*, with an accurate description of its contents. This meant it could not have been Holbrooke who leaked, as one of his minions commented to me, since he did not understand the details of the agreement. I later realized that I was suspected, though in fact I did not speak with any reporters at Dayton until the briefing Steiner and I gave after the signing. Suspicion was all that was required. I was told to get on the secretary's plane and go back to Washington that evening. Dayton for me was over.

## ANOTHER ROUGH WINTER

I was surprised, as nearly everyone was, when Dayton ended in success, but I also knew it meant more work for me on the federation. The agreement we had reached on separating the federation government from that of the republic and dissolving Herzeg-Bosna would require constant tending and prodding from abroad. So too would many details—down to the color of the federation police uniforms. I was back in Sarajevo a few days after Dayton had ended. Now, though, the path was reasonably clear: the Dayton agreement on the federation had to be converted into legislation and the institutions of the federation nurtured, not the least with money. The Federation Parliament met often and at length, and I became a fixture at its sometimes dull, sometimes lively debates, listening through an interpreter whose understanding of the issues was limited and lobbying for the steps needed to build up federation institutions.

Snow was on the ground again and peace had supposedly arrived, but there was still shooting around the city. The embassy, inundated with congressional visitors whose support would be critical to obtaining essential resources, could no longer provide me with an armored car and a driver, as it had during wartime. I began walking and making my own appointments through "state protocol," a couple of Bosnian officers who tried to keep up with the schedules of the harried inhabitants of the Presidency building.

This worked well enough but gave me the occasional jitters. Walking back to the Holiday Inn one night with $3,000 in my pocket—there was no way to pay for anything in Sarajevo except with cash, and nowhere to get cash, so it had to be carried in—I was passing the ruined towers of a Bosnian conglomerate when a slow-paced firefight broke out between Muslim snipers in the towers and Serb snipers on the other side of the hotel in Grabavica. The foolishness of what I was doing suddenly seemed obvious, though by the next day I had forgotten that realization. Sometimes people think of this behavior—ignoring danger to get a job done—as courage, but in fact it more closely resembles forgetfulness. I was always careful, at least to obey whatever security rules the embassy imposed, but I rarely thought about the risks or regarded the work as dangerous. Those who did avoided it.

A word about the American embassy is in order. For the next six months, I became more or less the embassy's most frequent visitor. John Menzies, who had picked me up at the airport on my first visit more than a year before, had become first chargé and then ambassador. The embassy had moved out of the Holiday Inn and into its renovated building. The half-dozen American staff had lived for a year in their offices. This was a courageous, hardworking team, with the easygoing, devoted Menzies providing a sense of purpose and mission. Unfortunately, Washington treated them with a lack of respect that made their job doubly difficult: phone calls at all hours every night, constant demands on minor issues, poor equipment scrounged from castoffs of other embassies, and inadequate personnel. I remember more than once having to ask someone to stand up because I needed a chair to sit at a computer.

My own role in the embassy was odd. Not quite staff, not really visitor. I tried to stay out of the way, but all too often found I had to pitch in on non-federation work to help get the job done. I wrote the cable asking for Secretary of Commerce Ron Brown to visit, because a contact of mine warned that the French and the Swedes were taking the lion's share of new contracts in electric utility reconstruction. I also reported on Bosnian relations with Iran, because key officials would discuss the issue with me. Not everyone was pleased to have a fifth wheel around, and at one point I returned to Sarajevo unexpectedly and found my photograph had been put up on one of the computers as a screen saver, along with other disliked figures: Milosevic and Tudjman to be precise. I laughed it off—and took a copy of the photo home on a disk.

By mid-December 1995, I was eager to get out of Sarajevo in any event. The Croats and the Muslims were beginning to make progress, and I was afraid I would become part of the wallpaper—a familiar part of the surroundings that could be ignored. It was better, I thought, to go away, giving them a few things to get done, and come back in a week or two, the impending visit serving as a deadline for their efforts. It worked fairly well: though they as often as not fell short or missed deadlines, progress was still in the right direction.

On the day I was to leave, along with Air Force Lieutenant Colonel Tony Simpson, a heavy snowfall began. Off to the airport we went in any event. We spent the better part of two days there. The Norwegians who ran the passenger operation movement control (movcon) there explained laughingly that the French had neglected to begin plowing the runways until early in the morning, though any fool knew they should have been plowed almost from the first flake that dropped during the night. In addition, they failed to plow wide enough for the gigantic Russian Ilyushins used by the United Nations to land. NATO was already moving in, so there were dozens of planes landing and taking off (though none from the United States as yet). But we had permission to fly only on UN aircraft. Simpson worked long and hard to get us out, talking with pilots and even phoning a secretary in the U.K. Ministry of Defence we had met a couple of months earlier for permission to board a Royal Air Force plane. All to no avail. We finally left on a UN High Commissioner for Refugees flight to Ancona, took the train to Rome, and watched the Dayton signing from the luxury of the Ambasciatori Hotel.

On the morning that we had left for Rome, we had been awakened at the Holiday Inn by a louder volley of gunfire than I had ever heard before in Sarajevo, where the sound of distant mortars and machine guns had become background noise. I considered for a moment getting out of bed and looking out the window, but that seemed foolhardy. If I could hear it, I was alive. Why put yourself at risk looking out a window? I rolled over and went back to bed, as if the noise was no more consequential than my next-door neighbor's Harley on Saturday morning. I discovered later that the Serbs had drilled a round of antiaircraft fire into the facade of the hotel, just one empty room from where I was sleeping.

I had always stayed at the Holiday Inn, but that winter decided to try a hotel favored at the time by the journalists, the Bosna. Tucked into the older (but not the oldest) part of the city, the hotel not only was hidden from Serb gunners but also had more heat and electricity than the precariously situated Holiday Inn. But it was also directly across from a noisy discotheque, and the journalists' jeeps would be idling outside by 5:00 A.M. That left little time for peaceful sleep, in a room narrow enough for me to touch opposite walls standing in the middle.

In front of the Bosna one snowy morning, just after I had managed for the first time to change dollars to deutsche marks in Sarajevo, I happened to run into the finance minister, Neven Tomic. As we stood knee-deep in the snow I could see that he was clearly not in an accommodating mood. He asked me to come see him in an hour.

I rounded up a German colleague, Christian Clages, who was working on the federation, and crossed the street to the Finance Ministry. Tomic was furious. With so much work being done on the federation's finances, the Muslims had the day before convened a session of the Republic Parliament, a parliament of a republic that had supposedly gone out of business with the signing of the Dayton agreements. The Republic Parliament had granted financial benefits worth several billion dollars to the members of the Bosnian Army, ignoring entirely the HVO as well as the IMF and the World Bank. Jadranko Prlic called while we were with Tomic and gave me an earful. I could do little at the time, but the incident reminded me of how much the federation problems were two sided, and how important it was to get to work on building up a real defense ministry.

By late January or early February 1996 the new federation government had been formed and approved in the Federation Parliament. I was in Sarajevo a great deal during that period, trying to ensure that the new institutions were up and running, including the cantons and municipalities as well as the ministries, police, customs authority, and courts. A lot of the work was "troubleshooting"—removing obstacles one by one as they arose. One day it would be the removal of checkpoints on the road to Mostar, another it would be municipal boundaries for those towns that were divided by the Dayton Interentity Boundary Line that divided the federation from Republika Srpska or voting procedures for people no longer living where they had before the war. Washington was always impatient with the slow pace and the constant unraveling of agreements.

An example will help to illustrate. The Germans, eager as usual to be part of the federation game, scheduled another meeting in Petersberg for late winter 1996, outside Bonn, in the hope that they could take credit for resolution of some of the difficulties then facing the federation. The most dramatic was the question of a federation flag and a coat of arms. The Federation Parliament had held a contest for their design, one that had produced two or three attractive proposals selected by a committee of Croats and Muslims. But the committee did not want to take the political heat for choosing the winner and left it up to Croat president Kresimir Zubak and Bosniak vice president Ejup Ganic of the federation.

Zubak refused to accept any of the contest winners, and there ensued a lengthy and acrimonious debate. The Bosniaks, as was their wont, claimed to be flexible; the Croats insisted that the coat of arms include the entire Croat "checkerboard," rather than merely a few squares. In the midst of this heated discussion, the Croat party chief suddenly proposed the coat of arms of the last king of Bosnia, who he knew was a Catholic. The Muslim prime minister, Hasan Muratovic, remembered that this coat of arms was on the base of a statue in Vienna: an arm holding a sword, he said, noting that the international community might object to the sword. In which case, he suggested, they could use only the arm, cocked in a classic clench-fisted gesture that Europeans use for rude purposes. We all laughed as the prime minister demonstrated the gesture, but it was the only good moment in a long and tortuous discussion. It later turned out that the Muslims accepted the coat of arms of the last king: the sword was a curved Turkish scimitar, but the Croats of course rejected it and denied having proposed it.

At this point, with no prospect for positive results in Petersberg, Steiner decided to postpone the meeting. I had warned Washington that he would do so, several days before in a cable analyzing in detail all the unresolved issues we were then working on. But it turned out that the secretary of state was annoyed at the Europeans for threatening to postpone a Bosnia donors' conference because peace implementation was not going well enough. This additional postponement of the Petersberg meeting angered Warren Christopher. Assistant Secretary for Europe John Kornblum told everyone it was my fault, without mentioning that I had warned Washington what was about to happen and had been sent no instructions to resist the postponement.

This was typical. Most people in Washington cared more for what was happening there than for the reality on the ground in Bosnia. Each issue was confronted with an "action plan," one that would establish bureaucratic primacy, but no one ever worried about checking that something was being done to follow through. This approach came closest to disaster during early 1996 when the "Serb suburbs" of Sarajevo, as they were known to the media, were to be handed over to the federation, as provided for in the peace agreement. This happened in the middle of a massive bureaucratic battle: Robert Gallucci, an ambassador at large, had been appointed to lead Dayton implementation, which Kornblum refused to give up. Kornblum had the usual "action plans" prepared, but nothing was really done because priority was given to the bureaucratic fight. I was in Sarajevo during this period and sat in on a meeting with the High Representative's office (the international group charged with overseeing Dayton implementation) and Ambassador Menzies. It was clear that the international community was ill prepared for the turnover, a fact that was reported to Washington. Michael Steiner, by then the number two in the High Representative's office, tried to prevent the Serb exodus from Sarajevo by getting agreement that the Serb police be allowed to stay during the transition. The Serbs then used the police to chase their own population out. The "Serb suburbs," none of which had a Serb plurality before the war, burned.

## SPRING DEFENSE

With peace came the very real need to move further in integrating the Muslim and Croat military establishments, the project John Sewall and I had already worked up until we were stopped in August 1995. When the governments of the republic and the federation were separated the next winter, Vladimir Soljic, the Herzeg-Bosna minister of defense, became minister of defense of the federation. Hasan Cengic became vice minister.

Cengic was to me a great challenge. A Muslim cleric who headed the Islamic Center in Zagreb before the war, he was not seen in Sarajevo during the war but was at the hub of Muslim efforts to acquire arms, principally from Iran, Turkey, and Malaysia, in violation of the UN embargo. This he did with considerable success. He was reputed to be a mysterious figure according to the Croats, a Muslim extremist who had surely enriched himself with arms dealing. They might know, since all the arms he smuggled into Bosnia during the war came through Croatian and Croat-controlled territory, where a quarter to a third of the total was said to be skimmed off.

At first, it was even difficult to find Cengic. After several abortive attempts, I complained to Ganic, who arranged a meeting. The bearded cleric with piercing eyes sat nervously at a table in his office, using a translator despite his more than serviceable command of English. He wore a tie, an obvious concession to his new position and to the need to deal with the likes of me, as he had been described to me as always wearing the buttoned-up collarless shirt familiar as the uniform of Iranians.

As uncomfortable in his new position as he was in his tie, Cengic of course assured me that he supported the federation and would do his best to make it work. He also made it clear that he was not pleased that President Izetbegovic, with whom he had spent time in prison, had chosen this approach. It would be difficult; he resented the Croats' skimming off arms during the war, and blamed Soljic for it. Cengic would be a stickler, he made clear, for Muslim interests.

I expected nothing less and knew that Soljic felt the same way about Croat interests. At that point, they faced three fundamental issues: Who would be commander in chief of the federation armed forces? How integrated would the HVO and the Bosnian Army become? How would the Defense Ministry be organized?

I had already met repeatedly with the "defense experts," a group of Bosniak and Croat officials who had been charged with resolving these issues. Their proposed resolutions had met with political resistance. From my perspective, it was a godsend to have political heavyweights like Soljic, who was tied closely to Croatian defense minister Goyko Susak (they went to grade school together!), and Cengic, who was then notoriously close to Alija Izetbegovic and well connected with General Rasim Delic and others both by professional and family ties. But first I had to get them into the same room.

This proved difficult but not impossible. After several false starts and complaints by me to Zubak and Izetbegovic, Soljic and Cengic appeared on opposite sides of a table in the minister's conference room, each with his own retinue of experts, to expound their sharply differing points of view. Izetbegovic must remain commander in chief of the Bosnian Army, even after it became part of the federation forces, Cengic said; Izetbegovic had no business commanding a federation force, the Croats claimed, since he had no position in the federation. They wanted Zubak, president of the federation, as commander in chief of the Federation Army. Soljic wanted to protect Croats from being drafted into the Bosnian Army; they should be allowed to choose, he thought, either the HVO or the army. Cengic viewed this "right to choose" as an unacceptable challenge to the authority of the state. He wanted complete integration, down to the unit level, in a unified federation force (under Izetbegovic's command), something Soljic was clearly not prepared to accept.

These were not easy meetings, and they were often made more difficult by events occurring outside the meeting room. At one point, I had to detour away from the main issues because Cengic thought two Muslims had been kidnapped by the HVO. It turned out they had driven their truckload of supplies across the Interentity Boundary Line that divided the federation from Republika Srpska into an area known for black marketeering. There the Serb authorities arrested them. But before we had sorted all this out, the Muslims had seized several Croats whom Cengic was threatening to do in if the Croats did not release the two Muslims unharmed. I had some very tough words with Cengic about this kind of misbehavior. Though he appeared to ignore me, his translator told me after the meeting that I had done well. The Croats were released the next day.

Cengic and Soljic did not disagree as much as they thought, but it took awhile to convince them. Both were strong nationalists, each interested in protecting his own "nationality." The more I listened, the more I thought they sounded alike: mirror images of each other. Soljic wanted the Croat President of the federation, Zubak, not to be subordinated to Izetbegovic, the president of a republic that was going out of business. Cengic would not tolerate Izetbegovic being subordinated to Zubak, or left out of the chain of command. Soljic wanted to ensure that no Croat was drafted against his will into the Bosnian Army; Cengic was no happier about the prospect of a Muslim being drafted into the HVO. Cengic wanted full integration, but only if the Federation Army was clearly under Izetbegovic's command. Soljic resisted integration, but could tolerate it if Zubak was in charge.

The question of commander in chief was resolved first. I told the Croats that they could not hope to choose the commander in chief of the Bosnian Army any more than the Muslims could choose the commander in chief of the HVO. The best they could hope for was equal treatment, which fortunately had been provided for in the Dayton Constitution. This put the Croat member of the collective presidency of Bosnia and Herzegovina (presumably Zubak, though not yet chosen) on an equal level with the Muslim member of the collective presidency (presumably Izetbegovic). Izetbegovic would no longer be on a "higher" level and they therefore need not continue to oppose his role in the command structure. He would remain commander in chief of the Bosnian Army, just as Zubak would remain commander in chief of the HVO, with neither subordinated to the other.

This was workable, however, only if the Croats and the Muslims agreed to a more integrated chain of command below the level of the presidency. Both sides agreed, to my dissatisfaction, to exclude the president and the vice president of the federation from the chain of command. The Defense Ministry would be fully integrated, as would be the Joint Staff, as John Sewall had proposed, with separate components at the corps level and below. Some integrated special units would also be possible. As the presidency exercises its command authority over armies directly only in wartime, this arrangement—while peculiar—represented a major advance over the past.

The question of the draft proved extraordinarily complicated. While Soljic and Cengic had parallel interests—to avoid any member of their ethnic group being forced to serve in the other's army—they could not agree on how to achieve this goal. Cengic refused to concede to Soljic any right of draftees to choose; he wanted an appeals procedure that would in practice guarantee the same result, but without doing any damage, in his eyes, to the authority of the state.

We were close to resolving this issue when "train and equip" intervened and took the matter out of my hands. At Dayton, Holbrooke had promised the Muslims arms supplies and training to enable them to defend themselves against the other half of their country, controlled by the Serbs. The arms were to go to the federation. This program had trouble getting off the ground because the United States insisted on controlling it but at first did not want to supply any arms. By the spring, the Pentagon had agreed to supply weapons and the Islamic states had agreed to provide money. The program was put in the hands of Jim Pardew, a retired U.S. Army colonel who had been on Holbrooke's Dayton team.

There was no way I could compete with Pardew, who had several hundred million dollars of the arms and training that the Muslims and the Croats wanted. I continued to mediate the defense issues into May, when we held a meeting on the federation at Blair House. This was what Kornblum termed a "Federation Forum," namely a U.S.-only effort to support the federation, with some support from the Germans. He preferred this formula to the broader-based Friends of the Federation, believing that it would give him the clout needed to solve the federation issues he thought I had not resolved quickly enough.

Pardew nailed together an agreement of sorts at Blair House, though it included points on integration of the HVO and the ABiH that the Croats immediately disowned. It was enough for "train and equip" to proceed. I realized it was time to move on—successes of this sort were not my style. When the Bureau of Intelligence and Research called to ask me to direct its European office, a job that entailed thinking and writing about the Balkans but did not require me to go there, I accepted.

I made one more trip to Bosnia, for the next meeting of the Federation Forum in June 1996. Much pomp, some ceremony, but no serious progress. Cengic showed up toward the end of the meeting and made it clear that any progress I had made in our many hours of talks had been blown because of Kornblum's refusal to have him in Washington for the Federation Forum meeting. He became totally obstructionist, and Washington convinced Izetbegovic to fire him a few months later.

## Lessons Learned

The Bosnian Federation was still shaky when I left, and I suppose it will always be, if it survives at all. But all things are relative. When I began, it existed only on paper. When I left, it had its own institutions: government, ministries, budgets, taxes, constitutional court, cantons, and municipalities. Some of these were truly functional, others not. But the direction was clear: more and more Muslims and Croats would resolve their differences within these institutions. Under constant international pressure, to be sure, but increasingly with a sense that their destinies lay in the same country.

The parties to the mediation efforts I undertook were not the tightest limit on my capacity to resolve conflicts: it was instead the lack of confidence and support—or at times interest—in Washington. I do not regret the effort—it was useful, and someone somewhere in Bosnia has reason to thank me for it. That will have to be enough of a reward.

Beyond that, relatively few problems arose specifically from the multi-party character of the mediation I was involved with. Friends of the Federation, UN and UNHCR officials in Bosnia and Croatia, European Union and High Representative officials, even Stabilization Force (SFOR) commanders and many others were generally supportive of the federation-building efforts I was engaged in, which were after all nothing but implementation of an already signed agreement. There were no vital interests for the United States or other major players in the details of how most of the federation issues were resolved. No one in Washington, Paris, or Bonn cared how the federation municipalities were formed, or what color the police uniforms were. It mattered only that the issues be resolved, sooner rather than later. While many people questioned whether the federation would last, most were willing to pitch in and help, if only because the alternative was a return to three-sided warfare.

I worked especially closely with the Germans, Michael Steiner and Christian Clages in particular. This was due in part to a remarkable convergence of views. Steiner's instincts were more American than European—he truly believed a multiethnic Bosnia could be created despite the war. We were both approached repeatedly by the Croats about implementation of an agreement, made at the time of the Washington Agreement in March 1994, for division of Bosnia's ambassadorial posts between Croats and Muslims. I discovered only casually that Steiner was ignoring these pleas as assiduously as I was—the idea of ethnically divvying up the embassies was unappealing to both of us. Ignoring the Croat push—which would have led among other things to replacement of the Jewish ambassador in Washington—was our admittedly small protest against the many ethnically based provisions of the federation agreements.

More generally, U.S.-European relations on federation-building were helped by division of labor. While military matters were left entirely to the United States, the Europeans in March 1994 took on the southern Bosnian city of Mostar, the site of some of the worst fighting between Croats and Muslims, as their exclusive project. They set up a municipal administration, headed by the courageous and amusing Hans Koschnik, and poured money into reconstruction in an effort to showcase a distinct European contribution to the Croat-Muslim peace. The results were meager: well past Dayton, the city remained divided, though there has been gradual improvement, especially in freedom of movement and in the physical infrastructure. The Americans would occasionally try to tinker with Mostar—unsuccessfully at the first anniversary of the federation in March 1995 and a year later at the first Dayton implementation meeting in February 1996 in Rome, when a maddeningly trivial issue concerning the geographical definition of the central district of the city was resolved under extraordinary pressure from Holbrooke. But for the most part the Americans regarded Mostar as a European responsibility and left it to the Europeans to decide how to go about things. This was certainly true at Dayton, where I was briefed regularly by the Germans on the Mostar negotiations but purposely avoided attending the meetings.

My bigger problems were obviously with other U.S. mediators, who tended to ignore what I was doing at best and interfere at worst. As attention shifted away from the problems of the federation to ending the Serb-Muslim war, I found it more and more difficult to capture resources or influence the shape of the outcome, as illustrated by my failure to convince the powers that were at Dayton to allow the federation central bank to be formed as a transitional measure. This was to some extent understandable: there were higher priorities and I had to adapt to them. What was annoying was the failure to take the federation into account in the broader picture, unless forced to do so. Washington's focus was constantly on the next day's headlines, no matter how lofty the rhetoric about building up multiethnic democracy. The federation provided mostly negative headlines—it was always on the verge of collapse or otherwise an embarrassment or hindrance—so Washington looked elsewhere for its triumphs. The slow progress that was made just was not sufficient to gain points with the press.

There were, of course, many setbacks, but in retrospect what really worked were those things that had a constituency in the international community. Virtually nothing was "self-enforcing" because the agreements had been imposed on unwilling parties. In the spring of 1996, for example, Steiner and I persuaded the Croats and the Muslims to agree to remove all the roadblocks and checkpoints within the federation. With the support of the NATO troops, who much preferred open roads, this happened overnight. We also persuaded the Croats and the Muslims to agree to divide the customs revenues between the federation and the central government, but nothing really worked until the European Union took its customs monitors, who during the war had been deployed on the border between Serbia and Bosnia to enforce sanctions, and put them on the Croatian-Bosnian border, where they managed over a period of months to direct most of the customs revenues into the right accounts. The American Bar Association set up the Federation Constitutional Court. UNHCR was the critical ingredient in almost all successful repatriation operations (as well as many unsuccessful ones).

The peace between Croats and Muslims is still a fragile one, though the many institutional forms it now takes are clearly more durable than the empty words of the past. What we have succeeded in doing in part is to channel their conflicts into institutional frameworks. Their mutual distaste and distrust are still strong, but not lethal. When the prime minister and deputy prime minister of the federation visited Washington in 1998, I asked—as the first person to be paid a full-time salary working on the federation—why we should have confidence in them now, after so many false starts and half-fulfillments. Amused by this reminder of ancient history, they responded that more than six thousand people now work for the Bosnian Federation. Institutions, not intentions, are what count.

## NOTE

The views and opinions expressed in this chapter are solely the author's and do not necessarily reflect those of the U.S. Department of State.

# Background to Chapter 22

## The United Nations in Angola: Post-Bicesse Implementation

The long and costly war between the MPLA and UNITA turned toward negotiation when neighboring Namibia reached a peace agreement (see chapter 10) and the Cold War came to an end. The Bicesse Accords officially ended the Angolan conflict and signaled that it was time to prepare for the next phase of the peace process. Although mandated only to observe and verify, the United Nations both facilitated the implementation of the Bicesse Accords and intervened in an active conflict to forge a new settlement. This impartial two-year effort led to free and fair elections; subsequently, however, the civil war resumed. Renewed UN mediation led to the Draft Protocol of Abidjan, which eventually became the Lusaka Protocol. Despite these efforts, the civil war still rages.

### MAJOR ACTORS

- MPLA (Popular Movement for the Liberation of Angola): the government of Angola, led by President José Eduardo dos Santos
- UNITA (National Union for the Total Independence of Angola): the opposition, led by Jonas Savimbi
- United Nations
- Troika: the United States, the Soviet Union, and Portugal

### IMPORTANT DATES

- 1975: Angola is granted independence

- May 1991: 50,000 Cuban troops complete their withdrawal from Angola under the guidance of UNAVEM I
- May 31, 1991: The Bicesse Accords, negotiated by the Troika, are signed by the MPLA and UNITA; UN Resolution 696 establishes UNAVEM II for a seventeen-month period
- February 7, 1992: Margaret Anstee is officially appointed the UN secretary-general's special representative for Angola and head of UNAVEM II
- September 29–30, 1992: 92 percent of voters turn out for national elections; UNITA, however, refuses to accept the results
- October 17, 1992: Elections are deemed "generally free and fair" by the United Nations and other impartial observers, but UNITA hostilities continue and increase
- November 26, 1992: First UN attempt (at Namibe) at mediation to end conflict and achieve reconciliation
- January 27–30 and February 26–March 1, 1993: Second UN attempt (at Addis Ababa) at mediation
- April 12 and May 21, 1993: Third UN attempt (at Abidjan) at mediation; failure to reach agreement on Draft Protocol of Abidjan
- June 30, 1993: Anstee ends her assignment
- September–October 1993: United Nations imposes sanctions and restrictions on UNITA
- November 1994: Lusaka Protocol is signed
- 1998: Peace process collapses and war resumes
- February 1999: United Nations withdraws its military observer mission (MONUA) and limits its activities to humanitarian relief

### Key Agreements Reached at Bicesse in May 1991

- Cease-fire
- Demobilization of two armies (estimated to total 200,000 troops), and the creation of new, unified armed forces totaling 50,000 men
- Extension of central administration to all areas of the country
- Development of a neutral police force
- Holding of free and fair multiparty elections
- Formation of a Joint Political Military Commission, consisting of MPLA and UNITA, with the Troika as observers

### Principal Outcomes

- Bicesse Peace Accords instituted a cease-fire and specified the conditions for consolidating peace
- Successful, multiparty elections were held in September 1992, but the losing side reverted to armed conflict, and successive attempts at mediation failed to stem the recurrence of war

# 22

# The United Nations in Angola
*Post-Bicesse Implementation*

MARGARET J. ANSTEE

From February 1992 to June 1993, I served as the United Nations secretary-general's special representative in Angola and head of the second United Nations Angola Verification Mission (UNAVEM II). The origins of that mission were as complex as the roots of the Angolan conflict itself and many players were involved, on both the national and international scenes.

## BACKGROUND

Angola, a huge and potentially rich country, had been the scene of conflict for nearly thirty years, beginning with the struggle for independence from the colonial power of Portugal in the 1960s. After the somewhat precipitate concession of independence in 1975, for reasons internal to the political situation of Portugal, the conflict between the various nationalist movements became polarized between the marxist Popular Movement for the Liberation of Angola (MPLA), which took over the reins of government, and the National Union for the Total Independence of Angola

(UNITA), as the formerly important National Front for the Liberation of Angola (FNLA) ceased to be a power to be reckoned with. That polarization was accentuated by the Cold War, with the Soviet Union and Cuba supporting the MPLA government, while the United States and South Africa helped UNITA. Because of its immense resources, Angola became a pawn in the struggle for control of southern Africa.

A solution became possible only with the thawing of the Cold War. The agreement with South Africa, negotiated by the then U.S. assistant secretary of state for Africa, Chester Crocker, included the withdrawal of the 50,000 Cuban troops on Angolan territory. The United Nations was entrusted with that task, which was successfully completed by UNAVEM I, ahead of schedule, in May 1991. In the meantime, the continuing improvement in international relations between East and West made possible an attempt to resolve the internal conflict in Angola. After a year of difficult negotiations, peace accords were signed between the MPLA and UNITA in Bicesse, Portugal, on May 31, 1991. They had been brokered by the two superpowers of the Cold War, the United States and the Soviet Union, and by Portugal, the former colonial power. The United Nations was not involved in those negotiations, except for the presence of a military observer in the very final stages.

The Bicesse Accords established a cease-fire and the conditions for consolidating peace in Angola. Their principal provisions encompassed the demobilization of two armies, estimated to total 200,000 men; the creation of a new, unified Angolan Armed Forces totaling 50,000 men; the extension of the central administration to all areas of the country; the development of a neutral police force; and the holding of free and fair multiparty elections within sixteen months, between September and November 1992.

One of the main features of the accords was that the onus for ensuring that its provisions were honored was placed on the two parties to the conflict: the government/MPLA and UNITA. This presupposed the existence of a "Boy Scout" spirit in circumstances that had hardly been conducive to its evolution. The United Nations, which had not been consulted in the matter before the deal was signed and sealed, was initially assigned a very marginal role, merely *observing* the actions of the two sides and *verifying* that they were implementing the terms of the accords.

This was the mandate given to UNAVEM II, set up by the UN Security Council on May 31, 1991, under its Resolution 696, for a period of seventeen months. It was initially a purely military mission, staffed by unarmed military observers under a chief military observer with the rank of major general. There was thus no *political* UN presence in place at that stage. It was not until December 5, 1991, that a civilian element was added to the UN role, when the Angolan government (MPLA) officially requested the United Nations to send observers to follow the electoral process and provide technical assistance. And it was only about that time, seven months into UNAVEM II's allotted life span, that the appointment of a political head for the mission, in the guise of a special representative of the UN secretary-general, was first mooted.

## MY MISSION

Even so, Boutros Boutros-Ghali did not ask me to consider taking the position until February 5, 1992, when he gave me twenty-four hours to make up my mind. I undertook a first exploratory mission to Angola from February 16 to 20 and, after a briefing in New York, I took up my position formally in Luanda on March 18, 1992. Ten months of the time allotted for the peace process had already elapsed, and there were barely six months to go before the elections were due to be held and the peace process was supposed to wind up, according to the timetable agreed on at Bicesse. All the other key international players—the three Troika representatives (Portugal, the Soviet Union, and the United States)—had been in place since May 1991 and all had been involved in the Bicesse negotiations. Ambassador Antonio Monteiro of Portugal had played a particularly prominent role as the right-hand man of Minister Durão Barroso, then secretary for foreign affairs and cooperation and later foreign minister of Portugal. Thus I found myself confronted by a very sharp learning curve.

All three of the observers, as well as the Russian ambassador, who kept a close eye on the situation, were extremely cooperative in helping me to meet this challenge and briefed me with all the information at their disposal, as well as their personal opinions, during my first mission in February. Indeed the warmth of their greeting made me suspect that they were only too glad to have someone with whom to share this very hot potato.

My mandate was not simply political. In addition to being the UN secretary-general's representative, I was head of UNAVEM II, which now comprised military, police, and electoral components and thus had important operational and management responsibilities. I was also in charge of all UN humanitarian activities related to the peace process. While those activities were nowhere near the level reached later when war again erupted, they were nonetheless considerable, encompassing World Food Program feeding programs and UNICEF health and social services for the troop assembly areas; the repatriation by the United Nations High Commission for Refugees (UNHCR) of some three hundred thousand refugees, driven abroad by the conflict; and the resettlement of about eight hundred thousand displaced people within the country.

The resources at my disposal—in a country as large as France, Spain, and Germany put together and in which two rival armies estimated to total two hundred thousand men were to be disbanded—were not imposing. UNAVEM II comprised 350 unarmed military observers, 90 unarmed police observers (later increased to 126), and 100 electoral observers, increased to 400 during the month of the elections. The total budget for seventeen months of operation was only $118,000. It had been impressed on me in New York that the UN Security Council wanted a "small and manageable operation." In vain I pleaded after my first mission that Angola was patently not small and did not look particularly manageable to me and that both the mandate and the resources were inadequate for the immense task ahead. The Troika shared that view (a somewhat ironic situation, because the Troika had negotiated the peace accords that limited the UN role). Minister Durão Barroso said as much in a meeting with the secretary-general in New York on March 31, 1992. The only practical effect of his expression of concern was that I received a sharp rap over the knuckles because it was assumed—wrongly—at UN Headquarters that I had put him up to it. Later, Ambassador Herman ("Hank") Cohen, then U.S. assistant secretary of state for Africa, made considerable efforts to help me augment UNAVEM's resources from nonbudgetary sources. None of that changed the basic problem of the paucity of means put at the United Nations' disposal in Angola, but it demonstrates that the other principal international players recognized the seriousness of the issue and tried to help.

## COORDINATION MECHANISMS

The principal mechanism for carrying out the Bicesse Accords was the Joint Political-Military Commission, usually known by its Portuguese acronym CCPM. The members were the two parties to the conflict, the government (MPLA) and UNITA, who took turns chairing the meetings and adopted decisions by consensus (the Boy Scout spirit). The three representatives of the Troika attended meetings by right, as observers. The United Nations was in a different, and lesser, category, the accords specifying that the UN representative could be "invited," as appropriate. In practice, it was taken for granted that I would attend all meetings.

Within the CCPM, the Troika and I almost always worked together smoothly. We shared the same objective—to make the peace process work and to ensure that the two sides honored their commitments—and the same concern that matters were not proceeding nearly fast enough. Our positions were discussed and coordinated in frequent meetings outside the CCPM. The Troika worked on two levels: representatives on the ground who followed day-to-day events, and senior officials in the foreign ministries of their respective capitals who made periodic visits to Angola to review the situation. Those high-level missions were timed to coincide with critical junctures in the timetable of the peace process and once or twice were mounted at short notice when unforeseen crises erupted. I was always the first person they came to see, and their high-level presence was usually helpful in prodding the two sides—at least temporarily—into speedier action.

Nonetheless, I found it necessary and expedient to maintain a clear distinction between our respective roles. It is imperative that a United Nations mediator not only be impartial but be *seen* to be impartial. Single-state mediators, however high-minded their motives, are inevitably prone to being perceived as promoting national interests by the suspicion-ridden parties to a conflict. In the case of Portugal, the long colonial legacy and the continued presence of Portuguese economic interests and a large number of Portuguese nationals colored the views of many, especially UNITA. In fact, until the war resumed after the elections, Portugal maintained an even-handed stance. The United States, the most powerful of the three, was seen as favoring UNITA, because of that country's long-standing support of Jonas Savimbi. Ironically, Russia appeared the most detached, simply because it had too many problems at home to take any leading role, but it was naturally regarded with mistrust by UNITA. For all those reasons, and even though we were often conveying similar concerns, I preferred to see the two leaders, President José Eduardo dos Santos and Jonas Savimbi, separately from the Troika, especially when the going got tough. In some ways, our separate representations reinforced the message. The important thing was that we always correlated our positions and worked well together in a mutually supportive way during moments of great crisis, such as UNITA's allegations of electoral fraud and threat to return to war in October 1992.

## THE SEQUENCE OF EVENTS

In the six months preceding the elections in September 1992, we were all deeply concerned about the snail-like progress of the peace process and the foot-dragging and gamesmanship exhibited by both sides. The cantonment and demobilization of troops and the creation of the joint Angolan Armed Forces (FAA) were all months behind schedule and the collection and custody of weapons and destruction of those no longer needed also posed thorny problems. The extension of the central administration to all areas of the country proceeded only in a largely symbolic and exceedingly limited manner while efforts to develop a neutral police comprising personnel drawn from UNITA as well as the government were frustrated by actions from both sides. Similarly, the free movement of people and goods continued to be severely restrained, when not impossible, particularly in UNITA-controlled areas; and hostile propaganda flourished virtually unabated. The government accused UNITA of concealing an army of 20,000 men (of which joint investigations by the CCPM, the Troika, and UNAVEM found no trace) whereas UNITA claimed that the government's newly created Emergency Police Force was a haven for its crack troops, once demobilized (efforts to get UNITA incorporated in that force also failed).

In contrast, after a slow and sticky start, preparations for the elections forged ahead. That was in large part due to the dynamism of the director general appointed to organize them, for like everything else under the Bicesse Accords, the responsibility rested with the Angolans, in this case the government. There were, however, serious lacunae in the area of logistics, especially air transport, that made it impossible to reach all eligible voters in the far-flung regions of that huge and war-devastated country.

I decided to overreach the UN mandate, which was merely to observe and verify all stages of the election, and to take a direct hand in solving the logistics problem. As a result of an intensive campaign in Luanda and in other major capitals, during which I begged and borrowed (but did not actually steal!), we put together, without any budget whatsoever, the largest air operation the United Nations has ever mounted for an exercise of this kind. The Troika, at both levels, was my enthusiastic ally and gave invaluable support, as did the European Union, South Africa, and some others. Had that air support not been mobilized, the elections could never have been free and fair, long before the actual voting took place, because it would have been impossible to register voters in remote areas—composed mostly, it should be said, of UNITA supporters.

The first miracle, then, was that the elections could be held in an acceptable and reasonably organized manner. The second was that the two days of voting—September 29 and 30, 1992—took place in absolute calm. Ninety-two percent of the registered voters turned out to perform their civic duty, many walking for days through the bush and waiting long hours under the broiling sun to do so.

The third miracle eluded us. Vote counting was slow, and when it appeared after a few days that UNITA was likely to lose, Savimbi jumped the gun, and without waiting for the final result, withdrew his generals from the FAA (which had been sworn in on the very eve of the election), cried fraud, and launched the long downward slide that was to end in renewed war. Had he been more patient, he would have found that his rival for the presidency, dos Santos, had not quite reached the required 50 percent and that a runoff election would have ensued. But even a meticulous investigation of the fraud claims, in which great pains were taken to involve UNITA fully at every level, and the endorsement by the Troika, the European Union, and all independent observers of my official declaration, on October 17, 1992, that the elections had been "generally free and fair," failed to move him.

That Savimbi was able to mobilize his forces again, in short order, was due to the failure to complete demobilization and the integration of the FAA fully before the election. Even those UNITA elements that had been demobilized had not moved far from the troop assembly areas, as they had no fixed homes to go to. The obvious question is, Why were the elections allowed to go ahead when demilitarization was so patently incomplete? The answer lies in the Bicesse Accords, which laid down the precise period by which time elections must be held. That was itself a compromise: UNITA had wanted elections within three months, the government (MPLA) not before three years. The United Nations, given its marginal role, had no right to decree a postponement, nor had the Troika or anyone else besides the two Angolan parties. Had the government, which was organizing the elections, attempted to do so, UNITA would simply have cried foul earlier and the violence would have begun sooner. As it was, the government had no interest in doing so. Initially a reluctant participant because it thought it would lose, the unexpected success of dos Santos's campaign on the hustings had persuaded it to the contrary. In the final run-up to the elections, both sides had convinced themselves of victory and were eager to have the matter resolved by the electorate.

## A CHANGE OF ROLE

Over the preceding six months since my arrival, and despite the narrowness of the role originally assigned to the United Nations, UNAVEM and I, as the secretary-general's special representative, had been increasingly called on to undertake key responsibilities lying well outside our mandate. Now, with the peace process on the verge of imminent collapse, the United Nations was thrust to center stage and became the main mediator. Although the Security Council did not modify our written mandate to reflect the new situation, the objectives of the mission changed: It was no longer merely to observe and verify compliance with the terms of the Bicesse

Accords, but was now the prime mover in a desperate attempt to halt the slide back into war. The Troika continued to be immensely important, but now in a supporting role, and in a similar fashion, other players intervened.

During the tense days immediately following the election, I was engaged in frantic shuttle diplomacy between dos Santos and Savimbi, who had retreated to his highland fastness in Huambo. My démarches were supported by a personal letter from the UN secretary-general, in which Boutros-Ghali, citing Savimbi's hero, General Charles de Gaulle, made an emotional appeal to him, as an old friend and fellow African, to exercise moderation and scrupulous respect for the verdict of the urns and for peace.

By the middle of October 1992, when the die in favor of war had not yet been irretrievably cast, a host of high-level mediators had swarmed into Luanda. The UN Security Council appointed an ad hoc commission composed of the permanent representatives of Cape Verde (heading the mission), Morocco, Russia, and the United States. They saw dos Santos and Savimbi but left ahead of schedule, filled with gloom and concern that the mounting violence would trap them in Luanda. They had also come to realize how inadequate UNAVEM's resources and mandate had been. U.S. ambassador Perkins exclaimed, "This was a UN operation done on the cheap—a totally false economy on the part of the international community."

The high-level segment of the Troika also flew in from Washington, Lisbon, and Moscow, and the Organization of African Unity (OAU) announced the imminent arrival of a mission headed by the presidents of Cape Verde and Zimbabwe that, perhaps wisely, did not materialize. But the most colorful arrival on this crowded scene was the South African foreign minister, Pik Botha, who appeared like a deus ex machina to resolve the situation. While South Africa could play a useful role as a longtime supporter of UNITA and was presumed to retain considerable influence with Savimbi, the problem was that Botha came as a lone player with his own agenda that did not jibe with that of the other mediators. After a first visit to Savimbi, Botha declared himself convinced that there had been electoral fraud, even though the investigation was still under way, and propounded a South African solution whereby a large role would be accorded to Savimbi and UNITA, virtually amounting to a coalition government, and there would be no second round of presidential elections; that is, the elections would, to all intents and purposes, be scrapped. That was not only unacceptable to the government but was repudiated by the Troika: the United States and Portugal threatened to withdraw from the process if the Bicesse Accords were not adhered to. Thus, Botha's initial intervention simply muddied already muddy waters.

The immediate aim of everyone was to bring about a face-to-face meeting between the two leaders. Botha was confident that he could succeed where the rest of us had failed. But after an extraordinary pantomime of ever-changing demands by Savimbi on the venue and security arrangements, in which I too was involved, and which entailed the use of the minister's own plane, he and Assistant Secretary Cohen waited for five hours in broiling heat at Luanda airport for a UNITA leader who never came. The minister returned to Pretoria a sadder and wiser man. Before he left, he had, on the basis of wider evidence, reversed his view on the fraudulence of the elections.

A positive outcome of Botha's intervention was that on October 23 he declared that the South African government accepted my finding that the elections had been generally free and fair and appealed to "all political leaders in Angola" to respect the results and renounce force. For its part, the Troika had returned from a meeting with Savimbi on October 20 in a state of deep depression. Assistant Secretary Cohen referred to the "Charles Taylor syndrome" ( by which I assumed he meant that, as Taylor had previously done in Liberia, Savimbi had retreated to the bush to pursue his ends by force) and remarked, only half jokingly, that the observer countries should bow out and leave everything to the United Nations.

The reality was that the Big League of mediators flew off to the four corners of the globe, leaving us lesser mortals to wrestle with a situation slipping daily further from the international community's grasp. My election declaration resulted in venomous attacks on me by UNITA's radio, Vorgan, including death threats. Savimbi still wanted to see me, but New York decreed that it was inappropriate and unsafe for me to go to Huambo until an apology was forthcoming.

The final blow came with the bloody battle for Luanda waged over the weekend of October 31–November 1. It erupted suddenly, minutes after the observers and I thought we had obtained at least a temporary respite of hostilities in the CCPM, when the British ambassador, John Flynn, was expecting to host a conciliation lunch for the two sides. None of the protagonists turned up and the eventual cease-fire was negotiated from the bowels of the embassy, where I was trapped by the fighting.

That turned out to be a blessing in disguise, as Great Britain was the current president of the European Union. The British ambassador thus had direct communication with all those countries, as well as with the American delegation. The latter, including the delegation's newly arrived chief observer, Ambassador Edmond De Jarnette, were in hiding, in danger of becoming hostages, as the American compound was surrounded by

UNITA forces. They could, therefore, take no part in the negotiations. Nor could the Russians, caught in similarly dangerous circumstances. Only Antonio Monteiro of Portugal and we were able to communicate with all concerned, including New York, Washington, London, and Lisbon, as well as the protagonists on the ground.

Ambassador Flynn played a critical role in a marathon telephone conversation with Savimbi that eventually brought about a truce, having the advantage of being seen as an independent mediator who had not been involved in the earlier negotiations. In the course of a rambling dialogue, Savimbi withdrew UNITA's scurrilous accusations against me, reiterated apologies, and asked that I visit him soon.

## SUBSEQUENT MEDIATION

Once a fragile peace was in place, and my direct communication with Savimbi restored, I renewed my efforts to mediate a longer-term solution. Ironically, in contrast to its original, marginal mandate, now, when things had gone badly wrong, the United Nations was pushed to center stage and obliged to take the lead role. Yet the formal mandate was never changed by the Security Council.

I also found myself in a difficult position personally. I had originally accepted a seven-month mission, to end after the elections had taken place. I had later been told that I was then expected to lead the mission in Mozambique. That plan came to naught when Savimbi resorted once more to armed struggle and I had to stay on in Angola to pick up the pieces. Nonetheless, I had told the secretary-general that I wished to be relieved of my functions as soon as he could find a successor. The primary reason was of a personal, family nature, but I had also realized from the outset that I had been landed with a "mission impossible," and it was now patently clear that the international community, particularly the Security Council, was not prepared to give the Angolan question the priority that might have given it some chance of success. The secretary-general agreed that I could leave by the end of 1992, but no successor had been found by then and he asked me to soldier on.

During the eight months from November 1992 to the end of June 1993, when I was finally able to relinquish my post, I chaired three successive attempts at mediation: the first in Namibe, in southern Angola, on November 26, 1992; the second, in two parts, in Addis Ababa, Ethiopia, from January 27 to 30 and February 26 to March 1, 1993; and the third, a marathon exercise in Abidjan, Côte d'Ivoire, from April 12 to May 21, 1993.

At each meeting, we appeared to make progress, but it was invariably canceled out by aggressive acts or noncompliance, in most cases by UNITA.

Thus, two days after both sides had signed a joint declaration at Namibe, manifesting their commitment to peace and to continuing negotiations, UNITA troops occupied the strategic towns of Uíge and Negage. It took me until the New Year to persuade the two sides to renew the talks. This time, it was the government that upset the applecart. On January 3, precisely one day after I had obtained that agreement, government forces attacked UNITA in Lubango, one of the few places where the two parties were still working together. Hard-liners were now gaining ground on both sides.

By the time we met in Addis Ababa, war had spread like wildfire throughout Angola. UNITA had the upper hand and had occupied a large part of the country, driving the government back to the coastal areas and to inland towns besieged by UNITA forces. A fierce and bloody battle was being waged for control of Huambo.

The results of the first meeting in Addis Ababa were not impressive, but at least the parties reaffirmed the validity of the peace accords and agreed to continue the dialogue. But the follow-up meeting was repeatedly delayed at UNITA's request, and when at last a new date was agreed for February 26, UNITA's delegation failed to show up, after keeping everyone else waiting for several days. The lame excuse was that the delegation's security had not been assured. That was clearly a pretext, for I had made elaborate arrangements to ensure the delegation's safe passage from an unspecified location in the Angolan bush. A series of UNAVEM planes, from helicopters to Beechcraft, had been laid on to ferry them to Kinshasa, where we had hired a Gulf Stream jet (for which we had no budget) to fly them across the African continent. At every stage, the delegation was to be accompanied by senior UNAVEM military officials, whose lives I was not likely to put in jeopardy, and I had obtained guarantees for all the flights from the Angolan government, which was even more anxious than we were that UNITA should turn up. The obvious explanation was that UNITA wanted to capture Huambo before engaging in further talks and it was taking longer than expected.

I had no option but to suspend the meeting on March 1, laying the blame on UNITA. Predictably, UNITA renewed its vicious attacks on me. Savimbi declared that UNITA would never again take part in negotiations conducted by me and requested my withdrawal, thus paradoxically ensuring that the secretary-general's action on my request to be relieved would be still further postponed. Predictably, too, Huambo fell and UNITA extended its inexorable advance all over Angola, leaving death and destruction in its wake.

During that fraught period the Troika was exceptionally supportive. It not only attended all the negotiations and used its good offices with both sides, but it also issued strong statements at critical junctures, for example, serving an ultimatum to UNITA when it constantly tried to postpone the second Addis Ababa meeting and blaming UNITA for the meeting's collapse when its delegation failed to turn up. All these statements threatened dire but unspecified consequences if UNITA did not mend its warlike ways, but the threats were never followed by action. The Troika also pulled out all the stops in support of my efforts to make the Addis Ababa negotiations a success, particularly the United States, which held bilateral meetings with representatives of both sides before the second session.

All that was most helpful, but it was as if a gulf existed between those of us operating on the ground and those dealing with the issue in the international stratosphere. True, at the end of December 1992, the secretary-general had tried unsuccessfully to use his good offices to hold a meeting between the two leaders, dos Santos and Savimbi, in Geneva, but what was really needed was firm and decisive action by the Security Council and that was signally lacking.

On December 22, 1992, the president of the Security Council made a statement that could only be described as anodyne, repeating all the old appeals, by now distinctly shop-soiled. Security Resolution 804 of January 29, 1993, adopted while the first session in Addis Ababa was still in progress, despite my appeals to wait for the results first, did contain some stronger language against UNITA, but it was still wishy-washy, providing no carrots or sticks that might induce the antagonists to come to agreement. And as if to reinforce the message to UNITA that the international community was unlikely to take any action to stem its aggression, the council was also significantly reducing UNAVEM's meager strength to its minimal expression.

After the collapse of the Addis Ababa talks, I briefed the Security Council in New York and proposed a number of actions. The reaction in informal consultations was encouraging, but Resolution 811, adopted on March 12, 1993, was disappointing. Although it at last pointed the finger unequivocally at UNITA, it was again a mixed bag of pious hopes rather than a harbinger of decisive action. That was largely due to the United States, which, despite having been a party to those tough communiqués in Addis Ababa and Luanda hinting darkly at retribution if UNITA did not comply, favored a less strongly worded resolution than would have been preferred by others. The U.S. Permanent Mission in New York explained that this was to avoid alienating UNITA and Savimbi, over whom the U.S. government considered that it still had leverage.

In Luanda, there had for several months been growing restiveness about the Security Council's approach, not only in the government, but also among the representatives of the Troika and of other influential countries. They could not understand why the United Nations did not "come off the fence" and roundly condemn UNITA and seemed to hold the UN Secretariat responsible for the failure to do so. In fact, I shared their view and was wryly amused that its strongest exponents came from countries that were members of the Security Council, which, rather than the Secretariat, was the arbiter of such matters.

By this stage, the only valid mediators on the scene were the Troika and the United Nations. The postponed OAU delegation—headed by President Robert Mugabe of Zimbabwe, who was accompanied by President Antonio Mascarenhas Monteiro of Cape Verde and OAU secretary-general Salim Salim—had visited Luanda on December 27 and 28, 1992, but achieved nothing because it had been unable to meet with Savimbi. During the negotiations in Addis Ababa, seat of the OAU, Salim Salim again offered his good offices, as did the president of Ethiopia, but to no avail, as both were held in deep suspicion by UNITA. In the case of the OAU the resentment went back twenty years, to the time of Angola's independence, when the OAU had speedily accorded recognition to the MPLA government.

After Security Council Resolution 811, the ball was squarely in the American court and the United States took the lead in trying to get UNITA back to the negotiating table, it being clearly understood, however, that any meeting that eventuated would be under UN auspices. The U.S. thesis was that the negotiations should be held in either Morocco or Côte d'Ivoire, since both countries had been long-term supporters of UNITA and could therefore wield some influence. In the end, the choice fell on Abidjan, where the U.S. diplomats held a preparatory and very difficult meeting with UNITA, with a government delegation available in the wings for consultations. As a result, it was agreed that formal negotiations under UN auspices would resume in Abidjan on April 12, 1993. The government was most unhappy about the venue, but the Troika pressured it into accepting the location on the grounds that President Félix Houphoüet-Boigny's influence would be critical, since he was one of Savimbi's oldest supporters and had bankrolled UNITA's activities for many years. I personally would have preferred Morocco, as I had served there, knew King Hassan II and members of the government, and was sure that they would be just as effective, if not more so, in tough talking to UNITA.

Just as everything looked set for talks in Abidjan, Vorgan unleashed another virulent attack on me, this time calling me a "prostitute," as well as corrupt, and repeating the death threats. The timing was clearly deliberate. The secretary-general, President Houphoüet-Boigny (as the host of the meeting), and the three observer countries insisted that a formal apology and personal guarantees for my safety should be forthcoming from the UNITA leader before the talks began and the first two made that clear to him directly. On the eve of the talks, when we were all already assembled in Abidjan, a rather lame message to that effect from Savimbi was delivered to me by his patently discomfited representative in Côte d'Ivoire.

Now began a marathon, last-ditch effort to save the peace process begun in Bicesse. A new and important mediator had come on the scene as well as the Troika and the United Nations: President Houphoüet-Boigny. Although frail from age and ill health, he followed the talks closely, requesting daily briefings from me and holding meetings with all concerned. His exceedingly able foreign minister, Amara Essy, was clearly under instructions to make the success of the talks his top priority, and indeed, one wondered what happened to the rest of Côte d'Ivoire's foreign policy during those long, fraught weeks. Eventually the minister moved into the hotel where the talks were held so as to be on call at all hours.

The United States sent a strong delegation, initially headed by Ambassador Jeffrey Davidow, later by Ambassador De Jarnette, and including several old Angola hands from the U.S. State Department. Ambassador Monteiro led an equally experienced Portuguese team. The Russian delegation was smaller, headed by Ambassador Yuri Kapralov, and when he had to leave in the middle of the talks, Russian participation, though supportive, was low-key. The OAU had an observer in the wings, who did not participate directly.

Our efforts were aimed not only at getting a cease-fire, as the most urgent step, but also at recasting the peace process entirely so as to put it on a sounder footing. Week by week, at a frustratingly slow pace, we hammered out a draft protocol of Abidjan, supported by a memorandum of understanding, encompassing every conceivable aspect in thirty-eight articles. The articles dealt with military matters, such as arrangements for a cease-fire, the withdrawal of UNITA troops from occupied areas, demilitarization, and the consolidation of the FAA; political issues, such as the formation of a government of national reconciliation, power sharing at all levels, the development of democratic and judicial institutions, and the conditions under which new elections would be held; a strengthened role for UNAVEM; the development of a neutral police force; human rights; the safe delivery of humanitarian aid, and so forth. In short, the protocol sought to rectify all the errors and omissions of the Bicesse Accords. UNAVEM in particular was to play a central role and call the shots. No date was to be fixed for elections until UNAVEM declared that the conditions were right.

The essence of the negotiations was that the government should make political concessions in exchange for military concessions by UNITA (which now occupied some 80 percent of the country) and vice versa. In this, the government proved by far the more amenable, while UNITA adopted an unmistakably filibustering technique. The negotiations took various forms: plenaries, separate meetings with each delegation held either by the observers or by me, and even face-to-face sessions between the government and UNITA with none of the rest of us present (the latter were surprisingly cordial but the results were minimal).

Both delegations returned to Angola for consultation, the government briefly, UNITA staying away six days instead of three. At one critical point, Foreign Minister Essy flew, in precarious conditions, to Huambo to see Savimbi and came back thinking he had his agreement to the protocol, only to find it was not so. The UN secretary-general and the Ivorian president also intervened with the UNITA leader but with great difficulty since he had taken to switching off his satellite phone in order to ensure that he alone could take the initiative. President Houphouët-Boigny left for medical treatment in France on May 14 a deeply disillusioned man; he was never to return alive or to fulfill his dying wish—to be the architect of lasting peace in Angola.

Despite all this, we came tantalizingly close to reaching agreement. The main stumbling block was over one article, admittedly a key one, on the withdrawal of UNITA forces from the places they had occupied. UNITA said it would do so only if I could guarantee the immediate deployment beforehand of a symbolic presence of 1,000 "Blue Helmets" (armed UN troops). That could very well have been a bluff, but the Troika representatives and I in Abidjan thought we should try anything that might save the talks and stop the war. But my pleas to New York fell on stony ground. I was told categorically that no troops would be provided until a cease-fire was in place, which confronted me with a chicken-and-egg situation, since UNITA would not agree to a cease-fire without the troops. Worse still, I was warned that, even if I managed to obtain a cease-fire, no UN troops could be provided to monitor it *until six or nine months later*, because of the overall crisis in peacekeeping. That left me, as the principal mediator, with no leverage whatsoever.

There were other unhelpful external factors. One was that UN Headquarters started negotiating the appointment of my successor, even though it had been agreed that, desirous as I was of leaving, it would not be politic to do so until the Abidjan negotiations had been completed, since otherwise I would become a lame duck. Savimbi rejected the proposed candidate, but the mere fact that UNITA was made aware of my imminent departure and that the news had leaked to the media made my position as mediator even more difficult. The other was the Clinton administration's announcement on May 19, at a most critical moment of the talks, of its long-awaited formal recognition of the Angolan government. The timing could not have been more bizarre. The original condition had been the holding of free and fair elections, so recognition had been expected much earlier and had, indeed, been strongly advocated to Washington months before by Ambassador De Jarnette. Then it would have been helpful. Now it could deal a deathblow to the negotiations.

In practice, it was a damp squib, for the talks were already virtually doomed. The UN secretary-general, from New York, and President Houphouët-Boigny, from Paris, made last-ditch efforts to save them by speaking with Savimbi and agreeing to his request for an extension of a few days, but it was to no avail: although the government offered important concessions, UNITA would not budge an inch. On May 21 I had no option but to "interrupt" the talks (I avoided any more final term).

In our postmortem on the Abidjan talks, Foreign Minister Essy and I agreed that their big lesson was that no one had any leverage over Savimbi anymore, not even his old supporters and allies. He now felt himself strong enough to "cock a snook" at the world at large, secure in his military gains and the conviction that the international community, represented by the member states of the United Nations and by the Security Council, was too weak, or too disinterested, to constitute a threat to his ambitions.

The three observers issued a strong statement blaming UNITA for the collapse of the talks, and I flew to New York, where the Security Council was to consider the situation. There, I tried unsuccessfully to persuade all and sundry that the best way to stop the killing and find a way forward was to deploy a modest contingent of Blue Helmets, with the initial mandate of protecting humanitarian operations, but whose functions could, by a rapid decision of the Security Council, be switched, or expanded, to monitoring the withdrawal of UNITA troops, if and when an agreement was reached, thus meeting UNITA's concerns. U.S. Ambassador Madeleine Albright reacted favorably initially, but Washington evidently thought otherwise. The Security Council adopted Resolution 834, which was more condemnatory of UNITA than in the past, long on exhortations that the interrupted talks should be resumed urgently but short on decisive action. The Troika issued another statement in Washington on June 8, but it, too, said nothing new.

Meanwhile, the appointment of my successor had been decided in the person of Maître Alioune Blondin Beye, a former foreign minister of Mali, and it was agreed that he would take over at the beginning of July. During my last weeks in Luanda in June 1993, I still tried to push my Blue Helmets solution. President dos Santos liked the idea and raised it with the new U.S. assistant secretary of state for Africa, Ambassador George Moose, when he visited Angola on June 21 to 23. Ambassador De Jarnette strongly supported my proposal, and Moose himself urged the president to get a strong resolution to that effect adopted by the African heads of state at the OAU summit in Cairo at the end of June that could then be carried to the Troika meeting in Moscow a few days later and thence to the Security Council when it resumed consideration of Angola on July 15. Unfortunately, that strategy was never put to the test because, for reasons that were never clear to me, the Angolan government did not follow through. Perhaps by then they were so disillusioned with the international community that a military solution seemed the only viable option remaining.

I was in New York for the next round of discussions in the Security Council on July 15, 1993, attended by a formidable array of African foreign ministers and other high-level representatives. This time, the council bit the bullet in its Resolution 851, which threatened an embargo on the sale of arms to UNITA unless the secretary-general reported by September 15, 1993, that an effective cease-fire had been established and that the peace accords and the council's resolutions were being fully implemented. By welcoming "the provision of assistance to the Government of Angola in support of the democratic process," Resolution 851 gave the nod, in suitably coded language, to those who wished to supply arms to the government, something that it had been forbidden to do to either side under the Bicesse Accords. The resolution also declared the Security Council's readiness to expand the UN presence in Angola "substantially" in the event of "significant progress in the peace process."

Here, Ambassador Albright's intervention was curiously nuanced. She warned that an expansion of UNAVEM could not be taken for granted so far as the United States was concerned, citing problems of costs and duration: "UN peacekeeping has become a growth industry." Those remarks seemed to reflect overall U.S. concerns about financing peacekeeping operations rather than an objective assessment of the needs of the Angolan situation and were symptomatic of the extraneous constraints that had bedeviled the United Nations' attempts to consolidate peace in Angola from the very outset, right up to Abidjan. They were all the more remarkable coming from the country that had taken the lead in trying to broker a solution.

Meanwhile, the war continued to rage unabated in Angola, more ferociously than at any time before Bicesse and largely forgotten by the rest of the world. In September 1993, the Security Council imposed sanctions on the sale of arms and oil to UNITA, but the sanctions were ineffective because of the porous nature of Angola's long frontiers, the willingness of certain partners to continue supplying UNITA, and the latter's enormous financial resources, derived from its control of the diamond-producing areas. The Security Council stopped short of applying travel restrictions, closing UNITA's offices abroad, and freezing its international assets—the only measures that might have had an effect. It was not until four years later, on October 30, 1997, that the council was at last constrained to those wider restrictions on UNITA, but by then it was too late.

Despite the intensive efforts of my successor, it was not possible to reach agreement on a cease-fire and a renewal of the peace process until November 1994. Ironically, the Lusaka Protocol was almost a mirror image of the document that we had prepared in Abidjan, with the details more elaborated. That the agreement that had eluded us then became possible seventeen months later owed less to international mediation than to the fact that the government, rearmed, had made spectacular advances on the battlefield and recaptured the cities and much of the territory occupied by UNITA. The government, and not UNITA, now had the military advantage.

UNAVEM III, set up to oversee implementation of the Lusaka Protocol, was endowed with all the faculties and funds so notoriously absent in UNAVEM II: a strong mandate, a central role in managing the process and calling the shots, and resources to match, including 7,000 Blue Helmets. Even so, the path to sustained peace has proved rocky and exceedingly slow. During 1998 it deteriorated at an even more alarming rate, and as of this writing, in March 1999, has relapsed once again into outright war, mainly because of UNITA's procrastination and prevarication in fulfilling its commitments under the Lusaka Protocol. Worse still, the United Nations has closed down its military observer mission, MONUA, the successor to UNAVEM III, and withdrawn the secretary-general's special representative, Issa Diallo. Thus, the United Nations no longer has a military or peacekeeping presence in Angola and its activities are limited to humanitarian relief. At least for the present, the two sides have been left to fight it out alone.

This is tragic news for ordinary Angolans. The four years of sporadic clashes since the Lusaka Protocol was signed had already claimed countless more Angolan lives, and some of those who came from other lands to try to further the path to peace and reconciliation have also perished. In June 1998, my successor, Maître Beye, joined their number, along with several of his UN colleagues, all killed in a fatal air crash in Côte d'Ivoire, on the last of his many journeys undertaken to try to stave off the threat of renewed war. At the end of the year, more UN personnel died when two UN aircraft, engaged in humanitarian relief, were shot down over UNITA-held territory in Angola.

Yet, despite all the international efforts over many years, the death toll of innocent, helpless Angolans seems likely to rise inexorably higher, while many more, fleeing the fighting, are made homeless, and several hundred thousand refugees cram already overcrowded cities. Now an outside observer, I am haunted by déjà vu; the same tragedy that I tried unavailingly to prevent is repeating itself all over again, each time with more suffering, and with diminishing hopes for a solution.

## CONCLUDING REFLECTIONS

The UN operation in Angola from 1991 to 1993 encompassed two of the three types of diplomatic intervention enumerated in chapter 1 (p. 11) of this book, though in reverse order to that specified there: it sought first to facilitate the implementation of a negotiated agreement (the Bicesse Accords), and then, when war broke out again, it had to intervene in an active conflict in order to try to bring about a new settlement.

The Angolan case shows clearly that the success or failure of the mediation process depends on many other factors besides the capacity of the mediators, and there are a number of sobering conclusions to be drawn. First and foremost, there can be no "quick fix" for long-standing, deep-rooted conflict, nor can it be done "on the cheap." If the international community decides to go in, it must be prepared for the long haul and to pay the price, or not go in at all. The "small-and-manageable" approach to Angola proved immensely costly, in money and prestige to the international community and in human lives and suffering to the Angolan people. If the United Nations is to be involved, then it must be a full participant in the negotiations leading to a peace agreement, including consideration of its own role, and it must be endowed with adequate mandate and resources. While no peace can be sustained without the full commitment of the antagonists, it is utopic to expect a Boy Scout spirit on their part, and a strong referee is essential. If elections are to be held, they should never take place until conditions are ripe, especially as concerns demilitarization of the conflicting parties, and should never be based on a "winner-take-all" formula. The losers must also have a stake in the future stability and prosperity of the country through a judicious system of power sharing. There must be confidence-building measures, especially in the development of sound democratic and judicial systems and a neutral police force; in the field of human rights; through economic and social measures fostering the reintegration of men who have known nothing but fighting by programs of vocational training and job creation; and by much greater involvement of local communities, most especially of women, in the peace process. That requires commitment and funding on the part of the international community in areas previously often neglected. All of these factors—or the absence of them—had as determining an effect on the Angolan peace process as the mediation itself.

In the mediation process over the period from Bicesse (May 1991) to Abidjan (May 1993), three stages may be observed:

*Stage 1:* The Bicesse Accords were negotiated exclusively by the three countries comprising the Troika—Portugal, the (then) Soviet Union, and the United States—with no participation by the United Nations. The time was propitious for a settlement, following on the withdrawal of Cuban troops from Angola and the agreement on Namibia, and even more important, because the government and UNITA had fought themselves to a standstill and there was a military stalemate that neither could break.

*Stage 2:* From June 1991 to September 1992 (the elections), the onus was on the two belligerents to police one another's fulfillment of the accords, with the Troika having the more important mediating role, while the United Nations had, in theory at least, a marginal and subsidiary function. In practice, the reality was rather different, especially after the appointment of a political head for UNAVEM II—the secretary-general's special representative—in February 1992.

*Stage 3:* With the resumption of hostilities in October 1992, and despite the intervention of a plethora of other would-be mediators (most notably, South Africa in the person of Pik Botha and the Organization of African Unity), the United Nations—and the secretary-general's special representative in particular—became the principal mediator, almost by default, with the Troika playing a strong supporting part. During the Abidjan negotiations, Côte d'Ivoire played an important but ultimately unsuccessful role. In the whole of that latter period, one of the main obstacles to a new settlement was UNITA's sustained military advantage over the Angolan government and its renewed conviction that it could win power by force of arms alone. It was no coincidence that the Lusaka Protocol of November 1994 became possible only when the tables were turned and government forces gained the upper hand, winning back large tracts of land and major cities that UNITA had occupied.

UNITA was then ready to negotiate again. Thus, the military situation affected the outcome as much as mediation.

Against that background, it is legitimate to ask whether the outcome would have been different had the original mandate and resources accorded to the United Nations been adequate to the task. My answer is that *timing is all-important*. In 1991–92, peace was in the air in Angola. I still believe that had UNAVEM II had the powers and resources given to UNAVEM III nearly four years later, peace might have been consolidated and the Angolan people could have been spared several more years of war and suffering. That can never be proved, but it is indisputable that, by the time the Lusaka Protocol was signed and UNAVEM III set up, all the old hatreds, suspicions, and mistrusts had been rekindled and intensified by months of renewed and savage war and the odds against achieving reconciliation immeasurably increased. Similarly, had the Security Council decreed sanctions against UNITA immediately after it had flouted the election results, rather than nearly a year later, and had those sanctions been wider, then the outcome might well have been different.

From an institutional viewpoint, the United Nations is well placed to lead mediation efforts. It has the advantages of being able to draw on the collective and individual help of all its member states and of being not only impartial but also *seen* as impartial. But it has the disadvantages of its actions being based on political compromise and so often long delayed and insufficiently decisive. Furthermore, the bureaucracy is heavy, there is insufficient delegation to the field, and the practice of appointing many staff on grounds of nationality and geographical representation, rather than qualifications, is often not conducive to effective operations. In contrast, individual countries can more easily take a decisive approach and may have more leverage with one or other of the parties through historical, economic, or political connections. By the same token, however, those same connections may expose the mediating country to charges of partiality in its dealings and of having an axe to grind.

The question of impartiality in mediation is in any case a tricky one. In general, it is obviously important to keep a neutral stance, but if any of the parties consistently breach the peace agreement, then that must be denounced, even though doing so may lessen the mediator's acceptability to the party criticized (vide UNITA's attack on me after I took it to task for not coming to the second round of talks in Addis Ababa). Sometimes an issue of principle may be involved. In Angola, UNITA first turned violently against me when I declared the elections to have been "generally free and fair," but there was no way I could modify that judgment. In short, impartiality is in the eye of the beholder: if you do what he wants, then you are impartial; if you do not, then you are biased and not to be trusted. There is a very fine line to be drawn by any mediator. The best test, perhaps, is when one is attacked by both sides, and every mediator must accept the inevitability of becoming an easy scapegoat, who will be blamed by either side when it suits it, regardless of the facts. It must also be recognized that the media are often not very helpful, criticizing the mediator for not crying foul publicly and failing to recognize the importance of quiet and even secret diplomacy as one of the main tools of mediation.

As my narrative has indicated, the United Nations was pushed into the leadership role in Angola as soon as things became sticky; in fact, the swing had begun once a political head of UNAVEM II—myself—had been appointed in February 1992. Leadership is not, of course, purely organizational. Much depends on the character, personal and professional attributes, and experience of the individual entrusted with the task. I had the advantage of many years of field experience in the developing world, including Africa, during which I had headed major operational missions, including some of an emergency nature, dealing with disasters or situations of civil conflict. I had also held senior positions at UN Headquarters and was very familiar with the workings of New York. For all that, I found my job in Angola immensely lonely and taxing. It was not merely that, perhaps with an exaggerated sense of responsibility, I felt that human lives depended on my actions and decisions, but that feedback and support from UN Headquarters declined with a change of leadership and a different style of management in the Department of Peacekeeping Operations in New York at the end of 1992 and the main attention focused on Bosnia-Herzegovina. During the negotiations in Abidjan, the U.S. and Portuguese representatives received regular comments from their capitals on the evolving draft protocol, whereas New York was silent until the refusal to provide Blue Helmets without a prior cease-fire that brought the talks to an end. At one point, I was barely constrained from sending a cable inquiring, "Is there anyone there?"

The matter of gender should perhaps also be mentioned here, because it became an issue in Angola. I was the first woman to be appointed as special representative of the UN secretary-general and head of a peacekeeping mission, and I am still the only woman to have had to deal with open conflict in that capacity. Contrary to conventional thinking, many of the people with whom I had to deal on both sides of the conflict welcomed my appointment, voicing the expectation that a woman would bring special qualities and more sensitive insights to bear. For myself, I harbored no illusions that feminine attributes, real or imagined, were likely to influence hard-bitten warriors. I simply applied myself to doing the best job possible that my training and experience had fitted me to do. I was not surprised that, when the peace process collapsed, many could not resist the easy jibe that it happened because a woman had been put in charge. Nor was I surprised that the attacks on me became sexually charged: Savimbi who had called me the "mother" of the process now dubbed me a "prostitute"! My own view is that a qualified woman is just as capable as a man of being an effective mediator, though she may have to try harder to overcome the imponderables of prejudice and perception. But neither a man nor a woman can succeed if there are insuperable obstacles to a positive outcome, such as lack of adequate support or political will.

At a meeting on Angola in 1997, an Angolan minister wryly conceded this in a public speech: "In 1993," he said, "quite a lot of people were saying that the peace process had failed because the person whom the United Nations sent to handle the situation was British, white, and female." He paused for effect and then went on: "But now for the last four years we have had someone who is African, black, and male and it still isn't working, so we have to look elsewhere than the person of the mediator for the causes of the continuing conflict!"

Multiparty mediation can be helpful, provided it shares the same objectives and serves to harness supporting forces that otherwise would not be available to the peace process. That is easier said than done unless one of the mediators, or mediating organizations, has a clear leading role. In Angola, the continuous mediating presence besides the United Nations was the Troika. As this narrative has sought to show, the relationship worked well on the whole, owing to a shared aim and generally similar perceptions of the evolving situation among the representatives on the ground, as well as the fortunate coincidence, not to be underestimated, of compatible personalities. The fact that two of the countries in the Troika were permanent members of the Security Council was a strength. I was also careful to hold regular briefings for the ambassadors of other countries resident in Angola and arranged special consultations with those representing members of the Security Council whenever a new council resolution was imminent, and the secretary-general invariably asked me to propose the main points for inclusion. My aim was to ensure a consistent and coherent approach on the part of the main governments concerned. Agreements reached locally were not necessarily reflected at the international level, however, because the capitals did not always follow the counsel of their field representatives but operated according to other lights, particularly Washington, on such matters as condemnation of UNITA, recognition of the Angolan government, and so on.

Mediators cannot function without leverage and that usually has to come through support from higher quarters. Just as Ambassador De Jarnette was frustrated by the delay in U.S. recognition of the Angolan government, so I was rendered powerless in Abidjan by the refusal to commit Blue Helmets and more so by the warning that, even if I did obtain an agreement, no UN troops would be sent to oversee it for many months.

By the same token, vain threats are not only useless but positively counterproductive. The numerous communiqués by the Troika, darkly hinting at dire consequences if UNITA did not shape up, but not followed by any action, and the succession of hand-wringing, increasingly condemnatory but ultimately toothless resolutions adopted by the Security Council from October 1992 to July 1993 merely confirmed UNITA's conviction that it could lead the international community by the nose with impunity. It is also true that there should be carrots as well as sticks. Thus, in Abidjan it would have been better to have tested UNITA's sincerity by acceding to its request for a symbolic presence of 1,000 Blue Helmets, while using the threat of full-scale sanctions as a deterrent. But it is difficult to expect such logical action from a body such as the UN Security Council, where political compromise is an inherent component. Each UN member state has its own interests to consider and the process of reconciling them is all too often inimical both to the adoption of clear, unequivocal mandates at the outset of peacekeeping operations and to decisive action if those operations go wrong.

As has been noted, other mediators appeared on the Angolan scene as the process evolved. The greatest congregation of would-be peacemakers occurred when things began to fall apart after the elections. It was not a case of " the more the merrier" but a demonstration of the law of diminishing returns when some new players came in with their own game plans that simply confused matters further, although in the end, there was no impact either way. To be effective, multiparty mediation must be consistent and mutually supportive, seeking the same objectives, even if it proves expedient to adopt varying tactics, according to the comparative advantage of each player.

In contrast, the British ambassador's involvement in negotiations during the battle of Luanda proved critically important, and the initiatives taken by Côte d'Ivoire during the Abidjan negotiations were most timely on account of that country's long involvement with UNITA. Thus, different mediators may prove useful at different stages in the evolution of a peace process. A word of warning is necessary, however, on the currently fashionable and convenient philosophy that regional actors should play the predominant role. That may work well in some places, but not universally. In Angola, the OAU could not gain a foothold since UNITA regarded it as antagonistic because it had officially recognized the MPLA government in 1976.

Tragically, the Ivorian efforts did not produce the desired effect. Nor did the strong pressure exerted on UNITA by its most powerful longtime supporter, the United States. It is always a dilemma to determine whether more drastic action will do more harm than good, but Washington made a serious misjudgment in realizing too late what was already apparent to us on the ground, namely that neither the United States nor anyone else had influence any longer over its former protégé and that Savimbi and UNITA were embarked on a course from which they would not easily be deterred, certainly not by watering down Security Council resolutions in the hope of retaining their goodwill.

One clear lesson from Angola that often seems to be overlooked is that mediation is never conducted in a vacuum. In today's media-dominated world, news travels fast, even to the farthest reaches of the African bush. I am convinced that Savimbi was encouraged in his decision to return to war after the elections by the international community's simultaneous inability to deal with Karadjic and the Serbs in Bosnia-Herzegovina in the autumn of 1992. There was thus a "copycat" effect that persuaded Savimbi that he too could "cock a snook" at world opinion with impunity.

An equally inescapable truth that must never be forgotten by any mediator, bilateral or international, is that even the most effective peacekeeping operations and the most persuasive mediation can fail if one or other of the parties to the conflict is hell-bent on achieving power at any cost and by any means and will stop at nothing to realize that ambition. That, sadly, seems still to be the case in Angola, four and a half years after the signature of the Lusaka Protocol. Without political will on the part of both antagonists, no mediation can be crowned with success. In Angola, the old rallying cry of the former Portuguese possessions in defiance of their colonial masters, *"A luta continua"* (The fight goes on), is acquiring a new and terrible meaning.

## Background to Chapter 23

# Mozambique: Implementation of the 1992 Peace Agreement

A successful multiparty mediation by Italy and the Community of Sant'Egidio over the course of two years resulted in a comprehensive General Peace Agreement between the Mozambican government and Renamo (see chapter 11). The implementation of this agreement was entrusted to the United Nations, which subsequently deployed a peacekeeping mission (ONUMOZ) with political, military, humanitarian, electoral, and civil police components. The UN operation culminated in free and fair elections won by Frelimo, with the result being accepted by all parties. Overall, the United Nations and its agencies can be credited with managing to secure one of the most successful transitions from war to peace in recent times.

#### MAJOR ACTORS

- Mozambican government: partner in the peace process
- Renamo (Resistência Nacional de Moçambique): the main opposition party, led by Afonso Dhlakama, partner in the peace process
- Frelimo (Frente de Libertação de Moçambique): the majority party led by President Joaquim Alberto Chissano
- Government of Italy: mediator for the peace negotiations
- Community of Sant'Egidio: mediator for the peace negotiations
- France, Portugal, the United Kingdom, and the United States: observers of the peace negotiations

- France, Germany, Italy, the Organization for African Unity, Portugal, the United Kingdom, and the United States: international members of the Supervision and Monitoring Commission
- ONUMOZ: UN peacekeeping operation led by UN Special Representative Aldo Ajello

**IMPORTANT DATES**

- 1990: Negotiations begin between Frelimo and Renamo mediated by the Italian government and Sant'Egidio
- October 4, 1992: General Peace Agreement (GPA) is signed in Rome by President Joaquim Alberto Chissano and Renamo's leader, Afonso Dhlakama
- October 5, 1992: Aldo Ajello is appointed by the UN secretary-general as his interim special representative to Mozambique
- October 13, 1992: Security Council Resolution 782 confirms the appointment of Ajello as special representative of the secretary-general (SRSG)
- October 15, 1992: Ajello and first group of military observers arrive in Mozambique
- November 4, 1992: Supervision and Monitoring Commission is formally established and holds its first meeting; subsidiary bodies are appointed in the following days, including Commissions for a Cease-Fire (CFC), for the Reintegration of Demobilized Soldiers (CORE), for the Formation of a New Army (CCFADM), for Police (ComPol), for Intelligence (ComInfo), for Territorial Administration, and for National Elections (CNE)
- December 16, 1992: Security Council Resolution 797 establishes ONUMOZ, including the UN Office for Humanitarian Assistance Coordination (UNOHAC), and military, political, electoral, and civil police components
- March 4, 1993: First contingent of the peacekeeping force arrives
- March 10, 1994: Demobilization of troops begins
- August 15, 1994: Demobilization is completed
- October 26, 1994: Dhlakama announces that Renamo will boycott the elections
- October 27, 1994: Voting begins across the country
- October 28, 1994: Dhlakama calls off boycott
- November 19, 1994: Election result is announced; Ajello declares elections free and fair
- December 9, 1994: Chissano is inaugurated as president

## KEY AGREEMENTS REACHED

- General Peace Agreement is recognized as the basic law prevailing over all other Mozambican legislation, including the Constitution
- Government and Renamo are recognized as equal partners in the peace process
- Supervision and Monitoring Commission replaces the government in all matters related to the implementation of the peace agreement
- United Nations is the driving force for the implementation of the peace agreement and chairs the main commissions, including the Supervision and Monitoring Commission
- A trust fund is established to help Renamo transform from a military organization into a political party
- A special fund, the Reintegration Support Scheme, is established to provide all demobilized soldiers with eighteen months' salary in addition to the six months' salary provided by the government

## PRINCIPAL OUTCOMES

- Consolidation of peace
- Demobilization and reintegration of more than eighty thousand soldiers
- Creation and training of a new, unified army
- Repatriation and resettlement of 4 million refugees and displaced persons
- Holding of free and fair elections, the result of which was accepted by all parties
- Establishment of a genuinely democratic system

# 23

# Mozambique
## Implementation of the 1992 Peace Agreement

ALDO AJELLO

On the evening of October 4, 1992, I was in Rome with the administrator of the United Nations Development Programme (UNDP), William H. Draper III, as part of a fund-raising mission to the Italian government. After a long day spent in useful but endless meetings, we decided to have dinner in a typical Roman restaurant. When we reached the Piazza di Santa Maria in Trastevere, we noticed that something special was going on in the church after which the piazza is named. There were lights and music and songs. We soon learned why. That very day, Joaquim Alberto Chissano, president of Mozambique and leader of Frelimo (Frente de Libertação de Moçambique) and Afonso Dhlakama, leader of the opposition movement Renamo (Resistência Nacional de Moçambique), had signed a General Peace Agreement that put an end to sixteen years of devastating war in

Mozambique. The Community of Sant'Egidio, which jointly with the Italian government had conducted the mediation between the Mozambican government and Renamo for two years, had offered its parish church—one of the most beautiful in Rome—as the site for celebrating this historical event.

Inside the church, Italians and Mozambicans of the two sides were singing together, celebrating the peace. I knew many of them well, and so it was a great joy to share with them that magical moment. I could not have possibly have imagined that only a few hours later I would be in charge of implementing that very peace agreement.

After dinner, I listened to a message on my answering machine from James Jonah, director of the United Nations Department of Political Affairs (UNDPA), who asked me to fly back to New York immediately because the secretary-general wanted to talk with me urgently. The following day, in Jonah's office in New York, I learned that the secretary-general had decided to appoint me as his special representative in Mozambique.

On what basis I was selected remains a mystery to me. When Jonah asked me basic questions about my professional background, I told him that the answers were in my curriculum vitae. His candid admission that he had not read it left me with the strange feeling that my name had been drawn in alphabetical order from among the senior Italian officials serving in the United Nations. At the time, I was a UNDP staff member with the rank of assistant secretary-general. I have since thought that if my name were Zjello I might not have been given this wonderful opportunity. The following morning, after a short meeting with the secretary-general, I was appointed interim special representative.

There has been considerable speculation over just what "interim" signifies. The term became part of my title after an agreement between the secretary-general and me. He wanted be sure that I was suitable for the job and I wanted be sure that the job was suitable for me. My "interim" status never made me feel insecure, nor did it affect my mission.

The Security Council approved the appointment on October 13, 1992, and just two days later, on October 15, I arrived in Maputo, the capital of Mozambique, accompanied by twenty-five UN military observers, a political adviser, and an administrative officer. My UNDP office in New York later agreed to second me an assistant and an acting executive director on a temporary basis. This extremely limited team comprised all the staff available to me for the following five months—a period that turned out to be very crucial to the peace process.

Our primary task was to assess the situation on the ground and to make recommendations to the secretary-general regarding the dimensions, structure, and mandate of the peacekeeping operation. At the same time we had to monitor the cease-fire and keep the peace process on track.

## ESTABLISHMENT OF THE PEACEKEEPING MISSION

The peacekeeping mission we recommended, the United Nations Operation in Mozambique (ONUMOZ), had four components—political, military, humanitarian, and electoral—supported by a strong administrative structure. A civil police component was added later.

The *political component*, as specified in the General Peace Agreement (GPA), consisted of a series of commissions. The key commission was the Supervision and Monitoring Commission (CSC), which was empowered to replace the government in all matters related to implementation of the agreement. This commission was assisted by a number of subsidiary bodies: the Cease-Fire Commission (CCF), the Commission for the Reintegration of Demobilized Soldiers (CORE), the Commission for the Formation of the New Army (CCFADM), the Commission for the Police (ComPol), the Commission for Intelligence (ComInfo), the Commission for the Territorial Administration, and the National Election Commission (CNE).

In accordance with the peace agreement, ONUMOZ was supposed to chair only the first three commissions: CSC, CCF, and CORE. All the others should have been chaired by Mozambicans. However, after the commissions chaired by ONUMOZ demonstrated that they were working effectively, at the request of the parties (the Frelimo government and Renamo) and the international observers, ONUMOZ agreed to chair the CCFADM to speed up the formation of the army.

The CSC was the engine moving the entire peace process forward. I chaired this commission in my capacity as special representative of the secretary-general. Its members were the two parties—which had to reach a consensus before any decision could be made—and various international partners: the Organization for African Unity (OAU), France, Germany, Italy, Portugal, the United Kingdom, and the United States.

The *military component* of ONUMOZ consisted of 350 UN observers and five infantry battalions with all the necessary logistical, transportation, and communication support structures (including a military engineering company and two field hospitals). The responsibilities of the military observers were to supervise the assembly and demobilization of both government and Renamo soldiers, to monitor the cease-fire, and to investigate any alleged violations of the peace agreement. The mandate of the armed contingent was to guarantee the security of UN personnel and to protect the main roads and corridors in order to allow the efficient delivery of humanitarian aid and the orderly return of refugees and displaced people.

The *humanitarian component* was coordinated by the United Nations Office of the Humanitarian Assistance Coordinator (UNOHAC), which had headquarters in Maputo and a series of suboffices at the regional and provincial levels. UNOHAC was established by the Security Council as an integral component of ONUMOZ under the overall authority of the special representative of the secretary-general. However, UNOHAC also had a second reporting line to the Department of Humanitarian Affairs (DHA), which often limited its flexibility in comparison with the rest of ONUMOZ. UNOHAC's mandate was to coordinate the humanitarian assistance of the UN organizations and, to the extent possible, of nongovernmental organizations (NGOs). Each of these organizations was invited to assign one representative to UNOHAC. The major target groups for humanitarian aid were Mozambicans who had remained in their villages and were severely affected by the war and the drought, refugees returning home, and displaced persons. Food was also to be provided for the soldiers being assembled. When UNOHAC was established there were an estimated 3 to 4 million displaced people and 1.4 to 1.8 million refugees.

The *electoral component* was relatively small. Its mandate was simply to monitor and observe. Organizing the elections was the responsibility of the National Election Commission, which performed impressively under the leadership of its chairman, Professor Brazao Mazula. Mazula and his team deserve full credit for the outstanding organization of the first democratic multiparty elections in Mozambique. ONUMOZ contributed to the electoral process through the provision of political advice and logistical support during the various phases of the electoral process: registration, campaigning, and polling. During the latter phase it organized and deployed a large number of international electoral observers and national party representatives. UNDP also provided effective technical assistance.

The *civil police* component was added at a much later stage as a confidence-building measure requested by Renamo. Despite the number of personnel deployed (1,059 police officers), its impact in the implementation of the peace agreement was marginal.

## THE GENERAL PEACE AGREEMENT

As we made our proposals for the establishment of ONUMOZ, our point of reference was the General Peace Agreement (GPA). This basic document was the outcome of two years of extensive negotiations in Rome between the Mozambican government and Renamo with the joint mediation of the Italian government and the Roman Catholic Community of Sant'Egidio, assisted by four countries (France, Portugal, the United Kingdom, and the United States) as observers.

On the positive side, there were a number of aspects of the peace agreement that are important to underline. The first was the process itself. The peace agreement was the outcome of a serious negotiation lasting two years, during which the two delegations (the Mozambican government and Renamo) worked together and discussed each point of the accord extensively. They had come to know each other well and had learned to work together harmoniously. This proved very useful in the early phase of the implementation. Often during a peace negotiation, the mediator tends to bypass sensitive issues and postpone them until the implementation phase, which is usually executed by someone else. However, during the lengthy negotiation in Rome, the two parties, guided by the mediator and the observers, not only discussed the most sensitive issues but also worked out solutions to the majority of them.

Second, several important points had been unambiguously decided within the agreement itself. These regarded the legal standing of the agreement, the status of the parties, the structures to be established, and the relative powers to be accorded. In legal terms, the peace agreement itself was to take primacy over any other legislation, including the Mozambican constitution. Also critical was the decision that the two parties were to be equal partners in the implementation of the peace agreement.

Third, a strong political structure had been established that accorded the commissions mentioned earlier genuine decision-making and operative powers. In this respect, the definition of the role to be played by the United Nations was especially important. The United Nations was not simply to be an observer, but the locomotive moving the entire process forward. If the United Nations had been solely an observer, as in Angola, it would have lacked the power to influence the course of events. Equally, it would have run the risk of acting as a scapegoat for anything that went wrong—an excellent recipe for jeopardizing the peacekeeping operation.

This latter point is especially relevant. As special representative of the secretary-general, I made use of all the powers accorded to me by the peace agreement. I was occasionally accused of exceeding these powers, but in reality I was working to ensure that the United Nations played the active role needed to keep the peace process on track. We took the initiative at the outset and maintained it until the end of the mission. In some cases the two parties tried to slow down the process and attribute the responsibility to others (preferably, the United Nations), but in the end they were forced to assume their own responsibilities, and this game did not last very long.

On the negative side, the peace agreement had overlooked several important issues that came to light as soon as implementation began. First, the agreement lacked a number of key provisions—notably the monitoring of police, power sharing after elections, and the creation of a neutral body to monitor the impartiality of the mass media.

Given the absence of a reference to civilian police in the peace agreement, we took the initiative of including *pro memoria* (for further consideration) monitoring of the police in the ONUMOZ mandate approved by the Security Council. This step was not immediately popular with the Mozambican government, but the issue was resolved much later at the first summit meeting between President Chissano and Dhlakama, who together decided to include it in the UN mission. Unfortunately, the problems concerning power sharing and the media remained unresolved and continued to create difficulties throughout the entire process and beyond.

Certainly the most negative element of the entire peace agreement was the timetable. Deployment of UN troops was to take place within the space of a few weeks; demobilization within a few months; and elections within one year. The timetable was unrealistic and unprofessional and should never have been accepted by the UN officials in Rome. It was also a source of embarrassment for several months, severely testing the credibility of the United Nations. It eventually took seven months for the United Nations merely to deploy the military component. Subsequently, long and hard negotiations were necessary for the full military demobilization of the two parties and the formation of the new army. Finally, it required two years to organize and hold the first democratic elections.

Fortunately, the United Nations was not alone in being troubled by the timetable. In fact, the delay in the deployment of the UN military contingent gave President Chissano the time he needed to negotiate its arrival with the government and Parliament. Several Mozambican leaders interpreted the deployment of UN troops as a challenge to national sovereignty. Indeed, following the approval of the mandate by the Security Council, the debate in Parliament was extremely tense, and the government was sharply criticized. In this context, the negotiation of the Status of Forces Agreement, which regulated the relationship between the government and ONUMOZ, was difficult. Hence, a longer time frame was critical for the government to solve its own problems.

Similarly, time was given to Dhlakama to solve his problems. The major difficulty for Renamo was that it did not have enough officials with the ability to deal with the complex political machinery specified by the peace agreement. In March 1993, when Renamo boycotted the work of the commissions and recalled its delegation to the bush, I did not insist on their immediate return from Marínguè to Maputo as the government had requested. I knew Renamo was organizing a series of seminars in Marínguè to train a team of new officials. The delay was equally useful to us as it gave us time to find suitable accommodation for the Renamo delegation and Dhlakama in Maputo. Given the strong centralization of decision making within Renamo, Dhlakama's physical presence in Maputo was essential. Without it the process would have been endless.

The respective difficulties encountered by the government and Renamo also gave me the opportunity to divert the attention of the media away from the alleged inefficiency of the United Nations to the reality of the problems faced by the two parties. Some members of the media criticized the "inaction" of that period. In fact, the first quarter of 1993 was well utilized as it allowed the United Nations and the two parties to resolve their problems and lay the groundwork for the smooth implementation of the peace process.

Every peace process has its own dynamic, and the job of the special representative of the secretary-general is to move forward within that dynamic. Abuses must be prevented, but it is critical to avoid the imposition of an arbitrary dynamic formulated in a political laboratory thousands of miles away. We had to adapt many rules and procedures to the reality in the field, rather than trying to adapt reality to the rules and procedures.

In the end, a new timetable was approved and flexibly implemented. Each time that a delay occurred due to a genuine difficulty on the part of one of the parties, we put no pressure on them, instead helping as best we could to solve the problem. On the other hand, when the delay was plainly the result of obstructionism, we acted with the necessary energy to keep the process going—even if this risked antagonizing one or both of the parties. In this very difficult and highly sensitive work I had the invaluable support of the diplomatic corps in Maputo and especially the international members of the CSC.

## CREATING THE COMMISSIONS AND MONITORING THE CEASE-FIRE

When I arrived in Maputo my first challenge was to establish the political structure conceived by the peace agreement as the basic mechanism to keep the political situation under control and monitor the cease-fire. It was immediately evident that Renamo was ill prepared for this. The Renamo office in Maputo was little more than a mailbox and had neither authority nor decision-making power. In order to communicate with Renamo, I had to go into the bush to meet with Dhlakama.

I called on Dhlakama two days after my arrival in Maputo. He received me in his headquarters—a hut in Maríngue—with his staff. They included Raul Domingos, chief negotiator in Rome; Vicente Ululu, who later became the secretary-general of Renamo; José de Castro, his foreign affairs minister; and two military commanders, General Matheus N'gognamo and General Erminio Morais. I was picked up at the airstrip by Raul Domingos on his cross-country motorbike. This journey from the airstrip to the headquarters was the unforgettable first in a long series of bumpy, hair-raising rides through the bush.

Dhlakama made it immediately clear to me that he mistrusted the government. He was not prepared to make any move until a significant number of UN troops were deployed. He had no intention of going to Maputo or sending a delegation there until the government had provided suitable accommodation for him and his large team. His most immediate preoccupation was to replace, as soon as possible, the troops from Zimbabwe and Malawi deployed in the Beira and Nacala corridors with UN troops. At the conclusion of my visit, the sole agreement we had reached regarded the number of assembly areas and the composition of the various commissions.

Despite the lack of more concrete results, I considered my first meeting with Dhlakama a success. Although his formal education was somewhat limited (he had attended a missionary school in his province of Zambezia), he showed an innate political skill, a strong desire to play a major political role, and a genuine desire for peace. Contact was established and a rapport of mutual trust had been created.

The durability of our rapport, together with the capability of ONUMOZ to keep the peace process on the rails and monitor the cease-fire, was heavily tested immediately after my return to Maputo. Renamo launched an attack and captured the towns of Angoche, Maganja da Costa, Memba, and Lugela. The fledgling and little more than symbolic UN mission (the commissions had not yet been established and I had only five civilian officials and twenty-five military observers) was suddenly confronted with a serious crisis.

In response, I made a decision that happily proved to be one of the most effective of the entire operation. I immediately called a meeting with all the ambassadors who had been involved in the Rome negotiations as mediators or observers (this group of ambassadors later became international members of the CSC and continued to work with me in various capacities until the end of the peace process). With their full support, I was able to call for the immediate convening of a meeting of the two parties, urging Dhlakama to dispatch a delegation despite the absence of the "suitable accommodations" he had stipulated as a precondition for his team to come to Maputo. The purpose of the meeting was to set up the commissions indicated in the peace agreement, especially the CSC, in order to manage the crisis produced by the attack. This was a risky gamble—had Renamo refused to send a delegation, my prestige and reputation would have instantly suffered. However, I judged that Dhlakama was interested in obtaining international recognition for his cause, and hence was likely to respond positively to a direct request from the United Nations.

This was indeed the case. Dhlakama sent a high-level delegation chaired by Raul Domingos. Within a few days we were able to hammer out a full agreement on the composition of the various commissions. The CSC, which was to begin functioning immediately, gave us the instrument with which to bring the crisis under control.

Soon afterward, I returned to Marínguè to see Dhlakama with the aim of consolidating my political success. This particular tête-à-tête proved to be one of the most significant. I pointed out to him that the time had come to change his strategy. It was common knowledge that he had muscle—he had demonstrated this for sixteen years. "Now the Mozambican people want to know if you also have wisdom," I told him. I then took a piece of paper and made a drawing of two boxes. One I marked "Frelimo," the other "Renamo."

"Frelimo has been the ruling party for many years," I said. "All the seats in the Frelimo box are fully booked, while the Renamo box, apart from the top leadership, is empty. This is therefore a great opportunity for young Mozambican intellectuals with political ambitions and, equally, an opportunity for Renamo. However, no bright young people will join Renamo if it is perceived as an organization of bandits. If you do not change this image, you will fail to attract this young generation and you will have no political future."

Dhlakama listened to me carefully and took notes on my comments. When I had finished he said only three words: "Wisdom, not muscle." He folded the drawing of the two boxes, put it in his pocket, and solemnly gave me his word: "No more attacks. Even if I am provoked, and I know I will be, I will not react." To the surprise of many observers, he kept his word throughout the entire peace process. In the ensuing months he and his team frequently mentioned the two boxes to me. I would not be surprised if this drawing could be found somewhere in Dhlakama's archives.

During this crisis two fundamental and critical truths had been established. The first was the importance Dhlakama attached to his being recognized by the international community. The second was the essential support of the diplomatic community in Maputo for my mission and its capacity to speak with a single voice. This support and unity of intent produced two important results. The first result was that neither the government nor Renamo had the opportunity to play one country off against another or the special representative. The second result was that the parties' perception of my role changed dramatically. I was subsequently viewed by the two parties not as the delegate of a bureaucracy in New York, but as a representative of the international community. Each time I had to take a tough position against either the government or Renamo in order to keep the peace process on track, it was clear that I spoke on behalf of the entire international community.

This coordinated approach of the international community was not a gift from the gods—it was the result of hard work. I held regular meetings with the international members of the CSC, the European Union, the group of African ambassadors, the "like-minded" countries, and the permanent members of the Security Council. The ambassadors who did not belong to any specific group were also briefed individually on a regular basis. In this way, all the key international players were briefed extensively and views were coordinated in advance of reporting. Hence, each representative was able to send a simultaneous report to his or her capital, reflecting a comprehensive and common political analysis of the situation. This usually generated a common reaction—exactly what I wanted to achieve.

The international members of the CSC played a special role and were fully involved in the decision-making process. I took no initiative without first securing their agreement. Even the draft reports to be presented by the secretary-general to the Security Council were discussed and agreed on with the ambassadors in Maputo before the reports were sent to New York. This group of ambassadors thus became genuine actors in the process, and invaluable allies and support for the special representative.

## ASSEMBLY AND DEMOBILIZATION OF THE TROOPS

Seven months after operations commenced, all the tools were in place for serious work to begin. The civilian and military components of ONUMOZ were fully established, consisting of some 7,000 people, and all the main commissions were in place and operational. Renamo's representatives had returned to Maputo and were temporarily settled at the Hotel Cardoso, rented for that purpose. These representatives were sufficient in number and quality to participate in all commissions and do their work effectively. Meanwhile, the government had signed the Status of Forces Agreement (SOFA), which provided ONUMOZ with the usual package of exemptions and privileges. Thus, it was time to start assembling, disarming, and demobilizing the troops.

As we moved into the assembly and demobilization phase, we encountered an entirely new set of obstacles. The first concerned the selection of the forty-nine assembly areas (twenty for Renamo, twenty-nine for the government) where all the soldiers were to assemble to be disarmed in preparation for their reintegration into civil life or appointment into the new army. Normally an area is selected for the basic facilities available, such as water supply, and for logistics, especially access by road. The soldiers had to be able to reach the area and to remain there for some weeks until their final destination had been decided.

Unfortunately, both parties were primarily guided by the need for strategic control of territory rather than by logistical suitability for demobilization, and proposed very inaccessible sites. Extensive, tough negotiations and a lot of patience were needed to induce them to accept a compromise. Even then, not all the sites finally approved were suitable, and we ran into difficulties in several cases.

The second obstacle concerned the equipping of the assembly areas, which was caused primarily by variations in approach within the UN system. In practice, the culture of peacekeeping operations differs from, and sometimes conflicts with, the cultures of development and humanitarian aid operations. The culture of development is exemplified by the tale of the man and the fish: "Instead of giving a man a fish, give him a fishing rod, and teach him how to catch a fish." A development approach therefore prioritizes self-help and the transfer of know-how and appropriate technology. The time frame for this to take place is less relevant.

Unlike development and humanitarian aid operations, time is of the essence for a peacekeeping operation. Time is money (the ONUMOZ operation cost nearly $1 million per day), and it is critical to maintaining political momentum. Hence, one usually has to move as quickly as possible. In Mozambique, the teams in charge of setting up and equipping the assembly areas were development officials. Their proposal was to provide the soldiers with raw materials and tools so that they could build their own shelters. The traditional African farm hut was deemed more suitable than military tents.

However, the soldiers, on reaching the assembly areas often after a long and strenuous march, did not appreciate this highly intellectualized and somewhat patronizing development approach. Exhausted, they were furious to find no accommodations ready and concluded that the United Nations was unreliable and disorganized. They resented that they were treated like peasant farmers rather than soldiers. In the end they had no choice but to build themselves huts. However, the soldiers incorrectly assumed they would be staying at the assembly area for a mere few days and built basic shelters that quickly proved unsuitable. This became a source of resentment and even mutiny. It was one of the more serious mistakes we made.

A similar problem we faced related to the provision of foodstuffs for the military. A nutritionist at the World Food Program (WFP) headquarters in Rome presented us with elaborate charts showing the number of calories required for the soldiers. However, this calculation was based on the nutritional requirements of refugees. I spent countless, precious hours trying to persuade WFP officials that, whether fair or not, the food requirements of a soldier armed with an AK-47 (and who knows how to use it) are greater than those of an unarmed refugee. I was guided less by the need to be fair than by the urgency to consolidate the peace process and prevent slippage. Thus, I had to put enough food into the stomach of each soldier to keep him peace loving. I knew that it was unfair to give more food to the soldiers than to the refugees, but it would have been more unfair to risk the reprisals of unhappy soldiers against the refugees.

For the same reason we had to provide job opportunities for demobilized soldiers and especially for officers and NCOs. These latter two groups represented the bulk of the middle class of Mozambique. In the process of building up a multiparty democracy and transforming a centrally planned economy into a market economy, the middle class is an essential actor. Reducing the standard of living of this part of the middle class would have been a serious error, and may have risked a proliferation of banditry or other illegal activities.

Generally speaking, in the cultures of development and humanitarian aid, priority goes to the most needy and vulnerable groups. By contrast, in a peacekeeping operation, priority should be given to the most dangerous groups, which tend to be the least needy and least vulnerable. In Mozambique, we managed to focus on carefully selected priorities and to invest sufficient resources to achieve a successful demobilization of the armed forces and their reintegration into civil life. Two tools proved essential for this process. One was the creation of a Technical Unit; the other was the establishment of the Reintegration Support Scheme (RSS).

Usually in a peacekeeping operation demobilization is the task of the UN military observers. However, in practice we found that these observers lacked the specific training to be effective. To remedy this situation, a special Technical Unit of civilians was created to take the lead. Its functions were (1) to prepare the assembly areas in coordination with the military observers; (2) to register the soldiers in coordination with military observers; (3) to prepare and deliver demobilization documents in coordination with the Ministry of Finance and military observers; (4) to establish of a database; and (5) to transport demobilized soldiers in coordination with the International Organization for Migration (IOM) and military observers.

The Technical Unit was directly accountable to the special representative and had a team present in the headquarters and in each assembly area. Each soldier to be demobilized was identified, registered on the database, and then issued an ID card and a package containing civilian clothing and some basics for his return to civilian life, such as simple farm tools and seeds. Every morning an updated list of the number of soldiers assembled and demobilized or selected for the new army was on my desk and shared with the press.

In accordance with the peace agreement, the government was to provide each soldier with six months' salary. It quickly became apparent that this sum was insufficient given the time required for their return to civil society. As it stood, implementation of the peace accord would have resulted in large numbers of demobilized soldiers without money or work and with easy access to a weapon. Hence, there would have been a serious risk of a return to violence, major disorders during the forthcoming electoral campaign, and a radical increase in banditry. To avoid this undesirable scenario, I decided, together with ambassadors of the donor countries, to supplement the six months' wages from government funds with funds from the international community. Therefore, an ad hoc Trust Fund was established to provide another eighteen months of wages to each soldier. This fund became the Reintegration Support Scheme (RSS) and was managed by UNDP.

The RSS achieved two results. It prevented violence and banditry and hence helped to establish a peaceful environment in which the electoral campaign could take place. Furthermore, it avoided what I would term the "Angola scenario." It became evident that, as in the case of Angola, both parties had held back a reserve of troops in military barracks and the bush as a safety net. When we announced that the international community would pay an additional salary of eighteen months to all soldiers swiftly demobilized, the first to show up for demobilization were those very reserve troops. Indeed, a battalion of government soldiers in Matola nearly mutinied so as not to lose their benefits and demanded demobilization on the spot within twenty-four hours. After negotiations, they eventually agreed to allow us three days to prepare the necessary documents.

This strong incentive also had the side effect of reducing the number of soldiers interested in joining the new army. In Rome, the two sides had negotiated on the assumption that large numbers of soldiers from each side would ask to be integrated into the new army. An agreement had been reached that an army of 30,000 soldiers would be established and trained—15,000 from each side. In the event, no more than 12,000 soldiers put themselves forward, and there was no way for parity to be respected as only a third of these were from Renamo. A few months after the completion of the peacekeeping operation, the new minister of defense confessed to me that he was very pleased with this unexpected side effect. In fact, the cost of sustaining an army of 30,000 soldiers would have been unbearable for a poor country like Mozambique.

It is generally recognized that demobilization was the most spectacular achievement of the United Nations Operation in Mozambique. A total of 80,000 combatants have been demobilized and reintegrated smoothly into civilian life. Achieving that result was a real challenge, especially given the political problems experienced at the beginning of the demobilization process (with Renamo) and at the end (with the government).

At the beginning, it was evident that Dhlakama's objective was to keep his troops in the bush as long as possible in order to preserve his bargaining power with the government. Keeping open both his military and his political options was the ideal solution for Dhlakama, but clearly impossible if the peace process was to proceed. Convincing him to change his mind was no easy task, but necessary. In fact, it was my firm resolution that no elections would take place without demobilization.

I started by reminding Dhlakama that the presence of the UN troops was his safety net, a kind of "life insurance" for him in his new role as a political leader. This life insurance was costing the international community $1 million a day, which meant very simply that the United Nations could not keep its troops in Mozambique for a long period. If he wanted the United Nations troops to be present to guarantee free and fair elections, they would have to take place no later than October 1994. If he wanted to opt for more time and hold the elections later, he could choose to do so, but the elections would have to take place without the presence of the UN troops. If the assembly and demobilization of soldiers did not start by a specified date in early 1994, the secretary-general would have been obliged to advise the Security Council to begin withdrawal of UN troops.

In fairness, Dhlakama's reluctance to cede his bargaining power and start the demobilization process was understandable. I therefore asked him to articulate his primary long-term concern, offering to see to what extent I could help address this concern. Dhlakama grasped the point. It was obvious that his primary interest was to assemble the financial resources that would allow him to compete fairly in the elections. This subject had already been discussed during the peace negotiations in Rome, but the agreement that had been reached was not viable in practice. It had been agreed that the Mozambican government should provide the financial resources for the transformation of Renamo from a military force into a political party. Clearly, it would have embarrassed Renamo to take funds from the Mozambican government, and it would have been equally difficult for some members of the government to provide funds for its political competitor. In any case, the government lacked the financial resources.

Following consultation with international members of the CSC and with the major donors, it was agreed that a special trust fund should be created within the United Nations. Funding by the donor community would provide Renamo with the necessary resources for building a political party. Following an assessment of the needs of Renamo, the sum of $19 million was considered appropriate for the establishment of the trust fund. Ultimately, we managed to gather $17.5 million. I considered this a significant achievement, given that the trust fund was unconventional, highly controversial, and rather distant from the concept of "politically correct."

The greatest single contribution came from the Italian government, whose special responsibility was singled out in the General Peace Agreement, because of its role as mediator. Important resources were also provided by other countries, including Portugal, South Africa, the Scandinavian countries, the United Kingdom, and the United States.

Once the trust fund was established and shown to be effective, Dhlakama was ready to initiate the demobilization. He made a firm commitment at the time of the successful visit to Mozambique of the UN secretary-general, Boutros Boutros-Ghali. Once again, despite a number of difficulties along the way, Dhlakama kept his word. The secretary-general's visit was also essential to the solution of other pending problems, including the composition and the chairmanship of the National Election Commission and approval of the electoral law.

Unfortunately, this was not the end of our problems. Once Renamo had stopped obstructing the demobilization process, the government began to do so. The Mozambican army, for different reasons, was equally reluctant to be demobilized. After independence, the army had become an entity unto itself outside the political control of the president and the government. Even former president, Samora Machel, with his unquestionable authority and strong charisma, did not succeed in putting the army under the full control of the political power. Despite being an able and sophisticated politician, President Chissano had neither the authority nor the charisma of Samora Machel. His leadership was based on an extraordinary capacity to mediate, but his style was not to give orders to the army. Instead, he would have to convince his defense minister and his generals that it was time to demobilize and move forward.

We realized that in order to allow President Chissano to do this, we had to build up the almost nonexistent constituency that was lobbying for immediate demobilization. Given the lack of support for demobilization within Frelimo, we had to build this pressure outside Frelimo, within the international community. In coordination with the international members of the CSC, we started to denounce every obstructive maneuver of the army and put constant pressure on the president and the government for immediate action.

This strong position taken by the special representative of the secretary-general and the international community created momentary serious tensions within the Mozambican government. In particular, it produced a series of violent reactions from the hard-liners. The favorite targets were U.S. ambassador Denis Jett and myself. However, in the end this gave President Chissano the space he needed to conduct his mediation and convince the army to demobilize. Once this decision was taken the process moved smoothly toward completion.

## THE ELECTIONS

Despite overcoming many obstacles, we realized that all was not over. On the eve of the elections, we needed a last dose of adrenaline when Dhlakama made the dramatic announcement that Renamo would not participate. He was convinced that massive fraud had been organized by the government. Three events had given him this idea. First, several days before the elections, a document was mysteriously faxed to a UN organization and immediately brought to my attention. Allegedly, the document originated from the Mozambican government and was written by the advertising company in charge of Frelimo's electoral campaign. It contained a detailed list of frauds that would have allowed Frelimo to win the elections comfortably. A copy of the document was sent to Renamo.

I immediately declared that I could not even consider the possibility that President Chissano and his government could be involved in the organization of an electoral fraud. Thus, the document had to be false. However, I promised that if a single fraud listed in the document materialized, I would be forced to invalidate the elections. I remain convinced that the document was false, but if by any chance a member of Frelimo thought that a fraud would help his party win elections, publication of the document by the mass media and my commitment should have made that person think again. Unfortunately, Dhlakama did not understand the implications of my declaration. Instead, he believed that I was covering for the government, and his mistrust increased.

Second, the activities of the National Election Commission (CNE) came under suspicion. Renamo had denounced various alleged irregularities, but the president of CNE did not fully investigate these. Once again, Dhlakama felt that he was the victim of a conspiracy. Finally, his suspicions heightened a few days later at the summit of the frontline states in Harare. President Mugabe invited Dhlakama to address the summit, but President Chissano refused to let him attend. Dhlakama spent the entire day in a hotel room waiting to be summoned. Finally, when the meeting was over, President Mugabe informed him briefly of the outcome of the summit. The message from the frontline states was clear and tough: they expected Renamo to accept the result of the elections; otherwise they would take appropriate measures including military intervention. No mention was made of elections being free and fair.

That was more than enough to feed Dhlakama's worst suspicions. His conclusions were quickly drawn: the government had organized massive fraud; the neighboring countries were ready to cover it up to ensure the stability of the region; the international community, anxious to see results from the huge amount of money it invested in the elections, would encourage the United Nations to declare the elections free and fair in any event. Dhlakama was surrounded by his hard-liners in Beira when he announced that Renamo would not participate in the elections. I reached him by phone the following morning. He was firm in his decision, but nevertheless provided me with the key for solving the last and most dangerous crisis of the entire peace process. "I know that the government has organized a fraud, and I refuse to legitimize it," he told me. "In any case I am not going back to the bush. I am not Savimbi. I am sure that the international community will understand my decision."

This last statement contained the magic words. In the ensuing hours the entire diplomatic corps in Maputo worked with me to mobilize the maximum number of heads of state and government to send an unequivocal message to Dhlakama that the international community did not understand his decision and that he was losing all the credibility he had accumulated over the past two years. That day Dhlakama returned to Maputo. I did not go to see him, knowing that he needed some time to digest all the messages and make up his mind. I sent him a message saying that I was ready to see him and work with him to solve the crisis, when he was ready to go back to the elections.

Subsequently, an ad hoc standing committee, composed of ONUMOZ, Renamo, and representatives of some international members of the CSC, went into permanent session. That night, at 2:00 A.M., a message arrived that Dhlakama was ready to go back to the elections. He wanted a declaration, signed by me and by the international members of the CSC, that every complaint presented by Renamo would be fully investigated and elections invalidated if any significant fraud were detected. A text was drafted during the night and signed the morning after. The crisis was over and the elections took place in an exemplary way. There was no fraud, only some minor irregularities owing mainly to lack of experience, which did not change the substance of the result. The result was accepted by all and Chissano was inaugurated a few weeks later as the first president of Mozambique democratically elected by the people.

## CRITICISMS

ONUMOZ's mandate was over, and the mission had been successfully accomplished. However, a number of criticisms have been made of the operation that must be properly addressed. These generally concern four different issues: the size and operation of the military component, the provision of funds to support Renamo's transformation into a political party, the effectiveness of the humanitarian component, and the approach to the problem of weapons.

First, the military component was accused of being oversized, inefficient, and unable to accomplish its mandate. I do not share this point of view. The size of the military component was decided following extensive consultation with the parties and with the military attachés of the mediator and observer countries (France, Italy, Portugal, the United Kingdom, and the United States).

At the time of the Mozambican peace process, the international political environment was dominated by the Angolan catastrophe. As a result, there existed a full consensus on the merit of a strong military deterrent. It is true that the level of the different units was uneven and that some viewed the mandate as UN self-protection, but the presence of a huge military component was helpful. It was a strong deterrent against any temptation to violate the cease-fire and it helped to reduce the level of localized banditry. In addition, and at my request, the military component performed duties that were not included in the ONUMOZ mandate. It provided logistic and transport facilities to the government and Renamo on several matters related to the implementation of the peace agreement, in particular, the assembly and demobilization of troops, the formation of the new army, and the electoral process. The military component gave me strong political leverage with the two parties.

Furthermore, the military component provided assistance to the population. Two military hospitals in Beira and Matola were regularly open to the civilians, and some roads were repaired. This assistance helped to build a positive image for ONUMOZ, which was therefore perceived by the Mozambicans as a friendly presence. In hindsight, the same result might have been possible with a smaller contingent, but when we designed the mission we thought it was wise to be on the safe side. Failure would have had much higher humanitarian, political, and financial costs, as witnessed in Angola, Rwanda, and Somalia.

Second, criticism was leveled at our decision to set up a Trust Fund to provide financial resources to transform Renamo from a military organization into a political party. In particular, we were accused of using an inappropriate instrument to "buy peace." In my view the criticism is unjust. The provision of such funds was clearly stated in the peace agreement that gave Renamo equal status with the government. However, in practical terms the two parties were far from equal. Whereas Frelimo had at its disposal the full machinery of the government, Renamo lacked everything, including basics such as housing, food, and clothes. Without the Trust Fund, it would have been impossible for Renamo to compete fairly on a political level. Therefore, we set up this valuable instrument to collect resources and deliver them to Renamo.

The provision of some funds in cash to Dhlakama was especially criticized. The sum of $3.9 million ($300,000 per month) was provided to Dhlakama during the final thirteen months. A great deal of thought went into this difficult decision. We realized that it was critical to keep Dhlakama strongly in control of his organization. Any splintering of Renamo into factions would have produced a warlord scenario and severely jeopardized peace. We therefore had to ensure that Dhlakama maintained his status as an African leader. Hence, when his supporters needed help, he had to have the ability to dispose of some funds independently; he would have lost face if he had to tell them to approach the UN administrator. We of course supervised how this money was spent. The terms of the Trust Fund required that, every month, I certified the behavior of Renamo toward the continuation of the peace process. This specific invention was an extraordinarily powerful tool in keeping the peace process on track.

Third, a number of criticisms were directed by the parties and the international community at the United Nations Office for Humanitarian Assistance Coordination: an excess of bureaucratic rules and procedures; UNOHAC's tendency to build overly heavy structures in Maputo and in the various provinces; and its inclination to exceed its mandate by getting involved in medium- and longer-term programs. In sum, the whole idea of an independent coordinating body such as UNOHAC was questioned.

Overall, I think UNOHAC did a very good job and achieved impressive results. However, some of the criticisms were legitimate—in particular, those concerning excessive bureaucratic rules and procedures. Unfortunately, this concerns not only UNOHAC but also the entire UN system. Far too many rules are overly complex and focus far more on transparency and accountability than on efficiency and timely delivery. In a peacekeeping operation, as pointed out earlier, time is money and political momentum. It can make the difference between success and failure.

This was best demonstrated by the implementation of the mine-clearance plan. On December 31, 1992, the CSC approved the list of the roads to be demined as a matter of absolute urgency to facilitate the delivery of humanitarian aid and the return of refugees. It took UNOHAC an unbelievable seven months to receive the necessary clearance and authorizations to start the mine-clearing activities. All the rules and procedures were meticulously followed, and transparency and accountability were assured, but the mine-clearance program was correctly labeled a perfect failure. Fortunately, alternative programs funded by bilateral donors reduced the negative impact of the failure.

This example demonstrates that the problem of a heavy bureaucracy is more widespread and cannot be solved simply through abandoning the concept of an office for the coordination of humanitarian assistance. The heart of the problem was again that the rules and procedures established for the delivery of development assistance were applied within a peacekeeping operation, ignoring the special nature of such an exercise. A peacekeeping operation requires a completely different set of priorities than those applied to standard humanitarian or development assistance programs. This difference makes the presence of an ad hoc coordinator even more necessary.

Coordination within the UN system has always been a very difficult (in fact, almost impossible) task. Effective coordination of the many UN agencies and programs would normally imply that the coordinator should have a clear line of authority or control of financial resources. Under present arrangements, the coordinator has neither. Hence, the concept of coordination we developed in Mozambique was innovative.

We worked hard to make the Office of the Humanitarian Coordinator a valid support for the UN organizations. In accordance with this approach, the office was supposed to provide services, not just to give instructions. One key task was to provide UN organizations and the NGO community with a regularly updated picture of the political and military situation. We also helped them solve any problems they might encounter with the government or Renamo while implementing their specific mandate. The director of UNOHAC and I briefed the UN family and NGOs on a regular basis. In addition, I organized on their behalf several crucial meetings with the government and especially with Renamo. The result was that I enjoyed a very high level of cooperation from all of them.

Fourth, ONUMOZ was criticized for its approach to the problem of weapons. This criticism is fair and I assume full responsibility for it. I realized early on that in the short period covered by the mandate of ONUMOZ, the collection of all the weapons in the hands of the military and civilians was an impossible task. There was a strong possibility that every adult male in Mozambique had an AK-47 under his bed. To attempt to collect all of them would have been a futile exercise, like collecting water with a sieve. We managed to collect weapons from the soldiers in the assembly areas and we also tried to identify and verify the most important arms caches. This latter task would have been much more effective without the delays imposed at the beginning, by Renamo and then by the government, on the demobilization process.

Unfortunately, at the end of the peacekeeping operation there was no time to complete the collection and verification of weapons. Conscious of these time constraints, I concentrated much more on political matters. War and peace are, after all, the result of political decisions. Weapons are never the cause of war, they are the instruments. If a political decision has been taken, finding weapons is easy (in Maputo, the cost of an AK-47 on the black market was between $15 and $20).

My primary objective was to create the conditions for a stable political environment that would render the weapons irrelevant. The new government, with the indispensable cooperation of the neighboring countries, would then complete the work.

Today, four years after the elections, Mozambique is exemplary as an active democracy enjoying an increasingly prosperous economy. There are still many problems to be solved in order to make the democratic process compatible with local culture and tradition, but I am convinced that the Mozambican leadership and people have enough wisdom to map out and follow the right course.

## CONCLUSIONS

What lessons can we draw from the Mozambican experience? I will draw out eight key points that seem most relevant.

1. *A strong will for peace on the part of all the parties involved in the conflict is an essential prerequisite for the success of a peacekeeping operation.* Otherwise, we confront the totally different scenario of peace enforcement, which requires a large military contingent with a specific mandate and a long training period. Peace enforcement does not guarantee that war will not resume after the withdrawal of UN troops. It is evident that the international community lacks the political will and is not prepared to provide the financial resources for such an exercise. The United Nations is equally reluctant to get involved in this way.

2. *A solid peace agreement provides the essential basis for a successful peacekeeping operation.* Lack of specificity in a peace agreement is a recipe for endless discussions and disputes during the implementation phase. In such a case, it would be difficult, if not impossible, to reach consensus, and the process would suffer endless delays. The additional time required in the negotiation phase to make a peace agreement more specific is largely compensated by gains in the implementation phase and creates a solid base for the success of a peacekeeping operation.

3. *A strong political structure should be established to manage the peace process.* While the government should continue its normal activity, the political structure should drive and monitor the entire process, prevent crises, or solve them when they explode. The existence of such a structure is essential to the confidence-building process. It gives parties an equal role in the decision-making process, reducing the advantage of the ruling party.

4. *The United Nations should be given an active political role in this structure as the engine of the process and not a passive role as an observer.* Being placed in the driver's seat, the United Nations constantly has the process in hand, being able to take initiatives, orient the process, and make it move. If one of the parties drags its feet, the United Nations is in a position to identify the party responsible and apply the necessary pressure for it to take immediate corrective measures. Conversely, as a mere observer, the United Nations risks receiving the blame for everything that goes wrong, without being able to influence the process.

5. *The international community should be an active player in the peace process.* It should speak with a single voice and be strongly coordinated with the United Nations. The special representative of the secretary-general should consider the coordination of the international community an essential part of his or her mandate.

6. *The preservation and consolidation of peace should be the top priority in a peacekeeping operation.* All the multilateral and bilateral organizations

operating in the country, including the humanitarian agencies, should act in coherence with this priority. An ad hoc office for the coordination of humanitarian and development assistance should be established in order to ensure this coherence.

7. *Rules and procedures should be applied with the required flexibility.* Imagination should be used to introduce the necessary innovations. Each time there is a conflict between UN rules and procedures and the reality on the ground, rules and procedures should be adapted to the reality, not vice versa.

8. *The special representative of the secretary-general must be carefully selected.* His or her role is absolutely vital for the success of the peacekeeping operation. He or she should be given full authority to take the appropriate decisions at the right time without being obstructed by overly heavy bureaucratic constraints. A peacekeeping operation cannot be directed from UN Headquarters. No matter how brilliant and competent the people sitting in New York may be, they will never have a true perception of what is going on and what is needed in the field.

In particular, the most important prerequisite in the selection of a special representative of the secretary-general is his or her political profile. In its essence, a peacekeeping operation is a political exercise. Military and humanitarian components are important, but they should complement and support the political side of the mission, following the priorities established on a political level. Familiarity with the UN machinery and management capacity are also important, but this familiarity can be supplemented through the appointment of a good manager with long-standing experience of the United Nations as deputy special representative. In this case, the special representative of the secretary-general and his deputy should be appointed at the same time to complement one another.

Finally, the special representative should have enough political sensitivity to be able to correct the imbalance that is implicit in every peacekeeping operation. During the war that precedes the deployment of peacekeepers, a kind of equilibrium exists on the ground between the government and the rebellion: neither side can win the war, and thus they are forced to negotiate an agreement. In the implementation phase of the agreement, this balance is heavily skewed in favor of the government. The ruling party keeps running the country and has the full control of the state machinery, while the rebellion often lacks even the basic instruments for effective political competition.

Conscious of its advantage, the government tends to use the peace agreement as a convenient tool to squeeze the rebellion and achieve on the political terrain the victory that it was not able to achieve on the military terrain. In this case, a typical defense mechanism for the rebellion is to obstruct the implementation of the peace agreement, which it starts to perceive as a trap. In turn, the typical reaction of the government is to push the rebellion into a corner, denouncing all its violations of the peace agreement and getting the full support of the special representative and the international community.

The special representative must be strong enough to resist such pressures and careful to avoid the evolution of a scenario in which one of the two parties is perceived as the good guy and the other one as the monster. He or she must be aware that this scenario is conducive to the resumption of war, not to the consolidation of peace.

In general, when one of the parties obstructs the peace process, we must analyze the reason why it is doing so and help it to find the right way out instead of pushing the party into the trap.

In conclusion, I do not believe that all these elements can be taken as a model to be replicated automatically in other missions. Every situation is different and should be addressed using an approach tailored to specific circumstances. However, some of the approaches that proved successful in Mozambique may be repeatable elsewhere. In this respect, a more in-depth analysis of the Mozambican case would be useful.

This analysis could usefully be done by the UN Secretariat, but also by all those countries interested in peacekeeping operations, in their capacity as potential players or as providers of human and financial resources. Without their support in the appropriate bodies of the UN system, no major decision can be taken and no substantive innovations can be introduced.

# Background to Chapter 24

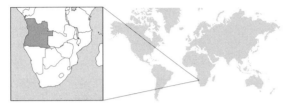

# Angola: The Lusaka Peace Process

The Cold War–driven conflict in Angola between forces backed by the United States and the Soviet Union turned toward a negotiated solution with the December 1988 agreement for the withdrawal of Cubans from Angola in exchange for free elections in Namibia (see chapter 10). After the end of the Cold War, the Angolan peace process began in earnest, with the Bicesse Accords signed in 1991 calling for a cease-fire, demobilization of troops, and elections (see chapter 22). However, violence soon resumed and the Lusaka process was launched in 1993 to end the humanitarian tragedy. The joint efforts of the United Nations and the Troika established an extensive agreement to begin a cease-fire, disarm UNITA, and form a coalition government codified in the Lusaka Protocol. However, distrust fueled the continuing tension between the two sides and armed conflict resumed, exemplifying the difficulty of imposing a settlement, especially when one of the parties is an unwilling or reluctant partner in the peace process.

## Major Actors

- UNAVEM (United Nations Angola Verification Mission)
- UN Special Representative Maître Alouine Blondin Beye
- Troika: Portugal, Russia, and the United States
- MPLA (Popular Movement for the Liberation of Angola): the government of Angola, led by President José Eduardo dos Santos

- UNITA (National Union for the Total Independence of Angola): the Angolan opposition, led by Jonas Savimbi

## IMPORTANT DATES

- September 1992: MPLA wins national elections (with 54 percent of votes, compared with the 34 percent won by UNITA); dos Santos wins presidential elections (with 49.6 percent of votes, compared with 40.1 percent for Savimbi)
- April–May 1993: Negotiations at Abidjan, Côte d'Ivoire, come close to reaching agreement on thirty-seven-point draft protocol
- September 1993: United Nations imposes arms and oil embargo on UNITA
- November 1993–November 1994: Lusaka negotiations take place
- May 1994: Government accepts mediator's proposal (the "May 28 proposals")
- August 1994: UNITA accepts proposal
- October 1994: Lusaka Protocol is initialed; government pursues military path against UNITA
- December 1995: President dos Santos visits President Clinton at the White House
- April 11, 1997: Government of National Unity and Reconciliation forms

## KEY AGREEMENTS REACHED

- UNITA's army to be dismantled and integrated into a national army and police force, while UNITA becomes a political party
- Leading role given to the United Nations in implementation

## PRINCIPAL OUTCOME

- Although the comprehensive Lusaka Protocol established the conditions for peace, UNITA continues to wage war; battlefield dynamics have proved to be more influential than international pressure

# 24

# Angola

## The Lusaka Peace Process

PAUL J. HARE

The Lusaka peace process, the latest effort to end Angola's long-running civil war, was launched officially in November 1993. The talks emerged from the ashes of an earlier peace initiative, the Bicesse Accords, which had paved the way for nationwide elections in Angola in September 1992. In the 1992 elections, the ruling MPLA party (Popular Movement for the Liberation of Angola) won 54 percent of the vote for the National Assembly, while UNITA (National Union for the Total Independence of Angola) won 34 percent. In the presidential election, José Eduardo dos Santos of the MPLA won 49.6 percent of the vote, while Jonas Savimbi of UNITA won 40.1 percent. According to the constitution, a runoff for the presidency was required because dos Santos failed to receive an absolute majority of the popular vote. However, the second round of presidential elections was never held. Although the United Nations special representative (UNSR), Margaret J. Anstee, declared that the elections were "generally free and fair," UNITA claimed they were fraudulent. Subsequently, the war resumed on an even more horrendous scale than before, with up to a thousand people per day dying from war-related causes, a humanitarian disaster of epic proportions, especially considering that the population of Angola numbered only 10 to 12 million people.

The UN Security Council condemned UNITA's resort to military force and demanded that its troops withdraw from the areas they had occupied following the elections. Three efforts were made to try to put the peace process back on track, but they all failed. During a final six-week marathon negotiating session in Abidjan, Côte d'Ivoire, in April–May 1993, the parties almost reached agreement on a thirty-seven-point draft protocol, but at the last moment, UNITA backed off, objecting in particular to one provision calling for the cantonment of its troops. Finally, in September 1993, the Security Council imposed an arms and oil embargo against UNITA and declared that additional sanctions would be imposed if UNITA did not comply with its resolutions. Sensing that the capital of Angola, Luanda, was beyond its military reach and that its forces might be overextended, and wishing to defuse its political isolation, UNITA signaled its readiness to resume peace talks. The stage was thus set for the Lusaka negotiations (November 1993 to November 1994), culminating in the Lusaka Protocol.

## THE ASSIGNMENT OF THE U.S. SPECIAL ENVOY

I was asked by the Clinton administration to become the U.S. special envoy for the Angolan peace process in October 1993. The decision was prompted by two considerations: First, under the leadership of the new UNSR, Maître Alouine Blondin Beye, exploratory talks with representatives of the government and UNITA were scheduled to be held in October 1993 to determine whether formal negotiations to end the civil war could resume. Second, a bipartisan congressional group had written to President Clinton in August 1993 requesting, among other things, that an American representative "with credibility to both sides" be appointed to end the tragic conflict in Angola. The representatives pointed out that the United States had important interests in Angola and the southern African regions that were being threatened by the ongoing Angolan civil war. They also felt that the United States should do whatever it could to end Angola's humanitarian tragedy.

On assuming this mission, I first sought to establish a constructive relationship with Maître Beye, a distinguished jurist, professor, and former foreign minister of Mali. Because relations between Washington and the then UN secretary-general, Boutros Boutros-Ghali, were frayed over Somalia and other hot spots, certain sensitivities came into play. Beye might wonder why the Americans were appointing a special envoy on the eve of the resumption of the talks. Was it to be interpreted as a sign of a lack of confidence in him and by implication the United Nations? Did the Americans have a special, possibly separate, initiative in mind? Suffice it to say, I made it as clear as I could to Beye during our first meeting in Lusaka in October 1993 that my *only* mission was to support his efforts to the best of my ability. We had no other agenda.

Following that initial meeting, our relationship quickly developed into a strong and permanent partnership (and friendship) that was to prove crucial in developing and sustaining a unified mediation effort in the months ahead. My dispatch following the exploratory talks in Lusaka summed up my first impressions of Beye and the role that the United States should play in the negotiations:

> I am impressed by the dynamic, deliberative approach that Maître Beye, the Secretary General's Special Representative, has brought to the talks. He has been even-handed and vigorously enforced discipline on both sides. In the process, he has rankled feelings. One member of the UNITA delegation said that he thought Beye's style undiplomatic, even brutal, a charge that I promptly rebutted. Beye has also been accessible and receptive to our suggestions and has instilled a team spirit among the Troika observers [representatives of Portugal, Russia, and the United States].
>
> The only viable negotiating track at this time is the effort led by Maître Beye. We must repeat must give it our full support, bearing in mind that American backing gives Beye more weight and influence over the Angolan parties. This approach has certain implications. It may mean we will not always get our way on specific issues, though I doubt it will be a substantial problem. We shall also have to keep our rhetoric and public declarations at a lower decibel level than that to which we are normally accustomed.

In looking back at that early message, I find no reason to revise my judgment. I believe the key to building relationships of trust and confidence with Beye, my Troika colleagues, and the representatives of the two parties was sharing information openly with them and being transparent in all our dealings. We had to show by word and deed that the United States had no hidden agenda and was not seeking a leadership role over the process. I underscored that point when my Troika colleagues and I briefed the UN Security Council in May 1994. At that time, I told the council that Beye was "our captain and that we [the Troika] were his lieutenants." I meant it.

From time to time, disagreements arose. Because of historical connections, Portugal and especially Russia tended to be progovernment. Although my American colleagues and I strove mightily to be even-handed, we were probably viewed at times as having a pro-UNITA tilt. I should note that, in the case of Portugal, the perceived bias of its government was basically overcome because of the outstanding diplomatic skills and integrity of its representative to the peace talks. The glue in keeping the mediation team together, however, was Beye. His authority was never disputed within the Troika. Whenever he was attacked by one of the parties, as inevitably happened in the course of the negotiations, we always stood at his side. Indeed, my message to Washington, quoted above, indicates an early effort by one of the parties to drive a wedge between Beye and me.

## PRINCIPLES GOVERNING THE LUSAKA PROCESS

The framework of the Lusaka negotiations was constructed out of the bits and pieces of the past, including the Bicesse Accords, the moribund Abidjan Protocol, and accumulated UN Security Council resolutions. At the same time, lessons drawn from past experience modified and shaped the approach to the negotiations. Those modifications affected negotiating objectives, procedures, and the question of resources. While precise interpretation of the principles varied among the parties and members of the mediation team, they were generally agreed to from the outset of the negotiations.

### Objectives

The first imperative of all the peace initiatives was the establishment of an effective cease-fire. However, Lusaka differed from Bicesse in its treatment of the two military forces. Under the Bicesse Accords, the two armies were essentially granted equal status with the objective of establishing a single, unified military force. At Lusaka, UNITA was called on to quarter all its troops in designated assembly areas under the supervision of UN peacekeepers. In a quid pro quo arrangement, the government's army, the Angolan Armed Forces (FAA), had to withdraw to defensive positions and barracks, but otherwise its military force remained intact. Also, at Lusaka, the parties recognized that the question of the status of the police force needed to be dealt with in greater depth than had been the case during the talks in Bicesse.

Another major difference related to the political content of the negotiations. Whereas Bicesse had focused on holding national elections, Lusaka deliberately put the issue to one side and concentrated instead on reaching agreement on the formation of a Government of National Unity and Reconciliation, in which representatives of UNITA would participate at the national and local levels. The objective was to avoid a "winner-take-all" scenario and to establish a base and a time frame for the former adversaries to work together and to begin to heal the wounds of war. As part of the new political arrangement, UNITA's deputies, elected in 1992, would take their seats in the National Assembly. A general amnesty would also be proclaimed.

In sum, the Lusaka Protocol rested on two major pillars: On the one side, UNITA's army would be dismantled and a substantial number of its troops and officer corps would be incorporated into the national army and police force. On the other side, UNITA would become a legally recognized political party and its representatives would hold positions in the government to foster a spirit of national reconciliation and to prepare the way for multiparty elections sometime in the future. Those essential goals did not change during the long course of the negotiations in Lusaka.

## Procedures

During the Bicesse negotiations, the Portuguese, assisted by the Americans and the Russians, had taken the lead in forging the agreement between the warring parties. Thus, the mediators were the former colonial power and the two Cold War adversaries and respective patrons of the MPLA and UNITA. The United Nations was hardly present at the table and was brought in as almost an afterthought. Subsequently, when the UNSR, Margaret Anstee, was named to help oversee the implementation of the accords, including preparing for the elections, her role was intended to facilitate rather than to direct the peace process.

Lusaka took a different tack. This time, the UNSR was put in charge of the negotiations. He was officially designated the mediator. The Portuguese, the Americans, and the Russians constituted the observer group, a mechanism inherited from the Bicesse period. The lead authority of the United Nations carried over to the implementation phase. Whereas under Bicesse, the body charged with overseeing the implementation of the accords (Joint Political-Military Commission) alternated chairmanship between the MPLA and UNITA delegations, the new overseeing body (Joint Commission) established under the Lusaka Protocol was to be chaired by the UNSR. There was no disagreement between the parties on the enhanced role that the United Nations would play in the peace process.

## Resources

The United Nations was criticized in many quarters, including by the UNSR at the time, for trying to implement the Bicesse Accords with inadequate resources. Given the resources available for other peacekeeping operations, that criticism was valid. If there was one point that the parties agreed on during the talks in Lusaka, it was the question of resources. Both sides wanted a strong peacekeeping force composed of military and police observers, infantry battalions, and associated units, such as engineers and communications personnel. In looking back and reconsidering the Bicesse experience, they tended to feel that they had been shortchanged by the international community, sometimes inferring that this was because they were Africans. The UN contingent in Lusaka also agreed that a substantial commitment by the international community was required if the peace accords were to be successfully implemented. The problem at times was to ratchet down their expectations of what was possible, given the budgetary constraints of the United Nations.

I shared the concern of the parties about the need for an effective peacekeeping force and stated my views in a dispatch that I sent to Washington in October 1993, before the formal negotiations had begun:

> It is imperative that the international community, and especially the United States, act with dispatch in the event an agreement is reached. This necessarily involves committing resources and money, bringing UNAVEM [the United Nations Angola Verification Mission in Angola] up to full strength immediately, and deploying soon thereafter a respectable peacekeeping force. Pre-planning and readiness will be critical in this regard. My initial estimate is that a peacekeeping force of 5,000 will be required.

At times during the negotiations, I wondered whether the United States would be prepared to rise to the challenge of funding a peacekeeping force because of anti-UN sentiments in Congress and the chronic inability of the U.S. government to pay its dues to the United Nations. In the end, the Clinton administration, along with the other members of the Security Council, approved a peacekeeping force of over 7,000 personnel. Much of the credit belongs to the then National Security Council adviser, Tony Lake, who took a keen interest in the Angolan peace process and was determined to do everything possible to make it succeed. The Lusaka Protocol also received broad bipartisan support in Congress. It is noteworthy that this consensus emerged despite the sharp differences that had prevailed between Republicans and Democrats during the Cold War over Angolan policy and despite the perceived failure of the UN operation in Somalia.

In summary, three overarching principles governed the Lusaka talks:

- the trade-off between the dismantling of UNITA's military machine and the participation of UNITA in all branches and levels of government institutions;
- the lead role of the United Nations during both the negotiating and implementing phases; and
- the commitment of substantial resources, including peacekeeping units, by the international community to the peace process.

Translating these general principles into a specific peace agreement proved to be a difficult, frustrating, and protracted exercise. As it turned out, the negotiations at Lusaka lasted one year, far longer than the mediator and the observers ever expected.

## NEGOTIATING HURDLES

Three factors, above and beyond specific issues, influenced the negotiations and made the process especially difficult. The first was the level of distrust that existed between the government and UNITA. During the weeks and then months of negotiations, one became familiar with the litany of treacheries that each side claimed the other had committed over the long course of the conflict. In fact, both the government and UNITA had a legitimate list of grievances accumulated over twenty years of civil war. The failure of the Bicesse peace process served only to heighten suspicions about the real intentions of the other side and made the negotiating effort vastly more complicated.

Because of the legacy of past failures, observers, experts, and analysts were also almost uniformly skeptical about the possibility of reaching a peace settlement in Lusaka. Again, the recent failure of Bicesse sharpened the skepticism. I can recall a meeting before I began my mission with the chairman of the House Subcommittee on Africa, Harry Johnston, who said somewhat humorously, though sympathetically, at the end of our conversation: "Mr. Ambassador, I believe they have just given you a poisoned chalice!" The sense of pessimism about what could be achieved in Lusaka permeated virtually all quarters of government in Washington that took an interest in the Angolan situation. Most bookmakers would have given, at best, one to ten odds that the talks in Lusaka would succeed. Although that view was justified in light of the history of failures since Angola's independence, it certainly did not make the task of the negotiators easier. Whatever was said from the vantage point of the field tended to be discounted as being overly optimistic or Pollyannish.

A third factor influencing the negotiations was the continuation of the fighting in Angola while the talks were being conducted in Lusaka. The Security Council and the negotiators in Lusaka constantly appealed to the parties to stop the fighting, but their appeals fell on deaf ears. Both the government and UNITA accused each other of conducting provocative military actions. In one instance, early in December 1993, the talks ground to a halt for about a week following an accusation by UNITA that the government had tried to assassinate Savimbi during an air attack in the central highlands. Although the charge was investigated and largely discounted (though the fact of an air attack was confirmed), it soon became clear that, until a formal agreement and cease-fire came into effect and UN peacekeepers were deployed to the field, it would be impossible to monitor the situation and sort out the claims and counterclaims of the two sides. Meanwhile, the Angolan people continued to suffer, though the international community did its best to staunch the bleeding by conducting an enormous humanitarian assistance program, largely by air, to all corners of the country. Nevertheless, at times, the delivery of foods and medicines to the outlying areas had to be stopped because of the fighting.

Beyond the posturing of the parties lay another military reality. Many observers estimated that UNITA controlled up to 70 percent of the territory following its military offensives after the 1992 elections. Key provincial towns, including Huambo in the central highlands and Uíge in the north, were captured, as well as the rich diamond areas in the northeast. The government was determined to redress this military imbalance. It recruited mercenaries (principally from previous supporters of UNITA in South Africa), increased the size of the army, trained elite commando units, and purchased massive amounts of arms and military equipment. Over time, the military balance began to swing in the government's favor, even though UNITA continued to strengthen its forces, mainly by bringing in arms and supplies from neighboring Zaire.

Against the backdrop of the bursts of fighting inside Angola, the desultory talks in Lusaka looked like a sideshow in the eyes of the Angolan people and much of the international community. The sense of malaise deepened as the talks dragged on at a snail's pace for weeks and then months. As both sides had access to large pockets of wealth—oil in the case of the government and diamonds in the case of UNITA—it seemed that the fighting might continue more or less indefinitely, even though no clear ideological differences separated the parties now that the Cold War was over. The struggle was principally, though not exclusively, about power.

## KEY NEGOTIATING ISSUES

Because the talks in Lusaka lasted over a year, it can be assumed there was a lot of quibbling over points big and small. In general, the government was determined to demonstrate its legitimacy, especially in the aftermath of the 1992 elections, and wanted that status to be reflected in the text of the agreement at every possible opportunity. UNITA's objective was to obtain the maximum amount of political, economic, and military space within the constitutional system. Ideally, it would have liked to rewrite the constitution by replacing the unitary state with a more decentralized model falling short of outright partition. Because the Lusaka group did not constitute a constituent assembly, that objective was declared off bounds by the mediation team, though the negotiators tried to accommodate UNITA's concerns to the extent they could by indicating areas where the constitution might be revised when UNITA rejoined the political process and the National Assembly.

Beyond these general points of difference, two key issues dominated the discussions in Lusaka, either of which could have derailed the talks: the disarming of UNITA's troops, and UNITA's participation in the government.

## The Disarming of UNITA's Troops

As the first order of business, the negotiators in Lusaka tackled the military issues on the agenda, such as arrangements for a cease-fire and the disengagement of forces. By and large, those were dealt with professionally and with dispatch. One issue, however, threatened to deadlock the talks. While UNITA accepted the proposition that its troops would enter designated assembly or quartering areas under UN supervision and protection, it balked at giving up its weapons to the peacekeepers. The UNITA delegation argued that, if its troops were disarmed, they would be left vulnerable and exposed to government attack. At a more fundamental level, the problem was psychological. UNITA had been founded as an armed liberation movement, and its soldiers had known no other way of life but to bear arms in the bush. Giving up their weapons conveyed a sense of surrender and shame. Beyond those considerations, disarmament also signified giving up the military base on which the movement had been built. Later, Savimbi would pose the rhetorical question that got to the heart of his concerns: "What leader has ever given up his army and survived?"

The mediator and the observers declared that UNITA's troops had to disarm when they entered the assembly areas. Although the mediator and the observers understood the psychological difficulties involved in the disarming process, they did not want to repeat the Bicesse experience, during which UNITA had left the assembly areas following the elections and resumed the war with its military machine largely intact. That position also conformed with the intent of the resolutions adopted by the Security Council. Moreover, the mediation team believed it would be fruitless to continue the negotiations until this issue was definitively resolved, lest they become entrapped in an elaborate charade.

At one point when the talks were stalled over this issue, the head of the UNITA delegation suggested to me that the question of disarming UNITA's troops should be set aside for the moment while other issues were discussed.

I replied that I did not see how that could be done. I had in mind other negotiating situations, such as Abidjan or the autonomy talks in the Middle East, where agreement had been reached on 90 percent or more of the package, but one or two core issues remained unresolved and ultimately led to the collapse of the talks. Beye and my fellow observers agreed there was no point walking down that path, even if it were to lead to an early end of the talks. While a calculated gamble, the approach was grounded on the assumption (or hope) that neither party wanted to be held responsible for the breakdown of the talks.

Ultimately, a face-saving formula was found. One member of UNITA's negotiating team, realizing that the mediator and the observers would not budge, said that the most important thing was to handle the turnover of arms in an honorable and dignified way. He suggested that UNITA's troops should first turn over their weapons to their commanding officers at the assembly areas, who would then give them to the UN peacekeepers. That would, he said, preserve dignity on all sides. This compromise was later incorporated into the text of the agreement and represented the first major breakthrough in the Lusaka negotiations.

## UNITA's Participation in the Government

When Beye and the observers in March 1994 finally turned to the second key element of peace agreement regarding UNITA's participation in the government, they were resolved that this core political issue should be discussed directly between the parties without the direct intervention or even presence of the mediation team. They believed that the issue was so sensitive and complicated it would be difficult for outsiders to know with any degree of assurance how to navigate through those shoals. They also knew that the question had been discussed between the government and UNITA delegations in Abidjan, although various interpretations had subsequently surfaced about what might have been agreed to between the two parties. The mediation team insisted this time that the heads of the two delegations should jointly inform the mediator and the observers of the progress in their bilateral discussions in order to avoid any misinterpretations or misunderstandings.

Although filled with good intentions, the approach foundered almost immediately. After meeting in a closed session, the heads of the two delegations reported that they had been unable to reach agreement. Both sides, it seemed, had staked out their maximum positions and had been unwilling to compromise or engage in serious discussions. As a result, the mediation team had little choice but to become involved in the nitty-gritty exercise of trying to decide which portfolios, down to the village level, UNITA should receive. The negotiations took six months.

The mediation team first discussed with the government delegation what would constitute an acceptable offer. From the outset, it was clear that one of the most contentious issues concerned the status of Huambo, the "Jerusalem" of Angola. Huambo city and province represented the bastion of UNITA's strength among the Ovimbundu peoples from whom the movement had traditionally drawn its principal support. Huambo is also the second-largest city in Angola, and at one point, Portugal had contemplated making it the capital of its empire in Africa. Huambo also had significance to the government, especially as the city had been captured by UNITA in early 1993 following a punishing fifty-five-day siege. In the course of that battle, the city had been pulverized, resembling downtown Beirut at the height of Lebanon's civil war.

Although I initially suggested that we should consider allocating the governorship of Huambo province to UNITA, my colleagues demurred, saying that the government would never accept relinquishing the province. We compromised by adding the municipality of Huambo to the list of positions to be offered to UNITA. After securing the government's agreement to the proposals, we presented them to UNITA. The latter stated that, although the proposals represented a considerable improvement over the original government offer, they were still deficient, especially in what was offered to UNITA at the provincial level and below. In particular, UNITA argued that it needed to be represented in areas where it had done well in the 1992 elections. The mediation team tried to incorporate some of UNITA's preferences in revised proposals. The number of municipal and communal positions was substantially increased. Two deputy governorships in the provinces of Huambo and Benguela were also added.

The government balked at the revised proposals, claiming that the package went too far, especially in offering to UNITA the deputy governorships in Huambo and Benguela provinces. As the government dug in its heels, cracks began to appear in the Troika. Some asked whether the government had been pushed too hard. Beye and the Americans, however, maintained that the revised proposals were fair and did not put the government at risk. In an effort to gain the government's acquiescence, President Clinton sent two letters to President dos Santos urging acceptance of the mediation proposals and promising full American support in implementing any peace agreement that was reached. Other intermediaries, including the UN secretary-general, supported the proposals. The government was also promised that it would not be asked to make any further concessions if the mediation proposals were accepted, regardless of what UNITA might subsequently say about the revised list. Finally, on the eve of a UN Security Council meeting at the end of May 1994, the government accepted the mediation proposals, which were subsequently referred to as the "May 28 proposals."

In this unending game of Ping-Pong, the revised proposals were then turned over to the UNITA delegation, which indicated that, although the revisions had gone a long way in meeting their concerns, still more was needed. Faced with yet another impasse, the mediator and the observers traveled to Huambo in June 1994 to take their case directly to Savimbi. Speaking in a positive vein, Savimbi declared that 90 percent of the work had been done, but added insistently that the governorship of Huambo remained a sine qua non for his party. During my private meeting with Savimbi, I gave him a letter from President Clinton urging acceptance of the proposals, and explained that, while I understood his concerns, he should also understand that we had gone as far as we could in exacting concessions from the government. I also suggested that perhaps what we should be looking at was not *which* party occupied the governor's chair in Huambo but *who* held the position.

Despite those and other efforts, including enlisting the support of Nelson Mandela, the impasse with UNITA continued for three months. During that time, influential figures in Washington argued that UNITA had a legitimate claim to Huambo, especially as the party had won the province in the 1992 elections. Although the argument had merit on the surface, it failed to take into account the tortuous path that had led to the "May 28 proposals" or the positions that President Clinton had stated in his letters to dos Santos and Savimbi. If any attempt had been made to change the proposals, it would have undercut the credibility and role of the mediator, not to mention my own position. Fortunately, the administration resisted the temptation to tinker with the proposals. Faced with a unified mediation position and the threat of sanctions from the Security Council, UNITA finally accepted the "May 28 proposals" at the end of August 1994.

## A Messy Ending

As previously mentioned, beginning in 1993, the Angolan government had undertaken strenuous efforts to redress the military balance and to recoup lost territory. Over time, those efforts succeeded and the government's military pressure on UNITA increased. Even after the initialing of the Lusaka Protocol at the end of October 1994 and the setting of the formal signing date two weeks later, the government continued its military operations with the objective of recapturing all of the provincial capitals before the Lusaka Protocol and the formal cease-fire came into force. Uíge and Huambo were taken during the first half of November, prompting an international outcry that those actions placed the peace agreement in severe jeopardy. Flush with success, some government "hawks" believed they had UNITA on the run and argued that the military campaign should be pursued to its conclusion. Although the "hawks" in the military were overruled by their civilian superiors, the question still remained whether UNITA would agree to sign the Lusaka Protocol. In the end, UNITA agreed to sign, though Savimbi declined to come to Lusaka for the signing ceremony, citing problems of security.

## IMPLEMENTING THE AGREEMENT

Implementing the terms of the Lusaka Protocol was jagged and slow paced—scarcely surprising given the nature and depth of the civil conflict in Angola. Nevertheless, substantial accomplishments were achieved. The Joint Commission functioned without interruption throughout and oversaw the implementation of the accords. More than 7,000 peacekeepers and military and police observers were deployed throughout the country. The cease-fire generally held. Fifteen assembly sites were constructed quartering more than 70,000 UNITA troops. Nine UNITA generals were incorporated into the national army, along with 11,000 troops. Many bridges were repaired and thousands of kilometers of roads de-mined. On April 11, 1997, the Government of National Unity and Reconciliation was formed, with four UNITA ministers and seven deputy ministers taking the oath of office. Two days earlier, the UNITA deputies had joined the National Assembly.

Despite these accomplishments, the peace process remained incomplete and finally collapsed in the second half of 1998. The principal cause was UNITA's refusal to allow the extension of state administration into the central highlands, specifically to Andulo and Bailundo. In a last-ditch effort to save the peace process, Maître Beye embarked on a mission to various countries in the region. It was a fateful decision. He and his colleagues died tragically when their plane crashed as it approached the airfield at Abidjan, Côte d'Ivoire. Shortly thereafter, at the end of June 1998, the Security Council imposed a third set of sanctions against UNITA because of its lack of compliance with the peace agreement. As government administrators and police were attacked and harassed in the countryside, it became increasingly clear that UNITA had retained significant military capabilities, even though it had previously stated it had disarmed. For its part, UNITA maintained that the government was carrying out a deliberate policy of attacking UNITA infrastructure and personnel under the guise of extending state administration. Faced with the steady deterioration of security in large parts of the country and the effective collapse of the Lusaka process, the Security Council terminated the UN mandate in Angola at the end of February 1999.

## SOME OBSERVATIONS

Although the Lusaka peace process did not ultimately succeed, several observations may be relevant to third-party mediation in other conflict situations.

### *External Intervention and Its Limitations*

In view of the profound distrust that existed between the two parties, the Lusaka Protocol would never have come to fruition without high-level international intervention. Beye put it this way, in remarks to his Troika colleagues: "It is not certain that the mediators will be able to bring peace to the Angolans, but it is perfectly clear that they will never achieve it without our help." At the same time, it is equally clear that only the Angolans will be able to achieve peace and reconciliation in their country. External intervention may produce a temporary respite and change the dynamic in a positive direction, but there are limits to what outsiders can accomplish. This proved to be the case in Angola.

### *Single Point of Mediation*

The type of third-party mediation will vary according to the circumstance. Regardless of the precise form it takes, it is critical that, whoever the mediator or mediators are, a clear and single source of leadership and direction is recognized. When there are too many would-be peacemakers, the result will be chaos and failure. In the case of the Lusaka peace process, the lead authority was put squarely in the hands of the UNSR. The supporting cast comprised the three observer countries. By and large, the mechanism worked, even though the Troika wobbled at times. The key factor in ensuring a coherent and directed mediation effort was that the UNSR's authority was never questioned. In this regard, the choice of mediator is crucial and can spell the difference between success and failure. In the case of the Lusaka peace process, Beye's diplomatic experience, intelligence, unflagging energy, and tenacity made him an outstanding choice. His African antecedents were also important for providing a better understanding of the motivations and sensitivities of the two parties to the conflict.

The problem with having multiple mediators or negotiators was demonstrated when regional actors were brought into the Lusaka process. While the regional actors supported the UN-led effort, complications arose when they became too intimately involved in the discussions. During the negotiations, the visit of the Zambian team to Huambo in July 1994 created the impression that there was a separate Zambian initiative to resolve the question of which positions UNITA would occupy in the government. Likewise, the effort to involve Nelson Mandela in persuading Savimbi to accept the mediation proposals backfired. Although this step was taken at the initiative of the mediators to break an impasse in the negotiations, UNITA tried to use the opportunity to open up another negotiating track, which led only to further delays. Later, during the implementation phase, the first, critical meeting between dos Santos and Savimbi was almost derailed by the South African invitation to Savimbi to visit that country on the eve of the Lusaka summit—an invitation that was not coordinated with the Angolan government or the mediators. Savimbi's visit to South Africa in January 1997 produced the impression that the South Africans had agreed to negotiate Savimbi's special status in the proposed new government, which again served only to complicate matters and to renew tensions between Angola and South Africa. The point here is that while it is important to marshal the support of regional and other actors for the peace process, it is critical that the core mediation team remains in control of negotiations.

### The Role of the United States

The United States brought some unique assets to the Lusaka peace process. Both the government and UNITA wanted a good relationship with and access to the American delegation. In the case of UNITA, the relationship dated back to the Cold War and, although circumstances had changed with the passage of time, a residue of trust remained. The government wanted to strengthen the relationship that had taken new form with the establishment of diplomatic relations in May 1993.

It is difficult to judge how effective the U.S. role was. The appointment of a special envoy gave one indication of America's interest in settling the conflict and playing an evenhanded role. The sending of presidential messages to the two parties at important turning points reinforced the sense of seriousness and conveyed from the highest authority exactly where the United States stood. Although the letters may not have had an immediate impact, they helped to draw "red lines" beyond which the parties could cross only at a certain risk.

American involvement increased during the implementation phase. The United States took a leading role in the UN Security Council in approving a substantial peacekeeping force. Always the major donor of humanitarian assistance, the United States pledged substantial economic assistance at the Brussels Roundtable on Angola in September 1995. In a further demonstration of high-level interest, President Clinton received President dos Santos at the White House in December 1995. On the ground, two talented and energetic ambassadors spearheaded the effort to implement the Lusaka Protocol. Their efforts were complemented by a number of high-ranking visits to Angola, including visits by the National Security Council adviser, the U.S. permanent representative to the United Nations, the deputy U.S. permanent representative to the United Nations, the assistant secretary of state for international organization affairs, the assistant secretary of state for African affairs, the deputy commander of the European Command, and two secretaries of state. Each visit was designed to support the UN-led effort, and each did indeed help to nudge the peace process along. For example, when the then U.S. permanent representative to the United Nations, Madeleine Albright, visited Angola in January 1996, she played an important role in obtaining Savimbi's commitment to begin quartering his troops.

### Why Did Lusaka Fail?

Despite the commitment of substantial resources and attention by the international community, and despite its efforts to draw on the lessons of the past, Angola has once again tumbled back into war. Could anything have been done differently to avert this outcome? It might be argued that the Lusaka Protocol itself was inherently flawed and was never acceptable to UNITA and Savimbi. According to this thesis, only a radical restructuring of Angola's political order giving UNITA much greater autonomy and political space in areas where it traditionally received support would have provided the necessary framework on which to build a more durable peace. This argument fails, however, to take into account two important factors. First, the elections of September 1992 had conferred legitimacy upon the elected government and had cast UNITA in the role of being in armed rebellion against an internationally recognized authority. Under these circumstances, the international community was not in a position to force the government to accept a significant diminution of its sovereignty, which would have come close to partition of the state. Second, it is highly questionable whether a peace agreement based on a highly decentralized political model would have been stable. If UNITA did not disarm under the terms of the Lusaka Protocol, it would have almost certainly not have disarmed under this scenario, making future conflict virtually inevitable, barring the presence of a substantial and well-armed peacekeeping force for an indefinite period.

Others claim that the implementation of the agreement was faulty: the UN peacekeepers arrived late, creating further, protracted delays in the implementation schedule; the Joint Commission turned a blind eye to UNITA's rearmament effort; the international community failed to enforce Security Council sanctions against UNITA. Of these and other charges, the most serious allegation is that the Joint Commission did not insist that UNITA send real soldiers and real weapons to the quartering areas. If the Joint Commission had taken a tougher approach, it is argued, either UNITA would have been compelled to comply or its real intentions would have been revealed at an earlier stage. Although this argument has merit, it does not take sufficiently into account the political context of executing an inherently difficult and incremental process. If it had appeared that the peace process would collapse over this issue, there would have been an outcry that the United Nations was being unfair to UNITA. Moreover, most observers accepted that UNITA would retain a residual military capability as a form of protection or insurance, even though it said it had disarmed. This had been, after all, the pattern in similar conflict situations. The surprise was that UNITA had not only retained its command-and-control systems but had also increased its inventory of sophisticated weaponry while the Lusaka Protocol was being implemented.

The basic problem in Angola is that Savimbi had the option of continuing the war because of UNITA's access to diamond wealth and because of the ineffectiveness of international sanctions. In the end, Savimbi chose the option of war over peace. That is the reason why the Lusaka peace process failed.

# PART V

# CONCLUSION

# 25

# Rising to the Challenge of Multiparty Mediation
## Institutional Readiness, Policy Context, and Mediator Relationships

CHESTER A. CROCKER, FEN OSLER HAMPSON, AND PAMELA AALL

This project on multiparty mediation started after the signing of the Dayton Peace Accords had ended a long series of mediations, marked by draining turf battles among different third-party institutions and between the United States and the Europeans. Witness to this sad history, our project was driven by a searing illustration of how bad things can get when third-party mediators vie for prominence and—intentionally or carelessly—undercut each other's efforts at peacemaking. It was also driven, however, by the knowledge that some multiparty mediations worked well. As the project developed, it brought to the surface some examples of deliberate cooperation among multiple third parties and other examples of a general agreement among interested third parties that one institution should take the lead. We also found institutions playing key roles at different phases of the conflict, adding in the end to the overall success of the peacemaking effort. In absorbing the wealth of experience and distilled insights contained in the preceding chapters, we came to recognize some important factors that influenced profoundly the course and viability of multiparty mediation. It is to these analytic conclusions and lessons learned that we now turn.

At this point, it is worth restating two important premises on which the project is based. The multiplication of mediators is less a matter of choice than a fact of life in today's world. This complexity has been brought on by the end of the Cold War and by the increasing involvement of a wide array of both state and nonstate actors in the more fluid and less structured relationships of the current era. We have also stressed that multiparty mediation means different things in different contexts: it can refer to simultaneous, sequential, and composite mediated interventions. Hence, the conclusions and the lessons suggested here refer to a wide range of possible institutional and mediatory contexts.

The ensuing discussion is organized as follows. In part 1 we discuss the evident reality that mediatory complexity can be both good and bad. We identify and comment on the opportunities as well as the challenges presented by multiparty mediation in our cases. We argue that multiparty and sequenced mediation can promote peacemaking in concrete ways. At the same time we note that multiparty mediated interventions have their own unique pathologies that are not adequately addressed in the current literature. From the foregoing cases, it is clear that too many mediators of varying competencies who are not working from the same script can actually make matters worse.

In part 2 we come back to the question of what determines who mediates in a multiparty setting. Recognizing that many factors govern this decision, we highlight two that seem particularly pertinent. The first has to do with certain operational and institutional factors of the mediation process itself, which we characterize as the "readiness" ("preparedness") aspects of mediation. We use the term "readiness" of the third-party mediator(s) in order to distinguish this quality clearly from those widely recognized, situational factors affecting the warring parties themselves—elements such as the existence of a mutually hurting stalemate that are usually associated with the concept of "ripeness." We argue that the case studies in this volume demonstrate that the operational and institutional context of the mediation process creates a set of constraints and opportunities for the mediator. These opportunities and constraints do not receive adequate attention in a literature that focuses mainly on the factors and the forces affecting the willingness of the parties themselves to engage in settlement talks.

The second factor in deciding who mediates has been recognized by some specialists in mediation—especially in the nonofficial world—but has failed to be fully appreciated by official and nonofficial institutions in planning their interventions. Turning back to the discussion in chapters 2 and 3, we reexamine the issue of comparative advantage among mediators. Although the case studies underscore the proposition that different mediators bring different kinds of resources and capabilities to the bargaining table, we also find that there are important, nonutilitarian sources of comparative advantage that have more to do with notions of identity, social relationships, and historical and cultural context than concrete resources per se. These translate into normative kinds of influence and sources of legitimacy that are associated with the logic of appropriateness as opposed to the logic of consequentiality. To understand why some parties—governmental or nongovernmental—make better mediators and are able not only to gain entry into a conflict but also to sustain a process of negotiation, we argue that one has to look beyond the kinds of resources and leverage these mediators bring to the table to their status, legitimacy, and broader political relationships with the parties concerned.

Part 3 moves away from a focused examination of the nature of multiparty mediation to look at the context of any mediation effort. The cases in this volume eloquently underscore the proposition that mediation does not occur in a policy vacuum. Rather, the fate of mediation appears to depend crucially on the political and policy foundations on which it rests and the degree of seriousness or ownership attached to it by the sponsoring entity or entities. With multiparty mediation, this implies that strategic goals and a sense of commitment should be shared if the exercise is to prosper. In the real world, however, mediations are undertaken by contemporary actors for a wide range of situational and sometimes transitory reasons, motives, and interests that we identify. Sadly, perhaps, mediators do not always act on the basis of a durable commitment to the sustained pursuit of a strategic goal. This "policy context" of mediation deserves far more attention than it typically receives.

And finally, we look at the implications of these conclusions for the practice of multiparty mediation.

We now turn to these three sets of conclusions, illustrating our points by necessarily selective reference to the wealth of case study material presented in this book. As noted in the initial chapters, we view these conclusions as pointing to areas for further testing and refinement and in hopes of encouraging an essential dialogue between practitioners and scholars.

## I. THE BALANCE SHEET:
### BENEFITS AND LIABILITIES OF MULTIPARTY MEDIATION

### The Benefits of Multiparty Mediation

Third-party intervention in conflict is a delicate matter, needing tact and persuasion as much as boldness and persistence. In the complicated world of modern conflict, it is not always possible for one institution or country to fulfill these requirements, and often more than one third party is necessary to prepare and establish a way to peace. This burden sharing, even in circumstances in which the organizations do not fully collaborate, often provides the means to avoid conflict or cement a peace agreement. The ability to support each other's efforts is one clear benefit of multiparty mediation. There are many others.

### *Gaining Entry at Different Stages*

In chapter 2 we offered a modified "contingency" model of mediation and negotiation that integrates the two main paradigms of mediation: the structuralist and social-psychological models. We hypothesized that individuals and institutions have different strengths and capabilities that, depending on the stage of the conflict, may be more appropriate to facilitating negotiations and establishing communications and dialogue among the parties. At the low end of the conflict curve, before the outbreak of major hostilities or large-scale violence, multitrack mediated interventions by nonofficial actors can be effective in defusing conflicts before they escalate.

At this stage, although the parties may be willing to talk to each other, they may nonetheless eschew high-level mediation by states or international organizations because they do not want to commit themselves to a formal dialogue with its attendant political costs and risks. In these circumstances, multiparty mediation can help to prevent the escalation of stakes by creating a set of parallel tracks for informal dialogue and communication. As the parties talk to each other in an informal setting removed from the political limelight, these dialogues can reduce tensions and encourage the development of trust and working relationships.

The chapters by Hasjim Djalal and Ian Townsend-Gault on the Spratly Islands and South China Sea and by Max van der Stoel on the Organization for Security and Cooperation in Europe (OSCE) provide useful illustrations of multiparty mediation as an instrument of conflict prevention. The South China Sea project was conceived as a series of nonofficial workshops, organized by a joint team composed of an Indonesian diplomat and a Canadian academic, that was sequenced over a period of almost ten years to discuss a range of joint scientific, environmental, and legal issues in the South China Sea. These workshops complemented a series of ongoing bilateral negotiations at the official level between various states in the region, making this a case of multiparty mediation involving simultaneous and sequential negotiations on two parallel tracks. Delegates, many of whom are government officials, participated in these nonofficial workshops in their individual capacities.

The success of these workshops in fostering dialogue, developing ideas for joint cooperation, and reducing tensions by placing issues once considered taboo on the negotiating agenda is due largely to the informal nature of the discussion and the functional and problem-solving manner in which issues have been addressed. The individuals responsible for organizing these workshops are high in what we call "expert" and "informational" power, but bring little to the table in terms of "coercive" or "reward" power.[1]

Likewise, the low-key manner in which the High Commissioner on National Minorities (HCNM) in the OSCE has tackled the problem of treatment of national minorities in Central and Eastern Europe and areas of the former Soviet Union underscores the importance of these intangible resources such as the "legitimate" power that comes with his office and the norms of the organization that he represents. In this case, the multiparty aspects of the mediation lie in the fact that the HCNM is acting on behalf of the OSCE—an international organization that is composed of member states that harbor different national interests but share certain normative concerns and political values. However, by maintaining an arm's-length relationship with the formal institutions of the OSCE, and by eschewing the formal language of "mediation," the commissioner has been able to gain entry into conflicts in ways that a formal mediation approach could not because it would raise the stakes and limit the flexibility of the parties to make concessions. Just as important, however, for this case of mediation as a strategy of conflict prevention, have been the commissioner's quiet style and consistent avoidance of publicity, which have raised confidence in his impartiality.

Many of the cases in the volume involve mediated interventions directed at ending ongoing violent conflict. Most of these conflicts have involved moderate to high levels of ongoing violence and hence tend to fall on the middle to upper ranges of the conflict curve. In chapter 2 we hypothesized that there are higher barriers to entry to mediated interventions in these conflicts because the parties are locked in a continuing struggle and the "we-they" images of the enemy have hardened. We also argued that in those situations where the conflict has yet to reach the point of a "hurting stalemate," coercive and/or reward power may be required to bring the parties to the table, hence the need for "mediators with muscle." Does this obviate or diminish the need for multiparty-mediated interventions of the simultaneous, sequential, or composite variety? Although the case studies in part 3 of the book cover a wide variety of conflicts and circumstances, they do suggest that multiparty and multilevel interventions can play a highly constructive role in ending violent conflict.

In some instances, composite or collective mediation by a group of states helps to furnish the requisite political will and "muscle" required to bring parties to the table and end violence. In other instances, the problem is not so much one of bringing sufficient pressure to bear on the parties, but of opening up new channels of communication that allow the parties to lead themselves toward a negotiated settlement. In these situations, sequential or simultaneous multiparty mediation in which a new or different mediating agent takes the lead is what is required. The case studies illustrate in different ways the wide potential uses of the varieties of multiparty mediation in different conflict settings. Together the case studies underscore the fact that in situations of protracted violence and conflict various composite, sequential, and simultaneous mediation strategies and approaches may also be called on to change attitudes, soften positions, break through the barriers to mutual recognition among parties (particularly when sovereignty concerns lies at the heart of the conflict and the parties refuse to officially recognize each other), create new openings, and build constituencies at the subnational, regional, and international levels that sustain the negotiation process.

### Opening New Avenues for Dialogue

When one avenue is blocked, the activities of another mediator or party providing "good offices" can create a new opening in the negotiation process. As Jan Egeland notes in his chapter, the process that led to the Oslo Accord was a multiparty effort to provide a new opportunity to bring together Israelis and Palestinians. The Norwegians were able to open up a confidential back channel that paved the way for Washington-led negotiations that involved high-level, direct face-to-face meetings between Israeli and Palestinian officials. The nongovernmental partner in these negotiations provided academic camouflage that gave the parties "their much-needed 'deniability,'" and the Norwegians' ability to deflect media attention allowed parties to take some risks without fear of exposure. It is worth noting that the Clinton administration gave its full backing to the Oslo peace process when an agreement was reached. As Egeland notes, a small country like Norway was able to play the role of third-party facilitator precisely because it was perceived by the parties as neutral and impartial; Norway did not assume the role of full-fledged "mediator" and did not seek the mandate to do so.

In Mozambique, the Community of Sant'Egidio was able to play a similar facilitative role in the nascent peace process because of its close relation to Jaime Gonçalves, the archbishop of Beira. He in turn played a leading role in encouraging a dialogue between Frelimo and Renamo. Working with Gonçalves, Sant'Egidio was able to provide both physical and psychological space so that direct talks between the government and the opposition could take place for the first time. During this process, Sant'Egidio kept other key actors, including the United States, states in the region, and the United Nations, closely informed about the negotiations. Sant'Egidio, although a volunteer charity organization, was able to use its relations with the important state actors to develop a powerful third-party constituency for the peace process, which gave the mediation a degree of political credibility it would have otherwise lacked.

Likewise, a series of ongoing workshops organized at the track-two level by a group of academics, as described in Paul Arthur's chapter, not only helped to recapture the political center in Northern Ireland, but also allowed for the building of personal relationships and trust at a time when the official peace process was breaking down. Discussions covered a wide range of issues, including how best to address the interests of the people of Northern Ireland in a new Europe after the creation of the European Union. The dialogue also generated a range of new ideas for the more formal, official peace process.

### Creating Leverage, Isolating Spoilers, and Sharing Costs and Risks

Multiparty mediation, particularly when undertaken by a coalition or collective body, not only provides a critical mechanism for sharing the costs and risks of mediation but also for multiplying sources of leverage. Luigi Einaudi in his chapter shows how four guarantor countries to the 1942 Rio Protocol between Peru and Ecuador were able to work together to help resolve the boundary dispute that escalated into full-scale warfare between the two countries in 1995. The guarantors were the only channel of communication between the two countries and no negotiation would have been possible without the guarantors. As Einaudi notes, "because the four guarantor states were powerful and successful countries, this automatically put pressure on the parties at least to appear to be working toward a settlement." At the same time, the "legitimacy of their actions and recommendations" came from the original Rio Protocol, which not only provided a legal framework but also gave broader political legitimacy and coherence to the peace process.

Aldo Ajello's ability to leverage his own resources was a direct result of his relationship with key embassies in Maputo. By putting together a "mini-Security Council" that brought together the ambassadors from France, Portugal, the United Kingdom, and the United States in the decision-making process, he was able to keep the international community squarely behind UN policies and actions. Consequently, he was able to determine how to use the leveraged resources they provided him and to decide when to act alone and when to act in concert.

Establishing a multiparty mediation team was also critical to American-led efforts in the Namibia-Angola peace negotiations in the 1980s. As noted in the chapter, the United States had limited leverage over Cuba, South Africa, and the Soviet Union, which had troops and military advisers in Angola. Even its superpower status did not provide the kind of leverage necessary to move the mediation forward. To break out of these constraints, the United States opted to borrow leverage by expanding the coalition of parties, at both regional and international levels, which could create access to the parties and add credibility and leverage to the U.S. effort. This broadening of coalition partners was also essential to isolating real and potential "spoilers" in the peace process, not only limiting their ability to reach out to allies but also reducing their bases of political support.[2]

General John de Chastelain's account of the work of the International Body in the Irish peace process shows that the parties to a conflict themselves may also quite consciously and deliberately try to multilateralize the negotiation process by bringing in an outside mediating team composed of individuals of different nationalities and backgrounds to handle the most intractable issues in the negotiation. This was certainly the case when the British and Irish governments announced the establishment of the International Body to "identify and advise on a suitable and acceptable method for full and verifiable decommissioning" of weapons. The members of the mediation team not only had the requisite political, technical, and negotiation skills, but also had the presence of former U.S. senator George Mitchell, who had close ties with official Washington and brought the prestige and weight of the United States to bear on the negotiations. This was to prove critical in facilitating the continuing engagement of President Bill Clinton.

### Catalyzing Systemic Change

In a number of cases, ongoing civil or "internal" conflicts are entangled in a wider complex of regional and/or great-power interests that sustain conflict processes and thwart the possibilities for a settlement. On such occasions, composite mediation efforts that involve key regional and/or global actors may be critical to restructuring relations at the wider subsystemic or even systemic level if there is to be any hope of reaching a negotiated settlement. Multiparty mediation efforts may serve as an important catalyst for advancing systemic change, particularly in those conflicts that threaten to spread across a region or strategic area. In his chapter on Cambodia, Richard Solomon shows how the five permanent members of the United Nations Security Council worked together in a combined multiparty effort to mediate the Comprehensive Peace Agreement for Cambodia. According to Solomon, the Cambodian settlement became an agent of broader, systemic change, serving to redefine relations between China and Vietnam, the United States and Russia, and the United States and all of Indochina. The mediators as parties to this wider process of structural transformation not only encouraged changes that were already beginning to occur but also acted as a catalytic force by providing a cover for the normalization of relations between Hanoi and Bejing. Other catalytic agents—the United Nations, the Association of Southeast Asian Nations (ASEAN), and Australia—were also important to moving the process forward and prompting the thaw in China-Vietnam relations that was critical to the settlement in Cambodia. This case points out that regional and international resources, when mobilized, can be critical factors in moving the conflict parties toward a negotiated settlement.

As James Baker also illustrates in his analysis of the road to the Madrid peace talks, the United States tried to capitalize on the dramatic new realities and reshaping of interstate relations in the region as a result of the cooperative, allied effort in the Gulf War against Iraq, coupled with the rapid decline of Soviet influence in the region with the collapse of the Soviet Union. Any new American initiative, Baker realized, was condemned to failure if it simply resurrected the diplomatic status quo. The United States, therefore, in its traditional role as mediator and broker of Israel's relations with its neighbors, launched an ambitious new set of negotiations on two tracks: one that would lead to an Israeli-Palestinian dialogue (with all the difficulties that entailed) and the other in the form of direct talks between Israel and its Arab neighbors. This tactical decision, Baker notes, not only enhanced American credibility, but also gave the parties the necessary cover to change their long-standing policies toward each other. Looking back on Madrid and the events that followed, Baker observes that "like a phoenix, the Middle East peace process was reborn in Madrid out of the ashes of the collapse of communism and of Saddam's ill-conceived invasion of Kuwait."

*Building Supportive Constituencies within Society*

Just as it may be necessary to build support upward, there is a similar need to work downward from the national level to the community level in order to engage local constituencies in the peace process. As Harold Saunders discusses in his chapter, a multilevel peace process in Tajikistan has helped develop a complementary peace process on different tracks. The nonofficial dialogue initiated under the auspices of a six-person American-Russian team helped pave the way for negotiations at a time when there was no contact between the government and the opposition. These informal discussions helped build trust and develop the agenda for subsequent negotiations at the official level. As part of their activities, dialogue members and organizers briefed top leaders in the government and the opposition as well as the U.S. government and the United Nations. Once formal negotiations were under way, the dialogue shifted its efforts to working with various civic groups on developing intercommunal mediation and negotiation mechanisms that supported the process of national reconciliation. Saunders describes the dialogue as a "mind at work in the middle of a country making itself." Similar kinds of constituency building are also evident in the various initiatives described by Paul Arthur.

## The Liabilities of Multiparty Mediation

There are costs to even the most successful multiparty mediation. Keeping a number of independent third parties on target, or just keeping them informed, demands much time and energy on the part of the principal mediator. Balanced against the benefits of an internationally supported peace agreement, these costs may be well worth the capital they consume. In other cases, however, these costs outweigh the benefits and can actually set back the peacemaking process. Too many parties can cause confusion and dilute responsibility among the various peacemakers; just as important, this multiplicity of efforts can waste the resources of the already overtaxed third-party institutions that respond to conflict. In these cases, the multiparty aspect of the mediation effort becomes a liability.

*Forum Shopping and Mixed Messages*

An obvious set of problems has to do with having too many "cooks" involved in the collective mediation enterprise. If there is no shared analysis of the problem, and no sense of a common solution, different mediators can undermine each other when they talk to the parties. Some situations call for a clear delegation of authority for conducting negotiations, particularly when negotiations are being conducted on separate tracks and with different constituencies. The danger of sending mixed or confusing signals rises with an increase in the number of mediators, and the international community will undermine its own efforts if the parties perceive that the mediators are working at cross-purposes. The inclination of the parties to go "forum shopping" also grows with the ever-present hope of finding a mediator who is sympathetic to their own particular interests and agenda.

As Fabienne Hara documents, the Great Lakes crisis produced all sorts of official mediations, particularly from the United Nations, the Organization of African Unity (OAU), the European Union (EU), the Arusha Group of states, the United States, and numerous nongovernmental organizations (NGOs). The sheer number of special envoys, each with his own special agenda and set of motivations, undermined official claims that the international community itself wanted peace. As Hara notes, many of these initiatives failed to solve the problems of communication gridlock and to some extent compounded the difficulties of reaching a settlement because they were too focused on narrow agendas without fully grasping the larger elements of the peace and the wide range of humanitarian, development, and human rights concerns that were central to it.

### Dropping the Ball

If forum shopping and mixed messages are symptomatic of the problems of having too many mediators on the ground at the same time, hand-off problems are all too frequently encountered when different mediators try to engage parties in negotiations over a prolonged period of time. Problems of hand-off are typically encountered in the transitional period between the successful negotiation of a peace settlement and its subsequent implementation. During this period, misunderstandings and conflicting interpretations about implementation are common. New problems may also surface that were not adequately addressed during the negotiation of the settlement, or that arise from the competition for scarce resources in the postconflict reconstruction of society and economy. The difficulties experienced by those responsible for implementing the settlement in question may be compounded by poorly defined mandates and inadequate resources for sustaining the peace process.

Margaret Anstee discusses these difficulties during the implementation of the Bicesse Accords in Angola in 1991–93. As the underfunded peace process began to collapse, in part because of the lack of Security Council backing, the United Nations mission was called on to undertake responsibilities lying well beyond its mandate. However, the mandate was not changed by the Security Council, which made matters increasingly difficult for the special representative. There were various subsequent mediated interventions by representatives from Washington, Lisbon, and Moscow and the Organization of African Unity in an effort to salvage the dying peace process. But coordination with those on the ground who were responsible for the day-to-day management of the peace process was weak. It became increasingly apparent that the Security Council was not prepared to give the kind of support and backing that was required to put the peace process back on track.

In contrast, the Lusaka peace process saw a more coherent division of labor among the members of the mediation team and those responsible for implementing the agreement. As Paul Hare observes in his account of these negotiations, one of the overriding elements governing the process was that the United Nations—and, by implication, the secretary-general's special representative, Maître Alouine Blondin Beye—would take the lead role both during the negotiations and thereafter during the implementation of the negotiated agreement. Hare's role, as U.S. special envoy, was to support the principal mediator. Maintaining this clear point of mediator focus—rather than allowing it to dissipate through various competing regional initiatives—was key to the effectiveness of this intervention.

However, this case also shows that a well-managed, coordinated process does not necessarily lead to a successful outcome. As Hare's own account of the Lusaka peace process testifies, even if the parties responsible for mediation and implementation work together as an effective team, the peace process can nonetheless fall apart. In the Angola case, UNITA leader Jonas Savimbi remained dissatisfied with the Lusaka negotiating framework and was determined to operate outside it.

### Buck Passing and Blame Avoidance

In any collective mediation undertaking of the composite or simultaneous variety there is always the danger that different mediators will duck the tough issues and try to pass the responsibility and blame when things go wrong. Just as there may be strong incentives to share the costs and risks of mediation and negotiation in the most problematic cases, there are also incentives to distance oneself from failures or the prospect of imminent failure. In the early years of the Balkan crisis, the United States was all too willing to stay clear of Yugoslavia and pass the buck to the Europeans after initial U.S. efforts to prevent the breakup of Yugoslavia had failed. It was only several years later, when public criticism of U.S. unwillingness to play a role intensified after the horrifying attack in August 1995 on a Sarajevo market, that the Clinton administration fully reengaged itself in the conflict, appointing Richard Holbrooke to serve as the U.S. mediator.

There are, of course, other illustrations of this problem. The Great Lakes crisis of 1996, which is the subject of Gordon Smith and John Hay's chapter, saw the appointment of Raymond Chrétien, Canadian ambassador to the United States, to serve as the secretary-general's special representative with a mandate to negotiate an end to hostilities in eastern Zaire and explore the potential for a longer-term UN presence in the region. Although Chrétien was careful to try to control from the start the large number of envoys from the European Union, the United States, several UN agencies, and regional actors, his task grew more complex as events began to overtake his own mandate. The Clinton administration, unwilling to engage in a humanitarian mission, asked Canada to take the lead in assembling a multinational humanitarian intervention in eastern Zaire. Although the impending deployment of a multinational force led by Canada provoked the local actors into a series of military moves of their own and prompted the sudden return by hundreds of thousands of refugees to their homes in Rwanda, it was apparent that Canada did not have the clout to orchestrate the diplomacy of such a multilateral intervention because it couldn't control the United States and France. As Smith and Hay wryly note, "Good intentions, reputation, and exceptional diplomatic skill can qualify a middle power to provide constructive mediation. . . . But leading a large Chapter VII multinational force imposes different demands, for which middle powers most of the time are less well equipped."

Even if there is an effective division of labor and negotiating authority in a composite, multiparty mediation effort, coalitions can work only if, as noted in the Namibia-Angola chapter, "the care and feeding of marginally useful partners" does not become a "distraction" and consume the diplomatic energy and attention of the negotiation enterprise. Some care is required in choosing one's coalition partners. At the same, a good deal of political self-restraint is required by those who want to contribute to the enterprise but who are clearly in a minor if supportive role.

## II. APPROPRIATE MEDIATORS: OPERATIONAL CONSIDERATIONS

Whether there is only one third-party mediator involved in a conflict or there are many, it is clear that some mediators do better than others in moving the parties toward peace. The introductory chapters discussed this issue in relation to the life cycle of the conflict (chapter 2) and institutional strengths and weaknesses (chapter 3). These chapters, and the ensuing case studies, serve to point out that the elements that govern the relationship between the mediator and the conflict are quite complex. However, two of these elements stand out as underappreciated but key factors in determining an appropriate match between the mediator and the parties to the conflict. The first factor pertains to the capabilities of the mediator's home institution—be it a government, an international agency, or a private, nonofficial organization—and how prepared it is to undertake the rigorous demands of a mediation effort. The second factor concerns the mediator's own identity and historical relationship with the conflict. It is to these two factors that we now turn.

## Mediator "Readiness" versus Conflict "Ripeness"

Much of the discussion in the scholarly literature about the various operational conditions that are conducive to successful mediation typically focuses on the attitudes and perceptions of the parties to the conflict, and how their own cost-benefit calculus and the "best alternative to a negotiated agreement" are affected by the military situation on the ground.[3] To be sure, there is some attention given in the scholarly literature to mediator incentives to become involved the negotiation process. In addition, as discussed in chapter 2, some of the most interesting work has looked at the different kinds of resources that different mediators bring to the bargaining table. However, the practitioner narratives in this volume underscore a major lacuna in much of the scholarly and policy literature on mediation. The operational and institutional environments within which different mediators have to work are for the most part ignored or not well understood.

In many cases mediators operate in an institutional environment where they are given few resources, receive precious little political guidance or support, are viewed by their bureaucratic colleagues as nuisances or distractions from other mainstream foreign policy tasks, and enjoy few allies or coalition partners. An example of this condition is found in the chapter on the implementation of the Bosnian Federation agreement. Daniel Serwer's attempts to focus the attention of his colleagues at the U.S. Department of State on the task of building the Bosnian Federation fell victim to bureaucratic infighting and a competing U.S. initiative to settle the total war. Although this situation is especially characteristic of the large bureaucratic environment of the U.S. government, where difficulties are compounded by Congress generally trying to second-guess the executive branch, it is also true of international organizations such as the United Nations, where there are many political masters and sources of potential opposition to the work of a special representative appointed by the secretary-general. When mediation is being undertaken by a collectivity, such as a group of states or a coalition of governmental and nongovernmental actors, getting the group to march to the same drummer presents its own challenges. This is particularly true when each member of the coalition is being buffeted by different kinds of internal and external institutional pressures and the levels of political commitment to negotiations vary.

Mediators appointed by or acting on behalf of nongovernmental organizations and private groups face many of the same problems, including inadequate resources and institutional support, and competition from other actors and interests. But they also confront their own set of difficulties: the problems of working on a crowded playing field when there are many other NGOs or private groups that are trying to do the same thing; the problems of engaging and working with governments and international organizations whose political and financial support and backing may be essential to keeping negotiations on track and moving them forward; and the problems of ensuring that their own involvement in what is essentially a highly charged political undertaking does not undermine their traditional roles and missions.

We use the term "readiness" to describe the moment when a mediator has assembled the requisite resources, political backing, and institutional support—both domestically and among coalition partners—to move the negotiation process forward.[4] Synchronizing these elements with the situation on the ground, which itself may be changing, presents one of the central challenges to any mediation effort, particularly when multiple third parties are involved. The fact of the matter is that the moment of mediator readiness can differ from the moment of ripeness, that is to say, the point at which the parties to the conflict are seriously willing to consider the negotiation option and to commit themselves to a political process. By the time the various partners to and members of a collective enterprise have organized themselves and given the mediator the tools and authority he or she needs to manage, manipulate, and sustain the negotiation process, the ripe moment for engaging the parties may have long since passed. The mediator then faces the daunting task of trying to re-create the conditions necessary to re-ripen negotiations while not losing his or her own institutional bases of support.

Mediator readiness was a key issue in the negotiations leading up to the Namibia-Angola peace settlement of 1988. Washington had limited leverage over the parties, which limited its ability to control the pace of negotiations and to enforce deadlines. These challenges were compounded by a volatile and fractious domestic political environment that threatened to undermine the mediation effort. Washington thus had to expend considerable energy and political capital at home on laying the foundation for a mediation effort. Just as important, it had to work closely with the other members of the Contact Group in a multiparty mediation effort, not just to bring the conflict situation to a point of ripeness, but also to develop and maintain a state of coordinated readiness to move ahead when the situation was ripe. The painstaking assembly of the multiparty mediation "team" was critical to the success of these negotiations, not only in securing the final peace agreement, but also in regaining momentum in earlier stages of the negotiations when they got bogged down.

Within the context of international organizations such as the United Nations, composite mediation—even when there is a single mediator who is acting on behalf of the organization—presents its own special challenges to achieving and securing readiness. Representatives of the organization may have difficulty serving in an intermediary capacity in a conflict because key members of the organization oppose its involvement in the conflict. Alvaro de Soto's persistent efforts in 1986 to engage first the United Nations and then the Organization of American States (OAS) in the search for a political solution to the El Salvador conflict were stymied by American resistance to multilateral activity in Central America. During the 1980s, the United States, a permanent member of the Security Council, considered the region to be its own "backyard" and was actively opposed to any kind of UN involvement in peacemaking or peacekeeping. It was only when U.S. attitudes began to change in the late 1980s that the United Nations was able to become more proactive, culminating in UN-led and -mediated peace talks in El Salvador. However, preparing his own institution to play an active role, convincing the parties that the United Nations was the most appropriate mediator, and keeping the mediation centered around the UN effort in the face of challenges both from the Contadora states and from the U.S. Congress required vision, vigilance, and pure hard work on de Soto's part. The ability to create and maintain the conditions for mediator readiness was, in this case, as important as the increasing willingness and interest of the Salvadoran government and the Frente Farabundo Martí para la Liberación de Nacional (FMLN) to sit down at the negotiating table.

Even when there is general support within an organization for a mediated intervention, the organization's own leverage and ability to successfully engage in negotiations with the parties to the conflict can be undermined by conflicts among the members of the organization about the goals and objectives of the mediated intervention. In her discussion of OAS-led negotiations in Haiti between ousted president Jean-Bertrand Aristide and the Cedras regime, Barbara McDougall underscores some of the difficulties experienced by the negotiating team because some members of the OAS were less enthusiastic than others about restoring Aristide to power. Other problems had to do with the group's inability to secure the cooperation and the support of key partners, such as France, which had its own special linguistic and cultural ties with the country's military leaders.

Other coalition undertakings have not been so fortunate in being able to attune third-party readiness with conflict ripeness. The chapter on the Great Lakes crisis of 1996 shows the ephemeral quality of this readiness when the international community is faced with supporting a mediation effort with more concerted action. Ambassador Raymond Chrétien's mediation mission in the Great Lakes crisis occurred within the context of a rapidly escalating humanitarian crisis of mammoth proportions. Once a decision was taken to intervene militarily in eastern Zaire in order to avert the humanitarian crisis, Canada faced the daunting task of coordinating and managing a coalition of largely unwilling and obstreperous partners. There were delays and much waffling as countries tried to wiggle out of their commitment to put troops on the ground. Although the threat of the impending deployment of the multinational force prompted Rwanda to unleash its chosen agent, Laurent Kabila, and to attack Hutu forces in the refugee encampments, thereby leading to the breakup of the camps and the flight of many refugees homeward to Rwanda, many died in the jungle or on the road home. In this particular case, the threat to use force—shaky though it was—proved to be the unwitting handmaiden of a failure of diplomacy, with massive consequences for the destabilization of Central Africa. There is perhaps no better illustration of the high costs and devastating results that an absence of mediator readiness—in this case on the part of the international community—can inflict on a conflict.

## Mediator Identities and Contextualized Relationships

What determines who mediates? We have already looked at the importance of institutional preparedness as a key element in determining who mediates. There is another critical factor in this equation, a factor that has more to do with historical, cultural, or philosophical relationships than with institutions. In chapter 2 we noted that much of the extant literature on mediation typically stresses the role of power and the different kinds of resources such as expert knowledge, skills in process management, and legitimacy as sources of influence and leverage in negotiation. Although we do not wish to diminish the importance of these resources, the practitioner accounts offered in this volume point to the fact that comparative advantage is also endowed by the mediator's own identity, image, and previous relationship to the parties. In other words, what mediators bring to bargaining tables may, in many situations, be less important than who they happen to be and why they had enough interest to show up. The implication being that for those who aspire to mediation among the parties in any given conflict, the question is not just "What do you have to bring to the table?" but also (and possibly more important) "Whom do you know and do you know them well enough to talk to them frankly?"

The importance of the mediator relationship has been a central component of the conflict resolution literature, particularly the literature that examines the role that nongovernmental organizations can play in responding to conflict. Both the problem-solving workshops of Herbert Kelman and the work on conflict transformation of John Paul Lederach offer concrete support of Jeffrey Rubin's argument that some sort of relationship of trust between the parties to the conflict and the third-party mediator or facilitator is essential to their ability to work together.[5] This attention to relationships, however, has not necessarily been incorporated into the practice of nonofficial conflict resolution, and the world is littered with examples of mediators who parachute into conflict zones, only to leave as quickly when the venture fails or funding runs out. On the official side, the same phenomenon exists, although it is rare that a country or international organization attempts to solve a problem without a historical basis for their involvement. It is not so rare, however, that an intervention attempt fails because of the nature of that relationship. Neighbors may not always make the best mediators because of their close relationship to the parties to the conflict, as Paul Hare points out in the chapter on the Lusaka agreement. At other times this close relationship does work, as it did in Peru and Ecuador. What makes the difference between these two cases is the nature and quality of the historical relationship.

There is, in effect, a kind of "informal matching" process between mediators and the mediated, which may or may not work to the advantage of those trying to gain entry in a conflict and initiate and sustain a process of negotiation. We observe that, in many cases, there is a natural fit between the various third parties that became engaged and the disputants themselves. This fit grows out of historical relationships, colonial legacies, and spheres of influence, or out of a long-standing presence in the country or other preexisting relationship with the parties, or out of a common personal background, language, or culture. In some cases, though obviously not all, this relationship did allow the third party or parties to exercise leverage and wrest concessions in the context of triadic bargaining, which characterizes many mediated interventions.

For example, to understand why the United Nations ended up being the "mediator of choice" in El Salvador, one has to look beyond its perceived "neutrality" by the various parties to the conflict, beyond the fact that the United Nations, in effect, represented "great-power" interests through the Security Council, thus ensuring that these powers would not be "spoilers" in the peace process, to the fact that the secretary-general himself at that time, Javier Pérez de Cuéllar, and his special representative came from the region and were willing to give the negotiations the priority, backing, and degree of political commitment they required. With a different cast of personalities the United Nations may not have been able to play such an effective role. Recall that concerns about Pérez de Cuéllar's impending departure from his post helped propel the negotiations to closure.

In other cases, the choice of mediator may seem an obvious matching. The role of the four guarantor nations of Argentina, Brazil, Chile, and the United States, which aided the Peru-Ecuador negotiations, provides such an example, at least at first sight. However, as Luigi Einaudi makes apparent, this mediating structure had not been able to play a role in the conflict until other factors were in place, especially a willingness on the part of the two presidents to talk about the border dispute. Once these factors were in place, the 1942 Rio Protocol provided a legal basis for the involvement of the guarantor states, but their ability to help the process depended equally on the long-term relationships built up over a fifty-year period. Without this relationship, the involvement of the guarantor states may have constituted interference rather than assistance.

In cases where the United States took the lead in multiparty mediation, U.S. military power and muscle were not always the critical ingredient in negotiations or in explaining why the United States decided to become involved and was accepted as mediator by the parties to the conflict. In the southern African case, mediation was carried out largely without "wallets and muscle." There was even some hesitation after the initial efforts of the Contact Group in 1978–80 on whether the new Reagan administration should even make the conflict in southern Africa a priority in its own foreign policies. When the United States decided to bite the bullet and take the lead, it put a great deal of effort into cultivating relationships and building trust with the various parties to the conflict so that the negotiations and concessions could follow. Ironically, the same is true in Cambodia where, following the U.S. withdrawal from Vietnam, the United States had largely relinquished its power and influence to the Chinese, Russians, and Vietnamese. But this very disengagement in some ways allowed the United States to take the lead, along with France, in the Permanent Five–led talks in Paris.

Identity and relationship elements are equally important to the mediation efforts of small powers and nongovernmental organizations. To understand why Norway became involved in taking the lead in direct negotiations between Israelis and Palestinians, one has to look to the network of relationships both personal and institutional that evolved among the leadership of the Norwegian Ministry of Foreign Affairs, the director of a nonofficial think tank, and the outgoing Swedish foreign minister Sten Andersson, who was a close friend of PLO leader Yasir Arafat and who recommended Norway as a possible candidate to host secret talks.

The multilevel peace process in Tajikistan was an initiative of the Dartmouth Conference Regional Conflicts Task Force. The Dartmouth group had been established during the height of the Cold War in the early 1960s. Over the years close personal relationships developed between the scientists and officials who participated in the talks led by the group. These relationships provided the basis for the dialogue initiative in Tajikistan that followed. In the case of Mozambique, the Community of Sant'Egidio engaged in the peace process not because it was a professional conflict resolution organization (it was not), but because Sant'Egidio had become involved in Mozambique in the early 1970s and the bishop of Beira, Jaime Gonçalves, had developed close personal ties with the Frelimo government and later with the Renamo opposition. Its role in mediation began in a very ad hoc way. Initially Sant'Egidio representatives were only observers to talks between the government and the guerrilla-based opposition. As Andrea Bartoli points out, "it was only after a few months that the observers were asked to act as full-fledged mediators."

The choice of George Mitchell to lead the International Body in the Irish peace process was also the result of his own personal ties originating from the considerable amount of time he had spent in Ireland and the fact that he was well known and trusted by leaders in Dublin, London, and Belfast.[6] In some ways, rather like the Community of Sant'Egidio, the International Body's involvement in the peace process began rather modestly—it was initially responsible for issuing a report on the decommissioning of weapons. As confidence in Mitchell and his colleagues grew, the International Body then became directly responsible for mediating the entire range of talks.

These critical elements of mediator identity and personal (or institutional) legitimacy help to explain the susceptibility of parties to particular mediators and why they are willing to consider the negotiation option. Once again, the practitioner accounts in this volume are highly suggestive about the rich mix of ingredients that go into a negotiated settlement. The theory of ripeness is based on a kind of rational choice theory, that is, a cost-benefit analysis, which suggests that parties will change course when they find themselves on a path where the costs (i.e., pain) of continued conflict begin to outweigh the potential costs of an agreement.[7] These analyses should be modified to take into account both normative and legitimizing aspects of a negotiated agreement. The motivations and the calculus of the parties are not simply utilitarian, but are intimately related to the parties' own sense of identity, personal honor, and perhaps even wider appreciation of certain social and political norms. When nontangible issues are at stake, the successful mediator is one who can devise resolving formulae and/or offer the appropriate *symbolic* rewards as these accounts suggest.

Robert Pastor forcefully underscores the intimate connection between mediator identity and the kinds of symbolic rewards mediators can offer to the parties to clinch an agreement. As negotiations went right down to the wire, Jimmy Carter told Raoul Cedras that Carter could not stop the impending invasion, but that if Cedras accepted the agreement it would be "an honorable decision" and that he (Carter) would be at Cedras's side and would publicly express his "gratitude and admiration" for the decision. Similarly, "Powell told Cedras that if he stepped down, Powell would make sure that it was with full military honors." Although Carter was subsequently criticized for being too fulsome in his praise of Cedras, the promise of these symbolic rewards closed the deal and averted a bloodbath.

John de Chastelain and Paul Arthur vividly recount the important symbolic impact of Gerry Adams's visit to New York and his subsequent visits to the White House and Congress on the Irish Republican Army (IRA) and the Irish peace process. These visits not only conferred legitimacy on the political aims and goals of the IRA, but also strengthened Adams's own position vis-à-vis more extremist elements in the IRA.

Similar kinds of normative and symbolic pressure can also be applied in a negative way, that is, by withdrawing (or by threatening to do so), to keep negotiations and a peace process on track. Aldo Ajello recounts how in the run-up to the elections in Mozambique the leader of Renamo, Afonso Dhlakama, announced that he was pulling out because he feared that the elections were rigged by the government. The fate of the entire peace process hung in the balance. When Dhlakama indicated that "the international community [would] understand his decision," Ajello was able to use the statement "to mobilize the maximum number of heads of state and government to send an unequivocal message to Dhlakama that the international community did not understand his decision and that he was losing all the credibility that he had accumulated over the past two years."

Dhlakama quickly got the message and the symbolic pressure tactics worked. Dhlakama agreed to participate in the elections in exchange for a written declaration that every complaint pressed by Renamo would be investigated by the Supervision and Monitoring Commission. The elections took place and the result was accepted by all.

Informal matching of mediator and mediated is crucial to understanding why some mediators are sought out by or offer their services to adversaries in certain kinds of conflicts. The key variables in such a matching process are history, culture, and the particular affinities and personal relationships that link the mediator with the mediated. But as we have also tried to suggest, in these situations mediator legitimacy and leverage also depend on the mediator's ability to confer or withhold key symbolic concessions and rewards and the political legitimacy that comes with them.

## III. THINKING STRATEGICALLY ABOUT MEDIATION

When the contributors to this book gathered to discuss their different experiences, they engaged in some exploration of the different roles that a mediator has to take on: organizer, educator, visionary, interpreter, conciliator, provocateur, risk taker, catalyst for change. Andrea Bartoli reflected on the growing professionalization of the activity, saying that as we learn more about what works and what does not work, we develop a fuller appreciation for how to conduct a mediation. Mediation, however, still tends to be presented as an isolated phenomenon that occurs between war and peace. It is seen as an important end in itself and a necessary component for altering the landscape so that other policy objectives can be achieved. It is much more rarely seen as forming part of a larger strategic picture, especially when it is conducted by an international organization or an NGO. The role of policymaker did not appear in the mediator roles mentioned above or in chapter 3. And yet, this is often a central part of mediators' work, whether they are official policymakers, such as James Baker and Barbara McDougall, or operate outside official circles, like Bishop Gonçalves and Paul Arthur.

These observations lead to two final recommendations that emerge from these preceding case studies for the field of multiparty mediation. The first is to understand how the mediation fits into a larger policy context, whether it is to restructure relationships within a region or to prevent conflict from erupting. The second is to think strategically about the requirements of multiparty mediation as part of the professionalizing of the field: to think clearly and ahead of time about coordination, commitment, representation, appropriate institutions, leadership, and the role that they play in any given peacemaking effort.

## Policy Contexts and Multiparty Mediation

There is a wealth of anecdotal evidence in these practitioner accounts that underscores the proposition that mediation does not occur in a policy vacuum. The activities and the choices of the mediator are both informed and shaped by the political goals and interests of the party (or parties) he or she represents. Sometimes these broader policy objectives are clear, as often they are not. Over the course of time, these policy objectives can also change—as a result of changes in political leadership or for some other reason—creating new windows of opportunity while perhaps closing others.

In multiparty mediation, a certain degree of policy convergence is usually desirable, especially when mediation is being undertaken by a coalition or on behalf of a composite body such as the United Nations or the OSCE. When broader policy objectives diverge, the result is likely to be confusion and a lack of coordination in negotiating efforts. It should also be noted that mediation is also sometimes a substitute for clear foreign policy objectives and a lack of strategic design or coherence. Mediation is sometimes a fig leaf for political inaction and policy disarray—that is, it is simply a means to be seen to be doing something while shifting responsibility and reducing the likelihood of being blamed for policy failures. Whatever the case may be, the practitioner accounts in this volume underscore the proposition that the content, the timing, and perhaps even the ultimate success or failure of mediated interventions depend crucially on the durability of their political and policy foundations than is perhaps credited in much of the policy and mediation literature.

### Mediation and Exit Strategies

Mediation efforts that are tied to wider exit strategies can lend coherence to multiparty mediation efforts provided that the various parties to the joint effort share similar strategic goals. Much has been written about the perceived "failure" of the peace process in Cambodia and the difficulties experienced by the parties once the United Nations left the country. Richard Solomon's chapter offers a useful corrective to this perception, noting that the Khmer Rouge movement "imploded" and that the "uneasy peace" in which Cambodians live today is far preferable to the three decades of revolution and political violence suffered by the country. At the same time, Solomon notes that the entire peace process was related to the "entente"-based foundations of the negotiations leading up to the Paris peace accords and motivated by the mutual desire on the part of China, Russia, Vietnam, and the United States to reduce their regional rivalries, exit from military commitments that were increasingly costly, and bring about a withdrawal of Vietnamese troops from Cambodia. The success of the peace process and the political settlement in Cambodia was thus intimately related to the shared policies of entente that made cooperation and support for the United Nations' peace plan and Permanent Five–led negotiations possible.

The desire for exit, paradoxically, was also a motivating factor, though obviously not the only one, behind U.S.-led mediation efforts leading up to the Dayton Peace Accords. The United States had become increasingly fearful that it would be forced to intervene militarily to rescue UN peacekeeping forces in UNPROFOR whose vulnerability to the Serbs had been demonstrated in a series of well-publicized harassment and hostage-taking crises. As Richard Holbrooke notes in his chapter, the UN-designated "safe areas" had also become centers of ethnic cleansing, notably in Srebrenica and Zepa where the most-notorious massacres of civilians had taken place. There were strong reasons to push for a political settlement in a region where human rights abuses and acts of genocide were mounting day by day and to extricate U.S. allies contributing peacekeeping troops to UNPROFOR from a difficult situation. The clarity in U.S. policy objectives—a clarity of purpose that had been lacking earlier—thus helped paved the way for the U.S. mediation team and the progress of negotiations leading to Dayton. At the same time, it also put a premium on early elections in the newly created tripartite state of Bosnia so as to allow for the subsequent removal of NATO troops that were responsible for implementing the military components of the accords. As Daniel Serwer argues in his chapter, the United States' own desire for a quick entry followed by a speedy exit once IFOR had fulfilled its peacekeeping functions created its own tensions and problems in the implementation of Dayton, which have continued to haunt the peace process even as NATO has been forced to continue with its peacekeeping presence in Bosnia under its reconstituted mandate with SFOR.

## Mediation and Regional Engagement

Multiparty mediation can also be related to a wider strategy of political engagement by external actors in a country or region. This commitment may be based on a desire to promote human rights, advance democratic political processes, foster domestic and regional political stability, and bring about much-needed political change. A genuine and sustained commitment to a policy of regional peacemaking can lend political support to multiparty mediation, particularly if early attempts to engage the parties are marked by failure and negotiations become deadlocked. This is because there is an appreciation or recognition that walking away from the problem will jeopardize the more general goals of the policy. The articulation and careful definition of these goals can also help to build domestic political support for multiparty mediation when different bureaucratic and institutional interests are at loggerheads or pursuing independent policies and initiatives of their own that are operating at cross-purposes. Likewise, the articulation of a broader set of political objectives can strengthen the incentives for cooperation in a multiparty mediation undertaking. This is particularly true when there are conflicting interests among coalition partners about timing and sequence or when linkages between the pieces of the strategic puzzle may not be apparent.

Although the United States had been involved in a Western-led peace process on Namibia since the mid-1970s, the efforts of the Contact Group to negotiate an end to the conflict were frustrated by the increasingly polarized situation on the ground. The incoming Reagan administration faced a number of options that included pulling out of the Contact Group and downgrading South African diplomacy. It was recognized early on that a key piece of the puzzle, the seeking of a negotiated withdrawal of Cuban troops from Angola that would assuage South African concerns about security threats to the north, was missing from earlier peace efforts. Some realized that until this issue was successfully addressed the situation would not be "ripe for resolution." The articulation of this linkage between the issue of Cuban troop withdrawals from Angola, which affected South Africa's fundamental security concerns, and the negotiated withdrawal of South African troops from Namibia to secure Namibia's independence became the cornerstone of the U.S. policy of constructive engagement. At the same time, these strategic goals were tied to a broader U.S. interest in promoting peaceful democratic change in South Africa that would see the dismantling of apartheid where engagement—as opposed to the isolation—of South Africa was seen as the key. Political support for these goals at the highest levels in the Reagan administration was essential to sustaining the negotiations and allowing the U.S. mediator to do his work, particularly when the going got tough. Better appreciation of this broader strategy among key U.S. allies and negotiating partners also lent support and momentum to the multiparty mediation enterprise.

### Mediation and Coercive Diplomacy

Mediation can also serve as part and parcel of a more general policy of coercive diplomacy, which imposes its own constraints on the timing and room for maneuver for the mediator(s) while simultaneously creating opportunities for the mediator to exercise leverage and bring pressure to bear on the parties so that a settlement is reached. Robert Pastor argues in his chapter that the Carter-Nunn-Powell initiative was indeed a case of mediation because (1) the team was composed of an unusual combination of two private citizens and a U.S. senator who were sent by the president but had substantial autonomy to conduct negotiations, and (2) the negotiations effectively involved four separate entities: the U.S. government, the Cedras regime and its supporters, ousted president Jean-Bertrand Aristide and his supporters, and the mediators themselves who operated in a quasi-official capacity insofar as they represented but did not speak for the U.S. government.

These negotiations took place in Port-au-Prince against the backdrop of an impending U.S. military invasion if talks failed. This fact was conveyed to Cedras and his generals early on in the negotiations. But once the threat was made, it was never used again. As Pastor vividly recounts, the rest of the time was devoted to listening and working through "a series of points that together made up the final agreement." Unbeknownst to the mediators themselves, as talks continued the countdown for the invasion had already begun. Pastor concludes that the threatened use of force can indeed change the balance of decision making and compel leaders to recalculate their options. Similarly, the use of deadlines (in this case the threat to invade if negotiations after a reasonable period of time failed) is a highly effective negotiating tactic, but that flexibility is also required if mediators are to have the time to gain concessions and forge an agreement. In this particular case, an extension of time was essential to wrapping up the details of an agreement and the conditions for President Aristide's return. But negotiations almost ended when Cedras and his generals learned that an invasion was already under way. Only by changing the location of the talks and finding a fall-back option were the negotiators able to keep talks going and reach an agreement.

Likewise, in his own account of the negotiations that led to Dayton, Richard Holbrooke underscores the importance of NATO bombing raids against Serbian positions in terms of the psychological impact they appeared to have had on Serbian leader Slobodan Milosevic as demonstrated by his willingness to come to the table and make key concessions.

### Mediation and Communal Constituency Building

As Paul Arthur and Harold Saunders illustrate in their respective chapters on Northern Ireland and Tajikistan, mediation or dialogue-based initiatives by various nongovernmental organizations and private groups can usefully serve as components of a wider intercommunal process of "constituency building." These initiatives at the track-two level, as noted previously, can open up new avenues for dialogue where none existed before and generate new ideas that feed into the broader political debate. Such face-to-face contacts are especially useful for building trust and breaking down the all-too-formidable barriers to communication and dialogue.

However, the low profile of such initiatives can also be a problem, as they can be undermined by officials who are unaware of the track-two initiatives and so launch competing dialogues of their own. Paul Arthur notes that this competitive arrangement occurred on at least one occasion during the Irish peace process when a British government–led initiative almost scuttled a set of dialogue partnerships that had been forged between various political parties and business communities in Northern Ireland. Sufficient levels of awareness, if not some degree of coordination or exchanges of information, are necessary if official and unofficial mediation and dialoguing activities are to be mutually reinforcing. Constituency-building and brainstorming dialogues appear to work best when ideas can percolate upward and feed into more formal, political dialogue and/or negotiations; that is, track-one and track-two negotiations are not entirely separate from each other and parties responsible for managing and facilitating the dialogue share common, "core" political objectives.

### Mediation and Conflict Prevention

Multiparty mediation can also contribute to conflict prevention and/or escalation avoidance. But again the political objectives and normative foundations on which such activities are based have to be clear and transparent to all concerned. Such activities also require clear political backing from their sponsors, which also means the provision of adequate resources to carry out and sustain the dialogue process. The case studies documenting the activities of the South China Sea initiative and the work of the OSCE respectively illustrate the utility of this approach as well as the opportunities and the limitations afforded by preventive diplomacy, albeit in two very different contexts. The South China Sea project demonstrates that such initiatives can only really take place if they have political support and credible sponsors (in this case the Indonesian and Canadian governments).

One of the problems with "unofficial" dialogues is that they can easily founder if sponsors lose interest, parties opt out, or sponsors are not persuaded that the dialogue process has led to concrete results. The benefits of a continuing process of discussion and "trust" building may be hard to measure or identify. The real value of the exercise may become apparent only

692 ───── CHESTER A. CROCKER, FEN OSLER HAMPSON, AND PAMELA AALL

after the process is terminated—due, for instance, to lack of funding—and relations among the parties deteriorate. Dialogue by itself may contribute to a reduction in tensions and an avoidance of conflict, but the value of this particular kind of activity is especially hard to measure because it rests on an assessment of a counterfactual situation, that is, the state of relations if there were no dialogue.

### Mediation and Peacebuilding

During the implementation of a peace settlement, those responsible for managing peacekeeping and peacebuilding operations often find themselves cast as the role of mediator among previously warring parties who now are having to carry out their "battles" on a political rather than a military playing field. The terms of a peace settlement, which often set strict limits on the mandate and timetables of those third parties responsible for assisting with the implementation of the settlement in question, create their own set of constraints not all of which are conducive to peacebuilding and laying foundations that will make the settlement last. Military, humanitarian, and development objectives are frequently at odds, as are the institutions and the officials responsible for pursuing them.

As Aldo Ajello also observes in his chapter on the implementation of the 1992 peace agreement in Mozambique, the implementation phase of a settlement changes the balance of forces between government and opposition, tending to favor the ruling party that is running the country and controlling the administrative and political machinery and resources of the state. This creates strong incentives for the opposition to defect from the peace process. In this strained environment it is all too easy for those responsible for implementation to lose sight of the "big picture" and their broader political objectives. Ajello emphasizes that not only is the "political profile" of the special representative of the secretary-general in UN-led peacebuilding operations critical to success, but he or she must recognize that such operations are essentially a "political exercise." He concludes that although the military and humanitarian components are important, "they should complement and support the political side of the mission, following the priorities established on a political level."

### Mediation and Political Triage

In virtually all the cases of mediation examined in this volume, it is clear that mediation generally serves as a form of political triage in which the urgent and most pressing issues—at least over the short term—typically take precedence over matters that appear less urgent but may be more central to the overall success of the peace process in the long run. One of the frankest accounts of this problem is found in Alvaro de Soto's retrospective assessment of the Salvadoran peace accords. He observes that Secretary-General Pérez de Cuéllar's imminent departure from his post at midnight on December 31, 1991, created a real deadline on the mediator and the parties to reach an agreement because they were told that the priority given to the negotiations would likely plummet under his successor. Although this gave new impetus to an agreement, the resulting "casualty" in talks was the issue of reintegration of former combatants into society. Although de Soto admits that there is enough blame to be shared all around, a "better-forged agreement on reintegration questions . . . might well have lessened the postwar crime wave that bedevils El Salvador to this day. Many combatants demobilized in bitter disappointment that their leaders had settled for much less than the revolutionary goals set in some of their manifestos on the age-old agrarian question. . . . Quick fixes have a way of coming back to haunt the fixed as well as the fixers."

There is obviously no substitute for carefully mediated and planned peace agreements that are not just driven by deadlines and a sense of urgency for the quick fix, but by a clear strategic vision of the elements necessary to ensure that the settlement remains durable. As de Soto and others in this volume argue, this requires a careful handover to successor institutions responsible for implementing the settlement in question, but also some degree of involvement by those responsible for implementation in the details of the negotiations itself before a settlement is reached.

## RISING TO THE CHALLENGE OF MULTIPARTY MEDIATION: ORGANIZATIONAL IMPLICATIONS AND INDIVIDUAL LEADERSHIP

As we recognized at the beginning of this chapter, multiparty mediation has become part of the architecture of the response to violent conflict that, under the right circumstances, can bring the mix of persuasion, leverage, and incentive (or disincentive) structure necessary to keep a peace process on track. Multiparty mediation—in which institutions compete with each other, fail to communicate, or use the opportunity to avoid taking responsibility—can also throw a peace process off track. In trying to identify what makes the difference between an effective multiparty mediation and an ineffective one, we have identified out of the preceding case studies three factors that have not received much attention in either scholarly or practitioner literature: institutional and mediator "readiness," the context of the personal relationship between the mediator and the parties to the conflict, and the context of the larger policy that the mediation supports.

What does this mean for the institutions and individuals who embark on a third-party peacemaking effort? In simple terms, mediating entities have to assess in realistic terms not only their good intentions and available resources, but also their ability to activate those resources and to reach—meaning to engage—the warring parties. It also means that they must be sentient of the consequences of their actions, seeing how the success or failure of the mediation affects not only the particular phase of the conflict that they are involved in, but all succeeding phases. Individual mediators need to be supported by their institutions; their institutions need to be supported by the other third-party institutions with an interest in the mediation effort. And both individuals and institutions need to recognize that mediation in a multiparty setting requires leadership of a very different nature than was necessary in preceding decades and centuries. In acknowledging that it may take more than one mediator to handle a dispute and that some mediators may have a comparative advantage over others in carrying out various kinds of mediation tasks, depending on the level, intensity, and duration of violence, we are also cognizant of the very real practical and operational challenges for institutions and for individuals who are associated with multiparty mediated interventions.

## Organizational Implications

Turning first to the institutional aspects, we recognize that different organizational capacities, structures, and lines of authority may be required to ensure that mediation is effective and not undermined by the institutional deficiencies of the mediating individual or organization. There can be no "one-size-fits-all" approach to organizational and institutional problems, as has been argued by some.[8] The requirements for mediation with muscle, or coercive interventions, are different from process-oriented mediation. The former requires clear lines of authority between the mediator and the actors or institutions that are in a position to deploy force or carry through on threats and offers made by the mediator. The mediator's leverage tends to be undermined if parties feel that the mediator is an independent actor who has little capacity to make good on his or her promises or threats. The mediator's leverage is also undermined if other mediators are present who are communicating different signals, or are in a position to offer a more attractive package of offers or inducements.

On the other hand, mediation requires independence not only to facilitate early intervention by the mediator but also to allow him or her to respond quickly to rapidly changing events. To take advantage of what may be a suddenly emerging set of opportunities because the balance of forces has changed on the ground, mediators have to act quickly and to demonstrate flexibility. If mediators and their backup teams are hamstrung by superiors and work in an organizational environment or institutional setting that stifles initiative and creativity, their efforts will be suboptimal and parties will either turn away or turn to others who have a proven track record in process management.

Experience in such varied places as the former Yugoslavia, Somalia, Cyprus, Mozambique, Central America, and Central Africa points to the growing need for comprehensive thinking and coherence or unity of action. While it may be gratifying to professionals and specialists in various types of third-party intervention to imagine that they can operate unburdened by other third parties' baggage and free from heavy-handed coordination mechanisms, the reality is that chaotic interventions will produce at best random results. Practitioners of all sorts can agree, presumably, on some form of the Hippocratic oath to "do no harm" and rise to the challenges of incremental learning in complex diplomatic-political interventions just as they are starting to do in the field of military intervention in complex emergencies. There is, in other words, some obligation on third parties to avoid simply exporting their own confusion, organizational and fund-raising agendas, and eagerness to help and to be seen helping to peoples in conflict who already have enough problems.

Successful peacekeepers and peace enforcers will keep in view the necessity for a center of gravity and a critical mass of efforts focused on clearly defined goals. Obviously, such operational coordination does not just happen; nor can it be imposed by one set or type of practitioners on another. A start can be made, however, by recalling that more will be accomplished when there is a laserlike focus on solving the problem at hand as distinct from getting the credit for being involved.

## Leadership in Multiparty Mediations

Although there is a tendency in some academic literature to diminish the importance of leadership in mediation, as the essays in this volume amply demonstrate, leadership matters.[9] That being said, leadership in situations involving a multiplicity of independent third-party actors calls for a broad array of personal and professional skills. Oran Young reminds us that there are three kinds of leadership roles in the negotiation of international regimes and other arrangements: structural leadership (relating to the use of strategic leverage), entrepreneurial leadership (relating to skill in presenting issues so as to bring parties together for a common purpose), and intellectual leadership (relating to the use of ideas to shape perceptions and attitudes about policy options).[10] All three of these are needed by multi-party mediators.

There are two aspects to the leadership imperative in complex or multi-party mediation. First, those state or institutional actors that "have the lead" (however that may have occurred) face the obvious challenge of coping with complexity and establishing coherence. Gone are the days when the field marshal or the proconsul could serve as the perfect role model for the peacemaker. Hence, the leaders of these efforts need to find means of including people, sharing credit, borrowing leverage, learning how to help other third-party players to save or maintain face, and identifying their work at every step with a widely shared agenda. This is not simply a question of good manners and learning the diplomatic graces. It is a question of building relationships with the other constituent members of the mediating "group" so that it hangs together and remains firmly goal oriented.

There is a second dimension of leadership that is becoming increasingly evident in situations involving multilevel mediation among a wide range of actors. Before third parties decide to intervene in a conflict arena, there is (or ought to be) some minimal obligation on their part to do their homework, ascertain who else is already involved, reflect upon the issue of coordination and coherence, and generally avoid complicating the local situation. The phenomenon we loosely refer to as "the international community" is, of course, not a clearly structured entity that is organized to make decisions binding on all sorts of actors. Hence, much depends on states, intergovernmental bodies, eminent persons, NGOs, and academic specialists having the common sense and humility to think in terms of coordination and a division of effort. Harold Saunders's chapter on Tajikistan illustrates to a high degree that desirable element of self-awareness that is called for, even if the situation in Tajikistan has peculiarities that may have facilitated such an approach.

Coherence is a challenge at several levels. A central issue is defining the conflict and the challenges it poses, agreeing on the key issues or missing ingredients that need to be addressed if the conflict is to be moved toward settlement, and—flowing from this—selecting an approach for mediation. If this effort is not undertaken, or if the political consensus does not exist to organize the intervention coherently at regional and international levels, the consequences for conflict parties can be severe, as Fabienne Hara and others in this volume remind us.

Another way of looking at the leadership question is that there may be times when multiparty mediation arises precisely because of a failure of political will or a refusal to lead. In the absence of such a lead being taken, one can anticipate that conflict participants may (if security and other conditions permit) be subjected to the well-intentioned efforts of a wide variety of external players. In the absence of leadership, the impact of sequential, simultaneous, and composite mediation may turn out to be random, as the external environment imposes its own "chaos" on that of the conflict itself. This is especially likely in conflicts that entail some requirement for the application of leverage and power, which are not provided, or are provided unevenly or inconsistently.

As we noted in the beginning of this volume, independent institutions find it difficult to fall into formation or even collaborate when acting as third parties in a conflict. Under these circumstances, the personal skills of the mediator become very important in persuading the institutions—including his or her own—to work together and support the peace process. The cases in this volume have illustrated a range of leadership techniques. Alvaro de Soto and Aldo Ajello maintained a single point of mediation in situations in which many state interests, any one of which could have derailed the negotiation, were involved. Paul Hare illustrates the special situation of a UN envoy from a small country backed discreetly by a superpower. Max van der Stoel illustrates an independent leadership on behalf of a regional organization by a strong-willed, senior foreign affairs veteran. James Baker exemplifies a particular formula of personalized, hands-on superpower leadership, driving the Middle East parties and other participants forward in Madrid. Luigi Einaudi and Richard Solomon illustrate the possibilities of superpower leadership from within a group, and Barbara McDougall, Jan Egeland, and Gordon Smith and John Hay underscore the particular challenges of leadership for middle powers working in a regional context.

The cases have also described a great variety of personal approaches, from Richard Holbrooke's forceful inducements to the ability of Minister Hasjim Djalal, former president Jimmy Carter, and members of the Community of Sant'Egidio to inspire confidence and cooperation on the basis of their own standing in the international community. In the same vein, John de Chastelain's chapter provided a powerful testimony to the impetus—also based on moral standing—that a seamless coalition of three leaders from three different countries could provide to a historically intractible negotiation. Paul Arthur and Harold Saunders, working with a different level of society, show the same characteristics of quiet leadership as George Mitchell and his colleagues used: patience, persistence, and a limitless capacity to listen. And finally, Margaret Anstee, Daniel Serwer, and Fabienne Hara illustrate that much can be accomplished by dedicated individuals even under the most adverse situations.

Looking at these different approaches, we see that each of these cases was characterized by a mix of Oran Young's categories of structural, entrepreneurial, and intellectual leadership. The answer to the question of what constitutes effective leadership in a multiparty intervention may be complex, but it is clear that part of the answer lies in the characteristics of the mediator. Although every case has its singularities, effectiveness in some sense hinges on the capacity to make the mediator's constituents and partners comfortable and to gain their confidence. In multiparty mediations, effective leadership depends on personal credibility, standing, passionate commitment to the goal at hand, vision, thoughtfulness, and cross-cultural sensitivity. It also depends on a deep grounding in the relevant histories and cultures; creativity in sharing tasks; agility in moving out of the way when others are leading; and an ability to reach, support, and inspire not only the parties to the conflict, but all interested parties.

The cases in this book illustrate the potency of these characteristics, but they also illustrate their limitations. Arriving at peace is a chancy operation and securing peace is even more difficult. The best mediator, acting alone, can be readily shrugged off when someone does not want peace. Creating conditions conducive to negotiations and promoting and consolidating peace take work at many levels by many actors, both inside and outside a conflict. This is why multiparty engagement in peacemaking is important. With the right individuals and institutions, multiparty engagement is a compelling force for peace and a key to that elusive goal, a lasting political settlement.

## Notes

1. See the earlier discussion of these terms in chapter 2.

2. For a broader treatment of this issue, see Stephan John Stedman, "Spoiler Problems in the Peace Process," *International Security* 22, no. 2 (fall 1997): 5–53.

3. For further discussion of this concept, see Roger Fisher, William Ury, and Bruce Patton, *Getting to Yes* (New York: Penguin Books USA, 1991).

4. The term *readiness* is discussed in Bertram I. Spector, "Negotiation Readiness in the Development Context: Adding Capacity to Ripeness" (paper presented at the annual conference of the International Studies Association, Minneapolis, March 19, 1998). In his treatment, readiness refers to the parties' readiness to negotiate and is related to the concept of ripeness. In our discussion, readiness refers to the capability of the mediators to engage in the conflict.

5. Herbert C. Kelman, "The Interactive Problem-Solving Approach," in *Managing Global Chaos: Sources of and Responses to International Conflict,* ed. Chester A. Crocker and Fen Osler Hampson with Pamela Aall (Washington, D.C.: United States Institute of Peace

Press, 1996), 501–519; John Paul Lederach, *Building Peace: Sustainable Reconciliation in Divided Societies* (Washington, D.C.: United States Institute of Peace Press, 1997); and Jeffrey Z. Rubin, "Conclusion: International Mediation in Context," in *Mediation in International Relations: Multiple Approaches to Conflict Management,* ed. Jacob Bercovitch and Jeffrey Z. Rubin (New York: St. Martin's Press, 1992).

6. George J. Mitchell, *Making Peace* (New York: Alfred A. Knopf, 1999).

7. See Saadia Touval and I. William Zartman, *International Mediation in Theory and Practice* (Boulder, Colo.: Westview Press, 1985); I. William Zartman, *Ripe for Resolution: Conflict and Intervention in Africa* (New York: Oxford University Press, 1989); and Richard N. Haass, *Conflicts Unending: The United States and Regional Disputes* (New Haven, Conn.: Yale University Press, 1990).

8. For a deeper discussion of institutional structure, see Antonia Handler Chayes, Abram Chayes, and George Raach, "Beyond Reform: Structuring for More Effective Conflict Intervention," *Global Governance* 3, no. 2 (May–August 1997): 117–146.

9. Andrew Moravcsik, "A New Statecraft? Supranational Entrepreneurs and International Cooperation," *International Organization* 53, no. 2 (spring 1999): 267–306.

10. Oran Young, "Political Leadership and Regime Formation" *International Organization* 45, no. 3 (summer 1991): 281–308.

# Index

Macedonia, 35
interethnic relations in, 72–73
McGuinness, Martin, 494
Machel, Samora, 254–255, 256–257, 633
Mack, John, 483
McMichael, Gary, 460
Madrid peace conference (1991), 26, 205–206, 527, 532–533, 673
*See also* Middle East peace process; Oslo Accord
Mahuad, Jamil, 422, 424–425
Major, John, 439, 444, 455
Malawi, 256
Malaysia
claim of sovereignty over Spratly Islands, 112, 113
oil exploration by, 112
as player in Cambodian peace process, 289
Mali, in Burundi mediation, 146
Mandela, Nelson, 484, 494, 659
Manley, Michael, intervention in Haiti, 510–511
Maputo, 232, 260
Margerie, Emmanuel de, 286
Martin, Claude, 287
Mayhew, Patrick, 437, 440, 446
Mazen, Abu, 527, 533, 534, 535, 540–541
Mazula, Brazao, 622
Media, role of in Cambodian peace settlement, 307–310
Mediation. *See* Conflict mediation; Multiparty facilitation/mediation
Mediators
appropriateness of, 677–678
mediator identities and contextualized relationships, 681–686
mediator "readiness" versus conflict "ripeness," 678–681
changing role of, 52–54

comparative advantages of different kinds of, 29–33
delegations, asymmetry in, 533
domestic constituencies of, 53
emotional intelligence of, 265–266
flexibility and freedom of, posing a paradox, 30
"friends of" as a useful device, 382
impartiality of, 60, 382
imposition of settlement by, 52
as informal convenors or moderators, 53–54
legitimacy of, 226–227, 544–545, 684–685
motives of, 239
as neutral brokers, 206–207
qualities necessary for, 52
technical host, role of, 543–544
*See also* Conflict mediation; Multiparty facilitation/mediation
Menem, Carlos, 425
Menzies, John, 335, 336, 554–555, 576
Mexico
action on embargo of Haiti, 399
as "Friend of Secretary General" in El Salvador mediation, 365–366, 368
involvement in Contadora Group, 353–354
Mexico agreements (El Salvador mediation), 350, 361, 364–365
Meyer, Rolf, 452
Middle East peace process, 165–166, 183, 206–207, 530
breakthrough for peace, 201–204
dynamics of, 188–189
effect of Gulf War on, 191–194
end game, 204–206
important dates, 184
key agreements, 184
major actors, 183
new optimism, 198–201
outcomes, 184

# United States Institute of Peace

The United States Institute of Peace is an independent, nonpartisan federal institution created by Congress to promote research, education, and training on the peaceful management and resolution of international conflicts. Established in 1984, the Institute meets its congressional mandate through an array of programs, including research grants, fellowships, professional training, education programs from high school through graduate school, conferences and workshops, library services, and publications. The Institute's Board of Directors is appointed by the President of the United States and confirmed by the Senate.

*Chairman of the Board:* Chester A. Crocker
*Vice Chairman:* Max M. Kampelman
*President:* Richard H. Solomon
*Executive Vice President:* Harriet Hentges

# HERDING CATS

This book is set in Adobe Caslon; the display type is Gill Sans. Hasten Design Studio, Inc. designed the book's cover, and Day W. Dosch designed the interior. Maps were prepared by Michael Sonensen. David Sweet copyedited the text, which was proofread by M. Kate St. Clair. Sonsie Conroy prepared the index. The book's editor was Nigel Quinney.